September 19–20, 2012
Lund, Sweden

**Association for
Computing Machinery**

Advancing Computing as a Science & Profession

ESEM'12

Proceedings of the ACM-IEEE International Symposium on

Empirical Software Engineering and Measurement

Sponsored by:

ACM SIGSOFT and IEEE CS

Association for
Computing Machinery

Advancing Computing as a Science & Profession

Chairs' Welcome

The International Symposium on Empirical Software Engineering and Measurement (ESEM) is one of the most important forums for presentation of empirical research in Software Engineering. ESEM's 6th installment will take place in Lund, Sweden, on the 19th and 20th of September 2012.

This year there were 95 full papers, 60 short papers and 4 posters submitted to the conference, of which 24, 19 and 4 were accepted, respectively. These accepted papers cover a broad range of topics related to empirical studies. There are both papers presenting the results of empirical studies, and papers about empirical research methodology.

In addition to the research papers, there are also two keynote speeches. Prof. Mark Harman will talk about search-based software engineering, a truly empirical discipline, which he has founded. The Bishop of Lund, Dr. Antje Jackelén will talk about using metaphors to visualize the invisible; how metaphors and symbols are used in theology, and how they can be used in Science and Engineering.

The ESEM conference will be held as part of the annual Empirical Software Engineering International Week (ESEIW), which, in addition to ESEM, includes the ISERN meeting (International Software Engineering Research Network), the International Doctoral Symposium on Empirical Software Engineering (IDoESE), the IASESE Advanced School (which this year will focus on Evidence Synthesis of Qualitative Research), and three co–located conferences/ workshops (MetriSec, PROMISE and EAST).

As organizers we would like to thank all of those who have contributed to making this conference a success: the authors for submitting their papers, the Program Committee members for their important work in reviewing and selecting the papers as well as in promoting the conference, and all the delegates. We would also like to thank all the sponsors to this event.

We wish you a very warm welcome and hope that you will enjoy your stay in Lund, Sweden.

Per Runeson
Lund University, Sweden
General Chair

Martin Höst
Lund University, Sweden

Emilia Mendes
Blekinge Institute of Technology, Sweden
Program Co-Chairs
Full Papers

Anneliese Andrews
University of Denver, USA

Rachel Harrison
Oxford Brookes University, UK
Program Co-Chairs
Short Papers and Posters

Table of Contents

Session 5: Full Papers: Empirical Studies & Systematic Reviews

Session 6: Short Papers: Methods and Principles

Keynote Address 2

Session 7: Full Papers: Prediction

Session 8: Full Papers: Testing and Inspection

Session 9: Short Papers: Global Software Engineering and Development

Session 10: Full Papers: Requirements

Session 11: Full Papers: Software Quality and Evolution

Session 12: Short Papers: Defect Detection

ESEM 2012 Conference Organization

General Chair: Per Runeson (*Lund University, Sweden*)

Program Chairs: Martin Höst (*Lund University, Sweden*)
Full Papers Emilia Mendes (*Zayed University, United Arab Emirates*)

Program Chairs: Anneliese Andrews (*University of Denver, USA*)
Short Papers and Posters Rachel Harrison (*Oxford Brookes University, UK*)

Local Arrangements: Jonas Wisbrant (*Lund University, Sweden*)
Congrex (*Sweden*)

Publicity Chair: Maria Teresa Baldassarre (*University of Bari, Italy*)

Co-Publicity Chairs: Muhammad Ali Babar (*IT University of Copenhagen, Denmark*)
Carolyn Seaman (*University of Maryland, USA*)
Martin Solari (*Universidad ORT, Uruguay*)
He (Jason) Zhang (*National ICT Australia & University of New South Wales, Australia*)

Steering Committee Chair: Guenther Ruhe (*University of Calgary, Canada*)

Steering Committee: Martin Höst (*Lund University, Sweden*)
Emilia Mendes (*Zayed University, United Arab Emirates*)
Maurizio Morisio (*Politecnico di Torino, Italy*)
Nachi Nagappan (*Microsoft Research, USA*)
Per Runeson (*Lund University, Sweden*)
Martin Shepperd (*Brunel University, UK*)
Forrest Shull (*Fraunhofer Center for Experimental Software Engineering, USA*)
Giancarlo Succi (*Free University Bolzano/Bozen, Italy*)

Program Committee: Anneliese Andrews (*University of Denver, USA*)
Full Papers Muhammad Ali Babar (*IT University of Copenhagen, Denmark*)
Maria Teresa Baldassare (*University of Bari, Italy*)
Ayse Bener (*Bogazici University, Turkey*)
Stefan Biffl (*Technical University Wienna, Austria*)
Pearl Brereton (*Keele University, UK*)
Giovanni Cantone (*Università di Roma "Tor Vergata", Italy*)
Jeffrey Carver (*University of Alabama, USA*)
Marcus Ciolkowski (*Fraunhofer IESE, Germany*)
Reidar Conradi (*Norwegian University of Science and Technology, Norway*)

Program Committee
Full Papers
(continued):

Daniela Soares Cruzes *(Norwegian University of Science and Technology, Norway)*

Tore Dybå *(SINTEF, Norway)*

Sebastian Elbaum *(University of Nebraska, USA)*

Hakan Erdogmus *(Kalemun Research Inc., Canada)*

Davide Falessi *(Simula Research Laboratory & University of Rome Tor Vergata, Italy)*

Marcela Genero *(University of Castilla-La Mancha, Spain)*

Tracy Hall *(Brunel University, UK)*

Mark Harman *(University College London, UK)*

Martin Höst *(Lund University, Sweden)*

Andreas Jedlitschka *(Fraunhofer IESE, Germany)*

Ross Jeffery *(National ICT Australia, Australia)*

Natalia Juristo *(Universidad Politecnica de Madrid, Spain)*

Magne Jørgensen *(Simula Research Laboratory, Norway)*

Barbara Kitchenham *(Keele University, UK)*

Filippo Lanubile *(University of Bari, Italy)*

Angelis Lefteris *(Aristitele University of Thessaloniki, Greece)*

Chris Lokan *(University of New South Wales, Australia)*

Stephen Macdonell *(Auckland University of Technology, New Zealand)*

Kenich Matsumoto *(Nara Institute of Science and Technology, Japan)*

Emilia Mendes *(Zayed University, United Arab Emirates)*

Tim Menzies *(West Virginia University, USA)*

James Miller *(University of Alberta, Canada)*

Yoshiki Mitani *(IPA/Sec & NAIST, Japan)*

Audris Mockus *(Avaya Labs Research, USA)*

Sandro Morasca *(Universita' degli Studi dell'Insubria, Italy)*

Shuji Morisaki *(Nara Institute of Science and Technology, Japan)*

Maurizio Morisio *(Politecnico di Torino, Italy)*

Jürgen Münch *(University of Helsinki, Finland)*

Nachiappan Nagappan *(Microsoft Research, USA)*

Markku Oivu *(University of Oulu, Finland)*

Dietmar Pfahl *(Lund University, Sweden)*

Lutz Prechelt *(Freie University Berlin, Germany)*

Brian Robinson *(ABB Corporate Research, USA)*

Marc Roper *(University of Strathclyde, UK)*

Guenther Ruhe *(University of Calgary, Canada)*

Per Runeson *(Lund University, Sweden)*

Carolyn Seaman *(University of Maryland, USA)*

Helen Sharp *(The Open University, UK)*

Martin Shepperd *(Brunel University, UK)*

Forrest Shull *(Fraunhofer Center, USA)*

Dag Sjøberg *(University of Oslo, Norway)*

Marco Torchiano *(Politecnico di Torino, Italy)*

Additional reviewers (continued):

Jason Sun
Shah Syed Muhammad Ali
Paolo Tell
Federico Tomassetti
Adam Trendowicz
Antonio Vetro'

Andreas Vogelsang
Jinying Yu
Mansooreh Zahedi
Minghui Zhou
Liming Zhu

ESEM 2012 Sponsors & Supporters

Sponsors: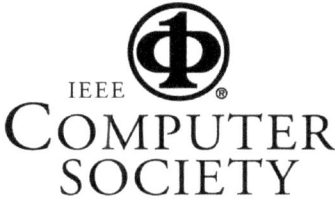

Supporters:  Nordic Council  LUND UNIVERSITY

 City of Lund

Dynamic Adaptive Search Based Software Engineering*

Mark Harman[1], Edmund Burke[2], John A. Clark[3] and Xin Yao[4]
[1]CREST Centre, University College London, Gower Street, London, WC1E 6BT, UK
[2]University of Stirling, Stirling, FK9 4LA Scotland, UK
[3]Department of Computer Science, University of York, Deramore Lane, York, YO10 5GH, UK
[4]School of Computer Science, The University of Birmingham, Edgbaston, Birmingham B15 2TT, UK

ABSTRACT

Search Based Software Engineering (SBSE) has proved to be a very effective way of optimising software engineering problems. Nevertheless, its full potential as a means of dynamic adaptivity remains under explored. This paper sets out the agenda for Dynamic Adaptive SBSE, in which the optimisation is embedded into deployed software to create self-optimising adaptive systems. Dynamic Adaptive SBSE will move the research agenda forward to encompass both software development processes and the software products they produce, addressing the long-standing, and as yet largely unsolved, grand challenge of self-adaptive systems.

Categories and Subject Descriptors

D.2 [**Software Engineering**]

General Terms

Search Based Software Engineering (SBSE), Evolution, Automatic Programming, Measurement, Testing

Keywords

SBSE, Search Based Optimization, Self-Adaptive Systems, Autonomic Computing

1. INTRODUCTION

Current software development practices achieve adaptivity at only a glacial pace, largely through enormous human engineering skill and effort. We force highly experienced engineers to waste their time and expertise adapting many

---

*This position paper is written to accompany Mark Harman's keynote talk at the 6th International Symposium on Empirical Software Engineering and Measurement (ESEM 12) in Lund, Sweden. It is joint work with Edmund Burke, John Clark and Xin Yao, funded by the EPSRC programme grant DAASE (EP/J017515/).

tedious implementation details. Often, the resulting software is equally inflexible: users often find themselves relying on their innate human adaptivity to compensate with 'workarounds'. This has to change.

To address the twin goals of adaptivity and automation, we advocate a development of the Search Based Software Engineering (SBSE) agenda that we call 'Dynamic Adaptive Search Based Software Engineering'. We seek greater software engineering automation through the development of hyper heuristics for SBSE. At the same time we seek greater adaptivity through the use of dynamic optimisation; optimisation embedded into the deployed software to re-tune its performance parameters and even to replace large portions of code with automatically re-evolved code.

2. SBSE

Search Based Software Engineering (SBSE) is the name given to a field of research and practice in which computational search (as well as optimisation techniques more usually associated with Operations Research) are used to address problems in Software Engineering [39]. The SBSE approach seeks to optimise software engineering processes and products using generic, robust, flexible, scalable and insight-rich computational search. SBSE provides a mechanism for managed automation of software engineering activities.

SBSE has proved to be a widely applicable and successful approach, with many applications right across the full spectrum of activities in software engineering, from initial requirements, project planning, and cost estimation to regression testing and onward evolution. Few aspects of development and deployment of software systems have remained untouched by the SBSE research agenda.

There is also an increasing interest in search based optimization from the industrial sector, as illustrated by work on testing involving Berner and Mattner and Daimler [49, 64], Ericsson [3], Google [69] and Microsoft [14, 50], and work on requirements analysis and optimisation involving Ericsson [70], Motorola [9] and NASA [20].

The increasing maturity of the field has led to a number of tools for SBSE applications, including AUSTIN (for C language test data generation, [49]), Bunch (for modularisation, [55]), Code-Imp (for automated refactoring, [56]), eTOC (for Java class testing, [63]), EvoSUITE (for Java test data generation, [26]), GenProg (for automated bug patching, [52]), MiLu (for higher order mutation testing, [46]), ReleasePlanner (for Requirements Optimisation, [58]), and SWAT (for PHP server-side test data generation [5]).

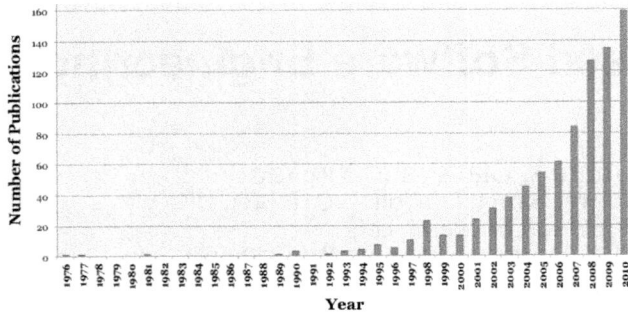

Figure 1: Yearly SBSE publication rates 1976-2010. Source: SBSE Repository [72].

Interest and research activity concerning SBSE has grown rapidly in the past ten years (see Figure 1) and there are now many excellent surveys and reviews on SBSE from which more information can be obtained. Rather than repeating this information, here are some pointers to specific SBSE surveys and reviews on:

- Requirements [71];
- Predictive Modelling [1, 34];
- Non-Functional Properties [2];
- Program Comprehension [32];
- Design [61] and
- Testing [2, 4, 33, 54].

In addition to this topic-specific SBSE literature, there are several more general SBSE surveys [18, 27, 31, 37, 40] and a review covering the relationship between other Artificial Intelligence techniques and SBSE [38]. There is also an SBSE tutorial aimed at those with no prior knowledge of SBSE who seek to adopt and apply search based optimization to software engineering problems of their own [42].

3. HYPER HEURISTIC SBSE

Current work on SBSE has produced significant advances in automated software engineering, particularly in the realms of testing, bug fixing and decision support. SBSE also shows great promise as a technique for handling non-functional properties and noisy, incomplete, and conflicting information concerning fitness.

Current SBSE automates specific problems in isolation, rather than the entire software engineering process. A dramatic increase in the breadth of automation lies within the grasp of the SBSE research and practitioner community. Such a 'holistic' optimisation-centric approach would ensure that SBSE achieves its full potential as a means to embed automated processes throughout the full range of software development and deployment activities.

To illustrate this vision for a more holistic SBSE, suppose we automate large parts of the development process using computational search: requirements engineering, project planning and testing could then become unified into a single automated activity.

To achieve a generic and holistic optimisation that connects diverse engineering activities, we turn to hyper-heuristic search [13] as a methodology for selecting or generating heuristics. That is, while most heuristic methods in the literature operate on a search space of potential solutions to a particular problem, a hyper-heuristic operates on a search space of heuristics. A Hyper Heuristic Search Based Software Engineering would address two important open questions in SBSE:

1. **To reach deeper, we need a holistic SBSE:** Why do we currently need to design special search based algorithms for each problem instance? This is unrealistic: every software engineer cannot be expected to be a computation search algorithm designer too.

2. **To reach wider, we need a generic SBSE:** Why do we currently optimise silos of software engineering activity? This is unrealistic: engineering decision making needs to take account of requirements, designs, test cases and implementation details *simultaneously*.

The Hyper Heuristic SBSE research agenda will raise fundamental questions. For example: how best do we draw the dividing line between adaptive automation for small changes and human intervention to invoke more fundamental adaption and to provide oversight and decision making? While automation is important, it is essential to understand the points at which human oversight, intervention, resumption-of-control and decision making should impinge on automation [35].

In the context of SBSE, this dividing line is the fine line between automated decision taking and automated decision support. Previous work on SBSE has tended to focus on automated decision making for those aspects of the development thought to occur later in the cycle, such as testing. The community has tended to reserve decision support for the early development cycle activities such as requirements analysis, and estimation. However, in a more holistic SBSE, there will be a far more intimate relationship between decision making and decision support, posing new methodological, engineering and pragmatic constraints and concerns.

Our vision of this new Hyper Heuristic Search Based Software Engineering is that it will provide the intellectual and technical tools to address the challenge of deeper, more holistic SBSE that cuts across the traditional software engineering boundaries such as requirements, design, modelling and testing. This vision is unashamedly experimental [67] and empirical [12]. It also aligns well with more agile and adaptive development practices, in which different software engineering activities such as design, re-factoring, testing and requirement elicitation are seen as iterative, integrated and inter-related activities, rather than as separate phases of development.

We also believe that the same Hyper Heuristic Search Based Software Engineering agenda will allow SBSE to reach a wider practitioner audience, by moving us from the bespoke to the generic. Instead of designing bespoke optimisation algorithms for specific instances, we advocate the design of 'reasonably good' hyper heuristic optimisers that have the generality to be applied more readily 'out of the box'. The results obtainable from a carefully crafted, specific, bespoke algorithm will surely out-perform those of a generic hyper heuristic SBSE algorithm.

We do not dispute this. Rather, we seek to surrender a little result quality for a lot of generality, believing that this balance of the meta objectives of quality and applicability will better address the factors that will influence uptake of SBSE. Our motivation is that ease of applicability will often trump quality of results, at least for the initial adopters, without whom there will be no take up. Has it not ever been thus in all technological development?

The hyper heuristic approach will require little tuning and will reduce the need for specific details, thereby significantly reducing the time to deployment and use. The key question will be whether sufficient optimisation power can be maintained so that the increased usability of the approach outweighs the reduction in result quality. This, in itself, is of course a twin-objective, cost-benefit optimisation trade off.

4. DYNAMIC ADAPTIVE SBSE

Self-adaptivity has been a goal of software and systems engineering research for some time, with work on architectures to support adaptive middleware [11, 59], Artificial Immune Systems (AIS) [45] for intrusion detection [47] and fault tolerance [68] and the vision of autonomic systems [29].

This research agenda is far from fully achieved; many authors still seek to address the outstanding grand challenge of self-adaptive systems, with large integrated projects such as the Self Managing Situated Computing project [25] and conferences and workshops, such as the Dagstuhl Seminar on Software Engineering for Self-Adaptive Systems [16].

SBSE has a potential to make a significant contribution to the realisation of this grand challenge. Unlike all other engineering optimization problems it is for *software* that optimisation has the most potential, because of the virtual nature of this extraordinary engineering material [36]. While computational search has been successfully applied to the design of engineering artefacts in civil, mechanical and electronic engineering, the search process cannot directly optimise these materials; the search ranges over a design space, guided by a simulation of a model of reality.

The search space and guidance are very different when we apply computation search to software. We find a new and potent possibility for search based optimisation: we can *directly* optimise the engineering material: the programs themselves. This opens up the possibility for in-situ, on the fly, optimisation to re-balance, re-configure, and even to *redevelop* the deployed software as it operates. This is the goal of Dynamic Adaptive Search Based Software Engineering.

The SBSE community has already developed techniques for tuning the performance of systems by identifying performance affecting parameters and treating them as configuration search spaces [19, 48]. There have also been exciting recent breakthroughs in the use of genetic programming to re-design aspects of systems to fix bugs [8, 65], to migrate to new platforms and languages [51] and to optimise non-functional properties [66].

These results can be thought of as early indications of the potential for Dynamic Adaptive SBSE. The work on parameter tuning shows that we can identify and tune performance parameters. If we can do this off-line, why not perform the tuning *on-line*. That is, compile into the deployed software an optimization algorithm that can identify and tune parameters that affect non-functional requirements. In this way, we would have self-monitoring, self-optimising systems.

By focusing on non-functional requirements we may partly escape the intricacies of requirements capture, with their inherent uncertainties. Functional requirements analysis is known to be plagued by difficulties of knowing exactly what the customer wants [15], something the customer may not even know themselves. Fortunately, the fitness function is often clear and unequivocal when it comes to non-functional requirements. The customer merely needs to state the non-functional requirements that matter (perhaps with acceptable tolerances, thresholds or ranges) and we can seek to optimise for these requirements.

By focusing on non-functional properties, we shall not be in a niche ghetto of 'optimisable software space'. The technological and business winds of change are clearly prevailing in a very non-functional direction. The advent of smart devices as an important computational platform, raises issues of power consumption, memory use and code size. The use of internet-enabled computing, in context aware mobile systems demands attention to bandwidth and response time. Cloud migration brings with it demands on throughput, heat dissipation and other service level properties.

Notice how this migration, from what might be termed the 'discrete' world of functional properties to the more 'continuous' world of non-functional properties, clearly illuminates the age-old debate about the difference between those two recalcitrant siamese twins: computer science and software engineering.

A focus on non-functional requirements such as power consumption, heat dissipation, throughput, response time, memory profile, bandwidth and information leakage will render a kind of Software Engineering more akin to traditional engineering disciplines. The inherent engineering character of software development and deployment will become more compelling than would have ever been thought by those who even ventured to doubt that there was such a thing as software *engineering* or that it could ever share the qualities of traditional engineering disciplines [22, 44, 43]. The rising importance of non-functional properties will also mean that software engineering will become ever more amenable to SBSE-style approaches.

Identification and optimisation of performance sensitive parameters will be one way to achieve Dynamic Adaptive SBSE. However, this will still leave the code largely unchanged. We will be extracting parameters, exposing them at the 'top level' and then searching for sensible settings, as the software executes. While this is likely to have many practical benefits, it merely scratches at the surface of the software.

Perhaps an even more exciting (yet demanding) challenge would be to seek a re-development of part of the software as deployed, while it executes, in situ, to replace the code with a better alternative. This dynamic adaptive SBSE would allow software to be more fundamentally adaptive. With this form of search-based adaptivity, we could hope that software systems would re-develop themselves, over time, to handle changing environments, platforms and contexts, while still seeking to meet the same overall functionality.

To some, such a vision of truly self-modifying code, might seem more of a nightmare than a dream: surely such code would be impossible to understand and to control? How would we ever apply source code analysis to such dynamically adapting code? Would the code not become unreadable?

However, with hindsight it may seem like merely another step on the pathway from assembler code to higher levels of abstraction. We already cede to the compiler a great deal of sovereignty over the code that it produces, seldom interfering with (or even enquiring about) the optimisation choices the compiler makes in producing object code.

With the advent of Dynamic Adaptive SBSE, we will make a further step towards the goal of greater abstraction. What we think of as source code today, may become the object code of tomorrow. In a world where non-functional, performance related requirements are 'optimised in' as the code executes, the programmer can move to a higher plain of abstraction. She will surely want to focus purely on the functional requirements of the system and will be happy to leave the optimisation of non-functional aspects to the SBSE compiler (and the 'on board re-evolver').

We hope to reach the point at which we are able to use Dynamic Adaptive SBSE to simultaneously meet the goals cherished by early pioneers of declarative languages [21] as well as the initial advocates of self-adaptive and autonomic computing [29, 59]: The program would be written in a purely declarative style. Why would anyone wish to code for performance-related details when these can be 'optimised in'? Initial results from new forms of SBSE-inspired genetic programming have indicated that this goal may be within our reach:

Bug fixing: With automated bug fixing, it is already possible to find and fix non trivial bugs [30]. The changes made by an automated patching system, are relatively small changes compared to the overall size of the program. One might think that they would simply be just that: a patch, deployed as a temporary measure to buy time for the more trusted code changers (the humans) to take over. However, there is recent evidence that there may be a longer-term future for such machine-generated patches [28].

Migration: Recent work on code migration using evolutionary improvement [51] showed that it was possible to automatically port the core computation of the unix utility `gzip` from a desk top platform supporting C code to a GPGPU platform supporting CUDA code. The automated re-evolution of the core computation of this utility demonstrates that it is not just patches that can be evolved, but larger pieces of code. It also indicates that it is possible to evolve new code for completely different architectures and languages than those for which the original code was designed. A key insight in this work is that the original program can act as an oracle for the functional requirements of the system to be re-evolved in this way [7].

Trading Functional and non-functional requirements: Previous work on searching for alternative balances between functional and non-functional requirements has also been promising. White et al. [66] showed how different versions of a pseudo random number generator could be evolved with a range of power-consumption characteristics. Crucially, in this work, functionality was sacrificed for non-functional properties. This may seem a curious approach to adopt after several decades of emphasis on correctness of functional requirements. However, for battery-powered platforms, power consumption is king:

$$correctness + flat\_battery = useless$$

A user might sacrifice the 'sacred cow' of complete functional correctness (did we ever attain that anyway?) should it come into stark conflict with longer battery life.

Indeed, do we not already do so when we switch off features of our smart phones to enable longer lifetime to the next re-charge?

The road to achieve our vision is not without challenges. There are fundamental obstacles to be overcome in computational search itself. It is still unclear whether it is even theoretically possible to evolve and adapt software from just a declarative description of functional requirements. There is a need to understand what is and is not possible using the SBSE approach and how efficient and effective such an approach is in evolving software dynamically.

5. EXPERIMENTAL VS. EMPIRICAL

The essence of science and engineering and their considerable achievements rest upon the careful construction of experiments, from which (often painstaking) observations are made. Experimentation is the foundation stone on which rests much of science, widely believed to be the principle driver behind the growth of scientific knowledge. Experimentation is the scientific credo enshrined in the Popperian view of science [60].

There has been much debate about the role of experimentation in computer science and software engineering too, with many arguing the case for experimental approaches [10, 57, 62]. However, there is a subtle distinction between purely experimental and empirical research in software engineering. This distiction is less important (and thus under-emphasied) in other science and engineering disciplines.

A scientific experiment is normally taken to mean the careful observation of one or more dependent attributes, under carefully controlled circumstances. The control of circumstances is crucial; one often uses the phrase 'under laboratory conditions' for such experiments.

By contrast, the term 'empirical' is typically used to define *any* statement about the world that is related to observation or experience. It is helpful to distinguish pure experimentation from the more general class of empirical investigation. Of course, a scientific experiment is an act of observation and experience; the experience of the scientist making those 'careful observations'. Therefore, any experimental approach is inherently empirical. Nevertheless, the controlled scientific experiment enjoys a special place in the scientific discovery process, because it is a way to determine and *measure* the effect of one quantity on another.

There is a long history of empirical observation dating back to the Babylonian astronomers, who provided data charting the movements of the heavenly bodies, from which present day astronomy continues to profit. As such, the concept of empirical observation considerably predates the scientific method of experimentation. Indeed, these ancient empirical stargazers were not only forerunners of present day astronomy, they were also astrologers, concerned as much with magic and mysticism as there were with reason and scientific experimentation [24].

Arbitrary empirical observations on their own, can provide no more than case studies in the observation of real world phenomena. While real world empirical observations have an important place in the testing of engineering artefacts in situ and in their final operation context, the first duty of scientist and engineer lies within the realm of pure experimentation, under laboratory conditions, where laboratory control serves as a mechanism for removing selection bias, confounding effect and miss observation.

6. SYNTHETIC DATA IN SOFTWARE ENGINEERING

In software engineering, pure experimentation often makes use of synthetically generated problem instances. For example, to understand the effect of a requirements analysis problem by generating instances of hypothetical requirements or the effects of a data mining approach by construction of a large number of different kinds of data set.

Curiously, in stark contrast to similar experimental work in longer-established scientific and engineering disciplines, pure experimentation is often frowned upon by computer scientists and software engineers. However, under properly controlled laboratory conditions it remains the primary way in which scientists can investigate the effects of the independent variables on the dependent variables — a principle widely accepted in all fields of science and engineering.

Therefore, it is important not to overlook the value of purely experimental studies. While laboratory conditions are not the same as real world conditions, they can be controlled. In empirical software engineering we need both laboratory controlled data and data based on real world empirical experimentation, not one or the other.

However, caution is needed. The empirical software engineering researcher might fall into the trap of using synthetic data as a *surrogate* for real data rather than as an *augmentation*; seeking to answer research questions that really should be answered using real data. When using purely experimental research for appropriate questions the experiment must be carefully designed.

Nevertheless, this does not mean that synthetic data has no role to play in empirical software engineering. For example, a data mining researcher might use synthetic data to investigate whether their algorithm could reveal interesting surprises about system behaviour. This is a question clearly best answered by real data: a 'surprise' found in synthetic data cannot really be a genuine surprise (by definition). However, synthetic data could be used to tests the scalability of the data mining algorithm.

Naturally, similar issues arise as with pure experimentation in other sciences and engineering; field trials are always required to augment laboratory testing. Fortunately, a 'best of both worlds' is also sometimes possible. Repositories may be large enough that one can find sufficiently many examples to cover a wide range of possibilities in the fine granularity required for experimental research questions. However, there are questions that can only be answered with experiments on synthetic data. For example, when exploring behaviour with corrupted, noisy and atypical cases, it may be not only necessary, but desirable to use synthetic examples.

6.1 The Role of Synthetic data in SBSE

Synthetic data can be useful as a means of experimenting with algorithms based on computational search. Such experiments cannot fully answer whether some SBSE approach will be useful in practice; evidence for this must ultimately accrue from empirical investigations using real world systems. The generation of synthetic data sets also requires care. For instance, the data must be reasonable and represent characteristics that may be found in the real world data sets that the techniques may encounter. Nevertheless, there are a number of experimental SBSE research questions that can be addressed using purely experimental analysis on synthetically generated data sets:

Scalability: How well does the algorithm scale with characteristics of the data? Scalability concerns resource consumption (typically space and time) of the search based algorithm as the characteristics of the input data vary. Scalability is a paramount concern in almost all software engineering applications. The input data variation is not necessarily merely a matter of the sheer size of the data set (though this is often important). The performance of some optimisation algorithms may also depend on other characteristics, such as density of dependence relations, correlations between elements and other non-size-based data characteristics. A purely experimental approach allows precise, fine-grained variation of data characteristics to explore the relationship between empirical algorithmic scalability and theoretical complexity bounds.

While general empirical and theoretical algorithm performance may be known for arbitrary problems, the specific software engineering problem in hand may exhibit peculiar scalability trends. Scalability is influenced by choices of representation and fitness function as well as the choice of search algorithm. An empirical scalability study can also determine the size and data characteristics at which an 'intelligent' search outperforms a purely random search, as has been done for requirements engineering problems [73].

Robustness: How resilient are the results on the presence of bias, noise, incompleteness and incorrectness in the inputs? Software engineering problems are often characterised by noisy, incomplete and even inconsistent data. SBSE has been argued to be well-suited to this paradigm [31]; search algorithms are naturally robust in the presence of incomplete and noisy data, and cope well with competing and conflicting objectives. However, the degree to which the choice of algorithms, fitness and representation cope with forms of bias, noise and incompleteness is often best assessed in laboratory conditions, where precise control can be exerted over the degree of challenge with which the algorithm is presented.

Algorithmic Performance Comparison: How do a set of search based algorithms compare for a problem over a wide range of data sets. There has been much recent progress in theoretical analysis of SBSE problems [6, 17, 41, 53]. Nevertheless, there remain many SBSE problems for which the only way to determine the best choice of search algorithm remains entirely empirical. In these situations one would certainly like to know how each algorithm performs on real world problems. These real world results can often be complemented by a more thorough purely experimental study, in which the factors that affect the choice can be explored in more detail. A study that exploits the full control afford by an experimental design unfettered by the availability of suitable real world data sets. Such a purely experimental approach necessitates the separate research problem of instance generation, a problem that has been considered in comparative studies of SBSE algorithms for requirements engineering [23].

Non-Functional Properties: How does the approach behave with respect to non-functional properties? Such properties of the search algorithm, such as its power consumption, response to change and communication bandwidth have not traditionally been the subject of intense investigation. However, in order to realise the Dynamic Adaptive SBSE agenda outlined in this paper, it will be necessary to compile (or otherwise embed) the search based computation into the deployed software to achieve search based adaptivity.

In this new paradigm of Dynamic Adaptive SBSE, non-functional characteristics of the search algorithms will be inherited by the software it is used to create. The complex interplay between several non-functional properties and the many problem characteristics that potentially influence them will mean that a full and thorough empirical evaluation will require a large and diverse body of data sets. Once again, the best way to ensure controllability of experimental method may be to create synthetic problem instances.

Adaptability: How well does a proposed SBSE approach cope with changes in the context or environment? The Dynamic Adaptive SBSE agenda will require algorithms and approaches that retain strong performance and result quality in the presence of changes in context and operating environment. Controlling for the operating environment of an approach is something that, almost inherently, calls for some form of laboratory experimentation, rather than a 'real world' evaluation; achieving laboratory control of experimental variables in a production deployed environment is unlikely to be realistic. Of course, results from such laboratory experiments should be augmented with field trials, but a field trial may not enable the researcher to report results for a wide variety of challenging contexts, which a purely experimental study can.

In many of the situations above, a purely experimental study alone will be insufficient and should be augmented with real world studies. Where real world data is abundant (for example when studying open source code as the subject of the empirical study), it may even be possible to find scale and variety in the available real world data sets sufficient to support a detailed experimental evaluation. However, in many situations, it is the very nature of the research questions asked that prohibits the use of real world data. For example, when attempting to assess scalability or robustness beyond what could reasonably be *currently* expected, the researcher must, to some extent, generate the experimental data set in order for it to be demanding.

7. THE DAASE PROJECT

The research agenda briefly outlined in this paper forms the focus of the DAASE project (DAASE: Dynamic Adaptive Automated Software Engineering).

DAASE is a major research initiative running from June 2012 to May 2018, funded by £6.8m from the Engineering and Physical Sciences Research Council (the EPSRC). DAASE also has matching support from University College London and the Universities of Birmingham, Stirling and York, which will complement the 22 EPSRC-funded post doctoral researchers recruited to DAASE with 26 fully funded PhD studentships and 6 permanent faculty positions (assistant and associate professors).

The DAASE project is keen to collaborate with leading researchers and research groups. We are also interested in collaboration with industrial parters and other organisations interested in joining the existing DAASE industrial partners which include Berner & Mattner, British Telecom, Ericsson, GCHQ, Honda, IBM and Microsoft. We have a programme for short and longer term visiting scholars (at all levels from PhD student to full professor) and arrangements for staff exchanges and internships with other organisations.

For more information, contact Lena Hierl, the DAASE Administrative Manager (crest-admin@ucl.ac.uk) or Mark Harman, the DAASE project director.

8. CONCLUSION

Dynamic adaptive search based software engineering is a development of the SBSE research agenda in which we seek to embed into the deployed code the optimisation techniques developed over the past decade of SBSE research. In so doing we seek to address the goals espoused by advocates of self-adaptive and autonomic computing, not merely to fix faults and cope with anomalies, but as a routine and natural means of on-line adaptivity to meet new challenges, environments and platforms. The approach may be particularly effective in the emerging world of more continuous non-functional properties.

We also look towards a Hyper-Heuristic future for SBSE, in which hyper heuristic search is used to improve the applicability and generality of SBSE techniques at the expense of some loss in quality of results. We argue that this may prove to be an important step in the wider practitioner uptake.

Both real world empirical studies and purely experimental studies (using laboratory-controlled synthetic examples) will be required to evaluate the practical aspects of Dynamic Adaptive SBSE. Theoretical analysis of problem characteristics, algorithm choices and solution space properties will also be needed to provide a sound scientific underpinning for this optimisation-based approach to dynamic adaptivity.

Acknowledgements: We would like to thank those whose ideas influenced this work (with apologies to those whom we may have failed to list here specifically): Enrique Alba, Nadia Alshahwan, Andrea Arcuri, Peter Bentley, Lionel Briand, Javier Dolado, Robert Feldt, Stephanie Forrest, Carlo Ghezzi, Rob Hierons, Mike Holcombe, Yue Jia, Bryan Jones, Kiran Lakhotia, Bill Langdon, Claire Le Goues, Spiros Mancoridis, Phil McMinn, Tim Menzies, Riccardo Poli, Marc Roper, Martin Shepperd, Paolo Tonella, Shin Yoo, Wes Weimer, Joachim Wegener, David White, Andreas Zeller & Yuanyuan Zhang. Thanks also to Lena Hierl for proof reading.

9. REFERENCES

[1] W. Afzal and R. Torkar. On the application of genetic programming for software engineering predictive modeling: A systematic review. *Expert Systems Applications*, 38(9):11984–11997, 2011.

[2] W. Afzal, R. Torkar, and R. Feldt. A systematic review of search-based testing for non-functional system properties. *Information and Software Technology*, 51(6):957–976, 2009.

[3] W. Afzal, R. Torkar, R. Feldt, and G. Wikstrand. Search-based prediction of fault-slip-through in large software projects. In *Second International Symposium on Search Based Software Engineering (SSBSE 2010)*, pages 79–88, Benevento, Italy, 7-9 Sept. 2010.

[4] S. Ali, L. C. Briand, H. Hemmati, and R. K. Panesar-Walawege. A systematic review of the application and empirical investigation of search-based test-case generation. *IEEE Transactions on Software Engineering*, pages 742–762, 2010.

[5] N. Alshahwan and M. Harman. Automated web application testing using search based software engineering. In 26th *IEEE/ACM International Conference on Automated Software Engineering (ASE 2011)*, pages 3 – 12, Lawrence, Kansas, USA, 6th - 10th November 2011.

[6] A. Arcuri. It does matter how you normalise the branch distance in search based software testing. In *International Conference on Software testing (ICST 2010)*, pages 205–214, Paris, France, 2010. IEEE Computer Society.

[7] A. Arcuri, D. R. White, J. A. Clark, and X. Yao. Multi-objective improvement of software using co-evolution and smart seeding. In 7th *International Conference on*

Simulated Evolution and Learning (SEAL 2008), pages 61–70, Melbourne, Australia, December 2008. Springer.

[8] A. Arcuri and X. Yao. A Novel Co-evolutionary Approach to Automatic Software Bug Fixing. In *Proceedings of the IEEE Congress on Evolutionary Computation (CEC '08)*, pages 162–168, Hongkong, China, 1-6 June 2008. IEEE Computer Society.

[9] P. Baker, M. Harman, K. Steinhöfel, and A. Skaliotis. Search based approaches to component selection and prioritization for the next release problem. In *22nd International Conference on Software Maintenance (ICSM 06)*, pages 176–185, Philadelphia, Pennsylvania, USA, Sept. 2006.

[10] V. R. Basili, R. W. Selby, and D. H. Hutchens. Experimentation in software engineering. *IEEE Transactions on Software Engineering*, 12(7):733–743, July 1986.

[11] J. S. Bradbury, J. R. Cordy, J. Dingel, and M. Wermelinger. A survey of self-management in dynamic software architecture specifications. In D. Garlan, J. Kramer, and A. L. Wolf, editors, *Proceedings of the 1st ACM SIGSOFT Workshop on Self-Managed Systems (WOSS 2004)*, pages 28–33, California, USA, October 31 - November 1 2004. ACM.

[12] L. Briand. Embracing the engineering side of software engineering. *IEEE Software*, 2012. To appear.

[13] E. K. Burke, B. McCollum, A. Meisels, S. Petrovic, and R. Qu. A Graph-Based Hyper-Heuristic for Timetabling Problems. *European Journal of Operational Research*, 176(1):177–192, 2007.

[14] C. Cadar, P. Godefroid, S. Khurshid, C. S. Păsăreanu, K. Sen, N. Tillmann, and W. Visser. Symbolic execution for software testing in practice: preliminary assessment. In *33rd International Conference on Software Engineering (ICSE'11)*, pages 1066–1071, New York, NY, USA, 2011. ACM.

[15] B. Cheng and J. Atlee. From state of the art to the future of requirements engineering. In L. Briand and A. Wolf, editors, *Future of Software Engineering 2007*, Los Alamitos, California, USA, 2007. IEEE Computer Society Press. This volume.

[16] B. H. C. Cheng, R. de Lemos, H. Giese, P. Inverardi, and J. Magee, editors. *Software Engineering for Self-Adaptive Systems (Dagstuhl Seminar)*, volume 08031 of *Dagstuhl Seminar Proceedings*. Internationales Begegnungs und Forschungszentrum für Informatik (IBFI), Schloss Dagstuhl, Germany, 2008.

[17] J. F. Chicano, J. Ferrer, and E. Alba. Elementary landscape decomposition of the test suite minimization problem. In M. B. Cohen and M. Ó. Cinnéide, editors, *3rd International Symposium on Search Based Software Engineering (SSBSE 2011)*, volume 6956 of *Lecture Notes in Computer Science*, pages 48–63, Szeged, Hungary, 2011. Springer.

[18] J. Clark, J. J. Dolado, M. Harman, R. M. Hierons, B. Jones, M. Lumkin, B. Mitchell, S. Mancoridis, K. Rees, M. Roper, and M. Shepperd. Reformulating software engineering as a search problem. *IEE Proceedings — Software*, 150(3):161–175, 2003.

[19] A. Corazza, S. D. Martino, F. Ferrucci, C. Gravino, F. Sarro, and E. Mendes. How effective is tabu search to configure support vector regression for effort estimation? In *6th International Conference on Predictive Models in Software Engineering (PROMISE '10)*, Timisoara, Romania, 12-13 September 2010. IEEE.

[20] S. L. Cornford, M. S. Feather, J. R. Dunphy, J. Salcedo, and T. Menzies. Optimizing Spacecraft Design - Optimization Engine Development: Progress and Plans. In *Proceedings of the IEEE Aerospace Conference*, pages 3681–3690, Big Sky, Montana, March 2003.

[21] J. Darlington and R. M. Burstall. A system which automatically improves programs. *Acta Informatica*, 6:41–60, 1976.

[22] E. W. Dijkstra. On a political pamphlet from the middle ages (A response to the paper 'social processes and proofs of theorems and programs' by DeMillo, Lipton, and Perlis). *ACM SIGSOFT, Software Engineering Notes*, 3(2):14–17, 1978.

[23] J. J. Durillo, Y. Zhang, E. Alba, M. Harman, and A. J. Nebro. A study of the bi-objective next release problem. *Empirical Software Engineering*, 16(1):29–60, 2011.

[24] P. Fara. *Science: A 4000-year history*. Oxford University Press, 2009.

[25] A. Filieri, C. Ghezzi, A. Leva, and M. Maggio. Self-adaptive software meets control theory: A preliminary approach supporting reliability requirements. In P. Alexander, C. S. Pasareanu, and J. G. Hosking, editors, *26th IEEE/ACM International Conference on Automated Software Engineering (ASE 2011)*, pages 283–292, Lawrence, KS, USA, November 2011. IEEE.

[26] G. Fraser and A. Arcuri. Evosuite: automatic test suite generation for object-oriented software. In *8th European Software Engineering Conference and the ACM SIGSOFT Symposium on the Foundations of Software Engineering (ESEC/FSE '11)*, pages 416–419. ACM, September 5th - 9th 2011.

[27] F. G. Freitas and J. T. Souza. Ten years of search based software engineering: A bibliometric analysis. In *3rd International Symposium on Search based Software Engineering (SSBSE 2011)*, pages 18–32, 10th - 12th September 2011.

[28] Z. P. Fry, B. Landau, and W. Weimer. A human study of patch maintainability. In *International Symposium on Software Testing and Analysis (ISSTA'12)*, Minneapolis, Minnesota, USA, July 2012. To appear.

[29] A. G. Ganek. Autonomic computing: Implementing the vision. In *Active Middleware Services*, pages 2–3. IEEE Computer Society, 2003.

[30] C. L. Goues, M. Dewey-Vogt, S. Forrest, and W. Weimer. A systematic study of automated program repair: Fixing 55 out of 105 bugs for $8 each. In *International Conference on Software Engineering (ICSE 2012)*, Zurich, Switzerland, 2012.

[31] M. Harman. The current state and future of search based software engineering. In L. Briand and A. Wolf, editors, *Future of Software Engineering 2007*, pages 342–357, Los Alamitos, California, USA, 2007. IEEE Computer Society Press.

[32] M. Harman. Search based software engineering for program comprehension. In *15th International Conference on Program Comprehension (ICPC 07)*, pages 3–13, Banff, Canada, 2007. IEEE Computer Society Press.

[33] M. Harman. Open problems in testability transformation. In *1st International Workshop on Search Based Testing (SBT 2008)*, Lillehammer, Norway, 2008.

[34] M. Harman. The relationship between search based software engineering and predictive modeling. In *6th International Conference on Predictive Models in Software Engineering (PROMISE 2010)*, Timisoara, Romania, 2010.

[35] M. Harman. Why source code analysis and manipulation will always be important. In *10th IEEE International Working Conference on Source Code Analysis and Manipulation*, pages 7–19, Timisoara, Romania, 2010.

[36] M. Harman. Why the virtual nature of software makes it ideal for search based optimization. In *13th International Conference on Fundamental Approaches to Software Engineering (FASE 2010)*, pages 1–12, Paphos, Cyprus, March 2010.

[37] M. Harman. Software engineering meets evolutionary computation. *IEEE Computer*, 44(10):31–39, Oct. 2011.

[38] M. Harman. The role of artificial intelligence in software engineering. In *1st International Workshop on Realizing Artificial Intelligence Synergies in Software Engineering (RAISE 2012)*, Zurich, Switzerland, 2012.

[39] M. Harman and B. F. Jones. Search based software

engineering. *Information and Software Technology*, 43(14):833–839, Dec. 2001.

[40] M. Harman, A. Mansouri, and Y. Zhang. Search based software engineering: Trends, techniques and applications. *ACM Computing Surveys*, 2012. To appear.

[41] M. Harman and P. McMinn. A theoretical and empirical study of search based testing: Local, global and hybrid search. *IEEE Transactions on Software Engineering*, 36(2):226–247, 2010.

[42] M. Harman, P. McMinn, J. Souza, and S. Yoo. Search based software engineering: Techniques, taxonomy, tutorial. In B. Meyer and M. Nordio, editors, *Empirical software engineering and verification: LASER 2009-2010*, pages 1–59. Springer, 2012. LNCS 7007.

[43] C. A. R. Hoare. The engineering of software: A startling contradiction. In D. Gries, editor, *Programming Methodology, A Collection of Articles by Members of IFIP WG2.3*. Springer-Verlag, New York, NY, 1978.

[44] C. A. R. Hoare. How did software get so reliable without proof? In *FME '96: Industrial Benefit and Advances in Formal Methods: Third International Symposium of Formal Methods Europe*, number 1051 in LNCS, pages 1–17. Springer-Verlag, Mar. 1996.

[45] S. A. Hofmeyr and S. Forrest. Immunity by design: An artificial immune system. *Proceedings of the Genetic and Evolutionary Computation Conference (GECCO '99)*, 2:1289–1296, 1999.

[46] Y. Jia and M. Harman. Milu: A customizable, runtime-optimized higher order mutation testing tool for the full C language. In 3rd *Testing Academia and Industry Conference - Practice and Research Techniques (TAIC PART'08)*, pages 94–98, Windsor, UK, August 2008.

[47] J. Kim, P. J. Bentley, U. Aickelin, J. Greensmith, G. Tedesco, and J. Twycross. Immune system approaches to intrusion detection - A review. *Natural Computing: An international journal*, 6, Dec. 2007.

[48] K. Krogmann, M. Kuperberg, and R. Reussner. Using genetic search for reverse engineering of parametric behaviour models for performance prediction. *IEEE Transactions on Software Engineering*, 36(6):865–877, November-December 2010.

[49] K. Lakhotia, M. Harman, and H. Gross. AUSTIN: A tool for search based software testing for the C language and its evaluation on deployed automotive systems. In 2nd *International Symposium on Search Based Software Engineering (SSBSE 2010)*, pages 101 – 110, Benevento, Italy, September 2010.

[50] K. Lakhotia, N. Tillmann, M. Harman, and J. de Halleux. FloPSy — Search-based floating point constraint solving for symbolic execution. In 22nd *IFIP International Conference on Testing Software and Systems (ICTSS 2010)*, pages 142–157, Natal, Brazil, November 2010. LNCS Volume 6435.

[51] W. B. Langdon and M. Harman. Evolving a CUDA kernel from an nVidia template. In *IEEE Congress on Evolutionary Computation*, pages 1–8. IEEE, 2010.

[52] C. Le Goues, T. Nguyen, S. Forrest, and W. Weimer. GenProg: A generic method for automatic software repair. *IEEE Transactions on Software Engineering*, 38(1):54–72, 2012.

[53] P. K. Lehre and X. Yao. Runtime analysis of search heuristics on software engineering problems. *Frontiers of Computer Science in China*, 3(1):64–72, 2009.

[54] P. McMinn. Search-based software test data generation: A survey. *Software Testing, Verification and Reliability*, 14(2):105–156, June 2004.

[55] B. S. Mitchell and S. Mancoridis. On the automatic modularization of software systems using the bunch tool. *IEEE Transactions on Software Engineering*, 32(3):193–208, 2006.

[56] I. H. Moghadam and Mel Ó Cinnéide. Code-Imp: A tool

[57] A. Newell and H. A. Simon. Computer science as empirical inquiry: symbols and search. *Communications of the ACM*, 19:113–126, 1976.

[58] A. Ngo-The and G. Ruhe. A systematic approach for solving the wicked problem of software release planning. *Soft Computing - A Fusion of Foundations, Methodologies and Applications*, 12(1):95–108, August 2008.

[59] P. Oreizy, M. M. Gorlick, R. N. Taylor, D. Heimbigner, G. Johnson, N. Medvidovic, A. Quilici, D. S. Rosenblum, and A. L. Wolf. An architecture-based approach to self-adaptive software. *IEEE Intelligent Systems*, 14:54–62, May 1999.

[60] K. R. Popper. *Conjectures and Refutations: The Growth of Scientific Knowledge*. Routledge, 2003.

[61] O. Räihä. A survey on search–based software design. *Computer Science Review*, 4(4):203–249, 2010.

[62] W. F. Tichy. Should computer scientists experiment more? *IEEE Computer*, 31(5):32–40, May 1998.

[63] P. Tonella. Evolutionary testing of classes. In *Proceedings of the 2004 ACM SIGSOFT International Symposium on Software Testing and Analysis (ISSTA '04)*, pages 119–128, Boston, Massachusetts, USA, 11-14 July 2004. ACM.

[64] J. Wegener and O. Bühler. Evaluation of different fitness functions for the evolutionary testing of an autonomous parking system. In *Genetic and Evolutionary Computation Conference (GECCO 2004)*, pages 1400–1412, Seattle, Washington, USA, June 2004. LNCS 3103.

[65] W. Weimer, T. V. Nguyen, C. L. Goues, and S. Forrest. Automatically finding patches using genetic programming. In *International Conference on Software Engineering (ICSE 2009)*, pages 364–374, Vancouver, Canada, 2009.

[66] D. R. White, J. Clark, J. Jacob, and S. Poulding. Searching for resource-efficient programs: Low-power pseudorandom number generators. In *2008 Genetic and Evolutionary Computation Conference (GECCO 2008)*, pages 1775–1782, Atlanta, USA, July 2008. ACM Press.

[67] C. Wohlin, P. Runeson, M. Höst, M. C. Ohlsson, B. Regnell, and A. Wesslén. *Experimentation in Software Engineering*. Kluwer Academic Publishers, 2000.

[68] S. Xanthakis, C. Karapoulios, R. Pajot, and A. Rozz. Immune system and fault-tolerant computing. *Artificial Evolution (Lecture Notes in Computer Science)*, 1063:181–197, 1996.

[69] S. Yoo, R. Nilsson, and M. Harman. Faster fault finding at Google using multi objective regression test optimisation. In 8th *European Software Engineering Conference and the ACM SIGSOFT Symposium on the Foundations of Software Engineering (ESEC/FSE '11)*, Szeged, Hungary, September 5th - 9th 2011. Industry Track.

[70] Y. Zhang, E. Alba, J. J. Durillo, S. Eldh, and M. Harman. Today/future importance analysis. In *ACM Genetic and Evolutionary Computation COnference (GECCO 2010)*, pages 1357–1364, Portland Oregon, USA, 7th–11th July 2010.

[71] Y. Zhang, A. Finkelstein, and M. Harman. Search based requirements optimisation: Existing work and challenges. In *International Working Conference on Requirements Engineering: Foundation for Software Quality (REFSQ'08)*, volume 5025, pages 88–94, Montpellier, France, 2008. Springer LNCS.

[72] Y. Zhang, M. Harman, and A. Mansouri. The SBSE repository: A repository and analysis of authors and research articles on search based software engineering. crestweb.cs.ucl.ac.uk/resources/sbse_repository/.

[73] Y. Zhang, M. Harman, and A. Mansouri. The multi-objective next release problem. In *GECCO 2007: Proceedings of the 9th annual conference on Genetic and evolutionary computation*, pages 1129 – 1137, London, UK, July 2007. ACM Press.

for automated search-based refactoring. In *Proceeding of the 4th workshop on Refactoring Tools (WRT '11)*, pages 41–44, Honolulu, HI, USA, 2011.

Challenges of Applying Ethnography to Study Software Practices

Carol Passos
Department of Computer
Science (DCC) - UFBA
40.170-110, Salvador-BA, Brazil
mcarolpassos@dcc.ufba.br

Daniela S. Cruzes
Department of Computer and
Information Science (IDI) - NTNU
NO-7491, Trondheim, Norway
dcruzes@idi.ntnu.no

Tore Dybå
SINTEF
NO-7465, Trondheim, Norway
tore.dyba@sintef.no

Manoel Mendonça
Department of Computer
Science (DCC) - UFBA
40.170-110, Salvador-BA, Brazil
mgmendonca@dcc.ufba.br

ABSTRACT

Ethnography is about the adoption of a cultural lens to observe and interpret events, actions, and behaviors, ensuring that they are placed in a relevant and meaningful context. Using this approach, it is possible to capture and analyze software development practices. Our aims are to illustrate the use of an ethnographic approach in a case study of agile software development adoption, to discuss the methodological challenges involved, and to provide support to others who conduct ethnographic studies of software practice. An ethnographic case study was conducted, employing participant observation, interviews, and document analysis. Difficulties and decisions were recorded and compared with those encountered in the literature. Finally, key challenges and guidelines to tackle them were discussed and documented. We identified five key challenges of applying ethnography to the study of software practices: (a) working in collaboration with and having something to offer to the participating company; (b) the insider/outsider dynamic of participant observation; (c) the balance between participant listening and participant observation; (d) the researcher's relationship with the participants; and (e) the rigor in qualitative work that involves the dilemma of the contextualization to be sufficiently broad and detailed. This study shows that ethnographic methods are indispensable when trying to understand software practice, and that the fundamental challenge for the researcher is to balance the role of participant observer with rigorous fieldwork.

Categories and Subject Descriptors

D.2 [**Software Engineering**]

General Terms

Management, Measurement, Experimentation, Human Factors.

Keywords

Qualitative Methods; Collaborative Ethnographic Research; Participant Observation.

1. INTRODUCTION

Ethnography is about telling a credible, rigorous, and authentic story, giving voice to people in their local context. This story is told through the eyes of people as they pursue their daily lives in their own communities [7]. Typically, the ethnographic story relies on verbatim quotations and descriptions of scenarios that allow an *inside* perspective of the context of the people under observation. Ethnography derives from traditional anthropology where time in the field is needed to get a comprehensive description and understanding of a setting, group, or culture under study [7].

Ethnographic research methods have played a substantial role in sociological research during the last half-century and are now used in many disciplines, especially those that involve social and human factors [3]. They have become widely used in the study of information systems and can be a highly useful methodology for addressing a range of research questions related to SE practices [2][10][15][17][21][22].

In particular, ethnographic methods are helpful in generating rich and detailed accounts of software project teams, their interactions with project stakeholders, and their approaches for delivering products, as well as in-depth accounts of their experiences. Ethnography is a way of getting close to the reality of a social phenomenon, of a software team's interactions, communications, and relationships. Additionally, since it aims to generate holistic social accounts, ethnographic research can identify, explore, and link social phenomena, which on the surface, seem to have little connection with each other.

However, applying an ethnographic approach to SE can be both challenging and demanding. The problems and objects of study in SE, by their very specific nature, require empirical methods suited to specific contexts. Certain phenomena, for example, require a specialist understanding of the concepts under study and extensive data collection that lasts for months and years, rather than days and weeks. Also, the ethnographic researcher needs to be aware of the effects on the behavior of the people being studied [12].

The aim of this paper is to present the methodological challenges of applying ethnography to a case study aimed at characterizing an agile project team's belief system and its origins, sources, and impacts on the team's software development practices [15]. In particular, we focus on the social interactions, communications, and relationships that arise as an intrinsic part of adopting agile software development practices. For that, we applied an ethnographic approach, employing participant observation, interviews, and document analysis. The main idea of our approach involved performing ethnography with its holistic and contextual vision, including some characteristics of action research, such as its collaborative and reflexive approach; used to recommend how to improve the studied practices to the company.

In particular, we address: (a) the advantages and challenges associated with working in collaboration with, and having results to offer to, the participating company (b) the insider/outsider dynamic of participant observation; (c) the balance between participant listening and participant observation; (d) the researcher's relationship with the participants; and (e) the rigor in qualitative work that involves the dilemma of the contextualization to be sufficiently broad and detailed. We relate our findings to relevant ethnographic theory, e.g., [3][7] [8][11][12][14][24][25] to contribute to a better understanding on how to apply ethnography to study software practices.

The rest of the paper is organized as follows: Section 2 introduces ethnography as a research method. Section 3 describes how we conducted the ethnographic case study. Section 4 discusses the challenges of applying ethnography as a research approach, implications for research and practice, and limitations. Conclusions and opportunities for further work are presented in Section 5.

2. BACKGROUND

Social anthropologists, to aid in the understanding of different cultures and environments, originally founded ethnographic research methods. Ethnography is about living in and immersing in the culture of the researched group for an extended period of time. It is about participating in social relations, seeking to understand actions within the context of an observed setting, and how people act and make sense of their environment. A key purpose of ethnography is to provide a detailed, in-depth description of everyday life and practice [8].

Ethnographic methods seek to understand practice in its own terms, while trying to minimize the impact of the researchers' backgrounds, prejudices, and assumptions. Ethnographers adopt a cultural lens to interpret observed events, actions, and behaviors, ensuring that they are placed in a culturally relevant and meaningful context. It is also important to participate in social relations and interactions to gather data by an active attitude in an observed setting.

Fieldwork is the most characteristic element of the ethnographic method. Typically, and concurrently with data collection, ethnographers devote a large amount of their fieldwork time to formally analyze and reanalyze their data [7]. While still in the field, interim reports, which are the beginnings of the ethnographically informed final report, are produced to enable feedback on the data-gathering cycle. Narratives can be made and revised to take into account the ethnographer's evolving knowledge.

In this context, the primary research technique is *participant observation* [6], which involves direct observation, participation in the life of the observed group, and collective discussions through an intensive involvement with people in their natural environment, usually over an extended period of time. It is a three-stage process in which the researcher first, gains access to a particular community. Second, lives and/or works among the people under study in order to grasp their world views and ways of life, and third, returns to make sense of the collected data through writing up an account of the community's culture [3]. The process of immersion may be unsystematic in the beginning, being somewhat uncontrolled and casual. However, even in the early stages of fieldwork, the ethnographer searches out experiences and events as they come to his/her attention. Thus, the participant observation technique becomes more refined, as the researcher understands more about the culture.

The acquisition of knowledge in ethnographic research is a cyclical process. It begins with a panoramic view of the community, closes in to a fine focus on details, and then goes back to the larger picture again, but this time with detailed information. The focus narrows and widens repeatedly during the process, because only by both deep diving and swimming on the surface can the ethnographer portray the cultural landscape in detail rich enough for others to comprehend and appreciate [7].

The traditional principles of participant observation and ethnographic fieldwork require a full immersion of the researcher in the chosen field of study, learning the day-to-day and extraordinary essence of social and cultural life by *being there* [18]. Ideally, the researcher does not disturb or change the natural setting.

For most anthropologists, ethnography involves actually living in the communities of the studied people, participating in their activities, interviewing them, drawing maps of the context, and collecting artifacts [9]. Critics of the approach are concerned about researchers getting over-involved with the people and environment under study, perhaps disturbing and changing the natural setting [18]. By contrast, some sociological ethnographers do not actually live with the people they study or spend most of their time with them. Instead, they focus on what happens in a particular institution when in operation; their participant observation is part-time, but sufficient to complete the research. In any case, ethnography must have a holistic view of the culture or group under study.

One can build a blueprint or roadmap to help the ethnographer conceptualize the steps to build knowledge and understanding. The goal is to find an effective problem-solving sequence [6]. The fieldwork approach shapes the design of all ethnographic work. The ethnographer typically begins with a survey period to learn the basics: language, history, structure, and function of the culture under study. After that it is possible to draw social and conceptual boundaries to identify or confirm themes, subjects, problems, and questions of interest to compose the research design. The next step is to start the fieldwork to observe, interview, read, ask insightful questions, and to write down what is seen and heard. Life histories of articulate individuals can be especially illuminating. The ethnographer must then crosscheck, compare, and triangulate the findings [3].

Proper organization from the very beginning of the work is a good practice. Keeping data organized and at hand allows the ethnographer to make interim reports and anticipate testing hypothesis throughout the investigation. Analysis and report writing are more efficient when the data is structured during fieldwork. During the analysis, it is possible to examine hypothesis and perceptions to construct or refine a conceptual framework about the studied group or culture [7].

Table 1. Ethnography vs. Action Research

	ETHNOGRAPHY	ACTION RESEARCH
Goal	Go Native In-Depth Understanding of Culture Generate Rich and Detailed Social Account	Process Improving Knowledge Advancing Problem-Solving
Focus	Culture and Values	Process and Practices
Main Technique	Participant Observation	No specific technique
Fieldwork	Holistic Comparative Contextual	Essentially Collaborative Reflexive Problem-Solving Driven
Final Product	In-Depth Description of Group's Life	Improved practice New knowledge

Some ethnographers spend as much time formally analyzing and reanalyzing their data and writing their ethnographies as they do conducting fieldwork. The final stage of analysis is the most creative step of ethnographic research, because the synthesis of ideas and field information often lead to useful insights through allowing the mind to wander and consider unusual combinations of thoughts. However, the researcher must always check whether the data will support the findings or invalidate them.

Research proposals, field notes, memos, web sites, interim reports, final reports, articles, and books are the tangible products of ethnography. The written work can be shared with participants, to verify its accuracy, and with colleagues for review and consideration. If the ethnographer is a collaborative researcher, he or she might share documents with community members, who can edit and co-write the ethnographic findings.

The decision of leaving the field should be based on more than one reason [6]. The best reason is the belief that enough data has been gathered to say something significant about it, but sometimes the proximity of a deadline is the determining reason. Different researchers require different levels of confidence about research findings and conclusions, but when the general picture reaffirms itself over and over again, it is probably time to leave the field and continue the job from outside.

After leaving the field, the ethnographic work continues with the final stages of analysis in which field notes, interim reports, papers, and so on are used to draw an overall picture of how the practice system works and which data will sustain or break the findings. Thus, ethnography is both a research method and a product, typically in the form of a written text.

Nowadays, a more collaborative perspective to ethnography is commonly required in organizational contexts. In contrast to traditional ethnography, contemporary collaborative ethnographic research has applied strategies, such as participatory action research [2][6][11][20][23], that aim not only to analyze but also to improve work practices. Dittrich et al., for example, adopted an ethnographically inspired action research approach, which combines qualitative social science fieldwork, with problem-oriented method, technique, and process improvement [5]. However, it is noteworthy that *ethnography* and *action research* are two different approaches (as showed in Table1). Ethnography focuses on the culture and values of a target group with the aim of generating rich and detailed accounts to produce an in-depth description of the group's life, while action research focuses on processes and practices and how to improve them in a problem-solving paradigm [11].

3. CONDUCTING AN ETHNOGRAPHIC CASE STUDY

We have being running a long-term case study, involving software development projects, which has gone through a main cycle of 18 months. This study is now undergoing another cycle, lasting approximately 12 months, with the aim of characterizing an agile project team's belief system and to investigate its origins, sources, and impacts on the team's software development practices [15]. In particular, we have been focusing on the social interactions, communications, and relationships that arise as an intrinsic part of adopting agile software development practices. To do this, we have been applying an ethnographic approach, immersing ourselves in the day-to-day project activities to delve deeper into the complexity of team's belief system and uncover meanings of behaviors, actions and events.

The case study was set in a medium sized software company[1] in Brazil, in which projects were applying, for the first time, agile methods based on Scrum[2]. The company provides software development and evolution services as well as information technology infrastructure management services for customers of both the public and private sectors.

We adopted an approach that aimed explicitly to help the company to improve the work practices under study, getting some characteristics of action research, but mainly based on more modern approaches of ethnography [2][8][11][12]. In our context, this participatory approach was required, so we worked collaboratively to support their process improvement initiative.

The first author of the paper performed the interviews, observations, and document analysis according to [13][18][19]. It is important to note that the first author is an employee of the company in leave for PhD study. Therefore, there was a pre-existent common language between the interviewer and the participants of the study.

The particular project studied involved a system for electrical energy management and lasted for one year. The project team followed a well-defined process for software development and used a project management application for stories and bug tracking. They also kept detailed records of the project status reports and the backlog of stories and changes to the software. Other important documents, including quantitative measures, were used for project tracking and monitoring (Table 2).

Table 2. Project Profile

Attribute	PGE Project
Team Size	5
Team Members	2 full time developers, 2 part time developers, 1 scrum master, 1 product owner + project manager
Language	JAVA
Tool Usage	Open Source Software
Development Methodology	SCRUM + PMI Approaches
Non-Functional Requirements	Reliability, Performance, Continuity, Availability
Reuse	High
Stability Requirements	Medium stability
Staff Turn-over	Considered high by the project manager
Interviews	2 with product owner + project manager 2 with scrum master

[1] SOLUTIS Tecnologias. http://www.solutis.com.br/
[2] Scrum approach. http://www.Scrum.org/

3.1 Interviews

After a literature review and evaluation of research objectives and questions, we opted for an interview-based qualitative data collection approach called War Story [13]. War Story questionnaires usually have warm-up, past experience, lessons learned, and reaction questions. We used an iterative approach in which we defined a questionnaire (see Appendix A), used it for a set of interviews, analyzed the data, and improved the process for the next round of interviews.

Warm-up questions aimed to put the interviewees in the right mindset, to focus them on the interview subject. Our version of the questionnaire had two warm-up questions that asked about the participants' background and experience, and the main challenges of the current software project.

Past experience questions intended to investigate how living experiences could influence the participants' current behavior, trying to cover the main aspects of a software project reality. Our questionnaire had four of these questions. These questions are about the respondents' past experiences, involving software process, communication plan, software engineering technical practices, and project monitoring.

Lessons learned questions tried to capture the beliefs that emerged or evolved from the project experiences. To keep the questionnaire simple and balanced for the research kick-off, we had three war story questions about lessons learned. They aimed to understand the basis of how the beliefs, personal values, and the paradigms of the participants came to be and also how they determined the participants' choices and actions during the project.

Reaction questions asked about the participants' reactions and personal opinions on the impacts of the use of technologies, methods, and process on the software project. The questionnaire had two reaction questions that directly asked about the impacts of new technologies and unexpected effects of known and new technologies on projects.

Besides the typical war story questions, we added a few questions to identify beliefs related to practices that affected project *productivity*, *quality*, *time*, and *cost*. Those attributes are usually quantitatively measured in software organizations, so they helped to link quantitative and qualitative findings (*Metric-based Questions*). We had four of them in the questionnaire.

The first author asked the respondents to retell and revive specific and directed stories that illustrated the experiences we were trying to capture. The resulting data contained a considerable amount of contextual information, which enabled connections between different, but related, stories.

3.2 Observation and Document Analysis

Field notes and recordings of relevant interviews on completion of observations in meetings provided rich insight into social relations, events, and practices. We established specific goals for our observation task and some guided questions to drive the researchers' work (Appendix B). During observations, we immersed ourselves in the setting, using an informal approach, which allowed us to probe emerging issues about unusual events in a naturalistic manner.

Additionally, we collected organizational documents and attended team meetings. We compared our field notes from interviews and observations with the practices and processes laid down in documents and information about tasks. We also used document analysis to map the company and project contexts (see Appendix C). By triangulating our data sources and our instruments, we addressed issues of validity and obtained comprehensive insights into the application of ethnographic methods.

3.3 Study Analysis and Results

The first author conducted four interviews with two people in the front lines of the project that introduced agile programming recently. Each person was interviewed twice, once at the beginning and once at the end of the project, six months later. These four interviews were complemented by meeting observations and document analysis. The first author attended and recorded 40 meetings involving the interviewed participants and all the team members.

All field notes, including transcripts and recordings of meetings and interviews, were categorized, tabulated, and then analyzed via cycles of pattern coding, which labeled keywords, phrases, and paragraphs to group and summarize segments of text into classes of findings.

We analyzed the relevant events of past and current projects that might influence team beliefs or practices, including the SCRUM methodology training. Considering these scenarios, we captured and classified the beliefs found and described their main attributes: origin, context, meaning, impact, participant, and frequency.

We represented our main findings in a mind map [15], which is a diagram used to represent concepts, ideas, beliefs, or other items linked to, and arranged around, a central key phrase or idea [1][4]. These mind maps were useful to visualize, structure, and classify the beliefs and to organize related information. We guided a validation of the findings with the participants of the study in a focus group discussion. The group's responses and perceptions were analyzed both individually and in aggregate.

An important part of the mind map showed the *common beliefs* shared by the Product Owner and Scrum Master [15]. For example, both of them agreed that a good automated software testing approach is essential to the success of any project. The origin of this belief of the Product Owner was the experience in the current project. But, for the Scrum Master, the origin was in his past experiences in another company. They also cited some negative impacts on the project practices due to the absence of the automated software testing approach. Thus, the resulting mind map contains classes to represent the related elements: belief, meaning, origin and impact.

The study showed that the beliefs originated from two main sources: past and current project experience. Some beliefs triggered the adoption of new technologies, but the decision of which technology to adopt was mostly based on expert opinion and the current software engineering community buzz around it. We found *conflicting beliefs* between the Product Owner and the Scrum Master, which hindered the adoption of practices.

Some *conflicting beliefs* were subtle. For example, the interviewees agreed that current effort estimation practice was limited, but digging further, we found that they disagreed on which practice should substitute it. An even more subtle problem was when the interviewees had a *common belief*, but did not act upon it. We named those *semi-beliefs*. An example was the applicability of software testing automation for the organization; both Product Owner and Scrum Master seemed to believe in testing automation, but they were not adopting it.

Lastly, there were cases of common *strong beliefs*. This was the case of component reuse. Both, the Product Owner and Scrum Master actively acted on the direction of implementing good reuse practices from the very beginning of the project. This type of common *strong beliefs* were strengthened and transferred to other people involved in the project.

4. CHALLENGES OF APPLYING ETHNOGRAPHY

During the case study we identified five key challenges of using ethnographic methods to study software practices. Some of these challenges have also been discussed in the social science literature [8][11][12][14] and in SE literature [2][10][17][22]. We related our findings to relevant ethnographic theory, [3][7] [8][11][12][14] [24][25] to contribute to an improved understanding on how to apply ethnography to study software practices.

4.1 Collaborative Ethnography

A more cooperative and participatory perspective to ethnography is commonly required in organizational contexts. The challenge is to redirect and reinvent ethnography along such lines as collaborative ethnography – the collaboration of researchers and subjects in the production of ethnographic results, involving a side-by-side work of all parties in a mutually beneficial research program.

In Software Engineering is intrinsic in order to not only analyze, but also improve work practices. When doing ethnography through participant observation, the researcher must assume an attitude toward *being there* enough to experience the environment and nuanced aspects of socio-cultural life. This, at first, does not *allow* a collaborative approach to the research. Therefore, a researcher aiming to conduct ethnography faces the challenge of not influencing the practices in its natural setting.

In our case, at first we were only going to interview and observe the team members about their beliefs, but we noticed that we also needed to give feedback to the team about their common and conflicting beliefs, so that they could act as a unit and resolve the conflicts that hindered the adoption of some practices. We then ran a focus group together with a feedback meeting on the results of the study. As a result of this meeting, the team was able to prioritize action to solve the problems in the team. When confronting with conflicting team's beliefs and trying to find solutions for the conflicts, it was important that the team members knew that we were impartial towards the beliefs of how they were impacting the team practices. Considering our ethnographer role and required skill for the study, we sought to communicate well and openly, also being honest, trusting, realistic, and objective on our research.

Engaging in a shared process with the practitioners freed access to some more subtle dynamics of the team processes and practices. As participant observers and interviewers we realized, for example, that the Scrum Master and Product Owner were concerned about story and task estimation. At that time, the stories were estimated by hours and the Product Owner was responsible for this task. The Scrum master clearly disagreed with this strategy. He believed that the team should be more autonomous to estimate task and stories using the story points technique. The task estimation practice was, therefore, not working well for the project, so together we listed some actions to be done to improve it.

We dealt with this challenge in a similar manner as reported in social science literature. We have adapted our approach to ethnography grounded in collaborative research practice and we have engaged in mutual knowledge exchange with the participants, based on Lassister [11] and Lewis and Russell's [12].

A resembling approach was adopted in some other SE studies. Boden et al.'s study [2] introduced the concept of Business Ethnography and illustrated their experiences of adapting and implementing a collaborative approach using a typical action research cycle: research, analysis, and feedback workshops with the aim of finding better ways of cooperating across temporal, spatial and organizational barriers. Robinson et al. [17] used the findings to uncover and understand problems and thereby delineate their solution spaces. Their study revealed potential solutions to some problems related to knowledge sharing, using the interview responses to provide a context in which the problems could be elucidated and possible solutions could be discussed.

4.2 Insider/Outsider Dynamic

The participant observation technique also requires the ethnographer to have both, an *insider* and *outsider* posture [12]. The challenge is to combine participation with observation, seeking to understand the social reality and also trying to see familiar settings with a professional distance that allows adequate observation and recording of data [7]. There is a need for a balance in the researcher's participation in the team.

In our context, we were able to identify some common and conflicting beliefs in the team. Some conflicting beliefs were subtle and our approach of being inside their world at one moment and offering an outsider's perspective in another moment definitely helped to identify and point out those conflicts between the involved stakeholders. For example, during the observation of the Scrum meetings, we could perceive that some issues related to Scrum, such as self-management team, generated conflicting beliefs between team members and the Product Owner. We had the opportunity to confirm this during a subsequent interview. This finding was only possible because we assumed an insider position, so we were able to see the interactions and relationships between the people under observation with an inside perspective of context.

Sometimes the researcher can assume the role of being only an insider and this attitude may hinder some important discoveries. In the initial interviews we did not explore some possibilities related to participants' responses because we thought we already knew the answer for them. Later, we realized that this was a mistake, because we had not properly obtained the participants' point of view. In an attempt to mitigate this, we performed complementary interviews to ask more details about origins and impacts of beliefs related to some practices.

On the opposite end, when the researcher is only an outsider, some mistaken interpretations can arise because the researcher does not manage to take an appropriate insider posture. The drawbacks of this situation also involve difficulties to overcome data access barriers. In our case study, we had full access to recordings of the project meetings because the participants were comfortable to give us confidential material. As insiders, they knew we were able to handle it and to interpret the data properly.

In some previous studies [2][12][17], as well as in our study, the ethnographers needed to know how to stand in-between their research subjects, contexts, and demands, and the ethnographic product. In our opinion, researchers must evolve their participant observation skills to accommodate an embedded analytic vision. In Boden et al [2], the researchers actively looked for a plurality of views to analyze the findings and their implications for the studied projects, taking into account their own roles in the projects, and constantly reflecting on them during the research, even in times when it was only possible to conduct remote interviews with team members of different sites. Lewis and Russell [12] identified and discussed the insider/outsider dynamic of participant observation as one of the key elements of embedded research practice. They conducted the research as some kind of team member and, even when they were not allowed to engage as a participant in clinical practice, for example, they did not stop to work alongside their co-workers in the community. Finally, Robinson et al [17] discussed their experiences and put the observations in the context of the study in order to maintain their perspective of strangeness and reduce the possibility of introducing bias.

4.3 Observation and Listening

Participant observation traditionally involves direct observation as the method of data collection. Other appropriate methods involve informal interviews, participation in the life of the group, collective discussions, analysis of personal documents produced within the group, self-analysis, results from activities undertaken off or online, and life stories.

Participant listening is an important technique employed by ethnographers, particularly among those who live in an interview society, where interviewing has became common practice. It is an appropriate way of participating and getting involved in software development contexts. The interviews allowed a deeper understanding of the obtained data through our observations [8].

In our context, beliefs are intangible. They are in the head of the team members. Usually beliefs are not externalized as part of their daily activities. It was very challenging to only observe the team members and try to understand what each person's beliefs were. We employed an interview-based qualitative data collection technique called *storytelling,* which adopts a specific story form, *the war story* [13]. Our war story questionnaire went beyond asking questions that allowed the team members to retell and revive specific and directed stories that illustrated the experiences we were trying to capture. So, it was possible to obtain personal opinions on the impacts of beliefs on agile team practices. Once we had identified the beliefs, we could observe their actions upon them.

For example, despite the fact that the Scrum Master and Product Owner shared the same belief of using tools for test automation, they did not adopt these tools in the project. We could observe that the Scrum Master and Product Owner did not seem to act according to their beliefs and, consequently, there were some negative impacts on project practices such as: no time left in sprint for bug correction; poor coverage and low effectiveness of the test and inspection practice; and greater effort to perform regression testing. In the interviews with the Scrum Master and Product Owner we identified that they did not really believe that tools for test automation were the appropriate solution for their test problems. Thus, the data collected in these interviews enabled connections between the participants' stories and our observations. Thus, we strongly recommend that SE researchers be both a participant listener and observer, because the data captured in the field can reflect more of what is heard than what is seen; casual conversations and formal interviews can be construed as part of what is observed in the field.

The same approach is advocated by several authors who argue that the practice of participant listening should sit alongside with participant observation as an equally valid way of gaining ethnographic knowledge [2][8][16][17]. In order to get a complete picture, the researchers deploying Business Ethnography [2] relied on intensive, individual interviews with all participants involved in the project alongside other ethnographic methods like on-site observation to complement the interviews, which helped them to get a rich understanding of the project context that is related to the different perspectives, intentions, and expectations of the participants. Forsey's hypothesis [8], that ethnography is at least as much about conversation as it is about observation, was confirmed when his thesis and subsequent monograph was not devoid of observational description, but the data presented reflected more of what he heard in the field than what he saw. In Reeves et al.'s research [16], ethnographers routinely used informal or conversational interviews during their observations, which allowed them to discuss, probe emerging issues, or ask questions about unusual events in a naturalistic manner. To answer the first research question of the study related to influence of social factors, Robinson et al [17] collected data from organisations using a combination of semi-structured interviews and ethnographic-based observation.

4.4 Relationship with the Participants

The relationship between researchers and participants in an ethnographical work is a core element for successful research. As the researcher immerses in the organizational context, this relationship tends to grow and improve gradually, as people get to know each other and become closer, or they gradually deteriorate. People in a relationship tend to influence each other, share their thoughts, beliefs and feelings, and engage in activities together.

In an ethnographic study, the researcher becomes a member of the community under study, since the researcher has an active role in the target projects. In this context, he or she could reasonably be described as a practitioner and as a research scientist at the same time. But being a member of the community under study has both challenges and advantages for the researchers. The main advantage is that researchers and practitioners share the same organizational culture and so researchers are accepted and have common vocabulary with the participants, therefore the participants can relax and focus on working in their natural way. The challenge lies in the tension involved in moving between two roles (researcher and practitioner), and maintaining a non-judgmental orientation and a perspective of strangeness. At the same time, ethnographers have to be flexible, patient, and persistent in their work to overcome data access barriers.

In our study, we had to be non-judgmental in order to avoid bias in collecting and interpreting data. For example, during the focus group meeting two project team members discussed some points related to conflicting beliefs. For the Scrum Master the team should avoid direct contact with the customer, but for the Product Owner this direct contact between the team and the customer could impact positively the team's commitment to the quality of the product delivered and sense of business value. We had to keep a neutral position throughout this discussion. We also sought to minimize our effect on the behavior of the subjects under study, trying not to get over-involved with the people and environment to not disturb the natural setting.

In Boden et al.'s study, the researchers were subjected to similar challenges as the practitioners [2]. Known problems of conducting research on global software development teams included getting access to the research field in the first place as well as dealing with constraints such as organizational hierarchies and conflicting interests that might hinder a deeper immersion of the researchers in the environment [2]. Reeves et al.'s research described the relationship between researcher and the participants and the ethical issues, related to informed consent agreements, which arose from this close relation [16]. In Robinson et al.'s study, the relationship between the researchers and the participants was particularly significant because ethical issues concerning formal contracts or informed consent agreements were problematic in their experience [17].

4.5 Rigor and Contextualization
In the context of ethnographic work, the researcher is the main instrument of the ethnographic study. It is more of a general style rather than following specific prescriptions in a procedure [18]. Rigorousness in data collection and analysis is essential in order to avoid bias.

One aspect of the rigorous approach is that all findings must be grounded in the data and it is important to look for disconfirming instances, seeking behavioral confirmation, not just what people say but what they actually do. One challenge is to deal with a substantial amount of data derived from the ethnographic process. We used tools to deal with the collected data, which helped to work on the data in several iterations. We attended and recorded 40 meetings involving the interviewed participants and all the team members. For each hour of recorded interviews, we spent an average of five hours transcripting with an average of 13 pages, and one hour of pattern coding to tag key words, phrases, and paragraphs. The data collected was then analyzed via cycles of pattern coding which grouped segments of data into 26 themes.

In terms of validity of the results, we checked the answers from the interviews with our observations during the project. When the conclusions were reached, we discussed them with the team members in a focus group meeting. With this practice we prevented inappropriate assumptions or interpretations.

For us, theory and ethnography should be conjoined to produce a concrete sense of the social, so we conducted our ethnographic study with an underlying theory, building a conceptual framework to represent graphically the beliefs, their origins, sources, and relationships with team practices. This theoretical research approach helped to define the problem and to limit the research scope and effort, establishing a baseline to begin observations and the research over time.

In pursuing rigor in the research also involves the dilemma of sufficiently broad and detailed contextualization. Contextualizing data involves placing observations and interviews into a larger perspective. Each scene exists within a multilayered and interrelated context [7]. Contextualization helps to provide a more accurate characterization of the software practices and helps to prevent misunderstandings that can happen especially when a setting is familiar. One example is that sufficient description and quotations were included in our reports to allow readers to understand our research context. However, no study can capture an entire culture or group context; even a comprehensive report has to omit a great deal.

In our case study, the participation of the first author in the Scrum meetings of the project helped us to realize that there were common strong beliefs, like component reuse, for example, in which both the Product Owner and Scrum master, actively acted on the direction of implementing good reuse practices from the very beginning of the project, even with several unfavourable conditions. Only with the contextual information about the origins and sources of their beliefs and the project environment was it possible to capture and understand how strong these beliefs really were.

In Robinson et al.'s study [17], rigorousness in data collection takes the form of three main principles: triangulation, seeking disconfirmation, and iterative development of understanding. The researchers employed triangulation by using data from different sources, for example, from interviews with different people having similar or different roles, from the artefacts, from observations of different roles and from informal conversations. They also focused on behavioural confirmation and searched for disconfirming instances during analysis and used both formal and informal feedback, presenting tentative findings to the participants.

5. DISCUSSION
This study highlights the methodological challenges involved in applying ethnography to study software practices. Here we discuss these challenges all together in order to support others who wish to conduct this type of study. Also in this section, limitations and implications for research will be presented.

5.1 Implications for Research in SE
Considering challenges 4.1 and 4.2, we highlight that it is not easy to immerse in a company with a dual objective of improving organizational problems and generating scientific knowledge. It demands an additional set of knowledge items and skills on the researcher in order to well conduct the process and provide relevant results. The researcher needs to formulate theories and ideas, prepare theoretical explanations, and establish collaboration with the people and the organization. In this scenario, it is important not to lose focus on the research goals and make constant reviews of the study plan and protocol. This is a product of the insider/outsider dynamic of participant observation, which requires the ethnographer to have both, an insider view as a practitioner and the ability of having an outsider's perspective as a researcher.

The study also shows a clear need for a particular way to deal with ethnographic research involving software development practices. SE contexts require a new approach that aims not only to analyze but also to improve work practices, engaging in a shared process with the practitioners. The researcher needs to demonstrate an ability to collaborate with the setting, understand the social reality and, at the same time, offer an outsider's perspective. Our study also highlights that it is important for the researchers to minimize their effects on the behavior of the people being studied. They should assume a collaborative posture and have something to offer to the participating company, but must avoid getting over-involved with its environment.

During the study, we made use of techniques that showed to be feasible, like a combination of interviews, observations, and document analysis. No doubt, the use of an interview technique contributed to meet challenge 4.3 through the balance of the practices of participant listening and participant observation, and the provision of a better perception of the participants' stories and their connection to the observations. The evidence suggests that researchers should consider the possibility of placing engaged listening on a similar footing to participant observation. After some casual conversations and formal interviews, the big picture can be construed as part of what was observed in the field, so it is relevant to say that the data captured in the field can reflect more of what is heard than what is seen.

In ethnographic studies the research instrument (the ethnographer) needs to be properly calibrated to ensure the validity of the findings. The premise of *going native* cannot result in discontinuation of the study or moving from the role of researcher to the role of advocate. However, some conflicting interpretations among the participants and researchers can emerge. To avoid this situation and overcome challenges 4.4 and 4.5, we adopted the practice of discussing and validating field notes with the participants. The participant's perceptions were analyzed both individually and on an aggregated basis in order to build the big picture of the findings and their relative importance. As mentioned before, this practice contributes to rigor and can mitigate inappropriate interpretations.

Considering the ethnographer role and required skill for this type of research, we recommend that the ethnographers seek to communicate well and openly, participate fully, work together with the participants, and be honest, trusting, realistic, and objective. Also, fieldworkers have to be flexible, patient, and persistent in their work to overcome the inherent barriers and difficulties of data collection and analysis.

Our findings indicate that researchers should balance the role of participant observer with rigorous fieldwork. Rigorousness in data collection and analysis is essential in order to avoid bias. It is also important to look for disconfirming instances. Methodological triangulation is a well-suited approach for this purpose as it can be used to perform a cross-examination. By combining multiple observations, theories, interviews, and empirical materials, researchers can overcome the weaknesses and intrinsic biases, address issues of validity and problems that occur during ethnographic studies, and obtain comprehensive insights into the application of ethnographic methods.

The final product of the ethnographic study will depend directly on the decisions of the researcher. These decisions are crucial to allow the production of relevant scientific findings, but also to reconcile them with the organization's business needs and meet challenge 4.1. Here, again, careful planning and execution has to be considered. In spite of that, it is still important to be flexible and adapt to occurrences of the daily project activities.

5.2 Limitations
The general critics of a methodological study based on a single case study also apply to an ethnographic study, among them one may list: uniqueness, difficulty to generalize the results, and introduction of bias by researchers.

In our study, we transformed the findings from empirical statements to theoretical statements, which involve generalizing data from observations and perceptions by discussing them in accordance with the ethnographic literature. In this respect, we related our findings to relevant examples of ethnographic research within the SE literature and compared them with the related ethnography theory.

Another limitation is that we were working with the findings of one particular project within one particular organization. The participants were professionals using typical development technologies in a typical working environment, e.g., the natural

setting demanded by ethnographic approach. Nonetheless, the case study's environment is quite context specific, since the participants belong to the same company.

In addition, the study shows that running ethnographic research in SE has some specific limitations. It is not easy to get involved in a software company with a dual objective of solving organizational problems and generating scientific knowledge. In a competitive industry like SE, to get information on projects, processes, and practices is not an easy task, because of confidentiality issues and the fact that empirical research is not a high priority for this industry. Hence, in order to achieve a successful research project, a combination of ethnography with other strategies, such as action research, can provide relevant results and overcome some intrinsic limitations.

We should say that we do not have a complete list of challenges, thus, further studies should be performed to point to other challenges of applying ethnography in SE contexts. Also, there is a risk that our findings could be influenced by factors that escaped our attention. One common view is that it is a good practice to discuss and validate findings with other researchers and with the participants to seek the completeness of the conclusions. We have done this partially among the researchers involved in this paper.

6. CONCLUSION AND FURTHER WORK
Applying an ethnographic approach can be both challenging and demanding, it requires a long time to collect data, sometimes years. Hence, it becomes necessary to take into account the influence of the researchers' presence and their effects, regarding the aim to support and collaborate with the participating companies, rather than just studying them.

In this study we identified five categories of challenges of applying ethnography in a case study involving an agile software project. Each challenge was described in terms of the current state of the practice and how we conceived the goals for future works.

Several ways of addressing the challenges were outlined. Together, the challenges suggest that there is a particular way to deal with software development practices, which requires approaches that aim explicitly to construct a cooperative workspace, encompassing the researchers and the project team.

It is important to emphasize the different types of observer roles and the degree of participation in order to, in some moments, be an outsider and, in others, an insider. Besides that, we recommended to use methodological triangulation to avoid bias due the close relationship with the participants.

Our next step is to conduct new ethnographic studies with other software projects. Through the synthesis of the evidence, we intend to contribute to provide rich narrative accounts of the ethnographic research activity, and elucidate more questions and issues that arise from the use of ethnographic methods to study the practice of software development.

7. ACKNOWLEDGMENTS
This work was partially supported by the scholarship from the CAPES Foundation, process number 5744-11-3 and by the National Institute of Science and Technology for Software Engineering (INES), funded by CNPq, grant 573964/2008-4.

The authors are grateful to all involved in this study, specially the interviewees for their insights and cooperation and to the SOLUTIS organization for supporting this work.

8. REFERENCES

[1] Attride-Stirling, J., "Thematic networks: an analytical tool for qualitative research," Qualitative Research 1(3): 385–405, December 2001.

[2] Boden, A., Müller, C., Nett, B."Conducting a business ethnography in global software development projects of small German enterprises". IST-53(9): 1012-1021, 2011.

[3] Crang M. and Cook I. "Doing ethnographies", UK: Sage, 2007.

[4] Cruzes, D., Dybå, T. "Recommended steps for thematic synthesis in software engineering". Proc. of ESEM'11, Banff-Alberta, Canada, September, 2011.

[5] Dittrich Y., Rönkkö, K., Eriksson, J. "Cooperative method development: Combining qualitative empirical research with method, technique and process improvement". EMSE 13(3): 231–260, 2008.

[6] Fægri T.E., Dybå T., M. Dingsøyr, T. "Introducing knowledge redundancy practice in software development: Experiences with job rotation in support work". IST 52(10): 1118–1132, 2010.

[7] Fetterman D. "Ethnography: step-by-step", 3rd ed. USA: Sage, 2010.

[8] Fotsey M.G." Ethnography as participant listening". Ethnography - 11(4): 558–572, 2010.

[9] Hammersley, M. "Ethnography: problems and prospects", Ethnography and Education, 1(1):3-14, 2006.

[10] Karn, J.S., Cowling, A.J." Using ethnographic methods to carry out human factors research in software engineering". Behavior Research Methods Journal. BRM-38(3), 495-503, 2006.

[11] Lassiter, L. "Collaborative Ethnography and Public Anthropology". Current Anthropology - 46(1):83-106, 2005.

[12] Lewis S.J., Russel, A.J. "Being embedded: A way forward for ethnographic research". Ethnography - 12(3): 398-416, 2011.

[13] Lutters, W.G., Seaman, C.B. "Revealing actual documentation usage in software maintenance through war stories". IST 1(49):576–587, 2007.

[14] Ortner, S.B."Access: Reflections on studying up in Hollywood". Ethnography - 11(2): 211–233, 2010.

[15] Passos, C., Braun, P., Cruzes, D., Mendonça, M. "Analyzing the impact of beliefs in software project practices". Proc. of ESEM'11, Banff-Alberta, Canada, September, 2011.

[16] Reeves, S., Kuper, A., Hodges. B. "Qualitative research methodologies: ethnography". BMJ, 337(10), 1336-1020, 2008.

[17] Robinson, H., Segal, J., Sharp, H. "Ethnographically-informed empirical studies of software practice". IST-1(49): 540–551, 2007.

[18] Robson, C. "Real world research : a resource for users of social research methods in applied settings", 3rd ed. USA: Wiley, 2011.

[19] Runeson P., Host M. "Guidelines for conducting and reporting case study research in software engineering". Empirical Software Engineering, 2008, 2(14):131–164.

[20] Santos, P. S. M. ; Travassos, G. H. . "Action Research Can Swing the Balance in Experimental Software Engineering". Advances in Computers, v. 83, p. 205-276, 2011.

[21] Sharp, H.,Souza, C., Dittrich, Y. "Using Ethnographic Methods in Software Engineering Research". Proc. of ICSE'10, Cape Town, South Africa, May, 2010.

[22] Sigfridsson A., Sheehan, A.. "On qualitative methodologies and dispersed communities: Reflections on the process of investigating an open source community". IST- 53(9): 981–993, 2001.

[23] Sjøberg D.I.K., Dybå T., M. Jørgensen M. "The future of empirical methods in software engineering research". In Future of Software Engineering, IEEE Press, pp.358–378, 2007.

[24] Willis, P., Trondman , M. "Manifesto for Ethnography". Ethnography - 1(1): 5–16, 2000.

[25] Wilson, W.J., Chaddha , A. "The role of theory in ethnography approach". Ethnography - 10(4): 549–564, 2009.

APPENDIX A:
INTERVIEW QUESTIONNAIRE

Warm-up questions:

1. What methodologies, software architectures, technologies, application domain, and types of client and size of projects have you worked with?
2. What are the main challenges of your current project?

Past experience questions:

3. Could you cite a past experience where the absence or presence of well-defined work process impacted (positively or negatively) the project's progress?
4. Could you cite a past experience where the absence or presence of risk and communication plans impacted (positively or negatively) the project's progress?
5. Could you cite a past experience where failures in software engineering practices impacted the project's progress?
6. Could you cite a past experience where the absence or presence of project monitoring process by metrics impacted (positively or negatively) the project's progress?

Lessons learned questions:

7. Could you tell me different and similar practices adopted in past projects and in the current project?
8. What best practices related to your expertise and experience were useful to apply to your current project? Could you tell me about their application?
9. What situation or risk have you tried to prevent or mitigate in the current project on account of experiences already lived? Cite and comment.

Reaction questions:

10. In what aspects is the software development methodology of the company impacting your project?
11. Have any unexpected effect or impact happened after your current project started to use this methodology? Cite and explain.

Metric-based questions:

12. What affects, positively and negatively, the productivity of your project? Cite and explain.
13. What affects, positively and negatively, the quality of your project? Cite and explain.
14. What affects, positively and negatively, the time schedule of your project? Cite and explain.
15. What affects, positively and negatively, the cost of your project? Cite and explain.

APPENDIX B:
OBSERVATION INSTRUMENT

Specific Goals to Record:

- personal values, paradigms, and folktales of the project team members.
- interactions between project team members.
- activities actually performed by the project team.
- practices adopted by members of the project team.
- impact of the practices of team members on the project.
- arguments for and against a particular practice.
- influence of a practice on another practice in the project.
- events that happened during the work of project team.
- exceptions during the work of project team.
- tools used by the project team members.
- time spent on activities performed by project team.
- metrics that show the practices adopted by the team.
- other phenomena relevant to the research.

Guided questions:

1. What activities are actually performed by the project team?
2. What practices are actually adopted by the project team?
3. How often these practices are adopted by the project team?
4. Are these practices being adopted properly by the project team?
5. Which profile adopts certain practices within the project?
6. How to understand the folklore behind the practices in the project team?
7. How to understand the meaning of folklore for the team?
8. How to understand the origin of folklore in the team?
9. How to perceive the impact of folklore on the project?
10. How to understand the influence of folklore on other folklore within the project?
11. How to characterize the folklore behind the practices in the project team?
12. How to track the impact of folklore on the project? (history, timeline, context, etc.)
13. How to measure the impact of folklore on the project?

APPENDIX C:
CONTEXT INSTRUMENT

Company Context:	Project Context:
ID:	ID:
Company Name:	Project Name:
Background:	Main Goal:
Creation:	Domain
Location:	Customer :
Segment:	Origin:
Services Offer:	Customer Type:
Annual Revenue:	Customer Segment:
Number of Employees:	Start Date:
Certifications:	Size (PF):
Standard Process:	Productivity(H/PF):
Project Team Context:	Time:
Member Name:	Technology Platform:
Role:	Methodology:
Role Description:	Tools:
Seniority:	Metrics:
Experience Time:	
Competences:	
Mini-CV:	

What Works for Whom, Where, When, and Why?
On the Role of Context in Empirical Software Engineering

Tore Dybå
Department of Informatics
University of Oslo and SINTEF
NO-7465 Trondheim, Norway
tore.dyba@sintef.no

Dag I.K. Sjøberg
Department of Informatics
University of Oslo
NO-0316 Oslo, Norway
dagsj@ifi.uio.no

Daniela S. Cruzes
Department of Computer and
Information Science, NTNU
NO-7491 Trondheim, Norway
dcruzes@idi.ntnu.no

ABSTRACT

Context is a central concept in empirical software engineering. It is one of the distinctive features of the discipline and it is an indispensable part of software practice. It is likely responsible for one of the most challenging methodological and theoretical problems: study-to-study variation in research findings. Still, empirical software engineering research is mostly concerned with attempts to identify universal relationships that are independent of how work settings and other contexts interact with the processes important to software practice. The aim of this paper is to provide an overview of how context affects empirical research and how empirical software engineering research can be better 'contextualized' in order to provide a better understanding of what works for whom, where, when, and why. We exemplify the importance of context with examples from recent systematic reviews and offer recommendations on the way forward.

Categories and Subject Descriptors
D.2 [**Software Engineering**]

General Terms
Management, Measurement, Experimentation, Theory

Keywords
Evidence-Based Software Engineering, Generalization, Theory, Empirical Methods, Sociotechnical System

1. INTRODUCTION
What is best? Pair programming or solo programming? Test-first or test-last? A multitude of studies have been performed to answer these and other similar questions of the type: "Is <technology x> better than <technology y>?" However, asking the general question of whether pairs outperform individuals in programming tasks, or whether test-driven development results in higher productivity, is meaningless. It is meaningless since these questions can be answered with "Yes" or "No" depending on the setting of the study. Still, posing research questions of this type, without considering contextual influences like the subjects of the study, the location, the time period, and the rational of the study, seems to prevail.

However, we cannot expect a technology to be universally good or universally bad, only more (or less) appropriate in some circumstances and for some organizations [19]. The settings in which practice takes place are rarely, if ever, the same. For example, one software organization will have a different environment or be influenced by different environmental factors to that of another software organization. The size of the organization, types of customers, country or geographical location, the age of the organization, all impose different influences in unique ways. Additionally, the human factors, which form the organizational culture and make one setting different from another one, also influence the way software development is performed. We know that these issues are important for the successful uptake of research into practice and that there are interrelationships among organizational systems, structures, processes, technologies, settings, and cultures. However, the nature of these relationships is poorly understood.

This dependence of a potentially large number of relevant context variables in any study is an important reason for why empirical software engineering (SE) is so hard. Because of this, we cannot a priori assume that the results of a particular study apply outside the specific context in which it was run [6].

In an effort to bring context information in empirical research in SE more into consideration, Kitchenham et al. [32] suggested the following general guideline: "Be sure to specify as much of the industrial context as possible. In particular, clearly define the entities, attributes, and measures that are capturing the contextual information." However, as Whetten pointed out, it is not of much help to have a long context description if it is short on explanation [48].

Such explanation relies on understanding and interpretation of research evidence in light of the features and characteristics surrounding it. Contrary to empirical SE's treatment of context as a stable set of attributes of the world, the problem is that these surroundings themselves are selected and interpreted in different ways. There is an implicit parallel with linguistics here; that the meaning of a word is determined by the words and sentences that surround it. This raises the question about what a SE context is, how it is selected, and by whom.

The aim of this paper is to address this question and to provide an overview of how context affects empirical SE research and how this research can be better 'contextualized.' The remainder of the paper is organized as follows: Section 2 provides an overview of the concept of context and describes important dimensions and implications of context. Section 3 describes relationships between empirical studies and context, with examples from test-driven development and pair programming. Section 4 points to a potential way forward by suggesting how SE research can be better contextualized. Section 5 concludes.

2. WHAT IS CONTEXT?

The word contextus is of Latin origin and stands for weaving together or to make a connection [38]. Approaches to context and contextual dimensions range widely, reflecting different philosophical stances and practical orientations. In linguistics, for example, context refers to how readers can infer the meaning of a passage by referring to its intratextual clues; something that transcends the text itself [11]. In other words, trying to make sense of a single word in a sentence or of a sentence in a paragraph by looking only at the specific word or sentence and isolating them from the rest of the text in which they are used can be problematic, even if one knows technically their various linguistic meanings. For instance, "I am attached to you" has very different meanings to a person in love and to a hand-cuffed prisoner [33]. So, to take something 'out of context' leads to misunderstanding; there is no meaning without context. On the other hand, even if one is not familiar with the specific meaning(s) of a word or sentence, one can infer their correct meaning by situating them in the greater text and connecting them with the rest of the text.

In management research, context refers to the circumstances, conditions, situations, or environments that are external to a specific phenomenon and that enable or constrain it [47]. Mowday and Sutton see context as stimuli existing in the external environment [36], while Johns takes this a step further and understands context as situational opportunities and constraints that affect behavior [30]. Moreover, Johns distinguishes between substantive and methodological contexts [29], where substantive context stands for the context individuals or groups face while methodological context refers to detailed information about the research study.

In this paper we focus on substantive contexts for empirical SE, taking into account omnibus and discrete context dimensions as suggested by Johns [30]. Omnibus context refers to a broad perspective, drawing attention to who, what, when, where, and why [30], [49], while discrete context refers to specific contextual variables [30]. Thus, context can simultaneously be considered as a "lens" (omnibus context) and as a "variable" (discrete context) [25]. However, as most empirical SE research to date has studied discrete contexts, focusing on context as a set of variables, this paper emphasizes omnibus contexts, applying a context "lens."

2.1 Omnibus Context

According to Johns [30], research will benefit more from the careful consideration of context by paying more attention to designing and reporting studies along the lines of good journalistic practice in which a story describes the who, what, when, where, and why to the reader (see Fig. 1), thus putting recounted events in their proper context. This corresponds to the typical situation in empirical SE, in which we study how an actor applies technologies to perform certain activities on a software system [41].

'What' constitutes the substantive content of the research, the factors (variables, constructs, concepts) or treatments that logically should be considered as part of the explanation of the phenomena of interest. Although it might seem obvious, and maybe not strictly part of the context, it is not always clear what is actually studied. A typical problem is the descriptions of measures of the constructs being studied and the justification for variable coding. For example, if software quality is the phenomenon of interest, then it would require quite a bit of justification if only defects are being measured and how they are coded.

'Who' refers to the occupational and demographic context, and concerns both the direct research participants and those who surround them. It is important that the study clearly identifies the population about which one intends to make claims, and selects and describes subjects who are representative of that population [6]. Usually, there is an assumption that the target population is professional software developers. One should, however, be aware that this group may be very diverse [1]. A typical example of the 'who' in controlled SE experiments, is the student vs. professional [28] and the personality of the subjects [10]. However, it might not be enough to just state the occupational context or personality of a subject since individual differences in skill also affect the outcome of empirical studies. Within many different domains of expertise, with increased skill, the number of errors in performance decreases and the speed with which a task is executed increases [8]. The performance may differ significantly between various categories of professionals. Description of the 'who', and especially the skill, is important, thus, since the similarity of the subjects of a study to the people who will use the technology impacts the ease of the technology transfer.

'Where' a research study is conducted can have a noticeable impact on its results. It refers to the various locations in which software development happens. An important distinction is whether the phenomenon occurs in an artificial laboratory or in a more realistic industry setting [42]. For example, a challenge when configuring an experimental environment is to provide an infrastructure of supporting technology (processes, methods, tools, etc.) that resembles an industrial development environment. Because the logistics is simpler, a classroom is often used instead of a usual work place. Conducting an experiment on the usual work site with professional development tools also implies less control of the experiment than one would have in a classroom setting with pen and paper. Nevertheless, there are many challenges when conducting experiments with professionals in industry that might also be due to location effect such as economic conditions and organizational and national culture.

'When' refers to the time at which the research was conducted or research events occurred. For example, it includes when the data was collected and reflects the role of temporal factors in the research. Time affects the sociotechnical relationships that surround all aspects of software development, and is especially important for researchers who deal with software product life-cycles. Key contextual conditions of time are also related to whether the study is cross-sectional or longitudinal. Repeated calls for longer duration of experimental tasks [43] and more longitudinal research [40] in SE underscore the importance of the temporal dimension in contextual influences.

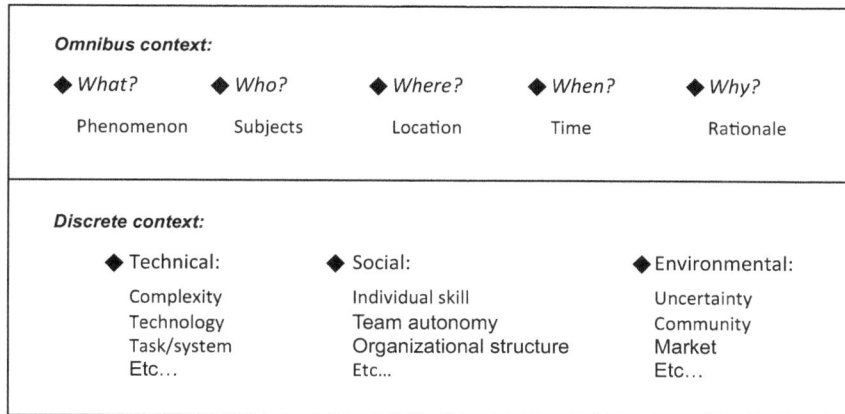

Figure 1. Important dimensions of SE context (adapted from [30]).

Time is also often a dependent variable in SE experiments, in which the goal is usually for subjects to solve the tasks with satisfactory quality in as short time as possible, as most software engineering jobs are subject of a relatively high pressure. However, if the time pressure on the participatory subjects is too high, then the task solution quality may be reduced to the point where it becomes meaningless to use the corresponding task times in subsequent analyses. A challenge is therefore to put a realistic time pressure on the subjects. How to best deal with this challenge depends to some extent on the size, duration, and location of the experiment. Methods for combining time and quality as task performance is currently being developed as a promising first step to measuring programming skill in both industry and research settings [8].

'Why' refers to the rationale for the conduct of the research or the collection of research data. Why data is collected can have a compelling contextual impact on organizational behavior and associated research. An experimental setting would, for example, ideally either reflect the subjects' organizational setting or would allow them to see some professional benefit from the experimental tasks, which would motivate them to put more effort and thought into the study. However, motivation can be a problem when subjects are asked to work on toy problems, are given unrealistic processes, or see some other disconnection between the study and their professional experience [6].

2.2 Discrete Context

Discrete context focuses on specific situational variables that directly influence behavior or moderate relationships between variables. Viewing software development from an open sociotechnical systems perspective [45], the lower portion of Figure 1 shows that the prominent dimensions of discrete context in SE research include technical, social, and environmental factors. Each of the variables within these dimensions may be treated as independent variables through selection or manipulation, or as moderator or mediator variables.

A moderator is a qualitative or quantitative variable that affects the direction and/or strength of the relations between an independent or predictor variable and a dependent or criterion variable [4]. Some moderator variables are categorical. Suppose, for example, that pair programming yielded high effect sizes on complex tasks but low effect sizes on simple tasks, with the

opposite pattern emerging for solo programming. Task complexity is then a categorical moderator. Other moderators are continuous. An example would be if pair programming produced moderate effect sizes no matter how complex the task is, but solo programming produced low effect sizes for developers with few years' experience and high effect sizes for developers with many years.

Mediators reflect a mechanism through which the independent variable causes the mediator, which then causes the outcome. For example, suppose that self-management (the independent variable) causes higher motivation (the mediator), which then leads to increased software quality (the dependent variable). However, more complex and subtle relationships may exist. For instance, the same variable can be both a moderator and a mediator in the same model, and mediators can be nonlinear or non-recursive, see [4].

The elements of the three discrete context dimensions (Fig. 1) can be seen as mediating the omnibus context. For example, knowing someone's occupation often permits reasonable inferences about his or her tasks, social, and physical environment at work, which, in turn, can be used to predict behavior and attitudes [30].

We will not consider the details of all possible discrete context variables, as several lists of a large variety and diversity of such variables have already been identified and proposed elsewhere (e.g., [12], [37], [50]). Therefore, the elements of technical, social, and environmental context in Figure 1 are not meant to be exhaustive, but argued to be *important*. This importance is inferred from a combination of the fact that they are interrelated, that they operate at multiple levels of analysis, and that they appear as fundamental elements in several empirical SE studies.

Along the technical dimension, for example, there is often a gap between researcher expectations and empirical results because one fails to acknowledge that potentially more powerful technologies may be more complex to use, or may require new skills in order to use correctly. It is self-evidently true that a technology is better when it is easier *and* faster to use than when it is not. However, what if a "faster" technology comes at the price of added complexity, which makes the technology harder to use properly. Then the faster technology would require more training to be used successfully. Without training, the faster and more complex technology would be associated with a higher proportion of incorrect uses, thereby making the faster technology appear worse than the existing alternative that is slow but easy to use correctly. More complex technologies frequently require more training than less complex technologies; at the same time, more complex technologies are adopted because they add to productivity [7].

Individual differences in skill are an important element along the social dimension that affects the outcome of empirical studies. When evaluating alternative processes, methods, or tools, skill levels may mediate the effect of using a specific alternative. For example, in an experiment on the effect of a centralized versus delegated control style, the purportedly most-skilled developers performed better using a delegated control style than with a centralized one, while the less-skilled developers performed better with the centralized style [1]. In another experiment, skill had a moderating effect on the benefits of pair programming [2].

Another important element along the social dimension is the complexity of team performance, which depends not only on the team's autonomy and competence in managing and executing its work but also on the organizational context surrounding it. For example, aspects of the organizational context such as reward systems, supervision, training, resources, and organizational structure can strongly affect team functioning. Likewise, relationships with the market and key stakeholders outside the team can influence task performance [35].

The environmental dimension refers to various characteristics outside the control of the organization that is important to its performance. These characteristics include the nature of the market, political climate, economic conditions, and the kind of technologies on which the organization depends. The environment of a particular software organization may range from stable to dynamic – from predictable to unpredictable. A study on process improvement strategies, for example, showed that there was no difference in the level of exploitation between small and large organizations regardless of the environment, but that there was a marked difference in the level of exploration. The results showed that small software organizations engaged in significantly more exploration in turbulent and uncertain environments than large software organization. Due to the increased complexity, increased convergence, and increased inertia of the large organizations, they are less likely to change in response to environmental changes than small organizations. They tend to generate the same response even when the stimuli had changed [15], [16].

The argument behind the usefulness of studying discrete context variables depend on the assumption that research findings are strongly a function of general empirical laws or processes. However, from a constructionist point of view, consistency of research results implies either the stability of the social constructions across the contexts in which the studies were conducted or an interpretive norm that leads to the perception of consistency [17], [27]. Similarly, inconsistency among research results might indicate an inconsistency among the interpretative norms of the research community. One of the most interesting implications of the constructionist perspective is that the perceived cumulativeness of scientific knowledge in SE is a function of the conventions of evidence and methodology in the research community.

3. CONTEXT AND EMPIRICAL STUDIES

It can often be problematic to transfer evidence generated from one context to another. Shull [39], for example, points to several recent studies showing that lessons learned from one project are simply not applicable to others. For example, a study of the prediction factors in the COCOMO model across 93 project datasets from one organization showed huge variations in the size of the effects those factors had on overall project effort. In some cases, the direction of the relationships changed from positive to negative depending on which projects were in the dataset being fit. Also, in another study on defect predictors for pairs of projects, only for four percent of the pairs did the factors that worked well for predicting defects in the first project also apply in the second [39].

In this section we will look further into three examples of the relationship between context and empirical studies of agile practices – two secondary studies and one primary study. The first one is a systematic review on test-driven development (TDD), the second is a meta-analysis of pair programming (PP), while the third is a large experiment on PP with professional developers. The systematic review and meta-analysis are typical examples of secondary studies which try to synthesize evidence from primary studies of the type: "Is *technology x* better than *technology y*?" without considering contextual influences. Our primary study example, however, shows how important contextual elements influence the main effects of the experiment.

3.1 Test-Driven Development

Attempts to aggregate the available evidence on agile practices like test-driven development (TDD) have shown wide disparities in how well these practices work in different contexts. Although advocates claim that TDD enhances both product quality and programmer productivity, skeptics maintain that such an approach to programming would be both counterproductive and hard to learn [46].

However, it is the productivity dimension that engenders the most controversial discussion of TDD. Although many admit that adopting TDD may require a steep learning curve that may decrease the productivity initially, there is no consensus on the long-term effects. One line of argument expects productivity to increase with TDD; reasons include easy context switching from one simple task to another, improved external quality (i.e., there are few errors and errors can be detected quickly), improved internal quality (i.e., fixing errors is easier due to simpler design), and improved test quality (i.e., chances of introducing new errors is low due to automated tests). The opposite line argues that TDD incurs too much overhead and will negatively impact productivity because too much time and focus may be spent on authoring tests as opposed to adding new functionality [46].

A systematic review that aggregated the available evidence about the effectiveness of TDD found that TDD does not have a consistent effect on productivity. The evidence from controlled experiments suggests an improvement in productivity when TDD is used. However, the pilot studies provide mixed evidence, some in favor of and others against TDD. In the industrial studies, the evidence suggests that TDD yields worse productivity. Even when considering only the more rigorous studies, the evidence is equally split for and against a positive effect on productivity. Ten studies resulted in higher productivity for TDD than otherwise, nine studies led to worse productivity for TDD, while six additional studies found no significant effect on productivity at all [46].

Based on a more detailed investigation of the results, the authors could not recommended any specific context that would benefit from the use of TDD. The results do not suggest to which domains TDD is applicable, to which kinds of tasks within a domain, or to which projects sizes and complexities it is applicable. Furthermore, the studies do not make it clear whether TDD is an applicable practice for developing embedded systems or for developing highly decentralized systems where incremental testing may not be feasible.

3.2 Pair Programming

Pair programming is one of the best documented and most popular agile practices, and it has been the subject of a relatively large body of empirical research from an industrial perspective [18], [26]. Like the TDD example, common to most of the PP studies is the general question of whether pairs outperform individuals in programming tasks without consideration of context.

Claims as to both the benefits and the adversities of PP abound. Advocates of PP claim that it has many benefits over individual programming when applied to new code development or when used to maintain and enhance existing code. Stated benefits include higher-quality code, shorter development duration, happier programmers, improved teamwork, improved knowledge transfer, and enhanced learning (see [18]). There are also expectations with respect to the benefits and drawbacks of various kinds of pairing, e.g., expert–expert vs. novice–novice pairing. However, the finding across decades of small group research is that groups usually fall short of reasonable expectations to improved performance (see [26]).

Motivated by the diverse claims regarding PP a meta-analysis on the effectiveness of PP, which extended the analysis presented by Dybå et al. [18], was undertaken, taking into account between-study variance, subgroup differences, and publication bias [26]. The meta-analysis included 18 studies, which showed a small positive overall effect of PP on quality, a medium positive overall effect on duration, and a medium negative overall effect on effort. The meta-analysis suggests that PP is not uniformly beneficial or effective, that inter-study variance is high, and that publication bias might be an issue. It showed large and partly contradictory differences in overall effects, specifically with respect to duration and effort.

Also, differences in research design and methodological rigor across the studies, makes it difficult to compare the findings. For example, some studies used student homework assignments as experimental tasks, some used repeated measure designs in which the same subjects worked individually as well as in pairs, while others employed quasi-experimental designs for the assignment of subjects to treatments. The approach to partner selection also differed considerably, ranging from self-selection by pairs to matching pairs on abilities or experience levels. Yet another source of variation is the unit of analysis employed in these studies. For example, certain studies used the programming team as the unit of analysis, whereas others used a dyad [3].

These issues point to a need for untangling the moderating factors of the effect of PP. The meta-analysis also concluded that the question of whether PP is better than solo programming is not precise enough to be meaningful, since the answer depends on other factors, for example, the expertise of the programmers and on the complexity of the system and tasks to be solved.

Indeed, expertise and task complexity are perhaps the most central situation-independent predictors of SE performance [8]. Situation-dependent factors, on the other hand, include more dynamic factors such as motivation, team climate, organizational issues, etc. Theory predicts that experts perform better on complex tasks than do novices because experts' level of understanding corresponds to the deep structure of a complex task [22].

The collaborative nature of PP also influences what social mechanisms (e.g., social loafing, social laboring, social facilitation, social inhibition, and social compensation) are applicable. However, these social mechanisms also depend on a host of other factors. In a meta-analysis of social loafing (the phenomenon that individuals tend to expend less effort when working collectively than when working individually), Karau and Williams [31] identified several conditions in which such loafing is eliminated (e.g., by high group cohesion) and some in which the opposite phenomenon, social laboring, could be observed (i.e., greater effort on group tasks). Social laboring seems to occur when complex or highly involving tasks are performed, or when the group is considered important for its members, or if the prevailing values favor collectivism rather than individualism [9].

Group performance also depends on whether a task is additive, compensatory, disjunctive, or conjunctive [9]. For example, for conjunctive tasks, all group members must contribute to the solution, but for disjunctive tasks it suffices that one group member has the ability to complete the task. However, it is not obvious what sort of task PP is in this respect.

Figure 2 is good example of the relationship between context and empirical studies. It shows the results of a large experiment, with 295 professional developers, performed by Arisholm et al. [2] that found moderating effects of both task complexity and expertise. Overall, the results showed that the pairs had an 8% decrease in duration with a corresponding 84% increase in effort and a 7% increase in correctness. However, the main effects of PP were masked by the moderating effect of system complexity, in that simpler designs had shorter duration, while more complex designs had increased correctness.

When considering the moderating effect of programmer expertise, junior pairs had a small (5%) increase in duration and thus a large increase in effort (111%), and a 73% increase in correctness. Intermediate pairs had a 28% decrease in duration (43% increase in effort) and a negligible (4%) increase in correctness. Senior pairs had a 9% decrease in duration (83% increase in effort) and an 8% decrease in correctness. Thus, the juniors benefited from PP in terms of increased correctness, the intermediates in terms of decreased duration, while there were no overall benefits of PP for seniors.

When considering the combined moderating effect of system complexity and programmer expertise on PP, there appears to be an interaction effect: Among the different treatment combinations, junior pairs assigned to the complex design had a remarkable 149% increase on correctness compared with individuals. Furthermore, intermediates and seniors experienced an effect of PP on duration on the simpler design, with a 39% and 23% decrease, respectively. However, the cost of this shorter duration was a corresponding decrease in correct solutions by 29% and 13%, respectively.

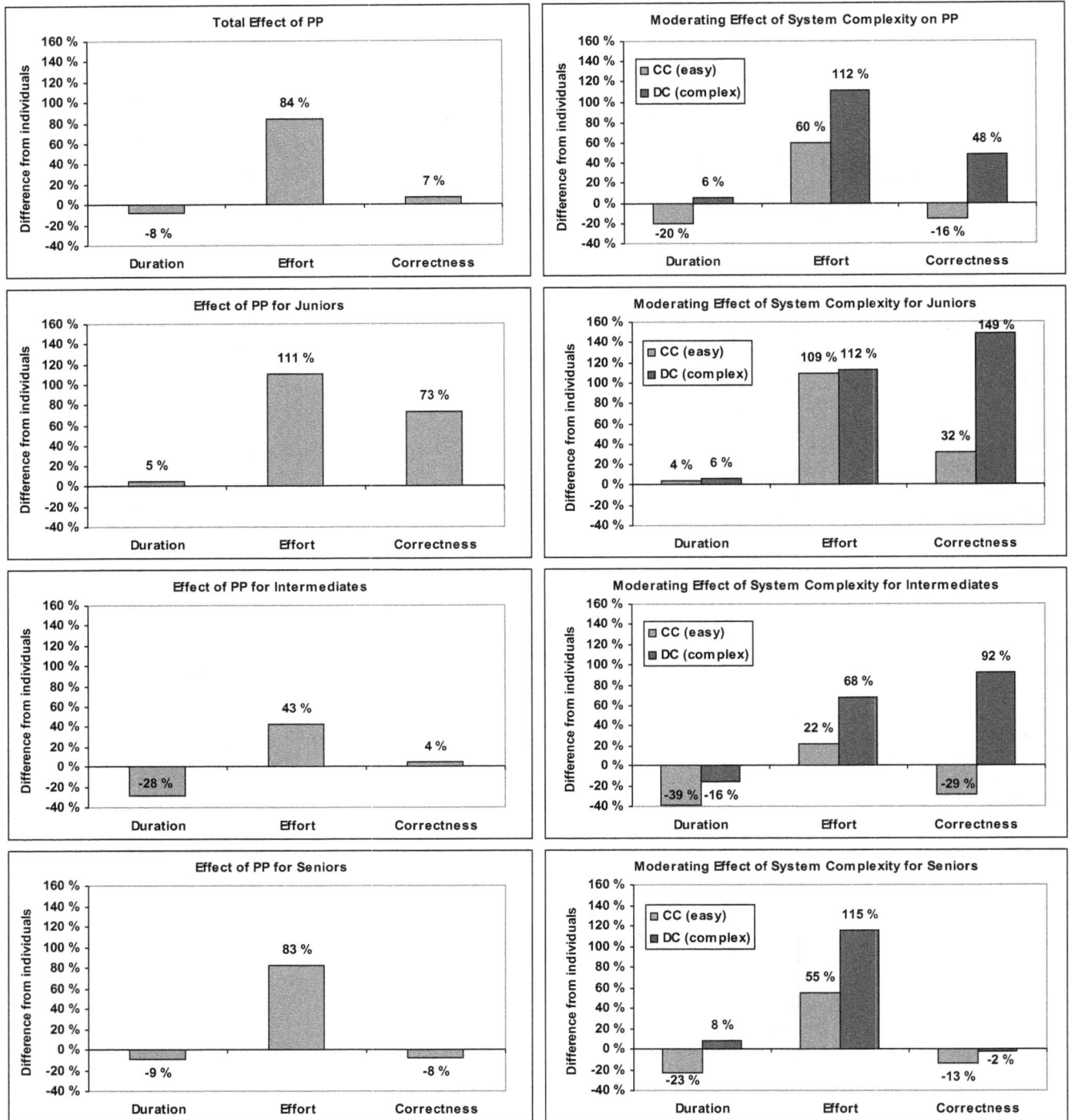

Figure 2. The moderating effects of programmer expertise (left column) and system complexity (right column) on the relation of pair programming on duration, effort, and correctness (Arisholm et al., 2007).

Hence, based on this experiment, the overall answer to the question of whether PP is "better" than solo programming is a clear "No". However, the more detailed examination of the evidence suggests that PP is faster than solo programming when programming task complexity is low and yields code solutions of higher quality when task complexity is high.

By cooperating, programmers may complete tasks and attain goals that would be difficult or impossible if they worked individually.

Junior pair programmers, for example, seem able to achieve approximately the same level of correctness in about the same amount of time (duration) as senior individuals. However, the higher quality for complex tasks comes at a price of a considerably higher effort (cost), while the reduced completion time for the simpler tasks comes at a price of a noticeably lower quality. These relationships give rise to a few evidence-based guidelines for the use of PP for professional software developers [18]: If you do not know the seniority or skill levels of your programmers, but do have a feeling for task complexity, then employ pair programming either when task complexity is low and time is of the essence, or when task complexity is high and correctness is important.

4. THE WAY FORWARD: CONTEXTUALIZING SE RESEARCH

The examples in the previous section clearly show that an obvious problem with current empirical SE research is in the stage of asking questions. The initial question posed, "Is <technology x> better than <technology y>?", e.g., "Is pair programming better than solo programming?" is meaningless. SE covers a highly diversified set of sociotechnical tasks, procedures, and systems based upon more or less well-defined theoretical formulations. Narrowing the question down to "Does pair programming lead to higher quality than solo programming" is no more meaningful than the general question, since the range of tasks and systems remain as diversified as within SE in general. Furthermore, this question fails to take into account the skill of the developers who may contribute to quality.

So, what is the appropriate question to be asked of empirical SE research? In all its complexity, the question towards which empirical SE research should ultimately be directed is the following:

> *What* technology is most effective for *whom,* performing *that* specific activity, on *that* kind of system, under *which* set of circumstances?

This question resembles the goal part of the goal-question-metric (GQM) paradigm, which is a systematic approach for setting project goals tailored to the specific needs of an organization and defining them in an operational and tractable way [5]. Relating it to the omnibus context in Figure 1, and the example of PP in Section 3.2, we find:

> What technology (PP vs. solo programming), is most effective (in terms of improvement in correctness), for whom (highly skilled developers), performing that specific activity (change tasks), on that kind of system (complex system designed with a delegated control style), under which set of circumstances (in the subjects' normal work environment for a full-day experiment)?

Posing the question in this manner, it becomes obvious that in order for knowledge to meaningfully accumulate across separate studies and provide a solid empirical foundation for subsequent research, it will be necessary for every empirical investigation to adequately describe, measure, or control a potentially large number of discrete context variables. However, as we will demonstrate, applying an experimental logic to this problem based on ready-made lists of discrete context factors is not a viable option.

The experimental logic, which underpins most empirical SE research, is to identify the 'dependent variable' that captures the 'outcome' or 'effect' that needs to be explained, and the 'independent variables' that have impact on, or explain variation in the dependent variable. A change in the independent variable (X) is said to 'bring about' change in the dependent variable (Y). The goal of an experiment is thus to isolate the critical causal condition, or treatment, (X_1) by experimental manipulation, with other potential influences $(X_2, X_3, X_4,$ etc.) being held in control. The influence of X_1 on Y can thus be observed and measured directly. Another strategy for achieving 'control' is by statistical means; by observing and including variables in *post hoc* analyses.

The quasi-experimental and analytical modelling traditions in empirical SE research build on these strategies in which variables do the explanatory work and causal complexity is managed via the progressive addition of subsets of variables (like in the PP example). The prevailing view on context in empirical SE has the same variable oriented logic.

However, if we were to evaluate only a small selection of discrete context variables that presumably would influence the main effects of a study using this logic, we would quickly find it difficult because of combinatorial complexity. As an example, Petersen and Wohlin [37] suggested a checklist for context documentation consisting of six facets: product, processes, practices and techniques, people, organization, and market, and a set of context elements describing each facet. However, Menzies et al. [33] criticize Petersen and Wohlin since "they offer no way to learn new contextualizations or ... no experimental confirmation that their contexts are the 'right' contexts" (p. 350), claiming that context is interesting only if it results in different and better treatments.

In total, Petersen and Wohlin suggested 21 context elements [37]. Even with simplified assumptions and a very conservative estimate for the number of legal values per context element, we get more than 4 billion combinations! Making matters even worse, Clarke and O'Connor [12] proposed a reference framework of situational factors for software development processes consisting of 44 factors and 170 sub-factors. Assuming only two legal values for each sub-factor this results in a minimum of:

$$2^{170} = 1.5 \times 10^{51} \text{ combinations of context factors.}$$

As a comparison, there are:

$$1.33 \times 10^{50} \text{ atoms in the world}^1,$$

which shows the absurdity of the variable oriented logic. Consequently, we need to shift focus away from a checklist-based approach to context in favor of a more dynamic view of software practice. Instead of viewing context as a set of discrete variables that statically surround parts of practice, we argue that context and practice stand in a mutually reflexive relationship to each other, with software practice, and the interpretive work it generates, shaping context as much as context shapes the practice.

On the one hand the traditional variables of empirical phenomena have to be supplemented by sociotechnical attributes and patterns that are intrinsic to the activity of software practice. On the other, the characteristics of research evidence as an interactive phenomenon, challenges the traditional notions of empirical SE

---

[1] http://education.jlab.org/qa/mathatom_05.html

research, suggesting a view of the relationship between evidence and context as a process that emerges and changes through time and space.

Given that in any study, there are an infinite number of contextual factors and combinations to consider, the decision as to which parameters along which to contextualize should be no different from the decision regarding which variables to control. Both decisions should be grounded in theory relevant to the phenomenon under study, or as Menzies et al. [33] formulated it: *"Rather than focus on generalities (that may be irrelevant to any particular project), empirical SE should focus more on context-specific principles."*

Therefore, we do not expect a single, precise, technical definition of context in SE. The term means quite different things within alternative research paradigms, and even within particular traditions seems to be defined more by situated practice, by use of the concept to work with particular analytic problems, than by formal definition [24]. Like Goodwin and Duranti [24], we do not see the lack of a single formal definition, or even general agreement about what is meant by context, as a situation that necessarily requires a remedy. We clearly dispute any attempt at providing a general framework or checklists of specific factors intended at describing the context of local, situated practice.

Instead, we encourage SE researchers to take a broad, omnibus, perspective to context in their studies and to actively take part in explaining how phenomena works, for whom, where, when, and why. Context is shaped by the specific activities being performed. It is crucial, therefore, to acknowledge that any definition of context can only be done in relation to a specific practice situation [17].

However, simply naming an organization, describing a site in detail, or doing a longitudinal study does not constitute a contextual contribution. Rather, these means of fostering context have to be used in a way that adds explanatory value to a study. So, if we are to move beyond simple assertions that the context is important, we need to articulate more clearly how contextual influences operate. Perhaps the best question to ask oneself is this:

> Does the inclusion of this information explain the constraints on, or the opportunities for, the phenomenon I am studying?

There are several ways to explore and exploit contextual impact in empirical SE research. Menzies et al. [33], for example, suggest that, rather than seeking general principles that apply to many projects, empirical SE should focus on ways to find the best local lessons for groups of related projects. Following Johns [30], we mention a few ways to explore and exploit contextual impact that are related to research design, measurement, analysis, and reporting. However, to succeed with such contextualization, a prerequisite is theoretical grounding and familiarity with the research site(s).

- *Perform cross-level comparative research* that explicitly demonstrate how higher-level situational factors such as environmental uncertainty and market conditions affect lower-level factors such as individual behavior and team autonomy.

- *Perform longitudinal research* that studies processes and examines how behavior unfolds over time or how software teams and organizations configure themselves to deal with recurrent problems.

- *Study critical events* that can punctuate context and make possible research and theory that form part of a larger whole, such as Moe et al.'s [35] study of the introduction of self-managing teams.

- *Collect qualitative data* that illuminate context effects and interactions that might affect behavior in a studied setting, or that can aid in making inferences about the situation.

- *Measure multiple dependent variables* that can uncover situational context when used in conjunction with one another or explain the gap in meaning, such as Dybå et al.'s [20] multiple measurement of software methodology usage.

- *Use analytic strategies* that are sensitive to the distributional properties of data, rather than simply exploring means, and contextual control variables that can explain interactions with main effects, as shown in the pair programming example.

- *Report contextual information* that has theoretical bearing on the study's results or that might be useful to others (e.g., meta-analysts) in the future [13], [14]. A good place to begin is to ensure that the elements of omnibus context are addressed in adequate detail: what was studied, who was studied, where were they studied, when were they studied, and why were they studied?

The last point is especially important to enable the identification of recurring themes or common contextual factors across studies. Systematic reviews conducted with respect to the determination of why study results differ (as they are likely to do), and the evaluation of the potentially contrasting insights from empirical studies will generally be more helpful than those that focus on identifying average effects [13]. Seemingly unpatterned and disagreeing findings from quantitative studies may have underlying consistency when omnibus context is taken into account. Qualitative data may also be useful in capturing developers' subjective evaluations of organizational- or project-level interventions and outcomes. In addition, qualitative findings can be used to develop theories and to identify relevant variables to be evaluated in future quantitative studies.

However, the presence of contextual variables does not mean they will shape software practice or be of theoretical interest. The context must act on, be noticed by, and be construed as important by individuals and groups before it can influence practice. Discovering that contextual variables are present but do not appear to be influential is often as important from a research perspective as confirming their power [36].

Maybe the most critical issue in contextualizing empirical SE research is our willingness, as researchers, to immerse ourselves in the context. Empirical studies in leading SE conferences and journals are often based on laboratory studies using students as subjects. About 90% of the subjects who take part in these experiments are students [44]. The applicability of most experimental results to an industrial setting may, therefore, be questioned.

When researchers move into the field, it is often to administer questionnaires to anonymous respondents who return them by mail, or by performing online surveys of organizational members or various online software communities. Thus, software practice is often studied without going near the organization and without talking to any of its members. Doing research so remote from the industrial context has costs, both in terms of the depth of understanding researchers can achieve and with respect to the inspiration that leads to new, relevant areas of inquiry.

In general, the more similar the research setting of a study is to the context in which the results will be applied, the more directly relevant the study is perceived. Fenton et al. [23], for example stated that *"evaluative research must involve realistic projects with realistic subjects, and it must be done with sufficient rigor to ensure that any benefits identified are clearly derived from the concept in question. This type of research is time-consuming and expensive and, admittedly, difficult to employ in all software-engineering research. It is not surprising that little of it is being done."*

In this situation, the most realistic research setting is found in action research studies, because the context of the study is the same as the context in which the results will be applied for a given organization, apart from the presence of the researcher(s). The context of industry-based case studies is also generally very similar to the setting of application, although researchers *may* study phenomena that might not be regarded as very relevant by the studied organization. Hence, more (high-quality) action research and case studies should be conducted. The increasing number of qualitative studies appearing in our leading journals may suggest a positive trend in this direction [21].

5. CONCLUSION
The aim of this paper was to provide an overview of how context affects empirical research and how empirical SE research can be better 'contextualized' in order to provide a better understanding of what works for whom, where, when, and why.

Empirical SE is concerned with different technologies, actors, activities, and systems, and therefore contexts, which demand higher levels of contextualization for accuracy in empirical generalization. Progress in this area is unlikely, however, if research is conducted with students in academic settings, through online surveys, or through short visits to companies during which questionnaires are distributed to convenience samples.

Contextualization requires immersion and a focus on relevant phenomena, which means that SE researchers need to invest considerable time within the practice they wish to understand. Action research and case studies applying qualitative and ethnographic methods are examples of approaches that will aid this immersion. Immersion will also enable us to move the discipline into a more useful direction that will counter the common criticism that much empirical SE research is irrelevant for software organizations and their members.

Empirical SE research only becomes comprehensible when one takes into account the larger sociotechnical frameworks within which it is embedded. It is all about context, interpretation, and evaluation. However, what counts as context will depend on the substantive problem under scrutiny; it cannot be captured by generalized lists of discrete variables. So, if we are to move beyond simple assertions that the context is important, we need to articulate more clearly how contextual influences operate.

6. REFERENCES

[1] Arisholm, E. and Sjøberg, D.I.K. (2004) Evaluating the Effect of a Delegated versus Centralized Control Style on the Maintainability of Object-Oriented Software, *IEEE Transactions on Software Engineering*, 30(8): 521-534.

[2] Arisholm, E., Gallis, H.E., Dybå, T. and Sjøberg, D.I.K. (2007) Evaluating Pair Programming with Respect to System Complexity and Programmer Expertise, *IEEE Transactions on Software Engineering*, 33(2): 65-86.

[3] Balijepally, V., Mahapatra, R., Nerur, S., Price, K.H. (2009) Are Two Heads Better Than One For Software Development? The Productivity Paradox of Pair Programming, *MIS Quarterly*, 33(1): 91-118.

[4] Baron, R.M. and Kenny, D.A. (1993) The moderator–mediator variable distinction in social psychological research: Conceptual, strategic, and statistical considerations, *Journal of Personality and Social Psychology*, 51(6): 1173-1182.

[5] Basili, V.R. and Rombach, D. (1988) The TAME Project: Towards Improvement-Oriented Software Environments, *IEEE Transactions on Software Engineering*, 14(6): 758-773.

[6] Basili, V.R., Shull, F., and Lanubile, F. (1999) Building Knowledge through Families of Experiments, *IEEE Transactions on Software Engineering*, 25(4): 456-473.

[7] Bergersen, B.R. and Sjøberg, D.I.K. (2012) Evaluating Methods and Technologies in Software Engineering with Respect to Developers' Skill Level, *Accepted to EASE'2012*.

[8] Bergersen, B.R., Hannay, J.E., Sjøberg, D.I.K., Dybå, T., and Karahasanović (2011) Inferring skill from tests of programming performance: Combining time and quality, *Proc. ESEM'2011*, IEEE Computer Society, pp. 305-314.

[9] Brown, R. (2000) *Group Processes: Dynamics within and between Groups*, Second Ed., Blackwell.

[10] Capretz, L.F. and Ahmed, F. (2010) Making Sense of Software Development and Personality Types, *IT Professional*, 12(1): 6-14.

[11] Chin, E. (1994) Redefining "context" in research on writing, *Written Communication*, 11(4), 445-482.

[12] Clarke, P. and O'Connor, R.V. (2012) The situational factors that affect the software development process: Towards a comprehensive reference framework, *Information and Software Technology*, 54(5): 433-447.

[13] Cruzes, D.S. and Dybå, T. (2011) Research Synthesis in Software Engineering: A Tertiary Study, *Information and Software Technology*, 53(5): 440-455.

[14] Cruzes, D.S. and Dybå, T. (2011) Recommended Steps for Thematic Synthesis in Software Engineering, *Proc. ESEM'2011*, IEEE Computer Society, pp. 275-284.

[15] Dybå, T. (2000) Improvisation in Small Software Organizations, *IEEE Software*, 17(5): 82-87.

[16] Dybå, T. (2003) Factors of Software Process Improvement Success in Small and Large Organizations: An Empirical Study in the Scandinavian Context, *Proc. ESEC/FSE'2003*, ACM press, pp. 148-157.

[17] Dybå, T. (2003) A Dynamic Model of Software Engineering Knowledge Creation, in A. Aurum et al. (Eds.) *Managing Software Engineering Knowledge*, Springer, pp. 95-117.

[18] Dybå, T., Arisholm, E., Sjøberg, D., Hannay, J., and Shull, F. (2007) Are Two Heads Better than One? On the Effectiveness of Pair-Programming, *IEEE Software*, 24(6): 12-15.

[19] Dybå, T., Kitchenham, B.A., and Jørgensen, M. (2005) Evidence-based Software Engineering for Practitioners, *IEEE Software*, 22(1): 58-65.

[20] Dybå, T., Moe, N.B., and Arisholm, E. (2005) Measuring Software Methodology Usage: Challenges of Conceptualization and Operationalization, *Proc. ISESE'2005*, pp. 447-457

[21] Dybå, T., Prikladnicki, R., Rönkkö, K., Seaman, C., and Sillito, J. (2011) Qualitative Research in Software Engineering, *Empirical Software Engineering*, 16(4): 425-429.

[22] Ericsson, K.A. and Charness, N. (1994) Expert Performance: Its Structure and Acquisition, *American Psychologist*, 49(8): 725-747.

[23] Fenton, N., Pfleeger, S.L. and Glass, R.L. (1994) Science and Substance: A Challenge to Software Engineers, *IEEE Software,* 11(4): 86-95.

[24] Goodwin, C. and Duranti, A. (1992) *Rethinking context: Language as an interactive phenomenon*, Cambridge Univ. Press.

[25] Griffin, M. (2007) Specifying organizational contexts: Systematic links between contexts and processes in organizational behavior, *Journal of Organizational Behavior*, 28: 859-863.

[26] Hannay, J., Dybå, T., Arisholm, E., and Sjøberg, D. (2009) The Effectiveness of Pair Programming: A Meta-Analysis, *Information and Software Technology*, 51(7): 1110-1122.

[27] Hedges, L.V. (1987) How Hard Is Hard Science, How Soft Is Soft Science? The Empirical Cumulativeness of Research, *American Psychologist*, 42(2): 443-455.

[28] Höst, M., Regnell, B., and Wohlin, C. (2000) Using Students as Subjects: A Comparative Study of Students and Professionals in Lead-Time Impact Assessment, *Empirical Software Engineering*, 5(3): 201-214.

[29] Johns, G. (1991) Substantive and methodological constraints on behavior and attitudes in organizational research. *Organizational Behavior and Human Decision Processes,* 49: 80-104.

[30] Johns, G. (2006) The Essential Impact of Context on Organizational Behavior, *Academy of Management Review*, 31(2): 386-408.

[31] Karau, S.J. and Williams, K.D. (1993) Social loafing: a meta-analytic review and theoretical integration, *Journal of Personality and Social Psychology*, 65(4): 681-706.

[32] Kitchenham, B.A., Pfleeger, S.L., Pickard, L.M., Jones, P.W., Hoaglin, D.C., El Emam, K. and Rosenberg, J. (2002) Preliminary Guidelines for Empirical Research in Software Engineering, *IEEE Transactions on Software Engineering*, 28(8): 721-734.

[33] Menzies, T., Butcher, A., Marcus, A., Zimmermann, T., and Cok, D. (2011) Local vs. Global Models for Effort Estimation and Defect Prediction, *Proc. ASE'2011*, pp. 343-351.

[34] Michailova, S. (2011) Contextualizing in International Business research: Why do we need more of it and how can we be better at it? *Scandinavian Journal of Management*, 27: 129-139.

[35] Moe, N.B., Dingsøyr, T. and Dybå, T. (2009) Overcoming Barriers to Self-management in Software Teams, *IEEE Software*, 26(6): 20-26.

[36] Mowday, R. and Sutton, R. (1993) Organizational behavior: Linking individuals and groups to organizational contexts, *Annual Review of Psychology*, 44: 195-229.

[37] Petersen K. and Wohlin, C. (2009) Context in Industrial Software Engineering Research, *Proc. ESEM'2009*, pp. 401-404.

[38] Rousseau, D.M. and Fried, Y. (2001) Location, location, location: contextualizing organizational research, *Journal of Organizational Behavior*, 22: 1-13.

[39] Shull, F. (2012) I Believe! *IEEE Software*, 29(1): 4-7.

[40] Sjøberg, D, Dybå, T., and Jørgensen, M. (2007) The Future of Empirical Methods in Software Engineering Research, *Proc. FOSE'2007*, pp. 358–378.

[41] Sjøberg, D., Dybå, T., Anda, B., and Hannay, J. (2008) Building Theories in Software Engineering, in F. Shull, J. Singer, and D. Sjøberg (Eds.) *Advanced Topics in Empirical Software Engineering*, Springer, pp. 312-336.

[42] Sjøberg, D.I.K., Anda, B., Arisholm, E., Dybå, T., Jørgensen, M., Karahasanovic, A., Koren, E.F. and Vokac M. (2002) Conducting Realistic Experiments in Software Engineering, *Proc. ISESE'2002*, pp. 17-26.

[43] Sjøberg, D.I.K., Anda, B., Arisholm, E., Dybå, T., Jørgensen, M., Karahasanovic, A., and Vokac M. (2003) Challenges and Recommendation when Increasing the Realism of Controlled Software Engineering Experiments, in R. Conradi & A.I. Wang (Eds.) *Empirical Methods and Studies in Software Engineering - Experiences from ESERNET*, Springer, LNCS 2765, pp. 24-38.

[44] Sjøberg, D.I.K., Hannay, J.E., Hansen, O., Kampenes, V.B., Karahasanović, A., Liborg, N.-K. and Rekdal, A.C. (2005) A Survey of Controlled Experiments in Software Engineering, *IEEE Transactions on Software Engineering*, 31(9): 733-753.

[45] Trist, E. (1981) The Evolution of Socio-Technical Systems: A Conceptual Framework and an Action Research Program, *Occasional papers No. 2,* Ontario Quality of Working Life Center.

[46] Turhan, B., Layman, L., Diep, M., Shull, F. and Erdogmus, H. (2010) How Effective is Test Driven Development?, in G.Wilson & A. Orham (Eds.), *Making Software: What Really Works, and Why We Believe It*, O'Reilly Press, pp. 207-219.

[47] Welter, F. (2010) Contextualizing Entrepreneurship: Conceptual Challenges and Ways Forward, *Entrepreneurship Theory and Practice*, 35(1): 165-184.

[48] Whetten (2009) An Examination of the Interface between Context and Theory Applied to the Study of Chinese Organizations, *Management and Organization Review*, 5(1): 29-55.

[49] Whetten, D.A. (1989) What Constitutes a Theoretical Contribution, *Academy of Management Review,* 14(4): 490-495.

[50] Xu, P. and Ramesh, B. (2007) Software process tailoring: an empirical investigation, *Journal of Management Information Systems*, 24(2): 293-328.

Systematic Literature Studies: Database Searches vs. Backward Snowballing

Samireh Jalali
Blekinge Institute of Technology
SE 37179 Karlskrona, Sweden
samireh.jalali@bth.se

Claes Wohlin
Blekinge Institute of Technology
SE 37179 Karlskrona, Sweden
claes.wohlin@bth.se

ABSTRACT

Systematic studies of the literature can be done in different ways. In particular, different guidelines propose different first steps in their recommendations, e.g. start with search strings in different databases or start with the reference lists of a starting set of papers.

In software engineering, the main recommended first step is using search strings in a number of databases, while in information systems, snowballing has been recommended as the first step. This paper compares the two different search approaches for conducting literature review studies.

The comparison is conducted by searching for articles addressing "Agile practices in global software engineering". The focus of the paper is on evaluating the two different search approaches.

Despite the differences in the included papers, the conclusions and the patterns found in both studies are quite similar. The strengths and weaknesses of each first step are discussed separately and in comparison with each other.

It is concluded that none of the first steps is outperforming the other, and the choice of guideline to follow, and hence the first step, may be context-specific, i.e. depending on the area of study.

Categories and Subject Descriptors

D.2 [**Software Engineering**]: Management—*Software process models*; K.6 [**Management of Computing and Information Systems**]: Software Management—*Software process*

General Terms

Experimentation, Measurement

Keywords

Systematic Literature Review, Snowballing, Agile Practices, Global Software Engineering

1. INTRODUCTION

Research literature may be divided into primary studies (new studies on a specific topic) or secondary studies (summarizing or synthesizing the current state of research on a specific topic). The secondary studies may be used to pinpoint gaps or to highlight areas that require more attention from researchers or practitioners.

Secondary studies require comprehensive searches in the published research literature. Kitchenham and Charters [11] proposed a systematic literature review (SLR) approach inspired by evidence-based medicine, which recommend starting with systematic searches in databases using well-defined search strings to find relevant literature. In the guidelines [11], it is recommended that snowballing from reference lists of the identified articles should be used in addition to the searches in the databases, i.e. to identify additional relevant articles through the reference lists of the articles found using the search strings.

However, the guidelines do not explicitly recommend forward snowballing, i.e. identifying articles that have cited the articles found in the search and backward snowballing (from the reference lists). In our experience, most systematic literature reviews (including our own) do not use snowballing as a complement to searching the databases. It is fully understandable given the amount of work needed to conduct a systematic literature review. The implication being that a review provides a limited set of all papers on the topic, i.e. a sample of the population.

Webster and Watson [4] proposed a slightly different approach to systematic literature studies in the field of information systems. They propose to use snowballing as the main method to find relevant literature. In their recommendation, they highlight both backward snowballing (from the reference lists) and forward snowballing (finding citations to the papers). The snowballing approach requires a starting set of papers, which they suggest should be based on identifying a set of papers from leading journals in the area.

Given that there exist different guidelines of how to conduct systematic literature review studies, we pose the following research questions:

1. To what extent do we find the same research papers using two different review approaches?

2. To what extent do we come to the same conclusions using two different review approaches?

The outcome of a systematic literature study is either a systematic literature review [11] or a systematic mapping study [20]. Database searches and snowballing are by no means the only options. The use of personal knowledge or contacts [6], or mixed methods [3] has also been discussed in the literature. The focus here is, however, on the first step of two recommended methods to identify relevant literature. Thus, we have limited our study to using either database searches or backward snowballing as the first step, in particular given that, in our experience, researchers are, all to often, forced to limit their search procedures given the time it takes to conduct a systematic literature study. However, we believe that if similar patterns are identified through applying partial methods (i.e. backward snowballing), the similarity is expected to increase if forward snowballing is also performed since the overlap in the included papers would be greater. The papers found are evaluated for relevance and quality, which gives a set of primary studies for each search approach (database search or backward snowballing), and these papers are the basis for further comparisons conducted in this paper.

Given that the number of published secondary studies increases [18], it is perceived as important to understand whether or not the first step in the searches impacts the actual outcomes of the systematic literature study, in particular since many published papers do not use all steps recommended in the guidelines. This is closely related to the need to ensure reliability of secondary studies, which means whether two independent studies on the same topic would find the same set of papers and draw the same conclusions [12].

Based on the need identified, we conducted two different literature reviews on Agile practices in Global Software Engineering (GSE) using different guidelines for the literature search, and in particular we only used the first step in the recommendation, i.e. database searches [11] or backward snowballing [4]. It should be noted that we included distributed development within a country in GSE too. The main reason being that many of the challenges experienced in a global setting also occurs in distributed development within a country, although some of the challenges are amplified when going global. Both studies have the same research questions. The first study is an SLR [9], and the second study applied a snowballing approach [4]. The differences between the search methods are discussed in more detail in Section 3.

The remainder of the paper is structured as follows. Section 2 summarizes related work, and Section 3 discusses the research method and introduces the two studies forming the input to the analysis. The results are presented in Section 4, and the discussions of the findings are given in Section 5. Finally, Section 6 presents the conclusions and the future research directions.

2. RELATED WORK

Inspired from medicine, in which systematic literature reviews is an approach for synthesizing evidence, Kitchenham et al. [7] introduced the concept of evidence-based software engineering (EBSE). A couple of years earlier Webster and Watson [4] suggested a structured approach in information systems to conduct systematic literature studies.

It should be noted that the research type in medicine and software engineering (SE) are not necessarily the same (e.g. controlled experiments vs. case studies). It implies different types of data, and different types of analyses of the data. Hence, the synthesis of the data collected from an SLR in

SE may not be as straightforward as in at least some parts of medicine.

However, a practitioner-oriented view was formulated based on the EBSE ideas [8], and researchers also suggested guidelines for conducting systematic literature reviews [11]. Furthermore, Brereton et al. [14] reviewed a number of existing literature reviews to examine the applicability of SLR practices to SE. They found out that although the basic steps in the SLR process are as relevant in SE as in medicine, some modifications are necessary for example in reporting of empirical studies in SE.

Although the number of literature review studies in SE has increased in the past five years [18], few studies exist which evaluate the reliability of literature search approaches for example to evaluate the repeatability of protocol-driven methods or to compare the results of literature searches conducted through different methods such as SLR and snowballing. In the following, we summarize the relevant research.

Greenhalgh and Peacock [6] conducted a study in order to describe where papers come from in a systematic review of complex evidence. They applied three different methods and found 495 primary sources related to "therapeutic interventions". Their conclusion was that protocol-driven search strategies by themselves are not the most efficient method regardless of the number of traversed databases, because some sources may be found through personal knowledge / contacts (e.g. browsing library shelves, asking colleagues), and snowballing is the best approach for identifying sources published in obscure journals.

In 2009, Skoglund and Runeson [15] investigated a reference-based search approach with the primary purpose of reducing the number of initial articles found in SLRs. Although the proposed method increased the precision without missing too many relevant papers for the technically focused reviews, its results were not satisfactory when the search area was wide or the searches included general terms. This implies that the choice of approach to searching is context-dependent.

Zhang et al. [13] conducted two participant-observer case studies to propose an effective way of identifying relevant papers in SLRs. The approach was based on the concept of quasi-gold standard for retrieving and identifying relevant studies, and it was concluded to serve the purpose and hence it can be used as a supplement to the guidelines for SLRs in EBSE. In a follow up validation study [3], a dual-case study was performed, and the proposed approach seemed to be more efficient than the EBSE process in capturing relevant studies and in saving reviewers' time. Further, the authors recommended an integrated search strategy to avoid limitations of applying a manual strategy or an automated search strategy.

MacDonell et al. [12] evaluated the reliability of systematic reviews through comparing the results of two studies with a common research question performed by two independent groups of researchers. In their case, the SLR seemed to be robust to differences in process and people, and it produced stable outcomes.

Kitchenham et al. [16] conducted a participant-observer multi-case study to investigate the repeatability of SLRs performed independently by two novice researchers. However, they did not find any indication of repeatability of such studies that are run by novice researchers.

In summary, too few studies have addressed the reliability of secondary studies. As discussed here, they have either compared different SLRs or mapping studies to check whether the same results are achieved [12] and [16], or investigated more efficient approaches of searching [6], [15] and [13]. As a complement to previous studies, we investigate the reliability of secondary studies using different search strategies. This is done by comparing the outcome of two studies on the same topic using different guidelines for finding the relevant literature. The research method used is discussed next.

3. RESEARCH METHOD

The main objective of this study is to examine whether two systematic review studies would provide the same result when the applied first step in the search strategy is different. Therefore, we planned two separate literature reviews.

The first study was conducted within 2009-2010 to capture relevant research about the most common Agile practices applied in different settings of global software engineering [9]. The second study was performed during 2010-2011 with exactly the same purpose and the same research questions [10]. The difference between the two studies was the way that the relevant papers and articles were extracted from the published research, i.e. the search strategy. The time between the two searches was a couple of months and the time between the syntheses was around eight months, and hence the details about specific papers found in the first search were not fresh in the mind of the researchers. Thus making the searches reasonably independent. An alternative would have been to have different researchers conducting the two studies. However, this would have introduced threats in relation to judgments of inclusion and exclusion of papers. The threat of having the same researchers involved was mitigated by time, i.e. by leaving several months between the two studies the researchers did not remember all the details of individual papers.

The first study (**S1**) follows the guidelines provided by Kitchenham and Charters [11] as far as it comes to conducting searches in the databases. S1 did not use snowballing from reference lists as recommended in the guidelines. In the second study (**S2**), a backward snowballing [4] approach was used. The starting set of papers for the snowballing approach was generated through a search in Google Scholar[1] on peer-reviewed papers published in 2009 rather than using our knowledge of relevant papers gained during S1. However, the purpose was to avoid the bias at this stage. This is further elaborated below.

The snowballing search method [4] can be summarized in three steps: 1) Start the searches in the leading journals and / or the conference proceedings to get a starting set of papers, 2) Go backward by reviewing the reference lists of the relevant articles found in step 1 and step 2 (iterate until no new papers are identified), and 3) Go forward by identifying articles citing the articles identified in the previous steps. Based on that S1 was focused on a specific time period, i.e. 1999-2009, it was decided to identify a starting set of papers from 2009 and then use backward snowballing based on the papers found. Given that researchers seem to focus on the database search, despite the guidelines [11], it was decided to only compare the first step for the searches, i.e.

---

[1]http://scholar.google.com/intl/en/scholar/about.html

the database search vs. the backward snowballing approach. It was done for two reasons:

1. It would make the systematic literature review using the guidelines more representative of the state of studies actually published. As a consequence we saw a need to not follow the guidelines [4] for snowballing perfectly either. Thus, trying to be as fair as possible in the comparison. It would have been unfair to follow the guidelines very closely in one case and then not in the other case.

2. It was realized that a more comprehensive use of the guidelines, i.e. following all steps recommended, would result in the outcomes getting closer to each other. With the first step, we refer to only doing the database search. However, for the papers found in the database search, we check relevance and quality to finally have a set of primary studies. The same procedure is done based on the other guideline [4], i.e. we only perform backward snowballing and identify a primary set of papers. Having done all steps recommended in the guidelines would undoubtedly mean that more papers would be included and if the searches being perfect they would end up with exactly the same set of papers. Thus, we wanted to compare the first steps in the different guidelines, since it is reasonable to believe that if these produce similar enough results, then a larger sample of papers would just increase the similarity. Thus, we are concerned with comparing the samples of papers obtained when conducting the first steps in the two different guidelines [11] and [4] respectively.

Furthermore, to make the studies as comparable as possible, we kept the search terms and keywords as similar as possible in both studies and also applied the same constraints on searches. This means that the same search terms were used in the database searches in S1 as in the Google Scholar search in S2. In addition, the same researchers were responsible for finding, evaluating, and analyzing the relevant papers in both studies in order to minimize the diversity in data collection and data analysis. Hence, the only (intended) difference between S1 and S2 is the search approach (the way we identified the relevant papers).

The assessment is performed through comparing the results of the two studies based on their primary papers and their conclusions. In summary, the research questions are:

- RQ1. To what extent do we find the same research papers using two different review approaches?

- RQ2. To what extent do we come to the same conclusions using two different review approaches?

In order to answer the research questions, we conducted an in-depth comparison of the two studies.

3.1 Details of Studies

S1: It was designed to be a systematic literature review following the guidelines by Kitchenham and Charters [11], although only doing the database searches and not snowballing. The study was conducted during 2009-2010 with the purpose of capturing the status of combining Agility with GSE [9]. The results were limited to peer-reviewed conference papers and journal articles published in 1999-2009.

The final set of papers (81 distinctive papers) was synthesized by classifying them into different categories (e.g. publication year, contribution type, research method and Agile practices used in GSE). More details of the S1 can be found in [9] and [2].

S2: It had the same purpose and research questions as the first study, and was conducted after we were finished with S1 (2010-2011) [10]. In this study, we followed the guidelines provided by Webster and Watson [4] regarding identification of a starting set of papers followed by backward snowballing. We searched in Google Scholar (only once) using similar search terms as in S1, and then limiting the search to 2009 to identify a starting set of papers for the backward snowballing. The main purpose with the search in Google Scholar was to minimize the researcher's bias in relation to S1 since an alternative was to begin with a set of relevant papers identified through S1. First, we evaluated the relevancy of the papers and then went through the reference list of the relevant papers in order to find additional sources. The process was stopped when we could not add any further relevant papers published in the time period 1999-2009. The analysis of the data was kept as similar as possible to S1. Some further details of S2 can be found in [10], since our objective is not to present the individual studies as such; the focus is on comparing the outcome of the two different first steps for the searches based on guidelines by Kitchenham and Charters [11] and Webster and Watson [4] respectively.

It has to be noted that the same criteria for inclusion process were applied in both studies e.g. gray literature was excluded from further analysis.

3.2 Comparison Approaches

The comparison is done in two different ways. First, we examined all papers identified in S1 and S2 regarding the papers included and the findings. However, due to the fact that the majority of the articles were identical, it was not surprising that the conclusions and the findings would be also similar in both studies. Therefore, we conducted a second comparison in which we excluded the papers, which were in common for both studies, and performed the analyses solely on the unique papers for S1 and S2 respectively. Then, we compared the findings from the two analyses. The major purpose of comparisons was to investigate similarities and differences between the extracted data for the same variables (e.g. research type) in database searches (S1) and backward snowballing (S2).

4. RESULTS

In the following, we present the differences and similarities between the findings of S1 and S2 given the different first steps for the searches.

4.1 Number of Papers

The first comparison relates to the number of papers found in the two studies. S1 resulted in 534 papers being identified from the databases. 81 papers were initially judged to be relevant. Thus, the data analysis began with 81 papers, but some articles were excluded. Papers were excluded if the report was incomplete (e.g. the results were missing), or if it was exactly the same study as another one in the list (e.g. if an empirical study formed the basis for both a conference paper and an extension published in a journal).

Finally, 53 papers were included in data analysis. In S2,

we found 109 papers initially. After an analysis of the relevance, we were left with 74 papers. At the end, 42 papers were included in the data analysis. Papers were removed based on the same criteria in both studies, and hence the main difference is the initial way of finding papers, i.e. the search strategy.

There is a huge difference between the numbers of papers we initially found (109 vs. 534), but it should be noted that we have checked the title of a lot of sources in snowballing too, i.e. when browsing the reference lists of the papers identified. The latter makes it hard to compare the numbers in the first step exactly. Nevertheless, 45 paper were the same in the initial set of papers identified. This overlap was surprisingly low (8% in S1 and 41% in S2). However, the situation changes when we look at the papers in the next step, i.e. those initially judged as relevant. In this step, 41 papers were identical, which should be compared with having 81 papers in S1 and 74 papers in S2 that indicates 51% and 55% overlap respectively. The final set of papers used for data extraction include 53 papers in S1 and 42 in S2 with 27 identical papers (51% overlap for S1 and 64% for S2) which is a slight majority of the identified papers between the two studies. Figure 1 visualizes the overlapping papers at the last stage and all stages are summarized in Table 1, where the unique papers in each study are shown separately as well as the papers in common. Discussions around the differences between the unique set of papers found in S1 and in S2 are provided in the Appendix.

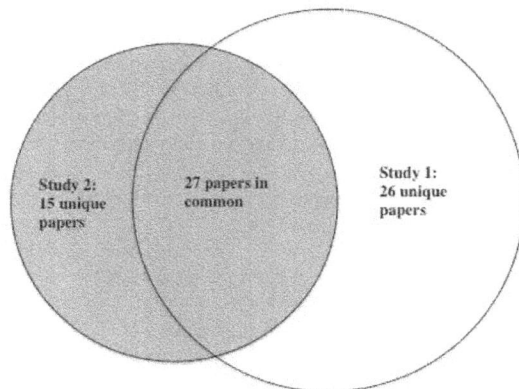

Figure 1: Venn Diagram for the Overlapping Papers

Table 1: Number of Papers in Two Different Studies

Study No.	Initial Papers	Relevant	Analyzed	Unique
1	489+45	40+41	26+27	26
2	64+45	33+41	15+27	15

The list of papers in common in S1 and S2 as well as list of unique papers for each separate study can be accessed in [19], in which the identical papers are denoted with M and are listed in Appendix A; the unique papers for S1 are denoted with D and are listed in Appendix B; and the unique papers for S2 are denoted with B and listed in Appendix C.

Table 4 in the Appendix summarizes the differences between unique set of papers found through database searches (S1) and backward snowballing (S2). For each paper, it represents: 1) the publication year, 2) the database that the paper has been found in, 3) the terms in the title that belong to the first set of keywords, 4) the terms in the title that are in the second set of keywords, 5) if the paper is expected to be found in the other study, 6) and notes or comments. Symbol "?" in the table indicates that the information is not available.

As Table 4 shows, 10 papers in S1 do not include terms from both set of keywords in their *title* and hence cannot be found in S2 (represented by "N" in the "expected" column). Two papers (denoted by "M") could be possibly found in S2 since they include names of Agile practices in their title (i.e. "TDD" in [D19], "user stories and acceptance tests" in [D3]) and it is also evident from the title that they are within GSE. Thus, 14 papers (out of 26) should have been possible to find in S2. The reason for missing them in S2 might be either due to researchers' error or because they were not cited by other relevant papers found in the backward snowballing.

In the list of unique papers found through backward snowballing (S2), six papers (out of 15) should have been possible to find, although they were not (see Table 4 in the Appendix). Therefore, we checked the complete list of papers found initially in S1 (including 534 papers). Two out of six papers were excluded in S1 in the later data analyses because the research was already published in another paper found in S1. One of the original papers is missing in S2 while one is included. This indicates that the researchers have evaluated papers in S1 and S2 in a slightly different way. Six other studies are published in different databases than databases of S1 and hence cannot be found in S1.

Three papers ([B4], [B1] and [B7]) use a slightly different terminology and hence they are not within the set of defined keywords in S1 (see Table 4 in the Appendix). Therefore, if the same terms are used in the abstract, they cannot be found in S1. For example, a study such as [B4] uses "extremely" in the title and we could guess that it refers to "Extreme Programming". However, it is surprisingly not found in S1 although by reading the abstract in S2, we judged it as relevant. This might indicate the different ways used by the researchers and the search engines to interpret the terms in the text. In the case of [B1], "remotely located" is used in the title, which could not be found in the searches in databases since the equivalent term of "remote team" was formulated in S1. It was found through backward snowballing because only by seeing these words in the title of the article, we could immediately recognize that "remotely located" means global or distributed. The examples illustrate the challenges in formulating search strings while in snowballing it may become evident to the researcher to include a paper when reading the title of a paper.

4.2 Distribution of Papers

The next step in the comparison is to compare the distribution of papers across the years.

4.2.1 First Comparison

As mentioned above, the first comparison includes all papers found in both studies, while the second comparison (see below) compare the unique papers in each of the two studies. As shown in Table 2, the number of papers found in S1 and S2 in each year (1999-2009) is not the same.

However, the pattern of distribution does not seem to be completely different and both indicate that the number of papers has grown in the past decade.

Table 2: Number of Papers over Years

	Year	1999	2000	2001	2002	2003	2004	2005	2006	2007	2008	2009
No. of	S1	0	0	0	1	2	10	6	12	14	20	17
Papers	S2	0	1	3	2	7	8	3	7	7	10	13

4.2.2 Second Comparison

The number of unique papers found by each study in each year is presented in Table 3. We have found no unique papers in S1 before 2004. Considering the number of papers in 2009, it is hard to conclude that the number of published papers is increasing in the past decade. In S2, the number of published papers seems to be constant over the years.

Table 3: Number of Papers over Years 2

	Year	1999	2000	2001	2002	2003	2004	2005	2006	2007	2008	2009
No. of	S1	0	0	0	0	0	4	3	0	9	7	4
Papers	S2	0	1	2	0	2	2	2	1	1	1	3

However, we should mention that this comparison is not fully fair because the total number of papers shall be compared against each other instead of considering only the unique ones. The question is whether the differences are due to the different search strategies.

4.3 Distribution of Research Types

Next, we wanted to compare the research types using the classification from Wieringa et al. [17]. In summary, the types are defined as follows:

Evaluation Research: Techniques, methods, tools or other solutions are implemented and evaluated in practice, and the outcomes are investigated.

Validation Research: A novel solution is developed and evaluated in a laboratory setting.

Solution Proposal: A solution for a research problem is proposed, and the benefits are discussed, but not evaluated.

Conceptual Proposal or Philosophical Paper: It structures an area in the form of a taxonomy or conceptual framework, hence provides a new way of looking at existing things.

Experience Paper: It includes the experience of the author on what and how something happened in practice.

Opinion Paper: The personal opinion on a special matter is discussed in an opinion paper without relying on related work and research methodologies.

4.3.1 First Comparison

Both studies have found a majority of papers to be reported as experience reports in which practitioners have reported their own experiences on a specific issue and the method applied to alleviate it [17]. It should be noted that the number of papers in S1 and S2 for each research type is different. This difference is, however, expected due to the fact that the number of papers found in S1 and S2 are different. In addition, the order of research types according to their frequency is different. The order in S1 is: 1) experience report, 2) evaluation, 3) opinion, 4) solution, 5) validation and 6) philosophical, and in S2 it is 1) experience, 2) validation, 3) evaluation, 4) solution, 5) philosophical and 6) opinion. It is surprising that we found no opinion paper in S2 while it was the third most frequent research type in S1.

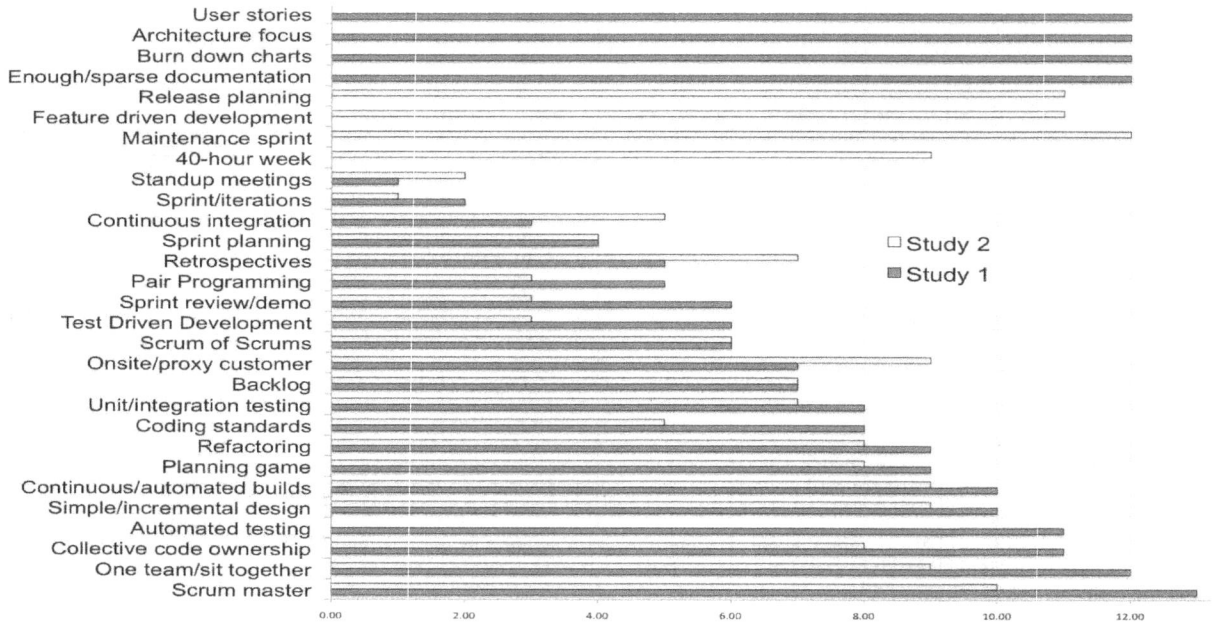

Figure 2: Agile Practices in S1 and S2 - Comparison 1

4.3.2 Second Comparison

When it comes to a comparison of the unique papers, the majority of the current research was found to be in form of experience reports in both studies. And in addition to the identified research types in S1, a solution paper is found in S2.

4.4 Countries Involved in GSE

It is also possible to compare the most common combinations of collaboration. The combinations include both global collaboration and distributed development.

4.4.1 First Comparison

In both studies, the collaboration between USA-India is found to be the most popular, and then distributed development within USA although the exact numbers are different.

4.4.2 Second Comparison

The same pattern as in the first comparison is found through the second comparison.

4.5 Most Efficient Practices

To identify the most efficient Agile practices used in a GSE was one of the main objectives of the literature review, and hence this is an important aspect to compare. If the studies identify completely different Agile practices, then the search strategy has indeed influenced the outcome of the literature review.

We would like to emphasize that it is not our intention to discuss the actual outcome in terms of which Agile practices are most efficient in a GSE setting. Our objective is to compare the outcomes from a search strategy point of view. Hence, the actual outcomes regarding Agility and GSE can be accessed in [9] and [10].

4.5.1 First Comparison

Considering the frequency of Agile practices in literature, we sorted the list of reported practices in both studies, where frequencies were counted based on the number of publications referring to a practice as being successful. We classified the practices based on their rank in a descending list. For example, if the highest frequency was found to be 18 for practice A, then practice A was assigned to class 1 together with all other practices having a frequency of 18. It means that the rank of each practice, in the sorted list, was considered as the class the practice belongs to. The practices with the same frequency have been assigned to the same class. The purpose of the classification was to be able to make a fair comparison, since the number of analyzed papers was different in S1 and S2. The result of the comparison is summarized in Figure 2 (the x-axis represents the classes for the practices).

If we take the 3 top classes of practices, S1 reported "standup meetings" (class 1), "sprint / iterations" (class 2), and "continuous integration" (class 3). S2 found "sprint / iterations" (class 1), "standup meetings" (class 2), and three practices of "pair programming", "sprint review / demo" and "test driven development" in class 3. Thus, top three efficient Agile practices in S1 and S2 are overlapping (2 out of 3 = 66%).

According to Figure 2, general agreement of the most efficient practices is high (see classes 1 to 8). However, the higher classes (9 and higher) are infrequent, which means that these practices are mentioned by few studies and hence the difference is simply due to random, i.e. whether specific papers mentioning these practices are included or not.

4.5.2 Second Comparison

In this comparison, both studies found 18 practices, in which 13 of them were identical and 5 unique practices were found in each study (summarized in Figure 3).

Similar to Figure 2, the most frequent Agile practices ac-

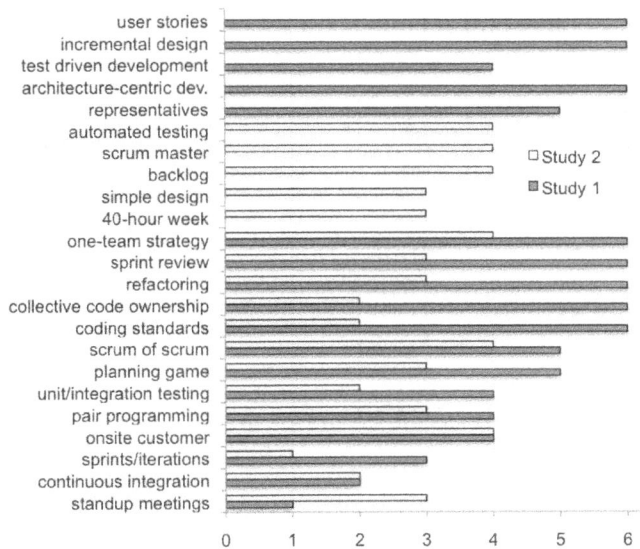

Figure 3: Practices in S1 and S2 - Comparison 2

cording to the literature (low numbers in Figure 3) show a very strong agreement.

4.6 Details for Agile - GSE Combinations

4.6.1 First Comparison

So far, we have presented and discussed which Agile practices were found most efficient in S1 and S2 as well as the countries involved in each combination of Agile method and distribution setting. For the purpose of comparison, we have assigned different scores to the combinations. If the practices and the countries found are the same for the Agile GSE combination in S1 and S2, we have assigned the score 4 to the combination; score 3 if only the practices are the same; score 2 if only the countries are identical; score 1 if neither practices nor countries are the same; and finally score 0 if the combination does not exist in the other study.

In this comparison, a majority of combinations are completely different. However, if we exclude the combinations, which were found in only one study (i.e. XP-open source in S2 and Agile-open source in S1), similar findings were identified for a majority of the combinations in both studies. Thus, it is clear that the comparison is very sensitive to individual studies.

4.6.2 Second Comparison

Unlike the previous comparison, most combinations seem to be completely different. However, it may be due to that the comparison is very sensitive to individual studies, and given that we have fewer studies here than in the first comparison, it may make it even more sensitive. It should be noted that the combinations of Agile with offshore, open source, and virtual team were found only in S1 whereas XP-open source, and XP-unclear were found only in S2. The latter combination means that the setting was unclear, although XP was used.

The higher the number shown in Figure 4 is, the higher is the similarity between the patterns in each comparison. Comparison 1 shows completely different pattern for 4 com-

binations out of 12, which indicates in 67% of the cases, the country involved, the Agile practices, or both have been the same for a specific combination of Agile and GSE.

In the second comparison, 7 patterns out of 11 are found to be completely different which is considerably different from results of comparison 1.

In the other words, we found exactly the same pattern (i.e. both Agile practices and the involved countries are the same in S1 and S2) for "three" distinctive combinations in comparison 1 and "one" combination in comparison 2. However, the number of combinations, which have the same score in both comparisons, is 6 out of 14, which implies 42% overlap. In addition, if we exclude the unique combinations, 6 out of 9 combinations have the same rank, which is 66% overlap.

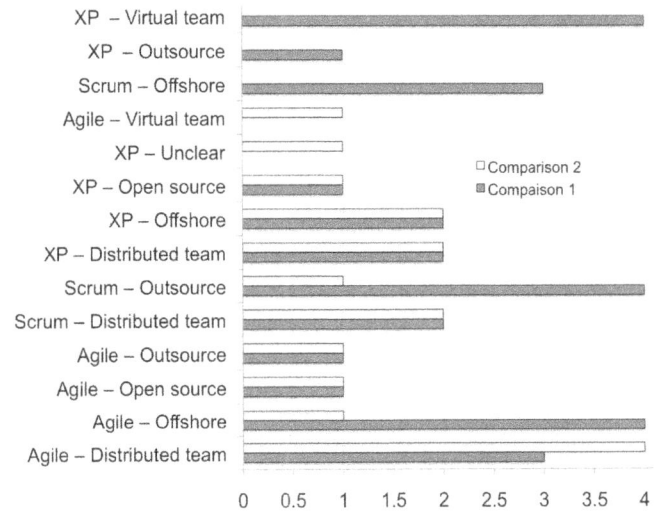

Figure 4: Patterns of Agile GSE Combinations

4.7 Limitations

In order to assure the reliability in this study, we tried to improve the reliability of the two systematic review studies in the first place (more details on this for each individual study can be found in [9] and [10]). Then considering the purpose of this study, which was to conduct a comparison, we tried to perform the comparison as fairly as possible.

Therefore, the researchers were the same in S1 and S2, and the analyses on the data were performed as similar as possible. Although we had more experiences of doing systematic reviews when we started S2, we tried to keep the gap between conducting searches as small as possible. So the data was collected with a few months difference for S1 and S2, although we synthesized them later for S2. The latter was done to ensure that the researchers did not remember all details when deciding on, for example, inclusion and exclusion of paper in S2. In addition, two researchers were involved in reviewing the comparisons and drawing the conclusions of this study.

In addition, the order of conducting the studies might have affected the results of each study and as a consequence the result of the comparisons.

5. DISCUSSION

5.1 Time and Effort Required

We cannot certainly claim that SLRs are more time consuming in formulating the search strings because snowballing requires some formulations too. However, SLRs require separate formulation for each database whilst snowballing does not explicitly require searching in more than one database. The number of initial papers in S1 was 534 and 109 in S2 which indicates greater time and effort spent to refine the searchers as well as identifying the relevant papers and discarding the irrelevant ones in the database searches approach (4.9 times more papers in S1 than S2).

5.2 Noise vs. Included Papers

Considering the term "Agile" which is a very general word and used in many papers in many disciplines, we found a lot of noise in S1. Due to this, we had to limit the search to abstract, title, and keywords. But still the number of irrelevant papers was much higher than the number of included and analyzed papers (85% noise). In the snowballing search, the balance seemed to be more reasonable (32% noise).

5.3 Judgments of Papers

In snowballing, most of the judgments were done based on the title of the paper when going backward through the reference lists (or forward in the citations if being applied). In some cases, we judged papers once more based on their abstract, i.e. it resulted in performing a stepwise judgment. In the SLR, the judgments were done on title and abstract at the same time. It should be noted that the papers with no relevant keywords in the title might be missed in snowballing. On the other hand, the papers that use different wordings (as in the example with cross-continent) might not be caught in an SLR.

5.4 Prior Experience

Prior experience of the researcher in the area of the studies as well as in performing the secondary studies may affect the results. The differences can be seen, for example, when judging the relevancy of the papers. An experienced person already knows several papers and knows several active researchers in the area, which may affect the reliability of the secondary study regarding the relevancy of included papers.

5.5 Ease of Use

We found the snowballing approach to be more understandable and easy to follow in particular it is believed to be easier for novice researchers. The SLR provides a lot of guidelines, which is good on one hand, but on the other hand novice researchers might find it confusing rather than helpful.

5.6 Identical Authors Risk

A potential threat in snowballing is that we might find several papers from the same authors since their previous research is usually relevant and is cited. Thus, the results of snowballing approach, might be biased by over presenting specific authors' research. On the other hand, database searches method performs searches on all papers in the database which eliminates this risk.

5.7 General Remark on Literature

It should be noted that a general problem with systematic literature reviews in software engineering is that in many cases existing papers are hard to classify and analyze since in many of the published studies, the contextual information is not well documented or the studies are not conducted in a realistic setting [1]. We have observed that insufficient contextual information hinders synthesizing the evidence from some studies (in particular industrial experience reports). Thus, we recommend practitioners and researchers working with industry to follow guidelines provided by Petersen and Wohlin [5] for documenting the contextual information.

6. CONCLUSIONS

In this paper, we evaluated two different first steps for conducting systematic literature studies. This was done by comparing two secondary studies on Agile practices in GSE, which were performed by the same researchers but using different search methods. First, we compared the studies against each other whether the same set of papers was found and if the included papers had resulted in the same conclusions. Secondly, we excluded the common papers from both studies and performed new analyses with the remaining unique papers for each study. Considering the fact that these comparisons did not indicate any remarkable differences between the two different studies, we compared the actual results found using the two different search methods applied. A summary of the findings is provided below. After comparing the two secondary studies in two different ways (with the common papers and with only the unique papers in each study), we did not find any major differences between the findings of the analyses. The figures and numbers were not the same, but the general interpretation of them is quite similar. We can summarize our findings as follows for the two research questions.

RQ1. To what extent do we find the same research papers using two different review approaches?
To answer the RQ1, we may observe that the papers found are different both in the number and the actual papers. In addition, the final set of papers used in data analyses, was also found to be different, although 27 papers were common. This is not really surprising given that we only used the first step in the two search methods, i.e. according to the different guidelines used. It is highly likely that the overlap would increase if we conducted snowballing from the papers found in the database searches, and also if we did forward snowballing when starting with backward snowballing. However, it is should be noted that a majority of the papers are the same despite only comparing the staring point for the comparison, i.e. database search vs. backward snowballing.

RQ2. To what extent do we come to the same conclusions using two different review approaches?
The answer to the RQ2 is more important, since it concerns the actual findings. Regardless of the differences in the actual numbers and figures, similar pattern were identified in both studies and hence similar conclusions were drawn. However, when excluding the same papers from both studies and analyzing only the remaining unique papers of each study, the identified patterns seem to be slightly different, which may be due to having fewer papers (a smaller sample). Therefore, it is not easy to draw any general conclusions with respect to the RQ2.

However, given the overlap, despite only conducting the first part in the guidelines, it indicates that the actual conclusions are at least not highly dependent on whether using database searches or snowballing. It is also quite obvious that the overlap will become larger if combining the two search strategies, although the downside being that it generates more work. Systematic literature studies are quite time consuming. Snowballing might be more efficient when the keywords for searching include general terms (e.g. Agile), because it dramatically reduces the amount of noise in database searches. Our personal experience confirms this. However, we recommend applying both backward and forward snowballing.

Although these conclusions, recommendations, and findings are based on our experiences with this comparison study as well as previous secondary studies, they seem to be in alignment with some previous studies [6] and [15], but contradictory with some others [14]. In anyway, more such comparison studies are required to be able to compare the methods fairly.

7. ACKNOWLEDGMENTS

This research was funded by the Industrial Excellence Center EASE - Embedded Applications Software Engineering, (http://ease.cs.lth.se).

8. REFERENCES

[1] M. Ivarsson, T. Gorschek (2011): A method for Evaluating Rigor and Industrial Relevance of Technology Evaluations. Empirical Software Engineering 16(3): 365-395.

[2] S. Jalali, C. Wohlin (2010): Agile Practices in Global Software Engineering - a Systematic Map. In 5th IEEE International Conference on Global Software Engineering, Princeton, USA, pp. 45-54.

[3] H. Zhang, M. A. Babar, X. Bai, J. Li, L. Huang (2011): An Empirical Assessment of a Systematic Search Process for Systematic Reviews. In the Proceedings of the 15th International Conference on Evaluation and Assessment in Software Engineering, pp. 56-65.

[4] J. Webster, R. T. Watson (2002.): Analyzing the Past to Prepare for the Future: Writing a Literature Review. MIS Quarterly 26(2): xiii-xxiii.

[5] K. Petersen, C. Wohlin (2009): Context in Industrial Software Engineering Research. 3rd International Symposium on Empirical Software Engineering and Measurement, pp. 401-404.

[6] T. Greenhalgh, R. Peacock (2005): Effectiveness and Efficiency of Search Methods in Systematic Reviews of Complex Evidence: Audit of Primary Sources. BMJ 331(7524): 1064-1065.

[7] B. Kitchenham, T. Dybå, M. Jørgensen (2004): Evidence-based Software Engineering. In Proceeding of the 27th IEEE International Conference on Software Engineering, pp. 273-281, IEEE Computer Society.

[8] T. Dybå, B. Kitchenham, M. Jørgensen (2005): Evidence-based Software Engineering for Practitioners. IEEE Software 22(1): 58-65.

[9] S. Jalali, C. Wohlin (2011): Global Software Engineering and Agile Practices: A Systematic Review. Journal of Software: Evolution and Process, published online: DOI: 10.1002/smr.561.

[10] S. Jalali, C. Wohlin (2011): Global Software Engineering and Agile Practices: A Systematic Review through Snowballing, Technical Report, http://www.wohlin.eu/GS_Search_Agile_and_Global.pdf.

[11] B. Kitchenham, S. Charters (2007): Guidelines for Performing Systematic Literature Reviews in Software Engineering. Version 2.3, Technical Report, Software Engineering Group, Keele University and Department of Computer Science, University of Durham.

[12] S. MacDonell, M. Shepperd, B. Kitchenham, E. Mendes (2010): How Reliable are Systematic Reviews in Empirical Software Engineering?. IEEE Transactions on Software Engineering 36(5): 676-687.

[13] H. Zhang, M. A. Babar, P. Tell (2011): Identifying Relevant Studies in Software Engineering. Information and Software Technology 53(6): 625-637.

[14] P. Brereton, B. Kitchenham, D. Budgen, M. Turner, M. Khalil (2007): Lessons from Applying the Systematic Literature Review Process within the Software Engineering Domain. Journal of Systems and Software 80(4): 571-583.

[15] M. Skoglund, P. Runeson (2009): Reference-based Search Strategies in Systematic Reviews. In the Proceedings of the 13th International Conference on Evaluation and Assessment in Software Engineering, Durham, England.

[16] B. Kitchenham, P. Brereton, Z. Li, D. Budgen, A. Burn (2001): Repeatability of Systematic Literature Reviews. In the Proceedings of the 15th International Conference on Evaluation and Assessment in Software Engineering, pp. 46-55.

[17] R. Wieringa, N. A. M. Maiden, N. R. Mead, C. Rolland (2006): Requirements Engineering Paper Classification and Evaluation Criteria: a Proposal and a Discussion. Journal of Requirements Engineering 11(1): 102-107.

[18] M. A. Babar, H. Zhang (2009): Systematic Literature Reviews in Software Engineering: Preliminary Results from Interviews with Researchers. In the Proceedings of the 3rd International Symposium On Empirical Software Engineering And Measurement, pp. 346-355, IEEE Computer Society.

[19] S. Jalali, C. Wohlin (2011): Systematic Literature Studies: Database Searches vs. Backward Snowballing. Technical Report, http://www.wohlin.eu/Database_Snowballing.pdf.

[20] K. Petersen, R. Feldt, S. Mujtaba, M. Mattsson (2008): Systematic Mapping Studies in Software Engineering. In the Proceedings of the 12th International Conference on Evaluation and Assessment in Software Engineering.

APPENDIX

Table 4 visualizes the differences between unique set of papers found through S1 and S2.

Table 4: Differences of Papers in S1 and S2

Study	Year	Ref.	Database	Keyword 1	Keyword 2	Expected	Comments
S1	2004	[D19]	ACM	?	Open Source	M	"TDD" in the title
S1	2004	[D15]	Inspec	XP	Distributed	Y	
S1	2004	[D22]	IEEE	XP	Outsourcing	Y	
S1	2004	[D7]	ACM	XP, Agile	?	N	
S1	2005	[D10]	ACM	?	?	N	
S1	2005	[D11]	IEEE	Agile	?	N	
S1	2005	[D13]	Compendex	Agile, XP	?	N	
S1	2007	[D18]	IEEE	Agile	?	N	
S1	2007	[D23]	AIS	Agile	Global, Distributed	Y	
S1	2007	[D1]	IEEE	XP	Offshore	Y	
S1	2007	[D2]	ACM	Agile	Offshore	Y	
S1	2007	[D3]	Compendex	?	Offshore	M	"User Stories", "Acceptance Tests" in the title
S1	2007	[D4]	Inspec	Agile	Global	Y	
S1	2007	[D8]	Inspec	Agile	Distributed Teams	Y	
S1	2007	[D9]	Compendex	Agile	Offshoring	Y	
S1	2008	[D12]	IEEE	?	?	N	"Continuous Integration" in the title
S1	2008	[D14]	AIS	Agile	Distributed	Y	
S1	2008	[D5]	IEEE	Scrum	?	N	
S1	2008	[D16]	IEEE	Agile	Distributed	Y	
S1	2008	[D20]	IEEE	Scrum	Offshore	Y	
S1	2008	[D21]	IEEE	?	Distributed	N	
S1	2008	[D24]	IEEE	Agile	Distributed	Y	
S1	2009	[D25]	Scopus	Agile	Distributed	Y	
S1	2009	[D26]	Scopus	Agile	Distributed	Y	
S1	2009	[D17]	Compendex	Scrum	?	N	
S1	2009	[D6]	IEEE	Agile	?	N	
S2	2000	[B14]	ACM	XP	Open-source	Y	
S2	2000	[B7]	IEEE	Daily Build	Distributed	M	"Daily Build" is not in the set of keywords of S1
S2	2001	[B8]	XP Proc.	XP	Distributed	N	
S2	2003	[B2]	Scopus	XP	Global Software Development	Y	
S2	2003	[B6]	Springer	Scrum, XP	Cross-continent	N	
S2	2004	[B12]	IEEE	XP	Global Software Development	Y	It was excluded in S1
S2	2004	[B15]	GSD Proc.	Iterative	Global Software Development	N	"Iterative" is not in the set of keywords of S1
S2	2005	[B9]	DSD Proc.	XP	Distributed	N	
S2	2005	[B13]	IEEE	XP	Distributed	Y	
S2	2006	[B4]	IEEE	XP	Distributed	M	"Extremely" refers to XP
S2	2007	[B3]	AIS	Scrum	Distributed	Y	
S2	2008	[B10]	IEEE	Scrum	Distributed	Y	It was excluded in S1
S2	2009	[B5]	MIPRO Proc.	Agile	Globally Distributed	N	
S2	2009	[B11]	Springer	XP	Offshore	N	
S2	2009	[B1]	IEEE	Agile	Remote	M	"Remote" is not within the keywords of S1

On the Definition of Dynamic Software Measures

Luigi Lavazza, Sandro Morasca, Davide Taibi, Davide Tosi
Dipartimento di Scienze Teoriche e Applicate
Università degli Studi dell'Insubria
Via Mazzini 5, I-21100, Varese, Italy
{luigi.lavazza, sandro.morasca, davide.taibi, davide.tosi}@uninsubria.it

ABSTRACT

The quantification of several software attributes (e.g., size, complexity, cohesion, coupling) is usually carried out in a static fashion, and several hundreds of measures have been defined to this end. However, static measurement may only be an approximation for the measurement of these attributes during software use. The paper proposes a theoretical framework based on Axiomatic Approaches for the definition of sensible dynamic software measures that can dynamically capture these attributes. Dynamic measures based on this framework are defined for dynamically quantifying size and coupling. In this paper, we also compare dynamic measures of size and coupling against well-known static measures by correlating them with fault-pronenesses of four case studies.

Categories and Subject Descriptors

H.4 [**Information Systems Applications**]: Miscellaneous; D.2.8 [**Software Engineering**]: Metrics—*complexity measures, performance measures*

General Terms

Measurement

Keywords

Dynamic measures, dynamic coupling, dynamic size, code coverage

1. INTRODUCTION

The vast majority of the measures for internal software attributes (e.g., structural size, structural complexity, cohesion, coupling) have been defined in a static way. However, the dynamic aspects of these attributes still remain to be largely investigated. For instance, just statically looking at the potential interactions between a software module and the rest of a software system may not tell the entire story, when assessing the coupling of the module. Suppose that

module A has fewer static connections with the rest of the system than module B does, but that module A at run-time interacts with the rest of the system much more frequently than B does. So, B may be considered to have a higher coupling than A from a static perspective, while the converse may be true from a dynamic point of view. When predicting the number of faults found due to integration problems, the dynamic interactions between classes may be more relevant than the static ones.

As another example, static size measurement does not capture the difference between heavily used and lightly used software code and may even take into account dead code. Routine A may be longer than another routine B, but it may turn out that fewer lines of code are executed in A than in B at run-time. Again, when estimating the number of faults found in a routine, dynamic size may be more relevant than static size, as one may reasonably hypothesize that the number of faults found increases with the number of lines of code exercised, rather than with the sheer number of lines of code.

Thus, it should be investigated whether dynamic measures may be used alongside static measures in the assessment of some software quality of interest or even if dynamic measures may be more useful than static ones. The distinction between static and dynamic internal software measures parallels, from a practical point of view, the distinction between static and dynamic analysis in software verification and validation. Both kinds of analysis may be useful when looking for software faults or when assessing some nonfunctional properties, like maintainability, performance, or usability.

The definition and use of a new measure for an internal software attribute entails two kinds of validation.

- Theoretical validation. We need to make sure that the new measure is adequate for quantifying the software attribute it is supposed to measure, so its values can be given a sensible interpretation. This activity can be carried out by using one of the available methods used in the Software Measurement literature, namely Measurement Theory. [8, 13] or Axiomatic Approaches [15, 6, 9].

- Empirical validation. It is necessary to check whether the new measure is practically useful, by showing that it is correlated to some variable of industrial interest. This activity can be carried out via empirical studies.

However, in the Software Measurement literature, measures have often been defined without undergoing a theoretical or an empirical validation. So, there exist literally thousands of measures for which there is no assessment as to whether they actually measure what they are supposed to measure or whether they are really useful. The end result is that the vast majority of measures has not survived the definition phase.

The contribution of this paper is therefore twofold, as we define measures for dynamic software attributes and address both kinds of validation.

- First, we introduce a framework that can be used for the definition of sensible measures for dynamic software attributes, based on Axiomatic Approaches [15, 6, 9]. As such, each dynamic software attribute may be associated with a set of necessary properties for the measures that purport to measure that attribute. These properties can guide software measurers in defining new measures for dynamic software attributes and assess the adequacy of existing ones. We have chosen size and coupling due to their importance in software development. Also, size allows us to investigate dynamic attributes for software modules in isolation, regardless of the existence of other modules, and coupling allows us to investigate dynamic attributes for modules related to other modules in a software system. The measures we define for dynamic size and coupling comply with the properties we proposed.

- Second, we have also applied these measures to a few software systems, to carry out an empirical investigation on whether these measures may be useful in practice for estimating fault proneness and compare their usefulness with static measures. Our results show that some dynamic measures can estimate fault proneness better than traditional static measures.

The remainder of the paper is organized as follows. Section 2 summarizes the basic concepts and notation used throughout the paper, which were introduced in previous work about static attribute measurement. Section 3 introduces dynamic aspects needed in the modeling of dynamic attribute measurement, via the notions of execution trace and its underlying module. Section 4 illustrates our proposed approach for the quantification of two specific dynamic software attributes: size and coupling. In Section 5, we define a few dynamic measures for size and coupling and we show that they comply with the properties required for dynamic size and coupling measures proposed in Section 4. Section 6 provides examples of use of the measures defined in Section 5. Related work is concisely reviewed in Section 7, both on coverage measures and measures that have been defined in the literature for various internal software attributes. Conclusions and an outline for future work are in Section 8.

2. STATIC ATTRIBUTES: BASIC CONCEPTS AND NOTATION

Here, we summarize the basic concepts and notation used in [9] for the Axiomatic Approaches for static attributes, as they are the basis for the proposal of this paper too. We basically view a system as a multigraph, where each arc is associated with a multiset of relationships, and each relationship has a type.

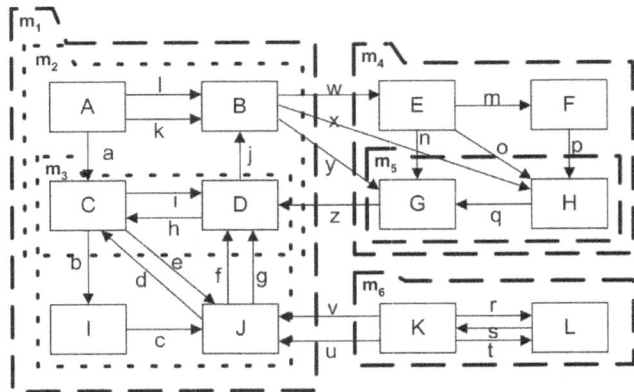

Figure 1: A UML-like Class Diagram

Definition 1. System. A system S is a pair $S = <E, R>$, where

- E represents the set of elements of S
- $R \in N^{E \times E \times T}$

where T is a finite set of types of relationships (N is the set of natural numbers, including 0).

Specifically, $<< a, b, t >, n > \in R$ associates $< a, b, t >$, i.e., a typed relationship between elements a and b, with a natural number n, which describes how many times the typed relationship $< a, b, t >$ occurs in the system.

This general representation may be adapted to different application cases. For instance, system elements (i.e., the nodes of the graph) may denote code statements, methods, classes, etc. The existence of a multiset of typed relationships associated with each arc of the graph allows one to model different kinds of interactions that may exist between system elements. For instance, suppose that a system element represents an OO class. Two OO classes may be linked by method calls or by variable uses at run-time, so different kinds of relationships may be needed. Also, each type of relationship associated with an arc may have a different cardinality. For instance, two OO classes may be linked by 5 variable uses and 20 method calls.

Figure 1 shows a system, in which we have used capital letters to denote elements and lowercase letters to denote relationships. For simplicity, all relationships in the graph have the same type.

In what follows, the same symbol (e.g., $\cup$ for union) may denote an operation between sets when sets of elements are involved, or an operation between multisets when multisets of typed relationships are involved. Even though these operations are different, no confusion will arise because there will never be an operation whose operands are a set of elements and a multiset of typed relationships.

Some software attributes require that parts of a system be identified. For instance, coupling may be defined for a specific part of the system (e.g., a class or a package) or an entire system. These parts of a system are actually subsystems that we call *modules*.

Definition 2. Module. Given a system $S = <E, R>$, a module $m = <E_m, R_m>$ is a system such that $E_m \subseteq E \wedge R_m \subseteq R$.

Thus, for maximum generality and simplicity, a module is simply a subsystem, with no additional characteristics (e.g., an interface).

Given a module m of a system $S = <E, R>$, the multiset of those relationships that involve one element within m and one element outside m is called the set of outer relationships of m and is denoted as $OuterR(m)$, with $OuterR(m) \subseteq R$. In Figure 1, UML-like packages [1] $m_1, m_2, m_3, m_4, m_5, m_6$, may be interpreted as modules. For notational convenience, it will be implied in the remainder of the paper that the set of elements and the multiset of relationships of a system or a module have the same subscript as the system or module, unless otherwise explicitly specified. For instance, it will be implied that m_1 has the set of elements E_1 and the multiset of relationships R_1. If no subscript appears in the name of the system or module, then no subscript appears in the name of its set of elements and multiset of relationships.

We now define an algebra for modules, based on set and typed multiset operations.

Inclusion. Module m_1 is said to be included in module m_2 (notation: $m_1 \subseteq m_2$) if $E_1 \subseteq E_2 \wedge R_1 \subseteq R_2$. In Figure 1, $m_5 \subseteq m_4$.

Union. The union of modules m_1 and m_2 (notation: $m_1 \cup m_2$) is the module $< E_1 \cup E_2, R_1 \cup R_2 >$. In Figure 1, $m_1 = m_2 \cup m_3$.

Intersection. The intersection of modules m_1 and m_2 (notation: $m_1 \cap m_2$) is the module $< E_1 \cap E_2, R_1 \cap R_2 >$. In Figure 1, $m_2 \cap m_3$ is the module whose elements are classes C and D and whose relationships are $< i, 1 >$ and $< h, 1 >$.

Empty module. Module $< \oslash, \oslash >$ (denoted by $\oslash$) is the empty module.

Disjoint modules. Modules m_1 and m_2 are said to be disjoint if $m_1 \cap m_2 = \oslash$. In Figure 1, m_3 and m_6 are disjoint.

Unconnected modules. Two disjoint modules m_1 and m_2 of a system are said to be unconnected if $OuterR(m_1) \cap OuterR(m_2) = \oslash$. In Figure 1, m_4 and m_6 are unconnected, while m_3 and m_6 are not unconnected.

Sets of axioms have been introduced based on these definitions. Each set of axioms describes the properties expected for the measures related to a specific software attribute, e.g., structural size, structural complexity, cohesion, coupling [6, 9].

3. EXECUTION TRACES AND DYNAMIC MODULES

Section 2 introduced the basic concepts used for the definition of static measures. In this section, we introduce the concepts related to the dynamic aspects of systems and modules in such a way that we can introduce sets of axioms for specific dynamic software attributes (see Section 4) in a way that is consistent with the axiom sets for static software attributes of [9].

In the context of a system, the dynamic view identifies a specific part of the entire system, i.e., a subsystem that we say is *executed* in a dynamic activity. We say that a part of a system is "executed" to encompass different activities like running some executable artifact such as software code and the inspection of some artifact. Even though it is usually classified as "static analysis" because it does not involve the

---
[1]Note that our definition of "module" is more general than the definition of packages in UML, which may not share classes.

machine execution of software code, the inspection of a software artifact is a dynamic activity for the software inspector that examines the software code (or any software artifact). Any subsystem is a module, based on the definitions of Section 2, so we say that a module is executed in a dynamic activity.

We assume that, during an execution, the elements and relationships of a system are exercised in a sequence, which we now formalize in the notion of execution trace.

Definition 3. Execution Trace. Given a system $S = <E, R>$ and a finite nonnegative integer number n, an execution trace tr is defined as follows:

- if $n > 0$, tr is a function

$$tr : 1..n \to E \cup R$$

  that associates a system element or relationship with any index value $i \in [1..n]$, in such a way that, if $tr(i)$ is a relationship, then $tr(i-1)$ is the start element of relationship $tr(i)$ and $tr(i+1)$ is the end element of relationship $tr(i)$; throughout the paper, such an execution trace is denoted either by its name tr or by the ordered sequence of its values;

- if $n = 0$, tr is the empty trace, which is denoted throughout the paper as ϵ.

For notational convenience, we denote

- the length n of execution trace tr as $|tr|$

- the set of elements appearing as components of an execution trace tr as $E_{tr} = \{e \in E | \exists i \in [1..|tr|] tr(i) = e\}$

- the set of component relationships of an execution trace tr as $R_{tr} = \{r \in E | \exists i \in [1..|tr|] tr(i) = r\}$.

For instance, in the system of Figure 1

$$tr = < A, a, C, i, D, j, B, C, e, J, f, D,$$
$$B, x, H, q, G, A, l, B, y, G, L, s, K >$$

is an execution trace (Formula 1).

Note that, based on the definition, a relationship may be included in an execution trace only if it is immediately preceded in the trace by its start element, and, whenever a relationship is included in the trace, it is followed by its end element. A similar requirement does not apply to elements, though. An element may not necessarily be immediately preceded by a transition in an execution trace, i.e., several nodes may be contiguously found in an execution trace. For instance, a software inspector may very well sequentially inspect a number of software classes in isolation without looking at the relationships that may exist between them. Another implication of the definition of execution trace is that there the first component of an execution trace is always an element, if the execution trace is not empty.

Given a module m and an execution sequence tr, some of the components of tr may belong to m, while others may not. We introduce the notion of dynamic module of a static module under an execution trace, to identify the part of the module that is involved in the execution trace.

Definition 4. Dynamic Module of a Module under an Execution Trace. The dynamic module of a static module

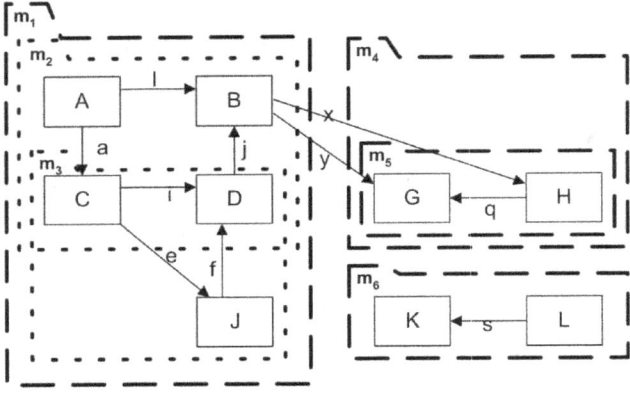

Figure 2: Dynamic Modules

$m = <E_m, R_m>$ under an execution sequence tr (notation $DynModule(m, tr)$) is composed of all of the elements and relationships appearing in both m and tr, i.e.,

$DynModule(m, tr) = <E_{DM}, R_{DM}>$, where $E_{DM} = E_m \cap E_{tr}$ and $R_{DM} = R_m \cap R_{tr}$ The underlying module $m(tr)$ of an execution trace tr is composed of all of the elements and relationships appearing in tr.

Also, an execution trace has an underlying static module composed of all the elements and the relationships that appear in the execution trace.

Definition 5. Underlying Module of an Execution Trace. The underlying module $m(tr)$ of an execution trace tr is composed of all of the elements and relationships appearing in tr.

For instance, Figure 2 shows the entire underlying module $m(tr)$ of the execution trace tr of Formula (1). The dynamic module of module m_1 in Figure 2 under execution trace tr of Formula (1) is the portion of Figure 2 strictly contained within the border of module m_1.

Like with modules, we now introduce an algebra that can be used to work with execution traces. We introduce the operations of that algebra intuitively and formally.

Inclusion. Intuitively, an execution trace tr_1 is included in execution trace tr_2 if it is possible to obtain tr_1 by eliminating elements of tr_2.

Formally, execution trace tr_1 is said to be included in execution trace tr_2 (notation: $tr_1 \subseteq tr_2$) if $\forall i, j \in 1..|tr_1|, \exists s, t \in 1..|tr_2|(i < j \wedge s < t \wedge tr_1(i) = tr_2(s) \wedge tr_1(j) = tr_2(t))$. Execution trace $tr_1 \subseteq tr_2$ is also said to be a subtrace of execution trace tr_2. As a consequence, given any trace tr, $\epsilon \subseteq tr$, i.e., the empty trace is included in all other traces. For instance, $<C, i, D, j, B, C, e, J, H, q, G, A, l, B, y, G> \subseteq tr$ for trace tr of Formula (1).

Union. Intuitively, the union of two traces tr_1 and tr_2 combines those two traces by interleaving the elements of tr_1 and tr_2 in a specified way.

Formally, the union of traces tr_1 and tr_2 according to indexing in (i.e., the function that specifies how the two traces are to be interleaved) is a trace tr_{12} (notation: $tr_{12} = tr_1 \cup_{in} tr_2$) such that the indexing schema in is a surjective function $in : [1..|tr_1| + |tr_2|] \rightarrow [1..n]$ for some integer value of n that provides an index in tr_{12} for each component of

either tr_1 or tr_2 in such a way that $\forall i \in [1..|tr_1|]tr_{12}(in(i)) = tr_1(i)$, $\forall i \in [|tr_1| + 1..|tr_1| + |tr_2|]tr_{12}(in(i)) = tr_2(i)$, and $\forall k \in [1..|tr_1| + |tr_2|], \neg\exists i \in [1..|tr_1|], j \in [|tr_1| + 1..|tr_1| + |tr_2|](in(i) = in(j) \wedge tr_1(i) \neq tr_2(j))$. As a consequence, tr_1 and tr_2 are subtraces of tr_{12}. Whenever the specific indexing chosen is immaterial, we use the abbreviated notation $tr_{12} = tr_1 \cup tr_2$. As an additional property, for any given indexing, we have $tr = tr \cup \epsilon$, i.e., the empty execution trace is the null element of this algebra of traces.

Note that, if a specific run-time execution of a software system is modeled by an execution trace, the effect of a set of run-time executions of the software system is still modeled by an execution trace, obtained as the union of the execution traces corresponding to the individual run-time executions. For instance, $<A, a, C, i, D, j, B, B, x, H, q, G, A, l, B, y, G> \cup <C, e, J, f, D, L, s, K> = tr$ for trace tr of Formula (1).

Concatenation. Intuitively, the concatenation of traces tr_1 and tr_2 is simply the trace obtained by adding trace tr_2 at the end of trace tr_1.

Formally, the concatenation of traces tr_1 and tr_2 is the trace $tr_{12} = tr_1 \cdot tr_2$ such that $|tr_{12}| = |tr_1| + |tr_2|$ and $\forall i \in [1..|tr_1|]tr_{12}(i) = tr_1(i)$ and $\forall i \in [|tr_1| + 1..|tr_1| + |tr_2|]tr_{12}(i + |tr_1|) = tr_2(i)$. So, a concatenation is a special case of union with a specific indexing, in which the components of tr_2 all appear in tr_{12} after the components of tr_1. This is the only operation in this algebra that is not commutative, as we may very well have $tr_{12} = tr_1 \cdot tr_2 \neq tr_2 \cdot tr_1 = tr_{21}$. For instance, $<A, a, C, i, D, j, B,> \cdot <C, e, J, f, D, B, x, H, q, G, A, l, B, y, G, L, s, K> = tr$ for trace tr of Formula (1).

Intersection. Intuitively, the intersection of traces tr_1 and tr_2 is the longest trace that is included in both tr_1 and tr_2.

Formally, the intersection of traces tr_1 and tr_2 is the maximal subtrace tr_{12} (notation: $tr_{12} = tr_1 \cap tr_2$) such that $tr_{12} \subseteq tr_1 \wedge tr_{12} \subseteq tr_2$. Specifically, tr_{12} is maximal in the sense that there does not exist another trace tr'_{12} such that $tr'_{12} \subseteq tr_1 \wedge tr'_{12} \subseteq tr_2$ and $tr_{12} \subseteq tr'_{12}$. As a consequence, the intersection of any trace with the empty trace is the empty trace ϵ. For instance, $<A, a, C, i, D, j, B, C, e, J> \cap <C, e, J, f, D, B, x, H, q, G, A, l, B, y, G> = <C, e, J>$ for trace tr of Formula (1).

Disjoint traces. Intuitively, two traces are disjoint if their intersection is empty.

Formally, traces tr_1 and tr_2 are said to be disjoint if $tr1 \cap tr_2 = \epsilon$. For instance, $<A, a, C, i, D, j, B> \cap <I, c, J> = \epsilon$.

Unconnected traces. Intuitively, two disjoint traces tr_1 and tr_2 are unconnected if their underlying modules are also unconnected.

Two disjoint traces tr_1 and tr_2 of a system are said to be unconnected if $OuterR(m(tr_1)) \cap OuterR(m(tr_2)) = \oslash$. For instance, $<A, a, C, i, D, j, B> \cap <H, q, G> = \epsilon$.

The algebra of traces and the algebra of their underlying modules are related, as we now show. Suppose that m is any module of a system S.

Inclusion: $tr_1 \subseteq tr_2 \Rightarrow DynModule(m, tr_1) \subseteq DynModule(m, tr_2)$.

Union: $\forall in, tr_{12} = tr_1 \cup_{in} tr_2 \Rightarrow DynModule(m, tr_{12}) = DynModule(m, tr_1) \cup DynModule(m, tr_2)$.

Intersection: $tr_{12} = tr_1 \cap tr_2 \Rightarrow DynModule(m, tr_{12}) = DynModule(m, tr_1) \cap DynModule(m, tr_2)$.

Disjoint traces $tr1 \cap tr_2 = \epsilon \Rightarrow DynModule(m, tr1) \cap DynModule(m, tr_2) = \oslash$

4. AN AXIOMATIC APPROACH FOR TWO DYNAMIC SOFTWARE ATTRIBUTES: SIZE AND COUPLING

Here, we focus on dynamic size and coupling, by providing definitions for what we believe are necessary properties for their measures. Therefore, we provide an axiom set for dynamic size and an axiom set for dynamic coupling. It can be shown that these two axiom sets are consistent with the necessary properties for static size and coupling of [9].

4.1 Dynamic Size

Dynamic size is based on the multisets of elements appearing in an execution trace of a module, as described by the following axioms. We denote a dynamic size measure for a given module m under execution trace tr as $DynSize(m, tr)$, to denote the dependence of the dynamic size of module m on the specific execution trace tr.

First, the dynamic size $DynSize(m, tr)$ of module m composed of two possibly overlapping modules, under execution trace tr, is not greater than the sum of the dynamic sizes of the two modules, each taken in isolation, under tr.

Dynamic Size Axiom 1. Union of Modules. Suppose we have two modules m_1 and m_2 and an execution trace tr. The dynamic size of $m = m_1 \cup m_2$ under tr is never greater than the sum of the dynamic sizes of m_1 and m_2 under tr, i.e.,

$$m = m_1 \cup m_2 \Rightarrow DynSize(m, tr) \leq$$
$$DynSize(m_1, tr) + DynSize(m_2, tr)$$

For instance, $DynSize(m_2 \cup m_3, tr) \leq DynSize(m_2, tr) + DynSize(m_3, tr)$ in Figure 2.

The basic idea is that the intersection of the two dynamic modules may or may not be taken into account twice when m is executed under tr. However, when the two dynamic modules are disjoint, dynamic size is additive.

Dynamic Size Axiom 2. Dynamic Size Additivity. Suppose we have two disjoint modules m_1 and m_2 and an execution trace tr. The dynamic size of $m = m_1 \cup m_2$ under tr is equal to the sum of the dynamic sizes of m_1 and m_2 under tr, i.e.,

$$m = m_1 \cup m_2 \Rightarrow DynSize(m, tr) =$$
$$DynSize(m_1, tr) + DynSize(m_2, tr)$$

Thus, $DynSize(m_2 \cup m_4, tr) = DynSize(m_2, tr) + DynSize(m_4, tr)$ in Figure 2.

Several properties can be derived from these axioms. We now list a few.

1. The dynamic size of the empty module under any execution trace is zero.

2. The dynamic size of a module under any execution trace is nonnegative.

3. Adding elements to a module cannot decrease its dynamic size under any execution trace.

4.2 Dynamic Coupling

Dynamic coupling is about the *amount* of relationships between the elements of the dynamic module (of a module under an execution trace) and the elements of the other dynamic modules under the same execution trace. We denote a dynamic coupling measure as for a given module m under execution trace tr as $DynCoupling(m, tr)$, to denote the dependence of the dynamic coupling of module m on the specific execution trace tr.

Dynamic Coupling Axiom 1. Monotonicity.
Adding a new relationship to a module m_1 or to its set of outer relationships $OuterR(m_1)$ does not decrease its dynamic coupling if the added relationship is added to an execution trace. So, if m_2 is a module such that $E_2 = E_1$ and $tr_1 \subseteq tr_2$ we have

$$OuterR(m_1) \subseteq OuterR(m_2) \wedge R_1 \subseteq R_2 \wedge tr_1 \subseteq tr_2 \Rightarrow$$
$$DynCoupling(m_1, tr_1) \leq DynCoupling(m_2, tr)$$

A module with no outer relationships has zero dynamic coupling under all execution traces, regardless of its internal relationships.

Dynamic Coupling Axiom 2. Null Value. The coupling of a module with no outer relationships is null under all execution traces.

When two modules are merged in a single module, the relationships that connect them to each other become internal ones, so the dynamic coupling of the new module is not higher than the sum of the dynamic couplings of the two modules.

Dynamic Coupling Axiom 3. Merging of Modules. The dynamic coupling of the union of two dynamic modules m_1 and m_2 under any specific execution trace tr is not greater than the sum of the dynamic couplings of the two modules under tr

$$\forall tr(DynCoupling(m_1 \cup m_2, tr) \leq$$
$$DynCoupling(m_1, tr) + Coupling(m_2, tr))$$

Thus, $DynCoupling(m_2 \cup m_3, tr) \leq DynCoupling(m_2, tr) + Coupling(m_3, tr)$ in Figure 2.

Coupling is additive for a system composed of two unconnected modules.

Dynamic Coupling Axiom 4. Unconnected Modules. The dynamic coupling of the union of two unconnected dynamic modules under an execution trace tr is equal to the sum of their couplings.

$$OuterR(DynModule(m_1, tr)) \cap OuterR(DynModule(m_2, tr))$$
$$= \oslash \Rightarrow \forall tr(DynCoupling(m_1 \cup m_2, tr) = DynCoupling(m_1, tr)$$
$$+ DynCoupling(m_2, tr))$$

Thus, $DynCoupling(m_4 \cup m_6, tr) = DynCoupling(m_4, tr) + Coupling(m_6, tr)$ in Figure 2.

As a derived property, the dynamic coupling of a module under any execution trace is nonnegative.

5. DYNAMIC MEASURES FOR SIZE AND COUPLING

We now provide a few examples of dynamic measures for size and coupling, which we use in the experiments of Section 6. Thus, an execution trace is related to a specific execution or a set of executions of a module. Here, we show that these measures are dynamic size and coupling measures according to the axiom sets of Section 4.

5.1 Dynamic Size Measures

Blocks: The number of blocks (i.e., the sequence of byte-code instructions without any jumps or jump targets) exercised by the test suite. A block is considered as exercised when its last instruction has been executed. A module in this case is statically modeled as a block control-flow, in which bytecode blocks are represented by the nodes of the graph (i.e., the elements of the system) and control-flow transfers between blocks are represented by the arcs of the graph (i.e., the relationships of the system). We now show that $Blocks$ is a size measure according to the axiom set in Section 4.1. First, given an execution trace tr and the corresponding $DynModule(m, tr)$, let us take two execution traces tr_1 and tr_2 such that $tr = tr_1 \cup tr_2$ and, therefore $DynModule(m, tr) = DynModule(m, tr_1) \cup DynModule(m, tr_2)$. The number of blocks in $DynModule(m, tr)$ is clearly never greater than the sum of the numbers of blocks in $DynModule(m, tr_1)$ and $DynModule(m, tr_2)$, since $DynModule(m, tr_1)$ and $DynModule(m, tr_2)$ may have some blocks in common. So, Axiom 1 is satisfied. Likewise, if modules $DynModule(m, tr_1)$ and $DynModule(m, tr_2)$ are disjoint, no overlap of blocks exist and the number of blocks in $DynModule(m, tr)$ is equal to the sum of the numbers of blocks in $DynModule(m, tr_1)$ and $DynModule(m, tr_2)$. So, Axiom 2 is satisfied too and $Blocks$ is a size measure according to the axiom set in Section 4.1.

Instructions: The number of bytecode instructions exercised. A module in this case is statically modeled as a control-flow graph, in which bytecode instructions are represented by the nodes of the graph and control-flow transfers between bytecode instructions are represented by the arcs of the graph. We can prove that $Instructions$ is a size measure in much the same way as we proved that $NumberOfBlocks$ is a size measure according to the axiom set in Section 4.1, by replacing blocks with instructions.

SLOC: The number of Java source lines of code exercised. A module in this case is statically modeled as a control-flow graph, in which source lines of code are represented by the nodes of the graph and control-flow transfers between source lines of code are represented by the arcs of the graph. We can prove that $SLOC$ is a size measure in much the same way as we proved that $Blocks$ and $Instructions$ size measures according to the axiom set in Section 4.1.

Methods: The number of distinct methods exercised. A method is considered as exercised if at least one statement of the method has been executed. A module is statically modeled as a sheer sequence of methods declared in a class, so methods are represented by the nodes of the graph. The node representing a method is linked to the next node (which represents the next method in the sequence) by an arc. The proof that $Methods$ is a size measure is analogous to the previous proofs.

Types: The number of distinct Java type exercised. A Java type is considered as exercised if it has been loaded and initialized. The proof that $Types$ is is a size measure is analogous to the previous proofs.

5.2 Dynamic Coupling Measures

We collected three dynamic coupling measures, defined in [4].

Distinct method invocations: The count, within a runtime session, of the total number of distinct methods invoked by each method in each object. By modeling each method as a module, each statement in the module as an element, and each control flow transfer within the method or to another method, the proof that `Distinct method invocations` is a dynamic coupling measure according to the axiom set of Section 4.2, can be carried out as follows: As for Axiom 1, adding a new invocation within the class or to its set of invocations of methods of other classes does not decrease its dynamic coupling if the added invocation is added to any execution trace. A class that is not linked to any other classes has no direct method invocations, so `Distinct method invocations` is null and Axiom 2 is satisfied. Let us now examine Axiom 3. If two classes c_1 and c_2 are merged into a single class c, the invocations of methods between c_1 and c_2 are no longer counted as contributing to the coupling of c towards the rest of the system in any execution trace, so the dynamic coupling of c is not greater than the sum of the dynamic couplings of c_1 and c_2. Finally, if, in a specific execution there are no methods invoked between c_1 and c_2, the number of distinct method invocations of c is the sum of the distinct method invocations of c_1 and c_2, and Axiom 4 is satisfied. So, `Distinct method invocations` is a coupling measure according to the axiom set of Section 4.2.

Dynamic messages: The count, within a runtime session, of the total number of distinct messages sent from one object of a class to other objects. Two messages are not distinct if their source and target classes, the method invoked in the target class, and the statement from which it is invoked in the source class are the same. The proof that `Dynamic messages` is a dynamic coupling measure can be carried out along the lines as the previous proof.

Distinct classes: The count of the distinct number of classes that a method uses within a runtime session. Here, we can use the same modeling as for `Distinct method invocations` and we can show that `Distinct classes` is a dynamic coupling measure in a similar way.

6. EXPERIMENTING DYNAMIC MEASURES

This section presents the results of four case studies we conducted to provide a first empirical validation of the dynamic measures we discussed above. Firstly, we present the methodology we follow, the environmental setup and the objectives of this experimentation. Secondly, we provide and we discuss quantitative results about size and coupling dynamic measures when compared against well-known static measures.

6.1 Methodology

We selected four open-source Java projects, specifically HttpUnit v1.7, Jakarta Commons IO v1.4, Log4J v1.2.16 and PMD v4.2.5 to evaluate dynamic size and coupling aspects.

HttpUnit is a tool to emulate the relevant portions of browser behavior and allows Java test code to examine returned pages either as text, an XML DOM, or containers of forms, tables, and links. The considered HttpUnit release consists of 19810 lines of code (SLOC) in 10 source packages, 286 classes and 3764 methods (after removing classes related to test cases and methods used to profile the source code of the application). In our experiments, we used all the 10 packages contained in the `src` folder of HttpUnit. However, two of them were excluded from the final computation due to the lack of test cases.

Jakarta Commons IO is a library of utilities (such as Input, Output, Filters, Comparators and Monitor classes) to assist with developing IO functionality. The considered Commons IO release consists of 2931 lines of code (SLOC) in 5 source packages, 74 classes and 422 methods (after removing classes related to test cases and methods used to profile the source code of the application). As for this experiment, we collected data for all the 5 packages contained in the `src` folder of Jakarta.

Log4J is a package to enable logging of an application context at runtime without modifying the application binary. The considered Log4J release consists of 11774 lines of code (SLOC) in 22 source packages, 181 classes and 1032 methods (after removing classes related to test cases and methods used to profile the source code of the application). As for this experiment, we collected data only for the 10 packages contained in the `src` folder of Log4J equipped with test cases.

PMD is a library to scan Java applications and look for possible bugs, dead / suboptimal / duplicate code, and over-complicated expressions. The considered PMD release consists of 49162 lines of code (SLOC) in 17 source packages, 642 classes and 4439 methods (after removing classes related to test cases and methods used to profile the source code of the application). As for this experiment, we collected data for all the 17 packages contained in the `src` folder of PMD. However, one package was excluded from the final computation due to the lack of test cases.

We focused on collecting different types of data referring to the static, dynamic size, dynamic coupling measures, and number of bugs for each case study at a package granularity. We collected the following static measures (by means of the Metrics plugin [3] v1.3.8): Number of Methods, Number of Classes, Afferent Coupling (Ca), Efferent Coupling (Ce), Package Instability (i.e., Ce / (Ca+Ce)) , Coupling Between Objects (CBO max and mean), and McCabe Complexity (max and mean.)

As for collecting dynamic size measures, we used the EclEmma Eclipse plugin [2]. EclEmma is a free Java code coverage tool for Eclipse that does not require modifying the source code of the applications. We used the test cases provided along with each application to exercise the system of each case study, and by means of EclEmma we are able to compute at run-time the measures we discussed in subsection 5.1. Specifically, we compute the percentage of blocks, instructions, SLOCs, methods and types exercised by the test cases.

As for collecting the dynamic coupling measures (i.e., dynamic messages, distinct methods, and distinct classes), we profiled each application by means of Aspect-Oriented Programming (AOP) and we exercised the system by means of each test suite. The test cases have been used to simulate the users' interactions with the application in order to exercise as much functionalities of the application as possible.

We used the AJDT Eclipse plugin (based on the AspectJ runtime library) [1] to define an aspect (i.e., a stand-alone module that contains cross-cutting concerns), a pointcut (i.e., a set of join points that are able to capture well-defined moments in the execution of a program, like method call, object instantiation, or variable access), and an advice (i.e., the code to run before, after, or around the specified join point) able to trace all the calling classes and methods, the called classes and methods, and the statements from which calls originate. The pseudo code of the most relevant part of the defined aspect looks like as follows:

```
public aspect DynamicCouplingAspect {
  pointcut executionTree():
      within(TestClass_a) ||
      ... ...
      within(TestClass_n) &&
      call (* *(..));
  Object around(): executionTree() {
      print(thisJointPointStaticPart.getSignature);
      print(thisJointPointStaticPart.getDeclaringType);
      ... ...
  }
  ... ...
}
```

As for collecting bugs data, we manually surfed the bug tracker system of each case study to identify all the valid bugs (i.e., open, closed, confirmed with the exception of unconfirmed bugs) that refer to the version of the target application. Each identified bug has been manually classified in the package it belongs to. To avoid biases, we try to reduce subjectivity in the manual analysis of each bug as much as possible, and we also try to replicate step by step the methodology we used for surfing each bug tracker. In any case, we are aware that bugs data are often non homogeneous due to different policies of each community in collecting, reporting and tracking bugs. For instance, the Jakarta Commons IO project uses the JIRA bug tracker, HttpUnit and PMD use the Sourceforge bug tracker, while Log4J uses the Bugzilla bug tracker system. For each package, we computed the

6.2 Objectives and Results

With these experiments, we are interested in collecting data to show:

Q1: whether there is a correlation between dynamic size and coupling measures with some relevant static measures;

Q2: whether dynamic measures are better than static measures in predicting some software quality aspects. In this paper, we limited our experimentation in investigating the fault-proneness aspect, thus we used as dependent variable the number of bugs of each application. We correlated dynamic measures and static measures with these bug data, and we compared the computed coefficients of correlation to understand the ability that dynamic and static measures have in predicting the fault-proneness of an application;

To answer question Q1 we used non parametric test, because distributions are generally not normal.

Table 1 reports the results of the Kendall's and Spearman's tests applied to Log4J dynamic size measures with all the seven static measures we listed above. We are not

Table 1: Correlation between static and dynamic size measures for Log4J (10 data points)

	Blocks	Instructions	SLOC	Methods	Types
Num. Methods	—	tau = 0.511 rho = 0.661	—	—	—
Num. Classes	tau = 0.688 rho = 0.794	tau = 0.777 rho = 0.903	tau = 0.733 rho = 0.854	—	—
CBO max	tau = 0.539 rho = 0.705	tau = 0.449 rho = 0.656	tau = 0.494 rho = 0.693	tau = 0.494 rho = 0.669	—

able to find any significant correlation for HttpUnit, PMD and Jakarta. Contrariwise, we found several correlations for Log4J (see Table 1). Due to the heterogeneity in the obtained results, no general conclusions can be derived.

Tables 2 to 4 report the results of the Kendall's and Spearman's tests applied to HttpUnit, PMD and Log4J dynamic coupling measures with all the seven static measures we listed above, respectively. For the Jakarta project no significant correlation could be found, but this is probably due to the small number of available datapoints (5). As a matter of fact, for Dynamic Messages vs. NumClasses and Distinct Methods vs. NumClasses fairly high values of Kendall's tau and Spearman's rho were found, but with p-value well above the chosen threshold (0.05).

As for the correlations between static measures and dynamic coupling measures, we can weakly state that dynamic messages, distinct methods and distinct classes correlate well with the number of methods, number of classes, efferent coupling, and McCabe (max) static measures (this can be derived by intersecting the HttpUnit results with the Log4J results). These results are limited to HttpUnit and Log4J, the only two projects that provide some correlations.

Table 2: Correlation between static and dynamic coupling measures for HttpUnit (8 data points)

	Dynamic Messages	Distinct Methods	Distinct Classes
Num. Methods	tau = 0.786 rho = 0.905	tau = 0.929 rho = 0.976	tau = 0.857 rho = 0.929
Num. Classes	tau = 0.786 rho = 0.905	tau = 0.929 rho = 0.976	tau = 0.857 rho = 0.929
Efferent Coupling	rho = 0.762	rho = 0.810	rho = 0.786
CBO max	—	tau = 0.618 rho = 0.778	—
Package Instability	tau = 0.643 rho = 0.833	tau = 0.643 rho = 0.810	tau = 0.714 rho = 0.881
McCabe max	tau = 0.593 rho = 0.711	tau = 0.667 rho = 0.795	tau = 0.593 rho = 0.730

Table 3: Correlation between static and dynamic coupling measures for PMD (16 data points)

	Dynamic Messages	Distinct Methods	Distinct Classes
CBO mean	—	rho = 0.538	—

To answer question Q2, we built models –via Ordinary Least Squares (OLS) regression– involving

Table 4: Correlation between static and dynamic coupling measures for Log4J (10 data points)

	Dynamic Messages	Distinct Methods	Distinct Classes
Num. Methods	tau = 0.556 rho = 0.721	tau = 0.644 rho = 0.794	tau = 0.629 rho = 0.754
Num. Classes	tau = 0.644 rho = 0.782	tau = 0.556 rho = 0.721	tau = 0.539 rho = 0.711
Afferent Coupling	tau = 0.540 rho = 0.657		tau = 0.523 rho = 0.640
Efferent Coupling	tau = 0.540 rho = 0.669	tau = 0.540 rho = 0.669	tau = 0.523 rho = 0.659
McCabe max	tau = 0.523 rho = 0.689	tau = 0.523 rho = 0.665	tau = 0.598 rho = 0.731
McCabe mean	tau = 0.584 rho = 0.760	tau = 0.674 rho = 0.815	tau = 0.705 rho = 0.826

- dependent variables representing defect density at the package level: the absolute number of bugs (NumBugs); the relative number of bugs (NumRelBugs), obtained as the ratio between the number of bugs of a package and the total number of bugs of the application; the number of bugs per LOC (BugsPerLOC); the ratio between the number of bugs and the number of classes (NumBugs/NumClasses); the ratio between the number of bugs and the number of methods (NumBugs/NumMethods).

- independent variables representing all the seven static measures and the dynamic measures of size and coupling.

We built both linear models and models obtained by applying OLS regression to log-log transformed data.

Not all the possible pairs of independent and dependent variables provided statistically significant models. The significant models obtained via OLS regression after log-log transformation are synthetically reported in Table 5.

In Table 5 we have reported for completeness also the models for Jakarta Commons IO, but we must remember that such model is based on 5 data points only, therefore it is not very reliable.

Table 5 shows that the number of distinct methods and distinct classes executed are the measures that in general correlate better with the various measures of defects for most projects, while static measures in general do not provide a reliable indicator on fault-proneness of a project (e.g., static measures provided heterogeneous results if comparing the models of the four case studies).

We are aware that the quality of the found models depends strongly on the quality of the partial results computed by

Table 5: Independent variables of log-log models (R^2 in parentheses)

Dep. Var.	Indip. Var. (R^2)			
	HTTPunit	Jakarta	PMD	Log4J
Num. Bugs	Distinct Methods(0.604) Distinct Classes(0.529) Pack. Instability(0.564)	Distinct Methods(0.928) Distinct Classes(0.932)	CBO max(0.466)	Distinct Methods(0.738) Distinct Classes(0.741) McCabe max(0.545) Num. Methods(0.887) Afferent Coupling(0.637) Efferent Coupling(0.817) Instructions Perc.(0.529) SLOC Perc.(0.493)
Num. rel. Bugs	Afferent Coupling(0.665)	Distinct Methods(0.928) Distinct Classes(0.932)	Afferent Coupling(0.698) Instructions Perc.(0.819) Methods Perc.(0.757)	Distinct Methods(0.732) Distinct Classes(0.735) McCabe max(0.542) Num. Methods(0.883) Afferent Coupling(0.646) Efferent Coupling(0.817) Instructions Perc.(0.544) SLOC Perc.(0.51)
Bugs per LOC		Distinct Methods(0.895) Distinct Classes(0.891)		Num. Methods(0.968) Blocks Perc.(0.604)
Num. Bugs / N.Classes		McCabe Max(0.869)	Methods Perc.(0.772)	Distinct Methods(0.816) Distinct Classes(0.906)
Num. Bugs / N.Methods			Instructions Perc.(0.517)	

each intermediate tool, on the accuracy of each community in collecting and reporting bugs data, and on the number of case studies and data points available. We are extending this work by collecting new data (at a class granularity instead of at the package granularity), to increase significantly the number of data points.

7. RELATED WORK

Several works exist on the measurement of static properties for software systems. In addition to classical works that define static measures such as lines of code, cohesion, coupling and other measures [14], a lot of recent works formally define static attributes [10, 9, 6] for object-oriented systems, while other works empirically evaluate the correlation among static attributes with subjective aspects such as maintainability and trustworthiness of object-oriented open-source software systems [5].

Recently, the introduction of profiling and probing mechanisms based on assertions, invariants, and aspects to monitor the dynamic behavior of software systems has shown how software systems often do not behave at run-time as expected at design-time [12]. Static measures are not able to detect misbehaviors and unexpected properties of the software, thus they need to be complemented with measures that work at run-time.

Starting from these considerations, some dynamic measures have been defined in the literature. For example, Yacoub et al. define dynamic object-oriented coupling measures based on executable Real-time Object Oriented Modeling (ROOM) [16]. These models are a specialization of sequence diagrams that allow execution simulations of the software system, thus providing a way to calculate the number of messages sent between two distinct objects in a given ROOM diagram. Unfortunately, the proposed approach works stati-

cally simulating the behavior of the system and the coupling measures defined in their work are not compliant with our axiomatic framework. In our work, we describe how to use aspect-oriented programming to instrument the source code of the system and how to collect traces at runtime to compute dynamic size and coupling attributes.

In [4], a set of dynamic coupling measures has been defined and validated against static size measures. We extended this work, by adding and formally defining, in an operational form, dynamic size measures, and we provide a set of experiments with the aim of demonstrating the potentialities of dynamic measures. We also show, by means of four case studies, how AOP can actually support the computation of dynamic measure.

In [7], the authors propose a way to estimate dynamic coupling metrics early in the software development lifecycle. They introduce the concept of "pseudo dynamic metrics", which are static metrics adjusted to reflect the operational profile of the expected software usage. They draw their approach starting from the assumption that dynamic metrics can only be computed at an advanced stage of the software development, because they need additional code to be wrote to detect dynamic behaviors. In our work, we demonstrated how it is simple to define advices and pointcuts able to monitor at run-time the behavior of the software system. Of course, our approach needs the availability of external inputs (such as test cases) that trigger and stimulate the system. We think that these external inputs are early available because test cases are normally coded in parallel with the development of the system, as software engineering guidelines and best practices suggest.

Other dynamic measures have been informally defined. For example, Munson et al. [11] obtained a sort of dynamic complexity (they call "relative complexity") starting from the static complexity of a software component and its frequency of execution. Our axiomatic framework for dynamic measures is open to new formal definitions. We are extending this work by formally defining other dynamic measures and the properties that characterize these measures.

In the research filed of software testing, a lot of work exists about how software systems are exercised at runtime by a test suite. This field studies coverage criteria to understand how good and adequate is a test suite in exercising all the criticisms of a software system. Several coverage and adequacy criteria have been defined in the literature. In [17] a comprehensive survey of these criteria is provided. For example, the Statement Coverage criteria reports whether each executable statement of the system is encountered when executing the test suite; the Condition Coverage criteria reports the true or false outcome of each boolean sub-expression, separated by logical-and and logical-or if they occur; the Path Coverage criteria reports whether each of the possible paths in each function have been followed. Several other criteria are available, and to the best of our knowledge, we think that these criteria should be investigated and adapted to collect dynamic software measures.

8. CONCLUSIONS AND FUTURE WORK

In this paper, we have proposed a framework for the definition of sensible measures of dynamic internal software attributes. The framework is based on Axiomatic Approaches and is consistent with previous work about static measures [9]. We have also provided examples to show how dynamic measures may be defined, collected, and used.

Future work will address several avenues of research, including:

- definition of axiom sets for other dynamic attributes like dynamic complexity and dynamic cohesion

- definition of additional measures and refinement of existing ones according to the axiom sets defined

- additional empirical studies (collecting data at the class granularity) to assess the practical usefulness of these measures.

9. ACKNOWLEDGMENT

The research presented in this paper has been partially funded by the IST project "QualiPSo," funded by the EU in the 6th FP (IST-034763); the FIRB project "ARTDECO," sponsored by the Italian Ministry of Education and University; and the projects "Elementi metodologici per la descrizione e lo sviluppo di sistemi software basati su modelli" and "La qualità nello sviluppo software," funded by the Università degli Studi dell'Insubria.

10. REFERENCES

[1] AJDT: AspectJ Development Tools. Web published: www.eclipse.org/ajdt/. Accessed: March 2012.

[2] The EclEmma Eclipse Plugin. Web published: www.eclemma.org. Accessed: March 2012.

[3] Metrics. Web published: http://metrics2.sourceforge.net/. Accessed: March 2012.

[4] E. Arisholm, L. C. Briand, and A. Føyen. Dynamic coupling measurement for object-oriented software. *IEEE Trans. Software Eng.*, 30(8):491–506, 2004.

[5] V. D. Bianco, L. Lavazza, S. Morasca, D. Taibi, and D. Tosi. An investigation of the users perception of OSS quality. In *International Conference on Open Source Systems (OSS)*, 2010.

[6] L. C. Briand, S. Morasca, and V. R. Basili. Property-based software engineering measurement. *IEEE Trans. Software Eng.*, 22(1):68–86, 1996.

[7] R. Gunnalan, M. Shereshevsky, and H. H. Ammar. Pseudo dynamic metrics [software metrics]. In *International Conference on Computer Systems and Applications (AICCSA)*, page 117, 2005.

[8] D. Krantz, R. Luce, P. Suppes, and A. Tversky. *Foundations of measurement*, volume 1: Additive and polynomial representations. Academic Press, New York, 1971.

[9] S. Morasca. Refining the axiomatic definition of internal software attributes. In *Proceedings of the Second International Symposium on Empirical Software Engineering and Measurement (ESEM)*, pages 188–197, 2008.

[10] S. Morasca. A probability-based approach for measuring external attributes of software artifacts. In *Proceedings of the Second International Symposium on Empirical Software Engineering and Measurement (ESEM)*, pages 44–55, 2009.

[11] J. C. Munson and T. M. Khoshgoftaar. Measuring dynamic program complexity. *IEEE Software*, 9(6):48–55, 1992.

[12] J. H. Perkins and M. D. Ernst. Efficient incremental algorithms for dynamic detection of likely invariants. In *Proceedings of the International Symposium on Foundations of Software Engineering (FSE)*, pages 23–32, 2004.

[13] F. Roberts. *Measurement theory, with applications to Decision Making, Utility and the Social Sciences*. Addison-Wesley, Boston, 1979.

[14] D. Stavrinoudis and M. N. Xenos. Comparing internal and external software quality measurements. In *Knowledge-Based Software Engineering, Proceedings of the Eighth Joint Conference on Knowledge-Based Software Engineering, (JCKBSE)*, pages 115–124, 2008.

[15] E. J. Weyuker. Evaluating software complexity measures. *IEEE Trans. Software Eng.*, 14(9):1357–1365, 1988.

[16] S. M. Yacoub, H. H. Ammar, and T. Robinson. Dynamic metrics for object oriented designs. In *IEEE International Software Metrics Symposium (METRICS)*, pages 50–61, 1999.

[17] H. Zhu, P. A. V. Hall, and J. H. R. May. Software unit test coverage and adequacy. *ACM Comput. Surv.*, 29(4):366–427, 1997.

Experimental Assessment of Software Metrics Using Automated Refactoring

Mel Ó Cinnéide
School of Computer Science
and Informatics
University College Dublin
mel.ocinneide@ucd.ie

Laurence Tratt
Dept. of Informatics
King's College London
laurie@tratt.net

Mark Harman
Dept. of Computer Science
University College London
mark.harman@ucl.ac.uk

Steve Counsell
Dept. of Information Systems
and Computing
Brunel University
steve.counsell@brunel.ac.uk

Iman Hemati Moghadam
School of Computer Science
and Informatics
University College Dublin
Iman.Hemati-
Moghadam@ucdconnect.ie

ABSTRACT

A large number of software metrics have been proposed in the literature, but there is little understanding of how these metrics relate to one another. We propose a novel experimental technique, based on search-based refactoring, to assess software metrics and to explore relationships between them. Our goal is not to improve the program being refactored, but to assess the software metrics that guide the automated refactoring through repeated refactoring experiments.

We apply our approach to five popular cohesion metrics using eight real-world Java systems, involving 300,000 lines of code and over 3,000 refactorings. Our results demonstrate that cohesion metrics disagree with each other in 55% of cases, and show how our approach can be used to reveal novel and surprising insights into the software metrics under investigation.

Categories and Subject Descriptors

D.2.8 [**Software Engineering**]: Metrics—*Complexity measures*; D.2.7 [**Software Engineering**]: Distribution, Maintenance, and Enhancement—*Restructuring, reverse engineering, and reengineering*

General Terms

Experimentation, Measurement.

Keywords

Software metrics, search based software engineering, refactoring.

1. INTRODUCTION

Metrics are used both implicitly and explicitly to measure and assess software [43], but it remains difficult to know how to assess the metrics themselves. Previous work in the metrics literature have suggested formal axiomatic analysis [45], though this approach is not without problems and limitations [18] and can only assess theoretical metric properties and not their practical aspects.

In this paper we introduce a novel experimental approach to the assessment of metrics, based on automated search-based refactoring. It is striking that many metrics purport to measure the same aspect of software quality, yet we have no way of checking these claims. For example, many metrics have been introduced in the literature that aim to measure software cohesion [9, 11, 26, 33, 20]. If these metrics were measuring the same property, then they ought to produce similar results. This poses some important but uncomfortable questions: how do the results of metrics that purport to measure the same software quality compare to one another? Can metrics that measure the same property disagree, and how strongly can they disagree? These questions are important, because we cannot rely on a suite of metrics to assess properties of software if we can neither determine the extent to which they agree, nor have any way to determine a likely worst case disagreement. They are also uncomfortable questions because, despite several decades of software metrics research and practice, there remains no answer, nor even an accepted approach to tackling them.

In this paper we address this problem by introducing an experimental technique to answer questions like these. Our approach applies automated refactoring to a program, repeatedly measuring the values of a number of metrics before and after applying each refactoring. In this way it is possible to make empirical observations about the relationships between the metrics. When a pair of metrics do not agree on the change brought about by a refactoring, we examine the causes of the conflict so as to gain a further (and more qualitative) insight into the differences between the metrics.

We evaluate our approach on five widely-used metrics for cohesion. We use a search-based, metric-guided refactoring platform, Code-Imp, that can apply a large number of refactorings without user intervention. Using Code-Imp, over 3,000 refactorings were applied to eight non-trivial, real-world Java programs comprising in total over 300,000 lines of code. For each refactoring, we compute before and after values for the cohesion metrics and analyse the results to obtain a quantitative and qualitative comparison of the metrics under assessment.

The primary contributions of this paper are as follows:

1. The introduction of a new approach to metric analysis at the source code level. This implements the approach to metric investigation using search-based refactoring first proposed by Harman and Clark [25], but which has hitherto remained unimplemented.

2. A case study showing how our approach reveals that seemingly similar metrics can be in conflict with one another, and can pinpoint the source of the conflict thus providing new insight into the differences between the metrics.

3. The identification of a number of undocumented anomalies in established cohesion metrics, thereby demonstrating the utility of our approach as a means of investigating metrics.

This paper is structured as follows. In Section 2 we describe our experimental approach in more detail and in section 3 we outline the platform we use in this paper to perform search based refactoring. In section 4 we describe our initial investigation into how a suite of software metrics changes in response to refactoring, which leads to Section 5 where a detailed empirical comparison between two particular cohesion metrics is presented. Section 6 describes related work and finally, Section 7 concludes and describes future work.

2. MOTIVATION AND APPROACH

The motivation for this work stems from a desire to "animate" metrics and observe their behaviour in relation to each other in a practical setting. A single software application allows only one set of metric measurements to be made. This is clearly not enough to make meaningful comparisons. A software repository such as CVS provides multiple versions of a software application and so serves as a better basis for comparison, and many studies have taken this approach [14, 2, 44]. However, a sequence of versions of a software application may vary wildly in terms of how great the gap is between each version. This lack of control over the differences between the versions is a significant confounding factor in studies that use software repositories to compare software metrics.

Our approach to this problem begins with the observation that individual refactorings in the style of Fowler [22] involve small behaviour-preserving program changes that typically have an impact on the values of software metrics that would be calculated for the program. For example, in applying the PushDownMethod refactoring, a method is moved from a superclass to those subclasses that require it. The superclass may become more cohesive if the method moved was weakly connected with the rest of the class. It may instead become less cohesive, if the moved method served to glue other methods and fields of the class together. It is impossible to state that the PushDownMethod refactoring leads to an increase or a decrease in cohesion without examining

Input: set of classes in program being refactored
Input: set of 14 refactoring types (e.g. PullUpMethod)
Input: set of metrics to be analysed
Output: metrics profile
$refactoring\_count = 0$
repeat
    $classes$ = set of classes in program
    while *!empty(classes)* **do**
        $class = classes$.pick()
        $refactoring\_types$ = set of refactoring types
        while *!empty(refactoring_types)* **do**
            $refactoring\_type = refactoring\_types$.pick()
            $refactorings$.populate($refactoring\_type, class$)
            if *!empty(refactorings)* **then**
                $refactoring = refactorings$.pick()
                $refactoring$.apply()
                if *fitness_function_improves()* **then**
                    $refactoring\_count$++
                    update metrics profile
                else
                    $refactoring$.undo()
                end
        end
    end
end
until $refactoring\_count == desired\_refactoring\_count$;

The functions used in this algorithm are defined as follows:
$Set<element>::pick$: removes and returns a it random element from a set
$Set<Refactoring>::populate(type, class)$: adds to the set all legal refactorings of the given type on the given class
fitness_function_improves: Tests if the applied refactoring has improved the software metrics. Details vary between investigation 1 and investigation 2.

Figure 1: The search-based refactoring algorithm used to explore software metrics

the context to which it is being applied. Furthermore, the impact the refactoring will have on the metric will depend on the precise notion of cohesion that the metric embodies.

The approach taken in this paper is to measure a set of metric values on a program, and then apply a sequence of refactorings to the program, measuring the metrics again after each refactoring is applied. Each refactoring represents a small, controlled change to the software, so it is possible to identify patterns in how the metric values change, and how they change in relation to each other. For N refactorings and M metrics, this approach provides a matrix of $(N + 1) \times M$ metric values. As will be demonstrated in sections 4 and 5, this matrix can be used to make a comparative, empirical assessment of the metrics and to detect areas of metric disagreement that can be subjected to closer examination.

An important issue in this approach is the manner in which the refactoring sequence itself is generated. The simplest solution is to apply a random sequence of refactorings to the program. However, most randomly-chosen refactorings can be expected to cause all software metrics to deteriorate, which is not of interest. In order to address this, we use the software metrics that are being studied to guide the refactoring process itself. In this way, we can ensure that a refactoring is applied only if it improves *at least one* of the metrics being studied. Crucially, each accepted refactoring will improve the cohesion of the program in terms of at least one of the metrics, though it may, in the extreme case, worsen it for all the other metrics.

This search-based approach to refactoring has already been used in many other studies [37, 38, 42, 27, 28, 41, 40, 29, 35, 32]. In this paper, we use search-based refactoring not to achieve a goal in terms of refactoring the program, but to learn more about the metrics that are used to guide the refactoring process. The search-based refactoring tool we use, Code-Imp, is described in more detail in section 3.

The search-based algorithm we use to perform the refactoring is defined in figure 1. It is stochastic, as the `pick` operation makes a random choice of the class to be refactored, the refactoring type to be used and the actual refactoring to be applied. It is only necessary to run this search once on each software application, as each refactoring applied is a complete experiment in itself. The purpose of this algorithm is to give each class an equal chance of being refactored and to give each refactoring type (PullUpMethod, CollapseHierarchy, etc.) an equal chance of being applied. This is important in order to reduce the risk that bias in the refactoring process affects the observed behaviour of the metrics. The details of the fitness function are not defined in this algorithm, as they depend on the exact nature of what is being investigated. The fitness functions will be defined in sections 4 and 5 where the experiments are described in more detail.

3. THE CODE-IMP PLATFORM

Code-Imp is an extensible platform for metrics-driven search-based refactoring that has been previously used for automated design improvement [37, 38]. It provides design-level refactorings such as moving methods around the class hierarchy, splitting classes and changing inheritance and delegation relationships. It does not support low-level refactorings that split or merge methods.

Code-Imp was developed on the RECODER platform [24] and fully supports Java 6. It currently implements the following refactorings [22]:

Method-level Refactorings

Push Down Method: Moves a method from a class to those subclasses that require it.
Pull Up Method: Moves a method from a class(es) to its immediate superclass.
Increase/Decrease Method Accessibility: Changes the accessibility of a method by one level, e.g. public to protected or private to package.

Field-level Refactorings

Push Down Field: Moves a field from a class to those subclasses that require it.
Pull Up Field: Moves a field from a class(es) to their immediate superclass.
Increase/Decrease Field Accessibility: Changes the accessibility of a field by one level, e.g. public to protected or private to package.

Class-level Refactorings

Extract Hierarchy: Adds a new subclass to a non-leaf class C in an inheritance hierarchy. A subset of the subclasses of C will inherit from the new class.
Collapse Hierarchy: Removes a non-leaf class from an inheritance hierarchy.
Make Superclass Abstract: Declares a constructorless class explicitly abstract.
Make Superclass Concrete: Removes the explicit 'abstract' declaration of an abstract class without abstract methods.
Replace Inheritance with Delegation: Replaces an inheritance relationship between two classes with a delegation relationship; the former subclass will have a field of the type of the former superclass.
Replace Delegation with Inheritance: Replaces a delegation relationship between two classes with an inheritance relationship; the delegating class becomes a subclass of the former delegate class.

Code-Imp parses the program to be refactored to produce a set of Abstract Syntax Trees (ASTs). It then repeatedly applies refactorings to the ASTs and regenerates the source code from the ASTs when the refactoring process is completed. Code-Imp decides on the next refactoring to perform based on the exact search technique in use and the value of the fitness function in use. The refactoring process can be driven using one of a number of metaheuristic search techniques, namely simulated annealing, hill climbing and a genetic algorithm. In this paper, only hill climbing is used.

The fitness function that guides the search is a computation based on one or more software metrics. Code-Imp provides two implementations for each metric related to the inclusion or exclusion of inheritance in the definition of the metric. Five cohesion metrics are used in this paper, namely Tight Class Cohesion (TCC) [8], Lack of Cohesion between Methods (LCOM5) [12], Class Cohesion (CC) [10], Sensitive Class Cohesion (SCOM) [21] and Low-level Similarity Base Class Cohesion (LSCC) [3]. The formal and informal definitions of these metrics are presented in Figure 2.

As with all automated approaches, the refactoring sequence generated by Code-Imp may not resemble the refactorings that a programmer would be inclined to undertake in practice. This issue is not relevant here as our focus is on the changes in the metric values, rather than the design changes brought about by the refactorings.

4. INVESTIGATION I: GENERAL ASSESSMENT OF COHESION METRICS

In this investigation we take a refactoring walk through the landscape of the range of cohesion metrics under consideration. Our goal is to gain an overall understanding of how the metrics change, and to seek out possible anomalous behaviour that can be investigated further.

As explained in section 2, random application of refactorings will usually cause deterioration in all cohesion metrics. We therefore use a search that cycles through the classes of the program under investigation as described in figure 1, and tries to find a refactoring on the class that improves *at least one* of the metrics being studied. The search will apply the first refactoring it finds that improves any metric. The other metrics may improve, stay the same, or deteriorate. Because

$$\text{LSCC}(c) = \begin{cases} 0 & \text{if } l=0 \text{ and } k>1, \\ 1 & \text{if } (l>0 \text{ and } k=0) \text{ or } k=1, \\ \sum_{i=1}^{l} x_i(x_i-1)/lk(k-1) & otherwise. \end{cases}$$

The similarity between two methods is the collection of their direct and indirect shared attributes.

$$\text{TCC}(c) = \frac{|\{(m1,m2)|m1,m2 \in M_I(c) \wedge m1 \neq m2 \wedge \text{cau}(m1,m2)\}|}{k(k-1)/2}$$

Two Methods interact with each other if they directly or indirectly use an attribute of class c in common.

$$\text{CC}(c) = 2\sum_{i=1}^{k-1} \sum_{j=i+1}^{k} \frac{|I_i \cap I_j|}{|I_i \cup I_j|}/k(k-1)$$

The similarity between two methods is the ratio of the collection of their shared attributes to the total number of their referenced attributes.

$$\text{SCOM}(c) = 2\sum_{i=1}^{k-1} \sum_{j=i+1}^{k} \frac{|I_i \cap I_j|}{\min(|I_i|,|I_j|)} * \frac{|I_i \cup I_j|}{l}/k(k-1)$$

The similarity between two methods is the ratio of the collection of their shared attributes to the minimum number of their referenced attributes. Connection intensity of a pair of methods is given more weight when such a pair involves more attributes.

$$\text{LCOM5}(c) = \frac{k - \frac{1}{l}\sum_{a \in A_I(c)} |\{m|m \in M_I(c) \wedge a \in I_m\}|}{k-1}$$

Measures the lack of cohesion of a class in terms of the proportion of attributes each method references. Unlike the other metrics, LCOM5 measures *lack* of cohesion, so a lower value indicates better cohesion.

In the above: c is a particular class; $M_I(c)$ is the set of methods implemented in c; $A_I(c)$ is the set of attributes implemented in c; k and l are the number of methods and attributes implemented in class c respectively; I_i is the set of attributes referenced by method i; x_i is the number of 1s in the *ith* column of the Method-Attribute Reference (MAR) matrix, $\text{MAR}(i,j)$ holds 1 if *ith* method directly or indirectly references *jth* attribute; $\text{cau}(m1,m2)$ holds 1 if $m1$ and $m2$ use an attribute of class c in common.

Figure 2: Formal and informal definitions of the metrics evaluated in this paper.

this fitness function is easy to improve, we obtain the long refactoring sequences that are required to draw conclusions about relationships between metrics.

The metrics formulae presented in Figure 2 show how to calculate the metric for a single class. To measure the cohesion of a number of classes, i.e., an entire program, we use the formula for weighted cohesion based on that proposed by Briand and Al Dallal [2]:

$$weight_c = \frac{l_c k_c (k_c - 1)}{\sum_{i \in Classes} l_i k_i (k_i - 1)}$$

where $weight_n$ is the weight assigned to the cohesion of class n, l_n is the number of attributes in class n, and k_n is the number of methods in class n. In the case where k_c equals 1, the numerator in the formula becomes l. This is the formula we use for LSCC. For other metrics we tailor this formula so it makes sense for that metric.

Most software metrics are ordinal in nature, so any formula that averages them is theoretically suspect. However, our experience suggests that these metrics are not far from being on an interval scale and so the risk in treating them as interval is slight in relation to the advantages that accrue. Briand et al. make a similar argument for the use of parametric methods for ordinal scale data [11].

System	Description	LOC	#Classes
JHotDraw 5.3	Graphics	14,577	208
XOM 1.1	XML API	28,723	212
ArtofIllusion 2.8.1	3D modeling	87,352	459
GanttProject 2.0.9	Scheduling	43,913	547
JabRef 2.4.2	Graphical	61,966	675
JRDF 0.4.1.1	RDF API	12,773	206
JTar 1.2	Compression	9,010	59
JGraphX 1.5.0.2	Java Graphing	48,810	229

Table 1: Software applications used in the first investigation

4.1 Results and Analysis

We applied this refactoring process to the eight open source Java projects presented in Table 1. In each case, the experiment was allowed to run for five days, or until a sequence of over 1000 refactorings was reached. In total, 3,453 refactorings were applied, as shown in Table 2. The applications were of high quality initially, so improvements to cohesion were time-consuming to find. JHotDraw proved the easiest program to refactor because its extensive use of design patterns and a rich inheritance hierarchy provided plenty of opportunity to refactor. Note that in this work we are using the refactoring process only to investigate the properties of the metrics. We make no claim that the refactored program has a better design than the original program.

	JHotDraw (1007)	JTar (115)	XOM (193)	JRDF (13)	JabRef (257)	JGraph (525)	ArtOfIllusion (593)	Gantt (750)	All (3453)
LSCC	96	99	100	92	99	100	99	96	98
TCC	86	53	97	46	61	72	84	71	78
SCOM	79	70	93	92	79	89	77	80	81
CC	100	98	100	92	99	100	100	99	100
LCOM5	100	100	100	100	100	100	100	99	100

Table 2: Metric volatility as a percentage. This shows the percentage of refactorings that caused a change in a metric. The number in parentheses is the number of refactorings that were performed on this application.

4.1.1 *Volatility*

One aspect of a metric that this investigation allows us to see is its *volatility*. A volatile metric is one that is changed often by refactorings, whereas an inert metric is one that is changed infrequently by refactorings. Volatility is an important factor in determining the usefulness of a metric. For example, in search-based refactoring, a highly volatile metric will have a very strong impact on how the refactoring proceeds while a relatively inert metric may simply be pointless to compute. In a software quality context, measuring the improvement in a system's design using a set of inert metrics is likely to be futile, as they are, by definition, crude measures that do not detect subtle changes in the property they measure. Table 2 shows the volatility of the 5 metrics in each individual system under investigation, and averaged across all systems.

The first observation is that LSCC, CC and LCOM5 are all highly volatile metrics. In 99% of the refactorings applied across all applications, each these metrics either increased or decreased. The relative lack of volatility of the TCC metric is largely due to the `cau` relation (see Figure 2), which holds relatively rarely for any given pair of methods.

The results for the JRDF application are notable. All metrics bar TCC are highly volatile for this application. Although JRDF is one of the larger applications, a total of only 13 refactorings could be applied to it, compared to the 1000+ refactorings that could be applied to JHotDraw, a similarly-sized application. The explanation for this lies in the nature of the applications. In JHotDraw, 86% of the classes are subclasses, whereas in JRDF this figure is only 6%. Since most of the refactorings Code-Imp applies relate to inheritance, an application that makes little use of inheritance provides few opportunities to refactor.

While there is some consistency across the different applications, the JRDF example illustrates that, given an individual metric, volatility can vary substantially between systems. We attempted normalising the volatilities against the overall volatility of each application, and, while this improved the consistency somewhat, a large variance remained. We thus conclude that volatility is dependent on a combination of a metric and the application to which it is applied.

4.1.2 *Probability of positive change*

Table 2 shows how volatile the metrics are, but it does not show whether the volatility is in a positive or negative sense. In Table 3 we present this view of the metrics. Recall that every refactoring applied in this investigation increases at least one of the cohesion metrics. It is remarkable then to note how often an increase in one cohesion metric leads to a decrease in another. Taking LSCC and ArtOfIllusion as an example, LSCC decreases in 42% of the refactorings (593 in

total). So for ArtOfIllusion, 249 refactorings that improved at least one of TCC, SCOM, CC or LCOM5, as guaranteed by the refactoring process, caused LSCC to worsen.

	LSCC	TCC	SCOM	CC
TCC	0.60			
SCOM	0.70	0.58		
CC	0.10	0.01	-0.28	
LCOM5	-0.17	-0.21	-0.46	0.72

Table 4: Spearman rank correlation between the metrics across all refactorings and all applications. Note that LCOM5 measures *lack* of cohesion, so a negative value indicates positive correlation.

This pattern of conflict is repeated across Table 3. As summarised in Table 4, TCC, LSCC and SCOM exhibit collective moderate positive correlation, while CC and LCOM5 show mixed correlation ranging from moderate positive correlation (LCOM5 and SCOM) to strong negative correlation (LCOM5 and CC).

In order to summarise the level of disagreement across the set of metrics, we also considered each pairwise comparison between each pair of metrics for each refactoring. For 5 metrics we have $(5 * 4)/2 = 10$ pairwise comparisons per refactoring. For 3,453 refactorings, this yields a total of 34,530 pairwise comparisons. Each pair is categorised as follows:

Agreement: Both metric values increase, both decrease, or both stay the same.

Dissonant: One value increases or decreases, while the other stays the same.

Conflicted: One value increases, while the other decreases.

Across the entire set of refactorings, we found the levels to be as follows: 45% agreement, 17% dissonant and 38% conflicted. The figure of 38% conflicted is remarkable and indicates that, in a significant number of cases, what one cohesion metric regards as an improvement in cohesion, another cohesion metric regards as a decrease in cohesion. This has a practical impact on how cohesion metrics are used. Trying to improve a software system using a combination of conflicted cohesion metrics is impossible — an improvement in terms of one cohesion metric is likely to cause a deterioration in terms of another metric.

4.2 Summary

This investigation has served to show the variance between software cohesion metrics in terms of their volatility and their propensity to agree or disagree with each other. Of course a cohesion metric that completely agrees with another makes no contribution to the cohesion debate. However, the conflict between the metrics indicates that the suite

	JHotDraw	JTar	XOM	JRDF	JabRef	JGraph	ArtOfIllusion	GanttProject	Average
LSCC	↑50 , 46↓	↑50 , 49↓	↑57 , 43↓	↑46 , 46↓	↑54 , 46↓	↑51 , 48↓	↑57 , 42↓	↑53 , 43↓	↑53 , 45↓
TCC	↑45 , 41↓	↑30 , 23↓	↑51 , 46↓	↑23 , 23↓	↑34 , 27↓	↑37 , 35↓	↑52 , 35↓	↑39 , 31↓	↑43 , 35↓
SCOM	↑38 , 40↓	↑34 , 36↓	↑50 , 44↓	↑46 , 46↓	↑37 , 42↓	↑36 , 53↓	↑44 , 33↓	↑40 , 40↓	↑40 , 41↓
CC	↑53 , 47↓	↑52 , 46↓	↑51 , 49↓	↑46 , 46↓	↑54 , 44↓	↑61 , 39↓	↑58 , 42↓	↑57 , 42↓	↑56 , 44↓
LCOM5	↑51 , 49↓	↑50 , 50↓	↑48 , 52↓	↑54 , 46↓	↑49 , 50↓	↑41 , 59↓	↑56 , 43↓	↑50 , 50↓	↑50 , 50↓

Table 3: Of those refactorings that change a metric, the percentage that are improvements and deteriorations, i.e., an uparrow indicates an improvement in cohesion.

of cohesion metrics do not simply reflect *different* aspects of cohesion, they reflect *contradictory* interpretations of cohesion.

In order to investigate this conflict further, we choose two cohesion metrics, LSCC and TCC, and analyse them in greater detail using search-based refactoring. The results of this are presented in the following section.

5. INVESTIGATION II: DETAILED ANALYSIS OF COHESION METRICS

The first investigation shows how search-based refactoring can be used to create a broad-stroke picture of how metrics relate to each other. In this second investigation we take two well-known cohesion metrics, LSCC and TCC, and explore their relationship more closely. We choose these two metrics as they are popular, low-level design metrics that have different characteristics. TCC was published in 1995 by Bieman and Kang [8], has stood the test of time, and was found to be rather inert in investigation I. LSCC was published in 2010 by Briand and Al Dallal [2], and hence represents a very recent interpretation of cohesion. In contrast to TCC, LSCC was found to be very volatile in investigation I.

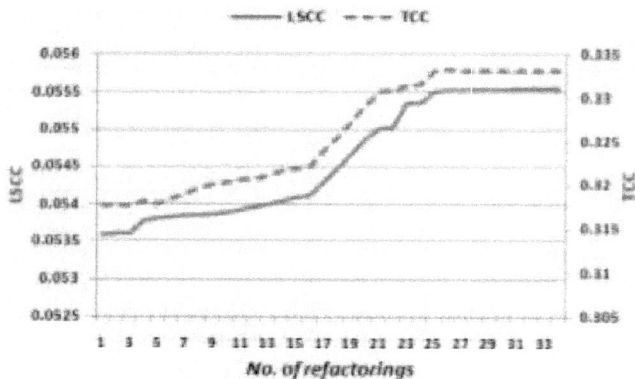

Figure 3: Graph of TCC improving as LSCC is improved by refactoring JHotDraw

In the definition of both these metrics [8, 2], the respective authors mention the issue of whether or not inheritance should be considered in calculating cohesion, but do not discuss it in detail. If inheritance is taken into account, then the cohesion of a class is calculated as if all inherited methods and fields were part of the class as well. In the view of the authors of this present paper, this is a critical issue. A class might appear to have two unrelated methods, but if they both access the same inherited methods or fields they

might in fact be very cohesive[1]. Hence we consider two versions of each of these metrics, the normal, 'local' versions termed LSCC and TCC, and the 'inherited' versions, which we term $LSCC_i$ and TCC_i.

We conducted two experiments to test the relationships between these metrics. In each experiment, we use one metric to drive the refactoring process, and measure the impact on another metric. The experiments are as follows:

1. increase LSCC measure TCC

2. increase TCC_i measure $LSCC_i$

The other obvious experiments, increasing TCC and measuring LSCC and increasing $LSCC_i$ measuring TCC_i were also performed. The results were in keeping with what we report below, but the details are omitted for space reasons. JHotDraw was chosen as the application on which to run these experiments as it proved in Section 4 to be the application that Code-Imp found easiest to refactor.

We alter the fitness function used to drive the search in these experiments. In our initial investigations in Section 4 the goal was to apply as many refactorings as possible to gain an overall view of the metric interactions. By contrast, in this section we wish to mimic a developer refactoring a program using a cohesion metric as guidance. If we use average class cohesion as the fitness function, we ignore the fact that, from a software engineering perspective, classes are not all of the same importance. For example, it is more useful to improve the cohesion of a frequently-updated class than of a stable class.

For these reasons we use a novel fitness function in the domain of search-based refactoring: a Pareto-optimal search *across the classes of the program being refactored*[2]. A refactoring that attempts to increase a metric is only accepted if it increases that metric for at least one class, and causes no decline in that metric for any other class. This is quite a limiting fitness function, but we argue that the resulting refactoring sequence is likely to be acceptable as a useful refactoring sequence in practice. The lengths of the refactoring sequences in these experiments are much shorter than those in Section 4, but are of sufficient length for trends to be observed.

---

[1]The Template Method design pattern [23] is an example of this. The subclasses contain several apparently unrelated methods. However, it is the inherited template method itself that provides the glue that makes these methods cohesive.
[2]Harman and Tratt first used Pareto optimality in search-based refactoring to avoid summing values for different metrics [27]. Our aim is to avoid summing values for the same metric on different classes.

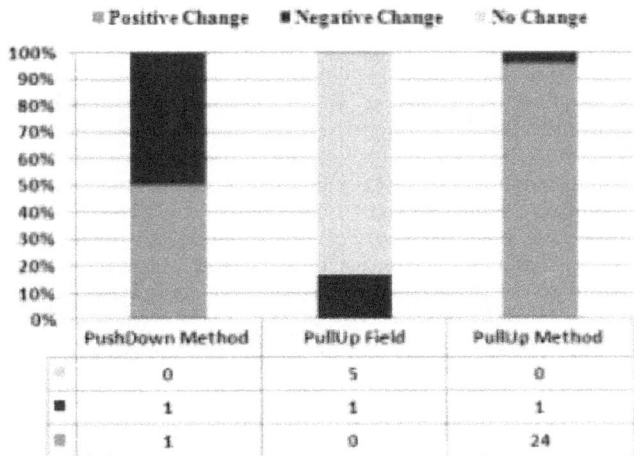

Figure 4: Impact of refactoring on the TCC metric in LSCC vs. TCC experiment on JHotDraw.

5.1 Increasing LSCC, measuring TCC

The result of refactoring JHotDraw to improve LSCC and measuring the impact on TCC is presented in Figures 3 and 4. 33 refactorings are performed and both metrics increase steadily and with little apparent conflict (Spearman rank correlation 0.8). However, when we look more closely at the refactorings in Figure 3, an anomaly becomes apparent. At refactoring 26, TCC drops slightly and remains constant for the next 5 refactorings, while LSCC steadily increases. We examine this area of disagreement more closely to determine what it tell us about the metrics.

This period of disagreement occurs during a sequence of PullUpField refactorings where the target class has no fields. TCC is undefined for a class with no fields, so moving a field to such a class appears to reduce cohesion by adding a class with zero cohesion to the program. On the other hand, we learn from this example that LSCC prefers to move a field that is loosely associated with a class (e.g. used directly or indirectly by only one method) to its superclass, if that superclass has a zero LSCC measure (no two methods access the same field). In practice, this would be viewed as a detrimental refactoring, so we have uncovered a weakness in the LSCC metric that it would reward such a refactoring.

5.2 Increasing TCC_i, measuring $LSCC_i$

The result of refactoring JHotDraw to improve TCC_i and measuring the impact on $LSCC_i$ is presented in Figure 5. 91 refactorings were performed and while there is some agreement in places, overall the graph shows extreme conflict (Spearman rank correlation -0.8).

Figure 6 provides a detailed view of the refactorings and their effect on the $LSCC_i$ metric. The most striking feature is that PullUp Field has a negative impact on $LSCC_i$ in every case. The negative impact occurs because a field is moved to a superclass where it has no interaction which reduces $LSCC_i$ for that class. TCC_i favours this refactoring because as part of pulling a private field up to a superclass, it must be made protected, and this causes more interaction between protected methods that use the field in the hierarchy structure. This use of PullUp Field in this case does

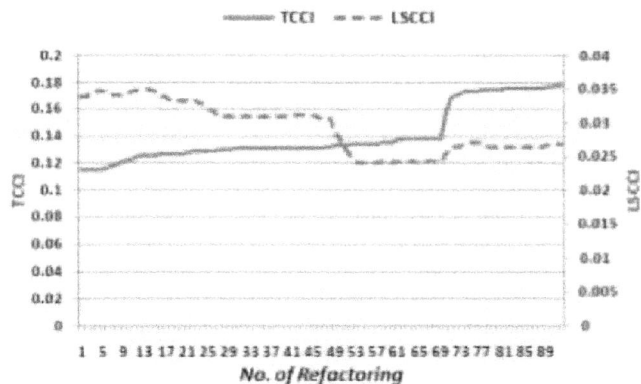

truly improve cohesion, so it is a strength of $LSCC_i$ that it would not recommend it.

Another area of conflict is the negative effect PushDown Method has on $LSCC_i$ in six refactorings. On inspecting these refactorings, we learn that TCC_i always prefers a method to reside in a class where it is used and access the fields it needs in its superclass (where they cannot be private of course), rather than reside in the superclass. However, $LSCC_i$ places more emphasis on keeping fields private, so it frequently prefers a method to stay in the class of the fields it uses except where the method is used by majority of the subclasses.

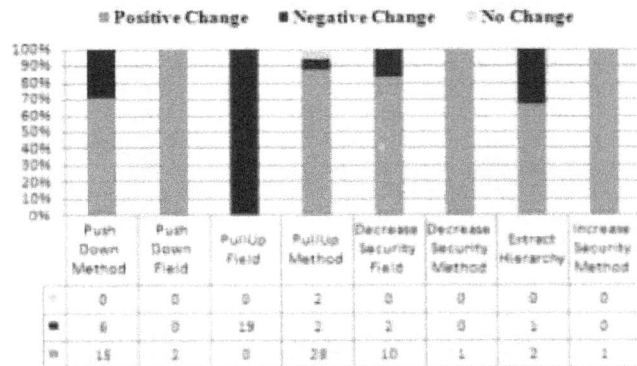

Figure 6: Impact of refactoring on the $LSCC_i$ metric in TCC_i vs. $LSCC_i$ experiment on JHotDraw.

5.3 Summary

In this section we used a Pareto-optimal search across classes in order to demonstrate how two metrics can be compared and contrasted in a detailed way. In both experiments, LSCC vs. TCC and TCC_i vs. $LSCC_i$, we found areas of agreement and conflict between the metrics. Examining the areas of conflict more closely shed light on aspects of the metrics that are not readily apparent from their formulae.

6. RELATED WORK

In this section we review related work in Search-Based Refactoring (section 6.1) and Software Metrics (section 6.2).

6.1 Search-Based Refactoring

Search-based refactoring is fully automated refactoring driven by metaheuristic search and guided by software quality metrics, as introduced by O'Keeffe and Ó Cinnéide [39]. Existing work in this area uses either a 'direct' or an 'indirect' approach. In the direct approach the refactoring steps are applied directly to the program, denoting moves from the current program to a near neighbour in the search space. Early examples of the direct approach are the works by Williams [46] and Nisbet [34] who addressed the parallelization problem. More recently, O'Keeffe and Ó Cinnéide [37, 38] applied the direct approach to the problem of automating design improvement.

In the indirect approach, the program is indirectly optimised through the optimisation of the sequence of transformations to apply to the program. In this approach fitness is computed by applying the sequence of transformations to the program in question and measuring the improvement in the metrics of interest. The first authors to use search in this way were Cooper et al. [13], who used biased random sampling to search a space of high-level whole-program transformations for compiler optimisation. Also following the indirect approach, Fatiregun et al. [16, 17] showed how search based transformations could be used to reduce code size and construct amorphous program slices.

Seng et al. [42] propose an indirect search-based technique that uses a genetic algorithm over refactoring sequences. In contrast to O'Keeffe and Ó Cinnéide [36], their fitness function is based on well-known measures of coupling between program components. Both these approaches used weighted-sum to combine metrics into a fitness function, which is of practical value but is a questionable operation on ordinal metric values. A solution to the problem of combining ordinal metrics was presented by Harman and Tratt, who introduced the concept of Pareto optimality to search-based refactoring [27]. They used it to combine two metrics into a fitness function and demonstrated that it has several advantages over the weighted-sum approach.

The work of Sahraoui et al. [41] has some similarities to ours, notably their premise that semi-automated refactoring can improve metrics. Their approach is to seek to gain insight into the refactorings that are chosen to improve a chosen metric. Our approach is the reverse of this: we use refactorings to gain insights into (multiple) metrics.

In recent work, Otero et al. [40] use search-based refactoring to refactor a program as it is being evolved using genetic programming in an attempt to find a different design which may admit a useful transformation as part of the genetic programming algorithm. Jensen and Cheng [29] use genetic programming to drive a search-based refactoring process that aims to introduce design patterns. Ó Cinnéide et al. use a search-based refactoring approach to try to improve program testability [35]. Kilic et al. explore the use of a variety of population-based approaches to search-based parallel refactoring, finding that local beam search could find the best solutions [32].

6.2 Analysis of Software Metrics

One criticism that is levelled at the use of software metrics is that they often fail to measure what they purport to measure [20]. This has led to a proliferation of software metrics [19], many of which attempt to measure the same aspect(s) of code. It is not surprising then that several studies have attempted to compare software metrics to better understand their similarities and differences. In this section, we focus on studies that have analysed cohesion metrics. The overriding problem with cohesion (and its measurement) has been that, unlike coupling, any metric claiming to measure cohesion is relatively subjective and open to interpretation [15]. Most cohesion measures have focused on the distribution of attributes in the methods of a class (and variations thereof). However, nuances of different object-oriented languages and the fact that the distribution of attributes can make it impossible to calculate cohesion metrics, means that no single, agreed cohesion metric exists.

The LCOM metric has been subject to detailed scrutiny [12] and revised several times to account for idiosyncrasies in its calculation. Comparisons between LCOM and other proposed cohesion metrics are a common feature of empirical studies [1, 2, 3, 7, 8, 14]. Most newly-proposed cohesion-based metrics have attempted to improve upon previous metrics by forming a link between low cohesion and high fault-proneness [2, 3] or intuitive notions of high cohesion and subjective developer views of what constitutes high cohesion [7]; others have tried to demonstrate a theoretical improvement [1, 14]. Comparison of cohesion metrics has been a consistent topic for research [30, 31, 44]. For example, the Cohesion Amongst the Methods of a Class (CAMC) metric [7] provides a variation on the LCOM metric by including the `self` property in C++ in its calculation, and has been validated against developer opinion.

Al Dallal and Briand [1] investigated the relationship between their proposed metric, Low-Level Similarity-Based Class Cohesion (LSCC), and eleven other low-level cohesion metrics in terms of correlation and ability to predict faults. Based on correlation studies they concluded that LSCC captures a cohesion measurement dimension of its own. Four open source Java applications consisting of 2,035 classes and over 200KLOC were used as a basis of their study.

Counsell et al. [14] proposed a new metric called the Normalized Hamming Distance Metric (NHD). The authors concluded that NHD is a better cohesion metric than CAMC. Their empirical data, obtained from three C++ applications, showed a strong negative correlation between NHD and other metrics. This contrasts with a more recent study by Kaur and Singh [31] who explored the relationship between NHD, SNHD [14] and CAMC. They observed that class size was a confounding factor in the computation of both CAMC and NHD.

Alshayeb discovered that refactoring had a positive effect on several cohesion metrics in his study of open source software [6]. However, in later work he reported that this effect was not necessarily positive on other external software quality attributes such as reusability, understandability, maintainability, testability and adaptability [5]. An information-theoretic approach to measuring cohesion was proposed by Khoshgoftaar et al. [4] and while this represented a fresh approach to cohesion measurement, their metric is subject to the same criticisms as previous metrics.

These studies have created a deeper understanding of software metrics and have shown that metrics with a similar intent do not necessarily provide similar results. However, understanding the underlying characteristics of a metric is just a first step in determining their usefulness. The approach detailed in this paper takes the next step by quantifying the extent of conflict between metrics to pinpoint the root cause of that conflict.

7. CONCLUSIONS AND FUTURE WORK

In this paper we use search-based refactoring for a novel purpose: to discover relationships between software metrics. By using a variety of search techniques (semi-random search, Pareto-optimal search on classes) guided by a number of cohesion metrics, we are able to make empirical assessments of the metrics. In areas of direct conflict between metrics, we examine the refactorings that caused the conflict in order to learn more about nature of the conflict.

In our study of 300KLOC of open source software we found that the cohesion metrics LSCC, TCC, CC, SCOM and LCOM5 agreed with each other in only 45% of the refactorings applied. In 17% of cases dissonance was observed (one metric changing while the other remains static) and in 38% of cases the metrics were found to be in direct conflict (one metric improving while the other disimproves). This high percentage of conflict reveals an important feature of cohesion metrics: they not only embody *different* notions of cohesion, they embody *conflicting* notions of cohesion. This key result refutes the possibility of ever creating a single, unifying cohesion metric.

In three areas of conflict between LSCC and TCC our analysis of the refactorings led to detailed insights into the differences between these metrics (see sections 5.1 and 5.2). This analysis also demonstrated that the decision of whether or not to include inheritance in the definition of a cohesion metric is not simply a matter of taste as has been hitherto assumed [8, 2] — LSCC and TCC largely agree while their inherited versions exhibit extreme conflict. Our goal in this work is not to resolve these issues, but to provide a methodology whereby they can be detected in order to aid further metrics research. In some cases, software design principles indicate which metric is best. In other cases, the developer can choose which metric best suits their needs.

We claim that this approach can contribute significantly to the ongoing metrics debate. It provides a platform upon which metrics can be animated and their areas of agreement and disagreement brought into clear focus. Future work in this area involves performing the analysis using a broader range of searches, e.g. using two metrics, try to refactor to increase their disagreement, or refactor to worsen a metric as much as possible, before refactoring to improve it again, as well as applying this approach to other metrics, most obviously coupling metrics. Another area for further research is the analysis of the refactorings that cause metrics to conflict. This analysis was performed by hand in this paper, but attempting to automate it is an interesting research challenge.

8. ACKNOWLEDGMENTS

This research is partly funded by the Irish Government's Programme for Research in Third-Level Institutions through the Lero Graduate School in Software Engineering.

9. REFERENCES

[1] J. Al Dallal. Validating object-oriented class cohesion metrics mathematically. In *SEPADS'10*, USA, 2010.

[2] J. Al Dallal and L. Briand. A precise method-method interaction-based cohesion metric for object-oriented classes. *ACM Transactions on Software Engineering and Methodology*, 2010.

[3] J. Al-Dallal and L. C. Briand. An object-oriented high-level design-based class cohesion metric. *Information & Software Technology*, 52(12):1346–1361, 2010.

[4] E. B. Allen, T. M. Khoshgoftaar, and Y. Chen. Measuring coupling and cohesion of software modules: an information-theory approach. *Proceedings Seventh International Software Metrics Symposium*, (561):124–134, 2001.

[5] M. Alshayeb. Empirical investigation of refactoring effect on software quality. *Information & Software Technology*, 51(9):1319–1326, 2009.

[6] M. Alshayeb. Refactoring effect on cohesion metrics. In *International Conference on Computing, Engineering and Information, 2009. ICC '09*, Apr. 2009.

[7] J. Bansiya, L. Etzkorn, C. Davis, and W. Li. A class cohesion metric for object-oriented designs. *Journal of Object Oriented Programming*, 11(08):47–52, 1999.

[8] J. M. Bieman and B.-K. Kang. Cohesion and reuse in an object-oriented system. In *Symposium on Software reusability*, Seattle, Washington, 1995.

[9] J. M. Bieman and L. M. Ott. Measuring functional cohesion. *IEEE Transactions on Software Engineering*, 20(8):644–657, Aug. 1994.

[10] C. Bonja and E. Kidanmariam. Metrics for class cohesion and similarity between methods. In *Proceedings of the 44th annual Southeast regional conference*, pages 91–95, Florida, 2006. ACM.

[11] L. Briand, K. E. Emam, and S. Morasca. On the application of measurement theory in software engineering. *Empirical Software Engineering*, 1:61–88, 1996.

[12] L. C. Briand, J. W. Daly, and J. Wüst. A unified framework for cohesion measurement in object-oriented systems. *Empirical Software Engineering*, 3(1):65–117, 1998.

[13] K. D. Cooper, P. J. Schielke, and D. Subramanian. Optimizing for reduced code space using genetic algorithms. In *Proceedings of LCTES'99*, volume 34.7 of *ACM Sigplan Notices*, pages 1–9, NY, May 5 1999.

[14] S. Counsell, S. Swift, and J. Crampton. The interpretation and utility of three cohesion metrics for object-oriented design. *ACM Trans. Softw. Eng. Methodol.*, 15(2):123–149, 2006.

[15] S. Counsell, S. Swift, and A. Tucker. Object-oriented cohesion as a surrogate of software comprehension: an empirical study. In *Proceedings of the Fifth IEEE International Workshop on Source Code Analysis and Manipulation*, SCAM '05, pages 161–172, Washington, DC, USA, 2005. IEEE Computer Society.

[16] D. Fatiregun, M. Harman, and R. Hierons. Evolving transformation sequences using genetic algorithms. In *SCAM 04*, pages 65–74, Los Alamitos, California, USA, Sept. 2004. IEEE Computer Society Press.

[17] D. Fatiregun, M. Harman, and R. Hierons. Search-based amorphous slicing. In *WCRE 05*, pages 3–12, Carnegie Mellon University, Pittsburgh, Pennsylvania, USA, Nov. 2005.

[18] N. E. Fenton. Software measurement: A necessary

scientific basis. *IEEE Transactions on Software Engineering*, 20(3):199–206, 1994.

[19] N. E. Fenton and M. Neil. Software metrics: Roadmap. pages 357–370. ACM Press, 2000.

[20] N. E. Fenton and S. L. Pfleeger. *Software metrics - a practical and rigorous approach (2. ed.)*. International Thomson, 1996.

[21] L. Fernández and R. P. na. A sensitive metric of class cohesion. *Information Theories and Applications*, 13(1):82–91, 2006.

[22] M. Fowler, K. Beck, J. Brant, W. Opdyke, and D. Roberts. *Refactoring: Improving the Design of Existing Code*. Addison-Wesley, 1999.

[23] E. Gamma, R. Helm, R. E. Johnson, and J. Vlissides. *Design Patterns: Elements of Reusable Object-Oriented Software*. Addison-Wesley, Reading, MA, 1995.

[24] T. Gutzmann et al. Recoder: a java metaprogramming framework, March 2010. http://sourceforge.net/projects/recoder.

[25] M. Harman and J. Clark. Metrics are fitness functions too. In *Proc. International Symposium on METRICS*, pages 58–69, USA, 2004. IEEE Computer Society.

[26] M. Harman, S. Danicic, B. Sivagurunathan, B. Jones, and Y. Sivagurunathan. Cohesion metrics. In 8th *International Quality Week*, pages Paper 3–T–2, pp 1–14, San Francisco, May 1995.

[27] M. Harman and L. Tratt. Pareto optimal search based refactoring at the design level. In *Proceedings GECCO 2007*, pages 1106–1113, July 2007.

[28] I. Hemati Moghadam and M. Ó Cinnéide. Automated refactoring using design differencing. In *Proc. of European Conference on Software Maintenance and Reengineering*, Szeged, Mar. 2012.

[29] A. Jensen and B. Cheng. On the use of genetic programming for automated refactoring and the introduction of design patterns. In *Proceedings of GECCO*. ACM, July 2010.

[30] P. Joshi and R. K. Joshi. Quality analysis of object oriented cohesion metrics. In *QUATIC'10*, pages 319–324. IEEE Computer Society, Oct. 2010.

[31] K. Kaur and H. Singh. Exploring design level class cohesion metrics. *Journal of Software Engineering and Applications*, 03(04):384–390, 2010.

[32] H. Kilic, E. Koc, and I. Cereci. Search-based parallel refactoring using population-based direct approaches. In *Proceedings of the Third international Conference on Search Based Software Engineering*, SSBSE'11, pages 271–272, 2011.

[33] A. Lakhotia. Rule–based approach to computing module cohesion. In *Proceedings of the 15th*

Conference on Software Engineering (ICSE-15)*, pages 34–44, 1993.

[34] A. Nisbet. GAPS: A compiler framework for genetic algorithm (GA) optimised parallelisation. In P. M. A. Sloot, M. Bubak, and L. O. Hertzberger, editors, *High-Performance Computing and Networking, International Conference and Exhibition, HPCN Europe 1998, Amsterdam, The Netherlands, April 21-23, 1998, Proceedings*, volume LNCS 1401, pages 987–989. Springer, 1998.

[35] M. Ó Cinnéide, D. Boyle, and I. Hemati Moghadam. Automated refactoring for testability. In *Proceedings of the International Conference on Software Testing, Verification and Validation Workshops (ICSTW 2011)*, Berlin, Mar. 2011.

[36] M. O'Keeffe and M. Ó. Cinnéide. Search-based software maintenance. In *CSMR'06*, Mar. 2006.

[37] M. O'Keeffe and M. Ó Cinnéide. Search-based refactoring: an empirical study. *J. Softw. Maint. Evol.*, 20(5):345–364, 2008.

[38] M. O'Keeffe and M. Ó Cinnéide. Search-based refactoring for software maintenance. *J. Syst. Softw.*, 81(4):502–516, 2008.

[39] M. O'Keeffe and M. Ó Cinnéide. A stochastic approach to automated design improvement. In *PPPJ'03*, pages 59–62, Kilkenny, June 2003.

[40] F. E. B. Otero, C. G. Johnson, A. A. Freitas, , and S. J. Thompson. Refactoring in automatically generated programs. *Search Based Software Engineering, International Symposium on*, 0, 2010.

[41] H. Sahraoui, R. Godin, and T. Miceli. Can metrics help to bridge the gap between the improvement of OO design quality and its automation? In *ICSM'00*, pages 154–162, Oct. 2000.

[42] O. Seng, J. Stammel, and D. Burkhart. Search-based determination of refactorings for improving the class structure of object-oriented systems. In *GECCO '06*, Seattle, Washington, USA, 8-12 July 2006. ACM.

[43] M. J. Shepperd. *Foundations of software measurement*. Prentice Hall, 1995.

[44] G. Succi, W. Pedrycz, S. Djokic, P. Zuliani, and B. Russo. An empirical exploration of the distributions of the chidamber and kemerer object-oriented metrics suite. *Empirical Software Engineering*, 10(1):81–104, 2005.

[45] E. J. Weyuker. Evaluating software complexity measures. *IEEE Transactions on Software Engineering*, 14(9):1357–1365, Sept. 1988.

[46] K. P. Williams. *Evolutionary Algorithms for Automatic Parallelization*. PhD thesis, University of Reading, UK, Sept. 1998.

Characterizing the Roles of Classes and their Fault-Proneness through Change Metrics

Maximilian Steff & Barbara Russo
Free University of Bozen-Bolzano
Bozen, Italy
{maximilian.steff,
barbara.russo}@unibz.it

ABSTRACT

Many approaches to determine the fault-proneness of code artifacts rely on historical data of and about these artifacts. These data include the code and how it was changed over time, and information about the changes from version control systems. Each of these can be considered at different levels of granularity. The level of granularity can substantially influence the estimated fault-proneness of a code artifact. Typically, the level of detail oscillates between releases and commits on the one hand, and single lines of code and whole files on the other hand. Not every information may be readily available or feasible to collect at every level, though, nor does more detail necessarily improve the results. Our approach is based on time series of changes in method-level dependencies and churn on a commit-to-commit basis for two systems, Spring and Eclipse. We identify sets of classes with distinct properties of the time series of their change histories. We differentiate between classes based on temporal patterns of change. Based on this differentiation, we show that our measure of structural change in concert with its complement, churn, effectively indicates fault-proneness in classes. We also use windows on time series to select sets of commits and show that changes over short amounts of time do effectively indicate the fault-proneness of classes.

Categories and Subject Descriptors

D.2.8 [**Metrics**]: Process metrics, Product metrics

Keywords

product metrics, fault-proneness, software architectures

1. INTRODUCTION

When we write software, we make mistakes. This seems to be an inevitable truth of software development. Knowing when, where and how defects (or faults) are introduced and when they occur is therefore a valuable asset in software development. Most approaches of fault detection and localization rely on mining historical data from various sources like version control systems of the source code, bug and feature trackers, and secondary sources like mailing lists. Version control systems generally provide information on who made which change when. Bug and feature trackers as well as most secondary sources augment the timeline of changes with information as to why which change was made. Historical data can have different levels of granularity. For example, the number of defects can be reported by line of code, method, class and so on. Not all data is available at every level, though. Defects in issue trackers, for instance, might not be (correctly) reported for all code versions. In previous work, we presented a method to measure structural change in software systems and derived a metric for the fault-proneness of classes [21]. We represented software structure at the class-level and our timeline was given by the releases of the systems we examined. Among the open questions we left was the issue of how our method would fare at a higher level of granularity. In this paper, we extend our previous work measuring with a finer measure of structural change and churn - changed lines of code per class - at the commit-level. We use two datasets, each covering about three years of development on the Spring Framework and Eclipse. At the commit-level, however, our previous metric is not able to reliably indicate fault-proneness anymore. To investigate the reasons behind this and qualify defective classes by their change history at the commit-level, we pose the following nested research questions:

RQ1 Are there different types of class change histories? Do they depend on the characteristics of software products?

RQ2 Do change history types indicate code defectiveness? Does this depend on characteristics of software products?

RQ3 Does local change history indicate top defective classes? What are the characteristics of the change history that are better observed in defective classes?

Structural change and churn are two complementary dimensions of complexity in software: complexity between and inside classes. In this work, we collect structural change and churn for each class over commits using bug-fixing commits as proxy for defects in that class. We observe these measures in time series. The new measures we are able to define over time series - length and stationarity - neatly separate the

Permission to make digital or hard copies of all or part of this work for personal or classroom use is granted without fee provided that copies are not made or distributed for profit or commercial advantage and that copies bear this notice and the full citation on the first page. To copy otherwise, to republish, to post on servers or to redistribute to lists, requires prior specific permission and/or a fee.
ESEM'12, September 19–20, 2012, Lund, Sweden.
Copyright 2012 ACM 978-1-4503-1056-7/12/09 ...$15.00.

time series into sets with consistently distinct defect densities for both structural change and churn. Finally, we show the advantage of using both structural change and churn in their complementary nature by further identifying the most fault-prone files and defects over files with these measures.

In the remainder of this paper, we will first have a look at relevant literature. After describing our method in detail, we proceed to describe our datasets and how we collected them. Then, we present the results of applying our previous method on these datasets, followed by an analysis of our new approach. We finish with limitations, a summary of our findings, conclusions and a few remarks on future work.

2. RELATED WORK

There is a wealth of methods for determining and predicting the fault-proneness of files or components in software development. We restrict ourselves to discussing studies that are directly related to our work.

Most relevant for our work are methods that include either product or process metrics. Process metrics have been introduced by Graves et al. [7]. They define process metrics as measurements taken on the change history of the code. The software repository is the prime source for these metrics. Graves et al. concluded that "process measures based on the change history are more useful in predicting fault rates than product metrics of the code." Thus, they introduced the differentiation between process and product metrics, the latter being measurements of the code and its structure. An example for the use of process metrics is the work by Zimmermann et al. [23]. They collected a set of measures on the method-, class-, and file-level for Eclipse and correlated these values on the file- and package-level to pre- and post-release defects. We will later use their results as a benchmark for our results.

Lately, the modeling of histories of process and product metrics as time series has garnered considerable attention. Ratzinger et al. [17] collected a number of metrics for three systems on every day for two months. The metrics included number of lines added and deleted, number of different authors of changes, and number of bugs. On the time series of these attributes they applied a genetic algorithm for feature selection to use in predicting the number of defects over the next two months. They obtained rather high correlation coefficients - between .716 and .946. One of their systems was Spring. They found that in Spring there are only few files with a single bug and very few with more than one. This uneven distribution of defects is an obstacle for defect prediction. For Spring they also found that the single best predictor was the number of times a file had been changed, followed by the number of authors of these changes. Kenmei et al. [10] collected bi-weekly snapshots over five years for three systems, one of which was Eclipse. From every snapshot they extracted the number of lines of code and identified the number of new change requests, i.e. bugs, from a bug tracker within that period. Then, they modeled and predicted the request density of requests per unit of size using ARIMA. While their results for JBoss and Mozilla are useful for predicting and identifying trends, they found it quite hard to do even one step ahead prediction for Eclipse. Couto et al. [1] used an approach similar to Kenmei et al.. Also using bi-weekly snapshots collected over several years, they collected a number of metrics including the CK suite of metrics from the code. They used Granger Causality [6] to find the causes for bugs in changes of the values of the metrics. For 64-93% of bugs they could identify a cause in the metrics. However, there was no single best predictor for any system nor any file. Ostrand et al. [16] built a negative binomial regression model using data like lines of code, a file's age and previous faults to predict the number of faults per file. They found that 20% of the files contained on average 83% on one and 84% of faults on another system. Menzies et al. [13] used their previous results on using static code attributes such as lines of code, Halstead and McCabe, and similar results to conjecture that moving away from maximizing the probability of detection over false alarms towards the approach taken by Ostrand et al. and others is, in fact, preferable. They conclude that current results essentially constitute a ceiling for what learners can achieve. Instead, better results can be achieved by maximizing the number of defects in as small a set of files as possible.

Reflecting on the above methods of analysis, we can identify several approaches to granularity. Measurements can be taken at the class- or package-level, the metrics themselves vary in their level of abstraction. Time-frames for each measurement range from single days (possibly already aggregating changes if several commits occurred that day) to indefinite spans of time given by the dates of releases. This causes two problems. First, if two classes were added to the system in the same commit, the length of their history is considered to be the same, no matter how many changes it includes. At a low granularity, i.e. using releases as time intervals, the change in a metric may degrade to a statistical artifact where the fact that it changed is more important than how it changed or what. Depending on the system, a change in a rarely modified file may be a very good indicator for a defect in that file, no matter what the change actually did. Second, at high granularity, it is apparently difficult to find a single best metric to predict fault-proneness. There are several possible explanations for this, for example that the level of abstraction of the employed metrics does not capture underlying relations or that confounding variables have a disproportionately high impact at this level of detail that they do not have at a lower granularity.

Śliwerski et al. [20] linked bug-fixes to the changes responsible for the bug using the commit history of Eclipse. One of their observations was that some classes were almost exclusively and repeatedly changed in bug-fixes. Classes have different characteristics and roles in a system. Thus, lumping them together disregarding their specificities may negatively impact the assessment of their fault-proneness. Ekanayake et al. [4] observed that they could track concept drift of software projects using defect prediction quality. On Eclipse and three other systems they found that defect prediction quality did indeed vary significantly over time. Specifically, they identified different periods of time where prediction quality was either stable or drifting. Furthermore, they could link periods of drift to an increase in the number of authors contributing code to the projects. Related to this observation is work on change bursts by Nagappan et al. [15] or Rossi et al. [19]. Nagappan et al. noticed that for commercial software periods of increased activity on the code could predict defects very well. Applying their method on Eclipse, however, they noted that change bursts work just as well as regular change activity as predictors. They attribute this to the open source nature of Eclipse. Rossi et al. investigated the relation between code churn, bug fixing activities, and software release dates to discover bursts in time-series of commits in several OSS projects. They found that there is an increase in code-related activities in the OSS community in the proximity of a software release but no specific activity in proximity of a bug fixing. Misirli *et al.* [22] investigated bugs in Eclipse in beta-releases and discovered that they have an interesting characteristic. They found that these bugs are concentrated in Eclipse files with few changes by few different people. This further indicates that there is value in differentiating files and the characteristics of their change behavior over time.

3. METHOD

In our previous work, we have presented and evaluated a measure for structural change as an indicator of fault-proneness of classes [21]. We use a graph kernel, specifically the Neighborhood Hash Kernel (NHK) [8], to measure structural distance between the graph representations of consecutive releases of a software system. In this section, we first describe these graph representations and how we extended them for our current work. Then, we briefly recapitulate how the NHK works and how we apply it as well as some notes about churn. This includes a description of our representation of structural changes and churn for each class over time. Based on these time series, we present our measurement of temporal change patterns and its implications for the analysis of the time series.

3.1 Graph Representation

The definition of structure for a software system depends on the programming language used and the level of granularity at which we consider the code. We restrict ourselves to the study of systems written in Java. In Java, we have the overall systems, its packages and its classes as the most important levels of granularity. For our purposes, we choose classes as the main entities for the representation of structure. The advantage of this choice is that classes essentially correspond to files in Java. Since version control systems typically manage files, we can easily map classes to files.

Thus, every class is a node in our graph representation of the structure of Java code. We have directed edges between two classes for any inheritance relationship, for every method call, and for every referencing of a public field. We distinguish between different method calls and field references so that the graph can be and typically is a multi-graph with several edges between nodes. For two classes, we collect all distinct method calls from each method in one class to each method in the other class. Previously, we had a single link between classes if there was any number of dependencies. Collecting the cardinality of each method call would entail parsing the structure of conditionals and loops in the code enclosing the call. Determining a definite number for the cardinality of an edge in the graph may thus not always be feasible which is why we do not consider cardinalities. We ignore all classes and relationships that are or go outside of the system. After all, we are interested in the development of the system and that has to exclude everything outside of that scope and beyond the reach of the system's developers.

3.2 Measuring Structural Change

The basic idea of the NHK is this. The name of each node is replaced with a unique bit label. Then we encode the neighborhood of each node into its label. We can repeat this encoding iteratively to include information about a bigger and bigger neighborhood in a node's label. This means that we calculate new labels for each node for each iteration. To compare two graphs, we count the number of labels they have in common for a given iteration, divided by the number of total labels for that iteration.

Originally, the NHK was used in applications in biology and chemistry where node names are not necessarily unique. Computing several iterations thus encodes local structure - neighborhoods - into each node and thus allows for efficient comparison of the global structure of the whole graph. In our case, node names are the classes' fully qualified names and are therefore distinct. Computing several iterations nevertheless yields an advantage. It lets us trace the impact of changes. When we compare the node labels of two graphs, the node labels of nodes whose dependencies are different will change in the first iteration. In the second iteration, the labels of nodes that have edges going to those nodes will change and so forth. This means that the NHK lets us trace change impact along the edges in the graph. For our purposes, we limit the calculation to three iterations, i.e. to nodes two steps removed from the original change. The predictive capabilities of dependencies and their change are firmly established in the literature (e.g. [11]). One more recent example of the influence of flawed classes on their clients in terms of defects is the work by Marinescu and Marinescu [12]. This supports the notion that impact of changes as represented by the NHK is valuable for determining fault-proneness of classes. We add changes in dependencies in our method and believe that they are even more valuable to identifying fault-prone classes.

For a set of graphs and their nodes we now have three values for each node in each graph. Since each graph represents the system at the time of a commit to the software repository, we can order the graphs by the time of the corresponding commit. Now we can compare the labels for nodes pairwise for two graphs and determine which labels changed due to the changes in that commit. We mark a 1 if the value changes and a 0 if it does not. We assign different weights for changes in the three iterations. If a label changes in the first iteration, we assign a weight of four, two for the second iteration and no weight for the third iteration. For every class we arrive at a vector with a length equal to the number of commits in the repository. Each entry in the vector reflects the change of that class in that commit. If a class is added or deleted in one of the commits we are considering, we do not consider it changed, though. Only if an existing class is changed in terms of dependencies we add the corresponding value to the vector for this class.

3.3 Measuring Size Change

Lines of code are a very simple and intuitive measure of size. However simple and intuitive, lines of code have also been the subject of countless studies and discussions, and a source of many problems when considering the fault-proneness of files (e.g. [18, 5]). Many problems stem from lines of code being an absolute value that makes comparison difficulty. Churn, thus, is a relative measure and is defined as the change of lines of code in a given period of time and has shown great value for the prediction of defect density (e.g. [14]).

Version control systems allow for the simple computation of added and deleted lines in the change to a file. Unfortunately, a modification in a line of code is represented as the deletion of the original line and the subsequent addition of the modified line. This causes several issues for the computation of churn. Some of these issues and a solution are discussed in [9]. We follow their approach to compute the churn for each commit. As with measuring structural change, we create a vector for each class with each entry being the churn value for that class for that commit.

3.4 Temporal Change Behavior and Defects

Typically, the change vectors for each class contain many zeros because most classes do not change most of the time. If a change occurs, it might introduce a defect into that class and necessitate a subsequent bug fix. Viewing only a single class, this chain of events is clear cut. From the point of view of the commit history of the repository, there may be many other commits in between the changes to that class. Assuming that these changes are not relevant for that class, we remove every 0, i.e. commits where the class was not modified, from its change vector.

There are different ways to analyze the properties of the resulting time series vectors. Since we are interested in how the values in the vectors behave over time, we employ the Augmented Dickey-Fuller test (ADF) [3] to check if the time series in the vector is stationary. A time series is stationary if its probability distribution and thus properties like mean and variance of the series do not change with time shift. Stationary time series allow prediction over time series periods and can reveal patterns in the evolution. The null hypothesis of ADF assumes non-stationarity of a time series. In our case, this tells us if there are different, non-periodical intervals in the time series of a class. For example, if there are periods where the class was changed but the churn values are low, and other periods where we have subsequent, high churn values for that class. To get stable results from the ADF test, we have to disregard all time series that have less than 30 values. We will see the implications of this cutoff in our analysis.

Assuming that we know in which commits a class was changed as part of a bug-fixing commit, we can create a second time series for each class. We create two bug vectors for each class, one for structural change and one for churn since these vectors may have different lengths. The bug vectors have the same length as the corresponding change vectors, we set every entry to 1 that corresponds to a bug-fixing commit and 0 otherwise. The bug vectors for churn cover all bug-fixing commits for a class. The bug vectors for structural change do not necessarily cover all bug-fixing commits because not every bug-fixing commit also changes the structure of the system. We do assume, however, that a structural change may cause a defect that does not require a structural change to fix. For this reason, we additionally insert all bug-fixing commits immediately following a structural change in the vector for structural change and the corresponding bug vector.

Since we have two pairs of vectors for each class, we have several options for testing stationarity. For the present study, our main interest is with consistently changing classes. Thus, we test both the metric vectors and the bug vectors for stationarity. In other words, we are interested in classes that have a stationary history of changes as well as a stationary history of bug-fixing commits. If either or both vectors are

non-stationary, we count the pair as non-stationary. Further distinguishing between these is matter of future work.

If a time series is non-stationary, we know that its mean and variance change for different sub-series. In our case, we can assume that these different time windows have different influence on the defect vector. In a period of small changes, we also expect there to be few bugs. In times of much activity, the chance of incurring defects is probably higher. Based on this observation, we can already make assumptions about different kinds of time series. Generally, short time series will have few bugs. Following Graves *et al.* [7], the number of changes to a file is a pretty good indicator for its fault-proneness. The fewer changes, the less fault-prone it is. With the help of ADF we can distinguish two different behaviors in longer time series, stationary and non-stationary behavior. If the behavior changes, say, periodically, the kind of period we are in at the moment influences our estimate of the corresponding file's fault-proneness within that time-frame. Similarly, predictions of the fault-proneness in the near future depend on the type of the current period. We propose a simple method to approach this issue. We shift small windows across the time series and sum the values in each window. Then, we correlate the value to the corresponding window on the bug vector for the same file. Changing the granularity like this allows us to consider short periods of time. The correlations we obtain then tell us if and how changes in short periods correlate to defects in the same time frame. We use windows of different size to explore how the vectors influence each other. Since our cut-off for the length of vectors to test in the ADF test is 30, we decided to use evenly sized windows equal or smaller than 30, namely 10, 20, and 30. Since longer histories provide us with more information, we let the windows slightly overlap by having the lower bound for each window increase by only half of the rate of the upper bound. The idea is to use more and more information about a class' history as it becomes available over time.

Our approach is, in a nutshell, to differentiate between different time series of structural changes for classes. This differentiation leads us to the realization that different properties of these time series require us to consider windows on these time series. Thus, we shift discrete, slightly overlapping windows of various sizes over the change and defect vectors, sum the values in each vector for each window and then correlate the values for change and defects for all classes.

4. DATA COLLECTION AND PROCESSING

4.1 Data Sources

We collected two datasets. The first dataset is the Subversion repository of the Spring Framework[1] for the development of version 3 of the system and the corresponding JIRA bug tracker. The second dataset is the CVS repository for Eclipse[2] and the corresponding BugZilla bug-tracker. The Spring repository covers the time from July 2008 to mid-October 2011 when we cloned it. We selected a comparable interval for the Eclipse repository and chose the time from January 2002 to December 2004. This is approximately the same time span covered by another, popular Eclipse data set [23]. In contrast to that dataset, however, we limited

---

[1]http://www.springsource.org
[2]http://www.eclipse.org

ourselves to one module in the repository, the JDT module. For both datasets, we restrict our analysis to the *trunk* since development activity for both projects mainly takes place in the *trunk* rather than *branches*. We do not consider refactorings, e.g. moving or renaming of classes. Doing so would probably increase the average length of our time series. However, we assume that a refactoring may also indicate a change in characteristic of class. To not bias our analysis, we therefore consider classes subject to refactorings as distinct entities. Also, we exclude all test files since they do not contribute to the core functionality of either system.

From the bug trackers we extracted all bug reports that affected versions developed in the respective time frames, i.e. bugs where we can assume that they were introduced during the time of our observation. From this subset, we selected all bug reports that were fixed within the respective intervals.

4.2 Data Processing

We converted the Eclipse repository to Subversion using cvs2svn[3] and then processed both Subversion repositories using SVNPlot[4]. Since Subversion only counts the lines added and deleted for every file per commit, we used Hofmann and Riehle's [9] technique to calculate churn values for each change to a file. To create graph representations for every commit in each repository, we had to build each commit into byte-code. Byte-code allows for easy and very fast extraction of classes and relationships between classes by using a library such as Apache BCEL[5]. Unfortunately, building commits typically fails because of unfulfillable dependencies to external libraries. For this reason we used PPA [2], a tool that creates partial builds from source code ignoring all dependencies to external libraries. From these partial builds we created our graph representations of their structure with a parser we wrote using BCEL. We save each graph to a database on which we then apply the NHK to calculate the structural distance between consecutive versions of the graphs.

Both bug trackers assign unique IDs to every bug report. Following common practice, we used regular expressions to find occurrences of these IDs in the commit messages of the repositories. For every match, we mark the commit as a bug-fixing commit. We cannot readily deduce bug-introducing changes or the actual location of defects, though. The actual location of a bug might be different from the place of the fix because the actual site may be too sensitive to changes. We use bug-fixing commits and the files therein as a proxy for the actual defects and their locations, following common practice. Since we use time series, we can assume that in most cases we will at least have a reasonable connection between bug-introducing and bug-fixing commits.

For each class, we have two pairs of vectors with structural change and churn, and their corresponding bug vectors. Each entry in the vectors represents a commit in which the class was changed according to our metrics. The change vectors contain those values, the bug vectors are boolean and indicate if the corresponding commit was a bug-fixing commit. As mentioned above, we added those commits to the vectors for structural change that only had churn but were bug-fixing commits and immediately followed a commit with structural change for the respective class. This is

Table 1: Summary Information of Spring and Eclipse.

		Spring	Eclipse
#classes	beginning	1,791	1,150
	end	2,709	2,278
	total	3,457	3,093
#dependencies	beginning	6,819	11,619
	end	12,169	21,627
	total	21,671	42,896
#commits	total	2,960	17,488
	structural	1,051	2,145
	bug-fixing	449	4,546
	struct. bug-fixing	147	803

based on the assumption that structural changes may cause defects but are not necessarily fixed in commits with structural change. Since they are presumably caused by a structural change, though, we still want to include them in that vector.

4.3 Summary Description of the Datasets

4.3.1 Spring

The Spring Framework is a Java application framework. The system connects several functionalities like an inversion of control container, support for aspect-oriented programming, or a model-view-controller framework for web applications. These functionalities are spread out among a large number of packages, indicating a high degree of modularization.

The period we are considering started in July 2008 when the development of version 3 of Spring started. After four milestone releases and three release candidates, Spring 3 was released in December 2009. The release of version 3.0 was followed by seven maintenance releases with minor version numbers. Meanwhile, development on version 3.1 started. Version 3.1 was released after two milestones and two release candidates in December 2011, just after the end of the time frame we consider.

Table 1 lists some figures describing the system, its structure and growth. The number of classes grows by about 50% while the number of dependencies doubles. Typically, we can expect a faster growth of dependencies than classes when adding new features. New classes have to be both connected among themselves and plugged into existing structures. This process may cause the breakdown of modularity. Comparing the values for density, average path length, and average in- and out-degree of its graphs, we found that the development team is upholding the modularity of the system. Furthermore, we observe that about 80% of classes that were in the system at one point are not there anymore in the end as shown by the number of total classes in the repository. We can attribute this to refactorings as well as deletions of obsolete classes. Given the growth in number of dependencies, the ratio of commits to commits that change the structure of the system is about 3:1, meaning every third commit changes one or more dependencies. This is also reflected in the ratio of bug-fixing commits to bug-fixing commits that change the structure.

[3]http://cvs2svn.tigris.org/
[4]http://code.google.com/p/svnplot/
[5]http://commons.apache.org/bcel/

63

4.3.2 *Eclipse*

As already mentioned, we retrieved the part of the Eclipse repository containing the JDT module and removed all tests and non-Java files. Eclipse started out as an Integrated Development Environment (IDE) but has since evolved into an extendable platform. The Java Development Tools (JDT) are a core part of the development environment, responsible for parsing and representing source code, among other things. Within JDT, there is a *core* package containing the most important features around which the rest of JDT is clustered.

In June 2002 and June 2004, Eclipse saw two major releases, 2.0 and 3.0. Our dataset covers an additional half year prior and past those two years. This includes version 2.1 and two minor versions leading up to it as well as three minor releases following it. In September 2004 we have one maintenance release following version 3.0.

In Table 1, we have a summary of some key figures of the system and repository data. The number of classes almost doubles in the span of three years while the number of dependencies grows by slightly less than 100%. However, we have a much higher turnover in dependencies, almost twice the number of the dependencies that are present in the end. Despite the turnover, the ratio between commits and structural commits is much smaller than in Spring, slightly more than 1:8. There are, however, many more commits than in Spring. Another difference is that Eclipse has many more bug-fixing commits. Similar to the ratio among commits, a smaller fraction of commits is structural. From these observations we can infer that Spring and Eclipse are indeed different in their internal structure.

As mentioned before, we assume that structural changes that cause a defect do not necessarily require a fix that changes the structure. For this reason, we chose to include bug-fixing commits without structural change in the vectors for structural change for each class. We tried two strategies, to add all bug-fixing commits and to add only bug-fixing commits preceded by structural changes. Surprisingly, we found the difference in total defects present in the different vectors to be very small (less than 5% difference). This means that classes that do have structural changes at all do not have many issues that require more than a single (non-structural) fix if any. This includes possibly interspersed non-structural changes which for this reason hardly occur neither. There is one major observation to be made. Changes in structure and changes in size are somewhat mutually exclusive (not considering the change in size that is a necessary consequence of structural change in any case) in Eclipse, specifically that we can distinguish sets of files for which one or the other holds true. This spells out the difference between classes that are themselves complex and classes that reuse functionality in other classes: one kind changes in size only, the other changes in structure as well. This observation is limited to classes with a considerable length of their history, though, in our case a history of more than 30 changes. It is interesting, however, that this difference is so pronounced for the more important classes of Eclipse. On the other hand, there are a few classes with histories shorter than 30 that have accumulated a lot of bug-fixes. In fact, for about a dozen classes, we find that they have been changed at most once not in a bug-fixing commit over a history of 20 or more changes. This corresponds to the findings in [20].

5. DATA ANALYSIS

5.1 Replicating our previous study

Spearman correlation between the sum of all values in the structural change vector, the churn vector, and the bug vector for each class is near 0 and significant for both systems. So there is no correlation. In our previous study, we used 74 releases of Spring and determined how many structural changes and bugs each class underwent and compared it to churn. We found rather strong correlations between change and defects, supporting similar results from the literature.

We explain this different outcome in two ways. At a low granularity, the fact that a class changed is already a pretty good indication of fault-proneness. Any change carries the risk of introducing a defect whereas the chance of having a defect in a class that did not change is considerably smaller. Even at a very high granularity, i.e. single commits, we find that large parts of Spring and Eclipse are essentially never modified structurally after their addition to the system (see Table 2 for the number of unchanged classes in each system in terms of structure). Typically, these classes have only an in-degree in our graphs, meaning that they are, for example, helper classes that provide functionality factored out for a single purpose from another class. Mistakes are rare in this kind of class. Very few classes do never have any churn, though. However, most classes have churn only in less than a handful of commits meaning that they reach their final state after few changes and are left unchanged afterwards. So we have a majority of classes that never or hardly ever change. This observation has to be kept in mind when analyzing the data.

On the other hand, we find that there is no correlation between structural change or churn and defects at a high level of granularity. Arguably, a large change does not necessarily have to be defective and vice versa. Other factors like the locus of a change in the overall system, the person who implemented the modification, and the purpose of the change play a role as well. So there is no straightforward relationship between the quantity and the quality of a change. Thus, any method using either quantity or quality of changes can benefit from using the other variable as well.

Another finding corroborates this argumentation. We calculated the similarity of the overall graphs for consecutive commits and wrote the values to a vector. In a second vector, we marked bug-fixing and non-bug-fixing commits. Using Granger Causality [6] (which was also used in [1] and is comparable to ARIMA used in [10]), we found that neither churn nor structural change Granger-caused defects for the overall system. So neither change at the class- nor at the system-level was correlated to defects at the scale of single commits.

However, if we evaluate our new scheme outlined in Section 3.2, we obtain very strong correlations. Stronger, in fact, than our previous results. Apparently, having longer histories requires a higher level of detail in terms of the dependency structure and where changes originate and how they propagate. On the other hand, though, when having longer histories it makes less sense to use correlations over the entire length of the histories. This insight is the basic reason for developing our new approach.

5.2 Evaluating our new approach

To answer our first research question, we analyze time

Table 2: Descriptive analysis of Spring and Eclipse time series. Length cutoff is 30, avg are rounded.

		Spring	Eclipse
	avg length	9	98
	#long	124	405
	#stationary	3	188
NHK	avg length stationary	70	408
	#non-stationary	121	217
	avg length non-stationary	55	155
	#short (< 30)	1381	753
	#0-length	1946	1875
	avg. length	4	13
	#long	19	284
	#stationary	0	18
Churn	avg. length stationary	-	166
	#non-stationary	19	266
	avg. length non-stationary	45	53
	#short (< 30)	3423	2596
	#0-length	15	213

series by their length. Table 2 lists the three different kinds of time series we derived: long, short, and 0-length time series. Long and short time series are defined by their length being greater or smaller 30 respectively. 0-length time series correspond to those classes that remain unchanged over all commits (i.e. with zero commits). Long time series are further classified into stationary and non-stationary. In the following, we preliminarily show that this classification of histories - long, short, stationary, non-stationary - can be used to characterize products' change history highlighting their differences.

Given the number of overall commits in Table 1, it is no surprise that there are fewer long histories in Spring than in Eclipse for both NHK and Churn. It is also no surprise that the average length of any type of time series for NHK is longer than the one for Churn. This is because the NHK time series values are positive also when neighbor classes change in structure whereas Churn times series values are positive only if they include churn of the class itself. What appears not to be obvious is that the number of unchanged classes is significantly greater with NHK. If compared with the total number of classes in Table 1, this indicates that half of the classes do not actually change their dependencies - and neither do their neighbors - whereas the majority of the classes have lines of code-changes at some point in time. If we further look at stationarity, we find very few (NHK) or no (Churn) stationary time series for Spring. This means that, in general, either class history is too short to draw any conclusions about stationary behavior or does not follow a stationary evolution - i.e. does not show a specific pattern - both for structural change and churn. For Eclipse, there are almost as many stationary as non-stationary NHK time series showing that there is a good number of classes whose dependency change behavior can be predictable over time. In addition, as structural changes always imply churn (but not vice versa) and as the number of stationary time series significantly drops for Churn, we can infer that the majority of classes with stationary NHK time series has either short or non-stationary Churn time series. This indicates that this majority of classes have predictable changes

in their neighborhoods while their own changes are much more rarely predictable. This observation has implications for the localization of bugs, as discussed in the next section.

The few classes with stationary churn times series include some of the core classes of JDT, classes representing code and project entities, various editors, and parsers. As such, Spring and Eclipse are very different in their internal structure and history. In Eclipse, there are a few core classes that are under constant (probably planned) development and many more that are directly affected and influenced by them. In Spring, on the other hand, development activity shifts between components. There are no classes that have stationary Churn time series. The few that have stationary NHK time series are classes that are well-connected in the dependency graph of the system through many out-going edges. They accumulate NHK values through the changes of their neighbors. All of them have been added during the development of Spring 3.0, i.e. they are classes added during the time of our observation. They are abstract classes or standard implementations of interfaces in the converter functionality, for the Spring Expression Language, and for the resolution of beans.

To answer our second research question, we analyze bug-fixing commits and their density in long and short time series to see whether different types of history indicate different activity of bug-fixing and, therefore, different class defectiveness. Tables 3 and 4 summarize this analysis. To read these tables we first need to make two remarks. First, the overall NHK totals for Spring and Eclipse exceed the total number of bug-fixing commits of Table 1. This is due to the fact that we include bug-fixing commits without structural changes if they immediately follow a structural change for a file. As files in a commit have all churn, the totals for Churn instead correspond to the total number of bug-fixing commits. Second, as bug-fixing commits typically change more than one file, time series for different classes might share the same bug-fixing commits. In Table 3 we removed bug-fixing commits that occur in more than one time series eliminating bug-fixing commits of non-stationary time series that are already present in stationary time series and bug-fixing commits of short time series that are already present in the non-stationary time series. With these assumptions, data in Table 3 and Table 4 demonstrate again a clear difference between Spring and Eclipse. For Spring, most bug-fixing commits are in short time series, but with a relatively low density. In NHK long time series, bug-fixing commits are more and more dense in non-stationary time series whereas for Eclipse bug-fixing commits are more and more dense in the stationary ones. Long Churn time series also show a different pattern in that for Eclipse bug-fixing commits are much more dense in stationary time series (Table 4).

Overall, bug-fixing commits for structural changes in Spring and Eclipse occur in a different manner in that Eclipse bug fixes occur more in short histories but are more likely in deterministic long histories (stationary time series) than in Spring. In absolute churn values, non-deterministic occurrences of bug fixes in long histories (non-stationary time series) are the norm in both software products - particularly in Eclipse - but in relative churn values (densities), bug-fixing commits in Eclipse are again much more likely to occur in deterministic histories (46.2). As such, history types can tell much about defective classes and the structure of the product surrounding them. First, we can say that files that

Table 3: Bug-fixing commits in time series

		Spring	Eclipse
NHK	stationary	12	735
	non-stationary	62	290
	short	216	1,594
	total	290	2,619
Churn	stationary	-	831
	non-stationary	100	2,424
	short	349	1,291
	total	449	4,546

Table 4: Densities of bug-fixes.

		Spring	Eclipse
NHK	stationary	4.0	3.9
	non-stationary	6.4	1.3
	short	.15	2.1
Churn	stationary	-	46.2
	non-stationary	5.3	9.1
	short	.10	.50

change frequently and over a long time experience more bug-fixing activities. This supports the claim that changed files are defective [7], in particular files that changed in structure. In addition, as evolving systems inevitable change to accommodate new features and functionalities and changes typically revolve around the core parts of the existing system, our findings indicate that the most important files are the most defective. Second, histories of changes reveal different structures of the systems and the way defects propagate in them. More deterministic long histories of structural changes in Eclipse can be due to the many more code dependencies that propagate defects.

As already mentioned, there are always exceptions. There are about a dozen files in Eclipse that have short time series for churn but are almost exclusively changed in bug-fixing commits. This was also noted in [20] where they found that bug-fixes are three times as likely to incur further, subsequent fixes in Eclipse.

5.2.1 Shifting windows on time series

With our previous analysis, we see that length and stationary nature of time series influences defect density. As such, we might hypothesize that defects might be indicated by the local nature of commits time series. Therefore, to answer our last research question, we investigate time series with commit windows of varying sizes and their correlation with bug-fixes. In this way, we are able to relate the local behavior of class change histories (structural, churn, long, short, stationary, or non-stationary) and code defectiveness. In other words, we discuss the local evolution of a class change to observe defect incidence that can be used to identify fault-prone classes. In particular, we analyze the correlation between churn and structural change with bug-fixing commits in the given windows. For each class, we have two change vectors and two corresponding bug vectors. We shift windows across each pair of vectors and sum the values in each vector for the window. We add these sums as entries to pairs of vectors for all classes in the given category. The correlation values are all in Table 5.

For Spring, we get two very different results. The correlation for stationary time series is strong, but there are only few stationary time series. The correlations for non-stationary time series are about as strong as comparable results from literature ([23]). Interestingly, the correlation values increase slightly with larger windows. This may indicate that different periods in those time series are sometimes rather long. As there are no stationary time series, we do not get any correlations for stationary time series and churn (Table 3). The non-stationary time series are either weakly correlated or not significant. As opposed to structural changes, churn does not only vary over time for single classes, the amount of churn is not even an indicator for defects.

The correlations for Eclipse deliver a much clearer picture. Stationary time series for churn and structural change are strongly correlated to bug-fixing commits as compared to [23]. The strength of the correlations decreases with increasing window sizes, though. This means that, in fact, consecutive changes to a file do immediately contribute to the fault-proneness of that file. The same holds true for non-stationary time series for churn. Here, the immediate influence is even more evident through the much weaker correlations for larger windows. For non-stationary time series, correlations between defects and structural change are slightly negative. This indicates that changes and defects are somehow not related locally and any possible relation can occur in longer windows. Similarly, we found small, slightly negative, or no correlation when we investigated short time series. For example, for Eclipse, the correlation between structural changes or churn and defects for a window size of 10 and 20 is negative and below -.18. For Spring, the correlation is positive but slightly above zero (0.09). In both cases, change is not directly related to local activity of bug-fixing and can even indicate a specific stage in the development process in which the focus is not on fixing bugs [4].

As hinted at above, we used windows of sizes 10 and 20 on the short time series. We found no or only weak correlations for structural change for either system. For these classes, churn was a better albeit not a good indicator. For Spring, we obtained significant correlations of .174 and .384 for the two window sizes respectively. For Eclipse, significant correlations are at .283 and .472, respectively.

Our condition for stationarity is rather strong since both the metric vector and the bug vector have to have stationary behavior. Thus, the rows for non-stationary behavior in Table 5 also include time series where either vector might be stationary. We found that a further distinction between those categories did not immediately lead to greater insights. A more in-depth investigation of different combinations of kinds of vectors would, however, change the low or non-significant correlations for what are now non-stationary vectors. We have a strong statement about the characteristics of stationary classes here. Relaxing the current, strong condition would probably also entail relaxing other conditions. This is matter of future work. This strong condition allows us to derive an implication of the impact of structural changes, though. In previous work, structural change was usually measured in terms of fan-in and fan-out for each class individually. We show that regular changes in neighborhoods of classes can also be a solid predictor of defectiveness. A relaxation of our condition for stationarity might shed further light on this.

66

Table 5: Correlations between windows of changes and bug-fixing commits, all significant. Omitted entries are either not significant (*) or too few to calculate correlation (-).

		window	Spring	Eclipse
NHK	stationary	10	**.745**	**.604**
		20	-	.594
		30	-	.581
	non-stationary	10	.483	-.043
		20	.481	*
		30	**.506**	-.064
Churn	stationary	10	-	**.608**
		20	-	.586
		30	-	.572
	non-stationary	10	.164	**.514**
		20	*	.452
		30	*	.381

5.2.2 Structural change and churn as complements

In the description of Table 3, we mentioned that we excluded bug-fixing commits from the count where they intersected with a different time series. As a final measure, we explore how structural change and churn complement each other. After all, we can assume that there are some classes that change often and extensively in terms of structure and churn. Since this is about the number of changes rather than their behavior over time, we consider stationary and non-stationary time series together.

For Spring, we have total of 124 long time series and 74 bug-fixing commits for structural change, and 19 time series and 100 defects for churn. Nine classes have time series in both sets and there are 39 bug-fixing commits in both sets of defects. Overall, we find 134 files with 135 defects. This amounts to about 30% of defects in 3% of the files, which are probably the most important files in the system. If we lower the length threshold for the time series down to 10, we get 75% of the defects in 15% of the files as a compound measure of structural change and churn.

In Eclipse, this result is even more pronounced. For a length threshold of 30, we get a total of 599 files with 3,384 defects (19% and 74%). However, the intersection of classes for structural change and churn is a mere 90 and the intersection of defects is 896. This means that in 90 classes we find 896 defects. According to Table 3, these are 90% of the defects in all structural change time series. This means that if we neglect the other about 300 time series, we have gained 9% of the files with 72% of the defects. For both Eclipse and Spring, there are strong correlations for most of the time series we gather in the intersecting sets. This means that for most files, we have strong correlations between small windows on time series of changes and incidence of defects.

6. LIMITATIONS

We consider two systems over about three years of development time. Nevertheless, the average length of the time series for one system, Spring, was too short to make as much use of our distinction of stationary and non-stationary time series as we did for Eclipse. This includes the issue that our approach requires a considerable amount of history and changes. However, this requirement is based on using the

ADF test. Replacing it with another measure for temporal change behavior may remedy this problem. Furthermore, we made several assumptions about the severity and impact of defects depending on where in the system they occur. It may be argued that defects in core classes are, on average, not as severe as in subordinate classes since they are more easily discovered. In any case, defects in core classes are typically more noticeable by users which makes them worse in this sense. We have mentioned before that the number of changes to a file is a good indicator for the defectiveness of that file. This is true if there are also periods of time where the file was not changed. Since we are considering only occasions where a file was changed in our change vectors, a boolean distinction for the occurrence of changes does not make much sense for us.

7. FINDINGS

In this section, we briefly recap the discussion of Section 5, highlighting the meta-level results we believe can be discussed and replicated for other software products.

We find that classes in two large software systems do, in fact, have varying temporal patterns in terms of structural change and churn. In particular, they are different in history length and stationarity. This differentiation then reveals different sets of files with different roles in the system and different defect incidence depending on the overall dependency structure of the systems. In particular, we find that the deterministic nature of histories is a promising instrument to discuss and identify core classes or classes prone to defects. In addition, we find that fine-grained correlations between changes and defects time series are strong, improving on our and previous results in the literature on defects in files. We also show that the two low-level measures that we employ (NHK and Churn) complement each other on both systems in identifying classes with a high fault-proneness.

8. CONCLUSION

Building on our previous work, we found that the level of granularity used for time and code artifacts in relation to defects oscillates between several extremes. We discussed the problems of different levels of granularity. Our method begins at a high level of detail and then differentiates between files based on the temporal characteristics of their changes. Then, after selecting sets of files, we accumulate sets of commits for these classes and correlate their changes to defects. We also outlined a possible way to navigate levels of detail in the dimensions of time, change, and files concerned. We started from a high level of granularity by using low-level code measures of structural change and churn on the one side and single commits as a proxy of time on the oder side. Unfortunately, the relationship between change metrics and defect incidence vanishes at this level of detail. Based on this observation, we hypothesized that the effect of this relationship must be better visible at file level and we analyzed the evolution of changes and defects for each class of the system. In the two projects we analyzed, we actually find that classes and their type of change history can describe structural differences, defect occurrences, and identify core classes. Based on this first result we hypothesized that difference in defectiveness would have been even more visible locally and we investigated the fault-proneness of individual files and how well defect incidence correlates to changes in short windows of commits. The correlations turn out comparably well and we find that we can use intersections of files for the two kinds of changes to further guide the study of defect incidence. This way, we can also harness our strong correlations to a bigger extent. Finally, we observed that it is not only how much a file is changed but also for how long and how it has been changed that might reveal its proneness to defects. How long and how a file is changed before it needs some maintenance also depend on the specfic structure of the software product, though.

There are some open issues to our work. So far, we differentiate between structural change and churn. As mentioned before, these two metrics measure the complexity in the relationships between classes and in classes themselves. As demonstrated by the intersections, they do complement each other, though. Thus, a possible extension to this work is considering them together somehow. Similarly, we do not consider effects classes have on each other outside of these metrics. Including, for example, logical couplings could improve our results. Further, different strategies for the windows could be explored. For instance, different types of classes might be better described using different window sizes depending on the type's characteristics. Finally, our approach to structural change does not include information on the extent of a change in terms of the number of dependencies that changed. This information could be added as a weight to our measure.

9. REFERENCES

[1] C. Couto, S. Christofer, M. Tulio Valente, R. Bigonha, and N. Anquetil. Uncovering Causal Relationships between Software Metrics and Bugs. In *CSMR'12*, Szeged, Hongrie, 2012.

[2] B. Dagenais and L. Hendren. Enabling static analysis for partial java programs. In *OOPSLA '08*, pages 313–328, 2008.

[3] D. A. Dickey and W. A. Fuller. Distribution of the estimators for autoregressive time series with a unit root. *Journal of the American Statistical Association*, 74(366):427–431, 1979.

[4] J. Ekanayake, J. Tappolet, H. Gall, and A. Bernstein. Tracking concept drift of software projects using defect prediction quality. In *MSR'09*, pages 51 –60, may 2009.

[5] K. El Emam, S. Benlarbi, N. Goel, and S. N. Rai. The confounding effect of class size on the validity of object-oriented metrics. *IEEE Trans. Softw. Eng.*, 27(7):630–650, 2001.

[6] C. W. J. Granger. Investigating causal relations by econometric models and cross-spectral methods. *Econometrica*, 37(3):424–38, 1969.

[7] T. Graves, A. Karr, J. Marron, and H. Siy. Predicting fault incidence using software change history. *IEEE Trans. Softw. Eng.*, 26(7):653 –661, July 2000.

[8] S. Hido and H. Kashima. A linear-time graph kernel. *ICDM'09*, 0:179–188, 2009.

[9] P. Hofmann and D. Riehle. Estimating commit sizes efficiently. In C. Boldyreff, K. Crowston, B. Lundell, and A. Wasserman, editors, *Open Source Ecosystems: Diverse Communities Interacting*, volume 299 of *IFIP Advances in Information and Communication Technology*, pages 105–115, 2009.

[10] B. Kenmei, G. Antoniol, and M. Di Penta. Trend analysis and issue prediction in large-scale open source systems. In *CSMR'08*, pages 73 –82, april 2008.

[11] B. A. Kitchenham, L. M. Pickard, and S. J. Linkman. Evaluation of some design metrics. *Software engineering journal*, 5(1):50–58, 1990.

[12] R. Marinescu and C. Marinescu. Are the clients of flawed classes (also) defect prone? In *SCAM'11*, pages 65 –74, sept. 2011.

[13] T. Menzies, Z. Milton, B. Turhan, B. Cukic, Y. Jiang, and A. Bener. Defect prediction from static code features: currentÊresults, limitations, new approaches. *Automated Software Engineering*, 17:375–407, 2010.

[14] N. Nagappan and T. Ball. Use of relative code churn measures to predict system defect density. In *ICSE'05*, pages 284–292, New York, NY, USA, 2005. ACM.

[15] N. Nagappan, A. Zeller, T. Zimmermann, K. Herzig, and B. Murphy. Change bursts as defect predictors. In *ISSRE'10*, pages 309 –318, nov. 2010.

[16] T. J. Ostrand, E. J. Weyuker, and R. M. Bell. Where the bugs are. In *ISSTA'04*, pages 86–96, 2004.

[17] J. Ratzinger, H. Gall, and M. Pinzger. Quality assessment based on attribute series of software evolution. In *WCRE'07*, pages 80 –89, oct. 2007.

[18] J. Rosenberg. Some misconceptions about lines of code. In *METRICS'97*, page 137, Washington, DC, USA, 1997. IEEE Computer Society.

[19] B. Rossi, B. Russo, and G. Succi. Analysis of open source software development iterations by means of burst detection techniques. In C. Boldyreff, K. Crowston, B. Lundell, and A. Wasserman, editors, *Open Source Ecosystems: Diverse Communities Interacting*, volume 299 of *IFIP Advances in Information and Communication Technology*, pages 83–93, 2009.

[20] J. Śliwerski, T. Zimmermann, and A. Zeller. When do changes induce fixes? In *MSR '05*, pages 1–5, 2005.

[21] M. Steff and B. Russo. Measuring architectural change for defect estimation and localization. In *ESEM'11*, pages 225 –234, Sept. 2011.

[22] A. Tosun Misirli, B. Murphy, T. Zimmermann, and A. Basar Bener. An explanatory analysis on eclipse beta-release bugs through in-process metrics. In *WoSQ '11*, pages 26–33, 2011.

[23] T. Zimmermann, R. Premraj, and A. Zeller. Predicting defects for eclipse. In *PROMISE'07*, May 2007.

Analyzing Differences in Risk Perceptions between Developers and Acquirers in OTS-based Custom Software Projects Using Stakeholder Analysis

Dana S. Kusumo[1,2,3], Mark Staples[1,2], Liming Zhu[1,2], Ross Jeffery[1,2]
[1]National ICT Australia
[2]University of New South Wales
[3]Institut Teknologi Telkom

{dana.kusumo, mark.staples, liming.zhu, ross.jeffery}@nicta.com.au

ABSTRACT

Project stakeholders can have different perceptions of risks and how they should be mitigated, but these differences are not always well understood and managed. This general issue occurs in Off-the-shelf (OTS)-based custom software development projects, which use and integrate OTS software in the development of specialized software for an individual customer. We report on a study of risk perceptions for developers and acquirers in OTS-based custom software development projects. The study used an online questionnaire-based survey. We compared stakeholders' perceptions about their level of control over and exposure to 11 shared risks in OTS-based software, in 35 OTS-based software developments and 34 OTS-based software acquisitions of Indonesian background. We found that both stakeholders can best control, and are most impacted by, risks about requirements negotiation. In general stakeholders agree who can best control risks (usually the developer), but there were different perceptions about who is most impacted by risks (the developer reported either themselves or both stakeholders; while usually the acquirer reported both stakeholders). In addition, both stakeholders agree that the acquirer is most impacted by the risk of reduced control of future evolution of the system. We also found disagreement about who is most impacted by the risk of lack of support (usually each stakeholder reported themselves). This paper makes two main contributions. First, the paper presents a method based on stakeholder analysis to compare perceptions of the respondents about which stakeholder is affected by and can control risks. Second, knowing stakeholder agreement on which stakeholder has high risk control should be helpful to rationalize responsibility for risks.

Categories and Subject Descriptors

D.2.9 [**Software Engineering**]: Management. K.6.1 [**Management of Computing and Information Systems**]: Project and People Management – *management techniques*.

Keywords: Risks, perception, Off-the-shelf (OTS), developers, acquirers, survey

1. INTRODUCTION

Custom software development is either in-house or contracted software development with specific requirements for an individual

customer [13] [22]. Off-The-Shelf (OTS) software is "a commercially available or open source piece of software that other software projects can reuse and integrate into their own products" [41]. This study focuses on OTS-based custom software development, which uses and integrates OTS software in the development of specialized software for an individual customer [8]. The relationship between acquirers and developers in OTS-based custom software development is depicted in Figure 1.

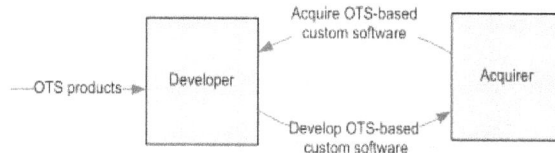

Figure 1. OTS-based custom software project

Risks associated with a software project affect all stakeholders [11] [33] [34] [46]. Here, we defined a risk as a deviation from the expected objective [48]. Risks arise from the start of the software acquisition process [33][34]. Most of the literature focuses on risks from the perspective of the software development organization, and little attention has been given to the software acquirer's perspective [18][33]. This paper covers both perspectives for OTS-based custom software projects.

One approach that accounts for different stakeholder involvement in a project is stakeholder analysis [10] [44] [46]. Stakeholders are defined as anyone who are affected by or can influence the system under development [10] [19] [44] [46]. Stakeholder analysis considers activities and issues such as: stakeholder identification, area of interest, stakeholder contribution and expectation, stakeholder influence, strategy to involve stakeholder and stakeholder responsibility [3] [16]. Responsibility is defined as "a duty, held by some agent, to achieve, maintain or avoid some given state, subject to conformance with organizational, social and cultural norms" [38].

Previous studies have reported that stakeholders tend to perceive the importance of certain risks as higher than others if they cannot control the risks, and also that different stakeholders tend to identify risk from other stakeholders' perspectives [20] [21] [35]. As different stakeholders perceive risk differently [21], therefore there are different perceptions of stakeholder's responsibility for risks. In addition, stakeholder perceptions vary based on either individual's or organization's background, experience, need and expectation [15]. To manage risks effectively, it is important to involve stakeholders [14] [34] aiming to take account differences in risk perceptions and to identify stakeholder responsibility for risks [14].

This paper focuses on investigating risks shared [34] by developers and acquirers and in particular differences in the perception of risks by the developers and acquirers. Another objective of this paper is to rationalize risk responsibility based on stakeholder analysis. It is expected that risk responsibility is able to provide a methodical and practical consideration to support risk management negotiation through dialogue, deliberation and communication [21]. Therefore this study addresses two research questions as follows, within the context of OTS-based custom software projects.

RQ1: How are OTS-specific risks perceived by developers and acquirers?

RQ2: How should risk responsibilities be defined between developers and acquirers?

Our study of these questions is based on a survey, with survey results analyzed using a new method based on stakeholder analysis [3][10][16][19][44][46].

The remainder of this paper is organized as follows. We first briefly review related work on stakeholder analysis in software development, and then describe our overall research design. We describe our method for analyzing differences in risk perceptions and collected data, before discussing the results and presenting conclusions.

2. STAKEHOLDER ANALYSIS IN SOFTWARE DEVELOPMENT

In software-related projects, stakeholder analysis has been used to identify stakeholders, and to identify their roles, their level of involvement [2][36][44] and their risks [11][23][46]. With regard to software project-related risks, Gotterbarn and Rogerson have developed a software development impact statement comprising a task and associated potential risk that impacts particular stakeholders [11]. The tasks are derived from a work breakdown structure (WBS) of the software project, and might be activities in the WBS or list of requirement specifications [11]. Woolridge et al. [46] has proposed a stakeholder risk assessment during requirements engineering process, comprising stakeholder identification, analyzing stakeholder influence on functional requirements, impact of functional requirements on stakeholders, and assessing and prioritizing stakeholder risks. The Riskit method [23] links risks, project goals and stakeholder to rank risks.

In OTS-based software development, there are studies [7][43] that map OTS-based software development risks to their related stakeholders. However, both software project-related risks and OTS-based software development project risks have not analyzed further differences in risk perceptions among stakeholders. This contrasts with our research which analyzes differences in the perception of risk between developers and acquirers in OTS-based custom software projects.

In the context of development of a socio-technical system, stakeholder responsibility can be modeled using a responsibility model [5][38][39][40]. A responsibility model describes responsibilities within a system under development, agents assigned to these responsibilities and resources used to discharge these responsibilities [38]. In addition, the responsibility should also be assigned to the stakeholder who has competences and capacity needed to discharge the responsibility [39][40].

3. RESEARCH DESIGN

We performed a structured online questionnaire survey to investigate different perceptions of risks of OTS-based software

projects (listed in Table 1) from the developer and acquirer perspectives. We posted the questionnaire online using Google Docs.

3.1 Survey Design

We performed a structured online questionnaire survey based on a prior definition of stakeholders [10][19][44][46] and developed a method based on stakeholder analysis [3][16] to analyze the survey data of differences in OTS-specific risks perceived by software developer and acquirer respondents (illustrated in Figure 2). However, the nature of this study is exploratory and does not test hypotheses.

The questionnaire targeted developers and acquirers of completed OTS-based custom software projects, using convenience sampling to identify potential respondents. Convenience sampling is reasonable to use in an exploratory study [12]. The sample population of the survey was 111 respondents which had a prior academic-industry relationship with the first author. The population consisted of software acquirers contracting OTS-based software to external software developers and software organizations developing OTS-based software for their acquirers of different organizations. The respondents comprised 35 software developers and 34 software acquirers of Indonesian background. We expected to explore differences in risk perceptions as the software developers and acquirers are in different organizations whose backgrounds, experiences, needs and expectations are different [15]. Furthermore, we excluded OTS software producer, who builds OTS software, because we wanted to focus on the software developers and acquirers, who are two key stakeholders in software development projects using and integrating OTS software.

In our survey we asked about risks that should be relevant not only to developers but also to acquirers of OTS-based custom software (described in Table 1). Based on our previous systematic mapping study [25], we focused on selection, integration, and maintenance related risks. As can be seen in Table 1, no studies identified risks to acquirers related to: not being adaptable to requirement changes, requirements not being negotiable, upgrading being unfeasible, lack of information about providers, and lack of support. These risks were nonetheless selected because acquirers may have interactions and contributions to these risks. We used 7 out of 13 of the risks of OTS-based software development reported by Li et al. [27] that acquirers might also control and be impacted by these following risks: selection effort ill-estimated (R1), not adaptable to requirement changes (R2), requirements not negotiable (R3), maintenance planning unfeasible (R7), upgrade unfeasible (R8), lack of information on provider (R9) and lack of support (R10). Respondents were asked who was affected by and who could influence the risks in Table 1. The respondents could choose one out of four options: "developer", "acquirer", "both" or "don't know".

3.2 Method for analyzing risk perspectives

Here we described our method to analyze the survey data of differences between perceived risks. The method compares perceptions of the respondents about which stakeholder is affected by and can control risks. The method extends the stakeholder analysis approach [3][16], and is illustrated in Figure 2. The method uses a template to compare risk perceptions (summarized in Table 2). As illustrated in Figure 2, the respondents (software developers and acquirers) completed the survey by choosing kind of stakeholder (developer, acquirer, both or don't know) impacted by and that can control each risk. All respondents' responses were mapped to the template (Table 2). Figure 3 models constructs used in the method to analyze the survey.

The method consists of four steps as in the template (in Table 2) and one additional step to rationalize risk responsibility as follows.

☐ Step 1/"Risks impacting stakeholders" counts the number of each kind of stakeholders affected by investigated risks

☐ Step 2/"Risks stakeholders can control" counts the number of kind of stakeholder who can control on investigated risks

☐ Step 3/"Mapping stakeholders from step 1 and 2 into risk control/impact matrix", maps the number of each kind of stakeholders from step 1 and 2 into a risk control/impact matrix, adapted from power/interest matrix [29][45]. This is illustrated in Figure 4. As this study focused to investigate different risk perceptions between developers and acquirers, the mapping process was only conducted for two kinds of stakeholders from step 1 and 2, developer and acquirer. Therefore if a respondent answering "both" to the survey question then they are included as both a developer and an acquirer. The mapping process is performed separately for developer and acquirer respondents.

In order to map the number of each kind of stakeholder (developer and acquirer) from step 1 and 2 into the risk control/impact matrix for each group of stakeholder respondents, a center point coordinate of the matrix has first to be defined for each risk under investigation.

A center point coordinate is an intersection point between centers of a horizontal (risk impact) and vertical (risk control) dimension of a risk control/impact matrix (as can be seen in Figure 4). The center of horizontal point is half of the number of respondents answering step 1 (risk impact). The center of vertical point is half of the number of respondents answering step 2 (risk control). The center point coordinate has a variable value depending on the number of respondents answering step 1 and 2. The following example demonstrates the mapping process of the developer respondents' risk perception about themselves. For example, for the risk of not being adaptable to requirement changes (R2) in Figure 5, the total number of developer respondents answering step 1 is 34 and step 2 is 35. Hence, the center point coordinate of the risk control/ impact matrix is (17, 17.5). The number of the developer respondents answering themselves impacted by (step 1) and can control (step 2) risk is 13 and 20 respectively. Furthermore the number of the developer respondents answering both stakeholders impacted by (step 1) and can control (step 2) risk is 20 and 11 respectively. Therefore, the total number of the developer respondents (the sum of both stakeholders and developer) perceive themselves impacted by risk is 33 and can control risk is 31. So for the risk of not being adaptable to requirement changes (R2), developers' perceptions on themselves can be mapped into high risk impact and control (Key Player (D)).

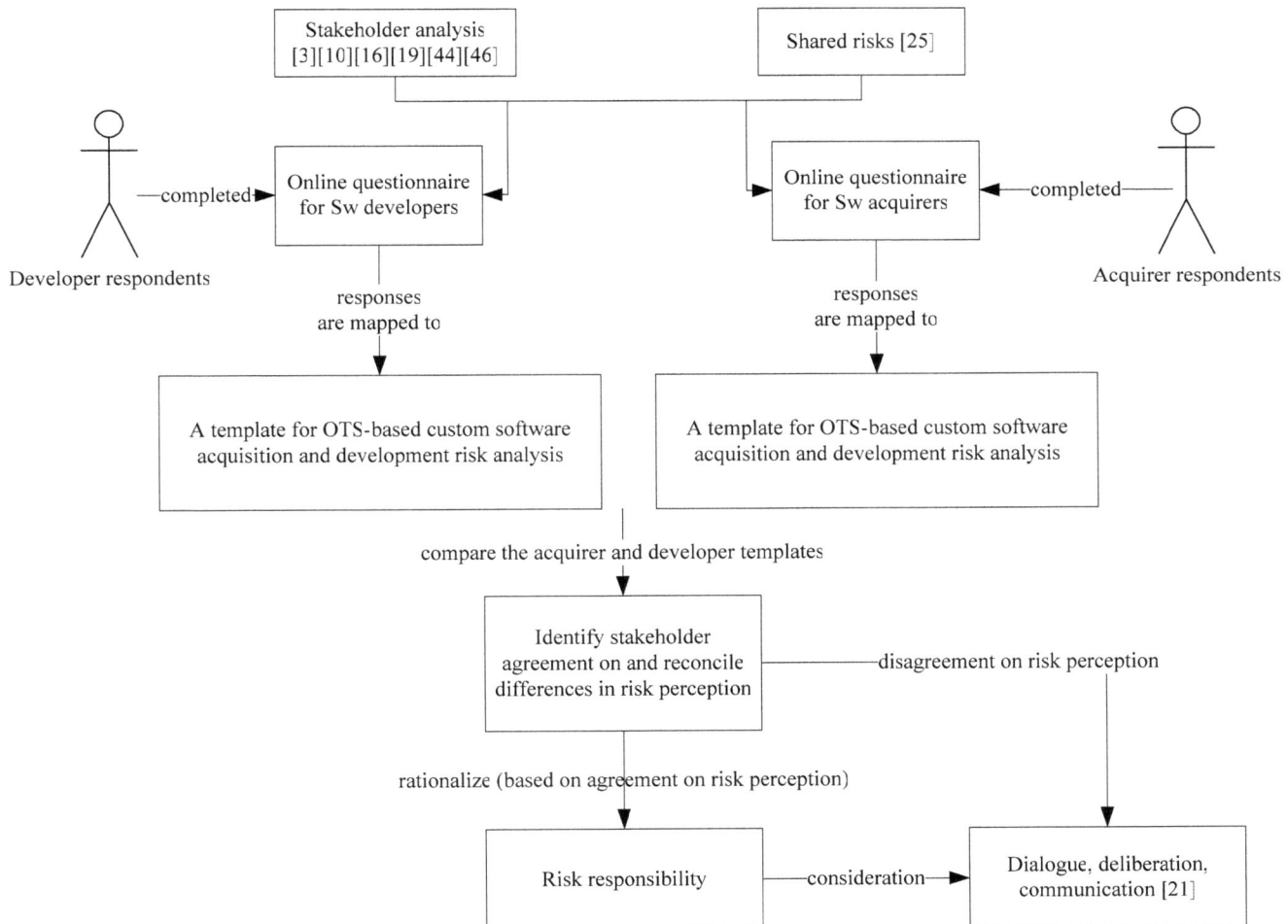

Figure 2. A method for analyzing differences in off-the-shelf risks between the developer and acquirer used in the survey

Table 1. OTS-specific project risks relevant to the developer and acquirer respondents

Stage	Risk		Perspective	
	ID	Item	Dev	Acq
Selection and integration	R1	Selection effort ill-estimated	[31][6][26][27]	[47]
	R2	Not adaptable to requirement changes	[27]	
	R3	Requirements not negotiable	[26][27][32]	
	R4	Complicated multi OTS components arrangement	[24][43]	[43][47]
	R5	Insufficient OTS component documents	[28][1]	[47]
	R6	Lack of OTS-driven requirements engineering process	[24][43]	[43][47]
Maintenance	R7	Maintenance planning unfeasible	[26][27]	[47]
	R8	Upgrade unfeasible	[24][26][27]	
	R9	Lack of information on provider	[26][27][32]	
	R10	Lack of support	[6][32][26][27]	
	R11	Reduced control of future evolution of the system	[42]	[43][47]

Table 2. A template to compare risk perceptions of OTS-based custom software acquisition and development

		Stakeholder	Risks			
			R1	R2	...	R11
Step 1	Risks impacting stakeholders	Developer				
		Acquirer				
		Both				
		Don't know				
Step 2	Risks stakeholder can control	Developer				
		Acquirer				
		Both				
		Don't know				
Step 3	Mapping stakeholders from step 1 and 2 into risk control/ impact matrix (see Figure 4)	Developer				
		Acquirer				
Step 4	Comparing risks using the risk control/impact matrix					

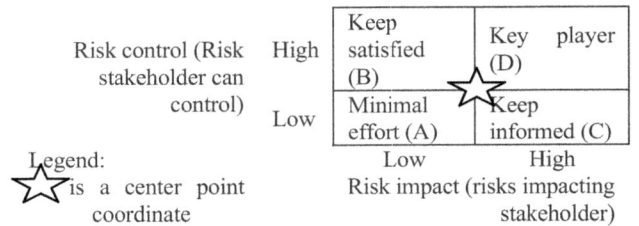

Risk control (Risk stakeholder can control)

High — Keep satisfied (B) | Key player (D)

Low — Minimal effort (A) | Keep informed (C)

Low   High

Risk impact (risks impacting stakeholder)

Legend:
☆ is a center point coordinate

Figure 4. Risk control/impact matrix, adapted from power/interest matrix [29][45]

☐ Step 4/"Comparing risks using the risk control/impact matrix" compares mapped risk control/impact matrix result between kind of stakeholders in Table 2, developer and acquirer. This comparison is performed separately for the developer and acquirer respondents. For example, as can be seen in Table 3, the risk of reduced control of future evolution of the system (R11) of the developer respondents has developer mapped into Key player (D) and acquirer mapped into Keep informed (C). Here, mapped risk control/impact matrix results of kind of stakeholders (developer and acquirer) are compared (D:C). The comparison result shows that developer respondents perceive themselves to have more control over the risk than their acquirers. Furthermore, the developer respondents perceive that both stakeholders (themselves and their acquirers) are equally impacted (high) by risk.

☐ Step 5/"Identify stakeholder agreement on and reconcile differences in risk perceptions between developer and acquirer respondents". This step aims to rationalize risk responsibility to mitigate risks based on stakeholder agreement of which stakeholder has high risk control. Stakeholder who has high risk control can be considered to be responsible on the risk as to

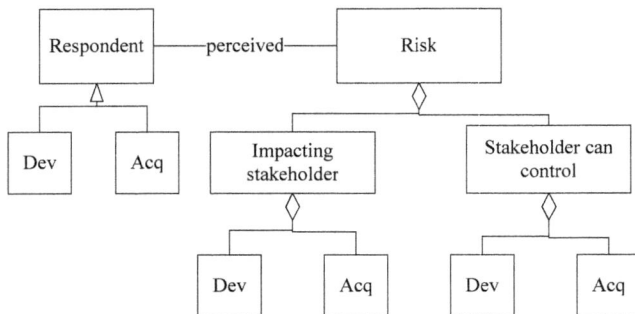

Figure 3. Relationship model of respondent, risk, risk control and impact to stakeholder

mitigate a risk as high influence [4][37] is needed to control key decisions and task implementation. Moreover, the consideration becomes stronger if both stakeholders also agree on high risk impact.

After the responses of developer and acquirer respondents are mapped to and compared using the template (as can be seen in Figure 2), the completed templates of the developer and acquirer respondents are then compared to identify stakeholder agreement on risk perceptions between developer and acquirer respondents. If there any differences in risk perceptions between the developer and acquirer respondents, stakeholder agreement will be decided from partial agreement between both stakeholder perceptions. In the following examples, reconciliations of different risk perceptions are demonstrated. In addition to the previous example, the acquirer respondents in Table 3 perceive the risk of reduced control of future evolution of the system (R11) mapping developer into Keep satisfied (B) and acquirer into Keep informed (D). Therefore, to identify stakeholder agreement of which stakeholder has high risk control, risk perceptions of the developer and acquirer respondents mapped into the risk control/impact matrix are compared (D:C for the developer respondents and B:D for the acquirer respondents). From this comparison, the developer respondents perceived themselves to have higher risk control compared to their acquirers; the acquirer respondents perceived both stakeholders to have high risk control. To reconcile this difference can be decided that the developers (as indicated in Part 2 Table 3) can best control the risk of reduced control of future evolution of the system (R11). Therefore it can be concluded that both developer and acquirer respondents agree the developer to have high risk control on the risk of reduced control of future evolution of the system (R11). This agreement might be used as a rationale to assign risk responsibility to the developer. In addition, the same procedure is then used to reconcile different risk impact perceptions between the developer (both stakeholders are most impacted by risk R11) and acquirer (the acquirer is most impacted by risk R11) respondents. The reconciliation indicates that both respondents agree that the acquirer has high risk impact compared to the developer; hence the acquirer is the stakeholder most impacted by this risk. Having known stakeholder agreement of which stakeholder has high risk control can be used to rationalize a consideration of risk responsibility in analyzing the different risk perceptions [21].

All of the previous steps are applied and completed for all risks in Table 1.

4. COLLECTED DATA

Of the 111 respondents invited by e-mail, 69 (62%) completed the survey. The respondents were 35 software developers and 34 software acquirers of Indonesian background. The questionnaire collected information about risks of completed OTS-based custom software projects from the developer and acquirer perspectives.

The developers' completed projects were in various domains: IT sector (15), banking or finance (8), public sector (8), e-commerce (3) and ERP (1). Of 35 completed projects, there were 2 different software developer companies that each participated in 2 different projects. All the developer respondents came from well-establish companies, i.e.: 8 multi-national software developing companies, 1 service provider and the remainder from medium and large software development companies. From 35 respondents, only one respondent came from a small company. The mean number of permanent software developers in the projects is 7 and median is 4. The mean

number of part-time software developers involved in the projects is 4 and the median is 3. The developer respondents had positions in the completed OTS-based custom software projects as project manager (13), developer (12), as project manager and software architect (3), software architect (3), as project manager, software architect and developer (2), as project manager and developer (1) and as software architect and developer (1). Only 1 developer respondent did not indicate his/her position. The respondents' level of education varied from 1 certificate, 26 bachelors (1 non computer science) and 8 master (1 non computer science) degrees in computer science.

The software acquirer respondents came from telecommunications (11), government (8), banking (3), automotive industry (3), university (3), plantation (1), insurance (1), private investment joint venture (1), engineering consultant (1), oil and gas (1), and energy company (1). From the telecommunications, automotive industry and university domains, we gathered more than 1 respondent working in different completed projects. The respondents representing the acquirers had positions in the completed OTS-based custom software projects as project manager (8), system analyst (5), user representation (5), IT architect (3), developer (3), IT staff (2), domain expert (2), client team leader (1) and project steering committee (1). Only 4 acquirer respondents did not describe their positions in the projects. The respondents' education consisted of 1 diploma, 23 bachelors (1 non computer science) and 10 master (2 non computer science) degree in computer science.

5. RESULTS

This section presents results of the survey organized by the developed method. Figure 5 and 6 present the questionnaire results mapped to step 1 and 2 of the method template (see Table 2). The results are organized as comparisons of the mapped risk control/impact matrix result between kinds of stakeholder (developer:acquirer) separately for each survey respondents (the developer and acquirer respondents) in Part 1 Table 3. Part 1 Table 3 follows step 4 in the method template (Table 2). Part 2 Table 3 shows stakeholder agreement on risk control and impact, and risk responsibility following step 5 in the developed method. Table 4 summarizes patterns of the comparisons from Part 1 Table 3.

It can be seen from Table 3 and 4, almost all the developer respondents perceive themselves to have higher risk control compared to their acquirers. The data in Table 4 show that for the developer respondents, there are 3 groups of comparison of risk mapped into the risk control/impact matrix. The first is D:D, which in Table 3 is the risk of requirements not negotiable (R3), the developer respondents perceive themselves and their acquirers to have the same high risk control and impact. For the second group, the developer respondents perceive themselves to have higher risk control compared to their acquirers, but perceive themselves to have equal risk impact as their acquirers (D:C in Table 3 and 4). Risks in this group are selection effort ill-estimated (R1), not adaptable to requirement changes (R2), complicated multi OTS components arrangement (R4), and maintenance planning unfeasible (R7) and reduced control of future evolution of the system (R11). The last group, the developer respondents perceive themselves to have higher risk control and impact compared to their acquirers (D:A in Table 3 and 4) as follows: insufficient OTS component documents (R5), lack of OTS-driven requirements engineering process (R6), upgrade unfeasible (R8), lack of information on provider (R9) and lack of support (R10).

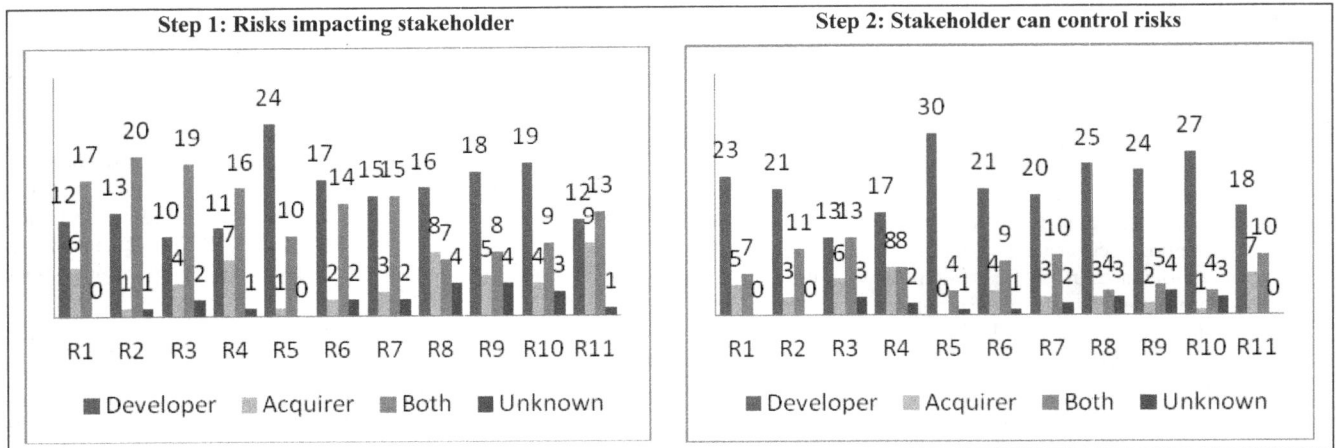

Figure 5. The developer respondents' responses mapped to step 1 and 2 of the template (35 respondents)

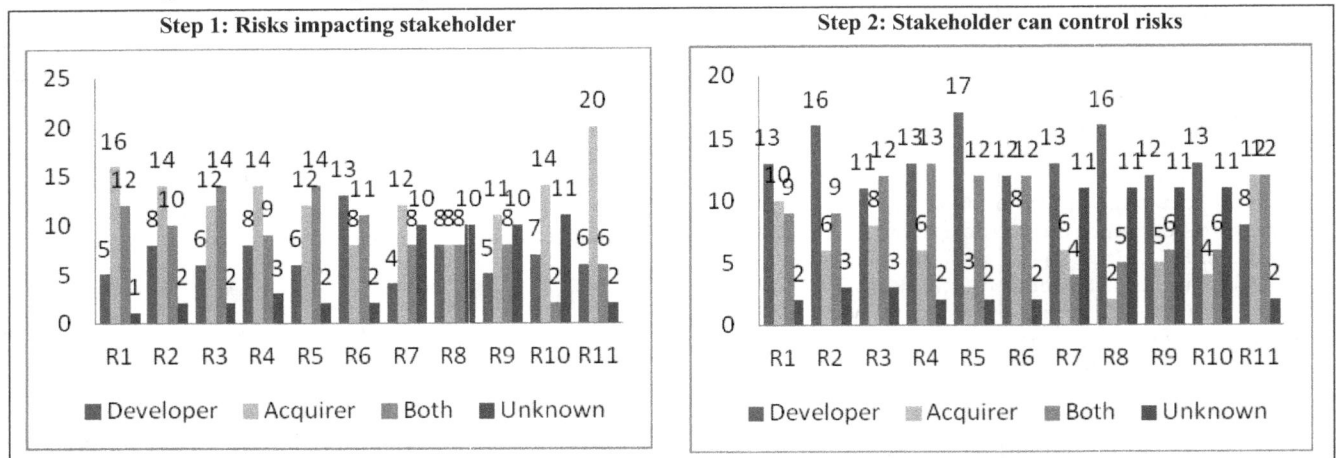

Figure 6. The acquirer respondents' responses mapped to step 1 and 2 of the template (34 respondents)

Table 3. Analyzing of different risk perceptions

Part 1										
Comparison of risk mapped into the risk control/impact matrix (developer:acquirer) from respondent perspectives										

	Risk (developer:acquirer)										
Respondents	**R1**	**R2**	**R3**	**R4**	**R5**	**R6**	**R7**	**R8**	**R9**	**R10**	**R11**
Developer	D:C	D:C	D:D	D:C	D:A	D:A	D:C	D:A	D:A	D:A	D:C
Acquirer	D:D	D:C	D:D	D:D	D:C	D:D	D:C	D:C	D:C	B:C	B:D

Part 2										
Stakeholder agreement on risk control and impact, and risk responsibility										

	R1	R2	R3	R4	R5	R6	R7	R8	R9	R10	R11
Stakeholder agreement on risk control	Dev	Dev	Both	Dev	Dev	Dev	Dev	Dev	Dev	Dev	Dev
Stakeholder agreement on risk impact	Both	Both	Both	Both	Dev	Dev	Both	Dev	Dev	-	Acq
Risk responsibility	Dev	Dev	Both	Dev	Dev	Dev	Dev	Dev	Dev	Dev	Dev

74

Table 4. Summary of comparison of risks mapped into the risk control/impact matrix between the developer and acquirer respondents (summarized from Table 3)

		Patterns of comparison of risk mapped into the risk control/impact matrix (developer:acquirer) from respondent perspectives				
		D:D	D:C	D:A	B:C	B:D
Respondent perspective	Developer	1	5	5		
	Acquirer	4	5		1	1

In Table 4, the acquirer respondents perceive 4 different comparison of risk mapped into the risk control/impact matrix. The first group comparison, the acquirer respondents perceive the following risks high in control and impact for themselves and their developers (D:D): selection effort ill-estimated (R1), requirements not negotiable (R3), complicated multi OTS components arrangement (R4) and lack of OTS-driven requirements (R6). In the second group, the acquirer respondents tend to report higher perceived risk control of the following risks to their developers, but the acquirer respondents tend to report higher perceived risk impact to both themselves and their developers (D:C): not adaptable to requirement changes (R2), insufficient OTS component documents (R5), maintenance planning unfeasible (R7), upgrade unfeasible (R8) and lack of information on provider (R9). In the third group, the acquirer respondents perceive themselves to have higher risk impact but lower risk control compared to their developers (B:C) on the risk of lack of support (R11). Finally, the acquirer respondents perceive themselves to have higher risk impact but equal risk control compared to their developer (B:D) for the risk of reduced control of future evolution of the system (R11).

Part 2 Table 3 shows stakeholder agreements on risk control and impact, including reconciliation results of different risk perceptions between the developer and acquirer respondents on the risks of R1, R4, R5, R6, R8, R9, and R11. With regard to risks R1, R4, R6 and R11, the developer respondents perceived themselves to have higher risk control compared to their acquirers and the acquirer respondents perceived both stakeholders to have high risk control and impact (for R1, R4 and R6) and to have high risk control (for R11). The differences between both stakeholders can be reconciled by agreeing the developer as a stakeholder who has risk control. For the risk of R5, R6, R8 and R9, the developer respondents perceived only themselves as most impacted by these risks (D:A in developer respondents row in Part 1 Table 3), and the acquirer respondents perceived both stakeholders as most impacted by these risks (developer and acquirer of the mapped risk control/impact matrix is either C or D in Part 1 Table 3). To reconcile these differences, it could be decided that the developers are most impacted by these risks (presented in Part 2 Table 3) as the developers always perceived to have high risk impact in these risks by both stakeholders. For risk R11, both stakeholders agree that the acquirer is most impacted by the risk (reduced control of future evolution of the system). This agreement is a reconciliation result of different risk perceptions between the developer (both stakeholders are most impacted by risk R11) and acquirer (the acquirer is most impacted by risk R11) respondents. For the risk of lack of support (R10), this study has found disagreement about who is most impacted by the risk (in R10 in Part 1 Table 3, the developer respondents perceive themselves have higher risk control and impact compared to their acquirer (D:A), while the acquirer respondents perceive themselves have higher risk impact compared to their developers (B:C)).

6. DISCUSSION
6.1 RQ1: How are OTS-specific risks perceived by the developer and acquirer?

Although a previous study has investigated different and common IT project risks as perceived by users and project managers [21], these risks are not specific to OTS-based custom software projects. Our study focused on OTS-specific project risks shared [34] by the developer and acquirer (listed in Table 1). In this section, we use Table 3 to compare risk perceptions mapped into the risk control/impact matrix between the developer and acquirer respondents. This comparison focused on risk control and impact perceived by the developer and acquirer respondents.

As indicated in Part 2 of Table 3, almost all stakeholders agree that the developer can best control risks (in Part 1 Table 3, all developer and acquirer respondents perceive that the developer has high risk control, and the mapped risk control/impact matrix is either D or B). There is only one risk, R3 (requirement not negotiable), where both stakeholders each claim to best control this risk (both respondents perceive high risk control and impact in the mapped risk control/impact matrix).

The developer respondents have two different groups of perceptions about which stakeholder is most impacted by risks. In the first group, developer respondents perceive both stakeholders as most impacted by risks (as shown in Part 1 Table 3, the risks of R1, R2, R3, R4, R7 and R11 whose developer and acquirer of the mapped risk control/impact matrix have high risk impact). In the second group, developer respondents perceive themselves as most impacted by risks (as shown in Part 1 Table 3, the risks of R5, R6, R8, R9 and R10 whose developer and acquirer of the mapped risk control/impact matrix has high and low risk impact, respectively).

The acquirer respondents perceive both stakeholders are most impacted by risks (developer and acquirer of the mapped risk control/impact matrix has high risk impact), except for their developers in R10 and R11. In regard to risk of lack of support (R10) and reduced control of future evolution of the system (R11), the acquirer respondents perceive themselves to have higher risk impact than their developers.

Comparing the developer and acquirer respondents' perspectives about which stakeholders are most impacted by risks, it could be concluded that for the risks of R1, R2, R4 and R7, both stakeholders agree (can be found in Part 2 Table 3) that they both are most impacted by the risks. For the risks of R5, R6, R8 and R9, there are different risk perceptions between the developer and acquirer respondents. From the results section, it is shown that the developers are most impacted by these risks (see Part 2 of Table 3). For the risk of lack of support (R10), this study has found disagreement about who is most impacted by the risk (Part 2 of Table 3). With regard to the risk of reduced control of future evolution of the system (R11), both stakeholders agree that the acquirer is most impacted by the risk of reduced control of future evolution of the system. The developed method provided a methodical and practical solution that support previous study [21] to analyze differences in the context of the risks of OTS-based custom software projects perceived by the developers and acquirers.

6.2 RQ2: How to define risk responsibility between the developers and acquirers?

As can be seen in Table 3, for only 3 out of 11 risks investigated, (R2, R3, R7) do both the developers and acquirers have exact risk comparison perceptions. It is interesting to analyze differences in the risks perceived by the developers and acquirers.

Understanding of differences in stakeholder perceptions about which stakeholder has high risk control is helpful to rationalize risk responsibility. High influence is needed to control key decisions and task implementation [4][37] to mitigate risks. This study provided a structured method to compare risk control and impact to identify stakeholder agreement on and reconcile differences in risk perceptions between developer and acquirer respondents. The outcomes of the method are risk responsibilities used to rationalize considerations to analyze different risk perceptions through dialogue, deliberation and communication [21]. Furthermore, this study indicated that the developed method supports responsibility models [5][38] [39][40] in rationalizing which stakeholder has responsibility. Having known the responsibility could eventually lead to the identification of roles [5][38] [39][40] to mitigate risks.

As shown in Part 2 Table 3, in all risks except requirements not negotiable (R3), both stakeholders agree that the developer is considered to be responsible on the risks. However, although the acquirer is not considered to be responsible on the risks, to better manage risk mitigation, the developer should inform, consult and involve the acquirer because the acquirer is also impacted (shown in Table 3, in some cases highly impacted) by the risks [29]. Furthermore, for the risk of requirements not negotiable (R3), both stakeholders should collaborate to discharge the responsibility [39] of risk mitigation. In the case of there is no stakeholder agreement on high risk control; the developed method cannot provide a consideration to analyze different risk perceptions (illustrated by Figure 2).

7. THREATS TO VALIDITY

We discuss construct, internal and external validity for the survey.

7.1 Construct validity

Construct validity is about the use of adequate definitions and measures of variables [9]. To prevent construct validity problems, we derived the questionnaire question from stakeholder definition [10] [19] [44][46]. We also used 7 risks from the previous empirical study [27] and 4 additional risks from the literature (can be seen in Table 1). The questionnaire used in this study was reviewed by 3 internal experts and pre-tested using a paper version by 6 industrial respondents.

7.2 Internal validity

Internal validity is concerned with whether research procedures, treatments or experiences of the research participants influence the researcher's ability to draw correct inferences from the data [9]. Providing related information on the beginning of the questionnaire is expected to give background and context information for the

respondents. In addition, this information may act as an initial filter to ensure that the respondents have needed knowledge and want to share his/her experience. There were less than 10 respondent inquiries before and after completing the questionnaire to ensure their understanding on the questionnaire questions. Furthermore, computer science educational backgrounds of almost all of the respondents increase confidence of this study for the respondents in understanding the survey questions.

7.3 External validity

External validity refers to the generalizability from this study [9]. This survey study did not have a big sample size and was only conducted in Indonesia; therefore it may not represent risks of OTS-based custom software development and acquisition in general. There were total 69 respondents, 35 representing software developers and 34 representing software acquirers. The respondents in the sample vary in organization sizes and acquirer/customer domains, which may reduce threats to external validity.

8. CONCLUSION

This study attempted to analyze differences in shared risks [34] of OTS-based custom software projects by comparing risk control and impact of two main stakeholders, the developers and acquirers. We performed an online questionnaire-based survey about OTS-based custom software project risks on Indonesian software developers and acquirers. To analyze the survey results, we developed and applied a method for analyzing differences in OTS-specific risks perceived by the developers and acquirers, based on stakeholder analysis [3][10] [16][19] [44][46].

This study has shown that both stakeholders can best control, and are most impacted by, risks about requirements negotiation. Developer respondents perceived themselves to best control risks, but perceived either themselves or both stakeholders to be most impacted by risks. Acquirer respondents agreed that their developers can best control risks, but perceived both stakeholders as most impacted by risks, except for risks of R10 and R11. For the risk of lack of support (R10), there was disagreement about who is most impacted by the risk (usually each stakeholder reported themselves). With regard to the risk of reduced control of future evolution of the system (R11), both stakeholders agreed that the acquirer is most impacted by the risk of reduced control of future evolution of the system.

The comparison method was developed to analyze the survey results. We use the method to rationalize a default position about which stakeholder should be responsible for risks based on stakeholders' agreement about which stakeholders have high control of each risk [4] [37]. In the context of a specific project, the method may be able to provide an explicit recognition of different risk perceptions, to inform risk management negotiation through dialogue, deliberation and communication [21]. The method can help stakeholders reduce gut feeling judgments and ensure that the risk mitigation decisions can be more objectively reviewed [17].The results show that responsibility for all risks (except requirements not negotiable) can be rationalized to be the responsibility of the developer. With regard to requirements not negotiable, we rationalized both stakeholders had responsibility of risk.

Even though we did not investigate actual risks from the developer and acquirer perspectives, a study of risk perception is an important approach to understand differences of actual risks between the developers and acquirers. The relationship between perceived and actual risk might be explained by adopting marketing concept [30].

Parasuraman et al. [30] reviewed marketing literature and found "service quality perceptions result from a comparison of consumer expectations with actual service performance" (p. 42). In our future work, we plan to improve the above method for analyzing differences in off-the-shelf risks by including differences of actual risks between the developers and acquirers and assigning level of risk impact and control (low/high) to rank risks through case studies. In addition, as our study based on stakeholder analysis, therefore further investigation on other related factor influencing risk responsibility is strongly recommended.

Overall, the developed method in this study added substantially to our understanding to provide a method-based consideration to analyze different risk perceptions [21]. The method used in this study may be able to be applied to other kinds of projects, to analyze differences in risk perceived by various stakeholders.

9. ACKNOWLEDGMENTS

NICTA is funded by the Australian Government as represented by the Department of Broadband, Communications and the Digital Economy and the Australian Research Council through the ICT Centre of Excellence program.

10. REFERENCES

[1] Admodisastro, N. and Kotonya, G. Architectural Analysis Approaches: A Component-Based System Development Perspective. In H. Mei, ed., *High Confidence Software Reuse in Large Systems*. Springer Berlin / Heidelberg, 2008, 26-38.

[2] Alexander, I. and Robertson, S. Understanding project sociology by modeling stakeholders. *Software, IEEE 21*, 1 (2004), 23-27.

[3] Andersen, E.S., Grude, K.V., and Haug, T. *Goal Directed Project Management: Effective Techniques and Strategies*. Kogan Page Business Book, London, 2009.

[4] Ballejos, L.C. and Montagna, J.M. Method for stakeholder identification in interorganizational environments. *Requirements Engineering 13*, 4 (2008), 281-297.

[5] Blyth, A. Using Stakeholders, Domain Knowledge, and Responsibilities to Specify Information Systems' Requirements. *Journal of Organizational Computing and Electronic Commerce 9*, 4 (1999), 287-296.

[6] Boehm, B., Port, D., Yang, Y., and Bhuta, J. Not All CBS Are Created Equally: COTS-Intensive Project Types. In H. Erdogmus and T. Weng, eds., *COTS-Based Software Systems*. Springer Berlin / Heidelberg, 2003, 36-50.

[7] Brereton, P. and Budgen, D. Component-based systems: a classification of issues. *Computer 33*, 11 (2000), 54-62.

[8] Carney, D. *Assembling Large Systems from COTS Components: Opportunities, Cautions, and Complexities. SEI Monographs on Use of Commercial Software in Government Systems*. Software Engineering Institute, Pittsburgh, USA, 1997.

[9] Creswell, J.W. *Research design: Qualitative, quantitative, and mixed methods approaches*. Sage Publications, 2009.

[10] Freeman, R.E. *Strategic management: A stakeholder approach*. Pitman, 1984.

[11] Gotterbarn, D.W. and Rogerson, S. Responsible risk analysis for software development: creating the software development

[12] Greer, D. and Conradi, R. Software project initiation and planning - an empirical study. *Software, IET 3*, 5 (2009), 356-368.

[13] Grudin, J. Interactive systems: bridging the gaps between developers and users. *Computer 24*, 4 (1991), 59-69.

[14] Heemstra, F.J. and Kusters, R.J. Dealing with risk: a practical approach. *Journal of Information Technology 11*, 4 (1996), 333-346.

[15] Hornik, S., Houn-Gee Chen, Klein, G., and Jiang, J.J. Communication skills of IS providers: an expectation gap analysis from three stakeholder perspectives. *Professional Communication, IEEE Transactions on 46*, 1 (2003), 17-34.

[16] Jepsen, A.L. and Eskerod, P. Stakeholder analysis in projects: Challenges in using current guidelines in the real world. *International Journal of Project Management 27*, 4 (2009), 335-343.

[17] Jorgensen, M. Practical guidelines for expert-judgment-based software effort estimation. *Software, IEEE 22*, 3 (2005), 57-63.

[18] Jorgensen, M. How to Avoid Selecting Bids Based on Overoptimistic Cost Estimates. *Software, IEEE 26*, 3 (2009), 79-84.

[19] Kaler, J. Differentiating Stakeholder Theories. *Journal of Business Ethics 46*, (2003), 71-83.

[20] Keil, M., Cule, P.E., Lyytinen, K., and Schmidt, R.C. A framework for identifying software project risks. *Communication of the ACM 41*, 11 (1998), 76-83.

[21] Keil, M., Tiwana, A., and Bush, A. Reconciling user and project manager perceptions of IT project risk: a Delphi study1. *Information Systems Journal 12*, 2 (2002), 103-119.

[22] Keil, M. and Tiwana, A. Relative importance of evaluation criteria for enterprise systems: a conjoint study. *Information Systems Journal 16*, 3 (2006), 237-262.

[23] Kontio, J., Getto, G., and Landes, D. Experiences in improving risk management processes using the concepts of the Riskit method. *Proceedings of the 6th ACM SIGSOFT international symposium on Foundations of software engineering*, ACM (1998), 163-174.

[24] Kotonya, G. and Rashid, A. A strategy for managing risk in component-based software development. (2001), 12-21.

[25] Kusumo, D.S., Staples, M., Zhu, L., Zhang, H., and Ross, J. Risks of Off-The-Shelf-based Software Acquisition and Development: A Systematic Mapping Study and A Survey. *16th International Conference on Evaluation & Assessment in Software Engineering*, (2012).

[26] Li, J., Conradi, R., Slyngstad, O.P.N., Torchiano, M., Morisio, M., and Bunse, C. Preliminary Results from a State-of-the-Practice Survey on Risk Management in Off-the-Shelf Component-Based Development. In X. Franch and D. Port, eds., *COTS-Based Software Systems*. Springer Berlin / Heidelberg, 2005, 278-288.

[27] Li, J., Slyngstad, O.P.N., Torchiano, M., Morisio, M., and Bunse, C. A State-of-the-Practice Survey of Risk Management in Development with Off-the-Shelf Software

impact statement. *Communications of AIS 2005*, 15 (2005), 730-750.

Components. *IEEE Transactions on Software Engineering 34*, 2 (2008), 271-286.

[28] Mahmood, S. and Khan, A. An industrial study on the importance of software component documentation: A system integrator's perspective. *Information Processing Letters 111*, 12 (2011), 583-590.

[29] Manowong, E. and Ogunlanas, S. Strategies and Tactics for Managing Construction Stakeholders. In *Construction Stakeholder Management*. Wiley-Blackwell, 2010, 121-137.

[30] Parasuraman, A., Zeithaml, V.A., and Berry, L.L. A Conceptual Model of Service Quality and Its Implications for Future Research. *Journal of Marketing 49*, 4 (1985), 41-50.

[31] Port, D. and Yang, Y. Empirical Analysis of COTS Activity Effort Sequences. In R. Kazman and D. Port, eds., *COTS-Based Software Systems*. Springer Berlin / Heidelberg, 2004, 169-182.

[32] Rose, L. Risk Management of COTS Based Systems Development. In *Component-Based Software Quality*. Springer Berlin / Heidelberg, 2003, 352-373.

[33] Rosendahl, E. and Vullinghs, T. Performing Initial Risk Assessments in Software Acquisition Projects. *Software Quality — ECSQ 2002*, 2002. 540-47984-8_18.

[34] Schmidt, C., Dart, P., Johnston, L., Sterling, L., and Thorne, P. Disincentives for communicating risk: a risk paradox. *Information and Software Technology 41*, 7 (1999), 403-411.

[35] Schmidt, R.C., Lyytinen, K., Keil, M., and Cule, P.E. Identifying software project risks: An international Delphi study. *Journal of Management Information Systems 17*, 4 (2001), 5-36.

[36] Sharp, H., Finkelstein, A., and Galal, G. Stakeholder identification in the requirements engineering process. *Database and Expert Systems Applications, 1999. Proceedings. Tenth International Workshop on*, (1999), 387-391.

[37] Smith, L.W. Project clarity through stakeholder analysis. *Crosstalk The Journal of Defense Software Engineering*, , December 2000.

[38] Sommerville, I., Lock, R., Storer, T., and Dobson, J. Deriving Information Requirements from Responsibility Models. In P. Eck, J. Gordijn and R. Wieringa, eds., *Advanced Information Systems Engineering*. Springer Berlin Heidelberg, Berlin, Heidelberg, 2009, 515-529.

[39] Sommerville, I. Models for Responsibility Assignment. In G. Dewsbury and J. Dobson, eds., *Responsibility and Dependable Systems*. Springer London, London, 165-186.

[40] Sommerville, I. Causal Responsibility Models. In G. Dewsbury and J. Dobson, eds., *Responsibility and Dependable Systems*. Springer London, London, 187-207.

[41] Torchiano, M. and Morisio, M. Overlooked aspects of COTS-based development. *Software, IEEE 21*, 2 (2004), 88-93.

[42] Vu Tran and Dar-Biau Liu. A risk-mitigating model for the development of reliable and maintainable large-scale commercial-off-the-shelf integrated software systems. (1997), 361-367.

[43] Vitharana, P. Risks and challenges of component-based software development. *Communication of the ACM 46*, 8 (2003), 67-72.

[44] Whitley, E.A. and Pouloudi, A. Stakeholder identification in inter-organizational systems: gaining insights for drug use management systems. *European Journal of Information Systems 6*, 1, 1-14.

[45] Winch, G.M. Managing Project Stakeholders. 321-339.

[46] Woolridge, R.W., McManus, D.J., and Hale, J.E. Stakeholder Risk Assessment: An Outcome-Based Approach. *Software, IEEE 24*, 2 (2007), 36-45.

[47] Yi Ding and Napier, N. Measurement Framework for Assessing Risks in Component-Based Software Development. Proceedings of the 39th Annual Hawaii International Conference on System Sciences, 2006 (2006), 230b.

[48] *AS/NZS ISO 31000:2009: Risk management - Principles and guidelines*. Standards Australia, 2009.

Using a Follow-on Survey to Investigate Why Use of the Visitor, Singleton & Facade Patterns is Controversial

Cheng Zhang, David Budgen and Sarah Drummond
School of Engineering & Computing Sciences
Durham University
Durham DH1 3LE, U.K.
{cheng.zhang2;david.budgen;sarah.drummond}@durham.ac.uk

ABSTRACT

Context: A previous study has shown that software developers who are experienced with using design patterns hold some conflicting opinions about three of the more popular design patterns: *Facade*, *Singleton* and *Visitor*.
Aim: To identify the characteristics of these three patterns that have caused them to generate such differing views.
Method: We employed a qualitative follow-on survey of those developers who had taken part in the earlier survey about design patterns.
Results: We received 46 usable responses from a possible total of 188, with nearly 85% of respondents having six or more years of experience with design patterns. Of these, 27 also provided comments and descriptions of experiences about the patterns, which we categorised.
Conclusions: All three patterns can easily be misused and in each case, the consequences of misuse are regarded as being particularly significant.

Categories and Subject Descriptors

D2.2 [**Design Tools and Techniques**]: Object-Oriented Design Methods

Keywords

design pattern; survey; empirical

1. INTRODUCTION

The concept of the *design pattern* forms a well-established and widely advocated mechanism for aiding the OO design process, with the textbook by the 'Gang of Four' (*GoF*) providing a widely-known and much-cited catalogue of patterns [4]. However, relatively little research has been done to identify how effective the concept actually is in practice, and to determine the conditions under which it might be appropriate (or inappropriate) to use specific patterns. In two previous studies we have:

- conducted a *Systematic Literature Review* (SLR) in the form of a mapping study, in order to identify how extensively the use of design patterns have been investigated through the use of empirical studies, and to identify any knowledge about their use and limitations that may have been identified [14];

- undertaken a *survey* of 216 experienced software developers to draw upon their experiences with using the 23 design patterns in the *GoF* [13].

We discuss the outcomes from these studies more fully in the next section. As might be expected, both the experiences and the opinions from the survey were quite varied. We did identify groups of patterns for which there was general agreement about their usefulness or otherwise. However, we also identified three patterns where significant differences emerged in the assessments of their value: *Facade*, *Singleton* and *Visitor*. (We might also note that within the patterns community, *Singleton* and *Visitor* have attracted considerable debate, and that one member of the *GoF* has gone on record to express doubts about the value of *Singleton*[1].)

A problem that was encountered in both studies was that of obtaining *causal* links that could provide a clear derivation of knowledge and opinions from experiences. In our survey we did ask for qualitative comments that could help with this, but this element received relatively few responses.

We therefore decided to investigate these three patterns more fully, to see if we could identify the characteristics that made them controversial. To do so, we conducted a second survey that asked respondents to express views about the characteristics of these three patterns. Since we were seeking to probe deeper into the reasons that lay behind the results of the first survey, the sampling frame used for this survey was the set of respondents to the first survey.

So, for this second survey, our research question was:

> "*What characteristics of these three patterns cause developers to hold widely differing views about their use?*"

A supplementary question we also asked was:

> "*Is a follow-on survey a useful way to investigate these characteristics?*"

Our second survey was conducted in early summer 2011. In the following sections we provide a little more background about the original studies, describe the design of this follow-on survey and its conduct, present our results and discuss how far they answer the research questions .

---

[1] http://www.informit.com/articles/article.aspx?p=1404056

2. BACKGROUND

This study forms the third in a sequence of three investigations into design patterns. We begin by briefly outlining the nature of a design pattern, and then describe the outcomes from each of the preceding studies that helped to motivate the question for the one described here.

2.1 Studying Design Patterns

The very nature of a design pattern makes it difficult to conduct empirical studies of its use or misuse, at least through the vehicle of conventional laboratory experiments. Essentially a pattern forms a *knowledge schema* through which the expertise of a group of designers can be recorded in such a way that it can be reused by others [2]. Hence the use of a pattern involves a creative activity, during which the pattern is interpreted within the context of the particular design task. This is turn means that for any experimental studies of design patterns, the experience and skills of the participants will form quite significant confounding factors.

There is therefore good reason to study design patterns by using a wide range of empirical study forms: experiments, case studies (especially in an industry setting), and surveys—and then to triangulate between the outcomes of these as fully as possible. We examine this range of options more fully in the discussion that follows.

2.2 The Mapping Study

A mapping study is a form of Systematic Literature Review that has as its research question the issue of determining the range and size of the set of studies addressing a fairly broad topic [6]. One of the aims of such a study is to determine whether there are enough primary studies available to provide scope to undertake an actual SLR with a much more focused research question. Obviously some blurring of the boundaries can occur—as was the case for our own mapping study where we did analyse and interpret the data for some of the patterns in more detail [14].

We conducted a systematic and thorough search over the period 1995-2009, which identified 611 candidate papers, although the number that met our inclusion/exclusion criteria was quite small. The final set for analysis included only 10 papers, describing 11 experimental studies. To augment this, we then re-examined the papers that we had classified as 'observational' (i.e. lacking experimental rigour) and included seven of these that offered reasonably good causal links between the reported observations and the conclusions. All of the studies involved patterns that were catalogued in the *GoF* (which includes 23 patterns in all), but only a sub-set of these were studied, and only three (*Composite*, *Observer* and *Visitor*) had been studied very extensively.

The added value provided by the observational studies, and particularly by one that was very clearly reported [11], suggested to us that a survey of experienced developers could potentially provide a fuller profile of the complete set of patterns from the *GoF*.

2.3 The First Survey

We conducted this over the summer of 2010, using an online data collection form (SurveyMonkey). Our respondents came from three groups.

- The authors of all of the papers that we identified as being about design patterns in our mapping study (not just empirical papers). We sent out 877 invitations, although returned e-mails indicated that only 681 of the addresses were still valid. We refer to this group as the *Authors*.

- People who were recommended by the Authors (our invitation to the Authors did ask them to pass it on to anyone who might have appropriate knowledge). We refer to these respondents as the *Snowball* group.

- Members of a research mail-list that was identified in the course of our survey, termed the *Mail-list* group.

After removing unusable responses, we were left with 206 responses: 128 Authors; 41 Snowball; and 37 Mail-list. Analysis of the demographic questions addressing such issues as years of experience with object-oriented development, and years of experience with patterns indicated that the profiles of the three groups were sufficiently close for them to be analysed as a single dataset. We also examined whether the respondents who categorised themselves as primarily working as developers had significantly different views from those who considered themselves as being primarily researchers and teachers (see below).

Respondents were asked to complete a 'rating' question by providing an assessment of 'usefulness' for all 23 of the *GoF* patterns (there was also an option for indicating 'no experience'). They were then asked to perform a 'ranking' exercise by identifying up to three patterns that they considered to be particularly useful, and also up to three patterns that they did not consider to be useful. As might be expected, there were more positive 'votes' than negative ones. We also provided an option for respondent's to comment on why they considered a pattern to be useful or not useful, and encouraged them to use this option to provide causal reasoning for their choices.

Our findings are reported elsewhere [13], where we review the assessments for all 23 of the patterns. The two patterns that were rated most highly, with relatively few reservations being entered, were *Observer* and *Composite*. At the other end of the spectrum there was a distinct group of patterns that were considered to be of little or no use, most notably *Memento* (with no positive votes at all), and *Flyweight* which had 21 negative votes and only two positive ones.

While the views of the different groups (developers versus the combined group of teachers and researchers) expressed in the *ranking* question were similar for most patterns, *Facade* is one where there was some difference. Developers all viewed it positively, with all of the negative votes coming from teachers and researchers. Developers also tended to be more negative about *Singleton*, although both groups held rather mixed views overall. The responses to the *rating* question were generally consistent with these profiles.

In assessing the validity of the outcomes we do need to recognise that our sample included many people with higher degrees, particularly among the teachers and researchers, and also a large proportion of people who had authored patterns. So this group may not be fully representative of the target population (software developers) for which they acted as a surrogate, and may have a more favourable (or critical) attitude towards design patterns.

Table 1 shows the number of 'votes' cast for the three patterns that we examine in this study. The figures in brackets indicate the percentage of the total of 389 positive and 113 negative votes that were made across the 23 patterns.

Table 1: Votes Cast for Each Pattern

Pattern	Positive Votes	Negative Votes
Visitor	26 (6.7%)	11 (9.7%)
Singleton	22 (5.7%)	14 (12.4%)
Facade	26 (6.7%)	7 (6.2%)
Total	74 (19.1%)	32 (28.2%)

While these three patterns attracted a broadly similar proportion of positive votes to many other patterns, they also attracted a disproportionately large number of negative votes. The qualitative comments also indicated mixed views, especially for *Singleton* and *Visitor* and were used as the basis for our second survey, described in the next section. The purpose of the second survey was to collect qualitative data that could identify the characteristics of these three patterns that led to such contrasting views about their value.

For the reader who may be unfamiliar with these three patterns, we provide a very brief summary of each of them below, to help with interpreting the comments we report.

2.3.1 The Visitor Pattern

This is a behavioural pattern that acts as an intermediary to the services provided by a composite set of objects, translating requests it receives into a set of requests to the objects. Its use makes it possible to add new functionality (for a client of these objects) simply by modifying/enhancing the *Visitor*. In exchange, the ability to modify the composite set of objects is made more difficult by its use, and the *Visitor* has to have knowledge about the 'state vectors' of those objects [3]. There are some implementational issues for *Visitor*, particularly with the use of 'double despatch' for many languages, which "lets visitors request different operations on each class of element" [4]. The use of this, along with the use of polymorphism, significantly complicates testing of systems that employ *Visitor* [1].

2.3.2 The Singleton Pattern

This is a creational pattern that "ensures a class only has one instance", with a single global access point. (A good example of a situation where this might be appropriate is for a spooler object managing a printer.) There are subtle issues with *Singleton* though, see reference [3] for a fuller discussion of these.

2.3.3 The Facade Pattern

Facade is a structural pattern that is intended to "provide a unified interface to a set of interfaces in a subsystem" [4]. Essentially, this can act as 'glue code' to hide individual components that are only of specialist interest and to provide a simple interface for a complex subsystem. *Facade* accepts a request from another object and delegates elements of this to appropriate objects in the subsystem, without the user needing to know that this is being done.

3. METHOD

Following up an initial study with a second, deeper, study that uses the same participants, or a subset of these, is categorised as a *multi-method study*. An example of this is to follow up a largely quantitative survey (such as our first survey) with a set of semi-structured interviews with selected participants, in order to obtain more in-depth explanatory

(qualitative) data, as described by Mingers [8]. This approach has the benefit that the researchers retain control of the sampling process—and so are able to identify the most appropriate interview candidates.

The nature of our first survey, where the sampling frame was determined largely by expertise, rather than by location, made the use of semi-structured interviews impractical. We therefore decided to employ a second, more qualitative follow-on survey of the group as a surrogate for using interviews, with its form reflecting this role. As a consequence, we retained little control of the sampling process, as well as being unable to probe and follow through on issues as deeply as would be possible using interviews.

For our follow-on survey, the population of interest (the sampling frame) consisted of those people who had taken part in our first survey. By re-surveying this group, we were able to probe more deeply on the issues of interest, while accepting that we would probably have a much lower number of responses (the norm for surveys is usually quoted as 10-20% [9]). Our first survey did include a question at the end to ask if respondents were willing to take part in any further study on design patterns. 11 respondents declined, leaving us with a sampling frame of 195 experienced pattern users.

In the rest of this section, we describe the design of the follow-on survey, and then report on how it was conducted.

3.1 Design of the Follow-on Survey

Guidelines for conducting semi-structured interviews suggest providing a short explanation of the purpose of the research at the start of an interview [9, 10]. Therefore, to help motivate possible respondents for the follow-on survey, we produced a four-sided 'executive summary' of the key outcomes from the first survey, extracted from the full report provided in reference [13]. This summary provided brief details of the demographic profiles and presented a chart showing the votes 'cast' in favour of, or against, the usefulness of each pattern in response to the ranking question. The purpose of the summary was to provide a context for the specific questions asked in the follow-on survey, and to show why these three patterns were considered as being of particular interest. A copy of the summary was attached to the e-mails sent to the respondents from the first survey who had indicated a willingness to take part in further study, inviting them to complete this further survey.

We again adopted an on-line model for applying the survey instrument, but since we aware that any potential respondent had already spent quite substantial time filling in the first survey, we aimed to keep this as short and focussed as possible. We therefore confined the demographic element to one question asking about length of experience with working with design patterns. Our reasons for doing so were two-fold: firstly, we were concerned that asking respondents to provide such material again would deter them from completing the survey, as they had already entered it once; and secondly, we expected to be able to retrieve much of this information from the data of the first survey, by matching the internet addresses used by the respondents to those recorded when they completed the first survey.

To provide a quantitative element we sought to determine how much consensus there was about the set of statements describing the characteristics of each pattern that we had extracted from the first survey. So, the respondents were first presented with each statement and asked to express a level

Table 2: Statements About Characteristics Used in the Questions for Each Pattern

Pattern	Statement provided from the first survey
Visitor	V1. "We conduct different analyses on Abstract Syntax Trees. *Visitor* can provide a unique way to do them and operations are completely independent."
Visitor	V2. "The ability to create many visitors for the same data model. This is very useful for web development. This combined with the MVC pattern means that we can create a lot of views with ease. For example, we have an HTML table printer, csv table printer etc., for the same table of information."
Visitor	V3. "The visitor is very useful in the context of language processors. I have used it primarily to support AST/ASG traversals. The time and effort involved in modifying a visitor hierarchy can be prohibitive but these factors are balanced by its nature suitability for tree/graph traversals."
Visitor	V4. "I prefer to use multiple despatch, however in systems with multiple dispatch you have to emulate it with a visitor. The resulting code using visitor is easy to get wrong, hard to maintain, and difficult to understand.
Visitor	V5. "Only useful to ship data structures and algorithm separately. But then, you have to fix either a set of data structures or a set of algorithms (depending on who visits who). So it can be a pain to manage."
Visitor	V6. "To avoid procedural dependencies of conditionals, I prefer to use idioms that utilize polymorphism to resolve the state of conditionals and the message to send as a consequence of that state. The visitor pattern requires too much awareness of handshaking to be practical. Supporting implementation details need to be invisible so they don't distract from the focus of the role being designed, and provide less opportunity for defects to be injected into the system."
Singleton	S1. "Singleton is natural for use in logging libraries and to maintain user configurations. It provides the convenience of a global variable (without the dirty feeling)."
Singleton	S2. Singleton is a basic pattern, but still it needs some discipline. In code analysis, global entities (e.g. symbol table) may need to have a single instance."
Singleton	S3. "I rarely have need of a Singleton as most domain objects are not unique. In maintenance, this is often used to hold global variables."
Singleton	S4. "Singleton is more an anti-patten and introduces global state."
Singleton	S5. "This pattern introduces 'temporal coupling' (the worst kind). I NEVER use this pattern. The last time I saw it and had to deal with it was 5 years ago and it was extremely painful to retrofit unit tests in that project, because of the Singletons."
Facade	F1. "Facade helps defining a proper architecture for a distributed system, by enforcing high cohesion and low coupling."
Facade	F2. "Make a good contract between lower level of application and upper level of application."
Facade	F3. "Nice pattern to help us deal with existing, problematic code. For third-party code, it enables us to rearrange (group, split, ...) a broken API so that it resembles what we want/need. For in-house legacy code, it's a way to extensively introduce tests by hiding dark sides of the existing implementation using an ideal interface."
Facade	F4. "Acts as a gateway between a subsystem and the rest of the system. Huge fan-in and fan-out, increasing coupling between parts of the system."
Facade	F5. "Used as simple passthrough classes rather than to actually make the life of a subsystem user any easier. Coupling is reduced but with no value added and at the expense of another class to maintain."

of agreement with it, based on a three-point scale (agree, no opinion, disagree). The set of statements are shown in Table 2. (We should note that each one was provided by a different respondent from the first survey.)

The main purpose of the second survey was to collect qualitative data that could identify the characteristics of these three patterns that led to such contrasting views. So, for each pattern we also invited the respondents to:

- add their own observations about that pattern, and any thoughts about why it attracts conflicting views;

- provide any examples of good or bad use of that pattern, based on their own experiences.

3.2 Conduct of the Follow-on Survey

Since the population to be surveyed was small, we did not attempt any sampling within this, and sent our request to all of the 195 respondents from the first survey who had indicated willingness to help further, providing them with the executive summary and inviting them to participate in the second survey. We also provided a follow-up message a few weeks later, as this is generally recommended as good practice with surveys, and one that can help improve the response rate. Seven addresses we used were no longer valid, reducing the size of the population to 188. We received 48 responses. One person completed only the first (demographic) question, while another answered 'no opinion' to all questions, and offered no comments. After excluding these, we were left with 46 responses, corresponding to a response rate of 24.5%.

No issues arose while conducting the survey.

4. RESULTS

4.1 Profile of the Respondents

The only demographic question included was about the degree of experience that our respondents had with using design patterns in general. The responses to this are shown in Table 3. From this we can see that 84.8% of respondents had six or more years of experience of working with patterns. (In the first survey, 67.4% of respondents had six or more years of experience with patterns.)

Table 3: Profile of Respondents' Experience with Using Design Patterns

Years of Experience	Frequency	Percentage
11 to 15 years	20	43.5
6 to 10 years	19	41.3
3 to 5 years	7	15.2
Total	46	100.0

We had originally expected to be able to undertake fuller profiling by matching up responses with those from the first survey, using the respondents' internet addresses, but because so many of these were allocated dynamically, this unfortunately proved to be impractical.

4.2 The Quantitative Responses

As noted above, these responses provided a measure of how far the respondents agreed with the statements selected from the original survey. A few respondents did not provide answers for a small number of these, and these 'null entries' were omitted from the analysis rather than treating them as if they were 'no opinon'. We examine the profile of responses for each pattern in turn.

4.2.1 The Visitor Pattern

Figure 1 shows the profile of the responses to the six statements about the *Visitor* pattern. Only three respondents

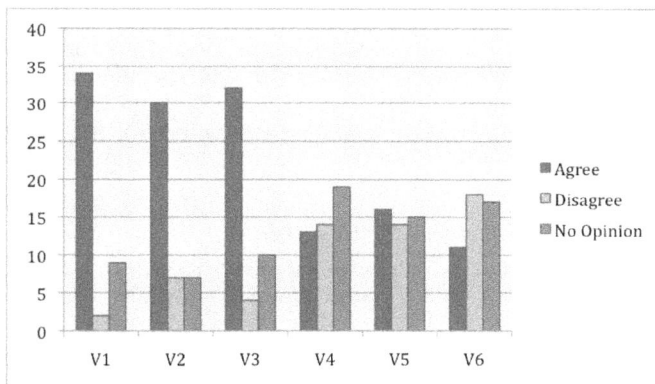

Figure 1: Responses to the Statements About Visitor

expressed 'no opinion' for all six statements. Two of these had 6–10 years of experience, the third had 3–5 years. Since V1–V3 are positive statements about the use of *Visitor*, and the overall profile for this pattern in the first survey was positive rather than negative, it is perhaps not surprising that these are well supported, with relatively few negative responses. Equally, V4–V6 were statements about the disadvantages of using *Visitor*, and here we see a much lower level of general agreement, with all three receiving more or less equal responses for each option.

4.2.2 The Singleton Pattern

The profile of responses for *Singleton* is shown in Figure 2. Only one respondent (with 6–10 years experience) expressed 'no opinion' for all five statements. S1–S2 are fairly

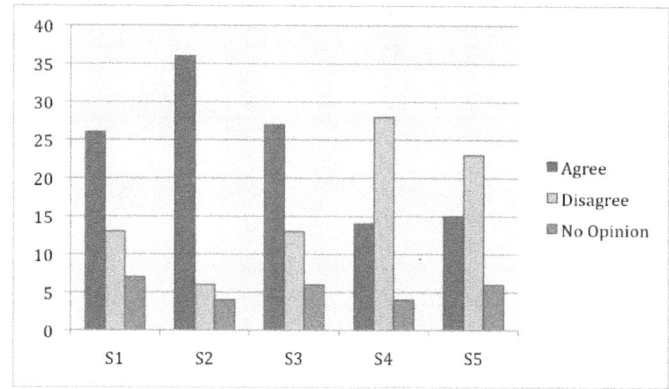

Figure 2: Responses to the Statements About Singleton

positive statements, S3 and S4 express different views about the use of *Singleton* to hold global data (regarded by many as misuse, a view expressed in S4, while S3 is more neutral), while S5 is decidedly negative about the pattern. Perhaps the most interesting answers are those to S3 and S4, which seem to imply that many respondents seem to consider the use of *Singleton* for holding global data as being an acceptable role.

4.2.3 The Facade Pattern

The profile of responses for *Facade* is shown in Figure 3. For this pattern, there were two respondents (both with 6–

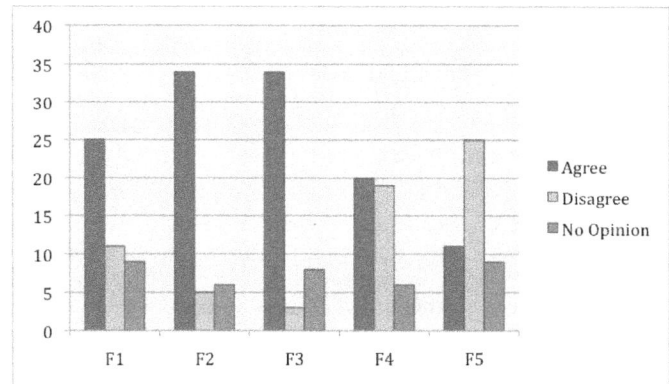

Figure 3: Responses to the Statements About Facade

10 years experience) who expressed 'no opinion' for all five statements and one (with 11-15 years) who did not respond to the questions about this pattern. Again, we see general agreement with the positive views expressed in F1–F3. Statements F4 and F5 express rather contradictory views about its effect upon coupling, and the responses show much more support for the view that coupling is increased by the use of Facade (F4).

4.3 The Qualitative Responses

We received a spread of comments and descriptions of experiences for each pattern. Table 4 shows the distribution

Table 4: Distribution of Qualitative Responses by Years of Experience

No. responses provided	Years of Experience			Total
	3-5 years	6-10 years	11-15 years	
6	1	4	7	12
5	0	1	2	3
4	0	2	0	2
3	0	0	4	4
2	0	1	0	1
1	1	2	2	5
0	5	9	5	19
Total	7	19	20	46

of the number of responses per respondent against years of experience (these were relatively evenly spread across the three patterns). From this, we can see that only 27 of the 46 respondents provided any qualitative responses at all. With one exception, it was also those with more experience who provided these responses.

When considering how to analyse these, we noted that, as observed by Seaman [10], there is "little guidance in the literature for the intellectual process of finding patterns and trends in qualitative data". For this study, we had six distinct datasets ('comments' and 'experiences' for each of the three patterns), and three reviewers. We adopted the following process for analysing each of the datasets.

1. All three of us individually read the responses and then wrote a short list of common issues (the categories).

2. We then met and merged our lists, generating an agreed set of short statements to describe each category.

3. Each of us independently coded the responses using the agreed set of categories.

4. Finally, we met and reviewed the merged codings, discussing any for which there were different interpretations, or where there are not at least two coders in agreement. Where necessary, we revised the wording of the statements describing the categories.

The process of discussion involved in steps 2 and 4 above proved to be a very important element. Responses often addressed multiple issues, and hence required us to assign multiple codes to them. Sometimes an issue was addressed indirectly (as might occur when reference was made to the comments provided from the first survey), and sometimes the structure of a response could be difficult to parse. A few were also considered to offer no clear or usable data and were discarded (see Table 5 for the distribution of these). For some responses, the distinction between a 'comment' (upon the statements provided) and an 'experience' (derived from the respondent's own use of the pattern) could also be indistinct, although we did manage to create separate lists for each.

The above process worked satisfactorily for all but the 'comments' received for the *Singleton* pattern. The initial set of statements we produced proved to be difficult to use. They were redrafted by one of us (DB), after which we successfully repeated steps 3 and 4 for the relevant responses.

To provide a check on this process we calculated *Kappa* (κ) values to provide an assessment of inter-rater consistency. As we had revised the *Visitor* categories during discussion, we omitted that group of ratings, and for simplicity,

Table 5: Distribution of Discarded Responses

Pattern	Category	Discards
Visitor	Comments	6
Visitor	Experiences	0
Singleton	Comments	6
Singleton	Experiences	2
Facade	Comments	4
Facade	Experiences	3

Table 6: Kappa Values for Inter-rater Agreement

Pattern	Form of response	Kappa value	Interpretation
Visitor	Experiences	0.64	Good
Singleton	Comments	0.69	Good
Singleton	Experiences	0.76	Good
Facade	Comments	0.68	Good
Facade	Experiences	0.45	Moderate

we also calculated the level of agreement between the two more experienced coders (DB and SD). The κ values for the remaining five sets of responses are shown in Table 6, and as can be seen, we generally achieved a good level of agreement in our coding.

In the rest of this section we review each set of responses.

4.3.1 Responses to the Comments for Visitor

We began by using a set of four issues, but when we discussed the coding these were restructured and extended into a set of seven. The responses provided good support for all of these. We have listed them in Table 7, and for each comment, the associated count indicates the number of responses related to that issue. (Since we were asking why the responses for the first survey were mixed, it is perhaps not surprising that these tended to emphasise any problems with the use of Visitor.)

4.3.2 Experiences with Visitor

Our original set of agreed statements identified four positive and four negative issues. However, in coding, we made little use of one of the positive issues and hence dropped this from the set, on the basis that the concepts concerned were adequately addressed by the other three. Table 8 summarises these.

As might be expected, these largely reflect the same issues that were identified in the original comments.

4.3.3 Responses to the Comments for Singleton

As noted above, our first attempt at coding these proved difficult to use and so we adopted a revised set of wordings

Table 7: Issues Identified in Comments About the Visitor Pattern

Code	Categories	Responses
VC1	Very specific and constrained application domain	5
VC2	Complexity impedes understanding and use	6
VC3	Structure constrains design options	2
VC4	Has a negative effect upon maintenance	4
VC5	Can increase encapsulation and abstraction	3
VC6	Complicated implementation	3
VC7	There may be better solutions	4

Table 8: Issues Identified in Experiences With the Visitor Pattern

Code	Categories	Responses
	Positive Issues	
VE1	Aids creation/use of data structures	4
VE2	Easy to extend functionality	3
VE3	Provides for good abstraction/separation of concerns	5
	Negative Issues	
VE4	Hard to change/extend structures	5
VE5	Complex to understand/use	6
VE6	Open to misuse in the wrong situation	3
VE7	Complication of use of double despatch in some languages	4

Table 9: Issues Identified in Comments About the Singleton Pattern

Code	Categories	Responses
SC1	Gets employed to provide global variables	8
SC2	Easy to understand but requires discipline in use	6
SC3	Needs care with implementation	3
SC4	Complicates testing and maintenance	4
SC5	OK for shared constants, but not for mutable data	2

for the categories, after which coding proceeded without any real problems. Table 9 shows these.

4.3.4 Experiences with Singleton

Again, although we originally identified eight categories (three positive, five negative), after coding and discussion, we decided that three of these (one positive, two negative) could either be subsumed within the others or was of too limited a scope to be worth retaining (i.e. only one respondent raised that issue). Our summary of these is given in Table 10.

4.3.5 Responses to the Comments for Facade

Facade attracted quite a number of comments although clearly, the respondents felt less strongly about this pattern than about the other two. Table 11 provides a summary of these. Although we originally identified six candidate categories, only three of these were addressed by more than one comment. These were noticeably less negative than those for the other two patterns.

4.3.6 Experiences with Facade

Again, we identified fewer categories for this pattern, as illustrated by Table 12. There were only three issues that were raised by more than one respondent.

Table 10: Issues Identified in Experiences With the Singleton Pattern

Code	Categories	Responses
	Positive Issues	
SE1	Useful for a limited role	4
SE2	Separates class and instance in the design	2
	Negative Issues	
SE3	Complicates testing	5
SE4	Gets misused to provide global variables	3
SE5	Increases maintenance/coupling	2

Table 11: Issues Identified in Comments About the Facade Pattern

Code	Categories	Responses
FC1	Concept of Facade is commonly misused or wrongly designed	7
FC2	Useful for integrating legacy code	4
FC3	Its use can reduce coupling	3

Table 12: Issues Identified in Experiences With the Facade Pattern

Code	Categories	Responses
	Positive Issues	
FE1	Means of encapsulating legacy code/data	3
FE2	Benefit of providing good abstraction	7
	Negative Issues	
FE3	Hard to maintain, loses structure	2

5. RELATED WORK

A survey about the effect of design patterns upon software quality that was conducted in 2007 by Khomh and Guéhéneuc is reported in [5]. They report upon the views of 20 respondents when asked about a set of ten quality attributes. In terms of comparison with this study, their paper reports in detail on only three patterns, none of which are those discussed here. They also provide a summary of the views about three attributes (expandability, understandability and reusability) for all patterns. Overall, we found little scope for any direct comparison with the our own results.

A recent paper by Williams [12] describes the use of a follow-on survey on a software engineering topic, which in this case is to probe views about agile development. However, this paper focuses on reporting the outcomes of the study, with no real discussion about the methodological aspects.

6. DISCUSSION

We first assess the threats to validity and then consider the implications for each pattern that arise from the results. Finally, we review our experiences from using a follow-on survey as our research approach.

6.1 Threats to Validity—the Survey

For a survey, two key issues that we need to consider are the design of the survey instrument itself and our sampling of the population.

Kitchenham and Pfleeger have identified a number of possible validity issues that can occur with a survey instrument [7]. For the first survey we were particularly concerned with *content validity*, and subjected our instrument to a review process to ensure that its questions were relevant. For a follow-on survey such as this, and particularly one that has the form of asking respondents whether or not they agree with a number of statements, this is less of an issue, especially as the statements were not designed by us, but extracted from the first survey. We therefore did not undertake a formal review process, and while the questions were simple, our failure to do so could be considered as a shortcoming. Overall though, we were unable to identify much guidance on how this type of second probe might be designed and evaluated. (In reference [8] the author notes that multi-method studies are not particularly common, even in

Information Systems research, which also seems to apply to follow-on studies of this form.)

Our survey population was well-defined and tightly constrained, with no sampling being needed (we simply mailed to all of the original respondents). As noted above, we were unable to profile the respondents to this survey as well as we had expected. However, having already established that the population formed a reasonably consistent group, and having obtained some limited data about the demographics pertaining to our sample, we have no reason to believe that it is unrepresentative of the population. However, there is one small caveat here, in that in reporting on our original survey [13], we did recognise that our sample in the first survey might not be wholly representative of the wider community of software developers who employ design patterns in any way. We should also note that although we received 46 responses, only 27 of these (59%) actually provided the qualitative information which formed the main reason for conducting the follow-on survey.

It is also possible that respondents may have been commenting upon statements that they had themselves provided in the first survey. However, as each of the statements we used was provided by a different person, it seems unlikely that this would create any significant bias.

6.2 Threats to Validity—the Analysis

The analysis process for a qualitative form of survey such as this also constitutes a potential threat to validity, not least because the open nature of the questions led to a wide range of responses. Our approach to analysis was obviously open to possible failings in both our *selection* of the categories and also our process of *assignment* to them.

As reported above, selection of the categories was a shared process, and when we reviewed the outcomes of our assignments to these, we did revise the categories where necessary. For the experience responses we actually reduced the number of categories used for each pattern (as a reminder, we did not retain any category with fewer than two responses assigned to it). For the comments, we extended the set of categories for *Visitor*, revised it for *Singleton* and reduced it for *Facade*. For all three, we were able to come to a good level of agreement about these assignments.

For assignment to categories we used a mix of independent coding and then discussion—with the discussion ensuring that we came to a shared interpretation of the more delphic responses (interpretation of these was often the reason why different coders might assign them to different categories). While it is difficult to assign a clear measure for the effectiveness of this process, we would observe that all of us did modify our position over various interpretations. (There were 22 cases where two of us changed our position to agree with the third. For 15 of these, the most experienced researcher in the team (DB) began in the minority position, while the remaining 7 were apportioned as 5 (CZ) and 2 (SAD).) In addition, as indicated in Table 6, we did usually achieve a good level of inter-rater agreement in our initial coding of responses.

6.3 Implications for the Three Patterns

For each pattern we have examined the statements taken from the original survey, as well as the quantitative and qualitative responses to this survey in order to seek an answer to our research question(s). We address these for each pattern in turn below.

6.3.1 Visitor

For the first survey, this was very much the 'middle case' among these three patterns. In terms of our main research question, the quantitative responses from this second survey showed good agreement with statements V1–V3 (the 'role' of the pattern), but a much wider spread for the other three (which tended to focus upon practical problems that could arise). If we turn to the qualitative responses, then similarly, the positive qualities identified are largely *design*-related (VC5, VE1, VE2, VE3), while many of the reservations about the pattern either relate to its *implementation* (VC6, VE4, VE7) or to its longer-term effects in terms of constraining design options (VC2, VC3, VC4, VC7, VE4, VE5). In contrast, we might note that the textbook by the *GoF* does recognise some implementation-related limitations, but does not discuss any design or maintenance issues related to its use.

The comments themselves have a strong flavour of rather conditional support for its use, as in the quotations below, which emphasise that, while useful, it needs to be viewed as a means to an end and one that is only really applicable to a limited range of situations.

- "I suspect that the issue is that there are sometimes other (perhaps better) ways to solve the 'visitation' problem."

- "Visitors are useful in languages that miss a language mechanism to extend existing encapsulations (such as Java)."

- "The visitor patterns applies to a relatively small number of supposed 'recurring problems' in OO design."

- "It is a pattern with limited application."

- "The visitor pattern tackles occasions when data structures drive the processes."

- "In programming languages without multiple despatch, visitor is the only way to achieve something similar."

Clearly too, the use of *Visitor* comes at a price, as indicated by the following.

- "Enforces a rigid view of algorithms and data structures."

- "For structures with complex relationships, or with elements of varying types, interfaces can likewise become cumbersome to design and implement."

- "Double despatch implementation can be cumbersome."

- "This is a complicated pattern that has its room in our toolbox, but [we] need to resist using it sometimes."

- "Poor: complexity, contorted data flow."

So maybe the comment from one respondent to the effect that "Visitor is useful when nothing else will do the job, but better avoided otherwise" sums up this set of comments well. Many of our respondents had clearly applied *Visitor* effectively, but were well aware that its use could imply substantial design trade-offs.

What therefore can we conclude from this? For both surveys, the responses clearly indicate that it is valued but that its use should carry a 'health warning', in that used outside of a well-constrained context, it is likely to increase complexity and complicate implementation, testing and maintenance. Essentially then, there is a clear message that this is a pattern where the price of misuse is particularly high.

6.3.2 Singleton

As indicated by its scores in Table 1, in the first survey this pattern appears to have polarised the views of our respondants more strongly than any other. This is reflected in the quantitative responses to the second survey, with few respondents having 'no opinion' and rather mixed responses to S3 and S4, where its use for global variables is raised. Turning to the qualitative responses, while there were some caveats about implementation issues and their consequences (see SC3, SC4, SE3, SE4 and SE5), the key concern seemed to be about exercising discipline when using it (SC2, SC3, SE1), a term also used in S2 (from Table 2) of course. While this might be reasonably be regarded as an issue for any pattern, in the case of *Singleton* there seems to be significantly different ideas about what that discipline should encompass, particularly with regard to global structures.

(The *GoF* textbook only discusses what they interpret as positive consequences of its use, but users seem to have more reservations, particularly regarding global structures.)

One respondent (bravely) stated that: "I quite like Singleton and have used it often in my development work...ensuring one and only one instance of queue, monitor, factor etc.". However, the comment that "Singleton solves a very specific problem with about as much grace as can be expected" is probably closer to a median view (if such a position is possible for *Singleton*). It was noticeable that the entries under the experiences of respondents cited only a very limited set of examples, to the extent that some really doubted that this really was addressing enough of a recurring problem to be classified as a pattern.

So, returning to our supplementary research question, we would suggest that if this pattern belongs in the toolbox at all, then it should be kept in a very specialist section. Unfortunately, the relatively simplicity of *Singleton* makes it a rather convenient example to use when teaching about patterns, but here there is a clear message that we should avoid using it as an example. Indeed, as one respondent observed: "the globals debate is never-ending", and maybe that debate is one that is best left to the experts.

6.3.3 Facade

While Table 1 indicates that this is the lest controversial of the three patterns considered in our study, it still attracted a significant 'negative' vote in the first survey. (But, as noted earlier, the 'negative' votes were all from teachers and researchers.) The quantitative responses showed general agreement with the original comments that dealt with 'role', but less so with those that dealt with consequences (there was particularly little support for F5). From the qualitative comments, as FC1 indicates, there was some feeling in this survey that the negative perceptions expressed in the first survey might arise at least partly from misuse, as well as a clear indication that it was particularly valuable for integrating legacy elements (FC2, FE1).

The individual comments about this pattern show rather less emotion than was engendered by the other two, and a number of respondents suggested that the negative views in the original list probably stemmed largely from a lack of understanding. Examples of positive views were:

- "Easy to misuse, I use it as a high level API, nothing else".

- "Reading the negative comments I get the feeling that the 'Facades' discussed are poorly designed."

- "I don't have bad experiences. However it is easy to use the patten inappropriately, but that is not an issue of the pattern, but of the designers using it".

The experiences quoted tended to be split between its use for legacy code ("when dealing with legacy systems...very useful to extract a cleaner interface" and "if it provides a coherent interface to a sub-system whose structure is then hidden, it has great value"), and its value in actual design ("simplified API for complex back-end systems to hide their details", "front controllers that serve as facades from the presentation to the application layer") — while accepting a possible cost in terms of maintenance ("gets hard to maintain after a while"). Again, if we consult the 'consequences' listed in the *GoF* text, the emphasis is placed upon the implementation benefits, and while users seem to agree about these, they also have some reservations about longer-term effects.

There are clearly occasions when Facade is appropriate, as indicated above (integrating legacy code, providing a good abstraction from complex structures). Indeed, the main concerns expressed are about the ease of misuse and the possible complications for maintenance. Again, while misuse can occur for any pattern, the consequences for Facade may be more significant than for many other patterns—although this may also reflect its relatively widespread use.

6.4 Use of a Follow-on Survey

To our knowledge, multi-method research has so far not formed one of the tools for empirical software engineering. Indeed, as indicated by Mingers in [8], it is relatively uncommon to find it used in IS research too. Although the use of a follow-on survey is not strictly a multi-method form, because we were using the follow-on survey as surrogate for interviews, our study could be considered to have been an approximation to that form.

If we return to our supplementary research question, this asks whether the use of a follow-on survey has successfully enhanced our knowledge about these three patterns, and helped answer the question posed in the title of the paper. We would argue that it has done so in two ways.

1. By helping identify those responses from the first survey that did not address a general issue. (A good example is statement S5 from Table 2. The respondents to the second survey did not consider temporal coupling to be of general concern.)

2. By providing reinforcement for issues that were considered important, and in some cases, clarification of what was important about them (such as for *Facade*).

Overall therefore, we would argue that this study has demonstrated the value of using a follow-on study to probe into the underlying rationale for any outcomes. Equally, we do recognise that in this case it was only possible because we were fortunate enough to have a relatively large number of responses to the first survey, without which, a more resource-intensive form such as semi-structured interviews would probably be the only option. Also, we cannot readily assess the effectiveness of using a follow-on survey as a surrogate for interviews when we lack any comparison with a similar study making use of (say) semi-structured interviews. Indeed, one of the limitations of using a follow-on survey was that it was not possible to probe as effectively as would be possible with an interview, as was demonstrated by the proportion of respondents who failed to provide any qualitative responses.

So while our answer to the supplementary question "is a follow-on survey a useful way to investigate these characteristics?" is positive, we do have to acknowledge that conducting a second survey is probably not the most effective way to follow up on a survey—although as here, it may well be the only pragmatic choice.

7. CONCLUSIONS

Design patterns form a useful element in the software designer's toolbox, by providing schemas that allow the exchange of design experience and knowledge. However, as demonstrated in our first survey [13], not all patterns from the *GoF* are considered to be of equal usefulness, and a designer needs to be aware of the consequences of using specific patterns. It is also noticeable that, whereas the *GoF* text focuses largely on implementation consequences, our respondents tended to be more concerned about consequential issues for such activities as maintenance and testing.

As discussed above, our study has demonstrated the value of performing a qualitative follow-on study to help explain the outcomes from a more quantitative study. This is particularly so for a topic such as this, since any form of knowledge schema is inevitably going to be difficult to assess and evaluate.

The title of our paper asks why the use of these three patterns is controversial, and the outcomes from this second study have provided some further insight into this.

- In the case of *Visitor*, there is a clear message about the consequences of using it outside of a limited context, with inappropriate use leading to negative effects for implementation, testing and maintenance for the reasons provided in our analyses of comments and experiences.

- For *Singleton*, the messages about this pattern are rather polarised as far as the acceptability of global structures is concerned, but taking the issues as a whole, it seems reasonable to recommend that, at the least, the use of this pattern as a teaching example should be avoided.

- While the use of *Facade* is less controversial, and although it can perform a valuable role for such purposes as integrating legacy code, there are still significant negative issues about its use, such as its effect upon maintenance, that the designer needs to consider.

What is important about this use of follow-on survey is that, through its use, we are able to provide a stronger rationale for making the above summaries, based upon the refinements to the evidence provided by the wider set of experts that we surveyed. So, while we cannot make definitive recommendations about when or when not to use one of these patterns, something that is probably not possible for any context, our survey does provide some further clarification about the situations where they could or should not be employed.

Acknowledgment

The authors would like to thank those respondents from the original survey who were kind enough to give further help by participating in this second survey. We also thank Gordon Rugg for suggesting the use of a multi-method approach.

8. REFERENCES

[1] B. Baudry, Y. L. Traon, G. Sunyé, and J.-M. Jézéquel. Measuring and improving design patterns testability. In *Proceedings of 9th International Software Metrics Symposium (METRICS'03)*, pages 50–59, 2003.

[2] F. Détienne. *Software Design – Cognitive Aspects*. Springer Practitioner Series, 2002.

[3] E. Freeman and E. Freeman. *Head First Design Patterns*. O'Reilly, 2004.

[4] E. Gamma, R. Helm, R. Johnson, and J. Vlissides. *Design Patterns: Elements of Reusable Object-Oriented Software*. Addison-Wesley, 1995.

[5] F. Khomh and Y.-G. Guéhéneuc. Do design patterns impact software quality positively? In *Proceedings of CSMR 2008*, pages 274–278, 2008.

[6] B. A. Kitchenham, D. Budgen, and O. P. Brereton. Using mapping studies as the basis for further research—a participant-observer case study. *Information & Software Technology*, 53(4):638–651, 2011. Special section from EASE 2010.

[7] B. A. Kitchenham and S. L. Pfleeger. Principles of survey research part 4: Questionnaire evaluation. *ACM Software Engineering Notes*, 27(3):20–23, May 2002.

[8] J. Mingers. The paucity of multimethod research: a review of the information systems literature. *Information Systems Journal*, 13(3):233–249, 2003.

[9] B. Oates. *Researching Information Systems and Computing*. SAGE, 2006.

[10] C. B. Seaman. Qualitative methods in empirical studies of software engineering. *IEEE Transactions on Software Engineering*, 25(4):557–572, 1999.

[11] P. Wendorff. Assessment of design patterns during software reengineering: Lessons learned from a large commercial project. In *Proceedings of 5th European Conference on Software Maintenance and Reengineering (CSMR'01)*, pages 77–84. IEEE Computer Society Press, 2001.

[12] L. Williams. What agile teams think of agile principles. *Communications of the ACM*, 55(4):71–76, 2012.

[13] C. Zhang and D. Budgen. A survey of experienced user perceptions about design patterns. Submitted for publication., 2011.

[14] C. Zhang and D. Budgen. What do we know about the effectiveness of software design patterns? Accepted for publication in IEEE Transactions on Software Engineering, 2011.

Empirical Analysis of User Data in Game Software Development

The Story of Project Gotham Racing 4

Kenneth Hullett*
UC Santa Cruz
Santa Cruz, CA, USA
khullett@soe.ucsc.edu

Nachiappan Nagappan
Microsoft Research
Redmond, WA, USA

Eric Schuh
Microsoft Game Studios
Redmond, WA, USA
{nachin, eschuh}@microsoft.com

John Hopson
Bungie Studios
Bellevue, WA, USA
jhopson@bungie.com

ABSTRACT

For several years empirical studies have spanned the spectrum of research from software productivity, quality, reliability, performance to human computer interaction. Analyses have involved software systems ranging from desktop software to telecommunication switching systems. But surprising there has been little work done on the emerging digital game industry, one of the fastest growing domains today. To the best of our knowledge, our work is one of the first empirical analysis of a large commercially successful game system. In this paper, we introduce an analysis of the significant user data generated in the gaming industry by using a successful game: Project Gotham Racing 4.

More specifically, due to the increasing ubiquity of constantly connected high-speed internet connections for game consoles, developers are able to collect extensive amounts of data about their games following release. The challenge now is to make sense of that data, and from it be able to make recommendations to developers. This paper presents an empirical case study analyzing the data collected from a released game over a three year period. The results of this analysis include a better understanding of the differences between long-term and short-term players, and the extent to which various options in the game are utilized. This led to recommendations for future development ways to reduce development costs and to keep new players engaged. A secondary goal for this paper is to introduce software game development as a topic of importance to the empirical software engineering community and discuss research results on a key difference area: data analytics on user data to customize user and development experiences.

Categories and Subject Descriptors

D.2.8 [**Software**]: Metrics, K.8.0 [**Personal Computing**]: Games

General Terms

Design, Measurement

Keywords

Game design, Game development, Game metrics

1. EMPIRICAL RESEARCH AND GAMES

Empirical research in software engineering has typically focused on software systems ranging from the traditional telecommunication systems to more recent web services. There has been little research on the software engineering aspects of digital games (a.k.a. video games, computer games, electronic games, etc.; referred to simply as games for the remainder of this paper). Games are increasingly becoming an important part of the mainstream software development industry. PricewaterhouseCoopers (PwC) report *Global Entertainment and Media Outlook: 2007-2011* estimates that the video game market will increase from $31.6 Billion in 2006 to $48.9 Billion in 2011[1]. Games require significant software engineering effort and have become increasingly complex as games get more sophisticated [3]. Many of the issues in the development, production, and testing of games reflect those of the general software engineering community, and in many cases represent the state of the art. Research communities exist for specialized aspects of game development, such as SIGGRAPH's game track [15] for graphics or AAAI's Artificial Intelligence and Interactive Digital Entertainment for game AI [2]. There are already workshops in this regard that have been held co-located to the International Conference of Software Engineering [12]. That said, games are a significantly wide field and in this paper our goals are twofold:

- Identify a specific area of research and characterize its operation in the gaming community

- Investigate via data analytics the ability to improve game design

There are several differences between software development for games compared to software development for traditional software

---

* Kenneth Hullett was an intern at Microsoft Research when this work was performed.

[1] http://www.businessweek.com/innovate/content/aug2007/id20070813_12 0384.htm

systems. It is beyond the scope of this paper to assess these differences. In this paper we focus on one particular aspect, the importance of user testing. In recent years there has been a rise in interest in the collection and analysis of game metrics, and how they can be used to inform the game development process. As games have gotten larger and more complex, the need for such metrics to make sense of player behavior has increased. The number of reachable states in a modern commercial game title is enormous; without some way to simplify and represent collected data development teams would be unable to act on it in a timely matter.

Telemetry, or the collection of metrics, has become increasingly common in game development. As games have become more complex traditional playtesting is no longer able to provide sufficient coverage of all possible gameplay states or reveal potential emergent elements. Playtesting refers to the user testing wherein data is collected from players playing the game to identify defects and improve customer experience. This makes long-term metrics collection the only viable means to understand players and how they interact with the game.

But just collecting data is not enough, the data has to be distilled and interpreted before it can be used to inform development decisions. A detailed accounting of players' in-game actions is difficult to interpret even for a developer who is intimately familiar with the game. Simply knowing what a player did at a certain time means nothing without the context of what they did previously, what they did afterwards, and how that relates to the larger patterns of behavior throughout the game.

Previous academic work studied data on smaller scales in limited domains, and case studies from industry have shown ways various types of data can be used in to aid the development process. Our aim is to unite and advance these traditions by presenting a case study of analysis of large-scale data collected from *Project Gotham Racing 4*, a popular commercially released game.

This paper presents our case study by explaining the domain, our analyses, the conclusions we drew, and recommendations we were able to make. Some areas we explore include:

- Factors that hinder a player's advancement
- Differences between long-term and short-term players
- Differences between multi- and single player usage
- How players interact with the game in their first ten races and how this relates to long term behavior
- Utilization rates of various game play options and factors that contribute to them

This paper is organized as follows. In Section 2 we discuss the related work. In Section 3 we explain the various sources of data in games via quantitative (testing) and qualitative (subjective evaluations) aspects to characterize the process on how the game industry handles these activities. In Section 4 introduce Project Gotham Racing 4. In Section 5 we describe the data collected and Section 6 the data analysis and results. Section 7 presents the recommendations. We present conclusions in Section 8.

2. RELATED WORK

A. Academic

Presented here are some examples of academic work that explore data analysis in games.

Dixit and Youngblood performed user tests and used the data collected to create visualizations showing where users' attention was focused during gameplay [4, 5]. This information was then used to determine the best places to put relevant information to improve recall. The implications for game design are to give designers a better idea of where to place important clues and other information so that players are most likely to see it.

Kim et al. presented TRUE, a system for collection and visualization of data from user studies, and presented a case study of its use in Halo 2 [8], a popular First-Person Shooter (FPS) game. Their studies specifically looked for unintended difficulty increases introduced during development. Their tests collected data on player deaths and surveyed the subject's opinions on difficulty. They were able to identify several unbalanced elements in the game and correct them before release.

Weber and Mateas used data mining techniques on large amounts of collected data to understand player strategies in the game *StarCraft*. Over 5000 replays of expert matches were used as training data for a machine learning algorithm that predicted player strategies [20]. This predictor became a component of an AI bot that played *StarCraft* better than most other available techniques, thus helping to improve game AI.

Weber et al. used analysis of large datasets generated by players of the game *Madden NFL 11* to understand player retention [19]. They selected gameplay features to use as input to a machine learning algorithm that tried to predict how many games a player would play overall. The selected features were then studied to make recommendations that would increase player retention in the game.

Lewis and Wardrip-Fruin presented a case study of large-scale data collection and interpretation of *World of Warcraft* repositories for better understanding of player behavior [9]. They analyzed how long it took players from each class to reach level 80 (the highest level) in order to empirically evaluate whether the game design is balanced, and confirm or refute common folklore surrounding the game.

Miller and Crowcroft also studied *World of Warcraft*, but instead looked at player movement [10]. They analyzed several gameplay traces that utilized the same battleground to find patterns in player traffic. They were able to identify distinct patterns of player behavior, including patrollers, who moved between multiple points along standard routes, and guards who tended to remain within a small area. This analysis is useful to developers by showing how players are interacting with the game environment.

B. Industry

Articles in industry-focused publications like Gamasutra are a good source of information for ways in which data is used in the game industry. Some key examples are presented in this section.

Russell examined the combat design in *Uncharted 2* [13, 14]. They reflected on the previous game in the series and drew useful lessons, as well as described the process by which they iterated on the design of their current game. Levels were playtested repeatedly, with both telemetry and observational data being collected. This data was used to informed design changes and improve the game.

Adent discussed the development of *Forza Motorsport 3* and how testing and data analysis contributed [1]. A key factor for that team was having a stable, playable build at all times. This enabled constant iterative development of the game. Constant playability allowed for a constant stream of data for the designers to study and make changes accordingly.

Van der Heijden examined the usability testing done for *Swords & Soldiers* [18]. They describe the key questions the developers hoped to answer, the set up and testing process, and what they learned. In particular they were interested in improving the interface design and used eye-tracking data to see where players' attention was focused.

Another example of usability testing is in Thompson's article on *Halo 3* development [17]. They describe the extensive playtesting performed to improve the playability and balance of the game. Large numbers of players were observed and data was collected about how well they performed, leading designers to make adjustments. Players were also asked subjective questions about their level of enjoyment.

Another game in the Halo series, *Halo: Reach*, was subjected to a large beta test – over 2.7 million players and 16 million hours of testing [11, 16]. The result was not only finding and fixing bugs, but also significantly tweaking the gameplay by adjusting factors such as weapon damage, reload times, shield recharge rates, etc.

3. SOURCES OF DATA

A. Internal Testing

One of the earliest sources of data for game development teams is from their internal testing. This includes informal testing by the developers themselves and more formal testing by the QA team.

1) Developers

The earliest testers of a game are the development team itself, and therefore are the earliest creators of useful data about the game. In the early development, teams create small prototypes to test and explore new ideas. While these prototypes are generally discarded once the main development cycle begins, the lessons learned are an important initial source of data about what works and doesn't work in the game.

Once the game is fully in development, the team will continuously be testing the game. Of particular interest to designers is the play balance of the game. Level designers will play levels to ensure that they have the correct difficulty level for where they appear in the game. Matching increasing difficulty to the players' increasing skill as they learn the game is key to keeping players engaged.

2) QA

The main objective of the QA team is to find bugs and report them to the development team. Statistics from reported bugs are used to make production decisions in much the same way as they are used in traditional software development.

Many bugs are straightforward problems that the programmers, designers, and artists can easily address, but the QA team will often find problems with the playability of the game, including play balance issues. QA testers are often highly skilled game players, and continuously evaluate aspects of the game for difficulty, play time, and balance. Data collected from this

playtesting can be used by the developers to make adjustments while the game is still in development.

B. External Testing

External testing is testing done by players from the community, rather than members of the development or QA teams. Releases of the game used for external testing are generally instrumented to collect data about the players' actions in the game.

1) Usability Testing

Usability testing is done with selected members of the target audience to better understand interactions with and reactions to the game. It is generally done under controlled psychological research protocols. To be effective, usability testing must be done late enough in the development cycle so that the game is representative of its final state, but not so late that it's costly to make changes.

In most cases, usability testing is the first time someone outside the organization plays the game. As the development and QA teams have been involved in the project for a long time, they are familiar with how the game is intended to be played and may not realize what is obvious or not to players. By putting a subject in a room and observing them play without instruction or interference, the development team can better gauge their expectations of how players will react to the finished game.

Typical outcomes of usability testing include the need for better tutorials to teach new players and clearer interfaces. Besides the qualitative assessment of players' reactions to the game, quantitative data about the players' specific actions can also be gathered.

2) Beta Tests

A beta test is a release of a nearly-complete version of a game to a limited set of players. Beta testers are generally selected from a pool of players of previous games.

In the past, beta tests consisted of sending copies of games to members of the pool, waiting for them to play, and receiving back questionnaire responses and comments. However, with the increasing ubiquity of internet connected game machines, the beta version can be downloaded directly to the tester's machine and play data can be reported directly to the development team.

Beta tests can also be contribute to the marketing of a game by giving players a preview of the game and building excitement about the release.

3) Long-term Play Data

While not actually testing per se, data gathered from players after a game's release can be an important source of data. Due to the increasing ubiquity of internet-connected game, development teams can easily collect player data indefinitely after release. If problems are found, teams can make changes and deliver a new version to players even after release.

Examples of useful data that can be obtained from long-term data are what achievements are earned, how quickly players progress, or favorite levels or game play modes. One well known example of long-term play data are the Halo heat maps published by Bungie Studios [17]. These show the locations of player deaths and kills by different weapons across all multiplayer maps. By examining these, the team can make adjustments for future releases.

Data from long-term play is particularly useful for maintaining play balance. A lack of balance may not have been appeared in earlier testing, but only becomes apparent after many months of play. An example would be an unanticipated dominant strategy. If, by observing play data, a team sees that a particular weapon has become favored, then they may want to adjust the balance to counter this.

Long-term data can also help teams plan the release of expansion content. When interest in a game starts to wane, developers can release new downloadable content that will entice players to continue playing. Also, examining at what point in their progress players start downloading new content can drive recommendation systems for future players.

C. Subjective Evaluations

1) Surveys

While much of the interest in game metrics is focused on quantitative data, qualitative data is also important. Survey data is generally collected along with the quantitative data collection during usability and beta testing. This data can be open ended, such as general questions about players' reactions to the game, or structured, such as rating various aspects of a game on a Likert scale.

2) Reviews

One source of expert data is reviews of games written by professional or non-professional journalists. The games industry is a large, international industry with hundreds of games released each year; game buyers consult reviews to determine what games are most worth spending their money on. By looking at reviews of their own and similar games, developers can decide what aspects to focus on to increase the likelihood of good reviews.

3) Online Communities

Gaming culture is increasingly involved and worldwide. Gamers don't play games in isolation; they comment upon and read other player's comments on various message boards and blogs dedicated to the subject.

Another aspect of online communities is expert players writing guides for new players. These guides, often called FAQs (from Frequently Asked Questions), are published at websites like GameFAQs.com [6]. Information found in FAQs includes complete walkthroughs of games, strategy guides, maps, and character creation guides.

By monitoring the online communities populated by their players, development teams can get a sense of how their game has been received by the gaming community and how their view of the game matches the design. If the walkthroughs miss some important aspect, then it was too hard to find. If the players'

assessment of the strength and weaknesses of various elements don't match the team's expectations, then their play balancing may need adjustment.

4) Post Mortems

It is becoming increasingly common for industry-focused publications to publish game developers' post mortems after a game is released. This is a summary of what went right and wrong in the development process. By studying areas of development that were problematic in other projects, developers can better anticipate and avoid problems in their own projects.

4. PROJECT GOTHAM RACING 4

We present an analysis of long-term play data from a commercially released game. For this case study, we looked at data from *Project Gotham Racing 4* (PGR4), an Xbox 360 game developed by Bizarre Creations and published by Microsoft Game Studios in 2007 (Example screen shot – Figure 1).

PGR4 is an auto racing game and is representative of many games in the genre. Players have the option to play either single or multiplayer races organized into various game modes and event types. Game modes include, for example, career mode, a single player mode where the player earns money by competing in races, which in turn allows them to unlock other races and vehicles, leading to continuous advancement. Other game modes are multiplayer quick races, arcade mode, and time attack challenges. There are ten of these in total. Event types are the 29 specific challenges a player may compete in within a mode. These include things like street race, cone challenges, and elimination races.

The game features 134 vehicles, both cars and motorcycles, organized into 7 classes, A–G. The primary division between classes is performance, with A-Class being the highest

Figure 1: A screenshot from *Project Gotham Racing 4*

performance and G-class being the lowest. Races are conducted on one of 121 routes spread out over 9 in-game locations. Locations are generally virtual representations of cities, such as Macau or Shanghai, while the routes are specific tracks laid out over the location.

In the time since its release, PGR4 has been played extensively by its audience. Telemetry data was collected from players who opted in whenever they played while connected to the Xbox Live service, regardless of whether they were playing in multi- or single player races.

5. DATASET

Several datasets were collected from PGR4. The primary one analyzed was the Start of Race dataset. This contained approximately 3.1 million entries, one for each time a player started a race, including both multi- and single player races. Data about both the race and the player were logged, including:

- Type of event
- Route selected
- Vehicle selected
- Number of vehicles in race
- Player's career rating
- Number of previous events completed by player
- Total kudos earned by player

A. Features

For our analysis we looked at usage patterns for five game features of interest to the development team:

- Game modes
- Event types
- Routes
- Vehicles
- Vehicle classes

As these are the main options available to the player, patterns in their usage present a picture of how players are playing the game and what is most important to them.

B. Subdivisions

We felt it would be beneficial to separately examine players grouped according to their level of engagement with the game. To this end we subdivided the data into four groups based on the total number of races for that player in the entire dataset. The four groups were:

- Regular: > 200 races
- Mid 2: > 85 & ≤ 200
- Mid 1: > 13 & ≤ 85
- Infrequent: ≤ 13 races

For most analyses, we specifically compared the two most extreme groups: the regular and the infrequent players. This allowed us to make statements about how the behavior of the most enthusiastic players compared to the least engaged.

C. Subsets

In addition to studying the entire dataset, we examined three subsets for additional insight. We looked at multiplayer and single player races separately, and looked at the first ten races for each unique player. The motivation behind looking at the first ten races was to understand how a player's initial experience affects their subsequent engagement by the game. Differences that exist between infrequent and regular players in their first ten races may contribute to the likelihood that a new player will ultimately fall into one group or the other.

6. ANALYSIS AND RESULTS

We drew five conclusions from our examination of the Start of Race dataset:

- Regular players play more multiplayer races
- Regular players play more in career mode
- Many options (game modes, event types, routes, and vehicles) are underused
- A- & F-Class vehicles are most popular classes of vehicles
- C-Class vehicles equally or more popular than B-Class, especially among regular players

A. Regular players play more multiplayer

Within both the entire Start of Race dataset and the first ten races, regular players showed a clear preference for multiplayer game modes and event types.

For regular players, NETWORK_PLAYTIME was the 2nd most popular mode, used in 27.6% of races overall (see Figure 2). In contrast, for infrequent players, NETWORK_PLAYTIME is 3rd, at 16.1%, behind 2 single player modes (OFFLINE_CAREER at 47.0% and PGR_ARCADE at 19.6%) (see Figure 3).

In terms of event types, the most popular for regular players in the entire dataset was NET_STREET_RACE at 26.6%. For infrequent players, it was second at 10.5%, significantly less than the single player event type of STREET_RACE at 54.8%.

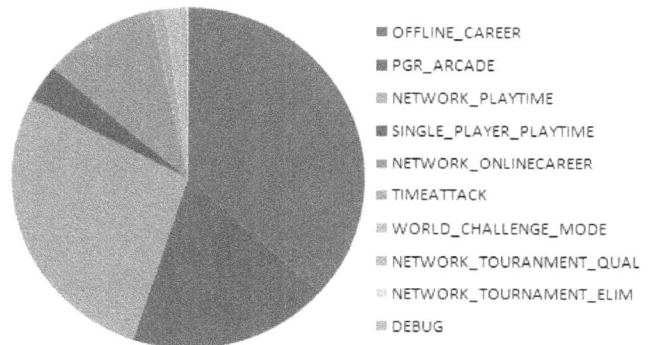

Figure 2: Game Modes, Regular Players

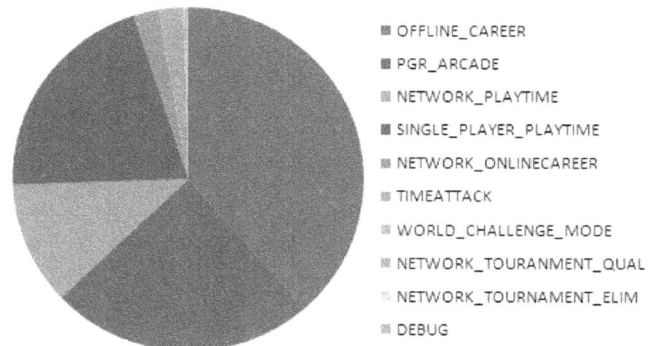

Figure 3: Game Modes, Infrequent Players

We see a similar pattern when looking at the first ten races only. 48% of races for regular player were in multiplayer game modes, compared to 20.8% for infrequent players. The most common multiplayer game mode, NETWORK_PLAYTIME, was significantly more preferred by regular players, 35.5% versus 7.6% for infrequent players.

For regular players NET_STREET_RACE was the most popular event type by an overwhelming margin: 39% of races, with single player STREET_RACE a distant second at 15.5%. For infrequent players, the single player event types of STREET_RACE and TIMEATTACK were vastly more preferred (24.9% and 20.8% respectively) over NET_STREE T_RACE (3rd at 9.4%).

- Regular players used the NETWORK_PLAYTIME game mode more than infrequent players
- Regular players used the NET_STREET_RACE event type more than infrequent players
- In their first 10 races, regular players used the NETWORK_PLAYTIME game mode more than infrequent players by a large margin
- In their first 10 races, regular players used the NET_STREET_RACE event type more than infrequent players by a large margin

B. Regular players play more career mode

When regular players do play single player races, they are more likely to do so in career mode than infrequent players.

In the entire dataset, OFFLINE_CAREER was the most popular game mode overall for regular players: 36.6%, followed by the aforementioned multiplayer mode NETWORK_PLAYTIME at 27.6% (see Figure 2). In contrast, the non-career modes of SINGLE_PLAYER_PLAYTIME and PGR_ARCADE were more preferred by infrequent players (20.6% v. 3.5% and 24.5% v. 18.46% respectively) (see Figure 3).

When looking at data from the single player races only, OFFLINE_CAREER was the most popular for both regular and infrequent players. 59.9% of single player races for regular players were in OFFLINE_CAREER and 47.5% for infrequent players. This may not seem like a large difference, but when we look at the primary non-career mode, SINGLE_PLAYER_PLAYTIME, the difference becomes apparent. Regular players used SINGLE_PLAYER_PLAYTIME in only 5.8% of single player races, while infrequent players used it in 24.2%.

We see a difference in the first ten races as well. Regular players prefer OFFLINE_CAREER career more than infrequent players (36.5% v. 22.2%). By contrast, infrequent players were more likely than regular players to play non-career modes TIMEATTACK (20.1% v. 0.5%) and PGR_ARCADE (26.4% v. 6.5%).

- OFFLINE_CAREER was the most popular game mode among regular players
- SINGLE_PLAYER_PLAYTIME was used more by infrequent players overall and in their first ten races
- Regular players used OFFLINE_CAREER more in their first ten races

C. Many options were underused

Our analysis showed that large amounts of the options available in the game were used in so few instances that they could have been removed from the game entirely. In four of the features we examined, 20% to over 70% of available options were used in less than 1% of races. This suggests that savings in development times and costs could be realized in future games by offering fewer options without negatively affecting the players' overall experience. When looking at the entire dataset,

- 22% (2 of 9) game modes,
- 41% (12 of 29) event types,
- 67% (81 of 121) routes,
- and 78% (104 of 134) vehicles

were used in less than 1% of races each.

1) Game Modes

As shown in Table 1, OFFLINE_CAREER (a single player mode) was the most commonly used game mode by far, with NETWORK_TOURANMENT_QUAL and NETWORK_TOURNAMENT_ELIM being used in less than 0.5% of races. If fact, the 7 least used modes account for only 15% of races overall.

Table 1. Game Modes

Game Mode	Races	% of Total
OFFLINE_CAREER	1479586	47.63%
PGR_ARCADE	566705	18.24%
NETWORK_PLAYTIME	584201	18.81%
NETWORK_ONLINECAREER	193091	6.22%
SINGLE_PLAYER_PLAYTIME	185415	5.97%
TIMEATTACK	43942	1.41%
WORLD_CHALLENGE_MODE	36581	1.18%
NETWORK_TOURANMENT_QUAL	13847	0.45%
NETWORK_TOURNAMENT_ELIM	2713	0.09%

When we look at just multiplayer game modes we see an even larger disparity: the top two modes account for 98% of all multiplayer races.

2) Event Types

When looking at event types, we again see a rapid drop off in popularity with the least popular types receiving only trivial usage. A reduced version of this data is shown in Table 2.

Table 2. Event Types (Reduced)

Group	Races	% of Total
STREET_RACE	795334	25.60%
NET_STREET_RACE	543491	17.50%
ELIMINATION	216042	6.95%

HOTLAP	195949	6.31%
...		
TESTTRACK_TIME	7484	0.24%
NET_CAT_AND_MOUSE_FREE_R OAM	3989	0.13%
CAT_AND_MOUSE	53	0.00%

Single player street races were the most popular event type, followed by multiplayer street races and elimination races (knock out stages in tournaments), whereas 12 of the 29 event types were used in less than 1% of races. The underutilization of event types is even more pronounced when looking at multiplayer races only (7 of 16 event types used in less than 0.1% of races).

3) Routes

While 67% of the available routes were used in less than 1% of races each, collectively they account for 36% of races. i.e., two-thirds of races occur on one-third of the routes. Developers would likely not support a proposal to eliminate such a large portion of potential gameplay, so we looked at even smaller percentages of use and found that

- 47 (39%) were used in less than 0.5%,
- 19 (16%) were used in less than 0.25%,
- and 8 (7%) were used in less than 0.1%

of total races.

The 47 routes used in less than 0.5% of races account for 13% of overall usage, a much more palatable percentage to consider removing, while still leaving 70+ routes available for players.

4) Vehicles

Similarly with routes, a wide variety of vehicles adds to depth of gameplay even if a significant portion is rarely used. Furthermore, the number of available vehicles in a driving game can be an important point in the marketing strategy.

The 104 of the 134 vehicles that are used in less than 1% of races each collectively represent 38% of usage. Furthermore,

- 72 (54%) were used in less than 0.5%;
- 50 (37%) were used in less than 0.25%,
- and 12 (9%) were used in less than 0.1% of total races.

The 50 vehicles used in less than 0.25% of races each represent less than 7% of the total races.

5) Vehicle Classes

We can also look at vehicles in terms of their classes. The vehicles in the game are grouped into 7 classes based on performance. As seen in Table 3, A-Class vehicles were used nearly twice as often as the next most popular class, while Classes B though F were close in popularity, ranging from 10-15% of all races.

Table 3. Vehicle Class

Vehicle Class	Races	% of Total
A_Class	908581	29.25%
F_Class	478944	15.42%
C_Class	465889	15.00%
B_Class	454594	14.63%
D_Class	386862	12.45%
E_Class	338938	10.91%
G_Class	69625	2.24%

Also, G-Class was considerably less popular, being used in about 2% of races overall. This suggests that the number of classes can be reduced. Players have little interest in the low-performance G-Class, and perceive little difference between the other classes except A-Class.

D. A- & F-Class vehicles most popular

As seen in Table 3, A-Class vehicles were the most popular by a considerable margin. They were also the most preferred in multiplayer (53.6%) and in the first ten races (32.5%). These are the highest performance vehicles, so we would expect them to be most preferred by regular players, and they were (36.2% v. 20.2% for infrequent players). However, they were still used significantly by infrequent players, being the second most popular in the first ten races (33%) and overall (20.2%) and most popular in multiplayer races (54.5%).

While in the overall dataset F-Class doesn't appear significantly more popular than B- through E-Classes, when we look at subsets of the data we see certain trends. Amongst infrequent players, F-Class was by far the most popular, 55.4% overall (see Figure 4) and 47% in single player races only. This seems like an obvious result as F-Class vehicles are the only ones initially available in career mode at the start of the game, but as shown above, infrequent players are less likely to play in career mode.

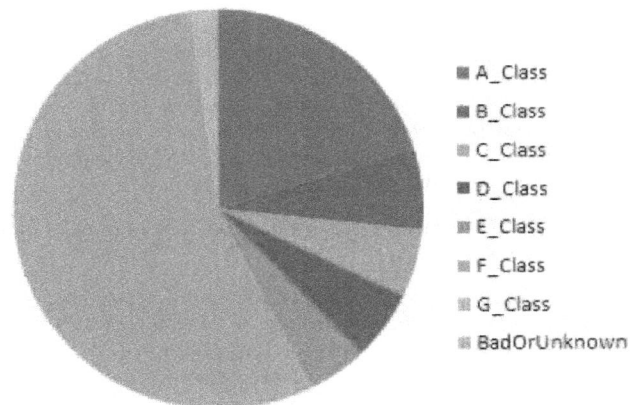

Figure 4: Vehicle Class, Infrequent Players

- A-Class vehicles were the most often used overall, in multiplayer, and in players' first ten races
- A-Class vehicle were the second most often used by infrequent players overall and in their first ten races
- F-Class vehicles were the most often by infrequent players

E. C-Class & B-Class equally popular

As seen in Table 3, C-Class was slightly more popular than B-Class overall. This may not seem significant, but when we look at the data for the first ten races, we see that C-Class was the second most popular class among regular players at 26% v. 13% for B-Class. This suggests that C-Class cars have characteristics that make them more appealing to players than the higher-performance B-Class vehicles.

> • In their first 10 races, regular players used C-Class vehicles twice as often as B-Class vehicles

7. RECOMMENDATIONS

The five conclusions we reached after examining the Start of Race dataset led to 4 recommendations for future development that would be applicable to many different games in the racing game genre, and could possibly be generalized to other games:

- New players should be encouraged to play in career mode
- New players should be encouraged to use F-Class vehicles in multiplayer
- Development time and costs could be reduced by having fewer available options
- Reduce the number of vehicle classes from 7 to 5

A. New players should be encouraged to play career mode

As discussed above, regular players are more likely to play in career mode, both overall and in the first ten races. This suggests that playing in career mode increases the likelihood that a player will continue playing the game for a much longer time. Players enjoy progression, and being presented with a series of increasing challenges and rewards, such as advancing through the stages in career mode, will cause them to be engaged and keep playing.

The data suggests that many new players come into the game, experiment with various game modes and event types in their first few races, and then stop playing. If they could be drawn into the challenge/reward structure of career mode they would be more likely to continue playing. The early career races are designed to be easy, so most players will start winning early, unlocking more cars and routes that they are then eager to try out.

B. New players should be encouraged to use F-Class vehicles in multiplayer

While infrequent players were shown to prefer F-Class vehicles in single player races, they had as high a preference for A-Class vehicles in multiplayer as regular players. Given that the learning curve for A-Class vehicles is quite steep, this may be a factor in infrequent players losing interest in the game. If, in one of their earliest experiences with the game, a player joins a multiplayer race with experienced players on a track they are unfamiliar with, picks one of the fastest cars available, and then crashes in the first turn, they are likely to become frustrated and stop playing.

Alternatively, new players could, by default, be sent to multiplayer races only with other new players, specifically on tracks that are available early in the single player game. The only vehicles available would be the F-Class vehicles, so they wouldn't feel compelled to select an A-Class vehicle merely to be competitive with other players. These initial experiences in multiplayer would be gentler, on tracks and using vehicles they are familiar with, and against other players of similar skill levels.

C. Development time and costs could be reduced by having available options

Our analysis showed that 20-70% of the available options were used in less than 1% of races each. As asset creation is a major expense in game development, reducing little-used options could significantly reduce costs and development time while having little impact on players' experience. Each vehicle in the game, for example, represents a significant investment: a 3d artist must model it, a texture artist must decorate it, a designer must to tweak its performance values, and testers must rigorously use it in a variety of conditions to make sure there are no problems. Creating new routes requires artists, designers, and testers, while new event types require engineering effort.

That being said, there are benefits to having little used content available in the game. It can extend the life of a game for players; they can explore rarely-used options when they grow tired of the game. A wide variety of options can lead to emergent play as players find uses for content that developers never anticipated. The amount of content can be useful in the marketing of a game; being able to say that you has more vehicles or event types than your competitors can drive sales.

While excessively pruning available content in future games might not be preferred, a reduction of 20% across the board could reduce costs and development times significantly while the back of the   box could still boast that the game contains more than 100 vehicles.

D. Reduce number of vehicle classes from 7 to 5

In addition to reducing the sheer amount of content, removing complexity from the game can reduce cognitive overhead for the player. In particular, the 7 vehicle classes are an unnecessary element that does not enhance the game experience for the player.

The analysis showed that G-Class vehicles were used in about 2% of races overall. These are mostly low-performance specialty and historic vehicles that are not generally of much use to players throughout the game. Any that developers feel are important enough to keep could be moved into other classes.

The analysis also showed little difference in preference for Classes B–E. While having stages of progression is important to the learning curve, fewer steps would achieve the same effect. In particular, C-Class is preferred over B-Class in some instances, suggesting there's little difference and the two could be combined.

The resulting 5 classes should offer sufficient ramp-up in difficulty for the player to progress though the game without any sudden increases.

8. CONCLUSIONS

This paper presented a series of analyses performed on data collected on players in the game *Project Gotham Racing 4*. We looked for patterns within large data sets that provide insight into player behavior. We learned there were key differences in how regular and infrequent players approached the game, and how what players do in their earliest exposure to the game can affect their desire to continue playing. We also found that much of the available options for gameplay were rarely used by players.

From the patterns in the data we made recommendations for future development. Many rarely utilized options could be removed with no negative impact on players. A more structured introduction would keep new players engaged and increase the likelihood that they will continue playing.

These conclusions could be applied generally to a wide variety of games in different genres. Developers who are inclined to add many options to their games should consider the result that players in PGR4 tended to focus mainly on the game's core features. Providing tutorials and a gentle early difficulty curve can help ease new players into a game and keep them playing. This paper also shows that simple analysis to begin with can greatly help advance the state of the art in software engineering in the games domain.

It is also important to call out several points.

a. Telemetry, or the collection of metrics, has become increasingly common in game development. The contribution of this paper is to show how data analysis, even exploratory, on data from games can have potentially far-reaching software engineering implications in the empirical community. There is the potential to evaluate how these new classes of software systems work with various empirical processes and practices.

b. The paper necessarily spends a lot of time explaining the domain of the analysis to provide context to the reader. A secondary goal of this paper is to introduce this topic of software engineering research for games to the broader software engineering community and expose the potential for research in games. We have presented the various sources of data available in game analytics. There are several open questions in the software engineering research for games community, ranging from the requirements engineering: how are requirements for games defined, where the major emphasis is based on user interaction and real-time feedback, the use of personas for requirements documents etc.; to testing and analysis: how can games be tested in the lab, simulating user behavior. We hope in coming years the software engineering community as a whole will embrace the games domain to investigate and address the important software engineering challenges facing games.

c. The paper is specific to Project Gotham Racing 4, though techniques similar to those outlined in this paper could be applied to any game dataset. As this case study involves an already released game, we were limited to making suggestions for future releases, but similar techniques could be applied to beta test data for a game in development. The larger the dataset, the more pronounced the patterns will be, but conclusions drawn from a pool of beta testers representative of the target audience are likely to be more insightful then those that can be gained through traditional playtesting. Similar analysis could be performed for different game genres, ranging from FPS (First Person Shooter) or strategy games to educational and physical activity games.

ACKNOWLEDGEMENTS

We would like to gratefully acknowledge the participants of ISERN in the special session on Games in 2009. Their encouragement was instrumental in submitting this paper to ESEM. Part of this paper, specifically Section 3, appeared as part of an ICSE NIER 2011 paper [7]. The rest of the paper has significantly newer results. We would like to thank the ICSE NIER reviewers who provided much encouragement and support which caused us to submit this paper. We would like to thank all the users who played PGR4, the data collection team in Xbox, Thomas Zimmermann, Christian Bird, Tom Ball, Jim Whitehead, and the broader ESEM and ISERN communities which have encouraged the publishing of research on Games.

REFERENCES

[1] Adent, D. *Forza Motorsport 3* and Predictable Development. Gamasutra.com. http://www.gamasutra.com/view/feature/6182/forza_motorsport_3_and_predictable_.php

[2] Annual Conference on Artificial Intelligence and Interactive Digital Entertainment. http://www.aiide.org/

[3] Blow, J. Game Development: Harder Than You Think. *Queue* 1, 10 (February 2004), 28-37, 2004.

[4] Dixit, P. N. and Youngblood, G. M. Optimal information placement in an interactive 3D environment. In *Proceedings of the 2007 ACM SIGGRAPH symposium on Video games*. 2007.

[5] Dixit, P. N. and Youngblood, G. M. Understanding information observation in interactive 3D environments. In *Proceedings of the 2008 ACM SIGGRAPH symposium on Video games*. 2008.

[6] GameFaqs. http://www.gamefaqs.com/

[7] Hullett, K., Nagappan, N., Schuh, E., Hopson, J. Data analytics for game development: NIER track. In *Proceedings of the International Conference on Software Engineering*. 2011.

[8] Kim, J., Gunn, D., Schuh, E., Phillips, B., Pagulayan, R., and Wixon, D. Tracking real-time user experience (TRUE): a comprehensive instrumentation solution for complex systems. In *Proceeding of the twenty-sixth annual SIGCHI conference on Human factors in computing systems*. 2008.

[9] Lewis, C. and Wardrip-Fruin, N. Mining game statistics from web services: a World of Warcraft armory case study. In *Proceedings of the Fifth International Conference on the Foundations of Digital Games*. 2010.

[10] Miller, J. L. and Crowcroft, J. Avatar movement in World of Warcraft battlegrounds. In *Proceedings of the 8th Annual Workshop on Network and Systems Support for Games* (NetGames '09). 2009.

[11] Nutt, C. *Halo: Reach* - The Beta Story. Gamasutra.com. http://www.gamasutra.com/view/feature/5875/halo_reach__the_beta_story.php

[12] Proceedings of the 1st International Workshop on Games and Software Engineering, ISBN: 978-1-4503-0578-5, New York, NY. http://dl.acm.org/citation.cfm?id=1984674&picked=prox

[13] Russell, B. A Deeper. Look into The Combat Design Of *Uncharted 2*. Gamasutra.com. http://www.gamasutra.com/view/feature/5883/a_deeper_look_into_the_combat_.php

[14] Russell, B. Designing Combat Encounters In *Uncharted 2*. Gamasutra.com. http://www.gamasutra.com/view/feature/5945/designing_combat_encounters_in_.php

[15] SIGGRAPH, Games Papers 2011. http://www.siggraph.org/s2011/for_submitters/game-papers

[16] Sofge, E. How *Halo: Reach* Was Created: Insider's Guide. PopularMechanics.com. http://www.popularmechanics.com/technology/gadgets/video-games/how-halo-reach-was-created-insiders-guide

[17] Thompson, C. *Halo 3*: How Microsoft Labs Invented a New Science of Play. Wired.com. http://www.wired.com/gaming/virtualworlds/magazine/15-09/ff_halo

[18] Van der Heijden, J. Successful Playtesting In *Swords & Soldiers*. Gamasutra.com

http://www.gamasutra.com/view/feature/5939/successful_playtesting_in_swords__.php

[19] Weber, B., John, M., Mateas, M., Jhala, A. Modeling Player Retention in Madden NFL 11. In Proceedings of *Innovative Applications of Artificial Intelligence*. 2011.

[20] Weber, B., Mateas, M. A data mining approach to strategy prediction. In *IEEE Symposium on Computational Intelligence and Games, 2009*.

Handling Categorical Variables in Effort Estimation

Masateru Tsunoda
Toyo University
2100 Kujirai, Kawagoe, Saitama
350-8585 Japan

tsunoda@toyo.jp

Sousuke Amasaki
Okayama Prefectural University
111 Kuboki, Soja, Okayama
719-1197 Japan

amasaki@cse.oka-pu.ac.jp

Akito Monden
Nara Institute of Science and
Technology, Kansai Science City
630-0192 Japan

akito-m@is.naist.jp

ABSTRACT

Background: Accurate effort estimation is the basis of the software development project management. The linear regression model is one of the widely-used methods for the purpose. A dataset used to build a model often includes categorical variables denoting such as programming languages. Categorical variables are usually handled with two methods: the stratification and dummy variables. Those methods have a positive effect on accuracy but have shortcomings. The other handing method, the interaction and the hierarchical linear model (HLM), might be able to compensate for them. However, the two methods have not been examined in the research area. **Aim:** giving useful suggestions for handling categorical variables with the stratification, transforming dummy variables, the interaction, or HLM, when building an estimation model. **Method:** We built estimation models with the four handling methods on ISBSG, NASA, and Desharnais datasets, and compared accuracy of the methods with each other. **Results:** The most effective method was different for datasets, and the difference was statistically significant on both mean balanced relative error (*MBRE*) and mean magnitude of relative error (*MMRE*). The interaction and HLM were effective in a certain case. **Conclusions:** The stratification and transforming dummy variables should be tried at least, for obtaining an accurate model. In addition, we suggest that the application of the interaction and HLM should be considered when building the estimation model.

Categories and Subject Descriptors

D.2.9 [**Software Engineering**]: Management – *Cost estimation*, K.6.1 [**Computing Milieux**]: Project and People Management – *Staffing*

Keywords

Model-based effort estimation, dummy variable, stratification, interaction, hierarchical linear model, mixed effects.

1. INTRODUCTION

Software development effort estimation is the basis of the project management. Model-based effort estimation methods have been studied well for its quantitative nature. The linear regression is

one of the widely-used methods. In model building, a past project dataset is used for parameter inference. A typical regression-based model is as follows:

$$\text{Effort} = \text{Size}^{\beta_s} x_1^{\beta_1} e^{\beta_2 x_2 + \beta_0 + \varepsilon}. \quad (1)$$

Size represents a functional size and other terms are attributes of a target project. β_k are parameters to be inferred, and ε is an error term. When β_s is greater than 1, the model signifies diseconomies of scale. When β_s is smaller than 1, it signifies economies of scale.

Log-transformed Eq. (1) is often used for parameter inference:

$$\log(\text{Effort}) = \beta_s \log(\text{Size}) + \beta_1 \log(x_1) + \beta_2 x_2 + \beta_0 + \varepsilon. \quad (2)$$

Attributes in a dataset can be classified into ratio (or ordinal) scale and nominal scale. For example, the functional size and effort are ratio scale attributes, and the programming language is the nominal scale attribute (categorical variables). In many studies on effort estimation models, categorical variables were handled with two ways: stratification [10] and dummy variables.

The stratification divides a dataset into subsets according to levels of categorical variables, and multiple models are built based on the subsets. Each model has parameters specific to a subset *j*:

$$\log(\text{Effort}) = \beta_{sj} \log(\text{Size}) + \beta_{1j} \log(x_1) + \beta_{2j} x_2 + \beta_{0j} + \varepsilon. \quad (3)$$

Dummy variables are used when a categorical variable is considered as predictor. A categorical variable is transformed into multiple dummy binary variables. Those are treated as ordinal scale. If a categorical variable is transformed into a dummy variable *y*, an equation takes the following form:

$$\log(\text{Effort}) = \beta_s \log(\text{Size}) + \beta_1 \log(x_1) + \beta_2 x_2 + \beta_0 + \beta_4 y + \varepsilon. \quad (4)$$

Dummy variables make difference only on the intercept (The model expresses either diseconomies of scale or economies of scale for all categories). Stratification is more flexible in this sense. However, stratification is disadvantageous in that its estimation accuracy may be low when an estimation model is built with small subset. In addition, these handling methods do not cover the model that a categorical variable has an effect only on economies/diseconomies of size.

The problems can be handled with two methods: the interaction and hierarchical linear model (HLM). The interaction [1] can handle the restriction on modeling of economies/diseconomies. The HLM [3] can mitigate the disadvantage. However, those method have rarely used in the literature. Furthermore, the effects of those four handling methods have not been evaluated comparatively.

The goal of this research is to give useful suggestions for handling categorical variable methods when building an effort estimation model based on the linear regression model. To achieve the goal, we set research questions as follows:

- RQ1. Are effort estimation accuracies of the models different from each categorical variable handling method?
- RQ2. (If the answer of RQ1 is "yes") Is there categorical variable handling method whose performance (the accuracy of the model built by the method) is the highest or the lowest in any case?
- RQ3. (If the answer of RQ2 is "no") Should we consider application of the interaction or HLM? (That is, are the accuracies of the models with the interaction or HLM higher than other methods in some cases?)

2. TREATING CATEGORICAL VARIABLE
2.1 Stratification
The stratification divides a dataset into subsets based on the values of a categorical variable. Estimation models are built with each subset. For instance, when a dataset includes a categorical variable denoting a programming language either "C" or "Java", the stratification divides the dataset into two subsets. Then, two estimation models are built with the two subsets. When a target project plans to use C, the estimation model for C is used.

The advantage of the stratification is building more flexible model than the dummy variable model. That is, with the stratification, the model of economies of scale can be built for some categories, and the model of diseconomies of scale can be built for the other categories. The disadvantage is that the estimation accuracy may be low when an estimation model is built with a small subset.

2.2 Dummy variables
Dummy variables are used to transform categorical variables into numerical variables. When a categorical variable has n categories, $n - 1$ dummy variables are defined. If a dummy variable corresponds with a category, its value is set to 1. If not, the value is set to 0. For example, when a categorical variable denotes a programming language either "C" or "Java", a dummy variable "C" is made. If a target project plans to use C, "C" is set to 1. If Java is used, "C" is set to 0. An estimation model using dummy variables is less flexible than a group of estimation models using stratified subsets. In the model, a categorical variable cannot have any influence on diseconomies/economies of scale.

The advantage of transforming dummy variables is that the number of required data points is smaller than the stratification, to build estimation model properly. As a rule of thumb, a linear regression model requires more than five times larger size of data points than the number of independent variables [14]. Suppose that a dataset includes b non-categorical variables and one categorical variable having a categories. The rule of thumb requires $5(a + b - 1)$ data points for dummy variables while $5ab$ data points for the stratification. The difference becomes larger as b becomes larger.

2.3 Interaction
The interaction [1] uses dummy variables so that a regression coefficient varies according to values of the dummy variables. The interaction assumes that a categorical variable itself has no effect to the dependent variable, but the combination of the categorical variable and another variable has the effect. The interaction introduces new variables made by multiplying an independent variable by dummy variables. For instance, when log(Size)

denotes functional size and y denotes a dummy variable, the new variable is log(Size)y. The resultant model includes the new variable as follows:

$$\log(\text{Effort}) = \beta_s \log(\text{Size}) + \beta_1 \log(x_1) + \beta_2 x_2 + \beta_0 + \beta_4 \log(\text{Size})y + \varepsilon. \quad (5)$$

The equation can be transformed as:

$$\log(\text{Effort}) = (\beta_s + \beta_4 y)\log(\text{Size}) + \beta_1 \log(x_1) + \beta_2 x_2 + \beta_0 + \varepsilon. \quad (6)$$

In the equation, the relationship between log(Effort) and Size is determined by $\beta_s + \beta_4 y$, and its value varies according to y. Thus, using the interaction, the model expresses diseconomies of scale and economies of scale.

To avoid multicollinearity between a main effect (log(Size)) and an interaction (log(Size)y), the average of main effect is subtracted from each value of main effect before building the model. This procedure is called as centering.

2.4 Hierarchical linear model
The hierarchical linear model (HLM) [3] is used in some research areas such as social science, to analyze the dataset where data points are cohesive with some groups (e.g. countries or schools). HLM builds an estimation model using models based on subsets divided by a categorical variable and the information gained from the whole dataset. HLM makes more flexible model than the dummy variable model.

The HLM considers the errors within categories and the errors between categories and builds models whose intercept and partial regression coefficients are different from each category. The HLM presumes models as shown in Eq. (2) for each category. An intercept and partial regression coefficients on the models are expressed by the following form:

$$\beta_i = \gamma_{i0} + \mu_i. \quad (7)$$

In the equation, γ_{i0} is the average of an intercept or a partial regression coefficient of the models, and μ_i is the errors between categories. ε in Eq. (2) is the errors within categories. Eq. (7) is set to any intercept and partial regression coefficient.

HLM first builds Eq. (2) model for each category using linear regression analysis, and estimates parameters in Eq. (7). After that, based on them, HLM uses empirical Bayes to decide the intercept and partial regression coefficients in Eq. (2) for each category.

3. EXPERIMENT
3.1 Datasets
In the experiment, we build effort estimation models using categorical variable handling methods, and compare estimation accuracy among them for evaluation. We used ISBSG dataset [8], NASA dataset [2], and Desharnais dataset [7]. These datasets recorded categorical variables that have at least three categories, and have relatively many data points.

Dummy variables were made for each categorical variable. We converted a categorical variable with n levels into n-1 binary dummy variables. ISBSG dataset and NASA dataset have multiple categorical variables. We stratified the datasets according to all combinations of values of the categorical variables. For example, when variable A has m categories, and variable B bas n categories, (m - 1) (n - 1) subsets are made at most.

The ISBSG dataset (Release 9) includes 3026 data points (projects) and 99 variables. We selected projects and variables based on the previous study [9], and excluded projects having a missing value (listwise deletion). We stratified the dataset and removed subsets which did not have at least 10 data points, because we applied 10 fold cross validation. As a result, 558 data points remained. Independent variables are: unadjusted function point and three categorical variables (development type, programming language, and development platform). Fourteen subsets and eight dummy variables were produced for the dataset.

The NASA dataset includes 93 data points. We stratified the dataset and 54 data points remained after removal of small subsets. Independent variables are: lines of code (estimated based on the function points [11]), productivity factors (six-level Likert scale), and three categorical variables (application type, system type, and development type). Three subsets and five dummy variables were produced for the dataset.

The Desharnais dataset includes 81 data points. We removed data points having a missing value, and 77 data points remained. We stratified the dataset, and all subsets remained. Independent variables are: adjusted function point, years of experience of team, years of experience of manager, and one categorical variable (programming language). Three subsets and two dummy variables were produced for the dataset.

3.2 Experimental Setting

As benchmark, we made a baseline estimation model for each dataset. The baseline models do not use any categorical variable. In the baseline estimation models, effort and size measurement were log-transformed. The handling methods were applied to the baseline models.

The interaction and HLM assumes that a relationship between effort and size measurement changes according to a categorical variable. For evaluation of the interaction, we added new variables made by multiplying functional size by dummy variables. For evaluation of HLM, we applied Eq. (7) to a partial regression coefficient of a functional size.

When a dataset had relatively many variables for sample size, we applied a variable selection based on AIC (Akaike's information criterion). The NASA dataset met the criterion in this experiment. HLM could not conduct variable selection because the HLM software we used did not support the function. Accordingly, we also performed the experiment with the NASA dataset removing productivity factors. We call it NASA FP dataset.

To evaluate the estimation accuracy, we used mean *MRE* (Magnitude of Relative Error) [6] (*MMRE*) and mean *BRE* (Balanced Relative Error) [12] (*MBRE*). Although *MRE* is widely used to evaluate effort estimation accuracy, it has biases for evaluating under estimation [4]. So we also adopted *BRE* whose evaluation is not biased, and gave weight to *BRE*. A lower value of each criterion indicates higher accuracy. The criteria were calculated for each treatment method according to 10 fold cross validation. We made training datasets and test datasets where the rate of each category is almost same as whole dataset.

3.3 Results

Table 1 shows estimation accuracy of the baseline models. Figure 1 shows the difference of *MBRE* between a model with a handling method and the corresponding baseline model. Figure 2 shows the difference of *MMRE*. A model with the highest positive difference is the most accurate one. The difference of *MBRE* for the stratification on the NASA dataset was outside the figure for

Table 1. *MBRE* and *MMRE* without categorical variables

	ISBSG	Desharnais	NASA FP	NASA
MBRE	166.1%	76.0%	150.5%	108.5%
MMRE	112.5%	61.5%	69.9%	78.4%

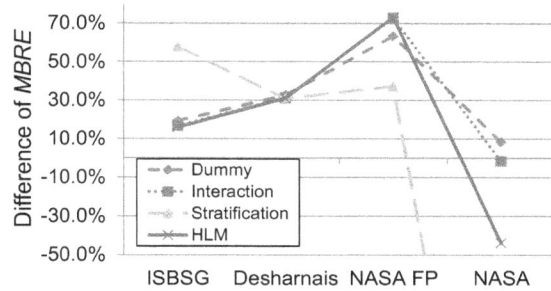

Figure 1. Difference of *MBRE* on each dataset

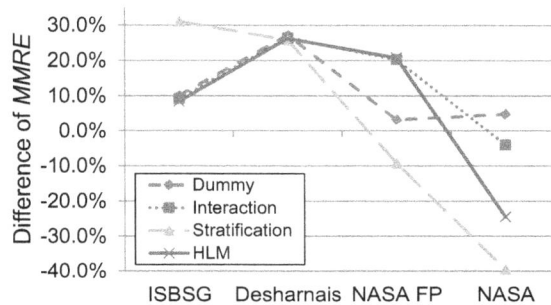

Figure 2. Difference of *MMRE* on each dataset

readability. The baseline models resulted in worse *MBRE* on the NASA FP dataset than on the NASA dataset. With the handling methods, the results had higher accuracy on the NASA FP dataset than on the NASA dataset (*MBRE* of HLM was 77.3%, and transforming dummy variables was 100.1%).

All but the stratification had similar tendency. The accuracy of HLM on the NASA dataset is not high. This would be because HLM did not conduct variable selection. On the contrary, the accuracy of the stratification was lower than those of the others in the NASA dataset (The difference of *MBRE* was minus 265.6%). Inclusion of many independent variables might cause the result. The stratification needs many data points when a dataset has many independent variables (see section 2.2). The result implies that choosing the stratification may result in lower performance when there are many independent variables. Note that the number of data points of each subset was enough in other datasets.

To answer RQ1 and RQ2, we confirmed the difference of estimation accuracy among the methods with the Friedman test. As a result, in the ISBSG dataset and the NASA FP dataset, the difference was statistically significant on both *MBRE* and *MMRE* (*P*-value was smaller than 0.05). We thus concluded that the answer to RQ1 is "yes" because estimation accuracy is different among the handling methods and that the answer to RQ2 is "no" because there is no handling method whose performance is always the highest or the lowest.

To answer RQ3, we confirmed the difference of estimation accuracy between alternative methods (HLM and the interaction) and common methods (dummy variables and the stratification) with the Wilcoxon signed rank test. The test did not show the statistical difference. However, on the NASA FP dataset, *MBRE* of HLM and the interaction were about 10% higher than transforming dummy variables (*MBRE* of HLM was 77.3%, the interaction was 77.5%, and transforming dummy variables was 87.2%). We think 10% difference is not ignorable. In addition, as shown in Figure 2, the difference of *MMRE* is large (The difference is about 17%). We thus concluded that the answer to RQ3 is "Yes (We should consider the interaction or HLM)."

4. RELATED WORK

There are few researches which used the interaction or HLM in the software engineering research area. However, they did not apply the methods to (ordinary) effort estimation model, and therefore their effects on effort estimation are not clear.

Moses et al. [13] proposed contingency (preliminary effort) estimation model, using hierarchical Bayesian model (Both the model and HLM have basically same mechanism). The model is not ordinary effort estimation model, since the independent variable is estimated effort, and the dependent variable is actual effort. Cataldo et al. [5] analyzed failures in feature-oriented software development using the logistic regression model with the interaction, and this is not effort estimation. Menzies et al. [10] showed the stratification is effective in some subsets. However, they used only one dataset and did not compare the stratification with the interaction and HLM.

5. CONCLUSIONS

In this paper, we set our research goal as giving useful suggestions to enhance the accuracy of an effort estimation model based on the linear regression analysis. We compared the estimation accuracy of linear regression models among four categorical variable handling methods. In our experiment, we applied transforming dummy variables, the stratification, the interaction, and HLM (hierarchical linear model). They were compared on three datasets in its effectiveness on estimation accuracy.

The experimental results showed that the most effective method is different for datasets. The finding suggests that the stratification and transforming dummy variables should be tried at least, for obtaining an accurate model. The experiment also suggested the interaction and HLM may have an effect in some cases. Therefore, the application of them should be considered when building the estimation model. We believe our suggestions are effective for many cases because the linear regression model is widely used for effort estimation. As future work, we will apply the handling methods to other datasets to examine how much the difference of handling methods is on the reliability of the results.

6. REFERENCES

[1] Aiken, L., West, S. 1991. *Multiple Regression: Testing and Interpreting Interactions*. SAGE Publications, Thousand Oaks, CA.

[2] Boetticher, G., Menzies, T., and Ostrand, T. 2007. *PROMISE Repository of empirical software engineering data* http://promisedata.org/?cat=11, West Virginia University, Department of Computer Science.

[3] Bryk, A., Raudenbush, S. 1992. *Hierarchical Linear Models for Social and Behavioral Research: Applications and Data Analysis Methods*. SAGE Publications, Thousand Oaks, CA.

[4] Burgess, C., and Lefley, M. 2001. Can genetic programming improve software effort estimation? A comparative evaluation. *Journal of Information and Software Technology* 43, 14, 863-873.

[5] Cataldo, M., and Herbsleb, J. 2011. Factors leading to integration failures in global feature-oriented development: an empirical analysis. *In Proc. of the International Conference on Software Engineering (ICSE 2011)*, 161-170.

[6] Conte, S., Dunsmore, H., and Shen, V. 1986. *Software Engineering, Metrics and Models*. Benjamin/Cummings.

[7] Desharnais, J. 1989. *Analyse Statistique de la Productivitie des Projets Informatique a Partie de la Technique des Point des Function*. Master Thesis. University of Montreal.

[8] International Software Benchmarking Standards Group (ISBSG). 2004. *ISBSG Estimating: Benchmarking and research suite*. ISBSG.

[9] Lokan, C., and Mendes, E. 2006. Cross-company and single-company effort models using the ISBSG Database: a further replicated study. *In Proc. of the international symposium on Empirical software engineering (ISESE 2006)*, 75-84.

[10] Menzies, T., Chen, Z., Hihn, J., and Lum., K. 2006. Selecting Best Practices for Effort Estimation. *IEEE Trans. Softw. Eng.* 32, 11 (Nov. 2006), 883-895.

[11] Menzies, T., Port, D., Chen, Z., Hihn, J., and Stukes, S.: Validation methods for calibrating software effort models. *In Proc. of the international conference on Software engineering (ICSE 2005)*, 587-595.

[12] Miyazaki, Y., Terakado, M., Ozaki, K., and Nozaki, H. 1994. Robust Regression for Developing Software Estimation Models. *J. Syst. Softw.* 27, 1 (October 1994), 3-16.

[13] Moses, J., and Farrow, M. 2003. A Procedure for Assessing the Influence of Problem Domain on Effort Estimation Consistency. *Software Quality Control* 11, 4 (November 2003), 283-300.

[14] Tan, H. B., Zhao, Y., and Zhang, H. 2009. Conceptual data model-based software size estimation for information systems. *ACM Trans. Softw. Eng. Methodol.* 19, 2, Article 4 (October 2009), 37 pages.

Discretization Methods for NBC in Effort Estimation: An Empirical Comparison based on ISBSG Projects

Marta Fernández-Diego
Department of Business Administration
Universitat Politècnica de València
46022 Valencia, Spain
(+34) 96 387 76 85

marferdi@omp.upv.es

José-María Torralba-Martínez
Department of Business Administration
Universitat Politècnica de València
46022 Valencia, Spain
(+34) 96 387 76 85

jtorral@omp.upv.es

ABSTRACT

Background: Bayesian networks have been applied in many fields, including effort estimation in software engineering. Even though there are Bayesian inference algorithms than can handle continuous variables, performance tends to be better when these variables are discretized that when they are assumed to follow a specific distribution. On the other hand, the choice of the discretization method and the number of discretized intervals may lead to significantly different estimating results. However, discretization issues are seldom mentioned in software engineering effort estimation models.

Aim: This paper seeks to show that discretization issues are important in terms of prediction accuracy while building a Naive Bayes Classifier (NBC) for estimating software effort.

Method: For this purpose, a NBC model has been developed for software effort estimation based on ISBSG projects applying different discretization schemes (equal width intervals, equal frequency intervals, and k-means clustering) and using different number of intervals.

Results: Regarding the NBC model built, the estimation accuracy of equal frequency discretization is only improved by k-means clustering with respect to Pred(0.25), although it reflects better the original distribution.

Conclusions: Further experimentation should determine the potential of clustering methods already highlighted in other fields.

Categories and Subject Descriptors

D.2.9 [**Software Engineering**]: Management – *cost estimation*;
G.3 [**Probability and statistics**]: Probabilistic algorithms (including Monte Carlo).

General Terms

Management, Measurement, Experimentation.

Keywords

Effort estimation, software projects, Bayesian networks, Naive Bayes Classifier, discretization methods, ISBSG.

1. INTRODUCTION

Even though there are Bayesian inference algorithms than can handle continuous variables, performance tends to be better when these variables are discretized that when they are assumed to follow a specific distribution [4]. Since this assumption is not always realistic, a discretization algorithm is needed to handle continuous variables.

For NBC, many discretization methods have been employed. Because of their simplicity, the unsupervised methods are appealing and remain the most common approaches. On one hand, it was found in [31] that equal-frequency interval discretization in conjunction with the NB learning scheme can give excellent results. On the other hand, why fixed k-interval discretization works for NBC was analyzed in [11]. However the choice of the discretization method and the number of discretized intervals may lead to significantly different estimating results.

This paper seeks to show that discretization issues are important in terms of prediction accuracy while building a NBC for estimating software development effort. However, these issues are seldom mentioned and comparison of different discretization methods are usually carried out generally and not in a particular field.

2. REVIEW OF DISCRETIZATION ISSUES IN BAYESIAN NETWORKS FOR SOFTWARE EFFORT ESTIMATION

Since the number of results when inputting the search terms "discretization", "Bayes" and "effort" grouped in pairs into several search engines (ACM Digital Library, IEEE Xplore, ScienceDirect, and Web of Knowledge) was insignificant, this section is based on a previous literature review of the use of Bayesian networks and NBC for effort estimation in software development projects. Then the discretization issues were highlighted from each retrieved paper. The aim was to identify which studies explicitly consider discretization issues.

From the literature review, Table 1 provides a chronological list of works using either Bayesian networks or NBC for effort and productivity estimation in software development projects, which has been contrasted with [23]. In total 22 papers were retrieved, related with the use of either Bayesian networks or NBC for effort estimation in software development projects. Most of the papers, 13 in total, explicitly consider discretization issues while 9 papers out of 22 do not mention the issue of discretization at all. However note that the discretization method can be implicitly guessed in three of these papers.

Table 1. Summary of Bayesian Networks and NBC for Effort Estimation in Software Engineering

Ref.	Year	Effort/ Prod	BN/ NBC	Expert / Data	Release	Number of projects	Discretization method	Number of intervals used in the discretization
[29]	2002	Effort	NBC	Data: ISBSG	R6	452	EW	10 intervals
[2]	2003	Prod	BN	Expert Data: COCOMO	1981	63	EW once logarithm transformation	Productivity: 7 intervals (Sturges' rule)
[27]	2003	Prod	BN	Data: COCOMO	1981	63	Expert	Productivity: 8 unequal intervals Other: 5 values
[5]	2004	Effort	BN	Expert: MODIST			Dynamic discretization (implicitly)	Up to 200 intervals for some variables
[28]	2004	Effort	BN	Expert				
[21]	2005	Effort	NBC	Two major companies in the northeastern US	1995	40	EF	Effort: 3 intervals using the Varis methodology and adjusting for sparse data
[20]	2006	Effort	BN	Expert				
[30]	2006	Effort	BN	Data: Older projects				
[15]	2007	Effort	BN	Data: Tukutuku		150	EF as suggested in [10]	5 intervals
[14]	2007	Effort	BN	Data: Tukutuku		150	EF as suggested in [10]	5 intervals
[22]	2007	Prod	NBC	Expert: MODIST Data: ISBSG	R9	1880	Dynamic discretization (implicitly)	
[25]	2007	Effort Prod	BN	Expert: MODIST Data: ISBSG	R9	1880	Dynamic discretization	
[1]	2008	Effort Prod	BN	Data: ISBSG	R7	20	EF	Productivity: 4 intervals
[16]	2008	Effort	BN	Data: Tukutuku		195	EF as suggested in [10]	5 intervals (expert)
[17]	2008	Effort	BN	Expert Data: Tukutuku		195	EF as suggested in [10]	5 intervals (expert)
[24]	2008	Prod	NBC	Expert Data: ISBSG / Jones	R9	2095	Dynamic discretization (implicitly)	
[26]	2008	Effort	NBC	Data: ISBSG Bank in Korea	R9	99 120		
[8]	2009	Effort	BN	20 Government organizations in the United Arab Emirates		27	EF	3 intervals
[9]	2009	Effort	BN	Expert Data: Motorola project, data from other papers			Dynamic discretization (implicitly)	
[3]	2010	Effort	BN	Data: ISBSG Greek telecom company	R7	22	EF	2 intervals
[12]	2011	Effort	BN	Data: ISBSG	R10			
[18]	2011	Effort	BN	Data: ISBSG	R10			

In the papers reviewed, the common approaches of handling continuous variables are the following:

- Discretize them creating equally likely intervals: [21], [15], [14], [1], [16], [17], [8], [3]

- Use the dynamic discretization algorithm [19] implemented in the AgenaRisk software: [5], [22], [25], [24], [9]. Dynamic discretization [13] allows not defining the fixed node states when the model is built.

- Use equal width intervals: [29], [2]

- Use intervals given by an expert: [27]

However one thing is mentioning dicretization issues and another different thing is the importance given to data discretization. Although some tools allow the use of parametric models to address the problem of specifying the conditional probability tables, the choice of the discretization scheme is still important since the assumption of parametric distributions for the continuous variables is not always realistic.

In this sense, in five papers ([2], [5], [25], [9], [3]) the validity of the results is questioned in such a way that the narrower the interval, the more accurate the estimate. In practice, the discretization chosen must be a tradeoff between the accuracy of the evidence added and computational feasibility [9]. However, in [3] the authors remind that the discretization is necessary not only because of the nature of the method but also because of the fact that it is safer to produce estimation in intervals. Moreover the importance of the generation of meaningful intervals, appealing and understood by software managers is highlighted in [2].

Besides, since the choice of the discretization and the number of interval used in the discretization do affect the results, Mendes et al. ([15], [14], [16], [17]) suggested further investigation. In such papers equal frequency intervals algorithm was employed, as suggested in [10]. Regarding the number of intervals, some studies have employed three, five, seven, eight intervals, which highlight the absence of strict rules. In [16] and [17], five intervals were chosen accordingly basically to expert knowledge, while the Sturges' rule was only applied explicitly in [2] for the choice of the number of intervals.

On the other hand, two papers detail their discretization option without addressing the accuracy problem. In [21], Varis methodology for discretization of continuous variables for Bayesian networks was used, resulting in a discrete effort distribution with three equally likely intervals. As opposed to this approach, in [1] the authors intuitively decided the number of intervals with approximately equal number of projects. Finally, note that only two papers ([2], [27]) refer the log-normal distributions of the dependent variable.

3. EMPIRICAL RESULTS

Given that the ISBSG is a large and heterogeneous dataset, a data preparation process was required before applying any analysis to get a minimum of homogeneity in the sample to be studied. These rules were adapted from [6] for our empirical experiment. Although the initial dataset comprised 5052 projects, preprocessing, missing data and outliers removal resulted in a final subset of 649 projects, 584 of them were used in the training set for building the model, while the remaining 65 projects, 10% of the total, were kept for the validation set.

The resulting NBC model for software effort estimation is showed in Fig. 1. Note that the nominal factors remained were re-categorized converting them into binary state variables [7].

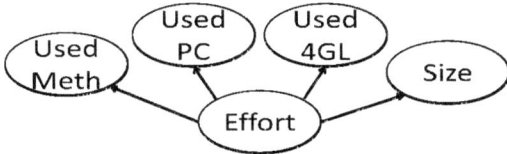

Figure 1. The resulting Naive Bayes Classifier (NBC).

As the dependent variable is a continuous one as well as one of the influencing factors, both variables have been categorized. For this, we take first the natural log transformation searching normality, and then follow different discretization schemes: equal width binning, equal frequency binning, and k-means clustering.

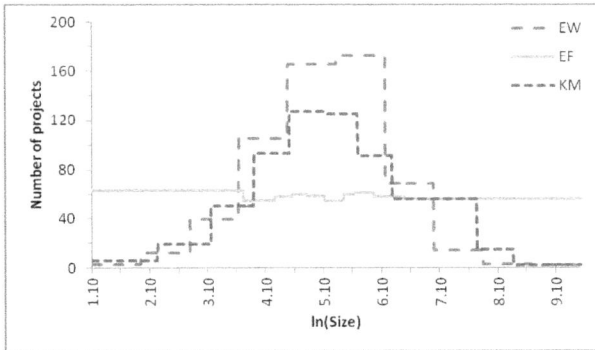

Figure 2. 10 bins discretization for "Size" once normalized.

Since we thought that different number of intervals for the continuous variables, i.e., the thinness of the discretization, would lead to different NBC accuracy results, the discretizations were performed with 3, 5, and 10 bins. Fig. 2 displays the number of projects as a function of log-transformed "Size" variable, where the number of bins is set to 10 for equal width, equal frequency, and k-means methods. We can see how the proposed k-means based intervals discretization offers a tradeoff between equal width and equal frequency discretization.

Table 2 to 4 summarize the values obtained for the different accuracy metrics regarding equal width discretization, equal

frequency discretization, and K-means clustering. The choice of the number of bins applied to each continuous variable independently led to nine NBC models. The values highlighted in bold font indicate the best estimation accuracy for each accuracy indicator.

Table 2. Accuracy Measures for EW Discretization

			Effort		
			3 Bins	5 Bins	10 Bins
Size	3 Bins	MMRE	1.4272	1.2958	1.2583
		MdMRE	0.7140	0.6908	0.7075
		Pred(0.25)	0.1077	0.1538	0.1538
	5 Bins	MMRE	0.9242	0.8002	0.8152
		MdMRE	0.4963	0.5261	0.5433
		Pred(0.25)	0.2308	0.2923	**0.3231**
	10 Bins	MMRE	1.0269	**0.7631**	1.0541
		MdMRE	0.5270	**0.4263**	0.4791
		Pred(0.25)	0.2154	0.2308	0.2308

Table 3. Accuracy Measures for EF Discretization

			Effort		
			3 Bins	5 Bins	10 Bins
Size	3 Bins	MMRE	0.7695	0.6397	**0.6211**
		MdMRE	0.5408	**0.3935**	0.4138
		Pred(0.25)	0.2154	**0.3385**	0.3077
	5 Bins	MMRE	0.8752	0.7450	0.7552
		MdMRE	0.6019	0.4593	0.4296
		Pred(0.25)	0.1692	0.2615	0.2923
	10 Bins	MMRE	0.8323	0.7877	0.7419
		MdMRE	0.5516	0.5126	0.4709
		Pred(0.25)	0.2308	0.2308	0.2462

Table 4. Accuracy Measures for K-Means Clustering

			Effort		
			3 Bins	5 Bins	10 Bins
Size	3 Bins	MMRE	0.8473	0.7552	**0.7333**
		MdMRE	0.5397	0.4747	0.4659
		Pred(0.25)	0.1692	0.3077	0.3077
	5 Bins	MMRE	0.9141	0.8884	0.8248
		MdMRE	0.6210	0.5237	0.5237
		Pred(0.25)	0.2154	0.2308	0.2615
	10 Bins	MMRE	0.8484	0.7612	0.9680
		MdMRE	0.5387	0.4215	**0.4188**
		Pred(0.25)	0.2000	0.3231	**0.3538**

In fact comparing the different discretization techniques, k-means clustering improves equal width discretization in absolute terms. However equal frequency discretization presents the best estimation accuracy results in terms of MMRE and MdMRE. The estimation accuracy is only improved by k-means clustering with respect to Pred(0.25), although it reflects better the original distribution.

4. CONCLUSIONS

This study worked on the latest release of the ISBSG dataset (R11). For the subset considered, the results suggest that equal frequency discretization performed on the natural log-transformed continuous variables can improve the accuracy results, in terms of most evaluation criteria.

On the other hand, the choice of the discretization thinness did produce different accurate estimates. However, the discretization method and the choice of the number of intervals are intrinsically linked, so experimentation is usually needed to determine an appropriate number of bins. Finally, the influence of the discretization is different depending on whether it concerns the dependent variable or the independent variable, which is reflected in the asymmetry of Table 2 to 4.

5. REFERENCES

[1] Bibi, S. and Stamelos, I. 2008. Estimating the Development Cost for Intelligent Systems. *Intelligent Interactive Systems in Knowledge-Based Environments Studies in Computational Intelligence.* Virvou, M. 25-45.

[2] Bibi, S., Stamelos, I. et al. 2003. Bayesian Belief Networks as a Software Productivity Estimation Tool. *1st Balkan Conference in Informatics, Thessaloniki.* (2003).

[3] Bibi, S., Stamelos, I. et al. 2010. BBN based approach for improving the software development process of an SME—a case study. *Journal of Software Maintenance and Evolution: Research and Practice.* 22, (Mar. 2010).

[4] Dougherty, J., Kohavi, R. et al. 1995. Supervised and Unsupervised Discretization of Continuous Features. *Proceedings of the Twelfth International Conference on Machine Learning* (1995), 194-202.

[5] Fenton, N., Marsh, W. et al. 2004. Making Resource Decisions for Software Projects. *Proceedings of the 26th International Conference on Software Engineering* (Washington, DC, USA, 2004), 397-406.

[6] Fernández-Diego, M., Martínez-Gómez, M. et al. 2010. Sensitivity of results to different data quality meta-data criteria in the sample selection of projects from the ISBSG dataset. *Proceedings of the 6th International Conference on Predictive Models in Software Engineering* (New York, NY, USA, 2010), 13:1–13:9.

[7] Fernández-Diego, M., Elmouaden, S. et al. 2012. Software Effort Estimation using NBC and SWR: A comparison based on ISBSG projects. *Proceedings of the Joint Conference of the 22nd International Workshop on Software Measurement (IWSM) and the 7th International Conference on Software Process and Product Measurement (Mensura)* (Assisi, Italy, 2012), 1–5.

[8] Hamdan, K., Bibi, S. et al. 2009. A bayesian belief network cost estimation model that incorporates cultural and project leadership factors. *IEEE Symposium on Industrial Electronics & Applications* (2009), 985-989.

[9] Hearty, P., Fenton, N. et al. 2009. Predicting Project Velocity in XP Using a Learning Dynamic Bayesian Network Model. *IEEE Transactions on Software Engineering.* 35, 1 (2009), 124-137.

[10] Ho, E.K.Y. and Knobbe, A.J. 2005. Numbers in multi-relational data mining. *Lecture Notes in Computer Science.* 3721, (2005), 544-551.

[11] Hsu, C., Huang, H. et al. 2000. Why Discretization Works for Naive Bayesian Classifiers. *Proceedings of the Seventeenth International Conference on Machine Learning* (2000), 309-406.

[12] Khan, J., Shaikh, Z.A. et al. 2011. Development of Intelligent Effort Estimation Model Based on Fuzzy Logic Using Bayesian Networks. *Communications in Computer and Information Science.* 257, (2011), 74-84.

[13] Kozlov, A. and Koller, D. 1997. Nonuniform Dynamic Discretization in Hybrid Networks. *Thirteenth Conference on Uncertainty in Artificial Intelligence* (1997), 314-325.

[14] Mendes, E. 2007. A Comparison of Techniques for Web Effort Estimation. *First International Symposium on Empirical Software Engineering and Measurement (ESEM)* (2007), 334-343.

[15] Mendes, E. 2007. Predicting Web Development Effort Using a Bayesian Network. *11th International Conference on Evaluation and Assessment in Software Engineering (EASE)* (2007), 83-93.

[16] Mendes, E. 2008. The Use of Bayesian Networks for Web Effort Estimation: Further Investigation. *Eighth International Conference on Web Engineering (ICWE 2008)* (Washington, DC, USA, 2008), 203–216.

[17] Mendes, E. and Mosley, N. 2008. Bayesian Network Models for Web Effort Prediction: A Comparative Study. *IEEE Transactions on Software Engineering.* 34, (Nov. 2008), 723–737.

[18] Nauman, A.B. and Aziz, R. 2011. Development of Simple Effort Estimation Model based on Fuzzy Logic using Bayesian Networks. *International Journal of Computer Applications.* 3, Special Issue on "Artificial Intelligence Techniques - Novel Approaches & Practical Applications" (2011), 31-34.

[19] Neil, M., Tailor, M. et al. 2007. Inference in hybrid Bayesian networks using dynamic discretization. *Statistics and Computing.* 17, (2007).

[20] Noothong, T. and Sutivong, D. 2006. Software Project Management Using Decision Networks. *Sixth International Conference on Intelligent Systems Design and Applications* (Jinan, 2006), 1124-1129.

[21] Pendharkar, P., Subramanian, G. et al. 2005. A probabilistic model for predicting software development effort. *IEEE Transactions on Software Engineering.* 31, 7 (2005), 615-624.

[22] Radliński, Ł., Fenton, N. et al. 2007. Modelling prior productivity and defect rates in a causal model for software project risk assessment. *Polish Journal of Environmental Studies.* 16, 4A (2007), 256-260.

[23] Radliński, Ł. 2010. A Survey of Bayesian Net Models for Software Development Effort Prediction. *International Journal of Software Engineering and Computing.* 2, 2 (2010), 95-109.

[24] Radliński, Ł., Fenton, N. et al. 2008. Estimating Productivity and Defect Rates Based on Environmental Factors. *Information Systems Architecture and Technology: Models of the Organisation's Risk Management* (Wrocław, Poland, 2008), 103–113.

[25] Radliński, Ł., Fenton, N. et al. 2007. Improved decision-making for software managers using Bayesian networks. *11th International Conference on Software Engineering and Applications* (Anaheim, CA, USA, 2007), 13–19.

[26] Seo, Y., Yoon, K. et al. 2008. An empirical analysis of software effort estimation with outlier elimination. *Proceedings of the 6th International Conference on Predictive Models in Software Engineering* (New York, NY, USA, 2008), 25–32.

[27] Stamelos, I., Angelis, L. et al. 2003. On the use of Bayesian belief networks for the prediction of software productivity. *Information and Software Technology.* 45, 1 (2003), 51-60.

[28] Stamelos, I. and Bibi, S. 2004. Software Process Modeling with Bayesian Belief Networks. *10th IEEE International Conference on Software METRICS* (September 2004).

[29] Stewart, B. 2002. Predicting project delivery rates using the Naive-Bayes classifier. *Journal of Software Maintenance: Research and Practice.* 14, (May. 2002), 161–179.

[30] Wang, H., Peng, F. et al. 2006. Software Project Level Estimation Model Framework based on Bayesian Belief Networks. *Proceedings of the Sixth International Conference on Quality Software* (Washington, DC, USA, 2006), 209–218.

[31] Witten, I.H. and Frank, E. 2005. *Data Mining: Practical Machine Learning Tools and Techniques.* Morgan Kaufmann.

Questioning Software Maintenance Metrics:
A Comparative Case Study

Dag I.K. Sjøberg
Department of Informatics,
University of Oslo, P.O. Box 1080
Blindern, NO-0316 Oslo, Norway

Dag.Sjoberg@ifi.uio.no

Bente Anda
Department of Informatics,
University of Oslo, P.O. Box 1080
Blindern, NO-0316 Oslo, Norway

Bente.Anda@ifi.uio.no

Audris Mockus
Department of Software,
Avaya Labs Research,
Basking Ridge, NJ 07920. USA

audris@avaya.com

ABSTRACT

Context: Many metrics are used in software engineering research as surrogates for maintainability of software systems. **Aim**: Our aim was to investigate whether such metrics are consistent among themselves and the extent to which they predict maintenance effort at the entire system level. **Method**: The Maintainability Index, a set of structural measures, two code smells (Feature Envy and God Class) and size were applied to a set of four functionally equivalent systems. The metrics were compared with each other and with the outcome of a study in which six developers were hired to perform three maintenance tasks on the same systems. **Results**: The metrics were not mutually consistent. Only system size and low cohesion were strongly associated with increased maintenance effort. **Conclusion**: Apart from size, surrogate maintainability measures may not reflect future maintenance effort. Surrogates need to be evaluated in the contexts for which they will be used. While traditional metrics are used to identify problematic areas in the code, the improvements of the worst areas may, inadvertently, lead to more problems for the entire system. Our results suggest that local improvements should be accompanied by an evaluation at the system level.

Categories and Subject Descriptors

D.2 SOFTWARE ENGINEERING

General Terms

Measurement, Experimentation

Keywords

Software maintenance, software metrics

1. INTRODUCTION

It is well known that software maintenance is costly and effort intensive. Therefore, software systems should be maintainable. However, how do we know which systems will be maintainable? What designs and implementations of a given set of requirements would be most maintainable? How can source code be improved to make it more maintainable?

To help answer such questions, much of software engineering research over the years has been devoted to *software maintenance*

metrics. Examples are the Maintainability Index [16], the CK metrics, including coupling and cohesion [5] and various code smells [9].

Previous research on the validation of these metrics and approaches has investigated systems that were functionally different. Differences in functionality make it difficult to isolate the effects of design choices from the functionality of the systems. In contrast, we are in a unique situation in that we have access to four industry-quality systems that are functionally equivalent. As a part of an investigation on the trade-offs between the costs of developing the systems and quality improvement, we assessed the maintainability of the four systems by using the metrics described above and the results of a particular maintenance study of these systems with six developers from two companies. In summary, the research questions of the study reported in this paper are as follows:

RQ1: Are commonly used software maintainability metrics mutually consistent at the system level?

RQ2: Are commonly used software maintainability metrics related to the actual maintenance effort observed in our study?

The remainder of this paper is organized as follows. Section 2 describes the four systems that are being the objects of this comparative study. Section 3 describes the maintenance metrics that were applied to the systems. Section 4 describes the results of the maintenance study on the systems. Section 5 discusses the results reported in the previous sections. Section 6 concludes.

2. THE FOUR SYSTEMS

The four systems available in this comparative case study were functionally equivalent (with the same requirements specifications) web-based information systems primarily implemented in Java. They were developed independently by four different companies at the costs of €18,000, €25,000, €52,000 and €61,000. The sizes of the four systems, named Systems A through D, are shown in the upper two rows of Table 1. The systems were developed as part of a study on the variability and reproducibility in software engineering [2].

3. SOFTWARE MAINTENANCE METRICS

This section describes the set of metrics that were selected because they are among the most used and well known.

3.1 Maintainability Index

The Maintainability Index (MI) has been proposed for assessing the maintainability of complete systems. The original three-metric MI uses a polynomial to combine the average per module of three traditional code measures (lines of code, cyclomatic complexity and Halstead Volume) into a single-value indicator of maintainability [16]. An improved four-metrics version of MI also includes the number of comments.

In conventional non-object-oriented systems, the values of the improved MI have been classified as follows: >85 indicate good maintainability; 65-85 indicate moderate maintainability; and 65 and below indicate poor maintainability with very poor pieces of code (big, uncommented, unstructured) [16].

To our knowledge, there are no heuristics for MI classification values for object-oriented systems. However, because classes are smaller in such systems than modules in conventional systems, researchers have argued that the thresholds for object-oriented systems should be higher [17]. This observation is consistent with the values that we found for our four systems. Table 1 shows that the MI values range from 113 (System A) to 120 (System D).

3.2 Structural Measures

The most common set of metrics for assessing code maintainability is structural measures (SM), including the CK metrics [5]. A previous study [3] used an adapted version of a subset of the CK metrics to evaluate the four systems that are also the subject of this study. The subset includes the coupling measure OMMIC (call to methods in an unrelated class), the cohesion measure TCC (tight class cohesion) and the measure of size of classes WMC1 (number of methods per class; each method has a weight of 1) and depth of inheritance tree (DIT). The values of the respective systems are shown in Table 1. By combining these and a few more metrics, the previous study ranked System D as the most maintainable one, System A slightly ahead of System B, and System C as the least maintainable system [3].

3.3 Code Smells

The concept of code smells was introduced as an indicator of problems with the software design [9]. Code smells have become an established way of indicating issues with software designs that may cause problems for future development and maintenance [9], [12]. However, a systematic review [18] found only five studies that investigated the impact of code smells on maintenance.

Nevertheless, we recently conducted a study [14] on the effects of 12 code smells on the maintenance effort in the four systems that are the subject of the study reported here. We found that only two smells negatively affected the maintenance effort (Feature Envy and God Class). However, this result was derived before we had adjusted for the file size and the number of changes. When we adjusted for these aspects, we found no effect. Still, to illustrate the use of code smells, we included the average number per KLOC of these two smells in the four systems in Table 1.

Note that the paper [14] identified the effects of various code smells on maintenance effort by analyzing the number of smells and the maintenance effort at the file level. We did not study the variation among the systems *per se*. Neither did we study whether refactoring of files to reduce smells, which may lead to reductions in size of the individual files, might increase the total system size and thus not improve the overall system maintainability. In contrast, the study reported here operates at the system level.

4. MAINTENANCE STUDY

Several maintenance metrics that were applied to the four systems were described above. However, how well do these metrics indicate actual maintainability (how easy it is to maintain the systems in practice)?

To find out, we conducted a controlled maintenance study on the four systems. We hired six developers for a total cost of €50,000 to perform three maintenance tasks each on two of the four functionally equivalent but independently developed Java systems. Three of the developers worked for a software company in the Czech Republic, and another set of three developers worked for a software company in Poland. We recruited the developers from a pool of 65 participants in an earlier study on programming skill [4] that also included maintenance tasks. Based on the results of that study, we selected these six developers because they could program reliably at medium to high levels of performance, reported high levels of motivation to participate in the study and were available to take part in new studies. In this case, the results of the former study became the pre-test measures for our study. In general, using pre-test measures to maximize the interpretability of the results is recommended [11].

The developers implemented two adaptive tasks that were needed to allow the systems to become operational again after changes had been made to the web platform. The developers also implemented a third task that was requested by the users. The amount of time that each developer spent on each file was automatically recorded by a plug-in to an Eclipse IDE. The study lasted three to four weeks in the Czech Republic and three weeks in Poland.

Each developer conducted the same three tasks on two different systems. There are two reasons for having the same developer maintain two systems. First, the relative impact of a system can be separated from the impact of the developer. Second, we could observe the developers' learning process when they implemented the same tasks the second time. These two rounds also correspond to two different settings commonly found in maintenance work: maintainers who are newcomers to a system and maintainers who are already familiar with it. Although the systems were assigned randomly to each developer, the four systems were maintained the same number of times (two) by each developer, and all of the systems were maintained at least once in each round.

The next lowest row of Table 1 shows the average amount of time that the developers spent on each of the systems. On average, the developers spent 39% less time on performing the tasks in the second round. We adjusted for this difference in the calculation of the average values in Table 1.

Usually in human-centric studies in software engineering, one measures the quality of the tasks performed by the subjects in addition to time (effort). Perhaps the most commonly used quality attribute is the number of defects. However, in our case, the acceptance tests showed that there were few defects in the systems after the maintenance tasks had been performed. Therefore, it was not meaningful to use defects as a quality indicator. Instead, we used the number of changes completed in the course of the task as an indicator of quality. The number of changes is typically found to be a good predictor of later defects, with more changes increasing the fault-proneness [10], [8]. Consequently, we also included the number of changes (revisions) performed to implement the tasks as the last control variable. The numbers were calculated using SVNKit [15], which is a Java library for obtaining information from Subversion the Subversion version control system.

The last row of Table 1 shows the average number of revisions per system. By combining the scores for effort and quality, Table 1 shows that System C is the most maintainable system. In contrast, System B has the lowest quality, and System A had the highest maintenance effort.

Table 1. Maintenance metrics and a maintenance study applied to the four systems
Legend: green indicates the best system and red the worst one

Category	Metrics	System A	System B	System C	System D
Size	Number of Java files	63	168	29	119
	Java lines of code (LOC)	8205	26679	4983	9960
Maintainability Index (MI)	LOC, # of comments, cyclomatic complexity, Halstead's volume	113	117	114	120
Structural measures (SM)	Coupling (OMMIC)	7.7	5.3	8.6	4.7
	Cohesion (TCC)	0.26	0.17	0.20	0.11
	Size of classes (WMC1)	6.9	7.8	11.4	4.9
	Depth of inheritance tree (DIT)	0.46	0.75	0	0.83
Code smells	Feature Envy (# per KLOC of code)	4.51	1.27	3.41	2.51
	God Class (# per KLOC of code)	0.12	0.19	0.60	0.20
Study of actual maintainability	Average effort (hours)	18	33	13	23
	Predictor of quality (avg. # changes)	148	125	76	124

5. COMPARISON AND DISCUSSION

Table 1 shows that none of the tailored maintenance metrics ranked the system that performed best in the maintenance study (System C) as the best one.

The Spearman rank correlations among the maintainability metrics and the observed maintenance effort and quality are shown in Table 2. High values of metrics MI, TCC and DIT are supposed to indicate high maintainability. (Note that higher DIT values are considered good at least up to three [6]. The DIT values in our study vary from 0 to 0.83 on average.) Therefore, to compare the variables directly with maintainability, expressed in the number of hours spent on the maintenance tasks, we inverted the MI, TCC and DIT.

The only two metrics that are highly correlated with effort are size and the inverse of cohesion (1/TCC). The remaining maintainability surrogate metrics are negatively correlated with the observed effort. Three of them, 1/MI, OMMIC and FE, have a high negative correlation.

The inconsistency among the metrics is striking. One reason for the inconsistency is that some metrics are strongly interdependent; that is, for a given system, improving the value of one metric may imply less favourable values for other ones. For example, achieving low coupling is more difficult if one also attempts to achieve high cohesion, and vice versa. Achieving high cohesion and low coupling among modules or classes would generally be easier if one were to increase their size, but then the overall maintainability would decrease because of the increase in the size of the module or class.

Similarly, some practices, such as the refactoring of God Classes, may lead to more files. Although this practice may decrease the size of what was originally a God-Class file, it would lead to a larger system overall. Thus, such apparent improvements induced by reducing the size of God Classes may make it more difficult to maintain the new refactored system.

The conformance between code size and the outcome of the maintenance study may not be surprising. Software engineering folklore states that reducing functionality will reduce maintenance problems. The systems in our study demonstrate the positive effect of reducing size (measured in number of files or total LOC) without reductions in functionality.

The answers to our research questions are as follows:

RQ1: The considered common maintainability metrics were not mutually consistent in the considered projects.

RQ2: Among the considered maintainability metrics, only size and the inverse of cohesion were strongly correlated with the actual maintenance effort observed in the study.

It is possible that metrics apart from size may play a role in reducing maintenance effort in large projects where it takes a long time (> 3 years) for developers to become fluent [19], but we see no evidence that they matter in our context.

Table 2. Spearman rank correlation matrix

	LOC	1/MI	OMMIC	1/TCC	WMC1	1/DIT	FE	GC	Hours	# chgs
LOC	1	-0.6	-0.8	0.6	-0.4	0.6	-0.8	-0.4	1	0.4
1/MI	-0.6	1	0.8	-1	0.4	1	0.8	-0.4	-0.6	0.4
OMMIC	-0.8	0.8	1	-0.8	0.8	1	0.6	0.2	-0.8	-0.2
1/TCC	0.6	-1	-0.8	1	-0.4	-1	-0.8	0.4	0.6	-0.4
WMC1	-0.4	0.4	0.8	-0.4	1	0.5	0	0.4	-0.4	-0.4
1/DIT	-0.5	1	1	-1	0.5	1	0.5	-1	-0.5	1
FE	-0.8	0.8	0.6	-0.8	0	0.5	1	-0.2	-0.8	0.2
GC	-0.4	-0.4	0.2	0.4	0.4	-1	-0.2	1	-0.4	-1
Hours	1	-0.6	-0.8	0.6	-0.4	-0.5	-0.8	-0.4	1	0.4
# chgs	0.4	0.4	-0.2	-0.4	-0.4	1	0.2	-1	0.4	1

Even though the study controlled for functionality and other factors, having only four sample points makes it difficult to make sweeping generalizations. The inherent inconsistency of maintainability metrics and the strength of the anti-correlations with observed maintainability, strongly suggest that, at least in the context of smaller scale projects, the size of the system may be the decisive factor determining actual maintainability.

6. CONCLUSIONS

The results of this comparative case study indicate that the existing software maintenance metrics are mutually inconsistent and that none of them, apart from size and the inverse of cohesion, are consistent with the results of a maintenance study of four systems that implemented the same functionality. Still, these metrics are used to validate a great number of technologies (processes, methods, techniques and tools) for supporting software maintenance. The choice of metrics, rather than actual maintainability, may determine the outcome of a study. For example, using the Maintainability Index, one could argue that hiring an expensive company with heavy processes (System D) improves maintainability. On the other hand, using size, one could claim that it is better to hire an inexpensive company with light processes (System C) because it will produce smaller systems that, consequently, are more maintainable.

Our results are consistent with the findings of a related systematic literature review [13]. The researchers of this study found that there was little evidence regarding the effectiveness of software maintainability prediction techniques and models.

Our study controlled for a number of factors including functionality, application domains and programming language, and the authors did not develop any of the metrics (lack of experimenter bias). Our contribution is the observation that at the entire system level, the simplest metric of size was the best predictor of maintainability.

Consequently, this study indicates that overall system size (as opposed to, e.g., file size or class size) as a measure of maintainability has been underrated in the software engineering community. However, the other "sophisticated" maintenance metrics are overrated. Researchers in software engineering should be cautious when using such metrics as surrogates for actual maintainability unless the metrics have been properly evaluated in the same context for which they serve as surrogates.

ACKNOWLEDGMENTS

We thank Aiko Yamashita for providing support with the data collection. This work was partly funded by the Research Council of Norway through the projects AGILE, grant 179851/I40, and TeamIT, grant 193236/I40.

REFERENCES

[1] B. Anda. Assessing Software System Maintainability using Structural Measures and Expert Assessments, Proc. 23rd Int'l Conf. on Software Maintenance, pp. 204-213, 2007.

[2] B.C.D. Anda, D.I.K. Sjøberg and A. Mockus. Variability and Reproducibility in Software Engineering: A Study of Four Companies that Developed the Same System, *IEEE Trans. Softw. Eng*, vol. 35, no. 3, pp. 407–429, 2009.

[3] H.C. Benestad, B. Anda and E. Arisholm. Assessing Software Product Maintainability Based on Class-Level Structural Measures, Proc. 7th Int'l Conf. on Product-focused Software Process Improvement, LNCS 3009, Springer-Verlag, pp. 94-111, 2006.

[4] G.R. Bergersen and J.E. Gustafsson, Programming Skill, Knowledge and Working Memory Among Professional Software Developers from an Investment Theory Perspective, *J. Individual Differences*, vol. 32, no. 4, pp. 201-209, 2011.

[5] S.R. Chidamber and C.F. Kemerer. A Metrics Suite for Object Oriented Design, *IEEE Trans. Softw. Eng.*, vol. 20, no. 6, pp. 476–493, 1994.

[6] J. Daly, A. Brooks, J. Miller, M. Roper and M. Wood. An Empirical Study Evaluating Depth of Inheritance on the Maintainability of Object-Oriented Software, *Empirical Softw. Eng.*, vol. 1, pp. 109-132, 1996.

[7] D. Darcy and C.F. Kemerer. OO Metrics in Practice, *IEEE Software*, vol. 22, no. 6, Nov./Dec. 2005, pp. 17–19, 2005.

[8] S.G. Eick, T L. Graves, A. F. Karr, J.S. Marron and A. Mockus, Does code decay? Assessing the evidence from change management data, *IEEE Trans. on Softw. Eng.*, vol. 27, no. 7, pp. 1-12, 2001.

[9] M. Fowler. Refactoring: Improving the Design of Existing Code. Addison-Wesley, 1999.

[10] T. Hall, S. Beecham, D. Bowes, D. Gray and S. Counsell. A Systematic Review of Fault Prediction Performance in Software Engineering, *IEEE Trans. Softw. Eng.*, 2011 (preprint).

[11] V.B. Kampenes, T. Dybå, J.E. Hannay and D.I.K. Sjøberg, A Systematic Review of Quasi-Experiments in Software Engineering. *Inf. and Softw. Tech.*, vol. 51, pp. 71-82, 2009

[12] M. Lanza, R. Marinescu and S. Ducasse, Object-Oriented Metrics in Practice: Using Software Metrics to Characterize, Evaluate and Improve the Design of Object-Oriented Systems. Springer-Verlag New York, Inc, 2005.

[13] M. Riaz, M. Mendes and E.D. Tempero. A Systematic Review of Software Maintainability Prediction and Metrics. 3rd International Symposium on Empirical Software Engineering and Measurement (ESEM 2009), Lake Buena Vista, FL, USA, 15-16 Oct. 2009, pp. 367-377, 2009.

[14] D.I.K. Sjøberg, A. Yamashita, B. Anda, A. Mockus and T. Dybå. Quantifying the Effect of Code Smells on Maintenance Effort. Submitted for publication in *IEEE Trans. Softw. Eng.* 2012.

[15] TMate-Sofware. SVNKit - Subversioning for Java. [Cited June 2010]; Available from: http://svnkit.com/.

[16] K.D. Welker, P.W. Oman and G.G. Atkinson. Development and Application of an Automated Source Code Maintainability Index. *Software Maintenance: Research and Practice,* vol. 9, pp. 127-159, 1997.

[17] K.D. Welker. The Software Maintainability Index Revisited, *CrossTalk*, August 2001.

[18] M. Zhang, T. Hall and N. Baddoo, Code Bad Smells: A Review of Current Knowledge, *Software Maintenance and Evolution: Research and Practice*, vol. 23, no. 3, pp. 179–202, 2011.

[19] M. Zhou and A. Mockus. Developer fluency: Achieving True Mastery in Software Projects. ACM SIGSOFT / FSE, pp. 137-146, Santa Fe, New Mexico, Nov. 7-11, 2010.

Evolution of Features and their Dependencies - An Explorative Study in OSS

Maximilian Steff, Barbara Russo
Free University of Bozen-Bolzano
Bozen, Italy
{maximilian.steff,
barbara.russo}@unibz.it

Günther Ruhe
University of Calgary
Calgary, Canada
ruhe@ucalgary.ca

ABSTRACT

Release Planning is the process of decision making about what features are to be implemented (or revised) in which release of a software product. While release planning for proprietary software products is well-studied, little investigation has been performed for open source products. Various types of feature dependencies are known to impact both the planning and the subsequent maintenance process. In this paper, we provide the basic layout of a method to formulate and analyze feature dependencies defined at the code level. Dependencies are defined from evolutionary analysis of the commit graph of OSS code development and syntactical dependencies. We demonstrate our method with an explorative study of an open source project, the Spring Framework. From the analysis of the development cycles of two major releases over forty-one months, we could correlate late, increased feature dependencies with an increased number for subsequent improvements and bug fixes.

Categories and Subject Descriptors

K.6.3 [**Software Management**]: Software maintenance, Software process

Keywords

release planning, feature coupling, case study

1. INTRODUCTION AND MOTIVATION

Release Planning (RP) is the process of deciding about the order of features to be implemented and delivered. A multitude of factors influence this process, ranging from considerations about the customer value of a given feature to its interdependencies with other features. Catering to all of these factors leads to a complex planning process. The majority of research work in this area has been dedicated to commercial software products with the inherent constraints of this setting, e.g. [1], [6], [7], [9] . The immense rise in popularity and wide-spread usage of Open Source Software

(OSS) warrants a closer look at the case of product development and release planning in this area.

In this work, we present an explorative case study to ground further research into the RP of OSS products. To this end, we follow the guidelines for conducting case study research by Runeson and Höst [8]. Our subject of study is the Spring Framework[1] (Spring for short), the premier framework for Java enterprise application development. We collect our data from two publicly available sources covering the development of two major releases of Spring, 3.0 and 3.1. The sources are the version control system of the code and the change request tracker of the team. Furthermore, we conduct interviews with a member of the core development team to gain further insight into their process and evaluate our observations.

The main contribution of the paper is three-fold. First, we give a new definition of feature dependencies using code and commit graph analysis. Second, for releases 3.0 and 3.1 of Spring, we study the time of occurrence and the impact of feature dependencies on subsequent adaptive and corrective maintenance activities. Third, we propose an agenda for future research derived from observations of this explorative case study.

The remainder of this paper is structured as follows. In Section 2, we review relevant literature. In Section 3, the research methodology is briefly outlined. In the main part (Section 4), the results of the explorative case study are presented. We describe the design of our case study and its results. We close with an outlook to future research.

2. RELATED WORK

RP in proprietary and OSS development differ in objectives and constraints. RP in OSS appears to have different value drivers that regulate the introduction of new features as, for example, relying on community feedback. Despite guidelines for RP being publicly accessible (e.g. for Eclipse [3] or Netbeans[2]), strategies for RP - as specification of general OSS project governance [5] - often reside in the tacit knowledge of key core contributors of these communities. To our knowledge, no specific model has ever been defined for RP in OSS projects and we suspect that any model would have been more ad-hoc for a specific community than systematic according to the definition of Svahnberg *et al.* [11]. For the Spring Framework and the Eclipse project we explored, we found in fact one common principle for RP: the

---

[1]http://www.springsource.org/
[2]http://www.netbeans.com/community/guidelines

core team identifies a few major themes - each comprising several major features thematically aligned - per major release and lets the community define at later stages (new) minor features and improvements more or less dependent on the previous ones. Thus, feature dependencies give some insight on the maintenance process in a single release and the strategies for RP across releases. In proprietary software, feature dependency is a key issue in RP. In the telecommunication domain, Carlshamre *et al.* [1] found 80% of the features being somehow dependent. In addition, features can have different types of dependencies in the same release: in implementation, effort, value, and user's usage [7]. Different dependencies might also occur in combination. Saliu and Ruhe [9] proposed a RP model based on implementation and value offering highly (implementation) dependent features into the same release maximizing the value created from features. In proprietary software, increases of feature dependency in different parts of a system have proven to be a significant predictor of future modifications due to bug fixes [4].

3. METHODOLOGY

Our work is an exploratory study based on the retrospective analysis of data collected from the code versioning system and issue tracker of the Spring Framework project and validated for RP strategy with repeated incremental interviews to one core member of the Spring Framework community. For data collection and presentation, we followed the process outlined in our previous work [10] where we mapped bug reports to the project's revision history. In the present paper, we have additionally repeated the mapping for features and improvements classifying them as 'major' or 'minor' according to their priority in the issue tracker. Overall, we were able to analyze three types of change requests, features, improvements, and bug fixes, and map about 80% of improvements and features to commits in the revision history. In the following, we define a change request "A" commit as a commit related to the change request "A" under this mapping.

To identify feature dependency, we have coupled features according to (1) files changed or (2) syntactically coupled in the corresponding commits. The first definition of feature coupling originates from logical couplings of code artifacts [2]:

Definition 1: Two Java classes (or Java source files) are logically coupled whenever they are changed in the same commit.

Definition 2: A logical coupling between change requests A and B occurs if at least one file was changed in both change request A commits and change request B commits.

The second definition is based on syntactical coupling of classes like inheritance or method calls.

Definition 3: A syntactical coupling between change requests A and B occurs if there exists a class a in the change request A commits and a class b in the change request B commits that are syntactically coupled through any kind of inheritance, method call or referencing of public attributes. The set of change requests connected according to syntactical (SC) or logical coupling (LC) defines two graphs:

Definition 4: $G_{LC} = (V, E)$, with V representing all change requests and E representing all logical couplings between them.

Definition 5: $G_{SC} = (V, E)$, with V representing change requests and E representing all syntactical couplings between them.

The two definitions of coupling contribute differently to feature dependency. For the Spring Framework project, we found that 80% and 45% of the features are connected to other features, improvements or bug fixes respectively with logical and syntactical couplings. In addition, couplings between features are more prevalent with logical couplings whereas coupling between features and improvements or bug fixes occurs about 25% more often with syntactical couplings. These differences can be also perceived by the different graph structures G_{LC} and G_{SC} in Figures 2 and 3.

4. EXPLORATIVE CASE STUDY

The goal of this case study is to gain a better understanding of the RP strategy of the Spring Framework project using the individual knowledge of a core member and the static analysis of feature coupling and evolution over the development lifecycle of the project. To this extent, we applied the Goal Question Metric (GQM) paradigm to structure our questions and to guide our analysis.

How is feature development planned over the whole release cycle? Our interviews outlined a very clear strategy for release planning. Release cycles for major releases typically last 1-2 years. A single cycle is divided into milestones, release candidates, and maintenance periods. Milestones are meant to introduce the major new features for the upcoming release. "The more significant the change, the earlier it gets developed in the milestone process [...] so we can maximize the feedback window on major feature prior the major release. [...] We blog and speak at conferences frequently about milestone features and encourage our more ambitious users to road test them as thoroughly as possible." Release candidates "ideally consist only of bug fixes but in practice do occasionally introduce new features or significant improvements." A number of maintenance releases focusing on bug fixing follows a major release while in parallel development begins on the next major release. For each major release, the team "aims for a cohesive set of themes and features" to be introduced or enhanced. Milestones are scheduled several months apart "to give plenty of time not only for feature development itself, but to collect user feedback." This flexible, intuitive approach to feature selection extends to release scheduling. "[Spring major releases] tend to be about delivering cohesive and stable feature sets, rather than being rigidly date-driven [...]." Simply put, "dates to matter to [them], but stability and completeness matter more." 2-4 milestones and typically 2-3 release candidates precede a major release. Development is supported with a variety of sources for feedback, use cases and ideas for further development. Planning and prioritization are done in an intuitive way, relying on personal communication inside the core development team. "Solutions are sought to be flexible and address 80% or better of the specific use cases we hear about." "Feature selection is also based on keeping a close eye on industry trends and predicting what would be useful to enterprise application developers that they may not have considered yet. We have a small team working on the core framework. We have a weekly call in which we discuss these topics and come to consensus about what's worth working on and what should get priority."

How much does coupling between features increase maintenance activities? We look at features with no

Table 1: Comparing original and coupled features regarding subsequent maintenance effort.

features	maintenance	total		3.1	
		avg	#	avg	#
original	improvements	1.84	32	1.5	18
	bugs	1.79	28	1.66	15
	code churn	2,289		2,029	
coupled	improvements	2.5	18	3.27	13
	bugs	2.08	13	2.8	5
	code churn	1,993		3,220	

Figure 1: Change Requests by Development Cycle.

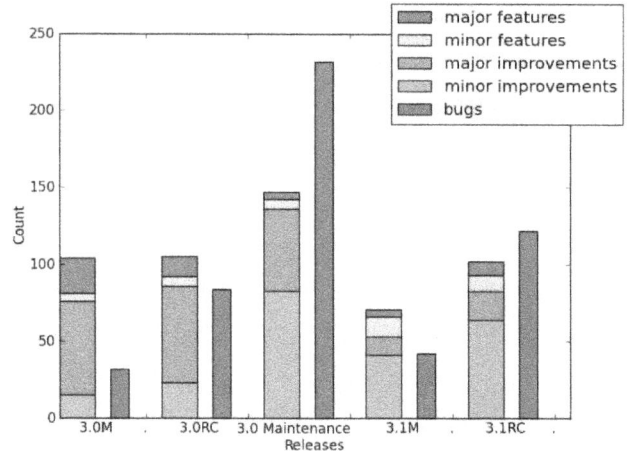

Figure 2: Logical Couplings, graph G_{LC}.

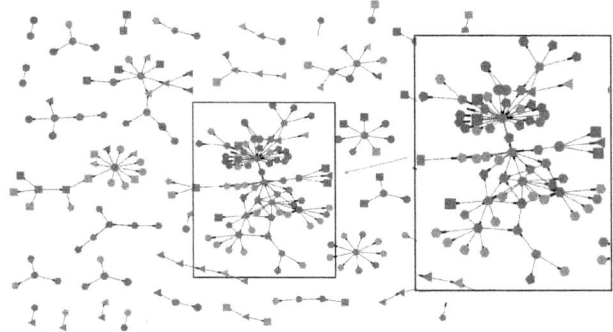

previous coupling (original features) and features that are coupled to them (coupled features) in the two graphs G_{LC} and G_{SC}. For both types of features, we count the number of adjacent nodes in the graph that are improvements or bug fixes. These numbers indicate the follow up activity connected to original features and their coupled feature(s) respectively. For logical couplings, we summarize our analysis in Table 1. We can see that, in general, there are fewer coupled than original features with subsequent maintenance activities although the average number of these activities is significantly larger for coupled features. This difference is even more pronounced if we look at Spring 3.1 only. This is also confirmed by the increase of more than 60% in code churn following coupled features. Figure 1 indicates that features and improvements in release 3.1 are mainly minor.

Is the development process in release 3.0 and 3.1 aligned with the strategy of RP defined by the team? To determine the alignment, we analyzed the change requests and in particular features over the different stages of the development process against the strategy outlined by the team in our first question. Figure 1 charts the number of change request commits over the different development stages for release 3.0 and 3.1. The chart illustrates that release 3.0 conforms to the strategy whereas 3.1 does only partially. Namely, we can see that the majority of features and improvements for release 3.0 are classified by the team as 'major' whereas the ones of 3.1 are 'minor'. In addition, for release 3.1 major features and improvements are in the release candidates stage rather in the milestone stage. On the contrary, the number of bug fixes is higher for 3.1 than for 3.0 in milestones and release candidates. We do not have data on the maintenance phase for release 3.1, thus we cannot compare the two stages. Just as an observation, we can see that a significant number of bug fixes occurs at maintenance of 3.0. This is not completely unexpected as in this stage the community starts using the new version widely and thus starts reporting bugs back to the team. In addition, bugs might have been opened in earlier stages and simply closed at maintenance.

How is feature coupling evolving over the whole release cycle? Figures 2 and 3 sketch the coupling structure of features (green), improvements (blue) and bug fixes (red) of releases 3.0 and 3.1 as discovered by logical and syntactical coupling, respectively. The more edges a node shape has, the older it is. For example a feature introduced in 3.0 M is a green circle, an improvement introduced in 3.1 RC is a blue hexagon. In G_{LC}, the majority of component centers are features meaning that features mainly determine later activities both in 3.0 and 3.1. In G_{SC} circles are the majority of the centers. This indicates that here, too, fea-

tures determine much of the later development, although there are fewer features in the graph. Looking at the overall graph structures, logical couplings are scattered across many more components in the graph, and there are only few large components. We also can see that logical couplings exhibit a higher degree of connectedness among changes within the same development cycle. Syntactical couplings give us fewer components and especially several star structures around features and an improvement from 3.0 M. Without going into more detail, we can clearly see the different nature of the two kinds of couplings. Consequently, they have different information to give. Counting the number of mutually contained files or the number of syntactical dependencies between the classes in the commits we are already able to identify peculiar structures. For example, three features - SPR-8386, 8387 and 7960 - have a particularly high logical and syntactical coupling strength. SPR-7960 presents a specific problem to be solved, SPR-8386 and 8387 pile on two layers of abstraction to generalize the solution to be applicable to both 7960 and more general to other possible applications by users. As this kind of solution shall have created a strong coupling among the above features, identifying the pattern confirms the validity of our approach.

Figure 3: Syntactical Couplings, graph G_{SC}.

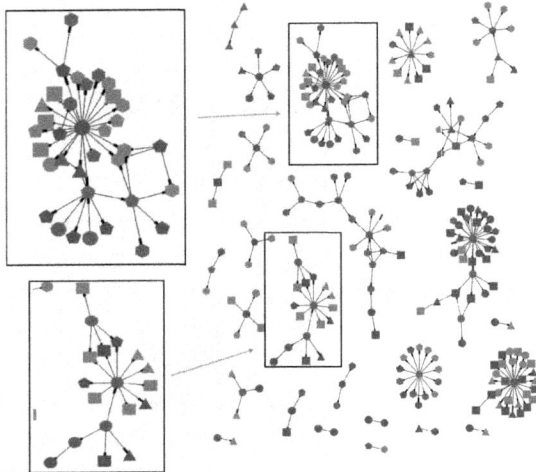

5. THREATS TO VALIDITY

While this is an explorative study with the primary focus on making observations and creating new research questions, we still need to mention some possible threats to validity. Naturally, we have to be cautious about the generalizability of our observations since we only examine one system, and of that only two release cycles. Our method of identifying features warrants scrutiny, there are other ways to define and identify features. Then, as hinted at before, we choose logical and syntactical couplings as proxy for feature couplings. As a consequence, we noticed that some features only modify existing files. This introduces a bias into our results in that feature coupling technically occurs inside the file and not among files as in the case of a feature adding files and another modifying these same files.

6. SUMMARY AND FUTURE RESEARCH

Given the nature of OSS, methods supporting RP close to the code are preferable. We sketched two definitions for feature couplings to explore the complexities of the planning process. We could analytically show that one method did indeed correlate feature couplings with an increased subsequent maintenance effort. We could also show that these methods provide two different perspectives on the planning and development process. Several notions derived from the raw data were confirmed during interviews. We believe this to be a promising starting point for conducting future research in different directions:
(1) Continuing with the analysis of Spring to describe the impact of feature couplings in later releases.
(2) Performing similar analysis for other OSS systems and explore the complementary contributions of the two coupling graphs, and ultimately assist in the planning process for new features.
(3) Finding the characteristics (if any) for feature couplings in OSS development when compared to proprietary systems.
(4) Studying the impact of weighted feature couplings and their usage to predict maintenance.
(5) Studying the schedule overlap in feature development and how it is related to subsequent maintenance.

OSS is not subject to as many of the constraints and influence factors as proprietary is. In the case of Spring, this is evident in the flexibility of the release scheduling and the intuitive approach to development and planning. In turn, the team is able to maintain a high standard of quality. However, even such a high-quality product could benefit from a more systematic and formally grounded aid in planning. Although every developer has rather specific responsibilities within the codebase, there are always seams and new parts non-responsible developers lack familiarity with. A recommendation tool could help schedule feature development to reduce overall feature coupling, which is expected to reduce overall development effort.

7. ACKNOWLEDGEMENTS

We are grateful to Chris Beams for the feedback and insights into development and process of Spring. Günther Ruhe was supported by a research fellowship of the Provincia Autonoma di Bolzano - Alto Adige (Mobility program for incoming researchers).

8. REFERENCES

[1] P. Carlshamre, K. Sandahl, M. Lindvall, B. Regnell, and J. Natt och Dag. An industrial survey of requirements interdependencies in software product release planning. RE'01, pages 84 –91, 2001.

[2] H. Gall, K. Hajek, and M. Jazayeri. Detection of logical coupling based on product release history. ICSM '98, pages 190–, 1998.

[3] E. Gamma. Agile, open source, distributed, and on-time: inside the eclipse development process. ICSE '05, pages 4–4, 2005.

[4] O. Giroux and M. P. Robillard. Detecting increases in feature coupling using regression tests. SIGSOFT '06/FSE-14, pages 163–174, 2006.

[5] C. Jensen and W. Scacchi. Governance in open source software development projects: A comparative multi-level analysis. In P. Ågerfalk, C. Boldyreff, J. González-Barahona, G. Madey, and J. Noll, editors, Open Source Software: New Horizons, volume 319, pages 130–142. 2010.

[6] F. Maurer, G. Succi, H. Holz, B. Kötting, S. Goldmann, and B. Dellen. Software process support over the internet. ICSE '99, pages 642–645, 1999.

[7] G. Ruhe. Product Release Planning: Methods, Tools and Applications. CRC Press, 2010.

[8] P. Runeson and M. Höst. Guidelines for conducting and reporting case study research in software engineering. Empirical Softw. Engg., 14(2):131–164, Apr. 2009.

[9] M. O. Saliu and G. Ruhe. Bi-objective release planning for evolving software systems. ESEC-FSE '07, pages 105–114, 2007.

[10] M. Steff and B. Russo. Co-evolution of logical couplings and commits for defect estimation. In MSR' 12, 2012.

[11] M. Svahnberg, T. Gorschek, R. Feldt, R. Torkar, S. B. Saleem, and M. U. Shafique. A systematic review on strategic release planning models. Information and Software Technology, 52(3):237 – 248, 2010.

A Hybrid Release Planning Method and its Empirical Justification

Mark Przepiora
University of Calgary
Calgary, Alberta, Canada
mark.przepiora@ucalgary.ca

Reza Karimpour
University of Calgary
Calgary, Alberta, Canada
reza.karimpour@ucalgary.ca

Guenther Ruhe
University of Calgary
Calgary, Alberta, Canada
ruhe@ucalgary.ca

ABSTRACT

Background: The use of Constraint Programming (CP) has been proposed by Regnell and Kuchcinski to model and solve the Release Planning Problem. However, they did not empirically demonstrate the advantages and disadvantages of CP over existing release planning methods.

Aims: The aims of this paper are (1) to perform a comparative analysis between CP and ReleasePlanner (RP), an existing release planning tool, and (2) to suggest a hybrid approach combining the strengths of each individual method.

Method: (1) An empirical evaluation was performed, evaluating the efficiency and effectiveness of the individual methods to justify their hybrid usage. (2) A proof of concept for a hybrid release planning method is introduced, and a real-world dataset including more than 600 features was solved using the hybrid method to provide evidence of its effectiveness.

Results: (1) Use of RP was found to be more efficient and effective than CP. However, CP is preferred when advanced planning objectives and constraints exist. (2) The hybrid method (RP&CP) greatly outperformed the individual approach (CP), increasing computational solution quality by 87%.

Conclusion: We were able to increase the expressiveness and thus applicability of an existing, efficient and effective release planning method. We presented evidence for its computational effectiveness, but more work is needed to make this result significant.

Categories and Subject Descriptors

D.2.1 [**Software Engineering**]: Requirements/Specifications—*tools*; D.2.9 [**Software Engineering**]: Management.

General Terms

Algorithms, Performance

Keywords:

Release planning, efficiency of use, user satisfaction, hybrid algorithm, performance evaluation

1. INTRODUCTION

Release planning is the problem of assigning features to subsequent releases in consideration of technological and resource constraints. The objective of planning is to find the most attractive composition of features delivered in releases to users and customers.

A variety of methods and techniques do exist to approach the various formulations of the release planning problem. A systematic literature review was conducted by Svahnberg at al. [1]. More recently, Regnell and Kuchcinski [2] proposed a solution for modeling the software release planning problem as a constraint satisfaction problem. The related solution method called Constraint Programming (CP) is a programming approach in which the state of discrete variables and their relationships are controlled using constraints [3]. Compared to procedural programming, constraints do not specify any sequence of actions, but rather the properties of a solution to be found. This is similar to declarative programming. Their CP formulation of the release planning formulation originally introduced in [4] includes relative and absolute stakeholder priorities among features, interdependencies, and release-specific resource constraints.

The results of Regnell and Kuchcinski [2] served as a proof-of concept to show the applicability of CP for a broad range of release planning formulations. Two main follow-up questions were derived from there: (i) How applicable is the formal notation used in CP from an application and user's perspective? (ii) How is the scalability of the approach to solve problems with hundreds of features?

To approach these questions, a comparative analysis was conducted between two solution approaches:

- CP: Constraint programming as implemented in MiniZinc

- RP: Formulation of release planning as integer linear programming problem and usage of special-purpose solvers as described in [5]

In this short paper, two research questions (RQ) are tackled:

RQ1: Perform an empirical analysis to compare CP against RP in terms of efficiency of use and user satisfaction.

RQ2: From the results of RQ1, combine the respective strengths of CP and RP and offer them in an integrated method.

In Section 2, we briefly report the results from two empirical studies comparing CP versus RP. As a result of the two studies, we propose a hybrid solution method for release planning called RP&CP. The hybrid method described in Section 3 is a two-staged solution approach which combines the higher flexibility in problem formulation (in terms of describing objectives and constraints) of CP with the advantages offered by RP. The results of the proof-of-concept analysis of RP&CP are given in Section 4. Outlook for future research is the content of Section 5.

2. COMPARATIVE ANALYSIS OF TWO RELEASE PLANNING METHODS

2.1 CONTEXT

The goal of our comparative analysis of two release planning methods with two associated tool implementations was to understand the principal advantages and disadvantages of each approach.

The tool used for CP is MiniZinc [2] which is a subset of a constraint modeling language called Zinc. In terms of complexity, MiniZinc is adequately high-level to formulate the constraint problems with reasonable effort. On the other hand it is simple enough to be adopted by existing solvers consistently.

The tool used for RP is ReleasePlanner [6], a web-based decision support system for release planning. The underlying solution method is based on algorithms (branch and bound, linear programming) combined with heuristics, all customized to the special structure of the problem formulation [5]. The RP problem formulation is limited to coupling and precedence constraints between features, linear resource constraints, and a (weighted) additive utility function aggregating stakeholder scores to features, given for a flexible number of planning criteria. While this formulation has been sufficient for solving a number of real-world cases, it appears desirable to enhance modeling capabilities both for the planning objectives (e.g., non-linear objectives) and constraints (e.g., general logical constrains such as "at least one feature from a given candidate set").

2.2 TWO EMPIRICAL STUDIES

Two empirical studies were conducted to compare two different aspects of the usages of CP versus RP. We do not intend to make a preference decision between the two systems. Instead, we were aiming to find out which approach (method and associated tool) is preferable in which situation. The preference criteria focused on are efficiency (referring to usage of resources) and effectiveness (referring to quality of solutions in dependence of effort spent).

2.2.1 EFFICIENCY

In [7], efficiency is considered to be a component of the usability of a system. It is defined as the capability of the software system to empower users to allot reasonable amounts of resources in relation to the effectiveness gained in a specified context of use. To measure the efficiency, eight frequently occurring tasks of the release planning process were considered:

- Adding a feature to feature repository (Task 1)
- Editing a feature already available (2)
- Defining a dependency between features (3)
- Defining available resources (4)
- Editing available resources (5)
- Inputting stakeholder votes (6)
- Editing stakeholder importance (7)
- Generating a solution (8)

In addition, we looked at

- Number of errors or failed commands and (9)
- Frequency of help or documentation use (10)

Experimental subjects were asked to perform the planning process for a benchmark problem introduced in [4]. Seven participants were recruited. The results of the measurements are summarized in Table 1. The unit of measurement for tasks 1 to 8 is *seconds*

(average) while the numbers for task types 9 and 10 represent *frequencies* (average).

Table 1. Efficiency evaluation results

	1	2	3	4	5	6	7	8	9	10
CP	186	154	135	147	197	154	161	147	3	6
RP	134	61	102	73	61	98	65	95	1	1

2.2.2 EFFECTIVENESS

In evaluating the effectiveness of each approach, we are interested only in exploring the computation that generates a release plan for a completely-defined project. The metric we use is best solution quality (that is, utility function value divided by maximum value) after 15 seconds of runtime, which we denote $q \in [0, 1]$.

Ideally, we would like to evaluate the performance of each approach as a function of the size of the input. However, the size of an RP project is determined by a number of parameters, some of which may have a greater impact on performance than others.

Our goal is to explore this space of parameters as fully as is feasible, and in particular we identified 7 parameters of importance: the number of planning items (N); the number of resources (M); the number of release periods (K); the number of weak precedence constraints (S); the number of strict precedence constraints (H); the number of pre-assignment constraints (L); and the "resource tightness" (T) of the project, that is, the ratio of sum total resource consumptions to sum total resource capacities.

We created a data set of 96 projects by creating a project of every possible combination of parameter values from the following list:

$N = \{30, 150\}$, $M = \{1, 5\}$, $K = \{1, 5\}$, $S = \{N/25, N/10\}$, $H = \{N/10\}$, $L = \{N/50, N/10\}$, $T = \{0.2, 1.0, 3.0\}$.

Item values were chosen uniformly from the interval [1000, 9000] and releases were weighted in decreasing order. Resource consumptions and resource capacities were chosen from uniform distributions as to result in the target resource tightness. Precedence constraints were generated from iteratively choosing random constraints. At each iteration, a cycle detection algorithm was applied to ensure that no logical contradictions were generated during problem generation.

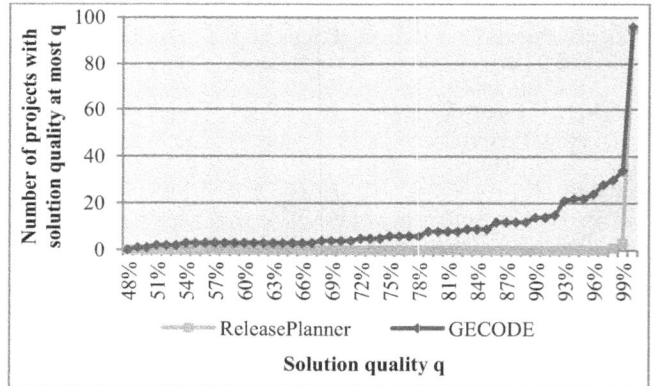

Figure 1. Cumulative frequency graph of solution quality.

In order for CP to be used to optimize the project as a whole, the RP parts must be converted into MiniZinc as well. To do so, we developed and implemented an RP to MiniZinc transformation in the form of a Java application that converts an input RP project into an equivalent CP in the MiniZinc format, following logical definitions that we briefly describe in Section 3.1.

The resulting CP may be solved using any MiniZinc solver, but in particular we considered GECODE[1], an open-source constraint solver which, according to the creators of MiniZinc, is currently the best-performing MiniZinc solver available.

We pre-computed the optimal solution for each project during previous research, and kept this information to allow us to determine the solution quality achieved by each solver. We solved each project using both solvers with 15 second time-limits using a 2.8GHz CPU and 4GB RAM, and recorded the utility values of the best solutions found by each solver within the allotted time.

Figure 1 shows a cumulative quality frequency graph for the solutions found by each solver. It can be seen that RP significantly outperformed GECODE in these tests, being able to solve all but 3 projects in the dataset to an optimality of at least 99% within the allotted time. GECODE was unable to do so in 34 cases, and in 14 cases achieved an optimality of less than 90%.

2.3 LIMITATIONS AND CONCLUSIONS
The results of the two empirical studies are not intended to provide a comprehensive and final comparison, but to motivate follow-up research. Users found RP easy to use while CP had mixed evaluations (for details, one may refer to [8]). Scores for RP showed that users can complete the intended task faster without extra help or training while getting started with CP needs some prior training. RP appeared to be clearly more effective, i.e., generating solutions of significantly higher degree of optimality.

Even in consideration of the existing threats to validity (including the small number of subjects having participated), there exists a clear pattern of usage of the two alternative systems. RP appears to be more efficient and effective in its use. It achieves high user satisfaction (which is confirmed from industrial users outside the survey made).

However, CP is the recommended preference in case of more sophisticated planning problems with more advanced planning objectives and constraints. Evaluation of real world software has shown that in addition to intrinsic constraints provided by classic feature models, many projects use custom constraints to model the intended domain [9]. CP has extensive and flexible support for defining relations and constraints between features. This makes it promising for industrial use while RP only supports two primary constraints, precedence and coupling that would not be sufficient for handling an industry level project like Linux.

3. A HYBRID RELEASE PLANNING METHOD
3.1 PROBLEM FORMULATION
The Release Planning Problem RPP can be described in an abstract way as the problem of defining an assignment (release plan) $x = (x(1) \dots x(N))$ of a given feature set $F = \{f(1) \dots f(N)\}$ with the following meaning.

- $x(n) = k$ if and only if feature $f(n)$ is assigned to release k
- $x(n) = 0$ if feature $f(n)$ is not offered at all

This assignment x is supposed to satisfy the following conditions.

- A utility function $G(x)$ is maximized.
- The assignment x satisfies a set X of constrains.

RP allows a weighted linear function for $G(x)$, which is composed from stakeholder scores related to different criteria. The constraint

set X^{RP} in RP allows couplings between features, pre-assignment of features, linear resource constraints as well as soft and strict precedence constrains (for details we refer to [5]). We call such constraints "RP constraints".

CP is not limited and allows any logical constraint as well as any formulation of objectives. We call such constraints "Non-RP constraints". Below we list a few examples of non-RP constraints that are easily-expressible using CP.

- Mutual exclusion, i.e. constraints of the form, "exactly one of feature a or feature b must be offered".
- Additive synergy between features, e.g. "if all features in the set A are offered, then the value of the plan is increased by C points".
- Productivity investments, e.g. "if feature a is completed in release k, then all resource consumption is lowered by C% in release $k + 1$ onward."

Such constraints motivate the following, hybrid approach, in which RP is extended with a module that allows project managers to implement non-RP constraints in their projects using a reusable template system.

3.2 CONSTRAINT DEFINITION
We have developed an expressive, domain-specific language based on MiniZinc used to define *templates* for commonly-used classes of constraints. Project managers may then *instantiate* these templates using a GUI without the need to comprehend the underlying code.

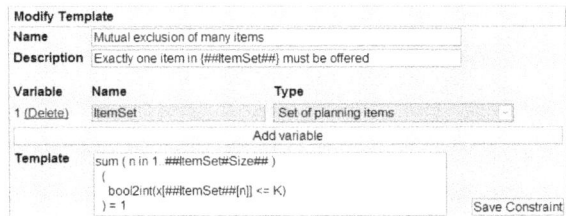

Figure 2. Template definition UI

This method enables the full expressive power of MiniZinc within RP without sacrificing usability for the project manager, since coding need only be performed once for each class of constraint that any manager wishes to use in the future.

We refer to our technical report [8] for a detailed usage scenario.

3.3 OPTIMIZATION
If the project manager does not choose to implement any non-RP constraints in his project, then the project resulting from this process is simply an RP project, and optimization can be performed using the existing, highly-effective RP solver.

But if the manager did add non-RP constraints to the project, then a hybrid algorithm is used. First, the relaxed problem is solved (ignoring the constraints outside X^{RP}) using the existing RP solver. Although the solution computed may in general violate the non-RP constraints of the project, we will use it as part of the CP search strategy as a starting solution.

To do so, the entire project, an RP project together with non-RP constraints, must be transformed into an equivalent CP expressed in the MiniZinc language. Non-RP constraints defined using the process in Section 3.2 are transformed naturally, as the template language is designed to easily translate into MiniZinc. On the other hand, in order to transform the remaining, RP-only portion of the project to MiniZinc, we use the tool we developed in Section 2.2.2.

---

[1] http://www.gecode.org/

Finally, parameters which instruct the MiniZinc solver to use the assignments from the RP solution as a starting point in its search strategy are added to the code. The project is then solved using a CP solver (as in Section 2.2.2, we used the GECODE solver).

4. PROOF-OF-CONCEPT ANALYSIS

To demonstrate the applicability of our hybrid method, we have used a real-world problem studied in [10], an RPP which includes 633 features.

Step 1: We began by computing release plans for the project using the RP solver. We saved the best solution found after 15 seconds. This solution had a 99.94% degree of optimality. We refer to this solution as the relaxed solution.

Step 2: We converted the RP project to the MiniZinc format using our tool, and added the following five non-RP constraints and objectives to the project in addition to its existing constraints:

- *At most one* of items 1, 2 and 3 may be released.

- *At least two* of items 9, 10 and 11 must be released.

- *Exactly two* of items 12, 13 and 14 must be released.

- If all of items 6, 7 and 8 are offered, then the utility function value is increased by 12,000 points (*non-linear utility G(x)*).

- If all of items 15, 16 and 17 are offered, then the utility function value is increased by 12,000 points (*non-linear utility function G(x)*).

We verified that the relaxed solution computed in Step 1 violated the first and third constraints above, which means that the CP solver may not simply reuse the relaxed solution as a solution to the non-RP constraints.

Step 3: Next, we computed solutions for this resulting project in two ways: (1) First, we used the CP solver alone, without modifying its default search strategy. (2) Second, we modified the search strategy to coerce the solver into using the relaxed, RP solution as a starting solution for optimization.

Table 2. Solution quality, CP-only vs. RP&CP

Method	Solution quality			
	5 seconds	15 seconds	5 minutes	30 minutes
CP	52.13%	52.89%	52.94%	52.94%
RP&CP	91.16%	98.83%	98.83%	98.83%

We computed solutions using 5-second, 15-second, 5-minute and 30-minute time limits on a personal computer with the same specifications as in Section 2.2.2, and recorded the utility function value of the best solution found during each run.

Step 4: The results of these computations are summarized in Table 2. We see that using CP alone achieved a solution quality of 52.89% after 15 seconds (improved only to 52.94% after 30 minutes), while the hybrid RP+CP computed a near-optimal solution after 15 seconds. This corresponds to an improvement of about 87%.

5. SUMMARY AND CONCLUSIONS

The underlying conjecture of this short paper was that a combination of two existing release planning would result in an even stronger (hybrid) approach. We performed two independent empirical investigations to evaluate the relative strengths and weaknesses of the two methods under investigation. We reported the design and implementation of the hybrid approach. From applying user-friendly templates, advanced logical constraints and non-linear planning functions could be easily expressed.

The results of the proof of concept evaluation are taken as first evidence that our conjecture is true. We were able to increase the expressiveness and thus applicability of an existing, efficient and effective release planning method RP. For future work, we plan to perform a broad evaluation of the hybrid approach with problems of varying size and structural characteristics. While RP has been industrially evaluated, we plan to do the same for the hybrid approach. Besides academic interest, the motivation to look into higher expressiveness came also from industrial applications. We will also look into the applicability of genetic search algorithms directly applied on top of RP. This would further simplify the process and eliminate the dependency from an additional solver.

6. ACKNOWLEDGMENT

This research was partially supported by the Natural Sciences and Engineering Research Council of Canada, NSERC Discovery Grant 250343-12. And thanks to all participants of the empirical studies.

7. REFERENCES

[1] M. Svahnberg, T. Gorschek, R. Feldt, R. Torkar, S. B. Saleem, and M. U. Shafique, "A systematic review on strategic release planning models," *Information and Software Technology*, vol. 52, no. 3, pp. 237-248, 2010.

[2] B. Regnell and K. Kuchcinski, "Exploring Software Product Management decision problems with constraint solving-opportunities for prioritization and release planning," in *Fifth International Workshop on Software Product Management (IWSPM)*, 2011, pp. 47-56.

[3] F. Rossi, P. Van Beek, and T. Walsh, *Handbook of constraint programming*. Elsevier Science, 2006.

[4] G. Ruhe and M. O. Saliu, "The Art and Science of Software Release Planning," *IEEE Software*, vol. 22, no. 6, pp. 47-53, Nov. 2005.

[5] A. Ngo-The and G. Ruhe, "A systematic approach for solving the wicked problem of software release planning," *Soft Computing*, vol. 12, no. 1, pp. 95-108, Aug. 2007.

[6] "ReleasePlanner." [Online]. Available: www.releaseplanner.com. [Accessed: 20-May-2012].

[7] A. Seffah, M. Donyaee, R. B. Kline, and H. K. Padda, "Usability measurement and metrics: A consolidated model," *Software Quality Journal*, vol. 14, no. 2, pp. 159-178, 2006.

[8] M. Przepiora, R. Karimpour, and G. Ruhe, Constraint Programming versus Specialized Tool Support: A Comparative Analysis for the Release Planning Problem," May 2012. [Online] Available: http://pages.cpsc.ucalgary.ca/~przepiom/esem2012/ [Accessed: May 20, 2012].

[9] T. Berger, S. She, R. Lotufo, A. Wąsowski, and K. Czarnecki, "Variability modeling in the real: a perspective from the operating systems domain," in *Proceedings of the IEEE/ACM International Conference on Automated Software Engineering*, 2010, pp. 73-82.

[10] S. bin Saleem, Y. Yu, and B. Nuseibeh, "An Empirical Study of Security Requirements in Planning Bug Fixes for an Open Source Software Project." TR 2012/01, Dep. of Computing, Faculty of Mathematics, Computing and Technology, The Open University, London, UK, 2012.

Plat_Forms 2011: Finding Emergent Properties of Web Application Development Platforms

Ulrich Stärk
Institut für Informatik
Freie Universität Berlin
Berlin, Germany
ustaerk@inf.fu-berlin.de

Lutz Prechelt
Institut für Informatik
Freie Universität Berlin
Berlin, Germany
prechelt@inf.fu-berlin.de

Ilija Jolevski
Technical Faculty Bitola
University St. Kliment Ohridski
Bitola, FYR of Macedonia
ilija.jolevski@uklo.edu.mk

ABSTRACT

Empirical evidence on emergent properties of different web development platforms when used in a non-trivial setting is rare to non-existent. In this paper we report on an experiment called *Plat_Forms 2011* where teams of professional software developers implemented the same specification of a small to medium sized web application using different web development platforms, with 3 to 4 teams per platform. We define platforms by the main programming language used, in our case Java, Perl, PHP, or Ruby. In order to find properties that are similar within a web development platform but different across platforms, we analyzed several characteristics of the teams and their solutions, such as completeness, robustness, structure and aspects of the team's development process. We found certain characteristics that can be attributed to the platforms used but others that cannot. Our findings also indicate that for some characteristics the programming language might not be the best attribute by which to define the platform anymore.

Categories and Subject Descriptors

D.2.0 [**Software Engineering**]: General

General Terms

Experimentation, Measurement, Languages

Keywords

Experiment, Web Development, Platforms, Comparison, Emergent Properties, Languages, Empirical Software Engineering

1. INTRODUCTION

A large part of applications developed today are web based applications. The possibility to deploy a web application on a web server and serve large number of clients has made the web one of the dominant platforms for software development.

For building web applications, many different technologies exist. But it is not only the technology (that is: the main programming language, HTML, CSS, JavaScript, frameworks, libraries, development tools) that defines a web development platform. Each platform also has it's own *platform culture* such as programming styles, preferred development processes, etc. We call the combination of those two aspects a *web development platform*.

When selecting the web development platform to be used for a project, there is however little to no objective evidence on when to use which platform. Depending on the platform they prefer, most people asked will claim that their respective platform is the best or make claims about alleged properties of some other platform. Examples of such claims are

- Ruby applications are slow
- Java teams are less productive
- Perl code tends to be small in size
- PHP is insecure
- Ruby does not scale well
- Java applications are well maintainable
- Perl code is hard to read

However, most of these claims are not based on strong evidence. They may be based on personal experience (perhaps exaggerated) or just be hearsay. The little evidence that is presented for such claims is either of dubious validity (e.g. comparing projects of different kinds) or limited relevance (e.g. focusing on a very narrow set of aspects only, such as pure performance benchmarks).

In order to provide objective empirical evidence about the real, rather then the alleged properties of different web development platforms, exhibited when used on a project level (if small), we conducted a quasi experiment where teams of professional software developers implemented the same specification under controlled conditions, each using a different web application platform.

This paper will investigate whether there are aspects in the development process or its results that can be attributed to the web development platform used.

2. STUDY SETUP

2.1 Methodology

When trying to determine the emergent properties of web development platforms, it is not enough to only look at the platforms' technologies. Rather, an empirical approach is needed: we need to observe the different web development platforms when used in a realistic, i.e. a project level, setting. We could have done this with a case study. It would however be hard to attribute observed differences to the web development platform used because we then could not exercise control over other variables that might be responsible for the effects we see. We therefore chose an experimental design.

We let teams of 3 professional software developers each implement the same small to medium sized specification. The complexity of the task (see below for details) and the fact that we let teams instead of individuals handle it ensured a setting as close to a real world project as feasible.

In a truly controlled experiment one would randomly assign the teams to the independent variable (the web development platform) while keeping everything else the same. While this ensures that human factors like experience don't influence the dependent variables (here: aspects of the development process) it is completely unrealistic in our case. A project manager wouldn't assign a team randomly to a platform. Rather he would either chose a team that is experienced with the given platform or chose a platform that a given team is most experienced with.

We had 4 teams each for the platforms Java, PHP and Ruby and 3 teams for the Perl platform. In addition we had one team working with JavaScript only, on the client as well as on the server side, which we believe will become a major trend in the coming years and therefore considered an interesting glimpse of the future. The JavaScript team's results will be treated separately in our evaluation.

All teams had to implement the same specification for a small to medium sized web application. The teams all worked in two large rooms of the same building on two consecutive days. During the experiment we conducted minimally invasive micro-interviews with all participants every 15 minutes to capture what type of activity each team member was doing how often.

In addition, the participants were allowed to ask the first author, acting as an on-site customer, questions regarding the specification document. Only questions regarding clarification of the meaning of requirements were answered.

2.2 Participants

Participants for the experiment were found by marketing the experiment as a contest, where teams of top class professional software developers would compete to implement the same specification for a web application, each using their preferred platform. By limiting admittance to high-class professional software developers we tried to keep within-platform variation between the teams low. Strong variation between the teams would make it hard to identify platform differences but the performance of high-class teams is likely to be similar.

Participation in the contest was rewarded by giving the teams an evaluation of their performance in comparison to other top-class teams. This evaluation provided well-performing teams with the best marketing material one can think of:

neutral, objective, fair and believable. Apart from the scientific evaluation, no other rewards were promised. With the help of sponsors, we eventually gave a prize of 1.000 EUR to one team per platform. This had not been announced before the contest, but had happened similarly after the 2007 instance of Plat_Forms, too.

We announced Plat_Forms three months before the actual experiment took place, i.e. in October 2010, and asked teams of three professional software developers to apply for admittance to the contest. Out of 24 applications we chose the following 16 participating teams under the condition that all platforms present at the contest would have at least 3 and at most 4 teams (with the exception of JavaScript as mentioned above).

The teams and their technologies were

- For Java:
  - Accenture with Spring Roo and Hibernate
  - Cordys (now Crealogix) with abaXX.Components including Hibernate
  - SIB Visions with JVx and JVx WebUI
  - Kayak.com with Spring MVC and Hibernate
- For Perl:
  - #austria.pm with Catalyst and DBIx::Class
  - Perl Ecosystem Group with Catalyst
  - Shadowcat Systems with Task::Kensho (built on top of Catalyst)
- For PHP:
  - Globalpark with Zend Framework
  - Mayflower with Zend Framework
  - Mindworks with Symfony
  - TYPO3 Association with FLOW3
- For Ruby:
  - Infopark with Rails
  - LessCode with Rails
  - makandra with Rails
  - tmp8 with Rails
- For JavaScript:
  - Upstream Agile with Node.js, express.js and sammy.js

The participants were between 22 and 45 years old (Java mean 34, JavaScript mean 28, Perl mean 31, PHP mean 31 and Ruby mean 34), and the majority spent 75% or more of their work time in the past 12 months with technical software development activities (as opposed to project management etc.). The participant's overall experience as professional software developers ranged from 4 to 19 years for Java (mean 11), from 3 to 6 years for JavaScript (mean 4.7), from 3 to 20 years for perl (mean 8.8), from 3 to 15 years for PHP (mean 8.6), and from 2 to 25 years for Ruby (mean 11).

A possibly more useful indicator for a participant's skill however is the number of programming languages that person has used, which assumes that more capable developers take the burden of learning a new language more often. We asked the participants to list the languages they have at some point regularly used and those that they have tried out at least once. Table 1 shows that the majority of our participants has regularly used 4 to 5 programming languages, that many of them know 9 or more, and that we likely have sufficient skill balance across platforms[1].

Platform	min	max	median
Java	4 (2)	12 (6)	9 (5)
Perl	7 (4)	17 (8)	9 (5)
PHP	6 (1)	12 (7)	9 (5)
Ruby	5 (3)	14 (10)	10 (5)
(JavaScript)	6 (3)	7 (4)	7 (4)

Table 1: number of all languages ever used (in parens: languages used regularly) per developer for each platform

The team characteristics also suggest that we achieved our goal of recruiting rather capable developers.

2.3 Task

The participating teams where all tasked with implementing the same specification for a web portal called *CaP: Conferences and Participants*. CaP is an application for organizing conferences, allowing unregistered users to browse conferences by categories and search for conferences. Registered users are able to create conferences, make friends with other users, and invite friends and others (whether signed up or not) to conferences. Official, verified organizers for conference series may create conferences in a conference series like ESEM, admin users can modify all data in the system.

The specification was divided in four parts. The first part dealt with the requirements for a HTML user interface and was organized around 9 use cases, each posing a number of requirements. Some of the use cases contained not-so-common requirements such as distance calculations based on a user's GPS coordinates, a simple query language for finding conferences and output of data in formats other than HTML, i.e. iCalendar, PDF and RSS. The second part specified a RESTful web service interface using HTTP for data transfer and JavaScript Object Notation (JSON) for the data exchange format. The third and fourth part dealt with non-functional requirements and development rules, respectively.

Requirements were all marked with one of three priority levels. *MUST* requirements represented functionality without which the system would be considered inacceptable. *SHOULD* marked important requirements without which the system would be considered incomplete but acceptable. Requirements marked as *MAY* were optional. Overall there were 204 requirements (114 MUST, 34 SHOULD, 56 MAY). The HTML user interface had 143 functional requirements, the web service interface 32. In addition, there were 23 nonfunctional requirements and 6 requirements regarding development rules and solution delivery. We strived to make the document precise and unambiguous as best we could. The participants confirmed that we were successful with this far beyond what they usually (or even ever) see in practice. This

---

[1]Remember the JavaScript team is noncompetitive, so it is not a problem that it appears a bit more junior

high requirements quality arguably makes the contest a bit less realistic but on the other hand avoids many mishaps and results interpretation ambiguities that might otherwise occur.

2.4 Execution

The experiment took place on January 18th and 19th 2011 at the CongressCenter Nürnberg in Nuremberg, Germany. 12 of the 16 teams worked in one large room, the other 4 teams worked in an adjacent smaller room. The contest started at 09:00 on January 18th with a short presentation on the task. Actual work began around 09:30. During 00:00 and 08:00 the next day, the teams were not supposed to work and the rooms were locked up for the night. This is contrary to what we did in the pilot study in 2007 were teams were free how they spent the night. In talks with the participants after the experiment in 2007 the wish for an explicit night break was expressed. Some participants did not feel reasonably well rested on the second day and felt that they could have delivered better results if a mandatory night break had forced them to have some sleep. Discussions with the 2011 participants revealed that the night break was perceived sensible because it forced them to get some needed rest.

On the second day, teams had time until 18:00 to finish their implementations and hand over their solutions. For the experiment each team was provided with about 18 m^2 of space, 4 tables, chairs, a multi strip for power and one ethernet cable for internet access. All other equipment, such as computers for development, additional power strips, desktop ethernet switches, etc. had to be brought by the teams themselves and were set up the day before the contest.

At the end of the experiment the teams handed over (on a USB stick) a virtual machine running their solution, a source code archive containing the sources for their solutions, and the complete version control archive created during the contest.

3. THREATS TO VALIDITY

The biggest threat to validity stems from the team selection. If we failed to recruit comparable teams, we cannot be sure if our observations are due to variations of the independent variable – the platform – or some artifact of the team selection. From a capability point of view it seems that we managed to find equally experienced teams. Two teams, however, are worth noting.

Team Java I told us after the contest, that they were using a technology that they don't regularly use in their projects and just recently started using for rapid prototyping. In addtion, the analysis of their development process showed that they spent a lot of time with up-front design and management activities, in particular with transferring requirements into their internal bug tracking system. This we believe reduced the completeness of their solution.

Team Perl O characterized itself in conversations after the contest as a team of three backend developers with no affinity towards HTML GUIs. This fact will most likely have had an effect on the team's solution's level of completeness which is measured in terms of requirements implemented on the HTML GUI.

Due to the nature of the task and the given time constraints, our results reflect a rapid prototyping work mode. It is unclear how well they generalize to production-quality software development. But given that we observed teams of professional software developers instead of students or individuals and that the assignment was much bigger than usually found in experiments, we believe that generalizability is higher than in most other controlled scientific studies.

The strong heterogeneity of technologies and frameworks makes it hard to effectively treat all solutions alike. This needs to be kept in mind for the size comparison.

4. RESULTS

The following subsections present an extract of some of the evaluations we have performed on the teams' solutions, namely

- Completeness: How many requirements (per priority level) did the teams manage to implement in the given time?

- Robustness: How well do the solutions react to weird, difficult, or dangerous inputs?

- Development process: How frequent are which types of development activities during the two days?

- Size and structure: How many files of which size and type comprise each team's solution?

Each subsection will start with a description of how we evaluated the corresponding characteristic, followed by the respective results.

We evaluated further charateristics, such as the team's version history, the origin and role of source files, more detailed characteristics of the development process, and many more. Due to space restrictions we will however only focus on the evaluations mentioned above. Some analyses, in particular a performance analysis, couldn't be carried out due to the varying level of the solutions' completeness (see the next section for details). A thorough security analysis is currently under way and a modularity and maintainability evaluation is in planning.

4.1 Completeness

We checked the implementation of each requirement twice for each team (by different judges). In order to avoid bias during the evaluation from changing the evaluation criteria over time, the requirements as specified in the requirements document were divided into blocks, each corresponding roughly to one of the nine use cases. Each block was then duplicated so that for the 16 solutions we got 288 blocks. These blocks were then randomly assigned to judges, such that each block would be evaluated by one judge but no judge would evaluate the same requirements for the same team twice.

The judges were graduate and PhD students with experience in web application development in Java, Perl, PHP, and Ruby.

They compared the teams' solutions with the expected behavior based on the requirements document and for each requirement assigned a value for its completeness with 0 meaning "not implemented", 1 "partially implemented", 2 "implemented, but in an especially bad way", 3 "implemented" and 4 "implemented, and particularly well done". Usually, a requirement would get a rating of 0 or 3 with 1, 2 and 4 being the exception.

For the 143 requirements concerning the HTML user interface, each evaluated by two judges for each of the 16 solutions, 4576 requirement implementations were compared to their expected behavior. In case the two judges came to a different rating for a requirement, they had to get together and discuss the implementation of the corresponding requirement until an unanimous rating was found. This happened in about 19% of the cases.

The 32 requirements concerning the web service interface were evaluated by a fully automated web service testing client comparing the actual implementation to the specification laid down in the requirements document and judging the differences by fixed criteria.

Figure 1 shows the number of all fully implemented requirements, i.e. those with a rating of 2, 3 or 4, by requirement priority. It includes requirements concerning the HTML user interface as well as those concerning the web service interface. Notably, of the six most complete solutions, four were delivered by Ruby teams. With the exception of Java team I, the Java teams showed similarly good results. Team I stated that they spent too much time with management tasks such as splitting up work and giving out work packages and were therefore lacking time in the end. Observations during the experiment and a relatively high number of incompletely implemented requirements (rating of 1) corroborate this.

Other notable outliers within their respective platforms are Perl team O and PHP team M. Team O was made up of three developers that classified themselves as back-end rather than front-end developers. According to information provided by this team, they finished most of the requirements on the back-end side but didn't spend enough time to wire everything together on the front-end side. Figure 2 shows that team O implemented almost as many requirements concerning the web service interface as concerning the user interface. This, plus the relatively high number of source lines of code (SLOC) per implemented requirement (see figure 6), corroborate the team's statement.

Team M used the Symfony framework, which borrows a lot of concepts from Ruby on Rails, and performed as well as the Ruby teams which were all using Ruby on Rails.

Figure 2 shows the same data as figure 1 but grouped by requirements category, i.e. user interface or web service interface. The results indicate that there is no platform-specific preference whether to implement a web service interface or a HTML user interface first for the same business logic. We expected that it would be easy for the teams to do both given that frameworks exist for each platform that help in automatically generating web service interfaces. But the decision what to focus on rather seems to be a team preference. One team (Perl team C) decided not to implement the web service interface at all and one team (Java team E) only implemented 1 of the 32 requirements.

4.2 Robustness

All solutions were tested on how they behaved when unexpected, erroneous or malicious input was provided and how they handled special situations. These tests comprised

- a naive test for cross-site-scripting attacks,

- a test how the solutions reacted to very long input,

- a test with multi-byte unicode characters for the input,

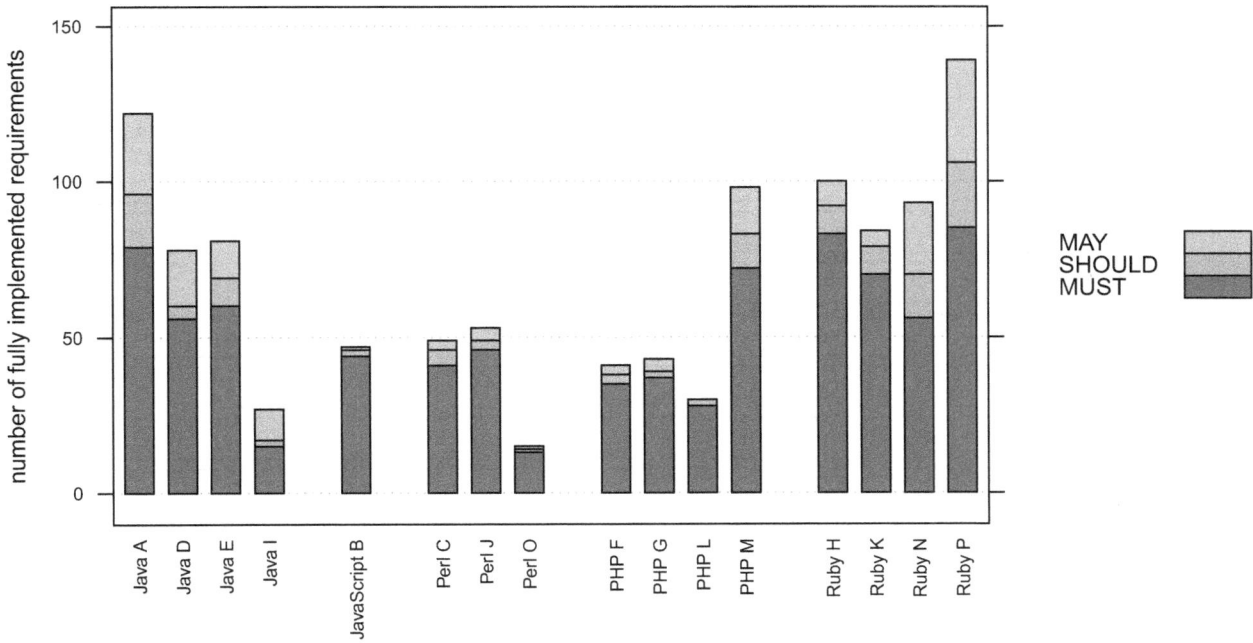

Figure 1: Number of fully implemented requirements by priority.

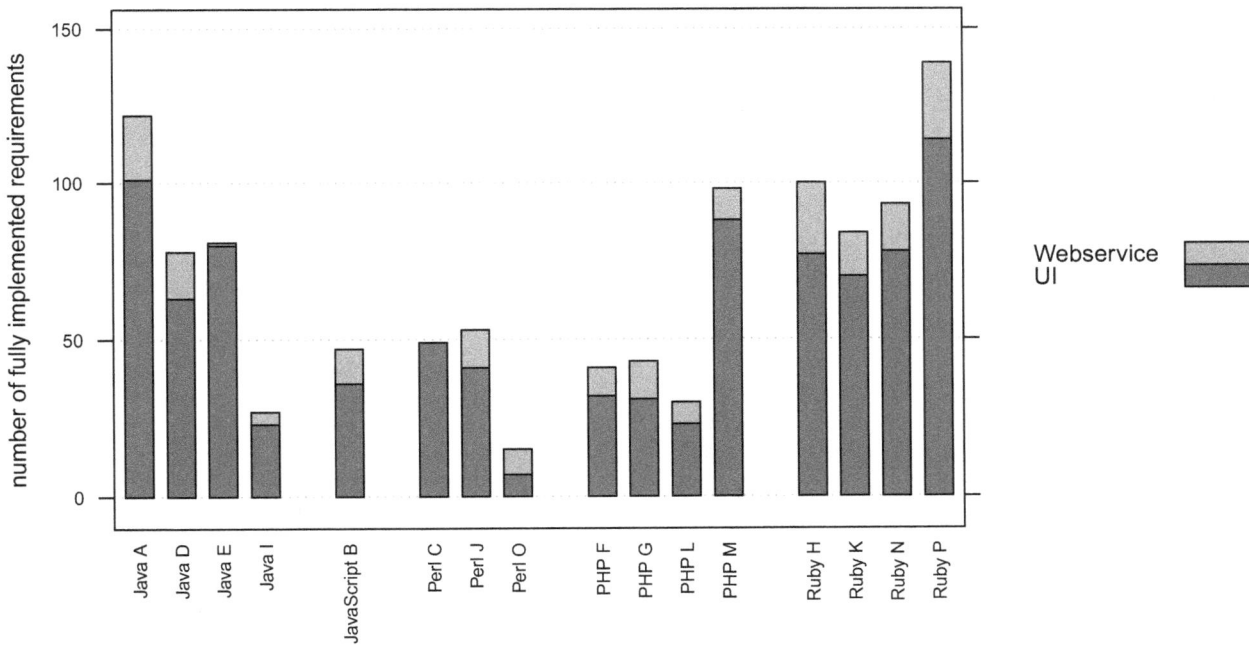

Figure 2: Number of fully implemented requirements by requirements category

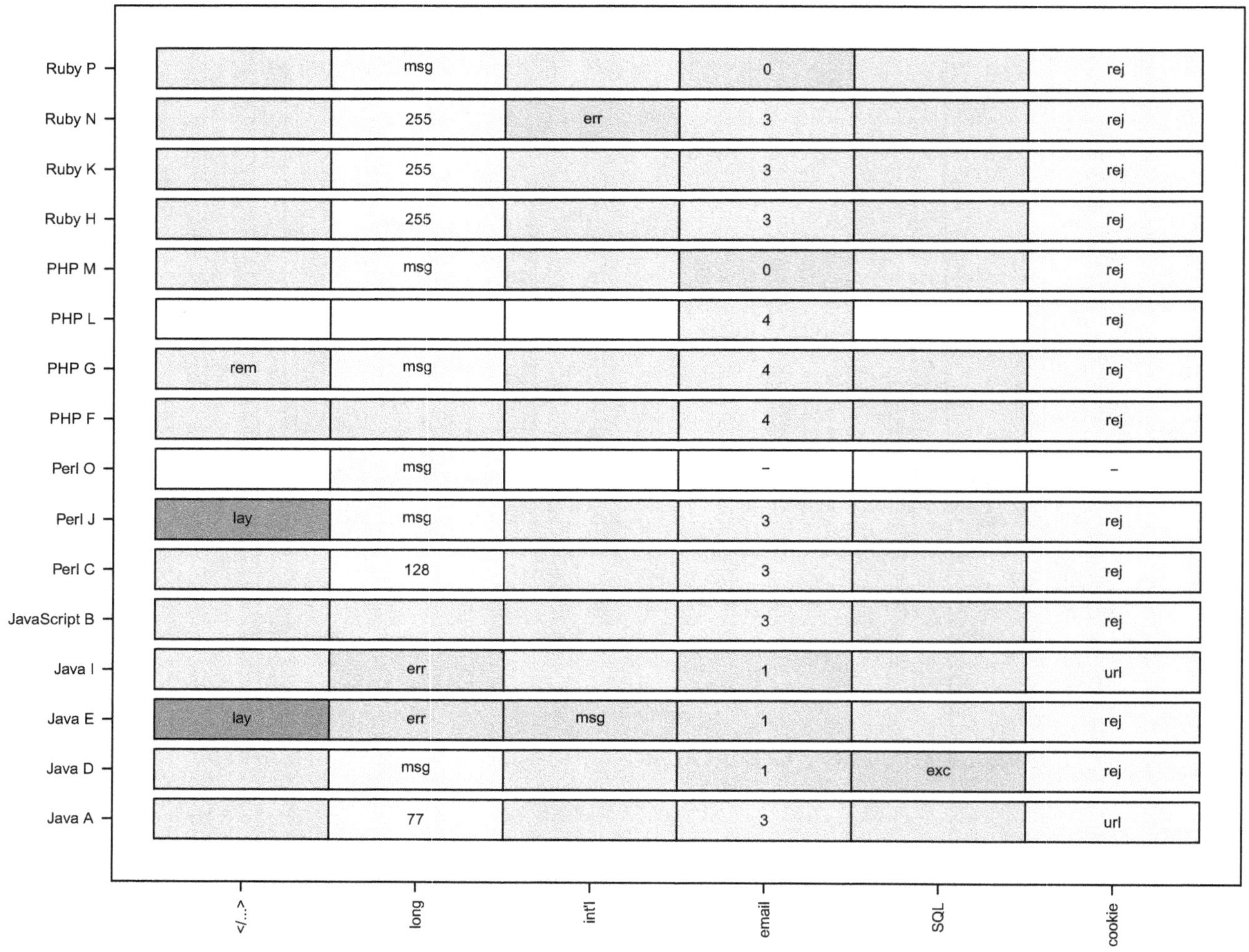

Figure 3: Solution Robustness. Solutions marked green are considered OK, yellow acceptable, soft red broken and bright red critical. Tests that could not be performed due to missing functionality are marked white.

	</...>	long	int'l	email	SQL	cookie
Ruby P		msg		0		rej
Ruby N		255	err	3		rej
Ruby K		255		3		rej
Ruby H		255		3		rej
PHP M		msg		0		rej
PHP L				4		rej
PHP G	rem	msg		4		rej
PHP F				4		rej
Perl O		msg		–		–
Perl J	lay	msg		3		rej
Perl C		128		3		rej
JavaScript B				3		rej
Java I		err		1		url
Java E	lay	err	msg	1		rej
Java D		msg		1	exc	rej
Java A		77		3		url

- a test of email address validation,

- a naive SQL injection test, and

- a test how the solutions reacted when cookies are turned off in the user's browser.

For the naive cross-site-scripting (XSS) test, two small HTML fragments were used for input on the user registration form. The first would, if not properly escaped, result in the input being displayed in bold. The second fragment consisted of various closing tags, resulting in a layout break if not escaped properly. While the first fragment might be considered acceptable since it doesn't pose any security risk and it might be a design decision to allow simple HTML for formatting purposes, a solution allowing for a successful manipulation of its layout most likely also allows for more harmful content to be injected into the HTML page, allowing for cross-site scripting attacks. Figure 3 shows in the "</...>" column, that 2 of the 16 solutions were vulnerable to our attack.

The long input test consisted of two strings, each 50,000 non-space characters long, separated by a space character. The concatenated string was used as input on the user registration form. Solutions that accepted the input and returned it as entered were considered OK. Solutions that silently truncated the input or rejected it with a user-oriented validation message were considered acceptable. Solutions that generated unhelpful technical error messages were considered broken. The "long" column in figure 3 shows that two of the Java solutions but no solution on any other platform was broken in this respect.

For the unicode test, several multi-byte unicode characters were input into the user registration form. Solutions that after registration correctly displayed the characters on the user interface were considered OK, those that did not or displayed a technical error message, were considered broken. All but one Ruby and one Java solution passed this test (see the "unicode" column in figure 3).

The email test aimed at testing the solution's email validation capabilities. We entered 5 different invalid email addresses during user registration: one was missing the domain part altogether, one was missing the top-level domain, and one was missing the second level domain. These three can all be detected using static tests, for example with regular expressions. Another two invalid email addresses were one with an invalid top-level domain and one with an unregistered second-level domain. The first can be detected using a static list of known top-level domains while the latter requires a DNS lookup. Solutions that rejected at least the three statically testable addresses were considered OK. If a solution did not reject at least those three, it was considered broken. The "email" column of figure 3 shows that three of the four Java solutions, one of the Ruby and one of the PHP solutions failed the email validation tests.

The "SQL" column in figure 3 shows the results of a simple test for a SQL injection vulnerability. For this test, a string containing SQL control characters was used as the input for different form fields, including fields where values from a drop-down box etc. were expected. If a solution simply escaped the input and displayed it as entered in the output, it was considered OK. Solutions that display a technical error message stemming from the underlying database system were considered broken. Only the solution of Java team D showed signs of a possible SQL injection vulnerability using this simplistic testing procedure.

The last test we performed was a login attempt with cookies turned off in the user's browser. All solutions either rejected the login or did URL rewriting for the session ID. Although the latter poses a higher risk for inadvertent session stealing by sharing a link containing the user's session ID with someone else, we considered that an acceptable trade-off between security and usability and considered both, login rejection as well as URL rewriting, acceptable. No solutions failed with an error message which would have been considered broken behavior.

It is noteworthy that with the exception of the team A solution, the Java solutions displayed the most robustness flaws. While the solutions on all other platforms show at most one severe flaw, all Java solutions except team A show at least two. Team Java E's solution even exhibits flaws in four categories, the highest value across all platforms.

4.3 Development Process

As mentioned before, the observation method used in the 2007 pilot study didn't reveal any platform specific characteristics of the development process because it was too coarse grained. We therefore conducted a micro-interview with each participant every 15 minutes. The participants were asked a single question: "What were you doing at the moment I arrived?" and answered using a fixed answering scheme.

The scheme allowed for 10 possible activities: program design, coding, debugging, testing, reading, discussing, absent, pausing, non-Plat_Forms work and other. For some activities, details were recorded: what file the participant was working on or what document he was reading and whether the activity was performed alone or together with a partner.

The interviews were characterized with one of 21 labels, such as "readtask", "design", "code", "mantest", "codeautotest", "runautotest" and "debug", resulting in 4656 data points overall, one for each of the 97 interviews conducted with each participant. The 97 interviews gave us a relatively fine-grained and detailed insight into how much time each participant spent with a certain type of activity.

The most interesting result is in the way the teams tested the behavior of their implementations. Figure 4 shows that an average Ruby team spent more time writing automated

tests than an average Java, Perl, and PHP team combined. On the other hand, the average Java team spent more time doing manual tests, i.e. manually testing the application in a web browser, than the average Perl, PHP, and Ruby team combined.

The high completeness of the Ruby teams' solutions (in comparison to teams on platforms that do not do less automated testing) also indicate that automated testing at least did not negatively influence productivity. It is remarkable also because automated testing is equally well supported on all other platforms. There really seems to be a cultural difference with regard to automated testing between Ruby teams and teams from the other platforms.

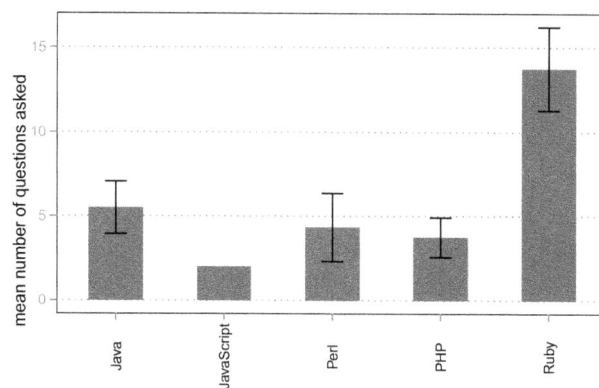

Figure 5: Mean number of questions posted to the on-site customer by platform. The bars indicate the standard error of the mean.

The Ruby teams also behaved remarkably in another way. During the contest, the participants were allowed to ask the first author (acting as an on-site customer) questions regarding the clarification of the requirements document. Figure 5 shows that the Ruby teams on average asked as many questions as the average Java, Perl, and PHP team combined. Note there is a correlation between number of questions asked and number of implemented requirements, so the many questions from the Ruby teams could indicate a cultural difference or reflect the additional questions that arise when delving deeper into implementing the requirements or some combination of both.

4.4 Size and Structure

From the source code and version archives turned in for each solution, we built file lists and classified each file according to its origin: manually written, generated, generated and subsequently modified, reused, and reused and subsequently modified. The teams were required to state the origin in the header of each file they touched. In combination with data from the version control systems we are confident that we assessed the origin of almost all files accurately.

Additionally, we classified the files according to their role: program code (server-side, client-side), binary files (e.g. images), templates, auxiliary files (such as build scripts), and data files (such as configuration files or files with sample data). External libraries that were included in the source distribution and that have not been modified during the experiment were ignored.

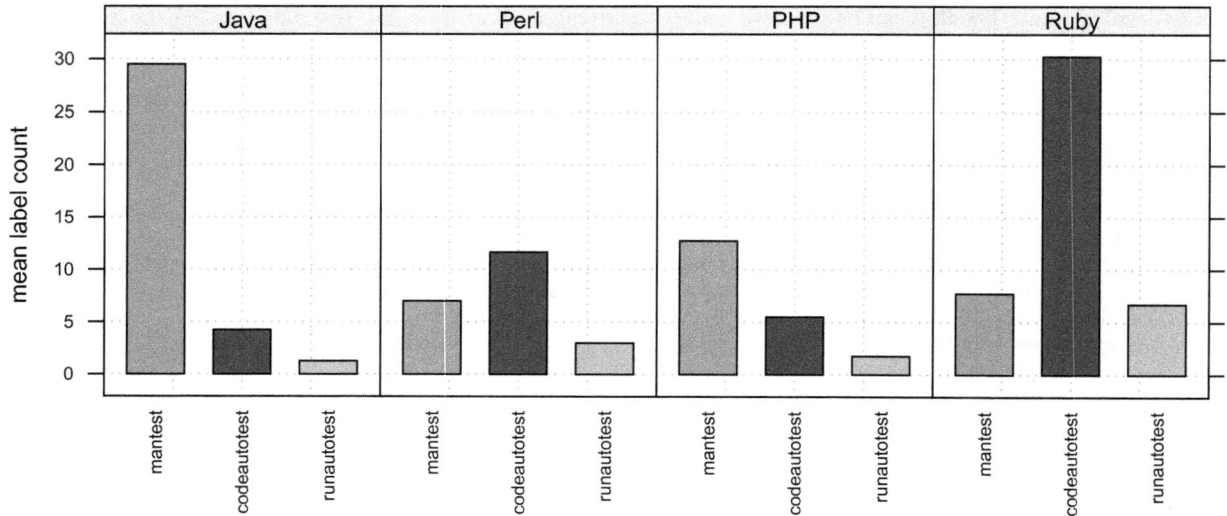

Figure 4: Mean count for activities concerning testing, per platform. The red bar indicates the frequency with which the interview determined manual testing, the blue bar indicates the frequency of writing an automated test and the orange bar the frequency of running an automated test.

We were not able to identify systematic platform-specific differences in the origin or role of the source files, with one exception: The Ruby teams and the teams using frameworks inspired by Ruby on Rails made extensive use of program code generation.

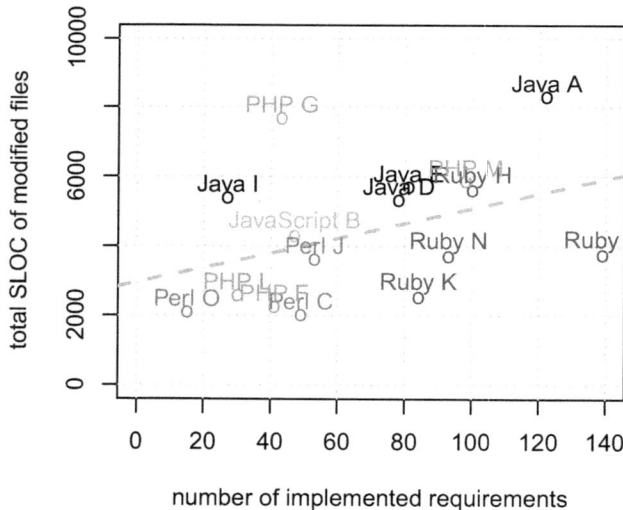

Figure 6: Source lines of code per implemented requirement. Includes files that were modified during the experiment (i.e. manually written, generated and subsequently modified, or reused and modified) and that were classified as either program code, template, or data files. The dashed line is a linear regression line.

We were, however, able to find a difference in the compactness of the solutions, as represented by the average number of lines of code needed to implement one requirement. Figure 6 shows that the Perl and Ruby solutions were more compact (i.e. required fewer lines of code per fully implemented requirement) than the Java and PHP solutions. The Java solutions tend to be bigger while the PHP solutions don't provide a clear picture with some being more compact and others less.

5. RELATED WORK

There are many informal comparisons of web development platforms which compare properties and programming styles mainly theoretically. For example, a broad comparison of Java- and Python-based frameworks can be found at [2] and [8]. Only few of the comparisons involve actual programming, and even if they do, they are different from the Plat_Forms setup in several aspects:

- They involve much less controlled conditions for the production of the solutions. In particular, authors can often put in an arbitrary amount of work during the course of several weeks.

- They often focus on only a single evaluation criterion, such as performance, length of the program code or expected maintainability.

- Some are prepared by a single author only, which raises the question whether we can assume that a similar level of platform-specific skills was applied for each platform.

Examples for such limited types of study are performance contests like the Heise Database contest [4] which compare only the performance aspect of the solutions and allow almost unlimited preparation time. Others are one-man shows

126

like Sean Kelly's video [3] comparing specifically the development process for a (rather trivial) application for Zope/Plone, Django, TurboGears (all from the Python world), Ruby-on-Rails, J2EE light (using Hibernate), and full-fledged J2EE (with EJB). This comparison, while impressive, is necessarily superficial and also visibly biased. The list could be extended, but none of these studies have the ambition to provide an evaluation that is scientifically sound, and few of them even attempt to review many of the relevant criteria at once.

An somewhat similar approach was used at Simula Laboratories in Norway: They hired multiple professional teams from different companies to perform the same complete custom software development project four times over [1]. Even though their goal was to investigate the reproducibility of SE projects, their setup is comparable to our setup for a single platform, except for their variable project duration. Since the systematically manipulated platform variable is missing, the Simula study is framed as a comparative case study. As a pronounced difference to Plat_Forms, the Simula study did not strive for the most similar teams, but rather picked four rather different project bids with respect to cost and then looked for predictable differences rather than for similarities.

The only work with which a direct results comparison is useful is the previous instance of Plat_Forms from 2007 [5, 6]. This execution used only three teams each per platform (for three platforms: Java, Perl, PHP) and also found some platform properties and many non-consistent properties. The 2011 setup incorporates two important learnings from 2007: First, having only three teams per platform makes the study vulnerable against individual, non-platform-related problems with any one team. This issue hit the 2007 Java results and we have hence opted for preferably four teams per platform in 2011. Second, the 2007 process observation was passive and could not discriminate enough interesting activity types to obtain any process-related result worth speaking of. We have hence opted for the micro-interviews in 2011 – with good success but also to the disgust of some of our participants.

As for the actual results, the findings of 2007 are only partially in line with those of 2011, which we will discuss in the next section.

6. DISCUSSION AND CONCLUSION

The goal of this work was identifying emerging properties of web development platforms, that is, characteristics that are largely consistent within the platform, yet different from other platforms. We have indeed found some of these:

- Ruby solutions tend to be compact (that is, have a relatively small source code).

- The same is true of Perl solutions.

- Java solutions tend to have large source code.

- Ruby teams spend much work on testing and have a strong preference for automated testing.

- Java teams also spend much work on testing, yet exhibit a strong preference for manual testing.

- The Ruby teams were consistently highly productive.

- The Perl teams were consistently less productive.

The compactness results can be partially attributed to the expressiveness of language and frameworks and partially may represent cultural differences in design style and programming style. The testing results are a fascinating cultural difference. The productivity results are an impressive proof of the Ruby platform's qualities at least for this type of small-scale, rapid-production project.

On the other hand, there are several lacks of platform consistency as well:

- The productivity of the Java and the PHP teams was rather non-uniform.

- The compactness of the PHP solutions was rather non-uniform.

- The robustness results were rather non-uniform for all platforms.

- The results are not fully in line with the results of the 2007 instance of Plat_Forms . In particular, PHP had then shown a very high and impressively consistent level of productivity, which is in obvious contrast to the 2011 results.

Our interpretation of these results is that the main programming language may no longer be a good indicator of platform: On all platforms (somewhat less for Ruby) there is a growing multitude of different frameworks with quite different characteristics in the last few years. On the other hand, there are groups of such frameworks that share similar ideas and approaches.

This may mean that similar frameworks in different languages provide more platform similarity than dissimilar frameworks in the same language. A convincing sign that this may be the case is the result of team PHP M: They use Symfony, a PHP framework that borrows heavily from the concepts of Ruby on Rails, and their productivity was much like that of the Ruby teams and much unlike that of the other PHP teams (which used different PHP frameworks).

This observation suggests it may be useful to perform the analysis with a different grouping of the solutions, namely by framework similarity rather than by main language. Unfortunately, (a) framework similarity is a gradual rather than a binary criterion and (b) it is unclear how to determine it or even which dimensions are even relevant for it.

We intend to perform such framework classification and re-analysis in the future. We will also perform a somewhat more sophisticated analysis of the security properties of our solutions, targeting the OWASP Top-10 [7] vulnerability types.

Acknowledgments

This work was possible only due to a grant from DFG. We thank all Plat_Forms participants for taking part in our experiment. We thank our student helpers who did the bulk evaluation work. For their financial support we thank our co-organizer Open Source Business Foundation and our sponsors Accenture, ICANS, and Microsoft.

7. REFERENCES

[1] Bente Anda, Dag I. K. Sjøberg, and Audris Mockus. Variability and reproducibility in software engineering: A study of four companies that developed the same

system. *IEEE Trans. Software Eng.*, 35(3):407–429, 2009.

[2] Rick Grehan. Pillars of python: Six python web frameworks compared, August 2011. http://www.infoworld.com/d/application-development/pillars-python-six-python-web-frameworks-compared-169442.

[3] Sean Kelly. Better web app development. 2006. Video on http://oodt.jpl.nasa.gov/better-web-app.mov, or on http://vimeo.com/12650821.

[4] Michael Kunze and Hajo Schulz. Gute Nachbarschaft: c't lädt zum Datenbank-Contest ein. *c't*, 20/2005:156, 2005. see also http://www.heise.de/ct/05/20/156/, english translation on http://firebird.sourceforge.net/connect/ct-dbContest.html, overview on http://www.heise.de/ct/dbcontest/ (all accessed 2007-05-01), results in issue 13/2006.

[5] Lutz Prechelt. Plat_Forms 2007: The web development platform comparison — evaluation and results. Technical Report TR-B-07-10, Freie Universität Berlin, Institut für Informatik, Germany, April 2007. www.plat-forms.org.

[6] Lutz Prechelt. Plat_Forms: A web development platform comparison by an exploratory experiment searching for emergent platform properties. *IEEE Transactions on Software Engineering*, 37(1):95–108, January/February 2011.

[7] J. Williams and D. Wichers. Owasp Top 10 – 2010. *OWASP Foundation*, 2010.

[8] Kelby Zorgdrager. Choosing the right java web development framework, July 2010. http://olex.openlogic.com/wazi/2010/choosing-the-right-java-web-development-framework.

Dispersion, Coordination and Performance in Global Software Teams: A Systematic Review

Nguyen Duc Anh
Department of Computer and Information Science (IDI), NTNU
NO-7491 Trondheim, Norway
anhn@idi.ntnu.no

Daniela S. Cruzes
Department of Computer and Information Science (IDI), NTNU
NO-7491 Trondheim, Norway
dcruzes@idi.ntnu.no

Reidar Conradi
Department of Computer and Information Science (IDI), NTNU
NO-7491 Trondheim, Norway
Reidar.Conradi@idi.ntnu.no

ABSTRACT

Effective team coordination is crucial for successful global software projects. Although considerable research effort has been made in this area, no agreement has been reached on the influence of dispersion on team coordination and performance. The objective of this paper is to summarize the evidence on the relationship among context dispersion, team coordination and performance in global software projects. We have performed a Systematic literature review (SLR) to collect relevant studies and a thematic analysis to synthesize the extracted data. We found 28 primary studies reporting the impact of five dispersion dimensions on team performance. Previously, only two primary studies considered and distinguished all of these dispersion dimensions in studying dispersed team performance. The dispersion dimensions affect team outcomes indirectly through influencing organic and mechanistic coordination processes. Empirical evidence show that geographical dispersion impacts negatively and temporal dispersion has a mixed effect on team performance. While studies with teams working across different time zones shows a tendency that the team performance is pessimistically perceived, studies that use direct measure on task performance shows a positive association to temporal dispersion. The paper provides implications for future research and practitioners in establishing effective distributed team coordination.

Categories and Subject Descriptors

D.2.9 [**Software Engineering**]: Management

Keywords

Systematic literature review, global software development, distribution, team coordination, communication, performance

1. INTRODUCTION

Global software development (GSD) has become a modern paradigm for developing and maintaining software intensive systems. On one hand, organizations are continually spreading and dispersing geographically to seek for mobility in resource, shortening time-to-market, technology innovation, increasing operational efficiency and reducing the negative effect of distance to customers [1]. An ACM report shows that 30% of US IT jobs are expected to be offshored by 2015 [2]. Open source software (OSS) have become popular with more than 160.000 projects registered in Source Forge[1] in the end of 2011, which doubled compared with that in the end of 2004. These figures illustrate for a wide and growing adoption of global development models in software intensive organizations and communities.

On the other hand, globalization is also accompanied by challenges of managing dispersed project activities. Many specialists and managers find global software projects too complex and time consuming to handle. There are an increasing number of problem reports caused by various dispersion dimensions, resulting in a high failure rate of GSD projects [3]. The common mentioned problems of dispersed projects are inadequate communication, different mental models, feedback delays, misunderstanding and lack of trust [4-7]. The claimed benefits of being dispersed and reported obstacles in managing global teams raise a question of cost benefit analysis when dispersing project teams and activities. Understanding the influence of dispersion on project outcomes is crucial to support decisions making on adopting a "going-global" strategy in new projects and improving performance of ongoing projects.

Global team is a concept with multi meanings, which at least consists of offshore team, outsourcing team, virtual team and open source community. Global teams operate in various types of dispersed environments where communication between team members is normally electronic, often asynchronous, with limited opportunities for informal and face-to-face contact [8]. Global teams can be dispersed in different branches of an organization (offshore insourcing), different organizations (outsourcing and partnership) and team members can jointly work in a virtual environment via common online infrastructures (open source and virtual team). In organization research, coordination is defined as an additional activity to manage different type of interdependencies between work tasks and task carriers [9, 10]. Team coordination occurs among project team members in a specific organizational context and follows a specific process to collectively perform the task. As software development activities are intensively interactive and normally complex, the ability to communicate ideas and manage task dependencies is determinant for the team performance, in term of development speed and task accuracy [11]. When software development tasks become larger and dispersed, the interdependencies among the tasks and task carriers become more complicated. This makes coordination in distributed team more difficult and more important than it in collocated team.

Given the significance as well as challenges of team coordination in dispersed context, a growing body of empirical research devotes to comprehend the relationship among dispersion, team coordination and project performance. Synthesis of these studies

[1] http://sourceforge.net

could provide a systematic view of commonalities and variations among primary studies, as well as new interpretive explanations that go beyond the scope of any primary study [12]. In this paper, we present the results of a systematic review of empirical studies of dispersion dimensions and team performance through the lens of team coordination. The main outputs of this SLR are (1) a list of dispersion dimensions and coordination aspects related to team performance, (2) a thematic map that characterizes state of the art on the influence of dispersion dimensions on team performance, (3) and an analysis of a set of context variables that may explain the heterogeneity in the influence directions.

The paper is organized as follows: section 2 presents related literature reviews. Section 3 describes our research methods while Section 4 presents our results and analysis. Section 5 describes our limitations. Section 6 discusses the findings and also conclusions of this paper.

2. PREVIOUS LITERATURE REVIEWS

Prior to this work, some authors have performed literature reviews on different topics in the context of GSD. Among them, there are three SLRs most relevant to our work [13, 14, 15]. Table 1 shows the differences between these works and our study in term of review's focus, scope, method and forms of final results.

Šmite et al. summarized the empirical evidence about the state of the art studies on GSD and discussed on the strength of evidence [13]. The review analyzed context setting of primary studies, such as number of sites, site locations, project life cycle, reasons for starting global collaboration and provided a list of good collaboration practices. Concerning team collaboration, the authors concluded that geographical, temporal and cultural dispersion have a significant effect on how dispersed team communication, coordination and control are done. However, they do not provide details about the effect direction and its influencing factors. In our study, we explored the impact of dispersion on team performance while considering the mediate effect of coordination mechanisms and contextual factors.

Steinmacher et al. reviewed studies about awareness support in GSD projects and its impact on team communication, coordination, and cooperation [14]. While Steinmacher explored antecedent factors that affect team collaboration, our study focuses on team collaboration as a mediator of the relationship between dispersion and team performance. Additionally, Steinmacher included both empirical, theoretical and tool review papers, while our review only focuses on empirical evidence.

Table 1: Related literature reviews

Study	#	Focus	Main Final Product
Šmite et al. 2010 [14]	59	Project type, research topic, reasons for starting global collaboration and good practices for GSD	List of best practices Descriptive statistic of study features
Steinmacher et al. 2010 [15]	42	Support of awareness on communication, coordination and cooperation in GSD	List of awareness aspect
Noll et al. 2011 [16]	26	Barriers and solutions for collaborating in GSD	List of barriers and solutions
This study	28	Relationship among dispersion, coordination and team performance in GSD	Thematic map List of influencing context factors

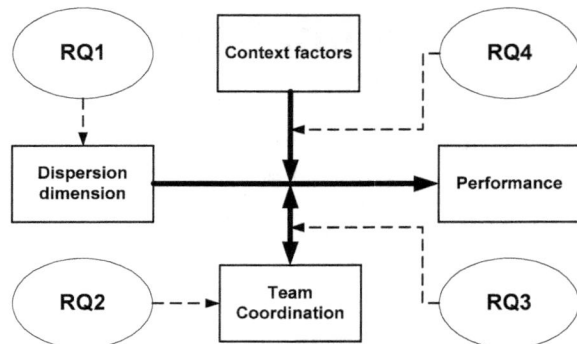

Figure 1: Research questions

Noll et al. reviewed studies about challenges and solutions for collaboration in software development teams [15]. The authors described key barriers to collaboration, such as geographic, temporal, cultural, and linguistic dispersion; and also solutions to overcome these barriers, such as site visits, synchronous communication technology, and knowledge sharing infrastructure. While this study performs a narrative summary of collaboration in distributed context, we thematically synthesize the direction of dispersion's influence on team performance and details of the influences through the lens of team coordination processes.

3. METHODOLOGICAL APPROACH

The main goal of this study is to summarize empirical evidences on the impact of dispersion on team performance mediated by team coordination. We planned, conducted, and reported the review results by following the SLR process suggested by Kitchenham [16].

3.1 Research Questions

The review objective is divided into four research questions as shown in Figure 1. We adopted the common input-process-outcome model to organize research questions and to provide the basics for integrating literatures [17]. The input part represents the starting conditions for teamwork, such as dispersion context of the projects. Although GSD is frequently mentioned in Software Engineering (SE) literature, it is not clear which dispersion aspects or dimensions are actually investigated and measured (RQ1). The process part represents the dynamic interaction among team members such as team coordination processes. The dispersion context of projects should have some influences on team coordination before it results in teamwork outcomes (RQ2). The outcome part represents team performance as consequences of a team's functioning in a specific context. Given concepts addressed in RQ1 and RQ2 as the basis, we investigated the relationship between dispersion, team performance and the mediate role of team coordination (RQ3). We also expected heterogeneous findings on the influences of dispersion dimensions on project performance among primary studies. Therefore, RQ4 searches for some possible explanations by investigating the study contextual factors. In short, the research questions investigated in this systematic review are:

RQ1: Which dimensions of dispersion are explored in relationship between the dispersion and team performance?
RQ2: How is team coordination investigated and influenced by the dispersion dimensions?
RQ3: How does the dispersion dimensions influence the teams' performance?
RQ4: Which contextual factors could explain the heterogeneity among empirical findings on the influence directions?

3.2 Search and Selection Strategy

The review process consisted of six phases, as shown in Figure 2. At first, we conducted an ad-hoc literature review on team coordination in global software projects. The goal was to understand the conceptual background and emergent issues for further investigation. A list of initial studies was identified to formulate the search string and to perform a validity check for the systematic search later. In the second step, we developed a review protocol, which specifies search terms, databases, search inclusion and exclusion criteria, quality assessment and a data extraction form. We conducted a pilot search and data extraction to test and refine the review protocol. The search terms were adjusted based on the search coverage and accuracy [18]. Besides, the data extraction form was also adjusted based on the extracted information from sample studies.

After refining the review protocol, the systematic search was carried out with a similar procedure of the pilot search. The search results were validated by its coverage of the initial papers. A screening process was performed to identify eligible studies (title and abstract, followed by full text review). After that, the quality of studies was assessed and studies with lowest quality scores were removed. In order not to miss any important papers, we performed an additional search by scanning the reference list forward and backward.

The search string consists of 3 parts: *(Coordination Or synonyms) AND (Dispersion Or synonyms) AND context*. The synonyms were identified in the context of SE and Information System (IS). As the ad-hoc review revealed that there is no distinguished use of terms "coordination", "collaboration" and "cooperation" in SE and IS literature, we considered them as interchangeable concepts. Several trial searches were conducted to determine which search string was most appropriate. The search was performed in two literature databases, namely Scopus and ISI. As common search fields in SLR, we searched in papers title, keyword and abstract with no restriction of the period of time. The final search string is:

> *(coordinati* or collaborativ* or cooperati*) AND (distributed or offshor* or "open source" or outsourc* or global or dispers*) AND (software or project or team) IN (Title or Abstract or Keyword)*

The selection process resulted in 28 papers studying impact of dispersion on team performance (See full list in Appendix). We included papers that: (1) investigate concepts, problems and solutions of coordination in GSD context; (2) and apply at least one of empirical methods to answer the proposed research questions.

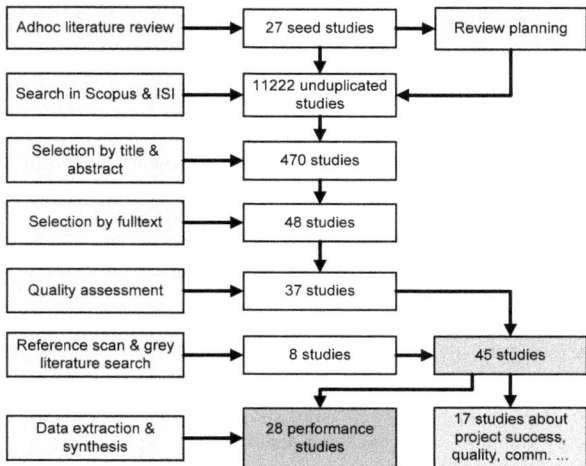

Figure 2: Search strategy and result

Table 2: Quality assessment checklist

Problem statement
1. Is the aim of the research sufficiently explained and well motivated?
Research design
2. Is the context of study clearly stated?
3. Is the research design sufficiently prepared beforehand?
Data collection
4. Are the data collection and measures adequately described?
5. Are the measures used in the study relevant for answering the research question?
Data analysis
6. Is the data analysis used in the study adequately described?
7a. Qualitative study: Are the interpretation of result clearly described?
7b. Quantitative study: Are the effect size reported with assessed statistical significance?
8. Are potential confounders adequately controlled or discussed?
Conclusion
9. Are the findings of study clearly stated and supported by the results?
10. Does the paper discuss limitations or validity?

We excluded 56 short papers (less than 6 pages) that do not provide sufficient information about data collection, analysis methods and interpretation of findings. We also excluded studies that either: (1) are not in SE or IS area; (2) are not about dispersed context; (3) investigate coordination-supported infrastructures or tools such as wiki-based systems and social network platforms; (4) do not have empirical validation; (5) or only focus on team coordination without relationships with project outcomes.

We devised a number of quality assessment questions to assess the rigorousness, credibility, and relevance of the relevant studies from Dybå and Dingsøyr's checklist [19]. The list of questions is shown in Table 2. Each question has three possible options: "Yes" (score 1), "Partially" (score 0.5) and "No" (score 0). For a given study, the quality score was counted by summing up the scores of all questions. To ensure the reliability of the findings of this review, we considered only the studies with quality score equal or greater than 5. We classified papers with score 5-6 as weak, 7-8 as medium and 9-10 as strong quality.

3.3 Data Extraction

The following information was extracted from selected studies: research design (research question, research design type, case study type, unit of analysis, sample size, data collection method, data analysis method, threats to validity); context setting (project description, number of site, site location, level of technology support), dispersion factor (name, explanation, measure), coordination aspect (name, explanation and measure), project outcome factors (name, explanation, measure), findings and implications. We distinguished studies that investigate multiple data sources in a period of time (case study) with studies that explore project repository without sufficient context description (data archive). We also distinguished between a study and a paper since a paper could report more than one study. Table 3 describes some characteristics of the 28 papers included in the SLR. Some studies adopt more than one research method and measurement approach.

Regarding to study design, survey is the dominant type with 46% of the studies, followed by data archive (32%) and case study (28%). Considering project type, 68% of the studies are about coordination in inner context, or offshore team within an organization. Five studies investigate outsourcing context and four studies explore coordination in OSS projects. Twenty three studies focus on developers level while 14 studies consider manager's viewpoints.

	P01	P02	P03	P04	P05	P06	P07	P08	P09	P10	P11	P12	P13	P14	P15	P16	P17	P18	P19	P20	P21	P22	P23	P24	P25	P26	P27	P28	Total	%
Study design (Section 3.3, 4.4)																														
Survey	♦	♦		♦						♦		♦	♦		♦		♦			♦		♦	♦			♦	♦		13	46%
Data archive	♦					♦	♦				♦			♦		♦		♦		♦			♦					♦	9	32%
Case study	♦	♦	♦		♦											♦												♦	6	21%
Interview									♦				♦				♦												3	10%
Experiment						♦																		♦					2	7%
Data analysis (Section 4.4)																														
Quantitative	♦	♦	♦		♦	♦	♦	♦		♦	♦	♦	♦	♦	♦	♦		♦	♦	♦	♦	♦	♦		♦	♦	♦	♦	25	89%
Qualitative				♦				♦									♦							♦					4	14%
Global type (Section 4.4)																														
Inner	♦	♦	♦		♦	♦	♦		♦	♦	♦	♦	♦	♦			♦	♦	♦		♦		♦	♦		♦			19	68%
Outsource				♦											♦		♦								♦		♦		5	18%
Open source							♦								♦					♦		♦							4	14%
Subject (Section 4.4)																														
Developer	♦	♦	♦		♦		♦	♦			♦	♦	♦	♦	♦		♦	♦		♦	♦	♦	♦	♦		♦	♦	♦	23	82%
Manager	♦		♦	♦		♦			♦	♦		♦		♦		♦	♦		♦		♦					♦	♦		14	50%
Student					♦																								1	4%
Quality (Section 3.3)																														
Strong		♦	♦	♦	♦		♦	♦					♦			♦	♦	♦	♦		♦				♦	♦	♦		19	68%
Medium						♦							♦																2	7%
Weak	♦								♦	♦					♦					♦			♦	♦					7	25%
Dispersion (Section 4.1, Section 4.3)																														
Geographical	♦	♦	♦			♦			♦	♦		♦	♦			♦	♦	♦				♦	♦			♦			16	57%
Temporal			♦	♦		♦		♦	♦			♦			♦				♦						♦	♦			8	28%
Organizational			♦	♦					♦			♦		♦					♦	♦			♦						8	28%
Work process				♦			♦		♦			♦				♦						♦					♦		7	25%
Cultural				♦					♦	♦		♦			♦														5	18%
Coordination (Section 4.2)																														
Organic	♦	♦			♦		♦		♦	♦	♦	♦	♦	♦	♦	♦	♦	♦	♦	♦	♦	♦	♦	♦	♦	♦			23	82%
Mechanistic			♦	♦	♦		♦	♦				♦					♦	♦						♦	♦			♦	11	39%

4. RESULTS

Thematic synthesis was used for synthesizing the results, following the recommended steps proposed by Cruzes and Dybå [20]. Firstly we identified the emerged dispersion dimensions from the papers. Secondly, we summarized empirical findings about their influence on team coordination on a thematic map. Lastly, we captured emergent themes that provide the guidance for comprehending the thematic map.

4.1 RQ1: Dimensions of Dispersion

There are five dimensions of dispersion emerging from the literature, namely: geographical, temporal, cultural, work process and organizational dispersion.

Geographical dispersion, which is also denoted as spatial distribution or physical proximity, is the most frequently investigated dimension of dispersion (57% of the papers). Geographical dispersion is commonly defined as the geographical difference in working places among project stakeholders. The metrics applied for this type of dispersion vary among primary studies. Most studies measure geographical dispersion by a dichotomous variable to differentiate team processes and outcomes between collocated and distributed teams (P1, P2, P7, P14, P18 and P19). Three studies consider degree of dispersions, e.g. number of sites (P3, P11 and P25) and three studies consider whether team member was located in the same room or different building, city, or country (P13, P20 and P27). Geographical dispersion introduces issues of using collaboration technology to alternate the face-to-face and synchronous communication (P20, P24 and P27).

Temporal dispersion is investigated in 28% of the papers. It occurs when a project' works are separated through different working hours, time zones, and work shift. The temporal dispersion introduces the issue of time synchronization when working time differences should be aligned with workflows (i.e. work is handed over at the end of the work day to a site whose work day is just beginning). Most of the studies measure temporal dispersion by the (degree of) difference in time zone among project team member (P3, P4, P6, P9, P13, P20 and P27). Temporal dispersion also accounts for situations where team members are located at the same site but in different shifts or even flexible hours (P8). In the open source context, P8 quantifies the temporal dispersion as a variance in developer's starting time.

Organizational dispersion occurs when the project work is shared across organizational boundaries, such as in a vendor-client relationship and ecosystem partnership (P4, P5, P15, P22 and P26). Organizational boundary also occurs between functionally independent units of the same organization (P9, P13). Organizational dispersion is investigated in 28% of the papers. This type of dispersion introduces issues of contractual obligations, cooperation and competition, goal conflicts, knowledge integration, different work process, different kind of coordination strategy and mechanism (P4, P9, P22 and P26). Organizational dispersion suffers from a relatively high level of conceptual ambiguity and was mainly qualitatively explored in these studies. Only one study uses boundary spanning subject, process and object as the quantitative measure for organizational dispersion (P26).

Work process dispersion (25% of the papers) refers to the difference in functional and process aspects of dispersed tasks (P9, P13, P17 and P28). Stakeholders in different working places can have different working environments, independently of being in the same time zone and the same organization. They may adopt different communicating and collaborating processes and may have different level of work infrastructure, such as computer, network, configuration, communication and development tools (P9, P13 P17 and P28). Besides, different sites can take charge of different project phase activities, such as one team for requirement analyst and the other team for development (P17, P28).

Cultural dispersion (18% of the papers) is normally mentioned as the difference in stakeholders' cultural background, such as language, mental model and subtle cognition (P9 and P13). Project stakeholders from different countries often have different perspectives on issues and different ways of communicating and resolving them (P4 and P10). For example, Western hierarchical relationships are more influenced by contractual agreements and an ideology of essential, while Indian hierarchical relationships are more oriented towards mutual obligations and emotional relationship (P4). In P10, cultural dimension is measured by power distance, individualism, masculinity, uncertainty avoidance, and long-term orientation. All the studies on cultural dispersion focus on the cultural differences in the nations or continents level, and no study explore the cultural differences in lower levels, such as regions and organizations.

It is noticed that in primary studies, these dispersion dimensions are overlap concepts and insufficiently explored in literature. While temporal and cultural dispersion could be embedded in the geographical dispersion, an organizational dispersion normally introduces work process dispersion. O'Leary and Cumming suggested a set of variables to quantify spatial-temporal and organizational distance [21].

4.2 RQ2: Coordination Mechanism

In social science, Thompson labeled two types of organizational structure, namely organic and mechanistic organization [22]. Organic organizations rely on lateral communication to exchange information rather than vertical communication to give direction. The coordination is based upon expertise and knowledge rather than on authority of position. Mechanistic organizations are characterized by high complexity, formalization and centralization. The organizations perform routine tasks and rely heavily on programmed behaviors. Based on Thompson's model, we organized the coordination aspects that are influenced by team coordination into two categories, namely organic coordination (82% of the papers) and mechanistic coordination (39% of the papers).

4.2.1 Organic Coordination

Organic coordination, or mutual adjustment, or social coordination mechanism, is the use of lateral communication means to coordinate activities [22]. Grounded from primary studies, organic coordination is influenced by dispersion dimensions via the frequency of communication and feedback, coordination delays and misinterpretation.

Frequency of communication and feedback: distributed team communication is much less frequently studied than collocated team communication (P2). Temporal dispersion limits the ability to communicate synchronously (P9) also creates difficulties in asynchronous communication (P20). However, the negative impact of distance on communication frequency is significant in early phases of projects and decreases somewhat over time (P2 and P5).

Coordination delay: time zone differences create discontinuity in dispersed tasks, which leads to a delay in asynchronous communication (P20, P27). Organizational differences introduce problems of complex escalation and delay in communication. Distributed communication differs from collocated communication in a way that it requires more people to participate, thereby introducing

delays (P2). As a surprising finding, P11 showed that distributed communication does not appear to introduce a significant amount of delay compared to collocated task completion time. In the study, modern shared workspace and task-driven communication is thought to account for mitigating coordination delay.

Misinterpretation: lacking of face-to-face contact, differences in working time and cultural background could make people misinterpret other's behaviors (P4, P9, P13). Differences in communicating language also cause remote members to switch to their native language. This leads to a mismatch in conversation style, and consequently difficulties in technical collaboration (P4, P15).

4.2.2 Mechanistic Coordination

Mechanistic coordination is the use of vertical communication means to coordinate activities in a programmed way, such as direct supervision and standardization, task organization, role assignment, schedules, plans, division of labor, project controls and specifications, routine meeting and status check (P6, P9, P17, P18, P26 and P28). Mechanistic coordination in distributed team is influenced by dispersion dimensions via team coordination structure, task scheduling complexity and coordination requirement gaps.

Team coordination structure: geographical and temporal dispersion introduce problems in organizing effective communication structure. Hierarchical structure of communication networks introduces the role of brokers who are in the connection with many other developers (P5). They are more likely to sustain collective actions, tend to reduce coordination gaps and increase coordination effectiveness. However, this centralization pattern also introduces a bottleneck since relying on a broker makes the entire issue tracking efficiency dependent on his (her) availability (P24). Democratic communication structure where team member freely communicate to each other is also problematic since it introduces complex communication paths and overloaded communication content (P12). High degree of network density creates redundant information flows, which may have a negative effect on the coordination performance (P16).

Task scheduling complexity: in the dynamic of task dependency and uncertain collaboration environment, lacking balance in adopting coordination mechanisms not only leads to coordination pitfalls, but also affects the remote team performance (P17). Team spanning through many different time zones are difficult to organize tasks, such as scheduling conference calls and setting up meeting for all relevant sites (P6, P27). Identifying roles and dividing tasks in distributed context, especially withwork process and organization dispersion, is much harder than those in homogeneous environment (P07). However, P8 showed that in the open source project context, time separation does not cause coordination problems but increase the total time available to projects by allowing developers to take the extra time to code appropriately.

Coordination requirement gap: geographical dispersion obstructs the identification of coordination requirements from team dependency. In comparison with collocated team, finding who should talk to whom in a collaboration is more difficult in distributed context (P01, P14, P19). Socio-technical congruence, which is defined as a match between coordination requirements established by task dependencies and the actual coordination activities carried out by developers, is harder to identify in distributed contexts (P19). Geographical distribution introduces more and larger coordination requirement gaps (P01). While knowledge broker would help to partially close the gaps, the remained problem is to align role assignment with informal communication structures and the dynamic nature of coordination requirements (P01, P19).

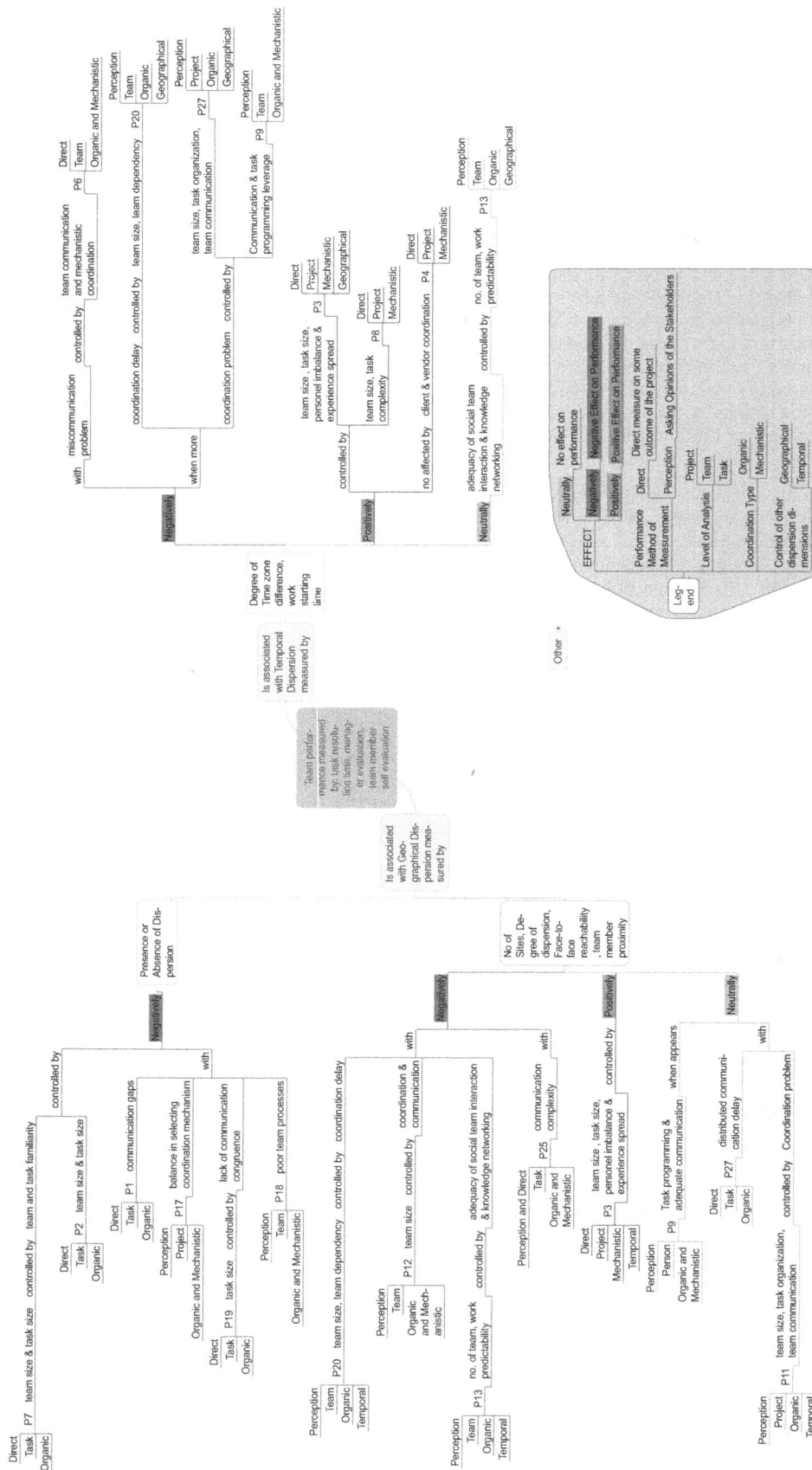

Figure 3: Impact of geographical and temporal dispersion on performance

4.3 RQ3: Dispersion and Team Performance

In this paper, we focused on the two main types of dispersion: geographical and temporal and the influence of them on the team performance. Figure 3 shows the final thematic mind map as a result of the synthesis. The map is read from the root and go down till the leaves as the below order:

> Team performance is associated with [*Dispersion measures*] [*Positively/Negatively/Neutrally*] with [*Coordination aspects*] controlled by [*Context factors*] in [*Study ID*]

In the included papers, team performance is measured in three main ways: (1) evaluation of project managers' on project performance (work on schedule and within budget) (P5, P6, P8, P9, P12, P13, P17, P18 and P20), (2) time to complete a shared task (P2, P7, P11, P14 and P19), (3) and amount of task (P1, P3, P6 and P25). The direction of influence of dispersion dimensions on team performance is decided by the direction of the dispersion variables in a statistical test model (correlation or regression models) from quantitative data or grounded conclusions from qualitative data in primary studies.

In summary, ten studies show a negative influence of geographical dispersion on team performance; one study shows a positive influence and three studies report a neutral effect. Regarding to temporal dispersion, four studies show a negative influence, three studies show a positive impact and one study report a neutral effect. We discuss these results in the following sections.

4.3.1 Presence or Absence of Geographical Dispersion

The presence or absence of the geographical dispersion was the measure of dispersion in six papers (P1, P2, P7, P17, P18 and P19). All of them reported a negative association between geographical dispersion and team performance.

In P2, the authors found that distributed work items take about 2.5 times as long to complete as similar items where all the work is collocated. In P17 and P18, the authors also found that distributed teams are less effective in communication and lower in performance than collocated teams are. The negative effect of geographical dispersion on the team performance is indirect via teamwork processes, such as communication and coordination process (P2, P18, P20 and P27) or requirements gaps (P1). This delay could be introduced by more relevant people than comparable same-site work items (P2), restricted flow of information across sites, lack of face-to-face contact, spontaneous communication, and shared social settings (P13). Consequently, it creates great difficulty in finding people and reducing the likelihood of obtaining useful information from them (P2). Distributed work introduces disparities in working practices, issues of trust among distributed development units, lack of face-to-face contact and constant feedbacks. Lacking balance in selecting coordination mechanisms not only leads to coordination pitfalls, but also affects the remote team performance (P17). The coordination problems are not only to identify interdependence between developers and tasks, but also the dynamic of coordination requirements when this interdependence changes over time (P19).

4.3.2 Degree of Geographical Dispersion

Eight papers (P3, P9, P11, P12, P13, P20, P25 and P27) measure geographic dispersion in terms of number of sites involved or the degree of dispersion. Four papers reported the negative effect (P12, P13, P20 and P25), one positive (P3) and three neutral effect (P9, P11 and P27) of geographical dispersion in team performance as shown in Figure 3.

In P12, P13, P20 and P25, authors found that geographical congruence had a negative effect on performance. Greater work place mobility, such as working in different sites, working from home or while travelling has a negative impact on team performance (P13, P20). An experiment with students showed that the average working speed of each individual site declines about 20 percent when each development site added (P25). Increasing the number of locations also complicates coordination and hampers the communication in the project status and feedback. The increased of number of site complicates coordination and hampers the communication in the project status and feedback (P25). This collaboration problem makes developers avoid conflicts by writing and maintaining code locally. Consequently, integrating or using code developed from other sites is more demanding (P2). In P12, geographical dispersion amplified the impact of teamwork quality on team performance. As the team members are more geographically dispersed, the influence of teamwork quality on team performance increases.

In P9, P11 and P27, authors did not find a significant relationship between the geographical dispersion and the performance. In P9, reducing or eliminating the impact of geographic dispersion was costly; but some participants stated that they had to invest more resources to overcome the difficulties of working over geographic distance. In P27, spatial separation alone was not directly associated with team performance; lower performance was primarily due to coordination problems created by a large time zone span. In P11, the authors concluded that the effect of distance is mitigated in collaborative environments such as Jazz, in which communication in large distributed work teams is facilitated by an ability to asynchronously comment on tracking activity of work items.

In contrary to the above-mentioned papers, P3 shows that when organizations distribute across geographical dispersion, such as increasing number of sites leads to increasing productivity at project level. However, the imbalance in personal experiences among development sites decrease productivity and geographical dispersion was found to have a negative impact on product quality (P3).

4.3.3 Degree of Temporal Dispersion

Eight studies investigated the influences of temporal dispersion on team performance (P3, P4, P6, P8, P9, P13, P20 and P27). Among them, four studies reported a negative effect (P6, P9, P20 and P27), three studies showed a positive effect (P3, P4 and P8) and one study reported an inconclusive result about the influence of temporal dispersion on team performance (P13).

Project managers tend to perceive the impact of temporal dispersion on team performance negatively (P6, P9, P20 and P27). Survey and interview of managers show that difficulties in maintaining awareness of distributed activities and lack of appropriate coordination mechanisms leads to negative effects on project performance in terms of time and budget overruns, lower system quality and customer satisfaction (P9, P20 and P27). The small time separation with some overlapping hours does not create substantial coordination problems, but greater time zone span is associated with more coordination problems, i.e. 9–12 hours span creates severe effects (P27). A complex model of time separation influence is presented in P6, which show that development speed decreased significantly with very small amounts of time separation (i.e., 2/3 overlap). Teams in the 1/3 overlap had lower levels of speed than full overlap, but the difference was less significant than for 2/3 overlap. The authors hypothesize that with more complex and equivocal tasks that require more frequent interaction, speed will be dramatically affected by time separation, but this effect may also be influenced by learning effects (P6).

In P13, temporal dispersion was not found to be significantly associated with team performance, including mutual trust among team members, effectiveness of communication and coordination, commitment and contribution of individual members, and quality and punctuality of team products. The given reason is that adoption of advanced working environment or evolution of communication pattern can offset the influence of dispersion dimensions.

In contrary to results from the above papers, P8 showed that temporal dispersion is positively associated with the speed and the quality of coding, in the context of OSS. Greater temporal dispersion allows project progress to be continually monitored, reflected, and revised around the clock, thereby leads to higher quantity-per-unit and quality of code. Temporal boundary is also found to have a positive effect on development speed in offshored context (P4). The given reason is that the difference in time zones may allow managers to leverage the "24 hour work-day" in making more effective use of calendar time on a project. These duration advantages are greater when the time separation is larger, i.e., India and US versus India and Singapore. In addition, a study of 246 industrial projects at the project level showed that when organizations distribute across spatial and temporal dispersion, they increased project level productivity (P3).

4.4 RQ4: Leveraging Effects of Context Factors

To explain for the differences in the influence directions among these papers, we explored some characteristics of the research methods and contextual factors by a data mining tool called Weka[2]. We applied C4.5 algorithm to build a classification tree of impact direction based on context factors [23]. The explored factors were: research method features such as performance measure type (perception based or direct measure), level of analysis (project, team or work item), sample size (small, medium or large), subject type and quality of study, context setting factors, such as level of technology infrastructure, dispersion range (project spread in 1, 2, or 3 continents) and global development type (inner, outsource or open source). The thematic map also reveals the adequate control level of task and team characteristics, which are basics for investigating team coordination (as shown in Figure 3).

The classification results show that sample size, subject type, dispersion range and global development type is not able to classify the direction impact. Level of communication technology support was disappointed to us since most of these papers were not clear about this factor, so we couldn't discuss the effect of this on the results. The only two factors that provided clusters with an acceptable homogeneity were performance measure and level of analysis. The summary of these two factors is shown in Table 4. Positive, negative or neutral impacts are marked by "(+)", "(-)" or "(O)" respectively.

On the *performance measure*, all of the investigated studies that use perception-based measurement show a negative or neutral impact of geographical and temporal dispersion on performance. Regarding to temporal dispersion only, performance measure type classify direction of the influences. Perception-based studies report a pessimistic view of the impact of dispersion on team performance while studies on direct measurement show positive results. This suggests that the psychological dispersion might not necessarily overlap with the physical dispersion, which confirms the "far-but-close" phenomenon in distributed working environments [24].

---

[2]http://www.cs.waikato.ac.nz/ml/weka

Table 4: Influencing context factors

Context factors	Geographical			Temporal		
	(+)	(-)	(O)	(+)	(-)	(O)
Total studies	1	11	3	5	3	1
Performance measure						
Perception	0	7	2	0	3	1
Direct measurement	1	4	1	5	0	0
Level of analysis						
Project	1	1	2	3	1	0
Team	0	5	0	2	2	1
Task	0	5	1	0	0	0

Concerning the *level of analysis*, 100% of studies (6 out of 6) that investigate team performance at task level report negative or neutral impacts of geographical dispersion on task resolving performance. 80% of studies (8 out of 10) that investigate team performance at team level show non-positive results. These results are observed in only 50% of studies (4 out of 8) at project level. The decrease of homogeneity of influence direction when increasing granularity level of analysis might indicate that the negative impact of dispersion dimensions is mediated by some team and project level context factors.

5. LIMITATIONS

In the process of selecting and aggregating results from primary studies, we faced various challenges related to quality of studies and heterogeneity of study context.

5.1 Challenges in Synthesizing Findings

Context factors are important to reason about the influence of dispersion dimensions on team coordination and performance. However, only few studies sufficiently and properly reported the context setting. Details about geographical and organizational context, such as site locations, involved parties and collaborative work processes are important to identify and isolate the influences of each dispersion dimensions. However, this information is often missing in literature. Besides, to understand the level of coordination practices, communication process and technology should be described as well. While availability of collaboration technology and its adoption level could be a mediate factor of team dispersion on performance, most of the primary studies do not give enough information about it.

Another challenge is to integrate results from quantitative studies and qualitative studies. The heterogeneity of primary studies does not allow quantitative summary methods, such as meta-analysis on the whole set of studies. Therefore, a qualitative thematic synthesis and a clustering analysis on temporal and geographical studies were selected. Besides, the variety of unit of analysis, measurement of dispersion and team performance make us difficult to interpret and generalize the findings to a larger extent.

5.2 Threats to Validity

Even though we have conducted a thorough process of searching and selecting primary studies, we are aware that the selection process may not captured all of the relevant studies, especially ones that have not been indexed in Scopus or ISI.

Another threat to SLR type of study is reviewer's bias in study selection and synthesis [16]. To reduce this threat, the selection process was conducted by the two first authors and constantly crosschecked. These two authors also jointly performed the synthesis. Conflicts were discussed until consensus was reached. Additionally, the third reviewer checked the paper selection and result of analysis from an outsider's perspective.

A threat to external validity of this SLR is generalization. The limited number of studies on each dispersion dimension (16 studies at most) does not allow us to conduct formal statistical analysis. However, consensus observations from these studies suggest important context factors that should be further investigated.

As mentioned in the challenges, we were limited to the context factors that are commonly reported in the studies. Therefore, it might be that the direction of dispersion's influence on team performance is explained by other factors, which is less visible from these studies.

6. CONCLUSIONS

This study identified five common dispersion dimensions in empirical studies about global software development team performance. These dispersion dimensions are often not clearly distinguished and comprehensively studied in the literature. While temporal, geographical and organizational dispersion are the most investigated types of dispersion, the amount of empirical studies that focus on work process and cultural dispersion are relatively small and mainly qualitative in research methods.

The synthesized evidence shows that dispersion dimensions do not directly impact team performance but indirectly via team co-ordination problems. The dispersion dimensions reduce communication frequency, created coordination delays and misinterpretation in lateral communication. They also introduce problems of team organizing, task scheduling and managing task-team interdependency in vertical coordination.

The analysis of studies on geographical and temporal dispersion shows that overall geographical dispersion has a negative impact on performance of distributed teams, in both subjective and objective measurement. The impact of temporal dispersion on team performance is negatively perceived by managers, while this impact is positive by direct measure at task level. Besides, studies at task level report more homogeneously negative impact of dispersion dimensions than studies at team and project level do.

The implications of this review for research are threefold. Firstly, inconclusive impacts of temporal and geographical dispersion on performance call for more research efforts on this topic. Future studies on GSD should take into account all type of dispersion dimensions to have a complete description of the context. Secondly, the review reveals a relatively small amount of study on open source context. As open source paradigm is getting more success as a distributed development model, coordination practices in OSS projects could provide useful lessons for commercial software projects. Future research should explore more on team performance in considering dispersion dimensions and the role of open source communication infrastructure on this relationship. Finally, the review discloses a significant amount of studies on geographical, temporal and organizational dispersions, while not so many studies have really focused on two other dispersion dimensions. This suggests an opportunity for future research on the relationship between cultural and work process dispersion on team performance.

The implications of this review for practice are also threefold. Firstly, since mechanistic coordination is as important as organic coordination in mediating and improving project performance, management level should not only build an informal communication community around the projects, but also construct an effective formal coordination mechanism and strategy. Secondly, project managers tend to have a pessimistic view on being distributed over physical spaces and time zones. Therefore, managers should look for more objective evidences on the impact measurement for a comprehensive view of cost-benefit when involving in global software projects. Finally, given significant role of team coordination in achieving project success, manager should invest on team configuration early in the project as a basis for facilitating coordination in later phases.

This review reports aggregated findings on the set of studies about team performance and mainly focus on geographical and temporal dispersion. Future extension of this work would explore the other three dispersion dimensions as well as synthesize the evidences on the influence of these dispersion dimensions on product quality, coordination effectiveness and team performance.

7. ACKNOWLEDGEMENT

We gratefully appreciate Professor James D. Herbsleb from the Institute for Software Research, CMU for valuable discussions on the systematic review.

8. REFERENCES

[1] J. D. Herbsleb, D. Moitra, "Guest Editors' Introduction: Global Software Development", *IEEE Software,* vol. 18, pp. 16-20, 2001

[2] ACM Job Migration Task Force, " Globalization and Offshoring of Software", *Association for Computing Machinery,* 2006

[3] M. Fabriek, M. Brand, S. Brinkkemper, F. Harmsen, and R. W. Helms, "Reasons for success and failure in offshore software development projects", European Conference on Information Systems, pp. 446-457, Galway, Ireland, 2008

[4] D. Damian and D. Moitra, "Guest Editors' Introduction: Global Software Development: How Far Have We Come?", *IEEE Software*, vol. 23, no. 5, pp. 17– 19, 2006

[5] N. B. Moe and D. Šmite, "Understanding a lack of trust in Global Software Teams: a multiple-case study", *Software Process: Improvement and Practice*, vol. 13(3), pp. 217–231, 2008

[6] D. Šmite, N. B. Moe, and R. Torkar, "Pitfalls in remote team coordination: Lessons learned from a case study", *LNCS*, vol. 5089, pp. 345-359, 2008

[7] J. A. Espinosa, J. N. Cummings, and C. Pickering, "Time Separation, Coordination, and Performance in Technical Teams", *IEEE Trans. on Engineering Management*, vol. 59, pp 91-103, 2011

[8] J. Lipnack and J. Stamps. *Virtual Teams, Reaching Across Space, Time and Organizations with Technology*, John Wiley & Sons, 1997

[9] B. Curtis, "Modeling coordination from field experiments", Conference on Organizational Computing, Coordination and Collaboration: Theories and Technologies for Computer-Supported Work, Texas, USA, 1989

[10] T. W. Malone and K. Crowston, "What is coordination theory and how can it help design cooperative work systems?", Conference on Computer-supported cooperative work, pp. 357-370, California, United States, 1990

[11] R. E. Kraut and L. A. Streeter, "Coordination in software development," *Communication of ACM*, vol. 38(3), pp. 69–81, 1995

[12] D. Cruzes and T. Dybå, "Research synthesis in software engineering: A tertiary study", *Information & Software Technology*, vol. 53(5), pp. 440-455, 2011

[13] D. Šmite, C. Wohlin, T. Gorschek, and R. Feldt, "Empirical evidence in global software engineering: a systematic review," *Empirical Software Engineering*, vol. 15(1), pp. 91–118, 2010

[14] I. Steinmacher, A. P. Chaves, and M. A. Gerosa, "Awareness support in global software development: a systematic review based on the 3C collaboration model", 16th Conference on Collaboration and Technology, pp.185–201, Maastricht, The Netherlands, 2010

[15] J. Noll, S. Beecham, and I. Richardson, "Global software development and collaboration: barriers and solutions," *ACM Inroads*, vol. 1(3), pp. 66–78, 2011

[16] B. A. Kitchenham, "Guidelines for performing Systematic Literature Reviews in Software Engineering", EBSE Technical Report, 2007

[17] J. R. Hackman and C. G. Morris, "Group Tasks, Group Interaction Process, and Group Performance Effectiveness: A Review and Proposed Integration", *Advances in Experimental Social Psychology*, vol 8, pp. 45-99, Academic Press, 1975

[18] O. Dieste and A. G. Padua, "Developing Search Strategies for Detecting Relevant Experiments for Systematic Reviews", pp. 215–224, ESEM, Madrid, Spain, 2007

[19] T. Dybå and T. Dingsøyr, "Empirical studies of agile software development: A systematic review", *Information and Software Technology*, vol 50, pp. 833-859, 2008

[20] D. S. Cruzes and T. Dybå, "Recommended Steps for Thematic Synthesis in Software Engineering", pp. 275–284, ESEM, Calgary, Canada, 2011

[21] M. B. O' Leary, and J. N. Cummings, "The spatial, temporal, and configurational characteristics of geographic dispersion in teams", *MIS Quarterly*, vol. 31(3), pp. 433-452, 2007

[22] J. Thompson, *Organizations in Action*, McGraw-Hill, 1967

[23] J. R. Quinlan, *C4.5: Programs for Machine Learning*, Morgan Kaufmann Publishers, 1993

[24] J. M. Wilson, M. B. O' Leary, A. Metiu and Q. R. Jett, "Perceived proximity in virtual work: Explaining the paradox of far-but-close", *Organization Studies*, vol. 29(7), pp. 979-1002, 2008

Appendix - Studies Included in The Review

[P1] K. Ehrlich, M. Helander, G. Valetto, S. Davies, and C. Williams, "An Analysis of Congruence Gaps and Their Effect on Distributed Software Development", Socio-Technical Congruence Workshop at ICSE, Leipzig, Germany, 2008

[P2] J. D. Herbsleb and A. Mockus, "An empirical study of speed and communication in globally distributed software development," *IEEE Transactions on Software Engineering*, vol. 29, pp. 481-494, 2003

[P3] N. Ramasubbu, M. Cataldo, R. K. Balan, and J. D. Herbsleb, "Configuring global software teams: a multi-company analysis of project productivity, quality, and profits," ICSE, Waikiki, Honolulu, HI, USA, 2011

[P4] A. Gopal, J. A. Espinosa, S. Gosain, and D. P. Darcy, "Coordination and performance in global software service delivery: The vendors perspective," *IEEE Transaction on Engineering Management*, vol. 58, pp. 772-785, 2011

[P5] J. Kotlarsky, P. C. van Fenema, and L. P. Willcocks, "Developing a knowledge-based perspective on coordination: The case of global software projects," *Information and Management*, vol. 45, pp. 96-108, 2008

[P6] J. A. Espinosa, N. Ning, and E. Carmel, "Do Gradations of Time Zone Separation Make a Difference in Performance? A First Laboratory Study", ICGSE, pp. 12-22, 2007

[P7] J. A. Espinosa, S. A. Slaughter, R. E. Kraut, and J. D. Herbsleb, "Familiarity, complexity, and team performance in geographically distributed software development," *Organization Science*, vol. 18, pp. 613-630, 2007

[P8] J. A. Colazo and Y. Fang, "Following the Sun: Temporal dispersion and performance in open source software project teams". *Journal of the Association of Information Systems*, vol. 11, pp. 684-707, 2010

[P9] J. A. Espinosa, W. DeLone, and G. Lee, "Global boundaries, task processes and IS project success: A field study," *Information Technology and People*, vol. 19, pp. 345-370, 2006

[P10] M. Sumner, J. Molka-Danielsen, "Global IT Teams and Project Success", Computer Personnel Research Conference, Vancouver, Canada, 2010

[P11] T. Nguyen, T. Wolf, and D. Damian, "Global software development and delay: Does distance still matter?", ICGSE, pp. 45-54, 2008

[P12] M. Hoegl, H. Ernst, and L. Proserpio, "How teamwork matters more as team member dispersion increases," *Journal of Product Innovation Management*, vol. 24, pp. 156-165, 2007

[P13] K. M. Chudoba, E. Wynn, M. Lu, and M. B. Watson-Manheim, "How virtual are we? Measuring virtuality and understanding its impact in a global organization," *Information Systems Journal*, vol. 15, pp. 279-306, 2005

[P14] M. Cataldo, P. A. Wagstrom, J. D. Herbsleb, and K. M. Carley, "Identification of coordination requirements: implications for the Design of collaboration and awareness tools," Computer supported cooperative work, Banff, Alberta, Canada, 2006

[P15] S. Narayanan, S. Balasubramanian, and J. M. Swaminathan, "Managing Outsourced Software Projects: An Analysis of Project Performance and Customer Satisfaction," *Production and Operations Management*, vol. 20, pp. 508-521, 2011

[P16] S. Feczak and L. Hossain, "Measuring coordination gaps of open source groups through social networks", International Conference on Information Systems, pp. 84-90, Missouri, USA, 2010

[P17] D. Šmite, N. B. Moe, and R. Torkar, "Pitfalls in remote team coordination: Lessons learned from a case study", *LNCS*, vol 5089, pp. 345-359, 2008

[P18] C. D. Cramton and S. S. Webber, "Relationships among geographic dispersion, team processes, and effectiveness in software development work teams," *Journal of Business Research*, vol. 58, pp. 758-765, 2005

[P19] M. Cataldo, J. D. Herbsleb, and K. M. Carley, "Socio-technical congruence: a framework for assessing the impact of technical and work dependencies on software development productivity", ESEM, Kaiserslautern, Germany, 2008

[P20] J. N. Cummings, J. A. Espinosa, and C. K. Pickering, "Spatial and temporal boundaries in global teams: Distinguishing where you work from when you work", *IFIP*, vol. 236, pp. 85-98, 2007

[P21] S. S. F. Merlo, and C. Francalanci, "The coevolution of organizatinoal structures in open sources and closed source projects", Organizational Communications and Information Systems Division, Illinois, USA, 2009

[P22] M. J. Liberatore and W. Luo, "The effect of client - Consultant coordination on is project performance: An agency theory perspective", Portland International Center for Management of Engineering and Technology, Portland, Canada, 2007

[P23] S. W. Chou and M. Y.He, "The factors that affect the performance of open source software development - the perspective of social capital and expertise integration", *Information Systems Journal*, vol. 21, pp. 195-219, 2011

[P24] A. Beckhaus, L. M. Karg, and D. Neumann, "The impact of collaboration network structure on issue tracking's process efficiency at a large business software vendor", HICSS, Hawaii, USA, 2010.

[P25] M. V. Rini van Solingen, "The Impact of Number of Sites in a Follow the Sun setting on the Actual and Perceived Working Speed and Accuracy: A Controlled Experiment", ICGSE, Princeton, NJ, USA, 2010

[P26] A. Gopal and S. Gosain, "The role of organizational controls and boundary spanning in software development outsourcing: Implications for project performance," *Information Systems Research*, vol. 21, pp. 960-982, 2010

[P27] J. Alberto Espinosa, J. N. Cummings, and C. Pickering, "Time Separation, Coordination, and Performance in Technical Teams," *IEEE Transactions on Engineering Management*, vol. 59, pp 91-103, 2011

[P28] N. Ramasubbu, S. Mithas, M. S. Krishnan, and C. F. Kemerer, "Work dispersion, process-based learning, and offshore software development performance," *Management Information Systems*, vol. 32, pp. 437-458, 2008

Survey on Agile and Lean Usage in Finnish Software Industry

Pilar Rodríguez   Jouni Markkula   Markku Oivo   Kimmo Turula

University of Oulu, Department of Information Processing Sciences
P.O.Box 3000, 90014 University of Oulu, Finland
{pilar.rodriguez, jouni.markkula, markku.oivo, kimmo.turula}@oulu.fi

ABSTRACT

Earlier empirical studies have demonstrated the interest that agile methods have generated in the software industry. Currently, lean approaches are increasingly adopted for complementing agile methods in software processes. With the goal of providing up-to-day results that can be used by organizations implementing or planning to implement agile and/or lean methods, we have conducted a study on the current stage of agile and lean adoption and usage in the software industry. For this purpose, we conducted an extensive survey among Finnish software practitioners in 2011, using the membership registry of *The Finnish Information Processing Association* (FIPA) as a sampling frame. 408 responses were collected from 200 software intensive organizations in the study. The survey included questions for identifying the rate of agile and lean usage in software organizations as well as the implementation of specific methods and practices, goals in adopting agile and lean, reasons for not applying these methods and effects of the agile and lean usage. The results of the survey reveal that a majority of respondents' organizational units are using agile and/or lean methods (58%). Furthermore, lean appears as a new player, being used by 24% of respondents, mainly in combination with agile (21%). The reasons and benefits for using agile and lean methods appeared to correspond in most parts to the findings of the earlier research. Generally, the experiences of using agile and lean methods seem to be rather positive, although challenges, such as obtaining management support and limitations for scaling agile in distributed settings, were also identified.

Categories and Subject Descriptors

D.2.9 [**Software Engineering**]: Management – *life cycle, productivity, programming teams, software process models.*
D.2.10 [**Software Engineering**]: Design – *Methodologies.*
A.1 [**Introductory and Survey**].

General Terms: Management, Design, Economics, Human Factors.

Keywords: Agile, lean, survey.

1. INTRODUCTION

Agile Software Development (ASD) can be seen as a reaction against traditional plan-driven methodologies, which were considered unable to meet the dynamism, unpredictability and changing conditions that characterize the current business environment for software intensive organizations [1]. Since the

Agile Manifesto[1] was published in 2001, the feedback on ASD has been relatively positive [2, 3, 4, 5, 6]. However, challenges such as how to scale ASD to large contexts have also been identified [7, 8, 9].

In more recent years, and mainly motivated by the agile community, the software industry has started to look at lean [10] as a new approach that could complement ASD. Lean Software Development (LSD) is aligned with many agile principles but considering a more holistic and enterprise system thinking [11]. The discussion, started as early as the 1990s [12], about the application of lean for software development has become again a trend. Thus, while progress towards LSD is mainly driven by industry pioneers, there is a growing body of literature documenting case studies [13, 14, 15] and investigating specific elements of lean in software development, e.g., flow [16, 17].

The universal application of the core lean principles in a creative activity as software development is under debate [15]. Furthermore, the relationship between ASD and LSD has not been clearly defined [18], limiting the current comprehension of the phenomenon. Nevertheless, we are interested in the fact that software organizations are moving towards agile and lean in the real-world industry context and in what we can learn from their experiences. In the past years, with a few exceptions (such as [8, 19, 20, 21], most of scientific research on ASD has been based on case studies and experimental works [1]. It is clearly recognized that these works provide detailed and valuable analysis of the usage of ASD for specific projects. However, they are limited for drawing general conclusions. Consequently, while the Agile Manifesto was formulated more than 10 years ago, little knowledge has been generalized about the usage of agile methods and its benefits and problems [1].

With the goal of contributing to provide more generalizable findings, and following the indications of studies analyzing the research agenda for ASD [1, 22], we have conducted a large-scale exploratory survey study for addressing the following questions: (a) What is the current state of adoption and usage of ASD and LSD methods and practices in the software industry? (b) What are the reasons why ASD and LSD are being adopted in some software development organizations? (c) Which are the impacts, in terms of benefits, of using ASD and LSD? (d) Which are the limitations and factors that can challenge the usage of ASD and LSD? and (e) Which are the reasons of some organizations for not using ASL and LSD?

The survey study, conducted in the Finnish software industry in 2011, collected more than four hundred responses of software practitioners. Large number of practitioners was from multinational companies with premises in several countries. Furthermore, the results of the study are especially interesting if it

---

[1] http://www.agilemanifesto.org/

is considered that Finland takes up the second position in the IT Industry Competitiveness Index 2011 of the BSA/Economist's report [23]. Therefore, although the generalization of the results is still limited, we consider the Finnish software industry as a suitable population for the study.

The paper makes the following contributions to research and practice: i) it provides more generalizable and up-to-date results on the state of ASD and LSD usage, using first-hand industrial insight on how ASD and LSD are being used in the real-world industry. The findings may be advantageously leveraged by other organizations considering whether/implementing agile and/or lean, through a better understanding of the methods and practices that their peers are using as well as their benefits and limitations in using ASD and/or LSD. ii) to our best knowledge, this study presents the first large scale explorative study analyzing the status of lean usage for software development, iii) moreover, the results of the study provide basis for future research by identifying the most applied methods and practices as well as the most experienced benefits and challenges on using ASD and LSD. These elements should guide the research agenda of other initiatives, such as case studies or experiments, which study in deeper detail the specific problems that organizations face when deploying ASD and LSD.

The rest of the paper is organized as follows: Section 2 reviews earlier studies on agile and lean usage. Next, section 3 describes the research setting, including the process for collecting the data as well as the design of the survey. Section 4 includes a systematic and extensive presentation of the survey questions and survey results. Finally, section 5 concludes the paper summarizing the results and presenting the limitations of the study.

2. EARLIER STUDIES ON AGILE AND LEAN USAGE

Most of earlier surveys on agile usage have been conducted by IT consultants. Although the results of this kind of studies can be used for guidance, their consideration as scientific contributions is questionable.

The last *"State of agile development"* survey [24] conducted by Version One between July and November of 2011 received 6042 responses (rate of response and design of the sample were not provided). The survey's findings showed that more than 80% of respondents' companies had adopted agile in some extent and nearly half of respondents indicated that their companies had practiced agile for over 2 years. Scrum was indicated as the most followed agile method (53% respondents were following it), followed by a hybrid usage of Scrum and Extreme Programming (14%). Only 2% of respondents indicated to be using lean. Regarding to agile practices, the survey found daily stand-up (78%), iteration planning (74%) and unit testing (70%) as the top followed practices. The top three reasons cited for adopting agile were to accelerate time to market, to increase productivity and to more easily manage changing priorities. Benefits that were actually experienced according to the respondents of this survey were the ability to manage changing priorities (84%) and improved project visibility (77%). Finally, the findings of the survey indicated the inability to change the organization's culture as the biggest barrier to agile adoption (52%), followed to the availability of personnel with right skills (40%). However, these results must be cautiously considered since Version One is a vendor of products and training on agile methods and, therefore, has vested interests in the results of the survey they conduct.

The Scott Ambler's February 2008 Agile Adoption Survey [25] collected 642 responses. The sample of the study was composed mainly by IT professionals in North America who were familiar with agile methods. 69% of respondents indicated that they were working in organizations that had some experience with agile. The results of the survey also indicated that collocated projects were more successful than no-collocated ones when using agile methods (82% and 71% rate of success respectively). Also, the respondents of the survey indicated that they had achieved benefits in productivity (88% of respondents answered somewhat higher or much higher productivity), quality (77% of respondents indicated somewhat higher or much higher quality of systems deployed) and business stakeholder satisfaction (78% of respondents indicated somewhat higher or much higher business stakeholder satisfaction).

A similar survey was conducted by Forrester Research from July to August 2009 [26]. The survey was fielded by 1298 application development and program management professionals who were readers of Dr. Dobb's magazine[2]. In this survey, 35% of respondents stated that agile most closely reflects their development process. However, 34% indicated that they continue to use either an iterative or waterfall process as their primary software development method. Regarding to the agile practices implemented, short iterations (79%), constant feedback (77%) and daily scrum meeting (71%) were the most implemented practices between the development professionals who had adopted agile. Oppositely, test-driven development (TDD) and system metaphor were the least implemented practices (42% and 15% respectively).

Regarding to studies published in scientific forums such as conferences and journals, most of them have focused on analyzing in detail specific elements in the usage of ASD, using research methods such as case studies [1]. Just as an example, Pikkarainen et al. [4] studied the impact of agile practices in communication through a case study in F-Secure. The results of the study indicated that agile practices had a positive impact on both communication inside development teams and communication outside team boundaries. However, it was found that the communication mechanisms that ASD provides for *"extended environments"* (with many stakeholder groups) are insufficient.

Some scientific studies have analyzed important factors in adopting and using ASD. Chow and Cao [19] studied critical success factors in agile software projects. Based on a confirmatory survey study, collecting data from 109 agile projects from 25 countries, Chow and Cao identified the following success factors: agile-friendly project team environment, high-caliber team capability, strong customer involvement, agile style project management process, agile style software engineering techniques and correct delivery strategy. Similarly, Misra et al. [21] carried out a survey-based ex-post facto study for identifying those factors that impact in the success of projects developed using ASD. The study, based on 241 responses, found personal characteristics of team members, society in which the organization operates, training and learning, customer satisfaction, collaboration and commitment, fast decision making, corporate culture and self-team control as important success factors. Other factors such as communication and negotiation capabilities or team distribution were not found as statistically significant. Contrarily, Hanssen et al. [9], using a tertiary review of the literature, found that although ASD is a more and more stable trend in global software engineering, the use of ASD in globally

---

[2] http://www.drdobbs.com/

distributed environments may have limitations. For example, lack of effective collaboration tools or the influence of cultural and linguistic diversity in communication and collaboration were seen as possible challenges. Thus, Hanssen et al. concluded that while some challenges seem solvable, other agile practices cannot be applied in a distributed setting.

Only few scientific studies have explored the level of agile adoption from an extensive perspective. Salo and Abrahamsson [27] investigated the use and usefulness of Extreme Programming (XP) and Scrum in European embedded software development organizations. The study is based on the data collected from a sample of 13 industrial organizations (from eight European countries) and 35 individual projects. Open office space (66% of systematically or mostly used responses), coding standards (60% of systematically or mostly used responses) and 40h week-sustainable pace (59% of systematically or mostly used responses) were reported as the most used XP practices. In addition, TDD and pair programming were found as the least "systematically or mostly" used XP practices. Regarding to Scrum, product backlogs and daily scrum meetings were the most used practices (24% and 21% of systematically or mostly used responses respectively). A significant finding of the study was the high percentage of "never" or "I don't know" responses that all Scrum practices received in this study. The authors interpreted this result as unfamiliarity with Scrum among a large proportion of respondents.

Vijayasarathy and Turk [8] conducted a survey study to assess the factors influencing agile adoption as well as benefits, challenges and limitations of agile development in 2008. The survey study, conducted among fifteen Yahoo online discussion groups on ASD, received 98 responses. Project turn-around time, complexity of software and stability of requirements were reported as the main drivers in organizational decisions to use agile. Regarding to benefits of using agile, better meet customer needs, improved software quality and increased flexibility in development were found as the top benefits. Also, the results of the study showed organizational resistance and management apathy as the main challenges in using agile, and limited support for distributed development environments and limited support for development involving large teams as limitations of agile methods.

Asnawi et al. [28] have recently investigated on agile methods usage in Malaysia. By interviewing 13 software development practitioners from seven organizations, they found that social and human aspects are more important than technical aspects when using agile methods.

With similar objectives than this study, Begel and Nagappan [7] presented the results of a survey study conducted at Microsoft in ESEM 2007. The goals of the study were to assess the extent to groups at Microsoft Research were using ASD and the benefits and problems associated with its usage. They found that 32% of the respondents were using ASD, being Scrum the most used method with 65% of respondents using it. Team coding standards and continuous integration were found as the top agile practices that teams followed, while pair programming and TDD were the least followed practices. Regarding to the benefits and problems associated to the usage of ASD at Microsoft Research, improved communication and coordination as well as the capacity to deliver quicker releases appeared as the most important perceived benefits. On the other hand, whether ASD scales to larger software teams and the inefficiency of too many meetings of methods such as Scrum were seem as the main problems. Although the results of this study provide valuable insight, the study is based on only one organization and its results cannot be generalized. Thus, Begel and Nagappan requested collaboration for replicating the study in a larger scale to provide more generalized knowledge on the status of ASD in software development organizations. Table 1 synthetizes the most important findings of previous studies regarding to ASD usage.

Table 1. Synthesis of previous studies on ASD usage

ASD usage rate	• Version One [24]:80% • Scott Ambler [25]: 69% • Forrester Research [26]: 35%
Most used agile practices	• Daily stand-up [24, 26, 27] • Iterative development [24, 26] • Coding standards [7, 27] • Continuous Integration [7], unit testing [24], constant customer feedback [26], 40 hours week [27] , product backlog [27] , open office space [27]
Least used agile practices	• TDD [7, 26, 27] • Pair programming [7, 27] • System metaphor [26]
Benefits	• Flexibility, ability to manage changing priorities [8, 24] • Improved software quality [8, 25] • Improved project visibility [24], improved productivity [25], reduced time-to-market [7], improved communication and cooperation [7], improved stakeholders -customer satisfaction [25], better meet customer needs [8]
Challenges and limitations	• Difficulties for scaling agile in the large [7, 8, 9, 25] • Difficulties for changing the organizational/ people culture [8, 24] • Difficulties for finding personnel with right skills [24], possible inefficiency of too many meetings in methods such as Scrum [7]

The research activity of LSD, viewed originally as just another agile method, is still an emerging area [18]. Thus, studies focused on LSD are quite scarce [13, 14, 15, 16, 17]. Although dedicated conferences and magazines, such as Leanssc, Less and Lean Magazine³, are emerging and contributing to increase the body of literature in the topic, there are not studies, at least at public level, that have analyzed the level of LSD usage.

As philosophies, lean and agile have different origins and some intertwined ideas. Agile focuses more on flexibility and the capacity to rapidly embrace change. While lean focuses on overall economic contribution from a more holistic enterprise perspective [29]. In the field of software engineering, discussions about software development and lean thinking started as early as the 1990s [12], well before the *Agile Manifesto* was formulated. Moreover, lean has been considered as one of the inspiring sources of the *Agile Manifesto* [30]. Therefore, it is reasonable that there exists a significant overlap and some confusion between agile and lean in software development, since both paradigms share numerous elements. Poppendieck considers lean thinking a *"platform upon which to build agile software development*

---

³ Leanssc: Lean Software and Systems Conference, http://www.leanssc.org/. Less: Conference on Lean Enterprise Software and Systems, http://less2011.leanssc.org/ . Lean Magazine, http://leanmagazine.net/

practices." [31]. Coplien and Bjornwig argue that although agile and lean have fundamental differences, yet complement each other by addressing different components of systems development [32]. As our approach in this study was essentially empirical, conceptual analysis and refinement of formal definition of agility or leanness, and their relationship, theoretically for software development was beyond the scope of this work. We were interested in the fact that software companies transitioning toward lean usually incorporate elements of agile and we wanted to empirically analyze how this phenomenon is happening and experienced by the organisations in the real-world software industry, in order to identify most important elements that impact their usage.

3. RESEARCH SETTING

The agile and lean usage survey was conducted among Finnish software professionals in June 2011, using Webropol Internet survey tool. In this section, we present the research setting of the survey, describing the data collection and survey design.

3.1 Data Collection

The target population of the survey was Finnish software practitioners. In Finland, there exists an independent association of Finnish ICT professionals and companies called *The Finnish Information Processing Association* (FIPA) [4]. It has about 16 000 professionals as personal members and the number of company members is more than 500. The membership registry of FIPA provided an excellent sampling frame for the survey, as large part of software professionals in Finland are members of it. FIPA provided from the membership registry a selection of 4450 e-mail addresses of software practitioners that suited to the focus of the survey. After piloting the questionnaire for checking its consistency and legibility, the Internet survey request was e-mailed to these persons and the survey was open for two weeks. During this time, 408 persons responded to the survey. These respondents represented 200 different organizations. The response rate was 9%.

3.2 Survey Design

The survey was designed to describe the extent of usage of agile and lean methods, principles and practices within the software practitioner's organization as well as to explore the reasons for adopting agile and lean, and effects in the adoption. The survey, including almost fifty questions, was designed based on the literature on agile and lean as well as earlier empirical studies of agile and lean adoption and usage. The survey questions consisted of the following sections: background information; usage of agile and lean methods; usage of specific methods, practices and principles; goals, challenges and effects in adoption; non-adopter's reasons and plans to adopt agile and lean methods.

Background information of the practitioners and their organization consisted of the following questions: position in the organization, years of experience in software development, name of the organization, number of employees in the organization, number of employees in the organizational unit, typical team size.

Usage of agile and lean methods consisted of the following questions: usage of agile and lean methods, duration of using agile and lean methods in the organizational unit, level of adoption of agile and lean methods in the organizational unit.

Usage of specific methods, practices and principles consisted of the following questions: usage of specific agile and lean methods, usage of specific agile and lean practices, usage of specific agile and lean principles.

Goals, challenges and effects in adoption consisted of the following questions: goals in agile and lean adoption, challenges in agile and lean adoption, limitations affecting agile and lean adoption, effects of adopting agile and lean in the organization.

Non-adopters reasons and plans to adopt agile and lean methods consisted of the following questions: reasons for not adopting agile and lean, plans to adopt agile and lean in the future, agile and lean methods planned to be adopted, reasons for adopt agile and lean in the future.

Although preliminary designed options were presented in the last three sections, the survey included open fields for indicating other options not included in the preliminary list.

4. RESULTS

This section presents the results of the survey. A preliminary analysis of companies' goals driving towards the adoption of agile and/or lean methods has previously been reported in [33]. The results are organized according to the sections of the survey and compared with the results of earlier studies on agile and lean usage.

4.1 Background Information

The number of practitioners answering the survey was 408. The respondents were working in various positions in their organizations. The main organizational roles of the respondents were developers (n=113) and project managers (n=99). Table 2 and Table 3 present the positions of the respondents in their organizations and the respondent's experiences in software development respectively.

Table 2. Positions in organization

Position[5]	n	Position	n
Developer	113	Scrum master	33
Project manager	99	Process manager	31
IT staff	79	Product owner	25
Architect	63	Product manager	23
Consultant/Trainer	52	President/VP/CEO/COO/CIO/CTO	22
Quality assurance/Tester	38	Sales/Marketing personnel	10
Operations/Support staff	35	Other	48

Table 3. Experience in software development

Years of experience	n	%
None	42	10,3
Less than 2	31	7,6
2-5	56	13,7
5-10	80	19,6
10-20	144	35,3
More than 20	55	13,5
Total	408	100,0

---

[4] http://www.ttlry.fi/english

[5] Since the same person can hold different positions, respondents were able to select multiple options

The respondents belonged to 200 different organizations. The majority of the organizations were companies, but there were also a few educational and governmental organizations. Some of the respondents (n=30) did not identify their organizations. Most of the organizations were big (46%, more than 1,000 employees) and middle size (45%, number of employees between 11-1000). The small organizations with 10 or less employees had 8% representation in the data. For one percent of the respondents the organization size information was missing.

The average size of the respondent's organizational units is presented in Table 4. In most of the organizations, the organizational unit size appears to be rather small, and three quarters of the organizational units include less than 100 persons.

Table 4. Size of the organizational unit

Employees	n	%	Cumulative %
1-10	93	23,8	23,4
11-50	141	35,4	58,8
51-100	66	16,6	75,4
101-200	44	11,1	86,4
201-500	28	7,0	93,5
501-1000	16	4,0	97,5
More than 1000	10	2,5	100,0
Total	398	100,0	

The typical size of working teams in the respondents organizational units are presented in Table 5 below. For ten percent of the respondents the team size information was missing.

Table 5. Team size

Team size	Frequency	%	Cumulative %
1-5	156	42,3	42,4
6-10	152	41,3	83,7
11-20	43	11,7	95,4
21-50	17	4,6	100,0
Total	368	100,0	

The size of the teams appears to be mostly smaller than 10 persons. Only less than five percent of the organizations have teams with more than 20 persons, and none of the organizations have teams bigger than fifty persons.

4.2 Usage of Agile and Lean Methods

Usage of agile methods in the respondents organizational unit was reported by 55% (n=225) and usage of lean methods by 24% (n=99) of the respondents. The usage of agile or lean methods or a combination of these, are presented in Table 6.

Table 6. Usage of Agile and Lean Methods

Agile and Lean usage	n	%
Only Agile	137	33,6
Agile and Lean	88	21,6
Only Lean	11	2,7
No Agile or Lean	172	42,2
Total	408	100,0

The majority of respondents' organizational units (58%) appears to be using agile and/or lean methods. Agile seems still to be more popular than lean, although they are also often used in combination (37% of agile and/or lean users). Only 2,7% of the respondents reported that they are using only lean methods. Earlier studies on the level of agile usage reported varying results, from 80% of respondents using agile in the survey conducted by Version One [24] to 32% in the survey conducted at Microsoft [7]. While the results of this study do not indicate as high level of agile usage as Version One, they reveal the strong position that agile methods are taking in software development. It is also significant that 24% of respondents reported to be using lean, when earlier studies have reported much lower levels of lean usage (2% by both [24] and [26]).

The time how long agile and lean methods have been used in the respondents' organizational units is presented in Table 7.

Table 7. Duration of Using Agile and Lean Methods

Usage time	Agile methods		Lean methods	
	n	%	n	%
Less than 1 year	32	14,2	22	22,2
1-2 years	78	34,7	50	50,5
2-5 years	99	44,0	18	18,2
More than 5 years	16	7,1	9	9,1
Total	225	100,0	99	100,0

Based on the data, agile methods seem to be used longer time than lean methods, as agile methods Median and Mode class is "2-5 years" and lean methods "1-2 years". According to the data 51% (n=115) have been using agile more than two years, in comparison to 27% (n=27) of lean usage more than two years.

There appeared also difference in the level of adoption of agile and lean methods. According the data, agile methods are used by all of the teams in 26% and by only some of the teams in 74% of the organizational units. The corresponding percentages of lean methods usage are 14% and 86%. These results show that agile methods are more widely spread in the organizations than lean.

4.3 Usage of specific methods, practice and principles

As a part of the survey, the popularity of different agile and lean methods, as well as agile and lean practices and principles were studied. The usage of specific agile methods, presented in Table 8, was measured by requesting the respondents to indicate which of the methods were in use in their organizational unit.

Table 8. Usage of specific agile methods

Methods	n	%
Scrum	196	83,1
Extreme Programming (XP)	43	18,1
Agile Modeling	27	11,4
Feature-Driven Development (FDD)	21	8,9
Kanban	11	4,7
Adaptive Software Development	10	4,2
Dynamic Systems Development Method (DSDM)	6	2,5
TDD	4	1,7
Crystal Methods	2	0,8
Other	18	7,6

Salo and Abrahamsson [27] reported that the respondents of their survey, conducted in 2008, were more familiarized with XP than with Scrum. The results of our study show that Scrum is clearly the most widely used method. These results could reveal a trend towards Scrum to the detriment of XP. It is remarkable that although kanban and TDD were not preliminary included as agile methods (kanban is usually associated with lean and TDD is more considered as a practice of XP than a method itself), both were identified as agile methods by the respondents in the open field that was included for collecting other methods not included as default. Otherwise, the "Other" methods were most typically in-house methods or modifications of well-known methods that were adapted to the organization's specific needs and practices.

The application of practices and principles were measured by five point scale, asking the respondents to indicate how frequently they were applied them in their organizational unit (value 1 indicating never and 5 indicating systematically). These results are reported correspondingly in Tables 9 and 10, where mean and mode presents the average frequency of application of the particular practice or principle.

Table 9. Usage of specific agile practices

Practices	n	Mean	Median
Prioritized work list	204	4,2	4
Iteration/sprint planning	203	4,1	4
Daily stand-up meetings	209	3,7	4
Unit testing	199	3,7	4
Release planning	196	3,9	4
Active customer participation	196	3,5	4
Self-organizing teams	194	3,5	4
Frequent and incremental delivery of working software	189	4,1	4
Automated builds	185	3,5	4
Continuous integration	182	3,8	4
Test-driven development (TDD)	179	2,7	3
Retrospectives	177	3,6	4
Burn-down charts	174	3,2	3
Pair programming	174	2,4	2
Refactoring	163	3,4	3
Collective code ownership	159	3,3	3
Other	9	1,8	1

Regarding to the agile practices in use, the results are well aligned with the results of earlier studies. However, it is significant that most of the practices are in general used without big differences in their usage, oppositely to the results of previous studies that reported non very much usage of practices such as TDD [7, 26, 27] and pair programming [7, 27].

Lean principles, presented in Table 10, were asked also from those respondents applying only agile, since they may be using them even if they are not aware of these principles belongs to lean.

Table 10. Usage of specific lean principles

Principles	n	Mean	Median
Focus on creating customer value	209	3,9	4
Eliminate waste and excess activities	199	3,4	3
Create a culture of continuous improvement	198	3,5	4
Do it right the first time	196	3,4	3
Respect and empower people	190	3,8	4
Minimize inventory or work in progress	189	3,2	3
Pull from demand	184	3,6	4
Focus on optimizing the whole system and not only local optimizations	181	3,3	3
Continuous flow of small batches in the development process	179	3,5	4
Make decisions as late as possible	175	3,0	3
Root source analysis is done after problems are discovered	174	3,2	3
Look simultaneously for multiple solutions	174	3,2	3
Create trusted relationships with suppliers	165	3,6	4
Create cadence	147	2,9	3

4.4 Goals, Challenges and Effects in adoption

The agile and lean users were also requested to identify their organisations' goals, challenges and experienced limitations in adopting agile and lean, as well as effect of the adoption in their organisational units. The goals were measured by requesting the respondents to indicate the specific goals in adoption and the results are presented in the Table 11. The challenges and affecting limitations were measured by using five point scale, asking the respondents to rate how signifficant the particular challenge or limitation has been and the results are presented in the Tables 12 and 13. Mean and median in these tables presents the average signifficance of the particular challenge or limitation in the adoption. The effects of adoption to the organisational units were measured also with five point scale indicationg the level of improvement. The result of the organisational effects are presented in the Table 14.

Table 11. Goals in agile and lean adoption

Goals	n	%
To increase productivity	158	66,9
To improve product and service quality	145	61,4
To reduce development cycle times and time-to-market	137	58,1
To improve process quality	113	47,9
To increase the ability to adapt to changes in the business environment	110	46,6
To improve team communication	100	42,4
To improve development flow	99	41,9
To reduce risks	86	36,4
To remove waste and excess activities	75	31,8
To decrease development costs	75	31,8
To improve customer understanding	65	27,5
To create transparency within the organization	63	26,7
To improve stakeholders' satisfaction	57	24,2
To improve organizational learning	45	19,1
To improve the management of business/product value	42	17,8
To establish team-wide project comprehension	33	14,0
To improve our understanding of the whole value stream	31	13,1
To achieve success others have achieved using lean methods	27	11,4
Other	6	2,5

The results in the Table 11 show the order of importance of different goals in agile and lean adoption. To increase the productivity and quality of the products/services as well as to reduce time-to-market are reported as the main goals in organizational decisions to use agile and lean methods. Moreover, to increase the ability to adapt to changes in the business environment, that has been reported in earlier studies as a key goal for adopting agile [8, 24] and should be essential in agile methods by definition [29], appears also in the top positions of our ranking.

Table 12. Challenges in agile and lean adoptipn

Challenges	n	Mean	Median
Top management commitment	201	4,0	4
Customer/supplier collaboration	192	3,9	4
Cultural change/translating agile/lean principles from development teams to the rest of the business	190	3,8	4
Measuring agile/lean success	190	3,6	4
Resistance to change	16	3,6	4
Defining business value	184	3,9	4
Need for specialized skills	183	3,1	3
Tailoring agile/lean practices	182	3,5	4
Lack of formal guidelines	176	2,8	3
Inadequate documentation	175	3,2	3
Scalability of agile/lean methods	174	3,6	4
Inadequate training	174	3,3	3
Synchronizing activities	172	3,4	4
Synchronizing activities	168	3,5	4
Loss of management control	168	2,8	3
Lack of big design up front	167	3,0	3
Fixed price contracts	161	3,3	3
Steep learning curve	159	3,1	3
Inappropriateness of existing technologies/tools	158	3,1	3
Achieving flow	157	3,5	4
Decreased predictability	155	3,1	3
Other	12	3,2	3

The results in the Table 12 show the order of significance of different challenges in agile and lean adoption. Top management commitment appears as the top challenge for adopting agile and lean methods. This result is opposed to the findings of the study by Chow and Cao [19], which rejected the strong management commitment as a critical success factor in agile software projects. Customer/suppliers collaboration is the second most important challenge that software organizations have for adopting agile and lean methods. Customer collaboration and commitment have been also identified as critical success factors in [19, 21].

Table 13. Limitations in agile and lean adoption

Limitations	n	Mean	Median
Limited support for developing large, complex software	189	3,3	3
Limited support for development involving large teams	185	3,1	3
Limited support for sub-contracting	181	2,8	3
Limited support for development involving legacy systems	179	3,1	3
Limited support for distributed development environments	178	2,9	3
Limited support for building reusable artifacts	176	3,0	3
Limited support for developing safety/mission-critical software	174	2,9	3
Other	16	3,3	3

The results in the Table 13 show the order of significance of different limitations in agile and lean adoption. One of the most controversial topics in the usage of agile methods is its ability to work in distributed environments. While [7, 8, 9, 25] have found that scaling agile to distributed environments could be a barrier for agile methods, [21] did not find statistical significance to assert that team distribution is a factor that impact in adopting agile. The results of our survey are aligned with those considering agile as a limited approach in distributed settings, since limited support for development involving large teams and limiting support for distributed development environment appear as important limitations in opinion of respondents of the survey.

Table14. Effects of adoption of agile and lean

Effect	n	Mean	Median
Improved team communication	204	4,0	4
Enhanced ability to adapt to changes	203	3,9	4
Increased productivity	201	3,8	4
Enhanced process quality	198	3,7	4
Improved learning and knowledge creation	197	3,7	4
Enhanced software quality	196	3,8	4
Accelerated time-to-market/cycle time	192	3,7	4
Reduced waste and excess activities	190	3,5	4
Improved customer collaboration	190	3,7	4
Improved organizational transparency	187	3,5	4
Improved customer understanding	188	3,7	4
Reduced risks	184	3,4	3
Improved alignment between IT and business objectives	180	3,4	3
Enhanced value creation	178	3,6	4
Improved stakeholder satisfaction	169	3,6	4
Reduced costs	163	3,2	3
Other	13	3,8	4

According to the results of the survey, respondents applying agile and lean reported benefits in almost of the aspects that theoretically should be improved using agile and lean methods. Improved communication, as already claimed by [4], increased ability to adapt to changes and increased productivity were the three most common benefits experienced by the respondents of the survey.

4.5 Non-adopter's reasons and plans to adopt agile and lean methods

The survey responses included also 137 practitioners in whose organizational units agile or lean methods were not in use. Those non-adopters were presented questions related to the reasons why they did not consider these methods appropriated for their software development activities. The results of these reasons are presented in Table 15.

Table 15. Reasons for not adopting agile and lean

Reasons for not adopting	n	%
Lack of knowledge and training	64	46,7
Too traditional organizational culture	59	43,1
Lack of support or commitment from the management	28	20,4
Fixed price contracts	25	18,2
Customers are not ready for agile/lean methods	22	16,1
Resistance to change	18	13,1
Inappropriate technology and tools	17	12,4
Incompatible business domain (please specify your business domain)	12	8,8
The burden of changing to agile/lean methods	10	7,3
Lack of quality assurance procedures	10	7,3
Unstable project requirements	9	6,6
Lack of progress-tracking mechanism	9	6,6
Our organization lacks customer understanding	7	5,1
Lack of scalability	6	4,4
Lack of support for reward system	6	4,4
Lack of big design up front	6	4,4
Limited support for building reusable artifacts	3	2,2
Limited support for distributed development environments	3	2,2
Decreasing predictability	2	1,5
Other	27	19,7

The results in Table 15 reveal that clearly the most common reasons preventing agile and lean adoption are lack of knowledge and training and organizational culture.

The future adoption plans were also charted, and those results are presented in the Table 16.

Table 16. Plans to adopt agile and lean in the future

Planned adoption	n	%
Within a year	14	10,2
Within two years	8	5,8
Not planned	52	38,0
Don't know	63	46,0
Total	137	100,0

Based on the result in Table 16, it seems that only a very few, organizational units of 22 respondents, have clear plans to adopt agile and lean in the near future. Majority of the organizations have not been thinking or planned yet utilization of agile and/or lean methods.

The agile and lean methods planned to be adopted in the future by those respondents that have future adoption plans, are presented in the Table 17.

Table 17. Agile and lean methods planned to be adopted

Planned methods[6]	n	%
Scrum	19	90
Lean Software Development	3	14
Agile Modeling	2	10
Extreme Programming (XP)	1	5
Dynamic Systems Development Method (DSDM)	0	0
Feature Driven Development (FDD)	0	0
Crystal Methods	0	0
Adaptive Software Development	0	0
Other	3	14

The reasons of those who are planning to adopt agile and lean methods are presented in the Table 18.

Table18. Reason for adoptin agile and lean in the future

Reasons for planned adoption	n	%
To increase productivity	14	64
To decrease development cycle times and time-to-market	10	45
To improve development flow	10	45
To improve product or service quality	9	41
To reduce risks	9	41
To improve process quality	8	36
To decrease development costs	8	36
To increase ability to adapt to changes in the business environment	8	36
To reduce waste and excess activities	6	27
To improve organizational learning	6	27
To improve stakeholders' satisfaction	6	27
To increase team communication	6	27
To improve customer understanding	4	18
To create transparency within the organization	4	18
To establish team-wide project comprehension	4	18
To improve the management of business/product value	3	14
To improve understanding of the whole value stream	3	14
To achieve success others have achieved using agile/lean methods	1	5
Other	1	5

Similarly to the reason of those respondents already using agile and lean methods, from the results of the Table 18, it can be seen that increasing the productivity and reducing development time are the most important reasons for considering agile and lean methods usage in future plans.

---

[6] Respondents were able to select multiple options

5. CONCLUSIONS AND LIMITATIONS OF THE STUDY

The goal of this study is to investigate the adoption and usage of agile and lean methods in the software industry. Using a large-scale exploratory survey, the study aims to analyze (i) the current state of agile and lean adoption and usage in the software industry, (ii) the usage of specific agile and lean methods, practices and principles and (iii) the goals, challenges and effects when agile and lean methods are adopted. Furthermore, the study investigates (iv) the reasons for no adopting agile and lean methods as well as the future plans of organizations that are not currently using them.

The results of the study are based on more than four hundred responses collected by a web-survey conducted in the Finnish software industry in 2011. Given the reported performance of Finnish IT industry (e.g. second highest productivity country in the world according to The Economist Intelligence unit [23] and the fact that large number of practitioners taking part in the survey belonged to multinational companies with premises in several countries, the conclusions can have interest to most of the existing software development communities.

The results of the study indicate that: (i) Most of respondents' organizational units were using agile and/or lean methods (58%). Moreover, lean appears to be used by 24% of respondents, mainly in combination with agile (21%); (ii) Most of agile practices are generally used without big differences in the usage between practices. Prioritized work list was reported as the most used agile practice and collective code ownership as the least used. Although lean principles appears to be less used than agile practices, principles such as eliminate waste and excess activities and focus on creating customer value are quite used by the respondents of the survey. (iii) To increase the productivity and quality of the products/services as well as to reduce time-to-market are reported as the main goals for adopting agile and lean methods. Furthermore, they are also reported as important benefits of the usage of agile and lean methods. Regarding to challenges and limitations, to get strong management commitments seem to be challenging organizations using agile and lean methods. The ability to work in distributed environments has also been reported as one of the main limitations of the usage of agile and lean methods. (iv) Finally, the most common reasons preventing agile and lean adoption are lack of knowledge and training and working in organizations with too traditional culture. Moreover, most of the non-adopter respondents have not been thinking or planned yet utilization of agile and/or lean methods in the near future.

As the survey included quite a large sample of software professionals in Finland, covered by well representative registry of FIPA, it provides a good descriptive view to the state of agile and lean usage and adoption in the software industry. However, the study has some limitations that should be taken into account when interpreting the results. At first, the study subjects were individual persons who represented different organizations. Although in order to study agile and lean usage more exactly in organizational level, it would be more appropriated to use organizations as sampling units, it has to be considered that organizations may have different units that may be at different levels of agile and lean usage. Therefore, it would have been impossible for a single person to answer for the whole company. Associated to this issue, the software professionals in the study were acting in varying positions and roles in the organizations. The persons in different organizational positions may have somehow different views to the organizational practices, as well

as varying knowledge about agile and lean methods, which might affect at some level to the reliability of the results. Furthermore, the inconsistency in how agile and lean are understood can impact the results of the study. Since definitions of agility and leanness are not clearly agreed and the study is explorative in nature, we did not want to restrict the usage of agile and/or lean to specific definitions. Thus, the survey was designed for whatever software practitioners understand to be using agile and/or lean is, starting with the questions *"Are you currently applying agile (lean) methods in your organizational unit?"* and going deeper with questions about specific methods, practices and principles that were in use. Finally, the sample included professionals from different types of organizations; additionally to software companies it included also a few educational and public organizations. Even if this can be seen as a richness of the study, limiting the research only to software companies might have given more exact view to the software business. Despite of its limitations, the study can be seen to provide valuable descriptive information about the contemporary state of agile and lean adoption in software developing organizations.

6. ACKNOWLEDGMENTS

This article is based on the work carried out in the ICT SHOK Cloud Software program financed by the Finnish Funding Agency for Technology and Innovation (Tekes) and Tivit OY. The graduate school on Software Systems and Engineering (SoSE), funded by the Ministry of Education in Finland and by the Academy of Finland, has also partially supported the work. We are especially grateful to FIPA (Tietotekniinan Liitto) for kindly helping us to distribute the survey to their members.

7. REFERENCES

[1] Dybå, T. and Dingsøyr, T. 2008. Empirical studies of agile software development: A systematic review. *Inf. Softw. Technol.* 50, 9-10 (August 2008), 833-859. DOI=http://dx.doi.org/10.1016/j.infsof.2008.01.006

[2] Layman, L., Williams, L. and Cunningham, L. 2004. Exploring Extreme Programming in Context: An Industrial Case Study. In *Proceedings of the Agile Development Conference* (ADC '04). IEEE Computer Society, Washington, DC, USA, 32-41.

[3] Melnik, G. and Maurer, F. 2006. Comparative analysis of job satisfaction in agile and non-agile software development teams, Inc. *Extreme Programming and Agile Processes in Software Engineering* (XP 2006), LNCS 4004, pp. 32-42.

[4] Pikkarainen, M., Haikara, J., Salo, O., Abrahamsson, P. and Still, J. 2008. The impact of agile practices on communication in software development, *Empir Software Eng* (2008) 13:303-337, DOI=http://dx.doi.org/10.1007/s10664-008-9065-9.

[5] Rico, D.F. 2008. Effects of Agile Methods on Website Quality for Electronic Commerce. In *Proceedings of the Proceedings of the 41st Annual Hawaii International Conference on System Sciences* (HICSS '08). IEEE Computer Society, Washington, DC, USA, 463-. DOI=http://dx.doi.org/10.1109/HICSS.2008.137.

[6] McHugh, O., Conboy, K. and Lang, M. 2011. The impact of agile practices on trust in software project teams, *IEEE Software*, 25 Aug. 2011. IEEE computer Society Digital Library. IEEE Computer Society, DOI= http://doi.ieeecomputersociety.org/10.1109/MS.2011.118.

[7] Begel, A. and Nagappan, N. 2007. Usage and Perceptions of Agile Software Development in an Industrial Context: An Exploratory Study. In *Proceedings of the First International Symposium on Empirical Software Engineering and Measurement* (ESEM '07). IEEE Computer Society, Washington, DC, USA, 255-264. DOI=http://dx.doi.org/10.1109/ESEM.2007.85.

[8] Vijayasarathy, L. and Turk, D. 2008. Agile software development: A survey of early adopters, *Journal of Information Tech. Management*, vol. 19, no. 2

[9] Hanssen, G. K., Smite, D. and Brede Moe, N. 2011. Signs of agile trends in global software engineering research: A tertiary study. In *Proceedings of the Sixth IEEE International Conference on Global Software Engineering Workshops*, DOI 10.1109/ICGSE-W.2011.12.

[10] Womack J.P., Jones D.T., Roos D. 1990. *The Machine that Changed the World: The Story of Lean* Production. New York: HarperPerennial.

[11] Poppendieck, M., Poppendieck, T.2007. *Implementing lean software development: From concept to cash.* Upper Saddle River, NJ: Addison-Wesley.

[12] Freeman, P. 1992. Lean concepts in software engineering, *IPSS-Europe International Conference on Lean Software Development*, Stuttgart, Germany, pp. 1-8.

[13] Middleton, P., Flaxel, A. and Cookson, A. 2005. Lean software management case study: Timberline. Inc. *Extreme Programming and Agile Processes in Software Engineering*, (XP 2005) Springer-Verlag Berlin Heidelberg, pp.1-9.

[14] Mehta, M., Anderson, D. and Raffo, D. 2008. Providing value to customers in software development through lean principles, *Software Process Improvement and Practice*, 13(1), January, 2008, pp.101-109.

[15] Staats, B., Brunner, D. and Upton, D. 2011. Lean principles, learning, and knowledge work: Evidence from a software services provider, *Journal of Operations Management*, 29(5), July 2011, pp.376-390.

[16] Mandic, V., Oivo, M., Rodriguez, P., Kuvaja, P., Kaikkonen H. and Turhan B. 2010 What is flowing in lean software development?, in *Proceedings of the 1st International Conference on Lean Enterprise Software and Systems* (LESS 2010), pp.72-84.

[17] Petersen, K. and Wohlin, C. 2011. Measuring the flow in lean software development, *Software: Practice and Experience*, 41(9), August 2011, pp.975-996.

[18] Wang, X. and Conboy, K. 2011. Comparing apples with oranges? Perspectives of a lean online community on the differences between agile and lean. *Thirty Second International Conference on Information Systems (ICIS 2011)*. Shanghai.

[19] Chow, T. and Cao, D. B. 2008. A survey study of critical success factors in agile software projects, *J. Syst. Softw.*, vol. 81, no. 6, pp. 961-971. DOI=http://dx.doi.org/10.1016/j.jss.2007.08.020.

[20] Livermore, J. A. 2008. Factors that significantly impact the implementation of an agile software development methodology. *Journal of Software*, Vol. 3, No. 4, April (2008)

[21] Misra, S. C., Kumar, V. and Kumar, U. 2009. Identifying some important success factors in adopting agile software development practices. *J. Syst. Softw.* 82, 11, 1869-1890. DOI=http://dx.doi.org/10.1016/j.jss.2009.05.052.

[22] Dingsøyr, T., Dybå, T. and Abrahamsson, P. 2008. A preliminary roadmap for empirical research on agile software development. In *Proceedings of the Agile 2008* (AGILE '08). IEEE Computer Society, Washington, DC, USA, 83-94. DOI=http://dx.doi.org/10.1109/Agile.2008.50.

[23] Business Software Alliance. 2011. Investment for the Future Benchmarking IT Industry Competitiveness Report.

[24] Version One. 2011. The sixth annual "State of Agile Development" survey (available: http://www.versionone.com/pdf/2011_State_of_Agile_Development_Survey_Results.pdf)

[25] Ambler, S. 2008. Results from Scott Ambler's February 2008 Agile Adoption Survey (available: http://www.ambysoft.com/surveys/)

[26] West, D. and Grant, T. 2010. Agile development: mainstream adoption has changed agility. Forrester Research.

[27] Salo, O. and Abrahamsson, P. 2008. Agile methods in European embedded software development organizations: a survey on the actual use and usefulness of extreme programming and scrum, *Software, IET*, vol. 2, no. 1, pp. 58-64.

[28] Asnawi, A. L., Gravell, A. M. and Wills, B. 2011. Empirical investigation on agile methods usage: issues identified from early adopters in Malaysia. Inc. *Extreme Programming and Agile Processes in Software Engineering* (XP 2011), LNCS LNBIP 77, pp. 192-207

[29] Conboy K. 2009. Agility from First Principles: Reconstructing the Concept of Agility in Information Systems Development. *Information Systems Research*, 20(3), September 2009, pp.329-354.

[30] Highsmith, J. 2002, Agile software development ecosystems, Addison-Wesley, Boston.

[31] Poppendieck, M. 2002. Principles of lean thinking, http://www.leanessays.com/2002/11/principles-of-lean-thinking.html (last accessed March, 11, 2012)

[32] Coplien J. and Bjornwig G. 2010. Lean architecture for agile software development. West Sussex, UK, John Wiley & Sons Ltd.

[33] Rodríguez, P., Markkula, J., Oivo, M., and Garbajosa, J. 2012. Analyzing the Drivers of the Combination of Lean and Agile in Software Development Companies, in *Proceedings of the 13th International Conference on Product Focused Software Development and Process Improvement* (PROFES 2012), pp. 145–159.

Analyzing Inspection Data for Heuristic Effectiveness

Forrest Shull*, Carolyn Seaman*,**, Madeline Diep*
*Fraunhofer CESE, 5825 University Research Court, Ste 1300, College Park, MD, USA
** Department of Information Systems, UMBC, Baltimore, MD, USA
{fshull,cseaman,mdiep}@fc-md.umd.edu

ABSTRACT

A significant body of knowledge concerning software inspection practice indicates that the value of inspections varies widely both within and across organizations. Inspection effectiveness and efficiency may be affected by a variety of factors such as inspection planning, the type of software, the developing organization, and many others. In the early 1990's, a governmental organization developing complex and highly critical software systems formulated heuristics for inspection planning based on best practices and their early inspection data. Since the development context at the organization has changed in some ways since the heuristics were proposed, it is important to assess whether the heuristics are still a suitable guideline to use. To investigate this question, we statistically evaluated the differences in effectiveness and efficiency between inspections that adhered to the heuristics and ones that did not. Our analysis revealed no significant difference in effectiveness or efficiency for most heuristics. We also learned that compliance with the heuristics is diminishing over time.

Categories and Subject Descriptors

D.2.8 [**Software Engineering**]: Metrics – *process metrics, product metrics.*

D.2.5 [**Software Engineering**]: Testing and Debugging - *Code inspections and walk-throughs.*

General Terms

Management, Measurement

Keywords

Inspection, planning, process improvement

1. INTRODUCTION

A long history of experience and experimentation has produced a significant body of knowledge concerning the effectiveness of software inspections. By inspections we refer to a family of techniques that involve visual inspection, by humans, of software artifacts for the purpose of finding anomalies [3]. Data and experience from many years and many types of organizations have shown that a properly conducted inspection can remove between 60% and 90% of the existing defects [9]. It is well established that inspections in the earliest phases of software development yield the most savings by avoiding downstream rework.

However, the value of inspections varies widely both within and across organizations. Inspection effectiveness and efficiency can be measured in numerous ways (defects found, defects slipped to testing, time spent, defects found per unit of effort, etc.), and may be affected by a variety of factors, some related to inspection planning (e.g. number of inspectors) and others related to the software and the developing organization (e.g. programming language used). The work described here is based on an analysis of a large body of data collected from inspections at a governmental organization developing complex and highly critical software system[1]. The organization was an early adopter of software inspections and has a long history of not only using inspections, but also continually studying, experimenting with, and refining their inspection processes.

In the early 1990's, software engineers at the organization developed a set of heuristics that inspection planners could use to choose values for inspection planning variables (e.g. number of inspectors, meeting length, and page rate) to maximize the effectiveness of the inspection (defined at the time as the number of defects reported). These heuristics include:

- Team size, the number of participants involved in the inspection, should be between 4 and 6. Teams of less than 4 people are likely to lack important perspectives, while larger teams are more likely to experience dynamics that limit full participation.

- Meeting length should be less than two hours. Participants' energy is likely to decrease after two hours with less than optimal results. Additional meetings should be scheduled if the inspection is not complete in two hours.

- Page rate, the number of document pages that the inspectors examine per hour of the meeting, will depend on the type of document. Inspections of requirements documents should examine less than 15 pages per hour; design and test documents less than 20 pages per hour; and code documents less than ten pages per hour. Giving a team too much material to look through will invariably result in a more superficial inspection.

Many things about software development have changed since the inspection planning heuristics were formulated. Languages, design notations, even the scale and type of problems tackled on the organization's projects are very different from what they would have been in the early 1990s. Inspections themselves remain a required part of development processes at the organization. So it makes sense to ask whether the original inspection planning heuristics are still relevant and valuable.

Furthermore, in the formulation and use of these heuristics, the outcome variable of interest has been the total number of defects found during an inspection. There have been both historical and practical reasons for this focus. During inspection planning, the

---

[1] Due to data sensitivity reason, we are unable to share the name of the organization.

total number of defects in the software to be inspected is unknown. It is also, practically speaking, unknowable, in this environment, due to the variety of verification and validation activities applied to the software and the difficulty in reconciling data from these activities with inspection data. Thus, managers and inspection planners have focused on maximizing the number of defects found in an inspection, and using that as a benchmark for comparing the effectiveness of different values for the inspection planning parameters (team size, meeting length, and page rate). However, in the current political and economic context, efficiency has become a competing goal. Because of that, it is important to also evaluate the heuristics with respect to the process efficiency that they provide.

To gain some insight into the effectiveness and efficiency of the heuristics over time, we conducted an initial analysis that attempted to validate the heuristics against the organization's existing inspection data. We differentiated the inspections that adhered to the heuristics to ones that did not, and statistically evaluated the differences in effectiveness and efficiency between them. Our analysis revealed no significant difference in effectiveness or efficiency for most heuristics. Our results also showed that newer inspections were less likely to follow the heuristics.

2. RELATED WORK

Software inspection has been an active research area for many years, but the portion of the inspection literature dealing with recommendations for inspection planning is primarily from the 1990's. In general, we found across this literature that:

- There is little agreement as to what the recommended team size is, although there is a tendency to keep it relatively small, especially for code inspections. In industry [1, 2, 7], inspection team size tends to be larger than the recommended team size in books or standards [3, 4, 6].
- A 2-hour meeting is the accepted norm [1, 2, 3, 7, 11].
- Comparing the suggested page rates to find a common recommendation is challenging due to the different units (e.g. LOC vs. pages) used to express the measure for different artifacts. We can, however, still observe several commonalities. For example, the page rates for code inspection tend to be within 150-200 LOC per hour [6, 11, 10], while the page rates for text-based documents range widely from 3-8 pages per hour [1, 11].

Additionally, there exist a number of studies evaluating the effect of planning parameters on the effectiveness and efficiency of inspections with the hope of finding the optimal planning parameters. For example, Porter et al. evaluated the impact of varying the team sizes on the effectiveness of code inspections, and reported that there is no difference in effectiveness observed between teams of size 2 and of size 4, but the effectiveness was better when compared with doing inspection individually [8]. Halling and Biffl found better inspection effectiveness when using a team size of 5 or 6 than when using team size of 4, but no significant difference between teams of size 5 and of size 6 [5]. Weller analyzed three years' worth of inspection data to evaluate the effectiveness and efficiency of inspection teams, and found that 4-person teams were twice as effective and more than twice as efficient as 3-person teams [10].

Our analyses also investigate the impact of planning parameters on the effectiveness and efficiency of inspections, but are unique because they are based on a data set from real inspections that span over a period of nearly 20 years, making it suitable for observing inspection performance over time.

3. DATA SET

The data set that was analyzed includes data on over 2500 software inspections of various types (e.g., requirement, design, code, and test). Each inspection in the dataset was conducted on a software development or maintenance project, sometime between 1988 and 2007. The data was reported by project personnel to quality assurance or process engineering personnel.

3.1 Variables

The dataset we obtained has numerous fields, which we have designated for our purposes as independent and dependent variables, described in the subsections below.

3.1.1 Independent variables

There is a very large number of attributes of inspections that could potentially affect the inspection outcome. Many, but not all, of these were represented in our dataset. These independent variables included the three inspection planning metrics, i.e. team size (number of participants), meeting length, and page rate, as well as a number of other important context variables.

The meeting length is reported in hours. An anomaly that we noticed in preparation for analysis was that a number of records reported very large meeting lengths, as high as 80 hours. In conversations with some of our contacts from whom our data were donated, we learned that some of these very long meetings were actually inspections that spanned multiple meetings, but for reporting purposes, the meeting lengths were summed. Since the meeting length heuristic is concerned with the length of contiguous time that the inspection team meets, for our analyses, we ignored inspections for which the reported meeting length was greater than 4 hours. We chose 4 hours as a reasonable limit on the length that a single contiguous meeting was likely to last. Also, it constituted a logical break in the data where only 194 records (8% of the total data set) were eliminated.

Page rate was a derived measure that normally did not appear in the raw data. Since some inspections reported the size of the inspected artifact in LOC, and others in pages, we used a scaling factor of 30 LOC per page to convert between the two (this is the standard conversion factor used in planning inspections at the organization). We then used the page measure (raw or derived) to calculate the page rate by dividing it by the meeting length.

In addition to these independent variables, our dataset also include several context variables, such as the application domains of the inspected software, project size, the division in which the project was performed, and the type of work artifact being inspected. However, the data that include these variables are too sparse to make meaningful analyses.

3.1.2 Dependent variables

The dependent variables for our study corresponded to the inspection outcomes, i.e. those attributes that describe how successful the inspection was. A large number of the inspections in our dataset reported the total number of defects found, which we designated as one of our dependent variables. In order to get an efficiency measure, we also looked at the defect count for each inspection normalized by total inspection effort ("defects per hour"). Total inspection effort, measured in person-hours, was calculated by multiplying the meeting effort by number of participants, and then added to the total preparation effort.

3.2 Limitations

We are grateful for the opportunity to analyze such an extensive dataset. However, in order to interpret the analysis results in the proper light, we must examine its limitations.

First, the data set cannot be assumed to be exhaustive, i.e. to include all software inspections conducted at the organization during the time period included. We have done a limited exclusion bias analysis (see Table 1) by comparing the part of the dataset available for analysis to the rest of the dataset, but it's not possible to know anything about the inspections that are not present at all in the dataset.

Second, we do not have access to quality assurance information, either of the inspection process used or of the data itself. There is a documented software inspection process, and we are aware that it is widely used, but there may be variations in that process among the inspections represented in the data set. Also, errors and misinterpretations in the recording of the data might exist, and we have no way to evaluate such errors, given the distance in time and situation between the point of collection and our analysis. One common inconsistency in collecting defect data is differing granularities. That is, one inspection team might count a group of small, highly related defects as just one defect, while another team might count a similar set of defects individually. However, we believe that the dataset is still much more homogeneous than a general dataset from a wider organizational and domain diversity.

4. ANALYSES

Out of the 2528 inspection data records (after excluding records with meeting length greater than 4 hours), only 547 of those inspections included data on both the number of defects found and the effort expended. Further, not all of those 547 records included values for all the other independent variables. Consequently, nearly all of the analyses described in this paper were based on a subset of between 472 and 547 inspections, depending on the variables involved.

Table 1 shows some basic descriptive statistics for the major variables of interest. It also shows a comparison between the statistics for the entire data set and those for the subset upon which most of our analysis are based. The purpose of this comparison is to identify potential biases in the analyzed subset.

Table 1 reveals that the inspections that have both defect and effort data (i.e. the ones that our analysis is based on) on average consume more effort (14.36 person hours as compared to 5.68), find more defects, include more participants, have longer meetings, and inspect more pages than the inspections for which we do not have the required data. Also, given that the full dataset contains 2528 inspection records, our analysis involves only about 20% of that data.

Recall that we want to evaluate whether the inspection planning heuristics that were originally proposed in 1992 are still effective in more current projects. To achieve this, we divided the data into an "historical" dataset that covered the period of the early 1990s when the original heuristics were formulated, and a "contemporary" dataset that covered the time period since then (up until 2007). As the dividing line, we used January 1, 1995. This was a rather arbitrary choice but had the advantage of dividing the entire set into two roughly equal parts (1041 contemporary inspections and 1487 historical ones). The relative sparseness of the contemporary set (1041 inspections over 11 years, as compared to 1487 inspections over 6 years) is an artifact of the data collection process (i.e. our dataset cannot be considered to be exhaustive), and is not evidence that the prevalence of inspections at the organization has decreased.

For each inspection in the dataset, we determined if it conformed to the recommended values of each inspection heuristic. For each heuristic, we compared the mean number of defects reported for inspections that complied with that heuristic (in-compliance inspections) to the mean for inspections that did not (out-of-compliance inspections). Since none of our variables were normally distributed, we used a non-parametric statistic, the Mann-Whitney test, to identify significant differences in the means. We summarize these results in Table 2.

Table 1. Distributions of major variables in the database

Variable	In whole dataset				Among records with defect and effort data			
	N	Mean	Min	Max	N	Mean	Min	Max
total effort (staff hour)	1850	5.68	0.2	119	547	14.36	0.2	119
#defects found	750	10.17	0	210	547	12.14	1	210
#participants	2479	2.62	1	17	522	3.6	1	9
meeting length (hour)	2347	0.55	0.05	4	499	0.874	0.1	4
#pages	1155	30.97	0.03	1000	513	37.13	0.03	1000
page rate (# pages/meeting hour)	1068	76.04	0.13	2667	472	65.36	0.13	2424

To examine the relationship between the heuristics and inspection efficiency, we applied a similar analysis using the defects per hour variable. The results of this analysis are summarized in Table 3.

5. RESULTS

Table 2 highlights several observations about the dataset. In the contemporary data, a much smaller percentage followed the suggested heuristics for inspection team size and page rate (10% and 15%, respectively), than historically.

Our results show that projects that followed the heuristics for team size detected significantly more defects on average for both contemporary and historical datasets. In fact, the difference is actually more pronounced in the contemporary data. Meanwhile, in term of efficiency, we see the opposite trend. In the historical datasets, projects that were in compliance with the team size heuristic were significantly less efficient than the projects that were out-of-compliance. The difference, however, seems to diminish in the contemporary dataset, although this may be due to the small number of projects that complied with the heuristics. It is interesting to note, however, an increase in efficiency in the contemporary dataset in general.

We also observe, counter to expectations, that in both the contemporary and historical datasets, inspections that conformed to the meeting length heuristic found fewer defects than those that exceeded the heuristic. This result is curious, but is probably affected at least in part by the fact that relatively few inspections did not conform to this heuristic. The opposite trend was also observed with regard to inspection efficiency. Projects that complied with the heuristic reported more defects per hour than the projects that were not in-compliance. This latter effect was not observed in the contemporary dataset.

The results pertaining to the page rate heuristic are also worthy of note. They indicate that the page rate heuristic is not only less effective, but also more difficult to comply with, in the contemporary dataset than historically. Historically, about 24% of the inspections were able to comply with the page rate heuristic (as compared to 15% of the contemporary inspections), and those inspections found significantly more defects. The contemporary inspections that conformed to the page rate heuristic found marginally more defects (4.4 vs. 4.1), but the difference is not significant. With regard to inspection efficiency, we observe a similar trend with the team size heuristic: in-compliance projects were found to be less efficient than the out-of-compliance ones in the historical datasets, but the efficiencies were similar between in- and out-of-compliance projects in the contemporary datasets.

Table 2. Testing effectiveness of original heuristics on historical and contemporary data

	In-compliance Inspections		Out-of-compliance Inspections		Inspections following heuristics significantly better?
	# of inspections	Avg. # of resulting defects	# of inspections	Avg. # of resulting defects	
CONTEMPORARY DATASET (1995 and later)					
Team size	23	38.7	206	6.5	YES (p<0.0005)
Meeting length	184	3.7	7	27.6	NO
Page rate	23	4.4	134	4.1	NO (p=0.5)
HISTORICAL DATASET (1994 and earlier)					
Team size	253	11.7	239	7.3	YES (p<0.0001)
Meeting length	460	8.5	29	22.7	NO
Page rate	115	15.6	355	7.4	YES (p<0.0001)

Table 3. Testing efficiency of original heuristics on historical and contemporary data

	In-compliance Inspections		Out-of-compliance Inspections		Inspections following heuristics significantly better?
	# of inspections	Avg. # of resulting defects/hr	# of inspections	Avg. # of resulting defects/hr	
CONTEMPORARY DATASET (1995 and later)					
Team size	19	2.32	126	2.36	NO
Meeting length	123	1.91	2	1.87	NO
Page rate	17	1.98	91	1.77	NO
HISTORICAL DATASET (1994 and earlier)					
Team size	202	0.94	175	1.85	YES (p<0.0001)
Meeting length	351	1.42	23	0.74	NO
Page rate	87	0.78	277	1.54	YES (p<0.0001)

6. CONCLUSIONS AND FUTURE WORK

These initial findings point to the conclusion that the original inspection planning heuristics are not as helpful to today's inspection planners as they could be. The results show that they do not always ensure a more effective or efficient inspection, and that, at least for some heuristics, teams are finding it less practical to comply with them.

There is still a need for guidelines and heuristics to help inspection planners make the most of their inspections. Because there is clear evidence that the heuristics can be improved upon, and because they lack a focus on inspection efficiency, we are examining the inspection data available for insight into the variables (not just the planning parameters) that are associated with higher levels of inspection efficiency. In other words, we are searching for a "sweet spot" or a "point of diminishing returns" at which the level of resources maximizes the outcome.

7. ACKNOWLEDGMENTS
The authors wish to thank our collaborators at the organization described in this paper who have made this work possible.

8. REFERENCES
[1] E.P. Doolan, "Experience with Fagan's Inspection Method," *Software – Practice and Experience*, vol. 22, no. 2, 1992, pp. 10.

[2] S.G. Eick, et al., "Estimating Software Fault Content Before Coding," *International Conference of Software Engineering*, 1992, pp. 59-65.

[3] M.E. Fagan, "Design and Code Inspections to Reduce Errors in Program Development," *IBM Systems Journal*, vol. 15, no. 3, 1976, pp. 30.

[4] T. Gilb and D. Graham, *Software Inspection*, Addison-Wesley Longman Publishing Co., 1993.

[5] M. Halling and S. Biffl, "Investigating the Influence of Software Inspection Process Parameters on Inspection Meeting Performance," *Software, IEE Proceedings -*, vol. 149, no. 5, 2002, pp. 115-121.

[6] IEEE, "IEEE Standard for Software Reviews," IEEE Std 1028-1997, 1998.

[7] J.C. Kelly, et al., "An Analysis of Defect Densities Found During Software Inspections," *Journal of Systems Software*, vol. 17, no. 2, 1992, pp. 7.

[8] A.A. Porter, et al., "An Experiment to Assess the Cost-benefits of Code Inspections in Large Scale Software Development," *Software Engineering, IEEE Transactions on*, vol. 23, no. 6, 1997, pp. 329-346

[9] F. Shull, et al., "What We Have Learned About Fighting Defects," *International Symposium on Software Metrics*. 2002, pp. 249-258.

[10] E.F. Weller, "Lessons from Three Years of Inspection Data in Software Development," *Software, IEEE*, vol. 10, no. 5, 1993, pp. 38-45.

[11] K.E. Wiegers, *Peer Reviews in Software*, Addison-Wesley, 2002.

Further Analysis on the Validation of a Usability Inspection Method for Model-Driven Web Development

Adrian Fernandez[1], Silvia Abrahão[1], Emilio Insfran[1], Maristella Matera[2]

[1]Universitat Politècnica de València
Camino de Vera, s/n, 46022, Valencia, Spain
+34 96 38773 50
{afernandez,sabrahao,einsfran}@dsic.upv.es

[2]Politécnico di Milano
via Ponzio, 34/5 - 20133, Milan, Italy
+39 02 23993408
matera@elet.polimi.it

ABSTRACT

Currently, there is a lack of empirically validated usability evaluation methods that can properly be integrated during the early stages of Web development processes. This has motivated us to propose a usability inspection method called WUEP that can be integrated into different model-driven Web development processes. In previous work, we presented the operationalization and validation of WUEP in a specific process based on the Object-Oriented Hypermedia (OO-H) method. In this paper, we present further analysis of the empirical validation of the operationalization of WUEP into WebML, which is one of the most well-known industrial model-driven Web development process. The effectiveness, efficiency, perceived ease of use, and satisfaction of WUEP was evaluated in comparison to Heuristic Evaluation. The results show that WUEP is more effective and efficient than heuristic evaluation in the detection of usability problems. The inspectors were also satisfied when applying WUEP, and found it easier to use than heuristic evaluation.

Categories and Subject Descriptors

D.2.4 [**Software Engineering**]: Software/Program Verification - *Validation*; D.2.9 [**Software Engineering**]: Management - *Software quality assurance.*

General Terms

Measurement, Design, Experimentation, Human Factors.

Keywords

Usability Inspection, Model-driven Web development, Controlled Experiment.

1. INTRODUCTION

Usability is considered to be one of the most important quality factors for Web applications, along with others such as reliability and security. The challenge of developing more usable Web applications has promoted the emergence of a large number of usability evaluation methods. However, most of these approaches only consider usability evaluations during the final stages of the Web development process. Works such as that of Matera *et al.* and [10] and Juristo *et al.* [9] claim that usability evaluations should also be performed during the early stages of the

development process in order to improve the user experience and decrease maintenance costs.

To address these issues, we have proposed a usability inspection method (i.e., Web Usability Evaluation Process – WUEP [7]), which can be instantiated and integrated into different model-driven Web development processes. In this type of processes, intermediate artifacts (i.e., models), which represent different views of a Web application, are used in all the steps of the development process, and the final source code is automatically generated from these models. In this context, inspections of these models can provide early usability evaluation reports to identify usability problems that can be corrected prior to the generation of the source code.

Besides the need of evaluation method we also envision the need of empirical studies to evaluate and improve any new proposed evaluation method. These studies can indeed provide useful information when a method is compared to others. Several empirical studies for validating Web usability evaluation methods exist (e.g., [5]). However, they focus on traditional Web development processes. There are few empirical studies based on the model-driven Web development processes (e.g., [10][1][6][13]). Among these studies, we presented in [6] an operationalization and validation of WUEP in a specific process followed by the Object-Oriented Hypermedia (OO-H) method. In this work, WUEP was compared against Heuristic Evaluation (HE) and the results showed that WUEP is more effective and efficient than HE in the detection of usability problems.

However, in other to verify the generalization of WUEP into another process this inspection method has been operationalized for use with the Web Modeling Language (WebML) [4], which is one of the most well-known industrial model-driven Web development process. This operationalization consisted in adapting the generic measures taken from the Web Usability Model [7] (that drives the inspection process followed by WUEP) to apply them to WebML artifacts as a way to predict the usability of Web applications early on the process. In this work, we present the results of a controlled experiment aimed at providing further analysis about the effectiveness, efficiency, perceived ease of use, and satisfaction of WUEP in detecting usability problems when integrated for use with WebML. WUEP was evaluated in comparison to Heuristic Evaluation (HE), which is a widely-used inspection method in industry.

This paper is structured as follows. Section 2 shows the evaluated usability inspection methods. Section 3 describes the controlled experiment. Section 4 shows the analysis of the results obtained. Section 5 discusses threats to the validity of the experiment, and Section 6 presents our conclusions and further work.

2. EVALUATED INSPECTION METHODS

The evaluated methods are two usability inspection methods: our proposal (WUEP), and the Heuristic Evaluation (HE) proposed by Nielsen [12]. Inspection methods are used by evaluators to evaluate artifacts (normally User Interfaces – UIs) with regard to certain principles in order to detect usability problems. These methods are commonly employed since they can be applied in several stages of a development process and not only when the software application has been completed and deployed.

The Web Usability Evaluation Process (WUEP) extends and adapts the quality evaluation process proposed in the ISO 25000 (SQuaRE) [8] with the purpose of integrating usability evaluations into model-driven Web development processes. WUEP employs a Web Usability Model that decomposes usability into sub-characteristics and measurable attributes. Measures with a generic definition are associated to these attributes in order for them to be operationalized at different abstraction levels (e.g., abstract UI) in any model-driven Web development process. The aim of applying measures was to reduce the subjectivity inherent to existing inspection methods. There are three roles involved in WUEP: evaluation designer, evaluation executor, and Web developer. The *evaluation designer* performs the establishment of evaluation requirements (e.g., scope, Web application selection, attributes selection, Web artifacts selection), the specification of the evaluation (e.g., operationalization of measures, rating levels for measures), and the design of the evaluation (e.g., number of evaluators, evaluation plan). The *evaluation executor* applies the evaluation plan designed in the execution stage (measures calculation, usability problem reports), and finally, the *Web developer* performs the analysis of changes in order to correct the usability problems detected.

The Heuristic Evaluation (HE) requires a group of evaluators to examine the UI in compliance with recognized usability principles called *heuristics*. HE proposes 10 heuristics that are intended to cover the best practices in the design of any UI (e.g., minimize the user workload, error prevention). There are two roles involved in HE: evaluation designer and evaluation executor. The *evaluation designer* determines the scope of the evaluation and defines the evaluation plan. The *evaluation executor* applies the heuristics to Web artifacts to identify and report the usability problems. HE was selected because i) it is widely-used in industrial settings and ii) it can be applied to intermediate artifacts (e.g., mock-ups) produced during early stages of Web development. It is worth to mention that there is no other inspection method for model-driven Web development processes with which to compare WUEP.

3. CONTROLLED EXPERIMENT

The controlled experiment was designed by considering the guidelines proposed by Wohlin *et al.* [14]. According to the Goal-Question-Metric (GQM) [2], the goal of the experiment is: to **analyze** the WUEP operationalization for the WebML development process, **for the purpose** of evaluating it **with regard to** its effectiveness, efficiency, perceived ease of use, and the evaluators' perceived satisfaction of it in comparison to HE **from the viewpoint** of a set of novice usability evaluators.

The context of the experiment is the usability evaluation of two Web applications performed by novice inspectors. This context is determined by the *Web applications* to be evaluated, the *usability evaluation methods* to be applied and the *subject selection*. The *Web applications* selected are a Web Calendar for meeting appointment management, and an e-commerce application for a Book Store. They were developed by a Web development company using the WebML model-driven development process.

Two different functionalities of the Web Calendar application (Appointment management and User comments support) were selected for defining the experimental object O1, whereas two different functionalities of the Book Store application (Book search and Book shopping) were selected for defining the experimental object O2. Each experimental object contains two Web artifacts: a Hypertext model (HM), specifying the structure of the applications through the WebML design notation, and a Final User Interface (FUI). We selected these four functionalities since they are relevant to the end-users and similar in size and complexity. The *usability inspection methods* to be evaluated were WUEP and HE, and only their execution stages were considered. Thirty *subjects* were chosen from a group of fifth-year Computer Science students from the Universitat Politècnica de València, who were enrolled on an Advanced Software Engineering course from September 2011 to January 2012.

The method has been applied to two **independent variables**: the evaluation method (WUEP and HE) and the experimental objects (O1 and O2). There are two **objective dependent variables**: *effectiveness*, which is calculated as the ratio between the number of usability problems detected and the total number of existing (known) usability problems; and *efficiency*, which is calculated as the ratio between the number of usability problems detected and the total time spent on the inspection process. There are also two **subjective dependent variables**: *perceived ease of use* and *evaluators' perceived satisfaction*. Both are calculated by closed-questions from a five-point Likert-scale questionnaire which also includes open-questions to obtain feedback from the evaluators.

The **hypotheses** of the experiment are:
- **H1-0:** There is no significant difference between the effectiveness of WUEP and HE / **H1-a:** WUEP is significantly more effective than HE.
- **H2-0:** There is no significant difference between the efficiency of WUEP and HE / **H2-a:** WUEP is significantly more efficient than HE.
- **H3-0:** There is no significant difference between the perceived ease of use of WUEP and HE / **H3-a:** WUEP is perceived to be significantly easier to use than HE.
- **H4-0:** There is no significant difference between the evaluators' perceived satisfaction of applying WUEP and HE / **H4-a:** WUEP is perceived to be significantly more satisfactory to use than HE.

The experiment was planned as a balanced within-subject design with a confounding effect, signifying that the same subjects use both methods in a different order and with different experimental objects (the subjects' assignation to the tasks was random). Table 1 shows the schedule of the experiment in more detail. In addition, before the controlled experiment, a control group was created in order to provide an initial list of usability problems by applying an *ad-hoc* inspection method, and to determine whether the usability problems reported by the subjects were real or false positives. This group was formed of two independent evaluators who are experts in usability evaluations, and one of the authors of this paper. Several documents were designed as instrumentation for the experiment: slides for training session, an explanation of the methods, gathering data forms, and two questionnaires.

Table 1. Schedule of the controlled experiment

	1st Day		2nd Day	
Training (15+20 m)	WebML introduction			
	Inspection using HE		Inspection using WUEP	
1st Session (90 min)	HE in O1	HE in O2	WUEP in O1	WUEP in O2
	HE Questionnaire		WUEP Questionnaire	
Break (180 min)				
Training (20 min)	Inspection using WUEP		Inspection using HE	
2nd Session (90 min)	WUEP in O2	WUEP in O1	HE in O2	HE in O1
	WUEP Questionnaire		HE Questionnaire	

4. ANALYSIS OF RESULTS

After the execution of the experiment, the control group analyzed all the usability problems detected by the subjects. If a usability problem was not in the initial list, this group determined whether it could be considered as a real usability problem or a false positive. Replicated problems were considered only once. Discrepancies in this analysis were solved by consensus. The control group determined a total of 9 and 11 usability problems in the experimental objects O1 and O2, respectively.

The quantitative analysis was performed by using the SPSS v16 statistical tool and $\alpha=0.05$. Table 2 summarizes the overall results of the usability evaluations. Mean and standard deviation were used as descriptive statistics also for the PEU and PSU subjective variables, being the five-point Likert scale adopted for their measurement an interval scale

Table 2. Overall results

	# Problems / Subject		False positives / Subject		Replicated Prob. / Subject	
		σ		σ		σ
HE	3.29	1.08	1.38	1.24	0.88	0.80
WUEP	**6.50**	1.14	**0.54**	0.66	**0.00**	0.00

	Duration (min)		Effectiveness (Effec) (%)		Efficiency (Effic) (prob / min)	
		σ		σ		σ
HE	**70.13**	13.52	33.04	10.85	0.05	0.02
WUEP	80.88	18.46	**65.32**	11.54	**0.08**	0.02

	Perceived Ease of use (PEU)		Perceived Satisfaction of use (PSU)	
		σ		σ
HE	3.38	0.73	3.63	0.67
WUEP	**3.80**	0.72	**3.92**	0.75

The overall results obtained have allowed us to interpret that WUEP has achieved the subjects' best performance in about all the analyzed statistics (see cells in bold), The only exception is the duration of the evaluation session, which however was longer for WUEP due to the longer time required to read the material containing the WUEP description As indicated by the results, WUEP tends to provide a low degree of false positives and replicated problems. The lack of false positives can be explained by the fact that WUEP tends to minimize the subjectivity of the evaluation. The lack of replicated problems can be explained by the fact that WUEP provides operationalized measures that are classified to be applied in one type of Web artifact.

Since the sample size is smaller than 50, we applied the Shapiro-Wilk test to verify whether the data was normally distributed. Our aim was to select which tests are needed in order to verify our hypotheses. Table 3 shows the results of the normality test, in

which '*' signifies that this variable is not normally distributed in this usability inspection method.

Table 3. Shapiro-Wilk Normality test results

	Effec.	Effic.	PEU	PSU
HE	0.219	0.722	0.414	0.281
WUEP	0.021 * (< 0.05)	0.296	0.072	0.053

The boxplots with the distribution of each dependent variable per subject per method (see Figure 1) show that WUEP was more effective and efficient than HE, and WUEP was also perceived by the evaluators as being easier to use and more satisfactory than HE. In order to determine whether or not these results were significant, we applied: the Mann-Whitney non-parametric test to verify H1 (since *WUEP_Effec* is not normally distributed), and the 1-tailed *t*-test for independent samples to verify H2, H3 and H4.

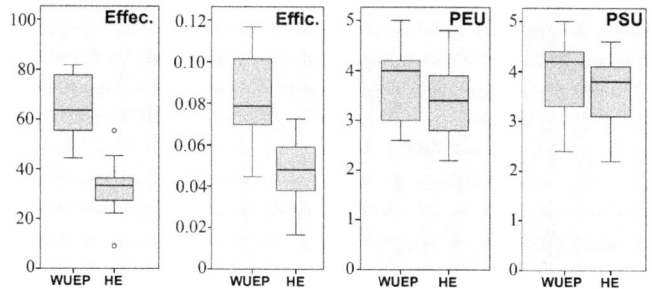

Figure 1. Boxplots for each dependent variable

The *p*-values obtained from the Mann-Whitney test for the *Effec.* variable was 0.000. The *p*-values obtained from the 1-tailed *t*-test test for the *Effic.*, *PEU* and *PSU* variables were 000, 0.026 and 0.086, respectively. These results therefore support the rejection of all the null-hypotheses and the acceptance of their respective alternative-hypotheses except from the H4 (0.086 > 0.05).

In order to strengthen our analysis, we used the method suggested in [3] to test the *effect of the order of methods* and the *order of experimental objects* (both independent variables). We used the Diff function: $\text{Diff}_x = \text{observation}_x(A) - \text{observation}_x(B)$, where x denotes a particular subject, and A, B are the two possible values of one independent variable. We created Diffs variables from each dependent variable (e.g., Effec_Diff(WUEP) represents the difference in effectiveness of the subjects who used WUEP first and HE second. On the other hand, Effec_Diff(HE) represents the difference in effectiveness of the subjects who used HE first and WUEP second). The aim was to verify that there were no significant differences between Diff functions since that would signify that there was no influence in the order of independent variables. The Shapiro-Wilk test showed that all the Diff functions were normally distributed, with the exception of Effic_Diff (HE) that was not. We therefore applied the parametric 2-tailed *t*-test in order to verify whether the effects were significant. Table 4 shows that all the *p*-values obtained were > 0.05. We can conclude that there was no effect with regard to the order of methods and experimental objects for any dependent variable.

Table 4. *t*-test results for Diff functions

Order of	Effec.	Effic.	PEU	PSU
Methods	0.095	0.291	0.173	0.560
Experimental Objects	0.989	0.932	0.709	0.560

Finally, a qualitative analysis was performed by analyzing the open-questions that were included in the questionnaire. This analysis revealed some important issues which can be considered to improve WUEP (e.g., the evaluators suggested that WUEP might be more useful if its evaluation process were automated by a tool (particularly the calculation of certain metrics).

5. THREATS TO VALIDITY

The main threats to the **internal validity** of the experiment are: learning effect, evaluation design, subject experience, and information exchange among evaluators. The learning effect was alleviated by ensuring that each subject applied each method to different experimental objects, and all the possible order combinations were considered. The evaluation design might have affected the results owing to the selection of attributes to be evaluated during the design stage of WUEP. We attempted to alleviate this threat by considering relevant usability attributes, although empirical studies that involve experts in the Web domain are needed to provide the evaluator designer with the most relevant usability attributes for each Web application family. Subject experience was alleviated due to the fact that none of the subjects had any experience in usability evaluations. Information exchange might have affected the results since the experiment took place over two days, and it is difficult to be certain whether the subjects exchanged any information with each other.

The main threats to the **external validity** of the experiment are: representativeness of the results, and duration of the experiment. Despite the fact that the experiment was performed in an academic context, the results could be representative with regard to novice evaluators with no experience in usability evaluations. However, the previous selection of usability attributes with their operationalized measures and the selection of the Web application might have affected the representativeness. To alleviate these issues, we intend to carry out a survey with Web designers to determine the relative importance of the usability attributes for different categories of Web applications. Since the duration of the experiment was limited to 90 min, only 3 representative artifacts were selected from the different types of artifacts available.

The main threats to the **construct validity** of the experiment are: measures that are applied in the quantitative analysis and the reliability of the questionnaire. Measures that are commonly employed in this kind of experiment were used in the quantitative analysis [5]. The reliability of the questionnaire was tested by applying the Cronbach test. Questions related to PEOU and PU obtained a Cronbach's alpha of 0.80 and 0.78, respectively. These values are higher than the acceptable minimum (0.70) [11]. The main threat to the **conclusion validity** of the experiment is the validity of the statistical tests applied. This was alleviated by applying the most common tests that are employed in the empirical software engineering field [11]. However, more replications are needed in order to confirm these results.

6. CONCLUSIONS AND FUTURE WORK

This paper presented a controlled experiment for validating a usability inspection method (WUEP) when integrated into the WebML model-driven development process. The effectiveness, efficiency, perceived ease of use and satisfaction of WUEP were compared against a widely-used inspection method: Heuristic Evaluation (HE). The results show that WUEP was more effective and efficient than HE in the detection of usability problems in WebML artifacts. The evaluators found it easier to use than HE. Although they were also more satisfied when applying WUEP, this last variable resulted not statistically significant.

These results confirmed our previous findings [6] when an operationalization of WUEP into the OO-H method was compared against HE. Although the experimental results provided good results as regards the usefulness of WUEP as a usability inspection method for Web applications, we are aware that more experimentation is needed to confirm these results. These results need to be interpreted with caution since they are only valid within the context established in this experiment. However, we have obtained valuable feedback from this empirical study with which to improve our proposal. As future work, we plan to replicate this experiment with subjects with different level of experience in usability evaluations (including practitioners) and by considering other kinds of Web applications such as mashups.

7. ACKNOWLEDGMENTS

This research work is funded by the MULTIPLE project (TIN2009-13838), the FPU program (AP2007-03731).

8. REFERENCES

[1] Abrahão, S., Iborra, E.,Vanderdonckt, J. 2007. Usability Evaluation of User Interfaces Generated with a Model-Driven Architecture Tool. Maturing Usability: Quality in Software, Interaction and Value, Springer, pp. 3-32.

[2] Basili, V., Rombach, H. 1988. The TAME Project: Towards Improvement-Oriented Software Environments, IEEE Transactions on Software Engineering 14(6), pp. 758-773.

[3] Briand, L., Labiche, Y., Di Penta, M., Yan-Bondoc, H. 2005. "An experimental investigation of formality in UML-based development", IEEE TSE, 31(10), pp. 833–849.

[4] Ceri, S., Fraternali, P., Bongio, A. 2000. Web modeling language (WebML): a modeling language for designing Web sites. 9th World Wide Web Conference, pp. 137–157.

[5] Conte, T., Massollar, J., Mendes, E., Travassos, G. H. 2007. Usability Evaluation Based on Web Design Perspectives. In Proc. of ESEM'07, Spain, pp. 146-155.

[6] Fernandez, A., Abrahão S., Insfran E. 2010. Towards to the validation of a usability evaluation method for model-driven web development, In Proc. of ESEM'10, Bolzano, Italy.

[7] Fernandez, A., Insfran, E., Abrahão, S. 2009. Integrating a Usability Model into a Model-Driven Web Development Process. In Proc. WISE'09, pp. 497-510, Springer.

[8] ISO/IEC. 2005. ISO/IEC 25000 series, Software Product Quality Requirements and Evaluation (SQuaRE).

[9] Juristo, N., Moreno, A., Sánchez-Segura, M.I. 2007. Guidelines for eliciting usability functionalities. IEEE Transactions on Software Engineering 33 (11), pp. 744-758.

[10] Matera, M., Costabile, M. F., Garzotto, F., Paolini, P. 2002. SUE inspection: an effective method for systematic usability evaluation of hypermedia. IEEE Transactions on Systems, Man, and Cybernetics, Part A 32(1): 93-103

[11] Maxwell, K. 2002. Applied Statistics for Software Managers. Software Quality Institute Series, Prentice Hall.

[12] Nielsen, J. 1994. Heuristic evaluation. Usability Inspection Methods, John Wiley & Sons, NY.

[13] Panach, I., Condori, N., Valverde, F., Aquino, N., Pastor, O. 2008. Understandability measurement in an early usability evaluation for MDD. In Proc. of ESEM'08, pp. 354-356.

[14] Wohlin, C., Runeson, P., Host, M., Ohlsson, M.C., Regnell, B., Weslen, A. 2000. Experimentation in Software Engineering - An Introduction, Kluwer.

Lessons Learned from Evaluating a Checklist for Reporting Experimental and Observational Research

Roel Wieringa
Dept. of Computer Science
University of Twente
The Netherlands
R.J.Wieringa@utwente.nl

Nelly Condori-Fernandez
Dept. of Computer Science
University of Twente
The Netherlands
n.condorifernandez
@utwente.nl

Maya Daneva
Dept. of Computer Science
University of Twente
The Netherlands
M.Daneva@utwente.nl

Bela Mutschler
University of Applied Sciences
Ravensburg-Weingarten
Germany
bela.mutschler@hs-
weingarten.de

Oscar Pastor
Universidad Poltécnica de
Valencia
Spain
opastor@dsic.upv.es

ABSTRACT

This short paper summarizes and discusses the result of an iterative construction and evaluation of a checklist for writing and reading reports about experimental and observational research.

Categories and Subject Descriptors

D.2.0 [**Software Engineering**]: General—*Miscellaneous*

General Terms

Documentation, Experimentation

Keywords

Unified checklist; Experimental and observational research

1. INTRODUCTION

In the past decades, several checklists for empirical research in software engineering (SE) have been proposed, mostly for experimental research [3, 4, 5, 15] but also for case study research [8]. The question that motivated the research summarized in this paper is: What are the differences and commonalities between these checklists? This question is relevant for teachers who want to recommend a checklist to their students and have to answer questions about which parts of which checklists are relevant for a particular research problem.

One obvious difference between checklists for experimental and for observational research is that the first refer to an experimental treatment and the second do not. But beyond

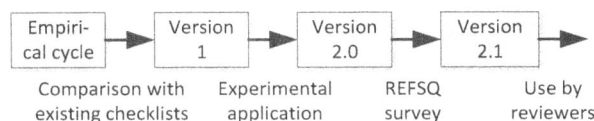

Figure 1: Iterative development of a unified checklist.

this, it is less obvious what are the differences between the checklists. Does the checklist of Jedlitschka & Pfahl [3] supersede all earlier experimental checklists? Is there a reason why it differs from the CONSORT [9] checklist? Why are there so many difference between the non-treatment part of the experimental checklists and the case study checklist [8]? Understanding the differences and commonalities between checklists would help students to interpret the checklists and apply them in an informed manner.

The effort to identify a common core of a cluster of checklists for reporting experimental and observational research has led in an iterative way to a new, unified checklist (figure 1). This short paper reports on the status of this iterative development. The effort started with the empirical cycle, which is a rational choice cycle in which the empirical researcher faces the problem to produce support for or against a knowledge claim about a population. This expresses a view of science as critical and rational knowledge acquisition [7]. The first author has used this as a framework for teaching empirical methods since 2007 [14]. Its use to define a checklist for empirical research based on extant checklists is described in [12]. In section 3, we review a number of lessons learned from evaluating the checklist. To save space, we frame the discussion in terms of Version 2.1 of the checklist (see figure 1).

2. VERSION 2.1 OF THE CHECKLIST

Version 2.1 assumes the research model of figure 2. This shows that there is an object of study (OoS), which represents elements of a population of interest. In statistical

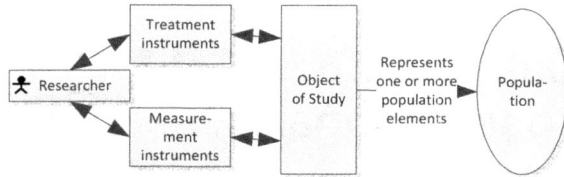

Figure 2: Research model assumed by Versions 2.0 and 2.1.

Data → Observations → Explanations → Generalizations

Figure 3: Analysis model assumed by Versions 2.0 and 2.1.

research, the population is the set of entities from which a sample is drawn; in case study research, the population is the set of cases similar to the case under study. Generalization from case studies is based on reasoning by similarity of structure [10], and is fallible, like all generalizations.

The researcher interacts with the OoS, usually mediated by instruments, through measurement interactions in which the researcher collects data from the OoS and aims to minimize influencing the OoS. In experimental research, the researcher additionally applies a treatment to the OoS, and aims to avoid any other interactions than the treatment.

Version 2.1 (table 1) asks for the relation of the research to a **context** of knowledge and practice in questions 1 and 14. The **research problem** is characterized by three items of information: a conceptual framework, research questions stated in terms of this framework, and a population about which the questions are asked. **Research design** follows the research model of figure 2 plus a question that asks how the report describes the reasoning from measurement to conclusions, and questions about the justification (i.e. validation) of design choices. A research report may include information about what actually happened during **execution** of the research design.

The questions under **Results Analysis** assume a list of abstraction levels as shown in figure 3. Each of the arrows represents a fallible inference that must be justified but also critically assessed. *Data* are the measurements taken, consisting of numbers, interview transcripts, etc. *Observations* are summaries of these, obtained by quantitative or qualitative analysis of the data. *Explanations* add some theoretical insight about what could have caused these observations; *generalizations* are claims beyond the OoS.

3. LESSONS LEARNED SO FAR

Version 1 (figure 1) had the same layout as Version 2.1 but has more questions. To construct it, three existing checklists were compared with each other by allocating their items to places in the empirical cycle. The checklists are referred to as JP [3], CT [9] and RH [8] henceforth. JP was selected because it is itself assembled from previous checklists in software engineering. CT was selected because it is the current end point of the development of a checklist for reporting experiments in a different field with a rich experimental tradition. RH was selected because it is the current state of

the art of checklists for case study reporting in software engineering. Version 1 is basically the union of all three checklists [13] and contains more questions than Version 2.1 The following observations about Version 1 are also valid for Version 2.1.

- The Population question does not occur explicitly as an item in these other checklists [13]. The two checklists for experiment reports consider this to be part of the description of the sampling procedure. RH take the position that case studies have no populations but that case study findings could be generalized analytically to similar cases [8, page 154]. We agree, and consider this set of similar cases to be the population, so this item is included in the unified checklist.

- CT and RH ask about possible explanations consistent with the observations; JP does not mention explanations. Explanations of observations relate observations to more general theory, and it is theory-building and -validation that advances scientific understanding [11]. So we have kept this item in our unified checklist.

- The two experiment report checklists (JP and CT) ask about generalizations from the observations; RH do not ask about this. However, RH support the idea of analytical generalization to similar cases, as we do [8, page 154], so we include this item in our unified list.

These observations capture the points in which Version 1, and hence Version 2.1, is *not* a common core but adds something with respect to at least one checklist. In addition, Version 1 contains detailed questions about validation and research execution. As explained below, these questions have been removed in Version 2.

We have evaluated Version 1 in a small experiment where seven PhD students and three senior researchers in three different research groups answered the checklist questions about a paper reporting about an observational case study and one reporting about an experiment [2].We give a brief summary of the conclusions.

- The number of questions answered by the subjects decreased when advancing through the 40 questions of the checklist. Our explanation is that Version 1 is too long.

- The answers and comments by the subjects showed us that important terms such as "Unit of Data Collection" (the term used for Object of Study in Version 1) and "treatment" are not understood by the subjects in the way we intended. For example, in our research model (figure 2), which was *not* made available to the subjects, a treatment is an intervention on the OoS by the researcher. This differs from the concept of a treatment that seemed to be used by some of the subjects, namely that a treatment is a level of an independent variable. The effect of an independent variable on a dependent variable can be studied observationally, by blocking on different levels of the independent variable. But these levels are then given to the researcher by nature rather than set by the researcher, as in our treatments. In Version 2, we tried to avoid this confusion by including figure 2 in the checklist.

The list is a classification of information items. Workshop papers present work started, not work finished, and typically contain a subset of the items listed below. Use your own judgment to decide what is acceptable.	
Items to consider	**Possible questions to consider**
Research context	
1. Motivation?	• Is the desired increment of knowledge of the paper clearly stated? • Is the current state of knowledge in this area adequately summarized? • Is the research goal motivated by a practical improvement goal?
Research problem	
2. Conceptual framework?	• Are relevant concepts common knowledge among the authors and readers of the paper? • Are relevant concepts that are not common knowledge, defined and motivated? • Are relevant concepts operationalized?
3. Research questions?	• Are research questions clearly stated?
4. Population?	• Is the target of generalization clear, i.e. for which population are these questions relevant?
Research design and justification	
5. Object of study?	• Is it clear what the object of study is, i.e. the sample, case(s) or model studied? • Is it clear how it was acquired or constructed? • Is it clear what structure it has? • Is validity of the OoS justified, i.e. is it clear why OoS is representative of the population (e.g. sample size, representativeness of the case or model)? • If people are involved, is ethics discussed (informed consent) ?
6. Reasoning?	• Is it clear what reasoning will be applied to extract observations from the data? (descriptive statistics, and/or qualitative coding of interviews, etc.) • Is it clear what reasoning will be used to answer the research questions? (statistical hypothesis testing, and/or qualitative analysis, etc.) • Is the validity of this reasoning justified?
7. Treatment specification?	• In experimental studies: Is the treatment (i.e. intervention by researcher) specified, including any instruments used? • Is the validity of the treatment discussed? • If people are involved, is ethics discussed (fairness, absence of harm)?
8. Measurement specification?	• Are measurements described, including measurement procedures and instruments? • Is the validity of these measurement procedures and instruments discussed? • If people are involved, is ethics discussed (privacy, respect for people)?
Research execution	
9. What happened?	• Is the report of what actually happened during research useful for the reader?
Results analysis	
10. Observations?	• Are the observations clearly described (graphs, box plots, interview summaries etc.)? • Limitations: Are the interpretations made in extracting observations from data critically assessed on validity?
11. Explanations?	• Are observations explained in terms of underlying mechanisms or of available theories? • Limitations: Are explanations assessed on plausibility?
12. Generalizations?	• Are observations or explanations generalized to the population? • Are population hypotheses tested? • Limitations: Is the plausibility of the hypotheses assessed?
13. Answers?	• Are the research questions answered explicitly? • Limitations: Is the plausibility of these answers assessed?
Research context	
14. Impact?	• Is future research discussed? • Are implications for practice discussed?

Table 1: Version 2.1 of the checklist, to be handed to PC members of a workshop.

- The validity questions in Version 1 were separated from the research design questions, even though they asked about the same items of information; and as stated above, the validity questions were very detailed and non-standard. This confused the subjects. In Version 2 we merged the validation questions with the design questions (as in table 1) and returned to the usual validation concepts: Conclusion, internal and external validity are about the three inferences in the ascent from data in figure 3; Construct validity is the discussion of the validity of the conceptual framework and its operationalizations.

Next, we have conducted a survey among participants of requirements engineering conference[1] in which we asked about understandability and perceived utility of Version 2 [1]. The outcome of this survey encouraged us to do a next evaluation. We have asked program committee members of a workshop[2] to use Version 2.1 when reviewing papers. Version 2.1 differs from Version 2 only in that the Context questions have been reduced to two in total.

4. DISCUSSION

Important differences between different checklists that we found are the absence of the concept of a population and generalization in the case study checklist (RH) and of an item asking for explanations in one experiment checklist (JP). In our proposal, these items are included, because we view research as the critical answering of knowledge questions about a population. The answers are never definitive and empirical research can only provide support that increases or decreases the plausibility of these answers.

So far our claim about this checklist is that this may be useful for readers of a paper to understand what the paper is about. Researchers may use our checklist as a reference point to compare or combine other checklists, or as an independent checklist to read or write papers. In addition, they can use it when they design an experiment of case study, possibly in combination with other checklists geared to those research designs. The checklist does *not* give criteria for evaluating the research reported in a paper: Our claim is that in order to understand what research a paper reports about, a reader, and therefore a reviewer, needs this information. *Judging* research is a different matter. It is difficult and even expert reviewers may differ in their judgment [6]. We intend to do additional evaluations by communities of experts as suggested by Kitchenham et al. [5].

5. ACKNOWLEDGMENTS

Dr. Condori-Fernandez is supported by the EU Marie Curie Fellowship Grant 50911302 PIEF-2010.

6. REFERENCES

[1] N. Condori-Fernandez, M. Daneva, and R. Wieringa. A survey on empirical requirements engineering research practices. In J. Dörr, editor, *Postproceedings REFSQ*, 2012. ISSN 1860-2770.

[2] N. Condori-Fernandez, R. Wieringa, M. Daneva, B. Mutschler, and O. Pastor. Experimental evaluation of a unified checklist for designing and reporting empirical research in software engineering. Technical Report TR-CTIT-12-12, Centre for Telematics and Information Technology University of Twente, 2012.

[3] A. Jedlitschka and D. Pfahl. Reporting guidelines for controlled experiments in software engineering. In *Proceedings of the 4th International Symposium on Empirical Software Engineering (ISESE 2005)*, pages 94–104. IEEE Computer Society, 2005.

[4] N. Juristo and A. Moreno. *Basics of Software Engineering Experimentation*. Kluwer, 2001.

[5] B. Kitchenham, H. Al-Khilidar, M. Babar, M. Berry, K. Cox, J. Keung, F. Kurniawati, M. Staples, H. Zhang, and L. Zhu. Evaluating guidelines for reporting empirical software engineering studies. *Empirical Software Engineering*, 13:97–121, 2008.

[6] B. Kitchenham, D. Sjøberg, P. Brereton, D. Budgen, T. Dybå, M. Höst, D. Pfahl, and P. Runeson. Can we evaluate the quality of software engineering experiments? In G. Succi, M. Morisio, and N. Nagappan, editors, *ESEM*. ACM, 2010.

[7] R. Merton. The normative structure of science. In *Social Theory and Social Structure*, pages 267–278. The Free Press, 1968. Enlarged Edition.

[8] P. Runeson and M. Höst. Guidelines for conducting and reporting case study research in software engineering. *Empirical Software Engineering*, 14:131–164, 2009.

[9] K. Schulz, D. Altman, and D. Moher. CONSORT 2010 Statement: updated guidelines for reporting parallel group randomised trials. *Annals of Internal Medicine*, 152(11):1–7, 1 June 2010.

[10] P. Seddon and R. Scheepers. Towards the improved treatment of generalization from knowledge claims in IS research: drawing general conclusions from samples. *European Journal of Information Systems*, pages 1–16, 2011. doi:10.1057/ejis.2011.9.

[11] D. Sjøberg, T. Dybå, B. Anda, and J. Hannay. Building theories in software engineering. In F. Shull, J. Singer, and D. Sjøberg, editors, *Guide to advanced empirical software engineering*, pages 312–336. Springer, 2008.

[12] R. Wieringa. Towards a unified checklist for empirical research in software engineering: First proposal. In T. Baldaresse, M. Genero, E. Mendes, and M. Piattini, editors, *16th International Conference on Evaluation and Assessment in Software Engineering (EASE 2012)*, pages 161–165. IET, 2012.

[13] R. Wieringa. A unified checklist for observational and experimental research in software engineering (version 1). Technical Report TR-CTIT-12-07, Centre for Telematics and Information Technology University of Twente, 2012.

[14] R. J. Wieringa and J. M. G. Heerkens. Designing requirements engineering research. In *Workshop on Comparative Evaluation in Requirements Engineering (CERE'07), Delhi*, pages 36–48, Los Alamitos, October 2007. IEEE Computer Society.

[15] C. Wohlin, P. Runeson, M. Höst, M. C. Ohlsson, B. Regnell, and A. Weslén. *Experimentation in Software Engineering: An Introduction*. Kluwer, 2002.

---

[1]www.refsq.org

[2]www.bpm.scitech.qut.edu.au/erbpm2012/

A Study of Reusability, Complexity, and Reuse Design Principles

Reghu Anguswamy
Software Reuse Lab, Virginia Tech.
7054 Haycock Road, Falls Church, VA, USA - 22043
Ph: +1-703.538.8371
email: reghu@vt.edu

William B. Frakes
Software Reuse Lab, Virginia Tech.
7054 Haycock Road, Falls Church, VA, USA - 22043
Ph: +1-703.538.8371
email: wfrakes@vt.edu

ABSTRACT

A study is reported on the relationship of complexity and reuse design principles with the reusability of code components. Reusability of a component is measured as the ease of reuse as perceived by the subjects reusing the component. Thirty-four subjects participated in the study with each subject reusing 5 components, resulting in 170 cases of reuse. The components were randomly assigned to the subjects from a pool of 25 components which were designed and built for reuse. The relationship between the complexity of a component and the ease of reuse was analyzed by a regression analysis. It was observed that the higher the complexity the lower the ease of reuse, but the correlation is not significant. An analysis of the relationship between a set of reuse design principles, used in designing and building the components, and the ease of reuse is also reported. The reuse design principles: *well-defined interface,* and *clarity and understandability* significantly increase the ease of reuse, while *documentation* does not have a significant impact on the ease of reuse

Categories and Subject Descriptors: D.2.13

[**Reusable Software**]: Component-based software engineering – *reusing components*

Keywords: Software reuse, reuse design, reusability, empirical study

1. INTRODUCTION

Studies from the software industry have analyzed benefits from software reuse such as improved software quality, productivity, and reliability [1-6]. Component based development for software reuse was presented as early as 1969 by McIlroy [7] suggesting that interchangeable pieces called software components should form the basis for software systems. Our study is based on analyzing the reusability of code components in an application. Reusability of a component was measured as the ease of reuse as perceived by the subjects reusing the component using a 5-point likert scale: (1 – not used, 2 – difficult to reuse, 3 – neither difficult nor easy to reuse, 4 – easy to reuse, 5 – very easy to reuse). The likert scale is similar to the one used in [8]. There have been no or little empirical studies similar to ours.

In a previous study [9], subjects built one-use stemming components [10]. The subjects were then trained on software reuse design based on a set of reuse design principles and converted their one-use components to be reusable.

The reusable components were found to be significantly larger (the median was 80% higher) in size than their equivalent on-use components. The three most commonly used reuse design principles identified in the study were *well-defined interface, documentation,* and *clarity and understandability.* We will now define briefly each of these principles.

Well-defined interface: An interface determines how a component can be reused and interconnected with other components. If the component's interface is simpler, it should be easier to reuse. There are three types of interfaces: application programming interface (API), user interface and data interface [11].

Documentation: It is essential for any future use or modification and critical for maintainability. Documentation should be self-contained, adaptable and extensible [11]. Stand-alone external documentation, interface documentation lilke Javadocs, or in-line code documentation are all considered *documentation.*

Clarity and Understandability: This is the degree to which a component is easily understood regarding functionality. Matsumoto [12] discusses definiteness as a characteristic to make components reusable. Definiteness represents the degree of clarity to which the module's purpose, capability, constraints, interfaces, and required resources are defined.

The common belief is that the larger the component the harder to reuse. Even in popular cost estimation models such as COCOMO II [13] which consider software reuse and reusing components, the cost is estimated higher for larger reusable components. Our study analyzes the relationship between the size of components and the ease of reuse. We also analyze the relationship between the reuse design principles and the ease of reuse.

2. HYPOTHESES

Hypothesis 1: The smaller the component the easier it is to reuse. Size is measured in SLOC (source lines of code).

Hypothesis 2: A component designed and built with a given reuse design principle will be easier to reuse than a component which is not built based on that reuse design principle. For this hypothesis, we analyzed individually the three most used reuse design principles [9] - *well-defined interface, documentation,* and *clarity and understandability.*

3. METHOD

Based on the faceted classification of types of software reuse by Frakes and Terry [14], the reuse design in our study involves development scope as internal, modification as white box, domain scope as vertical, management as ad hoc, and reused entity as code. A total of 34 subjects participated in this study.

3.1 Subject Demographics

Thirty-four subjects who participated were students of a graduate level course: *Software Design and Quality*. All were enrolled either at Master's or Ph.D. level at Virginia Tech., USA. Nine subjects (27%) already had a master's degree and the rest (73%) had an undergraduate degree. The subjects completed an online questionnaire hosted on surveymonkey (http://www.surveymonkey.com/s/37DLNPM) answering questions on their demographics. The questionnaire was completed by the subjects before they were given the assignment of reusing the components.

The subjects were asked to mention their roles in their respective organizations. They could choose multiple roles and 8 had at least 2 roles. Almost two-thirds (64.7%) were involved in development and programming. About one-fifth (20.6%) of the subjects were system architects. Five subjects (14.7%) were both system architects and software developers/programmers. 17.6% of the subjects were systems engineers. Two of them were system architects as well. 17.6% of the subjects were managers; one of them was only a manager, 2 were system architects as well and 2 were systems engineers as well. Four of them mentioned their role as 'other', 2 of them were data consultants, 1 a software consultant and 1 held a military position with no affiliation to software engineering.

Half of the subjects (50.0%) had more than 8 years of experience in programming as well as in the field of software engineering. Only 1 subject mentioned having no experience in software programming. Two subjects, including the subject having no experience in software programming had no experience in software engineering. Less than 15% of the subjects had none or very little experience (0-1year) in software programming and software engineering. 26.5% of the subjects had at least 2 years of experience in programming but less than 8 years. Since in the practical world, users with no experience in the software industry are also likely to reuse existing components, we have included such subjects in our study as well.

More than four-fifths (82%) of the subjects had mentioned they had no software reuse program in their organization. Only 19% of the subjects responded that they were trained to design and build components for reuse. Almost one-third (35.3%) had no experience in the field of software reuse and less than one-tenth (8.8%) had considerable experience (>8 years). One-fifth of the subjects had very little experience (0-2years) in software reuse.

3.2 Allocating and Reusing Components

In a previous study [9], one-use components and their equivalent reusable components were analyzed. In that study, the subjects were given an assignment to build a one-use software component implementing the s-stemming algorithm [10]. This was followed by training for the subjects on designing and building components for reuse. One hundred and one subjects then converted their one-use stemmer component to a reusable component. All the components were developed in Java. All the components compiled and executed successfully, and passed a suite of test cases. The s-stemming algorithm implemented was specified by 3 rules as given below (only the first applicable rule was used):

> *If a word ends in "ies" but not "eies" or "aies" then Change the "ies" to "y", For example, cities → city*
> *Else, If a word ends in "es" but not "aes", "ees", or "oes" then change "es" to "e" For example, rates → rate*
> *Else, If a word ends in "s", but not "us" or "ss" then Remove the "s". For example, lions → lion*

Twenty-five components from the sample of 101 components from study [9] was randomly selected for this study. From the pool of the selected 25 components, each of the 34 subjects in this study was randomly allocated 5 components. Total number of reuse cases

analyzed in this study is thus 170 (34*5). The subjects in this study are entirely different from the subjects of study [9]. Each component was reused at least 5 times but no more than 8 times.

In this study, the subjects were given an assignment to create a user-interface application that accepts an input string of characters in a text box. On the click of a button the stemmed string should be displayed in another textbox. The subjects were to use the 5 components to stem the string and display the result from the component in the output box. The subjects chose the way they wanted to reuse the components. Some chose to display the results from all the components on the user interface by the click of a single button while some gave the option on the user interface to choose the component to be used. The subjects also had the freedom to choose any operating system, programming language, and development environment. The subjects had to turn in the source code and the executables for the assignment. The subjects then completed an online questionnaire hosted on surveymonkey (http://www.surveymonkey.com/s/37CVND8). The results are discussed in section 4 (Results and Analysis).

3.3 Reuse design principles

In study [9], the subjects were given training on designing and building reusable components. Nineteen reuse design principles were taught to the subjects via class lectures. The subjects had reported the reuse design principles they used and were validated by the course grader. That study identified three most frequently used reuse design principles as – *well-defined interface, documentation, and clarity and understandability*. The distribution of the reuse design principles in the 25 components selected for this study is shown in Table 1. For example, 13 of the 25 components in our study were designed and built using a well-defined interface.

Table 1. Distribution of the reuse design principles

Well defined interface	13
Documentation	15
Clarity and understandability	13

4. RESULTS AND ANALYSIS

After completing the assignment on reusing the components, the subjects completed an online questionnaire hosted on surveymonkey (http://www.surveymonkey.com/s/37CVND8) giving feedback on the applications they built and on the components they had used. Thirty-four subjects participated in this study with each subject reusing 5 components resulting in a total of 170 cases of reuse. In the online questionnaire, the subjects rated each of the 5 components separately for a reusability score on a scale of 1-5 (1 – not used, 2 – difficult to reuse, 3 – neither difficult nor easy to reuse, 4 – easy to reuse, 5 – very easy to reuse). The distribution of the reusability scores is given in figure 1. Almost half of the reuse cases (48.8%) were either easy (score of 4) or very easy (score of 5). Twelve of the cases (7%) were not reused at all. About one-fifth (19.4%) of them were neither easy nor difficult (score of 3).

4.1 Complexity vs. reusability

The complexity of the components was measured in terms of their size in SLOC (source lines of code). SLOC is one of the first and most used software metrics for measuring size and complexity. In a survey by Boehm et al.[15], many cost estimation models were based directly on size measured in SLOC. COCOMO [16], COCOMO II [13], SLIM [17], SEER [18] are some of them. Complexity of software components has been measured based on SLOC in many empirical studies [19-22]. In this study, the smallest component had 37 SLOC and the largest component had 361 SLOC. Half of the components had SLOC between 77 (25th percentile) and 136 (75th percentile). Twenty of the components were between 50 and 150 SLOC.

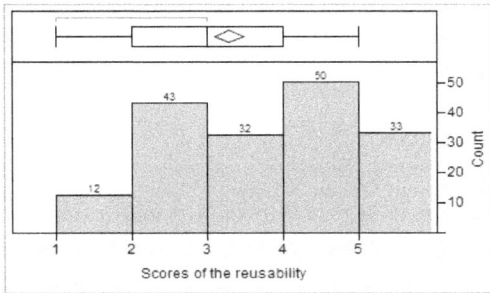

Figure 1. Distribution of the reusability scores

Each of the 25 selected components in our study was allocated to at least 5 subjects but no more than 8. The average reusability score for a component was calculated as the sum of all the reusability scores for that component divided by the number of reuses. For example, consider a component that was allocated to 5 subjects. The 5 subjects then reused the component and each subject gave the component a reusability score. Let the reusability scores of the component by the 5 subjects be 2, 4, 2, 3, and 1. The sum of the reusability scores is 12 (2+4+2+3+1). The average reusability score for the component is then 2.4 (=12/5). The mean of the average reusability scores was 3.2 and the median was 3.3 with a standard deviation of 0.8. Four components had an average reusability score greater than 4. The highest average score for a component was 4.4. Two components had average reusability scores less than 2. One component which had an average score of 1.4 could not be used by 5 of the 7 subjects who were allocated the component. Another component which had an average reusability score of 1.7 was the largest of the 25 components with 361 SLOC. It was allocated to 7 subjects but not reused by 2 subjects and the other 5 who reused it, all gave a score of only 2. This might be an indication that the larger the component the more difficult it is to reuse.

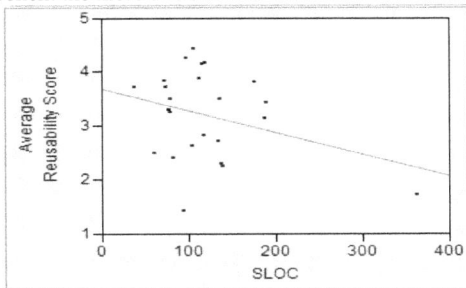

Figure 2. Bivariate fit of SLOC vs, the average reusability scores

Regression Analysis: A bivariate plot with a linear fit of the SLOC vs. the average reusability scores of the components is shown in figure 2. The regression equation of the line fit is: Average Reusability Score = 3.67 – 0.004*SLOC. The negative slope indicates a negative correlation i.e. the higher the SLOC the lower the reusability score for a component. The RSquare value was however very low at 0.102 indicating that only about 10% of variability in the reusability scores is explained by the SLOC. The F-ratio is also not significant: 2.63 with Prob>F at 0.1186.

4.2 Reuse design principles vs. reusability

The relationship between a reuse design principle and the ease of reuse was studied by comparing the boxplots of two groups of reusability scores. One group consists of the reuse cases where the component reused was built using a given reuse design principle and the other was not. Understanding and interpreting box plots can be found in [23]. If the notches of boxplots of different groups overlap, then there is no significant difference between the medians of the groups and if they do not overlap, there is significant difference between the medians of the groups with a confidence level of 95% [23]. The boxplots were generated using the statistical software R 2.14.2 (http://cran.r-project.org/).

Of the 170 cases of reuse 88 of them had a well-defined interface, the other 82 were without a well-defined interface. More than half of the reuse cases with a well-defined interface (47) had either a score of 4 or 5 indicating that they were easy to reuse. Figure 3 shows a boxplot comparison of the reusability scores of components with and without a well-defined interface. For the group with a well-defined interface the median was 4.0 and the group without a well-defined interface had a median of 3.0. The notches of the boxplots do not overlap and the notch is greater for components with a well-defined interface. This indicates that components with a well-defined interface have significantly higher reusability scores.

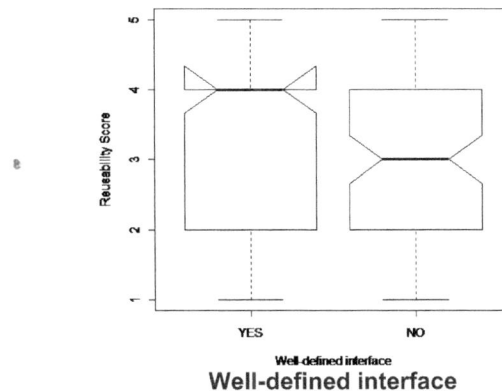

Well-defined interface

Figure 3. Box-plot comparison of the reusability scores of components with and without a well-defined interface

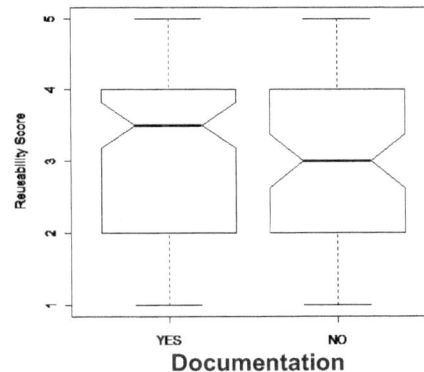

Documentation

Figure 4. Box-plot comparison of the reusability scores of components with and without documentation

Of the 25 components used in this study, 15 of them had documentation and of the 170 cases of reuse 103 of them had documentation. Figure 4 shows a boxplot comparison of the reusability scores of components with and without documentation. For the group with documentation the median was 3.5 and the group without documentation had a median of 3.0. The notches of the boxplots overlap. The notch is higher for components with documentation but not significantly as the notches of the boxplots overlap.

Of the 25 components used in this study, 13 of them used the reuse design principle of clarity and understandability. Of the 170 cases of reuse 92 of them used clarity and understandability. Figure 5 shows a boxplot comparison of the reusability scores of components with and without clarity and understandability. For the group with clarity and understandability the median was 4.0 and the group without clarity and understandability had a median of 3.0. The notches of the boxplots do not overlap and the notch is greater that for components with clarity and understandability. This indicates that components with clarity and understandability have significantly higher reusability scores.

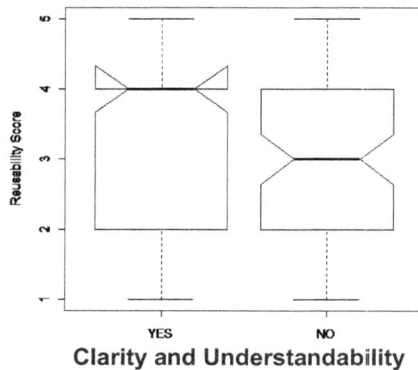

Figure 5. Box-plot comparison of the reusability scores of components with and without clarity and understandability

4.3 Threats to validity

The components used are only in Java. So, the results may not be valid for components in other languages. The components are also small in size. Future studies may involve larger components and in other languages as well. The subjects had varied degrees of experience from none to very high (>8 years). This may a reflection of the real world but is still a threat to external validity. Also, the subjects were given the source code as components and so had the choice to modify them if required. They had to reuse all the 5 components allocated to them. The reuse design principles that the subjects attributed to the components claimed to exhibit was based on the evaluation by the course grader.

5. CONCLUSIONS AND FUTURE WORK

In this study the relationship of reusability with complexity and reuse design principles was reported. Thirty-four subjects participated in the study with each subject reusing 5 components, resulting in 170 cases of reuse. The components were randomly assigned to the subjects from a pool of 25 components which were designed and built for reuse.

The relationship between the complexity of a component and the ease of reuse was analyzed by a regression analysis. It was observed that the higher the complexity the lower the ease of reuse, but the relationship was not statistically significant. An analysis of the relationship between a set of reuse design principles and the ease of reuse was also reported. Two of the three reuse design principles: *well-defined interface,* and *clarity and understandability* significantly increased the ease of reuse while *documentation* does not have a significant impact on the ease of reuse.

The impact of the development environment, OS and programming language on the ease of reusing code components may also be studied in future. Realizing that the components in our study are smaller in size and only in Java, similar studies may also be done for larger reusable components and in other languages as well. The

subjects had also answered open ended questions giving feedback on cases when they could not reuse the components. A content analysis may be done on the feedback. Complexity and reuse design principles are considered as independent factors in this study. These combined with more commonly used reuse design principles and subject demographics, such as experience in programming and software reuse, may be considered for a combined analysis to identify the combination of factors that affect reusability.

6. References

[1] R. van Ommering, "Software reuse in product populations," *IEEE Transactions on Software Engineering,* vol. 31, pp. 537-550, 2005.

[2] P. Mohagheghi and R. Conradi, "Quality, productivity and economic benefits of software reuse: a review of industrial studies," *Empirical Software Engineering,* vol. 12, pp. 471-516, 2007.

[3] P. Mohagheghi and R. Conradi, "An empirical investigation of software reuse benefits in a large telecom product," *ACM Transactions on Software Engineering Methodology,* vol. 17, pp. 1-31, 2008.

[4] W. B. Frakes and G. Succi, "An industrial study of reuse, quality, and productivity," *Journal of Systems and Software,* vol. 57, pp. 99-106, 2001.

[5] M. Morisio, *et al.,* "Success and Failure Factors in Software Reuse," *IEEE Transactions on Software Engineering,* vol. 28, pp. 340-357, 2002.

[6] W. C. Lim, "Effects of Reuse on Quality, Productivity, and Economics," *IEEE Softw.,* vol. 11, pp. 23-30, 1994.

[7] M. D. McIlroy, *et al.,* "Mass produced software components," *Software Engineering Concepts and Techniques,* pp. 88–98, 1969.

[8] S. R. Nidumolu and G. W. Knotts, "The effects of customizability and reusability on perceived process and competitive performance of software firms," *MIS Q.,* vol. 22, pp. 105-137, 1998.

[9] R. Anguswamy and W. B. Frakes, "An Exploratory Study of One-Use and Reusable Software Components," *24th International Conference of Software Engineering and Knowledge Engineering, SEKE'12,* San Francisco, USA, 2012. (ACCEPTED)

[10] W. B. Frakes and R. Baeza-Yates, *Information retrieval: data structures and algorithms,* 2nd ed. vol. 77. Englewood Cliffs, NJ: Prentice-Hall. , 1998.

[11] J. Sametinger, *Software engineering with reusable components.* Berlin Heidelberg, Germany: Springer Verlag, 1997.

[12] Y. Matsumoto, "Some Experiences in Promoting Reusable Software: Presentation in Higher Abstract Levels," *IEEE Transactions on Software Engineering,* vol. SE-10, pp. 502-513, 1984.

[13] B. Boehm, *et al.,* "Cost estimation with COCOMO II," ed: Upper Saddle River, NJ: Prentice-Hall, 2000.

[14] W. Frakes and C. Terry, "Software reuse: metrics and models," *ACM Comput. Surv.,* vol. 28, pp. 415-435, 1996.

[15] B. Boehm, *et al.,* "Software development cost estimation approaches — A survey," *Annals of Software Engineering,* vol. 10, pp. 177-205, 2000.

[16] B. W. Boehm, *Software engineering economics.* Upper Saddle River, NJ: Prentice-Hall, 1981.

[17] L. H. Putnam and W. Myers, *Measures for excellence*: Yourdon Press, 1992.

[18] R. Jensen, "An improved macrolevel software development resource estimation model," in *5th ISPA Conference,* 1983, pp. 88–92.

[19] N. E. Fenton and M. Neil, "Software metrics: roadmap," presented at the Proceedings of the Conference on The Future of Software Engineering, Limerick, Ireland, 2000.

[20] R. W. Selby, "Enabling reuse-based software development of large-scale systems," *IEEE Transactions on Software Engineering,* vol. 31, pp. 495-510, 2005.

[21] A. Gupta, "The profile of software changes in reused vs. non-reused industrial software systems," Doctoral Thesis, NTNU, Singapore, 2009.

[22] T. Tan, *et al.,* "Productivity trends in incremental and iterative software development," in *ESEM '09 Proceedings of the 2009 3rd International Symposium on Empirical Software Engineering and Measurement* Lake Buena Vista, Florida, USA, 2009, pp. 1-10.

[23] R. McGill, *et al.,* "Variations of box plots," *American Statistician,* pp. 12-16, 1978.

Seamless Integration of Order Processing in MS Outlook using SmartOffice: An Empirical Evaluation

Constanza Lampasona
Fraunhofer IESE
Fraunhofer-Platz-1
Kaiserslautern, Germany
+49 631 6800 2253
constanza.lampasona@iese.
fraunhofer.de

Oleg Rostanin
German Research Center for AI
Trippstadterstr. 122
Kaiserslautern, Germany
+49 631 4141252
oleg.rostanin@dfki.de

Heiko Maus
CC Virtual Office of the Future
German Research Center for AI
Trippstadterstr. 122
Kaiserslautern, Germany
+49 631 205 75 1110
heiko.maus@dfki.de

ABSTRACT

MS Outlook is currently the most widespread e-mail client in corporate environments. However, e-mail management with MS Outlook is usually decoupled from enterprise processes, making it difficult to synchronize e-mails and attachments with currently running processes. In this paper, we introduce SmartOffice – an extension for MS Outlook allowing the seamless integration of e-mail management with enterprise workflows, thus increasing the effectiveness of e-mail processing as well as coupling process-relevant e-mails and documents with the respective process instances. SmartOffice was integrated with a legacy system supporting the import management process of a large German retailer. We evaluated the SmartOffice integration in an empirical study in the context of the import process, using real data, and with the employees of the retailer's import office. We conducted a semi-structured interview, where one participant answered questions after solving three typical tasks and surveyed a group after a presentation and demonstration of SmartOffice's functionality. The results show that SmartOffice has high potential for being introduced in the process with high efficiency and high user acceptance. Although the number of participants was low, the results are considered very relevant from the perspective of the domain experts, since the study took place in an industrial setting.

Categories and Subject Descriptors

H.3.3 [**INFORMATION STORAGE AND RETRIEVAL**]:
Information Search and Retrieval – information filtering

H.4.1 [**INFORMATION SYSTEMS APPLICATIONS**]: Office Automation – *workflow management.*

H.4.2 [**INFORMATION SYSTEMS APPLICATIONS**]:
Communications Applications – *electronic mail.*

Keywords

SmartOffice, e-mail management, import process, retail, knowledge base, usefulness.

1. INTRODUCTION

According to the recently published studies of Pingdom [7], an average corporate user is sending or receiving 112 e-mails per day. BearingPoint states in [1] that e-mails increasingly contain business-critical information, e.g., orders, offers, inquiries, thus making employees' mail boxes valuable information sources – critical not only for individual workers but also in the scope of the enterprise. The information contained in business e-mails is highly relevant to enterprise business processes and needs to be accessed timely from running workflows. And vice versa, to speed up e-mail processing, quick access to relevant workflow information is required. Documents and e-mails used during process enactment document a process implicitly. Such process documentation can be used for continuous process analysis and improvement. Although solutions for integrated collaboration and process management exist (e.g., Lotus from IBM), their popularity and market share are continuously decreasing. Currently, MS Outlook is maintaining its leading position as an e-mail client and is widely used in corporate environments [2].

We considered the problem of efficiently integrating e-mail management performed with MS Outlook with the process of importing promotion articles from the Far East by a large German retailer in order to contribute to process analysis and controlling. The process of article import is extremely agile and requires communication via e-mail in all of its steps. Orders were originally managed by generating MS Excel spreadsheets from a centralized order database and maintained with status updates by process participants. E-mails and attached documents, e.g., order confirmation and test reports, cannot be connected with the import order information using the current practice. Process information is distributed over the computers of all process participants so that collecting process information and analyzing it is extremely difficult. During the project, a web-based application named Import Status List was developed to allow central maintenance of information about current orders, e.g., order number, article name, quantity, price, quality tests, manufacturer, and relevant documents. To address the problems of integrating e-mail communication with the Status List application, we developed the SmartOffice plugin for MS Outlook. It helps to easily map e-mails to running import processes and to quickly access the process information required for e-mail processing. It is important to note, that the maintenance of the status data is an obligation of the employees and their current job. The Status List replaces the spreadsheets and adds more convenience in maintaining this data. SmartOffice in turn uses this data and does not require maintaining additional data. This paper gives the necessary background information on SmartOffice and describes its evaluation.

2. RELATED WORK

Drezde et al. [4] introduce a plugin Activity Manager for Mozilla Thunderbird that allows semi-automatic classification of an e-mail as belonging to either a personal or a collaborative activity. Semi-automatic e-mail filing for personal information management (PIM) using a semantic desktop approach was considered in [8]. Scerri et al. developed an MS plugin, Semanta [9], which can assist users in extracting one or several *speech acts* from e-mail. Semanta helps to fill patterns for *speech acts*, e.g., action, object, and target, depending on the activity type. It builds upon the PIM ontology developed for the semantic desktop. All suggested systems are very generic, require considerable modeling effort for bootstrapping, are targeted at expert users, and do not consider processes. In contrast, SmartOffice aims at keeping modeling effort low, being integrated into the daily work environment, and being intuitive for non-experts.

3. SMARTOFFICE

SmartOffice is an extension of MS Outlook aimed at supporting office workers to cope with the large number of business process-related e-mails they receive every day. Its main features are: 1) proactive delivery of process-relevant information related to the current e-mail fully integrated into MS Outlook; 2) semi-automatic classification of e-mails and attachments via tagging, using concepts from the process-related knowledge base; 3) proactive delivery of desktop documents related to current e-mails; 4) evolutionary extension of the process-related knowledge base and implicit process documentation by automatic uploading of e-mails and attachments into the central knowledge base.

Figure 1 shows a screenshot of the SmartOffice plugin. The panel on the right side integrated into the MS Outlook e-mail inspector consists of 3 parts: 1) *Tag cloud* – shows e-mail classification using tags – references to concepts from the process-related knowledge base; in the domain of import we consider orders, manufacturers, and quality test types as concepts, for example;

using the tag cloud, the user can easily open the corresponding order in the *Status List* application; 2) *Categories* – proactive suggestions of concepts from the knowledge base the system considered as being relevant to the current e-mail, e.g., the order mentioned in the e-mail; the user can accept suggestions via drag&drop of the concept to the *tag cloud* or by attaching the concept using a context menu; if a suggestion is accepted, the concept appears on the e-mail's *tag cloud* and the e-mail is uploaded into the knowledge base together with its attachments. Concept suggestions can be expanded in SmartOffice, e.g., the user can see order details directly in MS Outlook. 3) *Document search* – the system proactively searches desktop documents and e-mails related to the current e-mail that could be helpful for processing that specific e-mail. SmartOffice is aimed to ease the problems of information overload when working with business relevant e-mail as well as the integration of e-mail communication into enterprise processes.

4. EMPIRICAL STUDY

4.1 Context and Research Goals

The study took place in cooperation with a large retailer. We evaluated how SmartOffice supports the import process at the retailer from the users' perspective.

We investigated whether SmartOffice has the potential to be used to support the import process of a retailer and to identify aspects that can be improved. Specifically, we had the following goals:

Characterize the usefulness (RG1), efficiency (RG2), quality of the provided information (RG3), usability (RG4), and intention to use (RG5) and evaluate the perceived usefulness (RG6) and ease of use (RG7) of SmartOffice within the import process at a retailer from the user perspective.

4.2 Participants

The participants were experienced retailer employees. Their tasks include planning the assortment of goods in the non-food sector, coordinating the import of planned products, organizing weekly promotions, and creating advertising flyers. Depending on their role, they are involved in various steps of the import process.

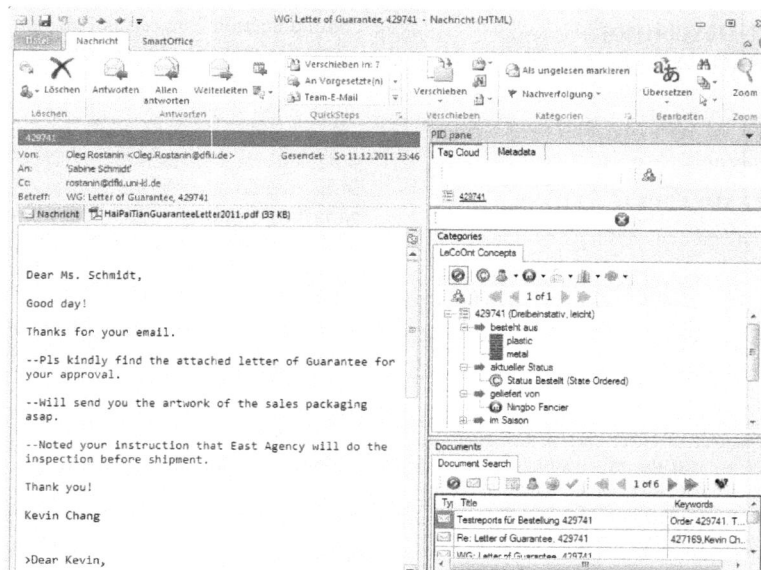

Figure 1 . SmartOffice plugin for MS Outlook

166

A key task in their daily duties is intensive communication with providers and colleagues via e-mail. E-mail is not only used to exchange documents, but important decisions are also made, communicated, and documented. Their e-mails are ordered in their personal inboxes and stored in folders (e.g., by provider or by season). The folder structure used depends on the employee's individual preferences. Each e-mail may contain one or more order numbers in the subject line or in the e-mail body, which is used to identify the reference to the corresponding orders.

Another important task for the import employees is keeping the status of the import process instances up to date. Currently, this is done by generating an Excel spreadsheet from a relevant excerpt of a centralized order database and communicating it to all process stakeholders via a network drive or e-mails. Thus, several Excel files need to be managed. To update an order status, the employee needs to search and access the corresponding file.

Vacation replacements use the substituted employee's computer. As a consequence, they have to deal with their e-mails following an unknown folder structure for e-mail organization.

4.3 Design

For this study, one person from the import office at the retailer was available for half a day, and another six people were available for one hour. In order to make the most of the opportunity of performing the evaluation with real users in their real work environment, our strategy was to conduct a semi-structured interview with the individual person and administer a questionnaire to the group.

4.4 Procedure

4.4.1 Semi-structured Interview

The procedure comprised three activities: 1) we provided training on how to use SmartOffice (20 minutes), 2) the participant conducted three different tasks and after each task answered questions about that specific task, and 3) afterwards we asked questions regarding SmartOffice in general and let the participant fill in the questionnaires. Each task was formulated in the text of the corresponding e-mail in MS Outlook:

T1: Find suppliers who delivered Buddha statues in the past.

T2: Assign the e-mail and its attachment to the corresponding import process instance in the status list.

T3: Reuse a test report from a past order for the current one.

4.4.2 Group Survey

During this part of the study, the group received a presentation and a demonstration of SmartOffice, where they were shown how to solve the same tasks as the ones that were solved during the semi-structured interview. The feedback was collected during a discussion and by answering a questionnaire.

4.5 Operationalization and Hypotheses

In a series of workshops, solution experts and an independent empirical expert derived items for measuring the evaluation goals. Four questionnaires were constructed: one for each of the three tasks (Q1, Q2, and Q3) and one for the whole group, which includes standardized items (Q4). The group survey included eight standardized items (Q5). The standardized items were adapted from [3], [5], and [6]. We used 5-point Likert

scales. For data analysis purposes, 1 was used for the lowest value for the concept and 5 for the best value for the respective concept. Table 1 shows the number of items used per concept and task. The questionnaires can be obtained from the authors.

Table 1. Items used per concept and task

	Task1 Q1	Task2 Q2	Task3 Q3	All tasks Q4	Presentation Q5
Usefulness	2	1	1	2	-
Efficiency	5	5	5	1	-
Quality of information	-	-	-	20	-
Usability	1	1	1	28	-
Intention of use	2	1	1	3	-
Perceived usefulness	-	-	-	4	4
Perceived ease of use	-	-	-	4	4
TOTAL	10	8	8	62	8

For the TAM items, we tested the following hypotheses:

H1: Median(Perceived usefulness) > 3

$H0_1$: Median(Perceived usefulness) $\leq$ 3

H2: Median(Perceived ease of use) > 3

$H0_2$: Median(Perceived ease of use) $\leq$ 3

4.6 Study Results

We tested the hypotheses using the one-sample Wilcoxon signed ranks test. Both $H0_1$ and $H0_2$ were rejected with a significance level of 0.01. Crombach's α was 0.24 for perceived usefulness and 0.70 for perceived ease of use. Table 2 summarizes the results from the closed questions.

Table 2. Results from closed questions

		Me- dian	Mean	Min	Max	St. Dev.
Semi-structured interview (N=1)	Usefulness	4	4.29	3	5	0.76
	Efficiency	5	4.67	3	5	0.62
	Quality of information	4	4.11	4	5	0.32
	Usability	4	4	2	5	0.69
	Intention of use	4	4.2	4	5	0.48
	Perceived usefulness	4	4	4	4	0
	Perceived ease of use	4	4.5	4	5	0.58
Group (N=6)	Perceived usefulness	4	4.08	3	5	0.72
	Perceived ease of use	4	4.25	3	5	0.61

The efficiency of SmartOffice was rated as very good (mean=4.67). This can be explained by the fact that many tasks are automatically performed without disturbing the person at work. SmartOffice's knowledge-based support also allows performing quick searches because there is no need to know anything about the folder structure used to organize e-mails. This makes the use of SmartOffice good for beginners and vacation replacements.

Only the efficiency item for evaluating the tagging functionality was rated neutrally as (neither efficient not as inefficient). This is explained by the huge number of e-mails involved in the process. Manual tagging may be worthwhile only for specific e-mails, for example, e-mails which lead to a change in status or an agreement between the employee and the provider. This was confirmed during the group survey.

The other concepts were rated as good. Document reuse was difficult for the example in the evaluation scenario. However, in the discussion, the concept for reusing documents was described as useful. The chosen example was not really applicable in practice because the kind of document selected for the study first needs approval by quality assurance in order to be reused. As a consequence, the specific task in the example was evaluated as easier to solve without the support of SmartOffice.

The only concern regarding the intention of use was that the whole scenario with SmartOffice provides the best results if all stakeholders involved use it continuously, i.e., maintain the status on the Status List and tag e-mails with the relevant attachments. This is true. However, considering the current process at the retailer, the employees currently also depend on the continuous maintenance of the Excel files. The only thing new is simply that, with SmartOffice, relevant e-mails containing documents are additionally tagged with the respective order number. The evaluation shows that, in contrast to the current practice with Excel files, the use of the Status List is perceived as more efficient for accessing order status information. Moreover, the proactive retrieval of information automatically identifies the order, which reduces the effort for tagging only relevant e-mails. If any relevant e-mail is not tagged, a fallback to the current practice can be used to process the order, i.e., the employee in charge needs to respond to a request of a colleague by manually searching the database.

We also found that, if the system goes into operation, its usability should be improved. For this, special user profiles need to be considered. These include various concepts and focused vocabulary used by different participant roles during specific phases of the process. Because the evaluation was focused on the import sector, only an import-specific vocabulary was used. The technical implementation as a filter (e.g., *show only the relevant vocabulary for the import sector*) is already implemented in SmartOffice. It would be necessary to set the filter depending on the role of the employee. It was also mentioned that in an e-mail, over a hundred orders can be listed as an interval. This must be identified by SmartOffice and implemented accordingly as a dialog that takes over the automatic tagging of all corresponding orders.

4.7 Threats to Validity

Explication of constructs: Not all items used were standardized (29 out of 88). This may be a threat to validity because their meaning may be misunderstood. To mitigate this threat, domain experts reviewed the operationalization.

Contamination: The interview and the group survey were carried out independent of each other in terms of time and space. Nonetheless, we could not control interactions outside the study, i.e., the participants could have known about the contents beforehand.

Low statistical power: Because of the low number of participants, the results have low statistical power. Nevertheless, the results are considered very relevant by the domain experts.

5. CONCLUSIONS

Overall, this evaluation of the SmartOffice prototype has shown that it has the potential to be used in practice. In particular, the positive attitude of the employees towards the whole system and the problem solving functionality shows the potential of embedding process knowledge into daily work, of process orientation, and of assistance through proactive information delivery. Furthermore, the underlying semantic domain models allow transferring SmartOffice to other business processes.

The results also show that, by embedding process knowledge into daily tasks, it is possible to control, monitor, and analyze the process at no extra cost. The participants accept this solution and would use it in their daily work; they are convinced that they would get a gain in efficiency by using the solution for their daily work. Therefore, the data required for process analysis would be available without significant additional effort. With this solution, data for process controlling and monitoring could be accessible. With the current practice, such data is stored in multiple places and is not available in real time.

6. ACKNOWLEDGMENTS
The work presented in this paper was funded by the German Federal Ministry of Education and Research (BMBF). It was performed in the context of the projects SWINNG, grant no. 01IC10S05, and ADiWa, grant no. 01IA08006. We acknowledge Liliana Guzmán for reviewing the questionnaires.

7. REFERENCES
[1] Bahr, T. 2008. *Herausforderungen und Trends im E-Mail Management - Eine Studie von BearingPoint.* http://www.competence-site.de/e-mail-management/ Herausforderungen-Trends-EMail-Management-Eine-Studie-BearingPoint.

[2] CampaignMonitor. *Email client popularity: June 2011.* http://www.campaignmonitor.com/stats/email-clients/

[3] Davis, F. D. 1989. Perceived usefulness, perceived ease of use, and user acceptance of information technology. *MIS Quarterly* 13, 3 (September 1989), 319-340.

[4] Dredze, M., Lau, T., Kushmerick, N. 2006. Automatically classifying emails into activities. *11th international conference on intelligent user interfaces.* ACM. 70-77.

[5] Hildebrand, K., Gebauer, M., Hinrichs, H., Mielke, M. 2008. *Daten- und Informationsqualität. Auf dem Weg zur Information Excellence.* Wiesbaden:Vieweg + Teubner.

[6] Kirakowski, J., Corbett, M. 1993. SUMI: The Software Usability Measurement Inventory. *British Journal of Educational Technology*, 24, 3 (Sept. 1993), 210-212.

[7] Royal Pingdom Blog. 2012. *Internet 2011 in numbers.* http://royal.pingdom.com/2012/01/17/internet-2011-in-numbers/.

[8] Sauermann, L. 2009. *The Gnowsis Semantic Desktop approach to Personal Information Management.* PhD-Thesis, University of Kaiserslautern, Dissertation.de, Berlin, 2009.

[9] Scerri, S., Davis, B., Handschuh, S., Hauswirth, M. 2009. Semanta - Semantic Email made easy. *Proceedings of the 6th European Semantic Web Conference.* 36-50.

Visualizing the Invisible – Symbols and Metaphors in Software Engineering?

Antje Jackelén
The Diocese of Lund
Sweden
antje.jackelen@svenskakyrkan.se

abstract>
ABSTRACT

Symbols and metaphors play a crucial role when we articulate our understanding of the world – be it everyday life, the life or science and technology or the life of religion and theology. How do we choose metaphors? How do we distinguish icons from idols? Do we always understand how symbols and icons work?

I will suggest that the experience that theologians have accumulated in the field of hermeneutics is an asset also in the area of science and technology. The critical engagement with the art of interpreting and understanding is necessitated by the potential of scientific concepts to build ideologies as well as by the role that metaphoric processes play – not only in communication with the general public but also in scientific research and self-understanding.

Dr. Antje Jackelén is Bishop of the Diocese of Lund in the Church of Sweden and Adjunct Professor of Systematic Theology/Religion and Science at the Lutheran School of Theology at Chicago, USA, where she taught 2001–2007. She was director of the Zygon Center for Religion and Science 2003–2007. Dr. Jackelén currently serves as president of the European Society for the Study of Science and Theology. She is the author of the books Time and Eternity (2005), The Dialogue between Religion and Science (2004), *Gud är större* (God is greater, 2011) and numerous articles, published in various languages.

Categories and Subject Descriptors

D.2.0 [**Software Engineering**]: General

General Terms

Human Factors

Keywords

Symbols, Metaphors

Copyright is held by the author/owner(s).
ESEM'12, September 19–20, 2012, Lund, Sweden.
ACM 978-1-4503-1056-7/12/09.

Method-Level Bug Prediction

Emanuel Giger
University of Zurich
giger@ifi.uzh.ch

Marco D'Ambros
University of Lugano
marco.dambros@usi.ch

Martin Pinzger
Delft University of Technology
m.pinzger@tudelft.nl

Harald C. Gall
University of Zurich
gall@ifi.uzh.ch

ABSTRACT

Researchers proposed a wide range of approaches to build effective bug prediction models that take into account multiple aspects of the software development process. Such models achieved good prediction performance, guiding developers towards those parts of their system where a large share of bugs can be expected. However, most of those approaches predict bugs on file-level. This often leaves developers with a considerable amount of effort to examine all methods of a file until a bug is located. This particular problem is reinforced by the fact that large files are typically predicted as the most bug-prone. In this paper, we present bug prediction models at the level of individual methods rather than at file-level. This increases the granularity of the prediction and thus reduces manual inspection efforts for developers. The models are based on change metrics and source code metrics that are typically used in bug prediction. Our experiments—performed on 21 Java open-source (sub-)systems—show that our prediction models reach a precision and recall of 84% and 88%, respectively. Furthermore, the results indicate that change metrics significantly outperform source code metrics.

Categories and Subject Descriptors

D.2.8 [**Software Engineering**]: Metrics—*complexity measures, process metrics, product metrics*

Keywords

method-level bug prediction, fine-grained source code changes, code metrics

1. INTRODUCTION

In the last decade, researchers have proposed a wide range of bug prediction models based on diverse information, such as source code metrics [3, 27, 48, 47, 32, 46], historical data (*e.g.*, number of changes, code churn, previous defects) [19, 34, 31, 23, 17, 16], and developers interaction information

(*e.g.*, contribution structure) [37, 40, 25]. Since most prediction models were evaluated on different systems—and frequently with different performance measures—researchers have also investigated which approaches provide the best and most stable performance across different systems [24, 30, 41, 9].

While having achieved remarkably good prediction performance, most of these approaches predict bugs at the level of source files (or binaries, modules, Java packages). However, since a file can be arbitrarily large, a developer needs to invest a significant amount of time to examine all methods of a file in order to locate a particular bug. Moreover, considering that larger files are known to be among the most bug-prone [3, 18, 36], the effort required for code inspection and review is even larger. In addition, Posnett *et al.* recently showed that there is a risk of inferential fallacy when transferring empirical findings from an aggregated level, *e.g.*, prediction models at the package- or file-level, to an dis-aggregated, smaller level, for instance, method-level—in particular when such models are used for inspection [38].

In our dataset, a class has on average 11 methods out of which 4 (~32%) are *bug-prone*, *i.e.*, are affected by at least one bug. Assuming that there is only knowledge that a file is *bug-prone*, but not which particular method contains the bug—as given by a file-level prediction model—a developer needs to inspect all methods one by one until the bug is located. Given the median precision of 0.84 achieved by one of our method-level based prediction models (see Table 4), a developer has roughly the same chance of picking a *bug-prone* method by randomly guessing after "eliminating" 6 out of those 11 methods (4/5 = 0.8). In other words, one needs to manually reduce the set of possible candidates by more than half of all methods until chance is as good as our prediction models in terms of retrieving a *bug-prone* method. Therefore, we argue that being able to narrow down the location of bugs to method-level can save manual inspection steps and significantly improve testing effort allocation. This is especially important if the resources for quality assurance are limited. In this paper, we investigate the following research questions:

RQ1 What is the performance of bug prediction models on method-level using change and source code metrics?

RQ2 Which set of predictors, among change metrics, source code metrics, and their combination, provides the best prediction performance at method-level?

RQ3 How does the prediction performance vary if the number of *bug-prone* methods (*i.e.*, positively labeled samples) decreases?

We investigate our research questions based on the source code and change history of 21 Java open-source (sub-)systems. The results of our study show that we can build prediction models to identify *bug-prone* methods with precision, recall, and AUC (*area under the receiver operating characteristic curve*) of 0.84, 0.88, and 0.95, respectively. Moreover, our experiments indicate that change metrics significantly outperform source code metrics for method-level bug prediction.

In contrast to previous work [23] which has also addressed bug prediction on entity-level, the goal of our models is to predict *bug-prone* methods in advance rather than suggesting further *bug-prone* source code entities that need to be changed in addition to that particular entity in which the bug is fixed. Furthermore, we use different methods and metrics to train the prediction models.

The remainder of the paper is organized as follows: Section 2 describes our dataset as well as the set of metrics and the tools to compute them. Section 3 presents our prediction models and reports on the results of the experiments. We discuss the potential benefits and applications of our approach in Section 4. We present work related to this paper in Section 6 and conclude with possible future work in Section 7.

2. DATA COLLECTION

To conduct our prediction experiments we collected a dataset consisting of code, change, and bug metrics for 21 software (sub-)systems (see Table 1). Building models to predict bugs at method- rather than at file-level requires that all metrics are available at the method level. In this section, we present the tools and methods necessary to assemble our dataset.

2.1 Dataset

We conducted our study with the source code and change history of the projects listed in Table 1: #Classes denotes the number of Java classes when checking out the source code at the end of the timeframe (*Time*) from the trunk of the specified repository path; #Methods denotes the number of methods (including Constructors), and #stmt refers to the number of source code statements. #MH is the number of *methodHistories* (see Table 3) and #Bugs denotes the number of bugs within the considered timeframe (*Time*). It is possible that #MH<#Methods since there is a substantial amount of methods that are never changed, *e.g.*, accessor-methods or default constructors.

2.2 Code Metrics

Code metrics (*i.e.*, product metrics) are directly computed on the source code itself. In the context of bug prediction the underlying rationale of these metrics is that larger and more complex pieces of code are more bug-prone because they are more difficult to understand and to change [9]. In the literature, two traditional suites of code metrics exist: (1) The CK metrics suite and (2) a set of metrics that are directly calculated at the method level that we named *SCM*. The CK suite, introduced by Chidamber and Kemerer [8], consists of six metrics that measure the size and complexity of various aspects of object-oriented source code and are calculated at the class level. It was successfully applied for bug prediction in prior work, *e.g.*, [3, 44]. This suite can be extended by additional object-oriented metrics, such as number of fields per class (*e.g.*, [48]). The *SCM* set of metrics is not lim-

Table 2: List of source code metrics used for the SCM set

Metric Name	Description (applies to method level)
fanIN	Number of methods that reference a given method
fanOUT	Number of methods referenced by a given method
localVar	Number of local variables in the body of a method
parameters	Number of parameters in the declaration
commentTo CodeRatio	Ratio of comments to source code (line based)
countPath	Number of possible paths in the body of a method
complexity	McCabe Cyclomatic complexity of a method
execStmt	Number of executable source code statements
maxNesting	Maximum nested depth of all control structures

ited to object-oriented source code, and includes measures such as lines of code (LOC) or complexity. When applied to files, these metrics are typically averaged, summed up over all methods that belong to a particular file, or the highest value in the file is selected [48, 47, 35, 26].

Since our goal is to build bug prediction models at the method level, we do not use the CK suite as it contains metrics which are not directly applicable to methods, *e.g.*, number of sub-classes. We choose instead the metrics listed in Table 2, whose good performance were shown in previous studies [30, 47, 20].

To compute the code metrics, we first obtained, for each project, the source code version at the end of the timeframe specified in Table 1. Then, using the EVOLIZER framework [14], we built a model of the source code that we use to compute fanIN, fanOUT, localVar, and parameters. Finally, using UNDERSTAND[1], we calculate the remaining code metrics for each method, *i.e.*, commentToCodeRatio, countPath, complexity, execStmt, and maxNesting.

Instead of *lines of code* (LOC) we use the number of declarative (localVar) and executable (execStmt) source code statements per method. We opted for this choice because LOC measures a textual aspect of source files, which is not suitable when changes at the method level are calculated based on the structure of the abstract syntax tree (see Section 2.3). However, our data shows that the number of source code statements ($= localVar + execStmt$) approximately corresponds to the LOC per method. In other words, there is roughly one source code statement per line of code.

2.3 Change Metrics

Version control systems (VCS), such as CVS, SVN, or GIT, contain data regarding the (source code) change history of a software project. VCSs store a log entry for each change providing detailed information about that particular change: The file(s) being affected by the change, a (revision) number to uniquely identify each change in correct temporal order, the name of the developer responsible for the change, a timestamp, and a manually entered commit message. Within current VCSs a file typically constitutes the atomic change unit, and hence, changes are solely recorded at the file level. Furthermore, source code files are handled as text files, ignoring their underlying syntactic and semantic structure.

However, to build prediction models at the method level, it is necessary to track changes at a finer granularity. For this purpose, change measures widely adopted for bug prediction

---

[1] http://www.scitools.com/

172

Table 1: Overview of the projects used in this study

Project	Version Control System Path	#Classes	#Methods	#MH	#stmt	#Bugs	Time[M, Y]
Compare	dev.eclipse.org:/cvsroot/eclipse:org.eclipse.compare	154	1720	2500	12776	563	May01-Sep10
jFace	dev.eclipse.org:/cvsroot/eclipse:org.eclipse.jface	374	4438	4043	23991	1275	Sep02-Sep10
JDT Debug	dev.eclipse.org:/cvsroot/eclipse:org.eclipse.jdt.debug	436	4434	4700	23517	900	May01-July10
Resource	dev.eclipse.org:/cvsroot/eclipse:org.eclipse.resources	270	3186	6167	20837	948	May01-Sep10
Team Core	dev.eclipse.org:/cvsroot/eclipse:org.eclipse.team.core	157	1510	1124	7833	288	Nov01-Aug10
Team CVS	dev.eclipse.org:/cvsroot/eclipse:org.eclipse.team.cvs.core	184	1830	2551	11826	769	Nov01-Aug10
Debug Core	dev.eclipse.org:/cvsroot/eclipse:org.eclipse.debug.core	173	1373	2218	6463	493	May01-Sep10
jFace Text	dev.eclipse.org:/cvsroot/eclipse:org.eclipse.jface	322	3029	3724	18821	777	Sep02-Oct10
Update Core	dev.eclipse.org:/cvsroot/eclipse:org.eclipse.update.core	262	2151	4185	14873	402	Oct01-Junt10
Debug UI	dev.eclipse.org:/cvsroot/eclipse:org.eclipse.debug.ui	770	6525	8065	43760	2761	May01-Oct10
JDT Debug UI	dev.eclipse.org:/cvsroot/eclipse:org.eclipse.jdt.debug.ui	390	2586	4231	20289	1822	Nov01-Sep10
Help	dev.eclipse.org:/cvsroot/eclipse:org.eclipse.help	112	562	536	3503	198	May01-May10
JDT Core	dev.eclipse.org:/cvsroot/eclipse:org.eclipse.jdt.core	1140	17703	43134	172939	4888	Jun01-Sep10
OSGI	dev.eclipse.org:/cvsroot/eclipse:org.eclipse.osgi	364	4106	5282	27744	1168	Nov03-Oct10
Azureus 3	azureus.cvs.sourceforge.net:/cvsroot/azureus:azureus3	362	3983	5394	40440	518	Dec06-Apr10
Openxava	openxava.cvs.sourceforge.net:/cvsroot/openxava:OpenXava	507	5132	4656	27662	331	Feb05-Apr11
Jena2	jena.cvs.sourceforge.net:/cvsroot/jena:Jena2	897	8340	7764	33542	704	Dec02-Apr11
Lucene	https://svn.apache.org/repos/asf/lucene/dev/trunk/lucene/src/java	477	3870	7754	23788	377	Mar10-May11
Xerces	http://svn.apache.org/repos/asf/xerces/java/trunk/src	693	8189	6866	56920	1017	Nov99-Apr11
Derby Engine	https://svn.apache.org/repos/asf/db/derby/code/trunk/java/engine	1394	18693	9507	116449	1663	Aug05-Apr11
Ant Core	http://svn.apache.org/repos/asf/ant/core/trunk	827	8698	17993	51738	1900	Jan00-Apr11

[17, 31, 37, 30, 7], such as *number of revisions* and *lines added/deleted*, are too coarse-grained and lack the semantic of individual code changes.

Fluri *et al.* proposed a tree differencing algorithm to extract *fine-grained source code changes* down to the level of single source code statements [12]. Their algorithm is based on the idea of comparing two different versions of the abstract syntax tree (AST) of the source code, and consists of the following three sub-steps: First, they match all individual nodes between the two versions of the AST using string and tree similarity measures. This matching is required to determine if a particular node was *inserted*, *deleted*, *updated*, or *moved* between two AST versions. In a second step, the algorithm generates a minimal set of these four basic tree edit operations, transforming one version of the AST into the other. Third, each edit operation for a given node is annotated with the semantic information of the source code entity it represents and is classified as a specific *change type* based on a *taxonomy of code changes* [14]. For instance, the insertion of a node representing an else-part in the AST is classified as *else-part insert* change type.

Combining the set of individual tree edit operations resulting from the AST comparison with the semantic information of each node allows us to track source code changes at the fine-grained level of individual source code statements. Moreover, we know not only which particular source entity was changed, but also the exact location of every change within the AST. For example, as illustrated in Figure 1 it is possible to determine that (1) the condition expression `obj != null` in body of method `foo()` of `Class A` was updated to `obj != null && !obj.equals(this)`, and (2) the parameter `int b` was added to the declaration of method `sum` from revision 1.2 to 1.3 of the corresponding file `A.java`. Furthermore, we are able to distinguish between changes that do affect source code entities and "textual" changes, such as license header updates or formatting.

Currently, this tree-differencing algorithm is implemented in CHANGEDISTILLER to work with AST structures of *Java* source code [14]. CHANGEDISTILLER accesses the VCS of a project and pairwise compares all subsequent revisions of every source file. All fine-grained source code changes are then stored in a database. Based on this, we extracted—at the method level—the change metrics (CM) listed in Table 3.

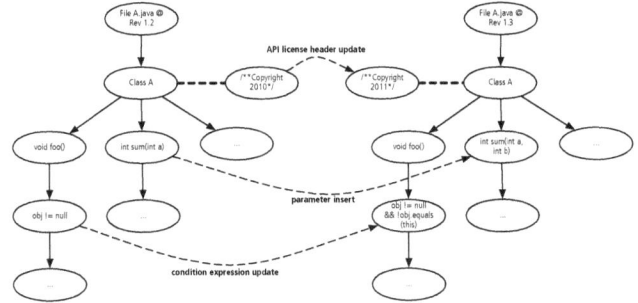

Figure 1: A schematic example of the fine-grained code change extraction based on the AST comparison of two file revisions as proposed in [12].

We selected and defined these metrics to provide an analogy to file-level based approaches [30]. For instance, *methodHistories* corresponds to the number of revisions of a file; the smt- and churn-metrics in Table 3 can be seen as analogue counterparts to the (textual) line based churn metrics. Other metrics, such as *cond*, are specific to the AST based change extraction.

2.4 Bug Data

Bug data of software projects is managed and stored in bug tracking systems, such as Bugzilla. Unfortunately, many bug tracking systems are not inherently linked to VCSs. However, developers fixing a bug often manually enter a reference to that particular bug in the commit message of the corresponding revision, *e.g.*,"fixed bug1234" or "bug#345". Researchers developed pattern matching techniques to detect those references accurately [43], and thus to link source code files with bugs. We adapted the pattern matching approach to work at method-level: Whenever we find that a method was changed between two revisions of a file (using CHANGEDISTILLER, see Section 2.3) and the commit message contains a bug reference, we consider the method to be affected by the bug. Based on this, we then count the number of bugs per method over the given timeframes in Table 1.

However, this linking technique requires that developers

Table 3: List of method level CM used in this study

Metric Name	Description (applies to method level)
methodHistories	Number of times a method was changed
authors	Number of distinct authors that changed a method
stmtAdded	Sum of all source code statements added to a method body over all method histories
maxStmtAdded	Maximum number of source code statements added to a method body for all method histories
avgStmtAdded	Average number of source code statements added to a method body per method history
stmtDeleted	Sum of all source code statements deleted from a method body over all method histories
maxStmtDeleted	Maximum number of source code statements deleted from a method body for all method histories
avgStmtDeleted	Average number of source code statements deleted from a method body per method history
churn	Sum of *stmtAdded − stmtDeleted* over all method histories
maxChurn	Maximum *churn* for all method histories
avgChurn	Average *churn* per method history
decl	Number of method declaration changes over all method histories
cond	Number of condition expression changes in a method body over all revisions
elseAdded	Number of added else-parts in a method body over all revisions
elseDeleted	Number of deleted else-parts from a method body over all revisions

consistently enter and track bugs within the commit messages of the VCS. Furthermore, we rely on the fact that developers commit regularly when carrying out corrective maintenance, *i.e.*, they only change those methods (between two revisions) related to that particular bug report being referenced in the commit message. We discuss issues regarding the data collection, in particular regarding the bug-linking approach, that might threaten the validity of our findings in Section 5.

3. PREDICTION EXPERIMENTS

We conducted a set of prediction experiments using the dataset presented in Section 2 to investigate the feasibility of building prediction models on method-level. We first describe the experimental setup and then report and discuss the results.

3.1 Experimental Setup

Prior to model building and classification we labeled each method in our dataset either as *bug-prone* or *not bug-prone* as follows:

$$bugClass = \begin{cases} not\ bug - prone & : \ \#bugs = 0 \\ bug - prone & : \ \#bugs >= 1 \end{cases} \quad (1)$$

These two classes represent the *binary* target classes for training and validating the prediction models. Using 0 (respectively 1) as cut-point is a common approach applied in many studies covering bug prediction models, *e.g.*, [30, 48, 47, 4, 27, 37]. Other cut-points are applied in literature, for instance, a statistical lower confidence bound [33] or the median [16]. Those varying cut-points as well as the diverse datasets result in different prior probabilities. For instance, in our dataset approximately one third of all methods were labeled as *bug-prone*; Moser *et al.* report on prior proba-

bilities of 23%–32% with respect to *bug-prone* files; in [27] 0.4%–49% of all modules contain bugs; and in [48] 50% of all Java packages are bug free. Given this (and the fact that prior probabilities are not consistently reported in literature), the use of precision and recall as classification performance measures across different studies is difficult. Following the advice proposed in [26, 27] we use the *area under the receiver operating characteristic curve* (AUC) to asses and discuss the performance of our prediction models. AUC is a robust measure since it is independent of prior probabilities [4]. Moreover, AUC has a clear statistical interpretation [26]: When selecting randomly a *bug-prone* and a *not bug-prone* method, AUC represents the probability that a given classifier assigns a higher rank to the *bug-prone* method. We also report on precision (P) and recall (R) in our experiments to allow for comparison with existing work.

In [26], Lessmann *et al.* compared the performance of several classification algorithms. They found out that more advanced algorithms, such as Random Forest and Support Vector Machine, perform better. However, the performance differences should not be overestimated, *i.e.*, they are not significant. We observed similar findings in a previous study using fine-grained source code changes to build prediction models on file-level [16]. Menzies *et al.* successfully used Bayesian classifiers for bug prediction [27]. To contribute to that discussion (on method-level) we chose four different classifiers: Random Forest (RndFor), Bayesian Network (BN), Support Vector Machine (SVM), and the J48 decision tree. The Rapidminer Toolkit [29] was used for running all classification experiments.

We built three different models for each classifier: The first model uses change metrics (CM, see Table 3) as predictors, the second uses source code metrics (SCM, see Table 2), and the third uses both metric sets (CM&SCM) as predictor variables. All our prediction models were trained and validated using 10-fold cross validation (based on stratified sampling ensuring that the class distribution in the subsets is the same as in the whole dataset).

3.2 Prediction Results

Table 4 lists the median (over the 10 folds) classification results over all projects per classifier and per model. The cells are interpreted as follows: **Bold** values are significantly different from all other values of the *same performance measure* in the *same row* (*i.e.*, classifier). Grey shaded cells are significantly different from the white cells of the *same performance measure* in the *same row*. To test for significance among the different metric sets we applied a *Related Samples Friedman Test* ($\alpha = 0.05$) for each performance measure (including α−adjustment for the pair-wise post-hoc comparison). These tests were repeated for each classifier. For instance, in case of SVM, the median recall value (R) of the combined model (CM&SCM), *i.e.*, 0.96, is significantly higher than the median recall values of the change (0.86) *and* the source code metric model (0.63). With respect to AUC and precision (P), this combined model performed significantly better than the code metric model (AUC: 0.95 vs. 0.7; P: 0.8 vs. 0.48) model but *not* significantly better than the change metric model.

From the performance values one can see two main patterns: First, the model based on source code metrics performs significantly lower over all prediction runs compared to the change metrics and the combined model. The AUC

Table 4: Median classification results over all projects per classifier and per model

	CM			SCM			CM&SCM		
	AUC	P	R	AUC	P	R	AUC	P	R
RndFor	.95	.84	.88	.72	.5	.64	.95	.85	.95
SVM	.96	.83	.86	.7	.48	.63	.95	.8	**.96**
BN	.96	.82	.86	.73	.46	.73	.96	.81	**.96**
J48	.95	.84	.82	.69	.56	.58	.91	.83	.89

values of the code metrics model are approximately 0.7 for each classifier—what is defined by Lessman *et al.* as "promising" [26]. However, the source code metrics suffer from considerably low precision values. The highest median precision value for the code metrics model is obtained in case of J48 (0.56). For the remaining classifiers the values are around 0.5. In other words, using the code metrics half of the methods are correctly classified (the other half being false positives). Moreover, code metrics only achieve moderate median recall values close to 0.6 (except for NB), *i.e.*, only two third of all *bug-prone* methods are retrieved.

Second, the change metrics and the combined model perform almost equally. Moreover, both exhibit good values in case of all three performance measures (refers to RQ1 introduced in Section 1). Only the median recall values obtained by SVM and BN for the combined model are significantly higher than the ones of the change metrics model (0.96 vs. 0.86 in both cases). Moreover, while AUC and precision are fairly similar for these two models, recall seems to benefit the most from using both metric sets in combination compared to change metrics only.

Summarizing, we can say that change metrics significantly outperform code metrics when discriminating between *bug-prone* and *not bug-prone* methods (refers to RQ2). A look at the J48 tree models of the combined metrics set supports this fact as the code metrics are added towards the leaves of the tree, whereas except for three projects (~14%) *authors* is selected as root attribute. *methodHistories* is for 11 projects (~52%) the second attribute and in one case the root. Furthermore, considering the average prior probabilities in the dataset (*i.e.*, ~32% of all methods are bug-prone), change metrics perform significantly better than chance. Hence, the results of our study confirms existing observations that historical change measures are good bug predictors, *e.g.*, [17, 30, 20, 24]. When using a combined model we might expect slightly better recall values. However, from a strict statistical point of view it is not necessary to collect code measures in addition to change metrics when predicting *bug-prone* methods.

Regarding the four classifiers, our results are mostly consistent. In particular, the performance differences between the classifiers when based on the change and the combined model are negligible. The largest variance in performance among the classifiers resulted from using the code metrics for model building. However, in this case these results are not conclusive: On the one hand, BN achieved significantly lower precision (median of 0.46) than the other classifiers. On the other hand, BN showed a significantly higher recall value (median of 0.73).

3.3 Prediction with Different Labeling Points

So far we used the absence and presence of bugs to label a

method as *not bug-prone* or *bug-prone*, respectively. Approximately one third of all methods are labeled as *bug-prone* in our dataset (see Section 3.1). Given this number a developer would need to spend a significant amount of her time for corrective maintenance activities when investigating all methods being predicted as *bug-prone*. We analyze in this section, how the classification performance varies (RQ3) as the number of samples in the target class shrinks, and whether we observe similar findings as in Section 3.2 regarding the results of the change and code metrics (RQ2). For that, we applied three additional cut-point values as follows:

$$bugClass = \begin{cases} not\ bug-prone & : \ \#bugs <= p \\ bug-prone & : \ \#bugs > p \end{cases} \quad (2)$$

where p represents either the value of the 75%, 90%, or 95% percentile of the distribution of the number of bugs in methods per project. For example, using the 95% percentile as cut-point for prior binning would mean to predict the "top-five percent" methods in terms of the number of bugs.

To conduct this study we applied the same experimental setup as in Section 3.1, except for the differently chosen cut-points. We limited the set of machine learning algorithms to one algorithm as we could not observe any major difference in the previous experiment among them (see Table 4). We chose Random Forest (RndFor) for this experiment since its performance lied approximately in the middle of all classifiers.

Table 5 shows the median classification results over all projects based on the RndFor classifier per cut-point and per metric set model. The cell coloring has the same interpretation as in Table 4: Grey shaded cells are significantly different from the white cells of the *same performance measure* in the *same row* (*i.e.*, percentile). For better readability and comparability, the first row of Table 5 (denoted by GT0, *i.e.*, greater than 0, see Equation 1) corresponds to the first row of Table 4 (*i.e.*, performance vector of RndFor).

We can see that the relative performances between the metric sets behave similarly to what was observed in Section 3.2. The change (CM) and the combined (CM&SCM) models outperform the source code metrics (SCM) model significantly across all thresholds and performance measures. The combined model, however, does not achieve a significantly different performance compared to the change model. While the results in Section 3.2 showed an increase regarding recall in favor of the combined model, one can notice an improved precision by 0.06 in case of the 90% and the 95% percentile between the change and combined model—although not statistically significant. In case of the 75% percentile the change and the combined model achieve nearly equal classification performance.

Comparing the classification results across the four cut-points we can see that the AUC values remain fairly constant on a high level for the change metrics and the combined model. Hence, the choice of a different binning cut-point does not affect the AUC values for these models. In contrast, a greater variance of the AUC values is obtained in the case of the classification models based on the code metric set. For instance, the median AUC value when using GT0 for binning (0.72) is significantly lower than the median AUC values of all other percentiles.

Generally, precision decreases as the number of samples in the target class becomes smaller (*i.e.*, the higher the percentile). For instance, the code model exhibits low preci-

Table 5: Median classification results for RndFor over all projects per cut-point and per model

	CM			SCM			CM&SCM		
	AUC	P	R	AUC	P	R	AUC	P	R
GT0	.95	.84	.88	.72	.50	.64	.95	.85	.95
75%	.97	.72	.95	.75	.39	.63	.97	.74	.95
90%	.97	.58	.94	.77	.20	.69	.98	.64	.94
95%	.97	.62	.92	.79	.13	.72	.98	.68	.92

sion in the case of the 95% percentile (median precision of 0.13). Looking at the change metrics and the combined model the median precision is significantly higher for the GT0 and the 75% percentiles compared to the 90% and the 95% percentiles. Moreover, the median precision of those two percentiles, *e.g.*, 0.64 and 0.68 in case of the combined model, might appear to be low. However, since only 10% and 5% of all methods are labeled as *bug-prone*, this is better than chance.

The picture regarding recall is not conclusive. On the one hand, there are improved median recall values for higher percentiles in case of the code metrics model. For instance, the median recall of the 95% percentile is significantly higher than the one of GT0 (0.72 vs. 0.64). On the other hand, recall slightly deteriorates for the other two models as higher cut-points for prior binning are chosen. However, one must keep in mind—as stated in Section 3.1—that using precision and recall for the comparison of classification models that were obtained under different prior probabilities (*i.e.*, in our case the different percentiles) might not be appropriate.

In short, we can say that (even) when the number of samples in the target class diminishes, collecting code metrics in addition to change metrics for building prediction models does not yield better results. Furthermore, the choice of a different cut-point for prior binning does not affect AUC and recall. However, we likely obtain lower precision values.

3.4 Summary of Results

Based on the experiments in this section we can answer our research questions posed in Section 1.

> *RQ1: It is possible to build method level bug prediction models achieving a precision of 0.85, a recall of 0.95, and an AUC of 0.95.*

Our experiments on 21 different software systems indicate that—using Random Forest—one can build a bug prediction model at the method level which achieves 0.85 precision, 0.95 recall, and 0.95 AUC. Employing different machine learning methods does not significantly impact the performance of the classification, which does not fall below 0.8 for precision, 0.89 for recall, and 0.91 for AUC. This result is similar to the findings of our earlier work performed at the file level [16]. Moreover, in an extensive experiment using 17 different classification algorithms no significant performance differences could be detected [26]. Hence, instead of using only classification performance as criteria, one might choose an algorithm resulting in a simple model consisting of a (few) readable rules, such as decision trees.

> *RQ2: While change metrics (CM) are a stronger indicator of bug-prone methods than source code metrics (SCM), combining CM and SCM does not improve the performance significantly.*

CM achieved significantly better prediction results with respect to AUC, precision, and recall (see Table 4). For instance, a Random Forest model using CM as input variables obtained a significantly higher median AUC value compared to the same model using SCM as predictor (0.95 vs. 0.72). This confirms prior work: Change metrics outperform measures that are computed from the source code [17, 24, 30].

While both—the CM based and the combined models—obtain significantly better results than the SCM based model, they are not significantly different among each other. We observed only a slight increase regarding recall when using both metric sets.

> *RQ3: Choosing a higher percentile for labeling does not affect AUC values.*

In addition to the commonly applied criteria "at least one bug" (see Equation 1) we used the 75%, 90%, and 95% percentiles (see Equation 2) of the number of bugs per methods as cut-point for a priori labeling. We obtained fairly high and consistent AUC values across all four percentiles in case of the CM and the combined models (see Table 5). Hence, we conclude that our models are robust with respect to different prior probabilities. Similar observations were made for recall. Not surprisingly, as the number of samples in the target class becomes smaller, *i.e.*, as higher percentiles are chosen as cut-points, precision tends to decrease. Consequently, when comparing prediction models that were trained with different target class distributions one should use AUC as performance measure as it is independent of prior probabilities [4].

4. APPLICATION OF RESULTS

The results of our study showed that we can build bug prediction models at the method level with good classification performance by leveraging the change information provided by *fine-grained source code changes*. In the following we demonstrate the application and benefit of our prediction model to identify the *bug-prone* methods in a source file compared to a file-level prediction model that performs equally well. For that, we assume a scenario as follows:

A software developer of the JDT Core plugin, the largest Eclipse project, and the Derby Engine module, the largest non-Eclipse project in our dataset, receives the task to improve the unit testing in their software application in order to prevent future post-release bugs. For this, she needs to know the most *bug-prone* methods because they should be tested first and more rigorously than the other methods. For illustration purpose, we assume the developer has little knowledge about her project (*e.g.*, she is new to the project). To identify the *bug-prone* methods, she uses two prediction models, one model to predict the *bug-prone* source files and our Random Forest (RndFor) model to directly predict the *bug-prone* methods of a given source file.

Furthermore, we take as examples release 3.0 of the JDT Core plugin and release 10.2.2.0 of the Derby Engine module. For both releases, she uses the two prediction models trained on the source code metrics *and* the versioning system history back to the last major release (*i.e.*, 2.1 in case of JDT Core and 10.2.1.6 in case of Derby) for calculating the change metrics. Furthermore, both the models were trained using *1 bug* as binning cut-point (see Equation 1) and 10-fold cross validation and then reapplied to the dataset. To better quantify the advantage of our method-level prediction model over the file-level prediction model, we assume that the file-level prediction model performs equally well in terms of AUC, precision, and recall.

Comparison.

We first discuss two exemplary methods of JDT Core 3.0 in the context of the above outlined scenario and then accordingly two methods of the Derby Engine 10.2.2.0 dataset. We selected these methods because they were ranked and classified as highly *bug-prone* by the RndFor model. Furthermore, they showed a large change history in their datasets. **JDT Core 3.0.** On average, 12% of all methods were *bug-prone*, and a class contained, on average, 13 methods in this release of Eclipse. The RndFor model resulted in an AUC of 0.9, precision of 0.82, and recall of 0.93.

In particular, the parent class of the method `Main.configure(..)`[2] had 26 methods in the release revision 1.151 out of which 11 (~42%) were affected by post-release bugs. Our model classified this particular method as *bug-prone* with a probability of 1.0. In fact, (among others) bug `74355`[3] was reported and fixed (rev. 1.162 with 3.1 M2 as target milestone) by changing two conditional expressions. After being guided to the class of this method by her file-level prediction model our developer would have a chance of 42% to guess one of the *bug-prone* methods in the first step. If not successful, her chances increase to 44% (=11/25) in the next step, in the third step to ~46% (11/24) and so on. On the other hand, given the precision of 0.82 achieved by our model[4], she arrives approximately at the same probability of selecting one of the *bug-prone* methods simply by chance after having ruled out 12 methods (*i.e.*, $11/(26 - 12) = 0.79$ vs. precision of 0.82). Therefore, our model could save up to 12 manual inspection steps.

`LocalDeclaration.resolve(..)`[5] was the only method out of six (as per revision 1.29) that contained a bug. This method was again confidently classified as *bug-prone* by our model with a probability of 0.97. In particular, bug `68998` was reported only a few days after the release and fixed in revision 1.31 for release 3.1. Similarly to the first example, our model correctly identified the affected method and, hence, could prevent a maximum of 5 manual method inspections. **Derby Engine 10.2.2.0.** The RndFor model created for this release obtained an AUC of 0.9, precision of 0.53, and recall of 0.7. This is a lower performance compared to the model of JDT Core. However, given the fact that only 12% of the methods were *bug-prone* and a class had on average 13 methods, this is better than chance, *i.e.*, predicting bugs at the file level.

The class `CreateIndexConstantAction`[6] had 6 methods as per release revision 429838. `executeConstantAction(Ac-`

`tivation)` was the only method being *bug-prone*. Our model correctly classified it with a probability of 0.9. Therefore, more than half of all methods need to be manually "eliminated" until guessing becomes as effective as our model regarding the identification of this particular *bug-prone* method (*i.e.*, $1/(6 - 4) = 0.5$ vs. precision of 0.53). An analysis of the revisions showed that, for example, bug `2599`[7] was fixed in revision 528033 for the upcoming release 10.3.1.4.

When class `TernaryOperatorNode`[8] was tagged for the release 10.2.2.0 with revision 480219, it contained 30 methods. After this release 6 methods (*i.e.*, 20%) were affected by bugs. One of those methods was `locateBind()`, *e.g.*, bug 2777 was fixed in revision 553735. Again, it was correctly classified as *bug-prone* with a high probability of 0.99. When comparing the prior probability of 20% to the precision of 0.53 our model denotes a major improvement and could save roughly up to 18 manual inspection steps (*i.e.*, $6/(30 - 18) = 0.5$).

Although these examples show a clear usefulness of our approach, there are some limitations to this scenario as it is illustrated above. For instance, in a corresponding real-life scenario a senior developer is not completely unaware of which particular methods contain most of the bugs. Hence, she will not have to rely on pure guessing when examining the potential candidate methods. Moreover, some methods, *e.g.*, accessor-methods, can be examined rather quickly. However, the scenario clearly shows the benefit of favoring our method-level prediction model over file-level prediction models. Moreover, we are convinced that due to the good performance of our models even senior software developers can benefit from them: Our models help to narrow down the search space for identifying the *bug-prone* methods. We plan to investigate these benefits with controlled experiments.

Regarding the practicability of our approach, the overhead of the more complex AST-based structural differencing compared to text differencing, *e.g.*, code churn, is negligible. For instance, the extraction process for the entire Eclipse Compare history takes 5min if the source code revisions are locally available. Currently, the time-critical factor is fetching all source code revisions from a remote repository. Hence, integrating our prediction models into a continuous integration environment, e.g., via svn hook, is part of the future work and would even speed up our approach since the fine-grained source code changes could be calculated locally, *e.g.*, for each commit or during nightly builds.

5. THREATS TO VALIDITY

The Construct Validity of our work, *i.e.*, how accurate we measure a particular concept, is mainly threatened by three facts: First, we establish the link between the change history of a project and bugs by searching for references to bug reports in commit messages. This method is only as reliable as such references are (manually) recorded when committing. In particular, bug reports that are not referenced in commit messages cannot be linked to any revision of the version control system. Therefore, this set of successfully linked bugs might not be a fair representation of all bugs [5]. We have reduced this threat by taking into account the bug fixing and commit policy as described in the documentation of a particular project. In Lucene, for instance, standard

---

[2] org.eclipse.jdt.internal.compiler.batch.Main.configure(String[])
[3] https://bugs.eclipse.org/bugs/show_bug.cgi?id=<bug_number>
[4] Precision can be seen as the probability that a randomly chosen method is relevant, i.e., contains a bug.
[5] org.eclipse.jdt.internal.compiler.ast.LocalDeclaration.resolve(BlockScope)
[6] org.apache.derby.impl.sql.execute.CreateIndexConstantAction

[7] https://issues.apache.org/jira/browse/DERBY-<bug_number>
[8] org.apache.derby.impl.sql.compile.TernaryOperatorNode

commit patterns are used for bug fixes (e.g. 'lucene-512'), which facilitates the bug-linking.

In addition, this threatens the usefulness of our approach—if bugs cannot be linked we will not be able to train any model. However, analyzing commit messages to establish the link between change history and bug reports is a common procedure and does also reflect state of the art [43, 9]. Moreover, prior studies found out that bug prediction models are to some extent resistant to such kind of noise [22]. Recently, research proposed a technique to re-establish links even if they are missing in the commit messages [45].

Second, CHANGEDISTILLER extracts *fine-grained source code changes* by comparing subsequent file revisions. Hence, varying commit behavior can influence how we measure code changes and link bugs. For instance, a developer might commit further changes in addition to a bug fix. In this case we would consider all methods that were changed to be affected by that bug. We mitigated this threat by considering a large number of projects in our experiments. Moreover, in our dataset on average a single method was changed per each revision with a reference to a bug report in its commit message—indicating that bug fixes are regularly committed in isolation. This observation is confirmed by prior studies that in most cases only small changes in a file are committed [39]. Moreover, in Eclipse a substantial amount of bugs are indeed fixed in one method [13].

Third, we took all references into account when counting the number of bugs. Therefore, it is possible that not all of these references represent bugs in their sense of meaning [1], *i.e.*, problems related to corrective maintenance. However, an inspection of bug references referring to JDT Core showed that most of those references are indeed real bugs [9].

The generalizability of our study, *i.e.*, its *External Validity*, is threatened by the dataset we use for this study. For instance, many of the systems belong to the Eclipse ecosystem. Similarly, Derby, Lucene, Ant, Jena, and Xerces are all projects of the Apache Foundation. Therefore, it is possible that our work suffers from the bias opposed by characteristics of the development process unique to these communities. We selected these systems because they are relatively large, actively developed, and were extensively studied before [48, 16, 9, 21, 20, 41], allowing us to contribute to an existing body of knowledge. In particular, Eclipse emerged to a "de facto standard" case study when analyzing open-source systems. Nevertheless, all projects are independently developed, come from different domains, and emerged from the context of unrelated communities. Moreover, although open source, Eclipse and (to some extent) Jena have an industrial background.

In addition, all tools used in this paper are publicly available, and Ghezzi and Gall offer our data collecting processes as web services [15] facilitating the extension of our work with data from other projects.

We modeled the relation between the two metric sets (see Table 2 and 3) and bugs in methods using different machine learning algorithms. The quality of our models were discussed by means of their classification performance and statistical significance testing. However, previous literature proposed further metrics, such as past bugs [48, 23], the age of files [30], or developer interaction measures [37, 33], as well as different approaches to measure those metrics, *e.g.*, entropy based [19], relative [31], or burst based [34]. As part of our future work we plan to conduct a comparative study

with an extended space of metrics including additional attribute selection and data mining techniques.

6. RELATED WORK

We discuss related work according to the type of metrics that were used to train the prediction models.

Change Metrics. The idea of change metrics (often referred to as *code churn*) is that bugs are introduced by changes [9]. Thus, the more changes are done to a particular part of the source code the more likely it will contain bugs. In [17], Generalized Linear Models were built based on several change metrics, *e.g.*, number of changes or average age of the code. A study showed that relative change metrics from the Windows Server change history are better indicators for defect density than absolute values [31]. The fault and change history in combination with a (negative binomial) regression model achieved good performance in predicting not only the location, but also the number of bugs [36]. Furthermore, the more complex source code changes are (as measured by entropy), the more likely they are *bug-prone* [19]. Nagappan *et al.* found that the number of subsequent, consecutive changes (rather than the total number of changes) is a strong predictor for bugs [34]. Bernstein *et al.* studied the extent to which measuring changes in different timeframes affects prediction performance [4]. In a prior study using the change history of Eclipse, we compared lines based code churn and fine-grained source code changes for bug prediction [16]. The latter metrics resulted in significantly better prediction performance. Shihab *et al.* predicted surprise defects in files that are rarely affected by changes [42]. An adaptive cache-like approach using fine-grained changes and past-defects to predict bugs at the entity-level (function, method) was proposed in [23]. The main difference to our work is that their approach suggests further source code entities that need to be changed while a particular bug is being fixed, rather than predicting *bug-prone* methods in advance.

A study on changes in general showed that a substantial amount of changes are *non-essential* changes, *i.e.*, they are not directly related to feature modifying changes [21], *e.g.*, adding and removing the keyword `this`.

Code Metrics. Using code metrics for predicting bugs assumes that a more complex piece of code is harder to understand and to change, and therefore, it is likely to contain more bugs [9]. Basili *et al.* investigated the impact of the CK object-oriented metrics suite to software quality [3]. The same metric suite was applied on a commercial system in [44]. A set of complexity and size metrics was used to predict post-release bugs in releases of Eclipse [48]. The usefulness of (static) code metrics to build prediction models was demonstrated using the NASA dataset [27]. In [26], an extensive study was conducted with the same dataset, focusing on evaluating different machine learning algorithms. The conclusion is that the difference between those algorithms is mostly not (statistically) significant. However, this *ceiling effect* is reported to disappear when focusing not only on maximizing detection and minimizing false alarm rates [28].

The practicability of lines of code (LOC) to predict defects was demonstrated in [46]. El Emam *et al.* showed that the size of a class is a confounding factor when building bug prediction models [11]. An extensive empirical study with 38 different metrics and multivariate models to predict the fault-prone modules of the Apache web-server is presented in [10]. Social-network measures were applied on the dependency graph of Windows Server [47] and open-source systems [19]: More central binaries are more defect-prone. **Social Measures.** Work on this subject investigates how the organizational and social context of the software development process affects its quality. Pinzger *et al.* related social-network techniques to the developer contribution network [37]. They found that if more developers contribute to a certain binary it will more likely be affected by post-release defects. Moreover, removing minor contributors from such a network affects prediction performance negatively [7]. Recent work showed that investigating code-ownership and interactions between developers at a fine-grained level can substantially contribute to defect prediction [40, 25]. Nagappan *et al.* showed that the organizational complexity of the development process is significantly related to defects [33]. Somewhat surprisingly, distributed development does not seem to affect software quality [6].

These metrics are rarely used in isolation but instead are often combined for building bug prediction models [2, 41]. The goal is to either achieve (significantly) higher prediction results or to study which of the metrics are better predictors for bugs [9, 33]. Although a general consensus has not been achieved, several studies showed—similarly to what we observed in this work—that change metrics potentially outperform code metrics [30, 20, 24].

7. CONCLUSIONS AND FUTURE WORK

We empirically investigated if bug prediction models at the method level can be successfully created. We used the source code and change history of 21 Java open-source (sub-)systems. Our experiments showed that:

- Change metrics (extracted from the version control system of a project) can be used to train prediction models with good performance. For example, a Random Forest model achieved an AUC of 0.95, precision of 0.84, and a recall of 0.88 (**RQ1**).

- Using change metrics as predictor variables produced prediction models with significantly better results compared to source code metrics. However, including both metrics sets did not improve the classification performance of our models (**RQ2**).

- Different binning values did not affect the AUC values of our models (**RQ3**). Moreover, with a precision of 0.68 our models identify the "top 5%" of all *bug-prone* methods better than chance.

- Conforming prior work, *e.g.*, [26], we could not observe a significant difference among several machine learning techniques with respect to their classification performance.

Given their good performance, our method-level prediction models can save manual inspection steps. Currently, we use the entire development history available at the time of data collection to train prediction models. It is part of our future work to measure changes based on different timeframes, *e.g.*, release, quarterly, or yearly based. Furthermore, we plan to investigate a broader feature space, *i.e.*, additional attributes, more advanced attribute selection techniques (rather than "feeding all data" to the data mining algorithms), *e.g.*, Information Gain [27], for prediction model building.

8. REFERENCES

[1] G. Antoniol, K. Ayari, M. D. Penta, F. Khomh, and Y.-G. Guéhéneuc. Is it a bug or an enhancement? a text-based approach to classify change requests. In *Proc. Conf. of the center for advanced studies on collaborative research: meeting of minds*, pages 304–318, 2008.

[2] E. Arisholm and L. Briand. Predicting fault-prone components in a java legacy system. In *Proc. Int'l Symp. on Empir. Softw. Eng.*, pages 8–17, 2006.

[3] V. Basili, L. Briand, and W. Melo. A validation of object-oriented design metrics as quality indicators. *IEEE Trans. Softw. Eng.*, 22:751–761, October 1996.

[4] A. Bernstein, J. Ekanayake, and M. Pinzger. Improving defect prediction using temporal features and non linear models. In *Proc. Int'l Workshop on Principles of Softw. Evolution*, pages 11–18, 2007.

[5] C. Bird, A. Bachmann, E. Aune, J. Duffy, A. Bernstein, V. Filkov, and P. Devanbu. Fair and balanced?: bias in bug-fix datasets. In *Proc. Joint Eur. Softw. Eng. Conf. and Symp. on the Found. of Softw. Eng.*, pages 121–130, 2009.

[6] C. Bird, N. Nagappan, P. Devanbu, H. Gall, and B. Murphy. Does distributed development affect software quality? an empirical case study of windows vista. In *Proc. Int'l Conf. on Softw. Eng.*, pages 518–528, 2009.

[7] C. Bird, N. Nagappan, B. Murphy, H. Gall, and P. Devanbu. Don't Touch My Code! Examining the Effects of Ownership on Software Quality. In *Proc. Joint Eur Softw. Eng. Conf. and Symp. on the Found. of Softw. Eng.*, pages 4–14, 2011.

[8] S. R. Chidamber and C. F. Kemerer. A metrics suite for object oriented design. *IEEE Trans. Softw. Eng.*, 20(6):476–493, June 1994.

[9] M. D'Ambros, M. Lanza, and R. Robbes. Evaluating defect prediction approaches: a benchmark and an extensive comparison. *Empir. Softw. Eng.*, pages 1–47, 2011.

[10] G. Denaro and M. Pezzè. An empirical evaluation of fault-proneness models. In *Proc. Int'l Conf. on Softw. Eng.*, pages 241–251, 2002.

[11] K. E. Emam, S. Benlarbi, N. Goel, and S. Rai. The confounding effect of class size on the validity of object-oriented metrics. *IEEE Trans. on Softw. Eng.*, 27(7):630–650, July 2001.

[12] B. Fluri, M. Würsch, M. Pinzger, and H. C. Gall. Change Distilling: Tree Differencing for Fine-Grained Source Code Change Extraction. *IEEE Trans. on Softw. Eng.*, 33(11):725–743, November 2007.

[13] B. Fluri, J. Zuberbuehler, and H. C. Gall. Recommending method invocation context changes. In *Proc. Int'l Workshop on Recomm. Syst. for Softw. Eng.*, pages 1–5, 2008.

[14] H. C. Gall, B. Fluri, and M. Pinzger. Change analysis with evolizer and changedistiller. *IEEE Software*, 26(1):26–33, January/February 2009.

[15] G. Ghezzi and H. Gall. Sofas: A lightweight architecture for software analysis as a service. In *Proc. Working Conf. on Softw. Architecture*, pages 93–102, 2011.

[16] E. Giger, M. Pinzger, and H. C. Gall. Comparing

fine-grained source code changes and code churn for bug prediction. In *Proc. Int'l Workshop on Mining Softw. Repos.*, pages 83–92, 2011.

[17] T. Graves, A. Karr, J. Marron, and H. Siy. Predicting fault incidence using software change history. *IEEE Trans. Softw. Eng.*, 26:653–661, July 2000.

[18] T. Gyimothy, R. Ferenc, and I. Siket. Empirical validation of object-oriented metrics on open source software for fault prediction. *IEEE Trans. Softw. Eng.*, 31:897–910, 2005.

[19] A. Hassan. Predicting faults using the complexity of code changes. In *Proc. Int'l Conf. on Softw. Eng.*, pages 78–88, 2009.

[20] Y. Kamei, S. Matsumoto, A. Monden, K. Matsumoto, B. Adams, and A. Hassan. Revisiting common bug prediction findings using effort-aware models. In *Proc. Int'l Conf. on Softw. Maint.*, pages 1–10, 2010.

[21] D. Kawrykow and M. P. Robillard. Non-essential changes in version histories. In *Proc. Int'l Conf. on Softw. Eng.*, pages 351–360, 2011.

[22] S. Kim, H. Zhang, R. Wu, and L. Gong. Dealing with noise in defect prediction. In *Proc. Int'l Conf. on Softw. Eng.*, pages 481–490, 2011.

[23] S. Kim, T. Zimmermann, J. Whitehead, and A. Zeller. Predicting faults from cached history. In *Proc. Int'l Conf. on Softw. Eng.*, pages 489–498, 2007.

[24] P. Knab, M. Pinzger, and A. Bernstein. Predicting defect densities in source code files with decision tree learners. In *Proc. Int'l Workshop on Mining Softw. Repos.*, pages 119–125, 2006.

[25] T. Lee, J. Nam, D. Han, S. Kim, and H. P. In. Micro interaction metrics for defect prediction. In *Proc. Joint Eur. Softw. Eng. Conf. and Symp. on the Found. of Softw. Eng.*, pages 311–321, 2011.

[26] S. Lessmann, B. Baesens, C. M. Swantje, and Pietsch. Benchmarking classification models for software defect prediction: A proposed framework and novel findings. *IEEE Trans. on Softw. Eng.*, 34:485–496, July 2008.

[27] T. Menzies, J. Greenwald, and A. Frank. Data mining static code attributes to learn defect predictors. *IEEE Trans. on Softw. Eng.*, 33:2–13, January 2007.

[28] T. Menzies, Z. Milton, B. Turhan, B. Cukic, Y. Jiang, and A. Bener. Defect prediction from static code features: current results, limitations, new approaches. *Automated Softw. Eng.*, 17(4):375–407, 2010.

[29] I. Mierswa, M. Wurst, R. Klinkenberg, M. Scholz, and T. Euler. Yale: Rapid prototyping for complex data mining tasks. In *Proc. Int'l Conf. on Knowl. Discovery and Data Mining*, pages 935–940, 2006.

[30] R. Moser, W. Pedrycz, and G. Succi. A comparative analysis of the efficiency of change metrics and static code attributes for defect prediction. In *Proc. Int'l Conf. on Softw. Eng.*, pages 181–190, 2008.

[31] N. Nagappan and T. Ball. Use of relative code churn measures to predict system defect density. In *Proc. Int'l Conf. on Softw. Eng.*, pages 284–292, 2005.

[32] N. Nagappan, T. Ball, and A. Zeller. Mining metrics to predict component failures. In *Proc. Int'l Conf. on Softw. Eng.*, pages 452–461, 2006.

[33] N. Nagappan, B. Murphy, and V. Basili. The influence of organizational structure on software quality: an empirical case study. In *Proc. Int'l Conf. on Softw. Eng.*, pages 521–530, 2008.

[34] N. Nagappan, A. Zeller, T. Zimmermann, K. Herzig, and B. Murphy. Change bursts as defect predictors. In *Proc. Int'l Symp. on Softw. Reliability Eng.*, 2010.

[35] T. Nguyen, B. Adams, and A. Hassan. Studying the impact of dependency network measures on software quality. In *Int'l Conf. on Softw. Maint.*, pages 1 –10, 2010.

[36] T. Ostrand, E. Weyuker, and R. Bell. Predicting the location and number of faults in large software systems. *IEEE Trans. Softw. Eng.*, 31(4):340–355, 2005.

[37] M. Pinzger, N. Nagappan, and B. Murphy. Can developer-module networks predict failures? In *Proc. Symp. on the Found. of Softw. Eng.*, pages 2–12, 2008.

[38] D. Posnett, V. Filkov, and P. Devanbu. Ecological inference in empirical software engineering. In *Proc. Int'l Conf. on Automated Softw. Eng.*, pages 362–371, 2011.

[39] R. Purushothaman and D. Perry. Toward understanding the rhetoric of small source code changes. *IEEE Trans. Softw. Eng.*, 31(6):511–526, June 2005.

[40] F. Rahman and P. Devanbu. Ownership, experience and defects: a fine-grained study of authorship. In *Proc. Int'l Conf. on Softw. Eng.*, pages 491–500, 2011.

[41] E. Shihab, M. Jiang, W. Ibrahim, B. Adams, and A. Hassan. Understanding the impact of code and process metrics on post-release defects: a case study on the eclipse project. In *Proc. Int'l Symp. on Empir. Softw. Eng. and Meas.*, pages 1–10, 2010.

[42] E. Shihab, A. Mockus, Y. Kamei, B. Adams, and A. Hassan. High-impact defects: a study of breakage and surprise defects. In *Proc. Joint Eur. Softw. Eng. Conf. and Symp. on the Found. of Softw. Eng.*, pages 300–310, 2011.

[43] J. Śliwerski, T. Zimmermann, and A. Zeller. When do changes induce fixes? In *Proc. Int'l Workshop on Mining Softw. Repos.*, pages 1–5, 2005.

[44] R. Subramanyam and M. Krishnan. Empirical analysis of ck metrics for object-oriented design complexity: Implications for software defects. *IEEE Trans. Softw. Eng.*, 29(4):297–310, 2003.

[45] R. Wu, H. Zhang, S. Kim, and S.-C. Cheung. Relink: Recovering links between bugs and changes. In *Proc. Joint Eur. Softw. Eng. Conf. and Symp. on the Found. of Softw. Eng.*, pages 15–25, 2011.

[46] H. Zhang. An investigation of the relationships between lines of code and defects. In *Proc. Int'l Conf. on Softw. Maint.*, pages 274–283, 2009.

[47] T. Zimmermann and N. Nagappan. Predicting defects using network analysis on dependency graphs. In *Proc. Int'l Conf. on Softw. Eng.*, pages 531–540, 2008.

[48] T. Zimmermann, R. Premraj, and A. Zeller. Predicting defects for eclipse. In *Proc. Int'l Workshop on Predictor Models in Softw. Eng.*, pages 9–15, 2007.

Studying Volatility Predictors in Open Source Software

Brandt Braunschweig, Neha Dhage, Maria Jose Viera, Carolyn Seaman, Sreedevi Sampath,
A. Gunes Koru
Department of Information Systems
University of Maryland Baltimore County
Baltimore, MD 21250 USA.

{brandtb1, nehad1, mviera1, cseaman, sampath, gkoru}@umbc.edu

ABSTRACT

Volatile software modules, for the purposes of this work, are defined as those that are significantly more change-prone than other modules in the same system or subsystem. There is significant literature investigating models for predicting which modules in a system will become volatile, and/or are defect-prone. Much of this work focuses on using source code-related characteristics (e.g., complexity metrics) and simple change metrics (e.g., number of past changes) as inputs to the predictive models. Our work attempts to broaden the array of factors considered in such prediction approaches. To this end, we collected data directly from development personnel about the factors they rely on to foresee what parts of a system are going to become volatile. In this paper, we describe a focus group study conducted with the development team of a small but active open source project, in which we asked this very question. The results of the focus group indicate, among other things, that a period of volatility in a particular area of the system is often predicted by a pattern characterized by inactivity in a certain area (resulting in that area becoming less mature than others), increased communication between developers regarding opportunities for improvement in that area, and then the emergence of a champion who takes the initiative to start working on those improvements. The initial changes lead to more changes (both to extend the improvements already made and to fix problems introduced), thus leading to volatility.

Categories and Subject Descriptors

D.2.7 **[Software Engineering]**: Distribution, Maintenance and Enhancement, D.2.8 **[Software Engineering]**: Metrics, D.2.9 **[Software Engineering]**: Management

Keywords

Open source software, volatility predictors, focus group study, empirical study.

1. INTRODUCTION

Software systems tend to change and evolve over time as they continue to serve their intended purpose. Unfortunately, not all software change is useful or necessary. Examples of useful changes are refactoring or the addition of new product features in response to users' and other stakeholders' requests. However, changes in long-lived, large-scale systems in particular lead to deterioration of the underlying code structure, increasing the risk of new defects introduced during bug fixing, leading to more future changes. In many software systems there exist some modules that are relatively more change prone, and thus consume more project resources, as compared with other comparable modules. In this context, we use the term volatility to mean *relative change proneness* among software modules that are part of the same high-level function or subsystem (e.g., user interface modules).

Reducing unnecessary future changes that lead to decay of the software system can reduce maintenance costs. By reducing maintenance costs, more time and resources could be spent on other aspects of system development, such as incorporating new technology into old systems and meeting the society's needs for increased functionality. Therefore, it is important to identify and understand the important factors that contribute to highly volatile software modules.

Several studies in the past [15, 42, 48] have stressed the 80:20 rule, which states that the majority of the problems (around 80%), such as defects and changes, in a software system are rooted in a small percentage of its modules (around 20%). While earlier research has focused on identifying this smaller percentage of troublesome modules by looking at their structural characteristics, so that increased testing, inspection, and restructuring efforts can be concentrated on those modules in order to reduce future maintenance costs [23-25], the results from these studies are of limited actionability, as they only give some insight into structural causes of software volatility. Most of the time, the structural characteristics of a software system are affected by other context variables related to continuous development and maintenance activities, and they cannot be considered or manipulated in isolation. In contrast, the novel aspect of this paper is that *we are taking one step back up the causal chain that leads to software volatility by examining other, more actionable, software characteristics that indicate future high volatility.*

In this paper, we collect data from open source software (OSS) developers on the factors that they deem important indicators of future volatility in their systems. We are interested in a wide variety of important factors, including organizational, process, people and technical issues. We report on our methodology and experiences in conducting an online focus group with open source developers of a software system. To our knowledge, focus groups have rarely been used in research on open source software and developers. Focus group interviews are an attractive method for obtaining rich and in-depth knowledge regarding these factors. Finally, we present the results, which contain observations and comments from the developers on factors they consider important predictors of software volatility.

From the results, we find that certain people aspects (such as developer interest), development aspects (such as a drive to rewrite documentation), and design aspects (such as poor design or difficulty of coding) were all factors that contributed to volatility in software.

Section 2 presents the background and related work on the areas of software prediction for volatility. Section 3 presents our empirical methodology for planning and conducting the focus group. In Section 4, we present the results from our study. We discuss the results and conclude in Section 5.

2. BACKGROUND AND RELATED WORK

In this section, we discuss some of the related studies in the areas of organizational and human aspects of software quality, and relationships between structural measures and external attributes.

2.1 Organizational, Process, and Human Aspects in Software Maintenance Quality

Writers on software engineering have been advocating for more investigation of the role of "softer" factors in software development and maintenance for quite some time [12, 41]. There has been an increase in studies of such organizational and process factors in various aspects of software development [1, 13], and some of this work has focused on maintenance [37]. Little of this work focuses on the effect of such factors on software quality during maintenance. However, some recent studies in this area are promising, and our work builds on it in part.

Some recent work has specifically looked at the role of people and organizational issues in software quality. In particular, Cataldo et al. [9] have examined several types of "dependencies", including those between developers, based on the work that they are doing. They found that these types of dependencies were significantly associated with failure-proneness after delivery. Wolf et al. [54] also examined relationships between developers, using social network analysis, and their ability to predict build failures. Rahman and Devanbu [44] investigated the relationship between ownership and "implicated code" (code that has been changed to fix bugs). They found that implicated code is less likely to involve contributions of multiple developers, and the general experience of a developer had no effect on implicated code.

What could broadly be termed "process characteristics" have also been examined in terms of their relationship to various aspects of software quality. Mockus et al. [34] looked specifically at characteristics of the deployment process (e.g. deployment schedule, hardware and software configurations) and found that they have a significant effect on customer-perceived quality. Others have studied such process factors as code churn [36] and outcomes of early static analysis [35], both on pre-release quality. Another example of a proposed prediction model based on a limited set of process indicators is Hassan and Holt's [16] "top ten list" model, which predicts change-prone modules based solely on the recentness of their latest changes.

The literature in this area is still spotty and has not yet provided a cohesive view of the relevant relationships. In particular, none of these works, to our knowledge, attempts to throw the net as widely as we propose, nor attempts to ground the choice of factors in evidence gathered from developers, as we describe in this paper. Further, none addresses their role in software volatility.

2.2 Relationships between structural measures and external attributes

This group of related studies explored the relationship between structural characteristics of software modules and some of their externally observable attributes that are commonly associated with problems, such as change-proneness and defect-proneness. We focus in particular on the studies that addressed the relationship between structural measures and change-proneness.

Henry and Kafura defined a set of structural measures based on information flow among system components [17, 19] and found strong correlations between their measurement values and the number of changed source lines in the Unix operating system. Later, Kafura and Reddy were able to validate their measures even when they used subjective quality evaluations of experts as the response variable rather than objective measurements such as change or defect count [20]. However, Kitchenham et al. [21] were not able to validate Henry and Kafura's information flow measures, whereas, they found that change was related to some other measures such as fan-out, size, and number of branches. Basili and Hutchens observed positive correlations especially between their hybrid measure, syntactic complexity (SynC), and change using data from the development of 19 student projects [5]. Binkley and Schach reported high correlations between their measures and change as well, especially with their Coupling Dependency Measure (CDM) [6].

In the 1990s, object-oriented development gained popularity. Chidamber and Kemerer [10], Lorenz and Kidd [31], and Briand et al. [7-8] proposed several object-oriented measures. Li and Henry [29] obtained high correlation values between object-oriented measures and change for two systems that they studied. Recent variations on this line of research have investigated different analysis techniques for combining structural measures into models that describe or predict software change, including genetic algorithms [51] and time series analysis [18]. Other recent approaches include incorporating expert assessments along with the structural measures [3], and including in the model a measure of "popularity" [50].

A number of studies focused on stability by examining code and design metrics during the evolution of a software system [2, 28, 45]. One primary result of these studies is that the Chidamber and Kemerer (C&K) metrics, particularly the LCOM (lack of cohesion in methods) might have weaknesses in terms of their definitions and relationship with code stability. It was also suggested that CBO (coupling between objects) is a composite measure of dependency [28], and it would be useful to use the sub-metrics of CBO by distinguishing between the dependencies to data items and dependencies to methods. Posnett et al. [43] examined the role of design patterns on change proneness and found that when controlled for module size, the role of design patterns was minimal. Weyuker, Ostrand, and Bell built models to predict the effects of structural measures on defect proneness [38, 52-53]. They moved on to the investigation of whether developer differences have an effect on defect proneness. Their results confirm that including developer-related data at the module level improves the prediction performance [39, 53].

To summarize, the evidence for a relationship between structural measures and changes or defects was found to be strong in some studies, but weak or not supported in other studies, as discussed in well-referenced detail by Shepperd and Ince [46]. El-Emam et al. [14] stated that the confounding effect of size raises doubts on the results of the validation studies in the literature. As a result, it can be said that the functional form of the relationship between structural measures and changes or defects is not a straightforward one. Additional empirical studies are required to increase our understanding of the phenomenon.

3. STUDY DESIGN
Our goal in this study was to identify a diverse set of potential factors that help predict highly volatile software modules. In particular, our research question was *what are the major predicting factors for future highly volatile software modules?* We believe that working directly with current, active software developers would provide the best opportunity to elicit new factors. We chose to hold focus group interviews to suggest a large number of factors in a short period of time. We chose to work with OSS developers because of the opportunity to identify factors not previously identified in research with commercial software development, because of the increasing business interest in OSS development, and to gain experience with qualitative research methods with the OSS community.

In the remainder of this section, we first present background on focus group interviews, followed by our study plan and execution. In order to conduct our study, we defined criteria for participant selection, developed an interview guide, defined a method to solicit open source projects for participants, defined the incentive method, and selected the teleconference method.

3.1 Focus Group Interviews
Focus groups are a qualitative research method appropriate for finding participants' ideas and feelings, factors underlying those feelings, and to elicit ideas from group interaction [27]. The Focus Group Interview is a group interview of 5 to 8 people, selected according to certain criteria, to hold a discussion of a particular topic, guided by a moderator to keep the discussion focused on the topic and to encourage productive discussion among the participants [27]. A focus group does not seek consensus. Unlike an individual interview, which is a dialog between the researcher and an informant, the emphasis in a focus group is on a discussion among the informants. Group discussion allows informants to build on each other's contributions and hopefully develop ideas that would not be mentioned in individual interviews.

The focus group is a form of semi-structured interview and follows an interview guide developed by the researchers to encourage participation by the participants and elicit the information of interest. The moderator must be skilled to loosely follow the interview guide, encourage discussion to develop new ideas, encourage participation by all, but also keep the discussion to the topic and pace the discussion to the allotted time.

The participants for the focus group are selected according to well defined criteria, should be knowledgeable in the subject of interest [22], and should all share some common characteristic to support group discussion. The size of the focus group should be big enough to allow for a dynamic discussion but small enough that group does not sub-divide into multiple, smaller discussions [27].

The focus group is generally recorded and transcribed. The transcription is then coded and analyzed to identify concepts, relationships, and patterns present within and across multiple focus groups conducted during the study [33]. We are primarily interested in a content analysis to identify factors related to future volatility. We use the techniques of open, axial, and selective coding drawn from grounded theory [33]. Open coding focuses on identification and classification of concepts in the text. Axial coding builds on this to find relationships among concepts and to build structure. Selective coding analyses this structure for sense making.

Potential weaknesses of focus groups include poor moderation leading to unfocused discussion, dominant personalities limiting discussion, and researcher bias in developing questions and analyzing results. Focus groups necessarily have a small sample size and results may not generalize.

Focus groups can be conducted by telephone conference call [26]. The primary advantage of a telephone focus group is that participants need not be co-located, allowing participation by geographically distributed groups. Telephone focus groups also have some disadvantages, such as the lack of non-verbal communication among participants and possibly poor audio quality. It is also not possible for the moderator to know if participants are listening attentively or are distracted with other activities.

To our knowledge, there is no previous research conducting a focus group directly with OSS developers. Andreasen et al. [4] conducted a focus group study of usability in OSS projects. Participants were experienced in OSS development, but were employees of a software usability consulting company. Crowston et al. conducted an online, text based, forum discussion targeting OSS developers on the popular Slashdot developer web site. [11] Crowston posted a question to the forum and received responses from 72 people. Although this was a kind of group discussion, the participation was unrestricted, there was no moderation, and it was not interactive. Long [30] stated an intention to hold focus group interviews with OSS developers in future work, but that has not yet been published.

We foresaw, and tried to mitigate, the following problems when conducting focus group interviews with OSS developers:

- OSS developers are geographically distributed and are quite commonly in different countries. Although some project teams occasionally meet face-to-face (such as at OSS developer conferences), it is not generally possible to hold group discussions in person. Our focus group therefore had to utilize some form of teleconferencing technology.

- Similarly, OSS developers may be in widely different time zones making it difficult to find a suitable meeting time. Although this may have limited participation for some, due to the diversity of open source projects and developers, a sufficient number of developers were still able to participate.

- OSS developers and researchers may not share a common natural language. OSS developers are generally conversant in written English, but may not be skilled in spoken English. Our focus group was restricted to those who could speak English, which may have excluded some potential participants.

- OSS developers may not be interested in participating in research or a focus group discussion. We offered incentives to the project to encourage participation. The incentive was substantial, but was not enough to increase participation beyond just one project. Further, it was not enough to achieve the desired minimum of 5 participants. We do not have any basis for insight into whether a different or larger incentive would have had a different effect.

3.2 Study Plan
Our study was designed to solicit project participants from several OSS projects, such that we could create one focus group per

project. Within a focus group, we wanted all the individual participants to belong to the same OSS project, so as to have common experience to support the discussion. In order to select participants, we defined criteria both for the open source project and for the individual participants. For an open source project to be a candidate, it must:

- Be at least 5 years old. Because we are investigating volatility over time, we wanted the participants to have had an opportunity to experience this on their project.

- Have at least 10 active developers. A project with more developers would be more likely to experience some of the maintenance problems we are investigating. Also, this would increase the chances of having enough willing participants, since we were looking for at least 5 participants for the focus group.

- Have at least 4 developers willing to participate in the focus group (although 5 were required to receive the incentive.)

- Have had a release in the last 6 months. We wanted to work with active projects so the developers would have recent experience to discuss.

- Have available source code, bug tracking database, and mailing list archives. These resources could provide additional sources of evidence for topics discussed.

- Have a defined method of making donations for the benefit of the project (rather than to individuals.)

We developed a list of candidate open source projects meeting the above criteria that was created during one of the authors' prior studies in the area of defect prediction in OSS.

For individuals to participate, they must have been at least 18 years of age, speak English, have contributed to the project within the last 6 months and have been involved for at least 2 years. Because we desired a wide range of experience, we did not limit participants to programmers. We allowed potential participants to freely interpret "contributed" and "involved."

We asked for participants by first e-mailing an individual point of contact for each identified OSS project. If they did not respond we sent a reminder after one week. If we did not get a response within one more week and the project had a public mailing list, we sent an e-mail to the project mailing list asking for participants.

As an incentive, we offered a $150 donation to a project's defined contribution fund for participation in the focus group. This was contingent on having at least 5 participants start the focus group. (Participants could withdraw at any time without penalty.)

We considered two teleconferencing solutions: commercial telephone conference calling and Skype [47]. Both are free to participants and allow call recording. We preferred Skype due to lower cost, but held the telephone conference calling as an option if participants did not have access to Skype. Although Skype also supports a shared desktop and text chat, we limited use to voice only.

Skype does not have built-in call recording capability. We purchased a license for Pamela Call Recorder [40] to allow recording the conference call. Pamela Call Recorder is a Skype add-on which allows recording calls to the MPEG-2 Audio Layer III (mp3) file format.

The interview guide was developed with the following objectives:

- To have all participants introduce themselves (and their voices);

- To start with specific examples and then move to more abstract concepts;

- To have short, simple questions to minimally influence the informants. Probes were available to assist the discussion if necessary;

- To complete the focus group in one hour.

The interview guide can be found in the appendix.

We held a practice focus group to evaluate the Skype conference call technology and gain experience moderating a focus group. Participants were the researchers and other graduate students. The technology performed as expected. The interview guide was updated to improve flow based on feedback from the practice session.

3.3 Study Execution

We solicited 15 projects between April and September, 2011. Of these, 7 did not respond, 7 declined, and 1 accepted. Four declined because they did not have enough members, one because they did not have time to participate, and one stated that they received too many requests from researchers. Having only one participating project obviously limits the diversity of potential factors we can identify but still allows us to meet our goal of identifying new factors.

The project that agreed to participate in a focus group has existed for about 15 years. The project lists 21 people as members of the development team including programmers, testers, documentation editors, and project management. The software they develop contains approximately 200,000 lines of source code in multiple languages, predominately C++.

The project was only able to have 4 people participate in the focus group, which was too few to be eligible for the incentive, but they chose to participate anyway.

Three of the participants were primarily programmers. The other participant was primarily a tester and documentation editor. All had been involved in a new release of the software which became available the day before the focus group interview.

Before the focus group, by email, we asked participants how many years they had been active in the project, whether they were paid for work in the project, whether they were engaged in similar work outside of the project, for how long, and how much they were paid for the same. Table 1 shows the data gathered in response to these questions from the participants.

Table 1: Participant Information

ID	L1	L2	L3	L4
Years active in project?	8	15		5
Paid to work on project?	No	No		No
Active in other projects?	No	Yes	no response	No
Years of experience doing this kind of work?	n/a	25		n/a
Perform similar work commercially?	n/a	Yes		n/a

Because the participants were located in 4 different countries, we found the web site Event Time Announcer [49] helpful for coordinating the focus group start time. It allowed participants to convert to their own local time instead of having the researcher attempt to coordinate local time zones and local daylight savings rules.

The focus group was also attended by two researchers, one of them the moderator (the first author). The call was held by Skype and lasted slightly over one hour and all questions were covered. Overall, the sound quality was excellent. There was a noticeable delay between speaking and being heard which made negotiating turn-taking awkward but there were no problems understanding what was said. Rapport was good with participants complimenting others for their contributions to the project and encouraging participation in the discussion.

The call recording was transcribed with the aid of Express Scribe [32] and the transcription was checked by a second researcher. The transcription was then coded jointly by two collocated researchers (the first and third authors) using Microsoft Word with the final coding determined by consensus. The initial code list contained 9 codes derived from the research question and one was added during the coding process. The codes that were used are shown in Table 2. The coded transcript was then analyzed by another researcher (the second author) who created field memos for the five codes with the most data. Finally, participants were asked to comment on the primary findings via e-mail for validation. In the next section, we present the results from the analysis.

Table 2: Codes used for coding the transcript

Code	Definition
Volatility	Modules that change more frequently than others in the same project.
• Definition	Discussions of what volatility means or alternate definitions.
• Reasons for	Underlying causes or things that lead to a module being or becoming volatile (might not be observable.) (Contrast with prediction.)
• Good or Bad	Value judgments of volatility.
• Prediction	Events or conditions that are observed to precede code modules being volatile. (Contrast with reasons for volatility)
• Reduction	Discussions of ways to reduce volatility.
• Impact	Something of value affected by having volatile code.
• Confounding Factors	Apparent volatility as a side effect (such as tools to write documentation also checking in code.) (Added during coding.)
Change Characteristics	Characteristics of software changes. This has a broad interpretation and includes people, process, or technology oriented characteristics.
Change Impact	Something that results from changes made to the code (as a result of individual changes but not volatility.)
Good Stories	Quotable and referable chunks for future publications

4. FINDINGS

Recall that the overarching research goal of this study is to identify factors that software developers view as indicative of future volatility. Our intention was to identify a wide range of factors, including those not considered in prior work on prediction models for software maintenance. The types of factors that arose from the focus group findings are presented in two groupings in the subsections below. The first and largest group of factors has to do with the history of the software module, and includes factors that could be gleaned from examining various project archives. The second has to do with characteristics of the changes themselves, apart from the history of the modules.

4.1 Historical contextual factors

The volatility prediction factors that were most strongly suggested by the focus group participants all had to do with elements of the project history related to software modules. The first factor is related to developer interest, as evidenced by the topics of conversations that occur before the period of volatility. The second is a set of factors related to conditions under which the module was initially developed. The third has to do with the module's most recent level of activity.

4.1.1 Developer interest

The focus group participants stated that individual developer interest in particular code modules, usually expressed through emails or discussions or requests on the issue tracker, could be a predictor of volatility of a module. This predictor was mentioned more than any other specific factor during the focus group, as in *"...the other way to predict it is just by looking at what people are talking about on the developer mailing list."* It was pointed out that, since this is an OSS project, and the developers are generally users of the application, they choose changes to work on based on their own interests. Such changes must be *"either very useful or you have to need it personally. It may be just pure fun."* In contrast to commercial software, *"you can't really say that it's what the users want that drive it, it's really what the developer wants to work on."*

To illustrate this point, the focus group participants told a story. The area of the code they were talking about had *"been untouched for 10 years"* and was considered, at least by some developers, the *"best part and most stable part of [software name]"*. It had to do with the fonts used to render the output of the software. Since it was so stable and had been untouched for so long, one might think that it was going to remain so. However, a fairly new developer (not participating in the focus group) started discussing these fonts on the email list: *"After the first e-mail, or maybe the first two or three e-mails when it was clear he was serious, then I think we could predict he would keep on being serious about this and he would continue to make improvements."* The participants explained that, over the last few months, this developer had made numerous commits in this area, and so it had in fact become volatile. Further, they predicted it would continue to be since this developer had such an interest in it.

The participants also referred to instances where the interest of one developer "spread" to others. When two or more developers work together in an area, the rate of change increases even more because those developers use code change as a way of communicating about the change with each other.

4.1.2 Context of initial development

Various factors related to the initial development of a module were also cited in the focus group as indicators of future volatility. Some pieces of code were so difficult to get right in the first commit that they had to undergo a lot of change to finally perfect them. Some cases were described in this way: *"one of the initial commits to that module was bad, and needed a lot of bug fixing."* Another was more of a prototyping scenario: *"the initial implementation was done kind of as a prototype to get it working and as experience came along we realized that the architecture wasn't right and there needed to be a big shift in the architecture."*

This motivated a common pattern of development in which the initial version was created as a prototype and later modified excessively to suit the purpose. Further, new developers on this project were encouraged to split up their change into multiple small commits, each of which is reviewed and approved by more experienced developers. This pattern of small, highly iterative coding cycles also contributed to a module's apparent volatility.

Another factor that arose in the discussion was the inadequacy of the test suites that were sometimes developed along with a new module. When a module is introduced into the project, often it has errors in it that are not revealed by its associated test suite, thus delaying identification of the error, and in turn increasing volatility as the error is harder to remove. This implies that attributes of the initial test suite associated with a new module or function might serve as a predictor of future volatility.

This portion of the focus group discussion included a related conversation about the level of risk that is incurred with some of the development on this project. Participants described some commits or patches as a *"leap of faith"* if they were either not tested, or were tested and found to have some errors that were not fixed. While some participants felt that such risky commits should not be allowed, another argued that *"if you impose such a restriction, developing will get less fun and less experimental and you will ... possibly miss out on big radical changes. So there is a tradeoff between being prudent and making strict improvements or making big leaps and then try to clean up the mess afterwards."* Presumably, the *"clean up"* could be characterized as volatility.

4.1.3 Current level of activity

Two strong, but seemingly contradictory, findings emerged about whether current high level or low levels of activity in a module predict future volatility. First, the argument was made several times that areas of the code that had not been touched for some time were more likely than other areas to become volatile. Such untouched code could attract the interest of developers for several reasons. Participants explained that, because the software deals in large part with aesthetics (i.e. getting things to look good), many parts of the code undergo a lot of *"polishing"*. So developers, especially newcomers, are more likely to be able to find improvements to make among parts of the code base that had not been touched (i.e. *"polished"*) for some time. Further, such *"old"* code is less likely to have good associated regression test suites, and so working on them after a long time is likely to introduce errors that then go undetected for some time, and then require several tries to fix, resulting in more volatility.

On the other hand, one participant also stated that *"... if something becomes volatile then there is a more likely chance it will stay volatile."* While this seems contradictory to the point made by several participants that long-untouched code is more likely to exhibit volatility, this latter point makes sense as well. Volatile code does not tend to be volatile for only short periods of time.

These two observations lead to a potential pattern, or cycle, in which volatility occurs, at least in this project. The pattern is driven, at least in part, by developer interest, so it may be particular to OSS projects. First, a module or area of the code remains untouched for some time. In the context of this project,

that also meant that the capabilities implemented in this area of code, while entirely functional, may have become somewhat less aesthetically pleasing, at least in comparison to other parts of the code base that had undergone more recent improvement. That is, it became, by comparison, less "polished". So, at some point, a developer looking for something to work on (often a new developer looking for a way to contribute, or simply someone with no pending assignments) will notice this "unpolished" area, and start asking questions and sharing ideas with other developers. This generates some discussion among developers, and possibly interest in contributing to the changes as well. At some point, the discussion leads to actual changes in the code base, beginning the period of noticeable volatility. Changes lead to more changes, for many of the reasons discussed previously (inadequate regression test suites, code changes used as a form of communication, etc.), thus the period of volatility lasts for some time. Eventually, the volatility dies down, and the area of code remains untouched for some time, until its lack of polish again becomes noticeable and the cycle repeats itself.

4.2 Volatile changes

While most of the findings of the focus group were related to contextual and historical factors, as described in the previous section, there were a few interesting points made by the participants about factors that were related to the changes being made during volatile periods.

4.2.1 Modules at the intersection of multiple changes

One factor participants brought up, when asked what makes a particular module more volatile, was that increased volatility results when a module is at the intersection of several different changes made by different developers during the same period of time. This is further exacerbated when collisions between changes occur, which are more likely for bigger changes, with longer periods of time between commits. This would imply that modules with more dependencies with other modules, or which are more strongly coupled with other modules, are more likely to be volatile.

4.2.2 Non-code changes

The focus group participants related a story about a period of time in 2008 when there was a big push throughout the project to update all the documentation. Because they use the same source code management tool for code and documentation, the entire project would have appeared quite volatile during this period. Not only was this phenomenon not indicative of actual code volatility, it was actually pointing to the opposite phenomenon. In general, developers would only be motivated to do a major update to the documentation for code that is fairly stable and non-volatile.

5. CONCLUSIONS

We have described a small focus group study that was intended to explore factors in software maintenance that could predict areas of source code volatility. Our motivation for pursuing this line of research was that much of the current work in volatility prediction focuses on a fairly narrow set of variables (e.g., structural code characteristics, simple change characteristics) and we wanted to broaden the range of factors considered. Thus, we designed a very open-ended focus group study that was intended to capture, from the developers' point of view, any kind of potential indicator of volatility. A small group of developers from one open source project were convened to discuss their views on volatility (what it means, whether or not it's good or bad), how it might be predicted, what its impact is, and what steps could be taken to reduce volatility.

As hoped, our findings did reveal several potentially predictive factors that are not widely treated in prior literature. Most of these are related to the historical context of a module or area of code, and could be operationalized by defining metrics on historical development archives of various kinds. The new factors discovered are:

- The amount of discussion of the functional area represented by the module, among project developers. An increase in discussion of an area indicates that at least one developer is interested in making changes to that area, which in turn may lead to increased volatility.

- The degree to which the initial development of the function implemented in the module was risky, experimental, or a prototype. Initial commits of such functionality are often followed by a period of volatility.

- The quality of the test suite developed for the module when it is developed. Low test quality will result in defects that are introduced but not caught for some time. When they are finally caught and fixed, a period of volatility often follows.

- The experience level of the developer who initially developed the module. New developers are encouraged to develop new functionality in small, iterative cycles, with review from experience developers in between.

- The level of activity on the module in the recent past. Currently volatile modules will tend to remain so for some time, while modules that have seen no activity for some time are likely to become volatile.

- Documentation update. Modules will appear to be volatile during times when effort is being put into updating their documentation, possibly because they have become stable.

In addition, our findings support the continued examination of structural factors (e.g., coupling and dependencies of various kinds) and their role in predicting volatility. However, it should be noted that the evidence supporting these types of factors is far outweighed by the preponderance of evidence supporting historical and contextual factors.

It is clear that some of the factors we have discovered in this study are closely tied to the fact that the subject project was open source. Developer interest in a particular area would play much less of a role, one might assume, in a commercial project, for example. It is also clear that not all of these factors lead to volatility that is detrimental to the project. Encouraging new developers to engage in small, frequent commits to allow review by experienced developers is a good practice, at least for this project, and the resulting volatility is not always a negative outcome. Updating documentation, similarly, cannot be said to result in unwanted volatility.

By design, these potential factors are the opinions of the developers that participated in the study. Additional effort is required to validate them via other methods and determine how broadly applicable they may be. Also, not all factors are equally actionable. For example, a discussion of a module on a mailing list may be a valid predictor, but not afford an opportunity to reduce volatility. We intend to investigate these issues in future work.

The threats to external validity of this study are obvious and are related to its size and scope. There were only 4 participants from just one project in the focus group. The fact that the project was open source limits the applicability of some of the findings to closed source environments. We have attempted to limit the threats to construct and internal validity through careful design and implementation of the study plan. Multiple researchers were involved in each aspect of the study, including instrument design and coding. To validate the findings of the focus group with the participants, we emailed all the participants from our study asked them to comment on the findings. Two of the four members responded to our request. All but one finding were confirmed. One member felt that defects, and the resulting volatility, were not correlated with the size of the test suite for the module. One also emphasized that not all new work is preceded by a discussion on the mailing list.

This study contributes to research in prediction in software maintenance, i.e. prediction of volatility in general, and change- and defect-proneness in particular. We have gathered evidence justifying the investigation of several new factors in future prediction models, with the aim of further fine-tuning the predictability and manageability of the software maintenance process.

6. REFERENCES

[1] Acuna, S., Juristo, N. and Moreno, A. Emphasizing Human Capabilities in Software Development. *IEEE Software*, 23, 2 (March/April 2006), 94-101.

[2] Alshayeb, M. and Li, W. An empirical study of system design instability metric and design evolution in an agile software process. *Journal of Systems and Software*, 74, 3 (February 2005), 269-274. DOI=10.1016/j.jss.2004.02.002.

[3] Anda, B. C. D. Assessing Software System Maintainability using Structural Measures and Expert Assessments. In *Proceedings of the The 23rd International Conference on Software Maintenance (ICSM 2007)* (Paris, France, Oct. 2-5 2007). IEEE, Piscataway, N.J., 204-213.

[4] Andreasen, M. S., Nielsen, H. V., Schroder, S. O. and Stage, J. Usability in Open Source Software Development: Opinions and Practice. *Information Technology and Control*, 35, 3a (2006), 303-303.

[5] Basili, V. R. and Hutchens, D. H. An Empirical Study of a Syntactic Complexity Family. *IEEE Trans. on Software Engineering*, 9, 6 (1983), 664-672.

[6] Binkley, A. B. and Schach, S. R. Validation of the Coupling Dependency Metric as a Predictor of Run-Time Failures and Maintenance Measures. In *Proceedings of the International Conference on Software Engineering, ICSE'98* (Kyoto, Japan, April 1998). IEEE Computer Society, Los Alamitos, Calif., 452-455.

[7] Briand, L. C., Daly, J. W. and Wüst, J. K. A Unified Framework for Cohesion Measurement in Object-Oriented Systems. *Journal of Empirical Software Engineering*, 3, 1 (1998), 65-117. DOI=10.1023/A:1009783721306.

[8] Briand, L. C., Daly, J. W. and Wüst, J. K. A Unified Framework for Coupling Measurement in Object-Oriented Systems. *IEEE Trans. on Software Engineering*, 25, 1 (1999), 91-121.

[9] Cataldo, M., Mockus, A., Roberts, J. A. and Herbsleb, J. D. Software dependencies, work dependencies, and their impact on failures. *IEEE Transactions on Software Engineering*, 35, 6 (Nov.-Dec. 2009), 864-878.

[10] Chidamber, S. R. and Kemerer, C. F. A Metrics Suite for Object Oriented Design. *IEEE Trans. on Software Engineering*, 20, 6 (June 1994), 476-493.

[11] Crowston, K., Annabi, H. and Howison, J. Defining Open Source Software Project Success. In *Proceedings of the*

Twenty-Fourth annual International Conference on Information Systems (ICIS 2003) (Seattle, Washington 2003).

[12] Curtis, B., Krasner, H. and Iscoe, N. A Field Study of the Software Design Process for Large Systems. *Communications of the ACM*, 31, 11 (November 1988), 1268-1287. DOI=10.1145/50087.50089.

[13] Damian, D. Stakeholders in Global Requirements Engineering: Lessons Learned from Practice. *IEEE Software*, 24, 2 (March 2007), 21-27. DOI=10.1109/MS.2007.55.

[14] El Emam, K., Benlarbi, S., Goel, N. and Rai, S. N. The Confounding Effect of Class Size on the Validity of Object-Oriented Metrics. *IEEE Trans. on Software Engineering*, 27, 7 (July 2001), 630-650. DOI=10.1109/32.935855.

[15] Fenton, N. E. and Ohlsson, N. Quantitative Analysis of Faults and Failures in a Complex Software System. *IEEE Trans. on Software Engineering*, 26, 8 (August 2000), 797-814. DOI=10.1109/32.879815.

[16] Hassan, A. E. and Holt, R. C. The top ten list: dynamic fault prediction. In *Proceedings of the Proceedings of the 21st IEEE International Conference on Software Maintenance (ICSM'05)* (Budapest, Hungary, 25-30 Sept. 2005). IEEE Computer Society, Washtingon, DC, USA, 263-272. DOI=10.1109/ICSM.2005.91.

[17] Henry, S. and Kafura, D. Software Structure Metrics Based on Information Flow. *IEEE Trans. on Software Engineering*, 7, 5 (September 1981), 510-518. DOI=10.1109/TSE.1981.231113.

[18] Herraiz, I., Gonzalez-Barahona, J. M., Robles, G. and German, D. M. On the prediction of the evolution of libre software projects. In *Proceedings of the IEEE International Conference on Software Maintenance (ICSM 2007)* (Paris, 2-5 Oct. 2007), 405-414. DOI=10.1109/ICSM.2007.4362653.

[19] Kafura, D. and Henry, S. Software Quality Metrics Based on Interconnectivity. *Journal of Systems and Software*, 2, 2 (June 1981), 121-131. DOI=10.1016/0164-1212(81)90032-7.

[20] Kafura, D. and Reddy, G. R. The Use of Software Complexity Metrics in Software Maintenance. *IEEE Trans. on Software Engineering*, 13, 3 (March 1987), 335-343. DOI=10.1109/TSE.1987.233164.

[21] Kitchenham, B. A., Pickard, L. M. and Linkman, S. J. An evaluation of some design metrics. *Software Engineering Journal*, 5, 1 (January 1990), 50-58. DOI=10.1049/sej.1990.0007.

[22] Kontio, J., Lehtola, L. and Bragge, J. Using the focus group method in software engineering: obtaining practitioner and user experiences. In *Proceedings of the ISESE '04: 2004 International Symposium on Empirical Software Engineering* (Redondo Beach, California, 2004 2004). IEEE Computer Society, Los Alamitos, CA, 271 - 280.

[23] Koru, A. G. and Liu, H. Building effective defect-prediction models in practice. *IEEE Software*, 22, 6 (Nov.-Dec. 2005), 23-29. DOI=10.1109/MS.2005.149

[24] Koru, A. G. and Liu, H. Identifying and characterizing change-prone classes in two large-scale open-source products. *Journal of Systems and Software*, 80, 1 (Jan 2007), 63-73. DOI=10.1016/j.jss.2006.05.017.

[25] Koru, A. G. and Tian, J. An Empirical Comparison and Characterization of High Defect and High Complexity Modules. *Journal of Systems and Software*, 67, 3 (15 September 2003), 153-163. DOI=10.1016/S0164-1212(02)00126-7.

[26] Krueger, R. *Telephone Focus Groups*, (2011) Retrieved Feb. 09, 2011, From University of Minnesota: http://www.tc.umn.edu/~rkrueger/focus_tfg.html.

[27] Krueger, R. and Casey, M. A. *Focus groups : a practical guide for applied research*. Sage Publications, Thousand Oaks Calif., 2000.

[28] Li, W., Etzkorn, L. H., Davis, C. and Talburt, J. An Empirical Study of Design Evolution in an Object-Oriented System. *Information and Software Technology*, 42, 6 (April 2000), 373--381.

[29] Li, W. and Henry, S. Object-oriented metrics that predict maintainability. *Journal of Systems and Software*, 23, 2 (1993), 111-122.

[30] Long, J. Understanding the Role of Core Developers in Open Source Software Development. *Journal of Information, Information Technology, and Organizations*, 1 (2006), 75-85.

[31] Lorenz, M. and Kidd, J. *Object-oriented software metrics : a practical guide*. PTR Prentice Hall, Englewood Cliffs, NJ, 1994.

[32] Ltd, N. S. P. *Transcription Software. Foot Pedal Software Player*, (2011) Retrieved Nov. 2, 2011, From: http://www.nch.com.au/scribe/index.html.

[33] Miles, M. B. and Huberman, A. M. *Qualitative data analysis : an expanded sourcebook*. Sage Publications, Thousand Oaks, 1994.

[34] Mockus, A., Zhang, P. and Li, P. L. Predictors of Customer Perceived Software Quality. In *Proceedings of the 27th International Conference on Software Engineering (ICSE'05)* (St. Louis, USA 2005). ACM, New York, NY, USA, 225-233. DOI=DOI=10.1145/1062455.1062506.

[35] Nagappan, N. and Ball, T. Static Analysis Tools as Early Indicators of Pre-Release Defect Density. In *Proceedings of the 27th International Conference on Software Engineering (ICSE'05)* (St. Louis, USA 2005). ACM, 580-586. DOI=10.1145/1062455.1062558

[36] Nagappan, N. and Ball, T. Use of Relative Code Churn Measures to Predict System Defect Density. In *Proceedings of the 27th International Conference on Software Engineering (ICSE'05)* (St. Louis, USA 2005). ACM, New York, NY, USA, 284-292. DOI=10.1145/1062455.1062514.

[37] Nagappan, N., Murphy, B. and Basili, V. The influence of organizational structure on software quality. In *Proceedings of the ICSE'08: ACM/IEEE 30th Interntional Conference on Software Engineering* (Leipzig, Germany, 2008 2008). ACM, New York, N. Y., 521 -530. DOI=10.1145/1368088.1368160.

[38] Ostrand, T. J., Weyuker, E. J. and Bell, R. M. Predicting the location and number of faults in large software systems. *IEEE Trans. on Software Engineering*, 31, 4 (April 2005), 340-355. DOI=10.1109/TSE.2005.49.

[39] Ostrand, T. J., Weyuker, E. J. and Bell, R. M. Programmer-based fault prediction. In *Proceedings of the 6th International Conference on Predictive Models in Software Engineering* (Timisoara, Romania 2010). ACM, New York, NY, USA, 1-10. DOI=10.1145/1868328.1868357.

[40] PamConsult Gmb, H. *Welcome - Pamela for Skype*, (2011) Retrieved Nov. 1, 2011, From: http://www.pamela.biz/en/.

[41] Perry, D. E., Staudenmayer, N. A. and Votta, L. G. People, Organizations, and Process Improvement. *IEEE Software*, 11, 4 (July 1994), 36-45. DOI=10.1109/52.300082.

[42] Porter, A. A. and Selby, R. W. Empirically Guided Software Development Using Metric-Based Classification Trees. *IEEE Software*, 7, 2 (March 1990), 46-54. DOI=10.1109/52.50773.

[43] Posnett, D., Bird, C. and Dévanbu, P. An empirical study on the influence of pattern roles on change-proneness. *Empirical Software Engineering*, 16, 3 (June 2011), 396-423. DOI=10.1007/s10664-010-9148-2.

[44] Rahman, F. and Devanbu, P. Ownership, experience and defects: a fine-grained study of authorship. In *Proceedings of the 33rd International Conference on Software Engineering (ICSE '11)* (Waikiki, Honolulu, HI, USA, 21-28 May 2011). ACM, New York, NY, USA, 491-500. DOI=10.1145/1985793.1985860.

[45] Roden, P. L., Virani, S., Etzkorn, L. H. and Messimer, S. An Empirical Study of the Relationship of Stability Metrics and the QMOOD Quality Models Over Software Developed Using Highly Iterative or Agile Software Processes. In *Proceedings of the Seventh IEEE International Working Conference on Source Code Analysis and Manipulation (SCAM '07)* (Paris, France, 30 Sept. - 1 Oct. 2007). IEEE Computer Society, Washington, DC, USA, 171-179. DOI=10.1109/SCAM.2007.2

[46] Shepperd, M. and Ince, D. *Derivation and Validation of Software Metrics.* Clarendon Press - Oxford, Oxford University Press, Walton Street, Oxford OX2 6DP, 1993.

[47] Skype *Free Skype internet calls and cheap calls to phones online,* (2012) Retrieved Nov. 1, 2011, From: http://www.skype.com/.

[48] Tian, J. and Troster, J. A Comparison of Measurement and Defect Characteristics of New and Legacy Software Systems. *Journal of Systems and Software,* 44, 2 (December 1998), 135-146. DOI=10.1016/S0164-1212(98)10050-X.

[49] Time and Date, A. S. *Event Time Announcer – setup,* (2011) Retrieved Sept. 30, 2011, From: http://www.timeanddate.com/worldclock/fixedform.html.

[50] Vasa, R., Schneider, J. G. and Nierstrasz, O. The Inevitable Stability of Software Change. In *Proceedings of the IEEE International Conference on Software Maintenance (ICSM '07)* (Paris, France, 2-5 Oct. 2007), 4-13. DOI=10.1109/ICSM.2007.4362613.

[51] Vivanco, R. and Jin, D. Improving predictive models of cognitive complexity using an evolutionary computational approach: a case study. In *Proceedings of the 2007 conference of the center for advanced studies on Collaborative research (CASCON '07)* (Richmond Hill, Ontario, Canada 2007). ACM, New York, NY, USA, 109-123. DOI=10.1145/1321211.1321223.

[52] Weyuker, E. J., Ostrand, T. J. and Bell, R. M. Adapting a Fault Prediction Model to Allow Widespread Usage. In *Proceedings of the International Workshop on Predictor Models in Software Engineering (PROMISE 2006)* (Philadelphia, PA 2006).

[53] Weyuker, E. J., Ostrand, T. J. and Bell, R. M. Using Developer Information as a Factor for Fault Prediction. In *Proceedings of the PROMISE 07: Predictive Models in Software Engineering* (Minneapolis, MN, 20-26 May 2007), 8. DOI=10.1109/PROMISE.2007.14

[54] Wolf, T., Schroeter, A., Damian, D. and Nguyen, T. Predicting build failures using social network analysis on developer communication. In *Proceedings of the 31st International Conference on Software Engineering* (Vancouver, BC, Canada, 16-24 May 2009). DOI=10.1109/ICSE.2009.5070503

Appendix A: Focus group guide

Est. Time	Questions
0	(Record starting time, participant list, any problems starting)
+5 5	<Start the call. Review purpose of the study and their participation.> *Our names are <Names>. We are with the UMBC Information Systems department. Thank you all again for taking time to help us with our research effort.* *Let me just quickly review who we have on the call. We have <list the participants>. Can everyone hear everyone else OK? (Verify everyone says yes. Verify we have a consent form from everyone on the call.)* *As you know, we are looking at some software development issues and we think that your experience can help us. Before we start I wanted to repeat that your participation is voluntary and you can quit at any time. Of course anything you say is known to the others in on the call, but we will keep your comments confidential. We won't attribute anything you say to you by name or to the project.* *We would like to record this meeting so we don't have to rely entirely on our written notes. We are the only ones that will have access to the recording. Anyone can ask us to stop recording at any time. Do you mind if we start recording?*
+1 6	<Introduce the rules of the focus group.> *Thanks. The purpose of this meeting is really to develop new ideas and insights. We aren't trying to figure out which ideas are right or wrong, but to just get the ideas out in the open. We don't have to agree. We hope to have a good discussion with input from everyone.* *I will also try to be respectful of your time. If we seem to be spending too much time in one area I'll ask that we move on to make sure we cover the planned topics without running over time.* *Any questions?*
+1 7	<Provide needed background.> *Before I start with the first question, I wanted to quickly review some of the topics we are studying. The focus of this research is "highly volatile software modules". By "software module" we mean a class in an object oriented language, or a source file in a procedural language. By "highly volatile" we are talking about modules that are changed much more frequently than other modules in the same program. We are looking at the history of software modules and whether there are patterns that may predict volatility. We are considering anything about the change history that might tell you something such as the technology used, the reason for the change, the people,*

	and what may influence them. *Just to review then, we are looking for anything about the changes to the software that may predict a high frequency of future changes.* *Ok, but before we get there, I wanted to find out a bit more about you and the project..*
+3 10	1. <Basic, factual question to get people talking.> *To start, could everyone tell me briefly about your current role in the project?<Participant 1>, would you start?* (Record participant, dates, activities, roles) 1.1. (Repeat for each participant)

+10
20
	2. <Introduction; try to set mental context for discussion>
	Let's say I tell you about two modules from your project. They are about the same size. But the change log for the first one is many times the size of the second one. If that is all I told you about the two modules, what other differences would you infer?
	(Record variety of potential differences and how they manifest as change differences.)
	   1.1. <Probes:>
	      1.1.1. *How does that relate to (more/fewer) changes?*
	      1.1.2. *Would it tell you anything about the age of the modules?*
	      1.1.3. *Would it tell you anything about the code itself?*
	      1.1.4. *Would it tell you anything about programmer(s)?*
	      1.1.5. *Would it tell you anything about the design?*
	      1.1.6. *Would it tell you anything about the types of features implemented?*
	      1.1.7. *Would it tell you anything about process to make the changes?*
	   1.2. <If they can't identify differences>
	What other information, combined with the quantity of changes, would be revealing?
	(Record other information necessary.)

+10 30	3. <Problem identification> *In these examples of high volatility modules we've talked about, is this volatility a problem?* (Record discriminators, good vs. bad, consequences.)

	1.3. <Probes:>
	      1.3.1. *What issues does <that problem> lead to?*
	      1.3.2. *Who is affected by <that problem>?*
	      1.3.3. *What does <that problem> cost? Who pays for it?*
	      1.3.4. *Is <that problem> always a problem? What makes the difference?*

+10
40
	4. <Explore changes.>
	So far we have looked at cases where we already know the module is volatile. Let's look to the future. What kinds of changes might predict future volatility in a module?
	(Record changes, change characteristics, relationships, any correlation or causation.)
	   1.4. <Probes:>
	      1.4.1. *How might the complexity of the change predict volatility?*
	      1.4.2. *How might the people involved in the change predict volatility?*
	      1.4.3. *How might the organizations involved in the change predict volatility?*
	      1.4.4. *How might the process followed predict volatility?*
	      1.4.5. *How might time pressure predict volatility?*

+10 50	5. <Practices and influences on volatility.> *If I asked you to reduce the volatility of a module in the project, what would you change?* (Record the practices, the changes, and the reasons for the changes.)
+10 60	6. <Closing, identify significant characteristics.> *Thinking about everything we have talked about, what do you think might be the most reliable predictor of volatility in a module?<Participant 1>?* (Repeat for each participant)
+2 67	*Ok, I think this is all we have time for. This has been a very interesting discussion.* *Thank you again for taking the time to help us with this research. If you have a question or something comes up, don't hesitate to send us an e-mail.* *Goodbye.* (Record the time. Wait for all callers to exit.)

Predicting Defect Numbers Based on Defect State Transition Models

Jue Wang and Hongyu Zhang

School of Software, Tsinghua University
Tsinghua National Laboratory for Information Science and Technology (TNList)
Beijing 100084, China
cecilia.juewang@gmail.com, hongyu@tsinghua.edu.cn

ABSTRACT

During software maintenance, a large number of defects could be discovered and reported. A defect can enter many states during its lifecycle, such as NEW, ASSIGNED, and RESOLVED. The ability to predict the number of defects at each state can help project teams better evaluate and plan maintenance activities. In this paper, we present BugStates, a method for predicting defect numbers at each state based on defect state transition models. In our method, we first construct defect state transition models using historical data. We then derive a stability metric from the transition models to measure a project's defect-fixing performance. For projects with stable defect-fixing performance, we show that we can apply Markovian method to predict the number of defects at each state in future based on the state transition model. We evaluate the effectiveness of BugStates using six open source projects and the results are promising. For example, when predicting defect numbers at each state in December 2010 using data from July 2009 to June 2010, the absolute errors for all projects are less than 28. In general, BugStates also outperforms other related methods.

Categories and Subject Descriptors

D.2.8 [**Software Engineering**]: Metrics – *performance measures, process metrics, product metrics*. D.2.9 [**Software Engineering**]: Management – *software quality assurance (SQA)*

General Terms

Measurement, Reliability, Management

Keywords

defect state transitions, defect prediction, defect numbers, defect-fixing performance, Markov models

1. INTRODUCTION

For a large and evolving software system, the project team could receive defect reports over a long period of time. After a defect report is received and confirmed, a defect begins its lifecycle. A typical life cycle of a defect includes many states such as New, Resolved, and Closed. A defect can transfer from one state to an allowable state once it is handled by developers. Currently, the defect state transition process is often recorded and tracked by bug tracking systems such as Bugzilla and Jira.

We believe it is important to understand the defect state transition process as it records the defect-fixing activities of a project team. The number of defects transferring from one state to the other actually reflects the team's defect-fixing performance. By analyzing defect state transitions we can estimate the stability of a team's defect-fixing performance over time.

For projects that have stable defect-fixing performance, it is desirable to predict the distribution/number of defects at each state in future based on the project teams' past defect-fixing performance. For example, we can predict the number of defects that will remain unresolved and the number of defects that will be resolved in the next six months. Such information can help a project team better estimate software maintenance effort and allocate limited resources.

In this paper, we present BugStates, a method for predicting defect numbers at each state. In BugStates, we represent defect state transition processes as Markov-like models, specifically, the Discrete-Time Markov Chain (DTMC) model. Based on historical state transition data, we can calculate the likelihood of the occurrence of each transition and construct state transition models. We derive a metric from defect state transitions to measure the stability of a project team's defect-fixing performance. For teams that have stable defect-fixing performance, we apply Markovian method to predict the number of defects at each state based on the assumption that past defect-fixing performance can be used to predict future performance.

To evaluate the proposed BugStates approach, we perform experiments on six open source projects, including four major Eclipse projects (PDE.Build, JDT.Text JDT.UI and Platform.Debug), as well as the Lucene and Spring.NET projects. We collect their state transition data by mining the defect activity logs maintained by Bugzilla or Jira, and then construct Markov-like models. For the projects that exhibit stable defect-fixing performance, we predict the number of defects at each state in the next six months based on the models constructed using the past twelve months' data. For example, when predicting defect numbers at each state in December 2010 using data from July 2009 to June 2010, the absolute errors for all projects are between 0 and 28, which are relatively small comparing to the actual number of defects (0 to 547). Furthermore, our evaluation results show that the BugStates outperforms three other methods (arithmetic mean, G-O model and quadratic polynomial methods).

In recent years, many researchers have mined bug databases for defect prediction [13, 24, 26], bug triage [9], effort prediction [12, 19], etc. To our best knowledge, modeling and predicting defect state transition have not received enough attention. Our work dedicates to this topic and makes the following contributions:

- We show that we can measure the stability of the project team's defect-fixing performance by analyzing the data derived from a defect state transition model.

- We show that we can predict defect numbers at each state based on a state transition model constructed using the historical data.

We believe that BugStates can help project teams improve maintenance process and project management. The rest of the paper is organized as follows. Section 2 briefly introduces the background about defect state transitions and the Markovian method. Section 3 presents the proposed BugStates approach for modeling and predicting defect numbers at each state. Section 4 describes our experiments and results. Section 5 analyzes the threats to validity. Section 6 briefly describes related work and Section 7 concludes this paper.

2. BACKGROUND

2.1 Defect State Transitions

Currently, defects are often recorded and managed by bug tracking systems such as Bugzilla [3] and Jira [10]. Figure 1 shows the defect state transition process supported by Bugzilla [3]. The defect state transition process describes a defect's life cycle. All the major transitions are as follows. Once a defect is reported, if nobody has confirmed that the problem is real, the defect's status is UNCONFIRMED. If the defect is confirmed, a defect record is created and its status is set to NEW. A defect's state can be changed from NEW to ASSIGNED when the defect is assigned to a developer, and then to RESOLVED after the developer has resolved the defect. Once a defect fix is verified by a QA personnel, the defect enters the state VERIFIED and will be subsequently CLOSED. If the defect is not fixed successfully, the defect will be REOPENED and may enter other states again. The defect state transitions described above are probabilistic as a defect can enter any allowable state and independent from the earlier states that the defect entered before.

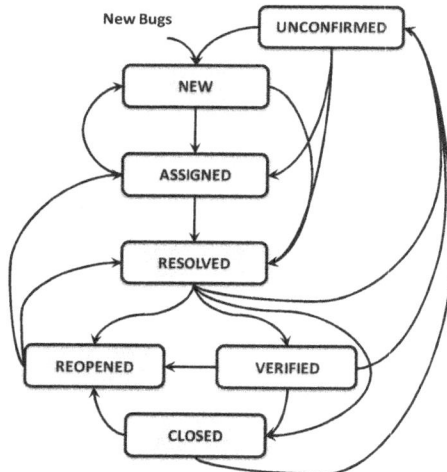

Figure 1. The defect state transition process of Bugzilla

Figure 2 shows the default state transition process supported by Jira [10], which is another widely-used bug tracking system. Unlike Bugzilla, there is no VERIFIED state in Jira. The NEW and ASSIGNED states are replaced by the OPEN and IN PROGRESS states, respectively. The other states remain the same with Bugzilla.

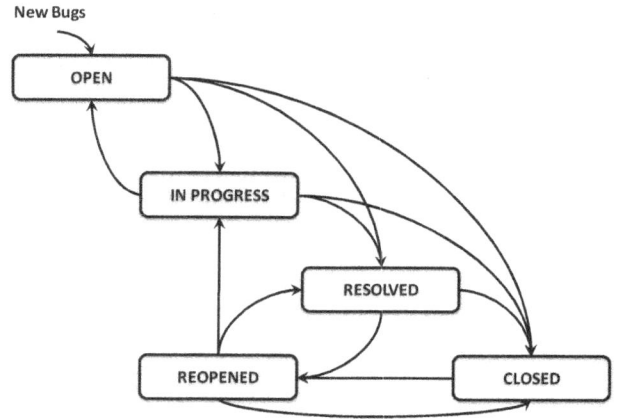

Figure 2. The default defect state transition process of Jira

2.2 Markovian Method

A Markov model is for modeling stochastic process with the property that the next state depends only on the current state [2, 11]. In this work, we consider discrete-time stochastic process and adopt the Discrete Time Markov Chain (DTMC) model. Formally, considering a stochastic process $X_1, X_2, X_3, \ldots, X_n$, where X_t is a random variable denoting the state of the process at discrete time t ($t = 0, 1, 2 \ldots$), the process is a Markov chain if the following property holds:

$$Pr(X_{n+1} = x | X_1 = x_1, X_2 = x_2 \ldots, X_n = x_n)$$
$$= Pr(X_{n+1} = x | X_n = x_n). \quad (1)$$

For a Markov model, its transition probability matrix P is defined as follows:

$$P = \begin{pmatrix} p_{11} p_{12} \cdots p_{1,x-1} p_{1,x} \\ p_{21} p_{22} \cdots p_{2,x-1} p_{2,x} \\ \cdot \\ \cdot \\ \cdot \\ p_{x,1} p_{x,2} \cdots p_{x,x-1} p_{x,x} \end{pmatrix} \quad (2)$$

where p_{ij} represents the probability from x_i to x_j. Then we have:

$$\alpha_{t+1} = P \cdot \alpha_t , \quad (3)$$

where α_t represents the state probability vector at time t, $\alpha_t(i) = Pr(X_t = i)$, α_{t+1} represents the state probability vector at time $t+1$.

In order to apply the Markovian method, a process must satisfy the property that the next state depends only on the current state. In software defect state transitions, a defect's state is changed by a developer when a certain defect-fixing action is completed. The defect's next state depends on its current state, not its previous states. Furthermore, a defect's next state cannot be known deterministically in advance. Therefore, the defect state transition process can be represented using Markov-like models (we use the term "Markov-like" as we did not rigorously prove that all defect state transition processes always hold the Markov property).

3. THE PROPOSED METHOD: BUGSTATES

3.1 Overall Structure

During software evolution new features could be added to the system and new defects could be reported to the project team. In this section we introduce the proposed BugStates method for measuring defect state transitions and predicting future defect numbers. Figure 3 shows the overall structure of BugStates. We first mine the historical defect records to obtain the state transition data. We then use the obtained data to construct defect state transition models. We measure the stability of defect-fixing performance using a distance metric derived from the transition model. If the defect-fixing performance is stable, we apply the Markovian method to predict distribution of defects among states at a future time. Based on the historical defect data we can also construct defect growth models and predict the total number of defects at a future time. Having estimated the defect distributions and the total numbers, we can then predict the number of defects at each state in future.

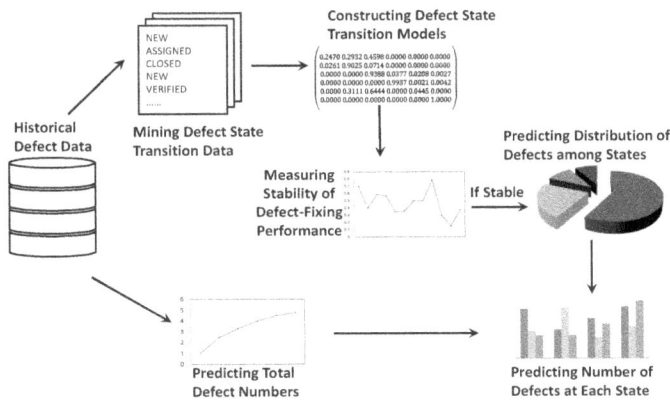

Figure 3. The overall structure of BugStates

3.2 Mining Defect State Transition Data

Typical defect tracking systems, such as BugZilla and Jira maintain an activity log for each defect. An activity log includes information such as a defect's previous states, current state, state change time, and developers assigned to this defect. Defect state transition data can be collected by mining the activity logs.

Table 1 gives an example of the activity logs for JDT.UI defect #280333, which is maintained by Eclipse Bugzilla. The bold lines mark the transitions of the defect's state. From the table we know that the defect is created at 07:40 on June 16, 2009, resolved as "Won't Fix" at 9:27 on the same day, re-opened on June 22, 2009, fixed on August 3, 2009, verified on August 6, 2009 and finally closed on August 10, 2009.

Table 2 gives an example of the activity logs for Lucene-Java defect #2060, which is maintained by Jira. The bold lines mark the transitions of the defect's state. The defect is resolved as "Fixed" on November 14, 2009 and closed on November 25, 2009. However, it was re-opened on May 30, 2010 and eventually closed on June 18, 2010.

To construct a defect state transition model, we collect data by analyzing activity logs (such as the ones shown in Table 1 and Table 2). In the bug tracking systems, these activity logs are typically presented as HTML pages. By crawling and parsing these HTML pages we can extract the state transition information for each

defect. We then count the number of defects at each state at each month, and calculate the probability of a defect transiting from one state to the other state, thus obtaining the defect state transition data.

Table 1. The activity log of defect #280333[1] for Eclipse JDT.UI

Who	When	What	Removed	Added
pwebs-ter	2009-06-16 07:40:50	CC		pwebs-ter
markus_keller	2009-06-16 09:27:01	CC		markus_keller
		Status	**NEW**	**RESOLVED**
		Resolution		WONTFIX
paules	2009-06-22 12:09:30	**Status**	**RESOLVED**	**REOPENED**
		Resolution	WONTFIX	
daniel_megert	2009-06-23 02:30:39	**Status**	**REOPENED**	**NEW**
		...	...	...
markus_keller	2009-08-03 07:59:13	**Status**	**NEW**	**RESOLVED**
		Resolution		FIXED
daniel_megert	2009-08-06 03:26:16	**Status**	**RESOLVED**	**VERIFIED**
paules	2009-08-10 08:24:07	**Status**	**VERIFIED**	**CLOSED**

Table 2. The activity log of defect #2060[2] for Lucene-Java

Michael McCandless made changes – 14/Nov/09 11:22		
Field	Original Value	New Value
Status	**Open**	**Resolved** (Resolution Fixed)
Uwe Schindler made changes – 25/Nov/09 16:47		
Status	**Resolved**	**Closed**
Michael McCandless made changes – 30/May/10 12:40		
Status	**Closed**	**Reopened**
...		
Uwe Schindler made changes – 18/Jun/10 08:03		
Status	**Resolved**	**Closed**

3.3 Constructing Defect State Transition Models

In defect state transition graphs such as the ones shown in Figure 1 and Figure 2, a defect's next state is only dependent on its current state. Therefore, the state transition process can be treated as a Markov-like model (more specifically, the DTMC model). Figure 4 describes the mapping from a Bugzilla defect state transition graph to a Markov-like model. In the mapping, each defect state is translated into a state labeled with a sequential number. Each arrow linking two states has a transitional probability from the start state to the destination state. Moreover, for each state in the Markov-like

---

[1]https://bugs.eclipse.org/bugs/show_bug.cgi?id=280333
[2]https://issues.apache.org/jira/browse/LUCENE-2060

model we add an arrow pointing to itself as a defect could remain in the same state at the next time interval. Note that in our method we only consider confirmed bugs (for our experimental subjects like Eclipse, all known bugs are confirmed bugs), therefore, for conciseness, we do not consider the UNCONFIRMED state in Figure 4.

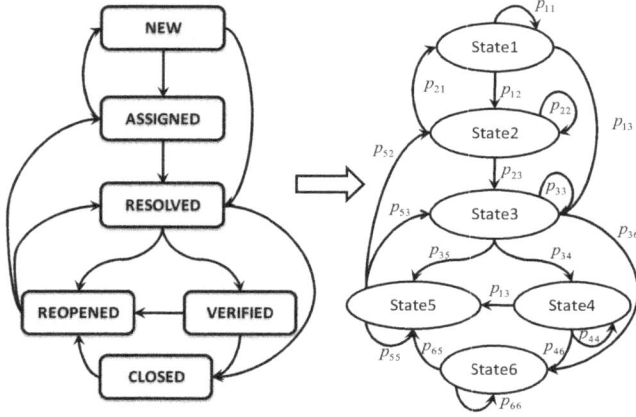

Figure 4. Mapping from Bugzilla defect state transition graph to Markov-like model

For the model shown in Figure 4, we can obtain the state transition probability matrix as follows:

$$P = (p_{ij}), \quad 1 \leq i \leq 6, 1 \leq j \leq 6, \quad (4)$$

where p_{ij} represents the probability from defect state i to state j, e.g. p_{13} represents the probability of a defect transferring from NEW to RESOLVED. Similarly, we can construct Markov-like models for Jira's defect state transition process.

3.4 Measuring the Stability of Defect-Fixing Performance

We derive a metric from the defect state transition matrix to measure the stability of a team's defect-fixing performance. Projects having stable defect-fixing performance should exhibit similar defect state transition matrix over time, while unstable defect-fixing performance would lead to large variances in defect state transitions.

To measure the stability of a project's defect-fixing performance over a time period, we first compute the defect state transition matrix that represents the project's average performance during the period. Then, we calculate the Euclidean distance between the current defect state transition matrix and the average defect state transition matrix. Formally, let P_m denote transition matrix in month m in a period T, and P_a denotes the average transition matrix during T, we calculate distance D between P_m and P_a by computing the average Euclidean distance for all the states as follows:

$$D = \frac{\sum_{i=1}^{n} \sqrt{\sum_{j=1}^{n} (p_{mij} - p_{aij})^2}}{n}, \quad (5)$$

where n is the number of states. We also use $D_{average}$ to represent the average D value during a time period T.

$$D_{average} = (\sum_{m=1}^{T} D_m)/T \quad (6)$$

The $D_{average}$ distance value is between 0 and 1, with a lower value indicating a more stable process. If $D_{average}$ exceeds a predefined

distance threshold (such as 0.25), we consider the defect-fixing performance instable. The actual threshold value can be specified by each individual team.

3.5 Predicting Defects Numbers at Each State

For a project that has stable defect-fixing performance, we can predict its future defect state transitions based on its current performance. Such ability can help the project team better estimate software maintenance efforts and plan the quality assurance resources.

To achieve the prediction, we utilize the characteristic of Markov model as given in Equation 3. Basically, we can predict the future defect state transitions based on the initial states and the state transition matrix. Our method consists of the following steps:

1) Predicting the distribution of defect among states

2) Predicting the number of defects at each state

3.5.1 Predicting the Distribution of Defects among States

We first gather statistics of the number of the defects at each state at an initial time t, we then compute the distribution of defects among the states (i.e., the state probability vector). For example, for Bugzilla, we define the number of defects in NEW, ASSIGNED, RESOLVED, VERIFIED, REOPEN, and CLOSED as n_1, n_2, n_3, n_4, n_5, and n_6, respectively. Then the sum of the defects is $S = \sum_{n=1}^{6} n_i$, and the state probability vector at time t is:

$$\alpha_t = (^{n_1}/_S, ^{n_2}/_S, ^{n_3}/_S, ^{n_4}/_S, ^{n_5}/_S, ^{n_6}/_S). \quad (7)$$

According to the Equation 3, we can infer the distribution of defects across the states at time $t+N$ as follows:

$$\alpha_{t+N} = P^N \cdot \alpha_t. \quad (8)$$

Equation 8 allows us to obtain the probability of defects at each state at a future time $t+N$.

3.5.2 Predicting the Number of Defects at Each State

Equation 8 only gives the probability of defects staying at a state. To estimate the number of defects at each state at a future time, we need to predict the total number of defects. Following typical software reliability engineering methods [15, 17], we can depict the growth of cumulative defect numbers based on historical data, apply non-linear regression analysis to fit the defect growth curve, and then use the fitted regression model to predict the number of newly reported defects at time $t+1$. More specifically, we treat the defect data as a time series:

$$f(1), f(2), \dots, f(t), \dots, \quad (9)$$

where $f(t)$ represents the number of defects at month t. The cumulative number of defects can be also represented as a series, which describes the growth of defects over time:

$$f(1), f(1) + f(2), \dots, \sum_{i=1}^{t} f(i) \quad (10)$$

In this research, we adopt the Goel-Okumoto (G-O) model [8, 17] to describe the growth of defect numbers over time. The G-O model is one of the commonly-used software reliability growth models, which is defined as follows:

$$m_t = a(1 - e^{-bt}), \quad (11)$$

where t represents the time (in month), m is the number of cumulative defects at time t, a and b are coefficients. We should note that our method does not depend on the G-O model. Other reliability growth models can be also integrated into our approach.

Having estimated the defect state probability vector α_{t+N} and the total number of defects m_{t+N} at time $t+N$, we can then predict the number of defects at each state as follows:

$$M_{t+N} = m_{t+N} \cdot \alpha_{t+N}, \qquad (12)$$

M_{t+N} is the vector representing the number of defects at each state at time $t+N$.

4. EXPERIMENTS
4.1 Subjects
To evaluate the proposed BugStates method, we perform experiments on six open source projects (Table 3), including four major Eclipse projects (PDE.Build, JDT.Text JDT.UI and Platform.Debug), as well as the Lucene-Java.Index and Spring.NET projects. The four Eclipse projects use Bugzilla as their bug tracking system. The other two projects use Jira. All these projects have evolved over a long period. In this experiment, we only consider defects reported from January 1, 2009 to December 31, 2010.

Table 3. The projects studied

Project	Description	Defects Reported in 2009	Defects Reported in 2010
PDE.Build[3]	build support for Java	227	139
JDT.Text[4]	Java editing support	248	235
JDT.UI[5]	user interface for the Eclipse Java IDE	663	472
Platform. Debug[6]	debug support for Eclipse platform	348	231
Lucene-Java.Index[7]	the index component of the Apache Java search engine	47	65
Spring.NET[8]	a port and extension of the Java based Spring Framework for .NET	66	39

4.2 Constructing Defect State Transition Models

For each defect in each project, we collect its state transition data by mining its activity log stored in the Eclipse Bugzilla[9] and Jira bug databases[10].To automatically extract the defect state transition information from an activity log, we developed a tool that can automatically grab the web page of the activity log, parse it and extract transition information between every two defect states. If a defect's state is not changed within a month, it has a transition to itself (staying at the same state). The tool counts the number of

---

[3]http://www.eclipse.org/pde/pde-build/
[4]http://www.eclipse.org/eclipse/platform-text/index.php
[5]http://www.eclipse.org/jdt/ui/index.php
[6]http://www.eclipse.org/eclipse/debug/index.php
[7]http://lucene.apache.org/java/docs/index.html
[8]http://www.springframework.net/
[9]https://bugs.eclipse.org/bugs/
[10]http://issues.apache.org/jira, http://jira.springsource.org

state transitions for each defect in each month in 2009 and then computes the total transitions in a year.

Having collected the state transition data, we then calculate the transition probability matrix P and construct a state transition model for the project. As an example, the transition matrix for the JDT.UI project ($P_{JDT.UI}$) for year 2009 is given below. The probabilities of some major transitions are as follows:

- From New to New: 24.70%,
- From New to Assigned: 29.32%
- From Assigned to Resolved: 7.14%
- From Resolved to Reopen: 2.08%.
- From Resolved to Verified: 3.77%

$$P_{JDT.UI} = \begin{pmatrix} 0.2470 & 0.2932 & 0.4598 & 0.0000 & 0.0000 & 0.0000 \\ 0.0261 & 0.9025 & 0.0714 & 0.0000 & 0.0000 & 0.0000 \\ 0.0000 & 0.0000 & 0.9388 & 0.0377 & 0.0208 & 0.0027 \\ 0.0000 & 0.0000 & 0.0000 & 0.9937 & 0.0021 & 0.0042 \\ 0.0000 & 0.3111 & 0.6444 & 0.0000 & 0.0445 & 0.0000 \\ 0.0000 & 0.0000 & 0.0000 & 0.0000 & 0.0000 & 1.0000 \end{pmatrix}$$

(NEW ASSI. RESO. VERI. REOP. CLOSED)

4.3 Measuring Stability of Defect-Fixing Performance
For the projects studied, we apply the method described in Section 3.4 to measure the stability of a project team's defect-fixing performance.

We measure the Euclidean distances between each month in 2009 (P_m) and the average value of 2009 (P_a). Figure 5 shows the distance values D for all the projects from January 2009 to December 2009. For the Lucene-Java.Index project, its distance values vary between 0.150 and 0.787, while for other projects, the distance values vary between 0.006 and 0.393. Clearly, the performance of Lucene-Java.Index project is less stable than the other projects.

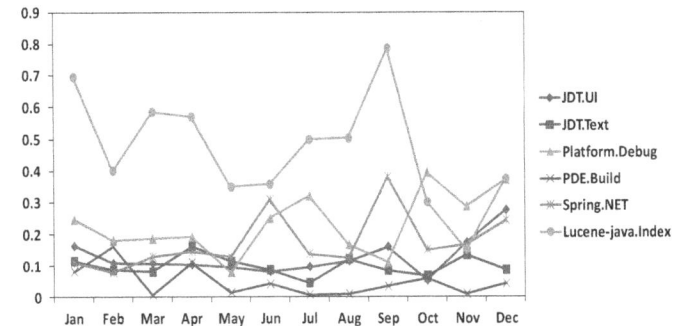

Figure 5. The Euclidean distances D for all projects in 2009

For JDT.UI, JDT.Text, PDE.Build, Platform.Debug, Spring.NET and Lucene-Java.Index, the computed average distance value $D_{average}$ in 2009 (12 months) is 0.127, 0.098, 0.048, 0.231, 0.175 and 0.464, respectively. We set the distance threshold as 0.25 in our experiments.

For all projects except Lucene-Java.Index, the $D_{average}$ value is below the distance threshold. Therefore, we consider the defect-fixing performance of these projects stable. The $D_{average}$ for the

Lucene-Java.Index project is 0.464, which is above the distance threshold and its defect-fixing performance is considered unstable.

4.4 Predicting Defect State Transitions

In this section, we evaluate the effectiveness of BugStates for predicting the number of defects at each state, on the projects that exhibit stable defect-fixing performance. We design the following experiments:

- *Experiment A:* Construct a state transition model using data from January 2009 to December 2009, and then use the model to predict the number of defects at each state from January 2010 to June 2010.

- *Experiment B:* Construct a state transition model using data from July 2009 to June 2010, and then use the model to predict the number of defects at each state from July 2010 to December 2010.

Basically, the above experiments use past twelve months' data to construct a Markov-like model, and then use this model to predict the number of defect at each state in the next six months.

To evaluate the accuracy of the predictions, we use the metrics AE (absolute error) and MAE (mean absolute error). AE is defined as the absolute prediction error $|y-y'|$, where y and y' are the actual value and its estimate, respectively. MAE is the average absolute prediction errors over the dataset:

$$AE = |y-y'|, \quad MAE = \frac{\sum_{i=1}^{n} AE}{n} \quad (13)$$

where n is the number of data points (in our experiments, n is the number of months being estimated). The smaller the MAE value the better the estimation.

4.4.1 Predicting the Distribution of Defects among States

Following the method described in Section 3.5, for projects having stable defect-fixing performance (all projects except Lucene-Java.Index), we predict the future distribution of defects among the states (a_{t+N}) based on the transition matrix (P) and the initial defect distribution (a_t).

In Experiment A, we first calculate the percentage of defects at each state at the end of December 31, 2009. These percentage values form the initial defect distribution vector. As an example, for the JDT.UI project, 7.99% of the defects at the end of 2009 are in the NEW state, 21.57% of the defects are in state ASSIGNED, and 51.89% of the defects are RESOLVED. The initial defect distribution vectors for all projects are given below.

	NEW	ASSI.	RESO.	VERI.	REOP.	CLOS.
PDE.Build	(0.3744	0.0044	0.5991	0.0088	0.0000	0.0132)
JDT.UI	(0.0799	0.2157	0.5189	0.1237	0.0015	0.0603)
JDT.Text	(0.0363	0.2472	0.4960	0.1250	0.0040	0.0645)
Platform. Debug	(0.3420	0.0344	0.2414	0.3420	0.0115	0.0287)
Spring.NET	(0.4394	0.0303	0.5152	N/A	0.0000	0.0152)

Having obtained the transition matrix P and the initial defect distribution vector a_t, we can then predict the future defect distributions by following the Equation 8. As an example, the resulting distributions of defects at the end of June 2010 are as follows:

	NEW	ASSI.	RESO.	VERI.	REOP.	CLOS.
PDE.Build	(0.2792	0.0071	0.6643	0.0106	0.0000	0.0389)
JDT.UI	(0.0152	0.1967	0.5034	0.1751	0.0108	0.0988)
JDT.Text	(0.0093	0.2437	0.4506	0.1742	0.0132	0.1090)
Platform. Debug	(0.2340	0.0289	0.2525	0.4040	0.0176	0.0630)
Spring.NET	(0.3238	0.0697	0.5220	N/A	0.0121	0.0723)

The above results show the predicted distributions of defects at each state on June 30, 2010. For example, for the JDT.UI project, 1.52% defects are at the NEW state, 19.67% defects are assigned, 50.34% are resolved and 9.88% are closed. Actually, on June 30, 2010, there are 3.10% defects at the NEW state, 20.50% defects are assigned, 50.11% defects are resolved and 10.04% defects are closed. The absolute prediction errors (AE) are between 0.2% and 1.6%, showing that the estimations are accurate.

Similarly, we perform the Experiment B to predict the distribution of defects from July 2010 to December 2010 based on historical data from the past 12 months. Figure 6 shows the comparisons between the predicted and actual values as of December 31, 2010. Clearly, the estimated values are all close to the actual data, the absolute prediction errors (AE) are within 17%.

Table 4 shows the MAE values of the predicted distributions for all twelve months of 2010. The average absolute errors between prediction and actual values range from 0.1% to 6.8%, showing that the predictions are accurate and consistent across all months.

Table 4. The MAE values for predicting defect distributions (all twelve months of 2010)

	NEW/ OPEN	ASSI./ INPRO.	RESO- LVED	VERI- FIED	REOP- ENED	CLOS- ED
PDE. Build	0.053	0.001	0.053	0.002	0.002	0.004
JDT. UI	0.023	0.009	0.009	0.016	0.010	0.003
JDT. Text	0.023	0.006	0.013	0.015	0.013	0.010
Plat. Debug	0.068	0.014	0.012	0.041	0.005	0.005
Spring. NET	0.052	0.025	0.034	N/A	0.002	0.008

4.4.2 Predicting the Number of Defects at Each State

Having predicted the distribution of defects among states, we then evaluate the effectiveness of the BugStates in predicting the number of defects at each state.

Following the method described in Section 3.5, we first predict the total number of defects by modeling the growth of defect numbers. For the projects studied, we calculate the cumulative monthly defect numbers from January 2009 to December 2009 (for Experiment A) and from July 2009 to June 2010 (for Experiment B), and then use Matlab to construct G-O models (Equation 11). Our results show that the G-O model can well represent the growth of defects over time, with R^2 values ranging from 0.968 to 0.997. Table 5 shows the coefficients of G-O models constructed in Experiment A, as well as the predicted and actual number of defects in June 2010.

Having predicted the defect distributions among states and the total number of defects, we can then predict the number of defects at each state using Equation 12. Figure 7 shows the predicted and actual numbers of defects at all states in December 2010. The prediction results are promising for all projects. For example, for the JDT.Text project, as of December 31, 2010, 188 defects are at the RESOLVED state and the predicted number is 185, the absolute prediction error (AE) is only 3. There are 123 defects at the ASSIGNED state and the predicted number is 113, the absolute prediction error is only 10. For all projects (except Lucene-Java.Index), the absolute prediction errors for all states are small, ranging from 0 to 28 (the actual numbers of defects range from 0 to 547).

Table 5. The G-O models constructed in Experiment A

	a	b	R^2	#Actu.	#Pred.	MRE
PDE. Build	354.2	0.0890	0.990	311	283	9.00%
JDT.UI	1572	0.0450	0.997	905	875	3.31%
JDT.Text	383	0.0860	0.997	350	302	13.71%
Platform. Debug	978	0.0350	0.988	509	460	9.63%
Spring. NET	9455	0.0004	0.968	88	83	5.68%

Table 6. The MAE values for predicting defect numbers (all twelve months of 2010)

	NEW/ OPEN	ASSI./ INPRO.	RESO- LVED	VERI- FIED	REOP- ENED	CLOS- ED
PDE.Build	17.33	0.083	14.17	0.75	0.67	1.58
JDT.UI	20.58	9.50	6.75	13.17	9.33	3.50
JDT.Text	8.83	7.58	7.58	3.92	4.25	5.42
Platform. Debug	30.75	7.08	14.42	25.08	2.58	4.58
Spring. NET	4.25	2.00	3.42	N/A	0.17	0.58

Table 6 also shows the MAE values for all twelve months of 2010. The average absolute prediction errors range from 0.083 to 30.75, which are relatively small comparing to the total number of defects. The MAE results show that the predictions are accurate and consistent across all months.

In summary, our experiments confirm that BugStates is effective in predicting the number of defects at each state in future, and that past defect-fixing performance can be used to predict future performance.

4.5 Comparisons

To further evaluate the effectiveness of BugStates, we compare it with the following three prediction methods:

- **Arithmetic mean**: this is a simple prediction method that uses the mean average number of changes in the defect state transitions ($\overline{\Delta x}$) in the past to predict the number defects at each state in the next n months:

$$y = y_0 + \overline{\Delta x} \cdot n, \qquad (14)$$

where y_0 is the initial defect number.

- **G-O model**: it is a classic software reliability model [8, 15]. Unlike Equation 11, here we use it to estimate the cumulative number of defects for each state:

$$y = a(1 - e^{-bn}), \qquad (15)$$

where a and b are parameters and n is the number of months.

- **Quadratic function**: this function assumes that the growth of defects follows a quadratic function. It is defined as follows:

$$y = an^2 + bn + c, \qquad (16)$$

where a, b and c are parameters, and n is the number of months. It has been found that for many Eclipse projects, the growth of the cumulative number of defects follows the quadratic function [25].

For the above three methods, we use the data from July 2009 to June 2010 to train the models, and predict the number of defects at each state in December 2010. For each method, there are in total 29 predictions for all states.

Table 7 shows the comparison results. A '+' sign indicates that the BugStates performed better than the related method in terms of the absolute prediction error (AE) in prediction; a '0' sign means that they achieved the same performance; and a '-' signs means BugStates lost. The numbers besides the '+' and '-'signs show the differences between the prediction results of BugStates and the related methods. For example, '-25' on the first row of the table means that BugStates predicts worse than the Arithmetic Mean method by 25 defects. '+29' means that BugStates predicts better than the G-O model by 29 defects.

In summary, among total 29 predictions, BugStates won the Arithmetic Mean method 17 times and only lost 9 times. Similarly, BugStates also won the G-O model (18/29) and the Quadratic function (18/29). The results confirm that, in general, BugStates can achieve better prediction results than the related methods.

Table 7. The comparisons between BugStates and other methods

Project	State	Arithmetic Mean	G-O Model	Quadratic Function
JDT.UI	NEW	-25	+29	+101
	ASSIGNED	+41	-4	+32
	RESOLVED	+172	+80	+82
	VERIFIED	-19	+7	+1
	REOPENED	-10	-11	-11
	CLOSED	+37	+13	+8
JDT.Text	NEW	-12	-15	+24
	ASSIGNED	+3	0	-8
	RESOLVED	+55	+10	0
	VERIFIED	+15	+18	0
	REOPENED	-3	-4	-3
	CLOSED	+26	+8	+20
Platform. Debug	NEW	+22	+52	+42
	ASSIGNED	0	+2	-2
	RESOLVED	-4	-6	+3
	VERIFIED	-12	-35	-17
	REOPENED	0	-4	-3
	CLOSED	+9	-3	+3
PDE.Build	NEW	+41	+21	+39
	ASSIGNED	0	+1	+1
	RESOLVED	+24	+5	-15
	VERIFIED	-1	+1	+1
	REOPENED	-1	-1	-1
	CLOSED	+17	+1	+8
Spring.NET	OPEN	+43	+38	+50
	IN PROGRESS	+1	-1	-1
	RESOLVED	+15	+32	+35
	REOPENED	+2	+2	+2
	CLOSED	+5	+6	+6
Summary	*Won (+)*	*17*	*18*	*18*
	Tie (0)	*3*	*1*	*2*
	Lost (-)	*9*	*10*	*9*

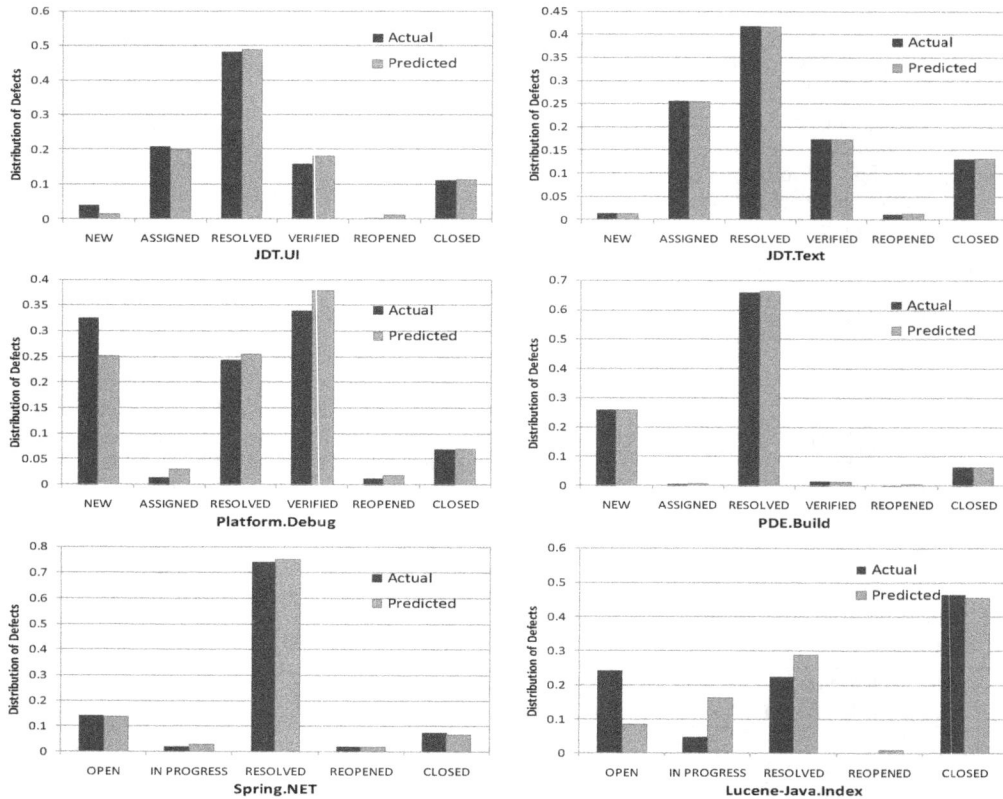

Figure 6. The actual and predicted distribution of defects in December 2010

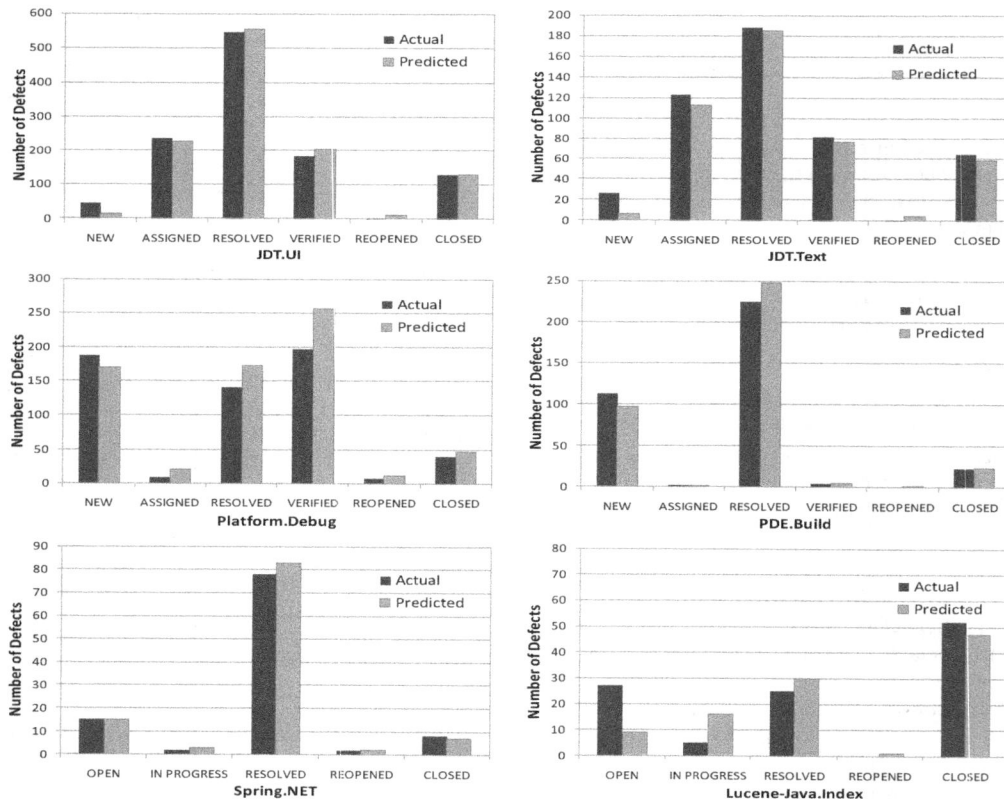

Figure 7. The actual and predicted number of defects in December 2010

198

4.6 Discussions

The proposed BugStates method can be applied to projects that are experiencing long-term evolution and have stable defect-fixing performance. For such projects, new features are constantly added and new defects are discovered, it is thus desirable to measure and predict the project teams' defect-fixing performance. Our experimental results show that it is reasonable to predict a team's future defect-fixing performance based on its past performance. The ability to have long term prediction of defect numbers can help a project team better plan limited maintenance resources and adjust their development schedule.

For projects that do not have stable defect-fixing performance, BugStates is less effective as the state transition probabilities are varying. Figures 6 and 7 show that for the Lucene-Java.Index project (which is the project exhibiting less stable performance), BugStates leads to larger relative prediction errors, especially for the OPEN and IN PROGRESS states. In practice, we suggest measuring the stability of the defect-fixing performance before applying the prediction method, as projects that have stable defect-fixing performance are expected to lead to consistent prediction results.

Table 8. The impact of distance thresholds on prediction results

	0.1	0.2	0.3	0.4	0.5
JDT.Text	√	√	√	√	√
PDE.Build	√	√	√	√	√
JDT.UI		√	√	√	√
Spring.NET		√	√	√	√
Platform.Debug			√	√	√
Lucene-Java.Index					√
min	0	0	0	0	0
max	24	34	59	59	59
Average MAE	6.014	6.278	7.733	7.733	7.349
Average MRE	0.106	0.086	0.133	0.133	0.170

To measure the stability of a project's defect-fixing performance, in our experiments, we set the distance threshold to 0.25. Table 8 shows the impact of different threshold values on the prediction results (for twelve months in 2010). If we set the threshold to 0.10, only the JDT.Text and PDE.Build projects meet the threshold. BugStates works well for these two projects. The maximum absolute prediction error is 24 and the average MAE value for all states is 6.014. If we set the threshold to 0.20, then the JDT.UI and Spring.NET projects also meet the threshold, with the maximum absolute error 34 and average MAE 6.278. When the threshold is increased to 0.5, all six projects are included. Although the average MAE value is slightly lower than the value achieved by threshold 0.4, the average MRE value is higher. In general, projects having stable defect-fixing performance (i.e., smaller $D_{average}$ values) can achieve better prediction results than projects exhibiting less stable performance (i.e., larger $D_{average}$ values).

5. THREATS TO VALIDITY

We have identified some threats to validities that should be taken into consideration when applying the proposed method:

- **Completeness**: In Eclipse Bugzilla database, there are some transitions that do not follow the defect life cycle (Figure 1). For example, some defects' states are transferred from NEW directly to CLOSED, but actually such transitions are not allowed. We

suspect that some developers omitted certain intermediate results when filling the activity logs, thus leading to the "undefined" transitions. If a project has less rigorous QA procedures and has many "undefined" state transitions, the accuracy of our prediction method could be affected.

- **Large evolving system**: The method we proposed is suitable for large software systems that are experiencing a long period of evolution and their project team's defect-fixing performances are stable. For a small or short-living system, the number of defects and state transitions are often small, thus making the statistical analysis inappropriate.

- **Open source data**: All datasets used in our experiments are collected from the open source projects such as Eclipse. The defect state transition behavior of Eclipse projects may be different from those of commercial projects. We will evaluate if BugStates can be applied to commercial projects. This is our important future work.

6. RELATED WORK

In recent years, there have been extensive studies on software defect prediction and analysis. Many methods collect historical defect data by mining software repositories (such as bug database and version archives), identify program features (such as complexity and process metrics), and then build classification models to predict the defect-proneness (defective or non-defective) of a new module. For example, Kim et al. [13] proposed the Change Classification (CC) technique, which learns buggy change patterns from history and predicts if a new change introduces bugs. Zimmermann et al. [24] proposed method for extracting defect information from the CVS/SVN repositories, and to predict defect-proneness of a file. In [16, 26, 27], the authors found that simple complexity metrics such as LOC can be used to predict defect-proneness of components. There are also studies on the distribution of defects over modules of a large software project [1, 5, 28], and on the automated bug localization [29]. In this work, we predict the distribution/number of defects at each state. To our best knowledge, modeling and predicting defect state transition have not been received enough attention.

Some researchers also studied defect life cycles and triage. For example, Koponen [14] studied the defects reported for the Apache HTTP Server and Mozilla Firefox projects from 2003 to 2005. They noticed that the defect life cycles in the two projects were much more straight forward because the states of the defects moved to RESOLVED directly from the initial state. In our study of Eclipse, we also found a few instances whose states were changed directly from NEW to CLOSED, but most of the defects follow the standard defect state transition procedures. Weib et al. [23] studied the lifecycle of defects and presented a search-based approach that can predict the defect-fixing effort. Jeong et al. [9] found that 37%-44% of defect reports for Mozilla and Eclipse are re-assigned to other developers. They constructed a Markov model based on bug tossing history and used it for defect triage. In this work, we mine the state transition information from the defect activity logs, and then use this information to measure and predict defect state transitions.

Our work is related to the field of software reliability engineering. Traditionally, in reliability prediction, the number of operational failures is predicted through a reliability growth model such as the Littlewood, S-Curve and Goel-Okumoto models [15, 17]. In our earlier work, we also proposed polynomial functions based method for predicting defect growth [25]. In recent years, people have also experimented with Markov-based software reliability prediction. For example, in [22] the authors applied Markov models to predict the reliability of a service-based software system. They proposed a hierarchical reliability model. A Markov model was created for analyzing the reliability of the composite services based on the system control structure and the operational scenarios. In [6], the authors also applied DTMC to model service compositions. They proposed a method called ATOP, which converted an activity diagram to a DTMC model and utilized probabilistic model checking techniques for quality prediction. In [4, 21], the authors proposed a user-oriented reliability model and an architecture-based reliability model using Markovian methods.

There are also studies on the measurement and prediction of defect-fixing performance. For example, Mockus et al. proposed quality metrics (such as percentage of defective files) to understand software maintenance effort quantitatively [18, 7]. Mockus also proposed regression models to estimate maintenance effort and its distribution over time [19]. Kim et al. [12] studied the life span of bugs in ArgoUML and PostgreSQL projects, and found that bug-fixing times have a median of about 200 days. Panjer [20] proposed to use machine-learning models to predict the time to fix a defect. In our work, we apply Markov model to represent the defect state transition process, and use the model to measure defect-fixing performance.

7. CONCLUSIONS

During software evolution, a large number of defects could be reported. Each defect has a life cycle, which is typically maintained by a bug tracking system such as Bugzilla and Jira. In this paper, we have proposed BugStates, a method for predicting defect numbers at each state. In BugStates, we model defect state transitions as Markov-like models. We measure the stability of a project team's defect-fixing performance by using a distance metric derived from the models. Furthermore, we can predict future defect numbers at each state based on the state transition models, that is, to predict a project's future defect-fixing performance based on its past performance. We have evaluated the proposed approach using data mined from defect records of six open source projects. The experimental results confirm the effectiveness of our method. We believe that our method can help project teams better understand and manage software maintenance activities.

In future, we plan to carry out large-scale evaluations of the proposed method on a variety of projects, including commercial projects. We will also analyze defect-fixing performance of different teams and investigate generic performance models.

ACKNOWLEDGMENTS

This research is supported by the NSF China grant 61073006, the 8th Open Lab Project of State Key Lab of Software Engineering (Wuhan University), and the National HGJ Project 2010ZX01045-002-3. We thank Dr Jun Sun at SUTD and Songzheng Song at NUS for their comments and help on an early draft of this paper.

REFERENCES

[1] C. Andersson and P. Runeson. 2007. A replicated quantitative analysis of fault distributions in complex software systems. *IEEE Trans. Software Eng.* 33 (5), 273-286.

[2] W. G. Belch, S. Greiner, H. de Meer, and K. S. Trivedi. 1998. *Queuing Network and Markov Chains.* John Wiley, Chichester.

[3] Bugzilla: http://www.Bugzilla.org/

[4] R. C. Cheung. 1980. A user-oriented software reliability model. *IEEE Transactions on Software Engineering.* 6(2), 118-125.

[5] N. Fenton and N. Ohlsson. 2000. Quantitative analysis of faults and failures in a complex software system. *IEEE Trans. Software Eng.* 26 (8), 797-814.

[6] S. Gallotti, C. Ghezzi, R.Mirandola, and G. Tamburrelli. 2008. Quality prediction of service compositions through probabilistic model checking. In *Proceedings 4th International Conference on the Quality of Software-Architectures* (QoSA'08). 119-134.

[7] D. German, A. Mockus. 2003. Automating the measurement of open source projects. In *ICSE '03 Workshop on Open Source Software Engineering.* Portland, Oregon.

[8] A. Goel and K. Okumoto. 1979. A time dependent error detection model for software reliability and other performance measures. *IEEE Trans. Reliability,* vol R-28, 206-211.

[9] G. Jeong, S. Kim and T. Zimmermann. 2009. Improving defect triage with defect tossing graphs. In *Proceedings ESEC/FSE 2009,* 111-120.

[10] Jira: http://www.atlassian.com/software/jira/

[11] E. Kao. 1996. *An Introduction to Stochastic Processes.* Duxbury Press.

[12] S. Kim and J. E. Whitehead. 2006. How long did it take to fix bugs? In *MSR '06,* 173–174.

[13] S. Kim, J. E. Whitehead, and Y. Zhang. 2008. Classifying Software Changes: Clean or Buggy?. IEEE Trans. Softw. Eng. 34, 2 (March 2008), 181-196.

[14] T. Koponen. 2006. Life cycle of defects in open source software projects. In *IFIP International Federation for Information Processing.* 195-200

[15] M. R. Lyu. 1996. *Handbook of Software Reliability Engineering.* McGraw Hill.

[16] T. Menzies, J. Greenwald, and A. Frank. 2007. Data mining static code attributes to learn defect predictors. *IEEE Trans. Softw.Eng.,* 33(1): 2–13.

[17] J. D. Musa. 1987. *Software Reliability: Measurement, Prediction and Application.* McGraw-Hill, New York.

[18] A. Mockus, R. T. Fielding, and J. D. Herbsleb. 2002. Two case studies of open source software development: Apache and Mozilla. *ACM Trans. Softw. Eng. Methodol.,* 11(3):309–346.

[19] A. Mockus, D. M. Weiss, and P. Zhang. 2003. Understanding and predicting effort in software projects. In *ICSE 2003.* 274–284, Portland, Oregon.

[20] L. Panjer. 2007. Predicting eclipse bug lifetimes. In *MSR '07.*

[21] W. L. Wang, Y. Wu and M. H Chen. 1999. An architecture-based software reliability model. In *Proceedings Pacific Rim International Symposium on Dependable Computing.*

[22] L. J. Wang, X. Y. Bai, L. Z. Zhou and Y. N. Chen. 2009. A hierarchical reliability model of service-based software system. In *Proceedings COMPSAC'09,* 199-208.

[23] C. Weib, R. Premraj, T. Zimmermann, and A. Zeller. 2007. How long will it take to fix this bug? In *Proceedings MSR 2007.* Minneapolis, USA.

[24] T. Zimmermann, R. Premraj and A. Zeller. 2007. Predicting defects for eclipse. In *Proceedings PROMISE 2007.* Minneapolis, USA.

[25] H. Zhang. 2008. An initial study of the growth of eclipse defects. In *Proceedings MSR 2008.* Leipzig, Germany, 141-144.

[26] H. Zhang. 2009. An Investigation of the Relationships between Lines of Code and Defects. In *Proceedings ICSM'09.* Edmonton, Canada, 274-283.

[27] H. Zhang and R. Wu. 2010. Sampling Program Quality. In *Proceedings ICSM 2010.* Timisoara, Romania.

[28] H. Zhang. 2008. On the Distribution of Software Faults. *IEEE Trans. on Software Eng.* vol. 34(2), 2008.

[29] J. Zhou, H. Zhang, and D. Lo. 2012. Where Should the Bugs be Fixed? in *Proceedings ICSE'12,* Zurich, Switzerland, 14-24.

Recommender Systems for Manual Testing

Deciding how to assign tests in a test team

Breno Miranda
Centro de Informática
Universidade Federal de
Pernambuco
Recife-PE, Brazil
CEP 50740-540
bafm@cin.ufpe.br

Eduardo Aranha
Departamento de Informática
e Matemática Aplicada
Universidade Federal do Rio
Grande do Norte
Natal-RN, Brazil
CEP 59078-970
eduardo@dimap.ufrn.br

Juliano Iyoda
Centro de Informática
Universidade Federal de
Pernambuco
Recife-PE, Brazil
CEP 50740-540
jmi@cin.ufpe.br

ABSTRACT

BACKGROUND: Software testing can be an arduous and expensive activity. A typical activity to maximise testing productivity is to allocate test cases according to the testers' profile. However, optimising the allocation of manual test cases is not a trivial task: in big companies, test managers are responsible for allocating hundreds of test cases among several testers. OBJECTIVE: In this paper we propose and evaluate 2 assignment algorithms for test case allocation and 3 tester profiles based on recommender systems. Each assignment algorithm can be combined with 3 tester profiles, which results in six possible allocation systems. METHOD: We run a controlled experiment that uses 100 test suites, each one with at least 50 test cases, from a real industrial setting in order to compare our allocation systems to the manager's allocation in terms of precision, recall and unassignment (percentage of test cases the algorithm could not allocate). RESULTS: In our experiment, the statistical analysis shows that one of the systems outperforms the others with respect to the precision and recall metrics. For unassignment, three of our six allocation systems achieved zero (best value) for the unassignment rate. CONCLUSION: The results of our experiment suggest that, in similar environments, test managers can use our allocation systems to reduce the amount of time spent in the test case allocation task. In the real industrial setting in which our work was developed, managers spend from 16 to 30 working days a year on test case allocation. Our algorithms can help them do it faster and better.

Categories and Subject Descriptors

D.2.4 [**Software Engineering**]: Software/Program Verification; D.2.5 [**Software Engineering**]: Testing and Debugging

Keywords

Recommender systems, Test allocation, Manual testing

1. INTRODUCTION

Testing is an essential activity that assesses the behaviour and the quality of a software. Given that this activity can be quite arduous and costly (testing is responsible for up to 40% of the total cost of a project [17]), all effort and tool support that optimises its costs are welcome.

This work is developed in the context of a company that outsources testing services to a mobile phone manufacturer. Due to some contractual reasons the company's name cannot be disclosed and, for this reason, from now on we call it **TTC** (*"The Testing Company"*). TTC performs black-box testing, mostly executed *manually*. One important activity at TTC is the test case allocation (Figure 1). Typically, a test manager has to allocate hundreds of test cases to be executed by the testers available at that moment. The manager's input to this task is a list of test cases and a list of testers. We call these lists the *allocation input*. The outcome of an allocation is a list of pairs (test case, tester) that indicates who should run which test case. We call this list a *test plan*. In the example of Figure 1, the test case TC01 is allocated to tester T04, the test case TC03 is allocated to the tester T01 etc.

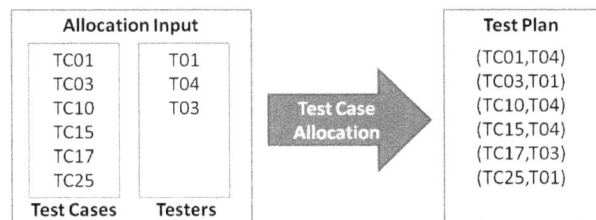

Figure 1: Test case allocation.

In order to perform this task, the test manager takes between 15 to 35 minutes, depending on the amount of tests to be allocated. And this task is executed routinely at TTC: around 10 times per week. This means that the time spent on this task per year varies from 16 to 30 working days. A bad allocation has also an impact on the execution time of the test suite and the effectiveness of it (fewer bugs found).

By allocating a test to an experienced tester, which is someone who has executed that test (or similar tests) in the past, the execution time may reduce. Analogously, a tester who has found bugs executing a particular test in the past is a good candidate to execute that same test again or other tests that are similar to that. At TTC the same test is run several times over a month, either for regression testing or in a different mobile phone model. Note that, in principle, bug finding should not depend on who is executing which test case. However, our context is that of manual execution. Test cases are written in English and are usually ambiguous and open to different interpretations. So, we believe a wise choice of a tester can make a difference on bug finding.

Since various test management tools such as Testlink[1], Qmetry[2], PractiTest[3] and Testuff[4] handle test case assignment in a very similar way to the TTC (each test case can be assigned to a different tester), we believe our approach can be generalised to other test companies with minor adjustments.

We implemented 2 assignment algorithms for test case allocation and defined 3 tester profiles based on recommender systems [10] (the same kind of system that recommends a book at Amazon.com). Each assignment algorithm can be combined with 3 tester profiles, which results in six possible allocation systems. We compared the allocation systems among themselves and with respect to the manager's allocation and to a random algorithm. Our comparison was done in terms of precision and recall (two well-established metrics from the recommender systems domain); and unassignment (percentage of test cases the algorithm could not allocate). *Precision* measures how often the approach makes an appropriate recommendation. In our context, an appropriate recommendation is achieved when our algorithms recommend a suitable pair (test case, tester) for a given test plan. *Recall* measures how many of appropriate pairs (test case, tester) are actually recommended by the algorithm.

The results showed that one of the systems outperforms all the others with respect to the precision and the recall metrics. All the allocation systems were superior to the random algorithm. The average precision (among the allocation systems) varied from 39.32% to 64.83% while the average recall ranged from 39.19% to 64.83%; For unassignment, three of our six allocation systems presented a better performance by achieving zero unassignment rate for all the allocation inputs. The average unassignment varied from 0% to 2.34% (for unassignment, the lower the better).

Recommender systems have been applied to almost all activities of Software Engineering. Several works describe recommender systems for allocating tasks to people [1, 8, 13, 14, 15], bug prevention and debugging [6]. Only a few are directly related to testing [11], and none (as far as we know) is related to allocating test case to testers.

The main contributions of this paper are:

- The application of recommender systems to test case allocation;

- The proposal of 6 allocation systems for allocating test cases to testers;

[1] http://testlink.org
[2] http://www.qmetry.com
[3] http://www.practitest.com
[4] http://www.testuff.com

- The implementation of a tool that mechanises this activity. Test case allocation with the support of a recommender system can be done faster than before. Moreover, new managers who are not familiar with the testers and the test cases can benefit from an initial allocation produced by the tool;

- An experiment in which all allocation systems are compared to the manager's performance in terms of unassignment, precision and recall.

The paper is organised as follows: Section 2 describes how recommender systems can be used to test case allocation. Section 3 explains the implementation details of our algorithms. A controlled experiment that compares our algorithms with the test manager's allocation and with a random allocation is presented in sections 4, 5, 6 and 7. Section 8 describes related work and Section 9 concludes.

2. RECOMMENDER SYSTEMS AND TESTING

Recommender systems [10] are information filtering systems that recommend *items* to users. Items are typically books or movies. In our case, the item is an allocation of a test case to a tester. We represent such allocation as a pair (test case, tester). Our typical user is a test manager. Our recommendations are made by comparing a particular test case with a tester's profile and evaluating their similarity.

We defined 6 allocation systems for assigning test cases to testers. They vary in the tester profile we use and in the algorithm that assigns a test to a tester.

We propose 3 profiles for a tester. The *expertise* profile measures if the tester has previous knowledge and experience in executing a particular test. This profile is built using the amount of times a tester has executed a given test in the past. The *effectiveness* profile captures the amount of valid bugs found by a tester in previous executions of a particular test. Recall that, at TTC, the same test can be executed several times due to regression testing, retesting or the arrival of new mobile phone models. The third profile is the *multi-objective* profile (*MO* for short). The *MO* profile combines *expertise* and *effectiveness* by assigning a different weight to each. Note that *expertise* and *effectiveness* can be seen as two extremes of the same spectrum, which can be fine tuned through the *MO* profile (the manager may decide to use 60% on *expertise* and 40% on *effectiveness*, for example). In our experiment, reported in Section 4, we used our recommender systems with 50% weight to *expertise* and 50% weight to *effectiveness* as an attempt to capture the manager's intentions during allocations: test execution should be fast (*expertise*) and effective (*effectiveness*).

We defined 2 different ways of assigning test cases to testers. Suppose we have to execute 50 test cases today and we have 5 testers available. It is often the case that the test manager does not distribute test cases to testers uniformly, i.e. it is often the case that the test manager will *not* allocate 10 test cases to each tester. Some testers are more experienced than others, some are busier (already allocated to another activity) than others, some are faster than others etc. Therefore, the distribution of test cases among testers is usually *not* uniform. One variation of our allocation algorithm takes as input (from the test manager) the amount of test cases each tester should execute (the tester's workload). We call this algorithm *manager-based*. Alternatively, the recommender system could assign freely test cases to testers without taking into account the manager's distribution. We call this assignment *blind*. Notice that the *blind* assignment also does not distribute test cases to testers evenly. It depends on the similarity between a test case and a tester (similarity is explained in Section 2.2).

All possible combinations of profiles and assignment algorithms are shown in Table 1. The 6 allocation systems are named after their profile and assignment algorithms: Exp-Manager, Eff-Manager, MO-Manager, Exp-Blind, Eff-Blind and MO-Blind.

Table 1: The allocation systems.

Allocation System	Profile	Assignment
Exp-Manager	*Expertise*	Manager-based
Eff-Manager	*Effectiveness*	Manager-based
MO-Manager	*MO*	Manager-based
Exp-Blind	*Expertise*	Blind
Eff-Blind	*Effectiveness*	Blind
MO-Blind	*MO*	Blind

All allocation systems shown on Table 1 share the same kernel for building the profile and checking similarity between a test case and a tester (details are described in sections 2.1 and 2.2).

We adopt the recommender system proposed by Bezerra and Carvalho [3] based on Symbolic Data Analysis [4] as their model of an item captures very closely our test cases and testers.

2.1 Test Cases and Tester Profiles

This section describes how we model test cases and tester profiles. We start by introducing the terms and concepts used in the TTC through simple examples.

A test case comprises an *id*, a *description* (a short description of the test case objective), and a sequence of steps and expected results. Additional fields may include, but are not limited to: feature ID, component, test case category, test case level, preconditions, etc. A *feature* is a clustering of individual requirements that describes a cohesive, identifiable unit of functionality [18]. For example, the "support of multiple contact lists" is a feature of Instant Messaging applications. At TTC, each feature has a unique identifier and each test case is associated to one or more features. A *component* is a grouping of various features from the same domain. Each test is also associated to one or more components. A *category* distinguishes a test case among different types of tests: "functional", "interaction", "performance", "stress", "load", "sanity", "localisation", "interoperability", etc. Each test case can be associated to one or more categories. In this work, we assume that our test cases contain feature, component, category and description. However, our approach is not limited by these particular attributes (it can be easily extended to different contexts).

Our system store all test cases in a structure similar to that shown in Table 2. For simplicity, we use values like F1, F2, ... for *features*, CMP1, CMP2, ... for *components*, CTG1, CTG2, ... for *categories*, and W1, W2, ... for words present in the test case *description*. The (fictitious) test case TC02 tests the features *F2*, *F4* and *F8*, and is associated to the components *CMP3* and *CMP5*; and belongs to the CTG4 and CTG6 categories. Each test case is represented

by attributes whose values have uniform *weights*. In the case of a textual variable, such as the *description*, it is preprocessed by the TF-IDF [16] method (a statistical measure used to evaluate how important a word is to a document). Each attribute has a total weight equal to 1 and each value of a non-textual attribute has its weight evenly distributed among their values. For example, components *CMP3* and *CMP5* of TC02 have, each one, $\frac{1}{2}$ weight. In the case of the textual variable *description*, the weight of each word computed from the textual value comes from the TF-IDF.

Table 2: Test cases and their attributes.

TC	Feature	Component	Category	Description
TC02	(F2,1/3), (F4,1/3), (F8,1/3)	(CMP3,1/2), (CMP5,1/2)	(CTG4,1/2), (CTG6,1/2)	(W3,0.425), (W7,0.575)
TC03	(F3,1/2), (F5,1/2)	(CMP4,1)	(CTG1,1)	(W1,0.197), (W6,0.333), (W8,0.470)
TC04	(F3,1/3), (F6,1/3), (F7,1/3)	(CMP2,1/2), (CMP5,1/2)	(CTG4,1)	(W1,0.531), (W3,0.243), (W8,0.226)
TC05	(F3,1/2), (F7,1/2)	(CMP2,1/3), (CMP5,1/3), (CMP7,1/3)	(CTG1,1/2), (CTG5,1/2)	(W1,0.631), (W9,0.369)

Now that we have defined how test cases are modelled, we describe how we build the tester's profiles. As mentioned in Section 2, we work with three profiles: *expertise*, *effectiveness*, and *multi-objective*.

The expertise profile captures how much experience a tester has with respect to a set of features, components and categories. Based on this profile we can calculate how similar a given test case is in comparison to a given tester. In what follows we illustrate how we construct the profile of a given tester, say, Tester03, which we assume has run test cases TC02, TC03 and TC04 in the past.

Table 3 shows the Tester03's *expertise* profile, which was built taking into account her execution history and the test cases displayed on Table 2. As Tester03 executed test cases TC02, TC03 and TC04, we calculate the weights of each *feature*, *component*, *category*, and *description* associated with those test cases. We have to calculate the weights for the features F2, F3, F4, F5, F6, F7 and F8, as they are present on test cases TC02, TC03 and TC04 (see Table 2). The weight of a given feature for a tester is the average of the weights of all features present on the test cases performed by her. For example, the weights for F3 are 0 (its weight on TC02), $\frac{1}{2}$ (its weight on TC03) and $\frac{1}{3}$ (its weight on TC04). Therefore, the weight of feature F3 for Tester03 is the average of those weights:

$$Tester03_{(F3)} = \frac{\left(0 + \frac{1}{2} + \frac{1}{3}\right)}{3} = \frac{5}{18}.$$

The weight of the remainder features, components, categories, and descriptions are calculated in the same way.

The *effectiveness* profile is also built for each tester. This profile takes into account all test cases that a tester found a bug by running it. The calculation of the weights for the features, components, categories, and descriptions is performed in the same way described above for the *expertise* profile.

The *multi-objective* profile is built by combining the expertise and effectiveness profiles by assigning a different weight to each.

Table 3: Tester03's expertise profile.

Tester	Feature	Component	Category	Description
Tester03	(F2, 1/9), (F3, 5/18), (F4, 1/9), (F5, 1/6), (F6, 1/9), (F7, 1/9), (F8, 1/9)	(CMP2, 1/6), (CMP3, 1/6), (CMP4, 1/3), (CMP5, 1/3)	(CTG1, 1/3), (CTG4, 1/2) (CTG6, 1/6)	(W1, 0.243) (W3, 0.223), (W6, 0.111), (W7, 0.191), (W8, 0.232)

2.2 Calculating Similarity

This section describes how to calculate the similarity between a test and a tester. The similarity degree is a number between 0 and 1. The closer to 1 the similarity is, the more advisable it is to allocate a given test to a tester. Let us calculate the similarity between the test TC05 (Table 2) and the Tester03 with respect to the expertise profile.

Let $C = \{CMP2, CMP5\}$ be the set of common components between TC05 and Tester03. Let $TC = \{CMP7\}$ and $T = \{CMP3, CMP4\}$ be the sets of components that belong exclusively to TC05 and Tester03, respectively. (see Figure 2). We will calculate four sums of weights: α, β, γ and δ. The sum α is the sum of weights from TC05 for the elements in C and the sum β is the sum of weights from Tester03 for the elements in C. Therefore, $\alpha = \frac{1}{3} + \frac{1}{3} = \frac{2}{3}$ and $\beta = \frac{1}{6} + \frac{1}{3} = \frac{1+2}{6} = \frac{1}{2}$.

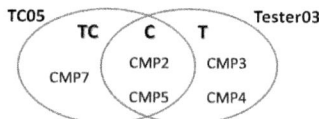

Figure 2: Components for TC05 and Tester03.

The sum γ is the sum of weights from Tester03 for the elements in T and the sum δ is the sum of weights from TC05 for the elements in TC: $\gamma = \frac{1}{6} + \frac{1}{3} = \frac{1+2}{6} = \frac{1}{2}$ and $\delta = \frac{1}{3}$.

Note that α and β are common components that capture the *agreements* between the Tester03's profiles and the test TC05, whereas the sums γ and δ capture the *disagreements* between the Tester03's profiles and the test TC05. The *dissimilarity* with respect to components is calculated through the following equation:

$$\frac{1}{2} \cdot \left(\frac{\gamma+\delta}{\alpha+\gamma+\delta} + \frac{\gamma+\delta}{\beta+\gamma+\delta} \right) = \frac{1}{2} \cdot \left(\frac{\frac{1}{2}+\frac{1}{3}}{\frac{2}{3}+\frac{1}{2}+\frac{1}{3}} + \frac{\frac{1}{2}+\frac{1}{3}}{\frac{1}{2}+\frac{1}{2}+\frac{1}{3}} \right) \cong 0.59.$$

The dissimilarities for feature, category, and description are calculated in the same way. In this case, the results (omitted here for simplicity), are approximately 0.50 for feature, 0.74 for category, and 0.73 for description.

The *total dissimilarity* is the average of the partial dissimilarities: $(0.59 + 0.50 + 0.74 + 0.73)/4 = 0.64$. The *similarity degree* is the complement of this value: $1 - 0.64 = 0.36$. Thus, the *similarity* between the Tester03 and the test TC05 is 36%. The work by Bezerra and Carvalho [3] describes in details all the equations used in our recommender systems.

3. THE TEST ALLOCATION SYSTEMS

Our allocation systems were developed in *Python* [12] using the *Eclipse* Integrated Development Environment [7]. We decided to use Python mostly because the communication with the test case repository through SQL queries is very simple. In what follows we describe how the recommendations are made both in the manager-based and the blind approaches.

The first step performed by the algorithms is to build up the test case descriptions (Table 2) and the testers profiles (Table 3). This step is achieved by communicating with the test case repository in order to collect data from previous test executions.

The second step takes as input (from the test manager) the allocation input: a list of test cases to be executed and a list of testers available for that execution. Then, the test manager selects the profile (*Expertise*, *Effectiveness* or *Multi-objective*) and the assignment algorithm (*Manager-based* or *Blind*) she wants to use. With this information, our system calculates the relevance (through the similarity degree) of each test for all the testers available. An example of the outcome of this step is shown in Table 4. We give as allocation input to the algorithms 5 test cases (TC01, TC02, TC03, TC04 and TC05) and 2 testers (T01 and T02). The algorithm computes the similarity of all pairs (test case,tester) and orders them by similarity. Our algorithms discard from this list all pairs (test case,tester) whose similarity is smaller than 5%. This decision was taken in order to avoid the algorithm from recommending testers not based on their profiles (if the similarity is too low, it means that the test case is poorly documented in the test case repository). Therefore, the pairs (TC02,T02), (TC04,T01) and (TC05,T02) are not taken into account during the production of the recommendation list.

Table 4: Similarities.

TC	Tester	Similarity	TC	Tester	Similarity
TC01	T02	65,78%	TC01	T01	33,63%
TC03	T02	62,75%	TC05	T01	13,46%
TC03	T01	59,65%	TC02	T02	2,44%
TC04	T02	57,19%	TC04	T01	1,45%
TC02	T01	55,17%	TC05	T02	1,45%

The third and last step is the test case allocation itself. The way this step is performed depends on the assignment algorithm selected by the manager.

Manager-based: if the manager chooses a manager-based algorithm, she is asked to provide the amount of test cases she wants to assign to each tester. Let us assume that the manager decides to allocate 2 test cases for T01 and 3 test cases for T02. The manager-based algorithm allocates one test case for each tester in each iteration over Table 4. So, in the first iteration, the (test case,tester) with the highest similarity is allocated: i.e. test case TC01 is allocated to tester T02. This pair is then removed from Table 4. The algorithm continues the first iteration and keeps searching for the next pair with highest similarity for a tester *different* from T02. This pair is (TC03,T01). This pair is allocated and is subsequently removed from the list. As both testers have been allocated to one test case each, this iteration is finished. The algorithm continues to search for pairs where: 1) the test case has not been allocated yet; 2) the tester has not reached her workload; and 3) the similarity is above 5%. In our example, T01 can take 1 more test case while T02 can still take 2 test cases. The final recommendation is (TC01,T02), (TC03,T01), (TC04,T02), and (TC02,T01).

Blind: In the blind algorithms, each test case is allocated to the tester that has the highest similarity degree with that test case without taking into account the workload. Apart from that, it works in the same way as the manager based. The pairs (TC01,T02), (TC03,T02), (TC04,T02), (TC02,T01), (TC05,T01) are recommended. Both manager-based and blind algorithms do *not* necessarily allocate all test cases. Recall that pairs (test case,tester) whose similarity are smaller than 5% are discarded. There are test cases that are poorly documented (attributes are missing) and therefore their similarity to all testers are below 5%. In addition to that, in the case of manager-based algorithms, the workload for each tester may prevent some test cases to be allocated despite having a similarity above 5%.

On performance. The first step of the algorithms is the construction of tables 2 and 3. This step takes less than 3 minutes running on an Intel T2050, 1.6GHz, 1GB of RAM. This step needs to run only in the first time we run the recommendation systems (say, at installation time). In subsequent runs, the system simply updates the tester's profiles. In this case, the time to update the profiles is negligible. The second and third step generate the similarities table (table 4) and the recommendations themselves; they take no more than 30 seconds for an allocation input with 300 test cases.

4. EXPERIMENTAL PLANNING

In this section we describe the planning, design and execution of our experiment following the guidelines of well-known books on experimental software engineering [9, 19]. We compared the performance of our algorithms with respect to the history of allocations done by the managers of TTC from November 2009 to September 2010, over a subset of 7 mobile phone models. Here, we assume that the managers performed the best possible allocations. We also include six random allocation approaches (varying the seed used) in the comparisons to confirm that our proposed approaches are better than simple random choices.

4.1 Goals

The research objective of this experiment is to: *Analyse* the performance of the proposed allocation systems *for the purpose of* comparison *with respect to* the rate of unassigned test cases and the adequacy of the achieved test allocation *from the viewpoint of* test managers *in the context of* manual test execution at TTC. An *unassigned* test case is a test case that the algorithm did not allocate to any tester. In order to achieve this objective, we defined the following goals for this study (following the Goal/Question/Metric method [2]):

G_1: Evaluate the unassignment rate of each recommender algorithm.

G_2: Evaluate and compare the effectiveness of each allocation system with respect to the following approaches: real manager's allocation and random allocation.

Before we introduce our research questions, we need to define some comparison concepts. Let TC_S and TC_M be test cases, and T_S and T_M be testers. Let (TC_S, T_S) and (TC_M, T_M) be allocations recommended by our system and by the manager, respectively. Whenever our system recommends an allocation exactly as the manager did, we say that

our system produced a *strictly correct pair*. In other words, whenever $TC_S = TC_M$ and $T_S = T_M$, (TC_S, T_S) is a strictly correct pair (same as the managers' allocation).

Since testers can have similar performance, the concept of a strict correct pair can be relaxed. In this way, we define the concept of an *approximately correct pair*. To understand it, let us assume that testers can be grouped according to their skills. Also, suppose that G_1 is the group of the most talented testers, G_2 is the group of the second most talented testers, and so on. The pair (TC_S, T_S) is an approximately correct pair whenever $TC_S = TC_M$ and T_S belongs to the same group of T_M (equivalent allocation).

We intend to assess our algorithms in terms of strictly correct pairs and approximately correct pairs. The assessment of the goals $\mathbf{G_1}$ and $\mathbf{G_2}$ is performed by the following research questions ($\mathbf{Q_1}$ to $\mathbf{Q_5}$) and metrics ($\mathbf{M_1}$ to $\mathbf{M_5}$).

$\mathbf{Q_1}$ **[unassignment]** What is the ratio of unassigned test cases with respect to all test cases allocated?

$$\mathbf{M_1} = \frac{\#\ of\ unassigned\ test\ cases}{\#\ of\ test\ cases\ in\ the\ allocation\ input}$$

$\mathbf{Q_2}$ **[strict precision]** What is the ratio of strictly correct pairs with respect to all recommended pairs?

$$\mathbf{M_2} = \frac{\#\ of\ strictly\ correct\ pairs}{\#\ of\ recomendations\ of\ the\ algorithm}$$

$\mathbf{Q_3}$ **[strict recall]** What is the ratio of strictly correct pairs with respect to all pairs recommended by the manager?

$$\mathbf{M_3} = \frac{\#\ of\ strictly\ correct\ pairs}{\#\ of\ recomendations\ of\ the\ manager}$$

$\mathbf{Q_4}$ **[approximate precision]** What is the ratio of approximately correct pairs with respect to all recommended pairs?

$$\mathbf{M_4} = \frac{\#\ of\ approximately\ correct\ pairs}{\#\ of\ recomendations\ of\ the\ algorithm}$$

$\mathbf{Q_5}$ **[approximate recall]** What is the ratio of approximately correct pairs with respect to all pairs recommended by the manager?

$$\mathbf{M_5} = \frac{\#\ of\ approximately\ correct\ pairs}{\#\ of\ recomendations\ of\ the\ manager}$$

The unassignment metric $\mathbf{M_1}$ computes the amount of unassigned test cases for each algorithm with respect to the total amount of test cases given in the allocation input. Strict precision $\mathbf{M_2}$ computes the total amount of strictly correct pairs with respect to the total amount of recommendations made. The strict recall metric $\mathbf{M_3}$ computes the percentage of strictly correct pairs recommended by the system with respect to all correct pairs, which are those pairs allocated by the manager. The approximate precision $\mathbf{M_4}$ and approximate recall $\mathbf{M_5}$ are analogous to the strict precision and the strict recall, comparing testers based on their experience (equivalence groups).

4.2 Participants

We evaluate our algorithms using historical data. However, in order to calculate the approximately correct pairs, we needed to identify the groups or classes of equivalent testers. To produce these groups, we asked two TTC's test managers to define them in cooperation. They are both equally experienced and happen to know all testers involved in the past allocations (each manager knows a subset of all testers involved, but the union of these subsets is the set of all testers).

4.3 Experimental Material

In order to carry out our experiments, we selected 100 allocation inputs (parts of test plans) from the past that have been manually allocated by the TTC managers in the period from November 2009 to September 2010. Not all allocation inputs in this period were used. We chose those that had more than 50 test cases and involved at least 2 testers. We chose 50 test cases because we think the allocation of 50 test cases (or more) is a problem hard enough for a human being to deal with by hand. The allocation input sizes varied from 50 to 585 test cases (our largest allocation input). The highest number of testers involved in our allocation inputs was 9. The scatter plot displayed on Figure 3 shows the amount of test cases (horizontal axis) and the number of testers (vertical axis) of each allocation input. This figure captures the main features of the allocation inputs we used in our experiment.

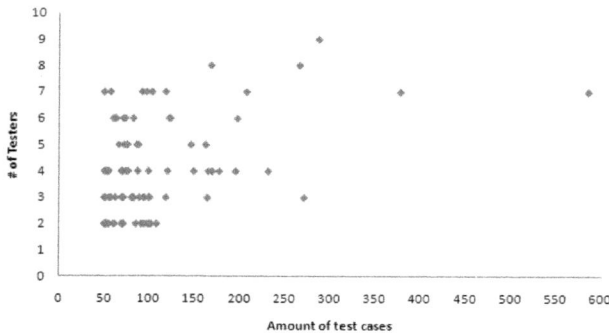

Figure 3: Amount of test cases and number of testers per allocation input.

The majority of the allocation inputs have between 50 and 200 test cases and 2 to 7 testers; just a few have more than 200 test cases and only one contains more than 500 test cases. Only 3 allocation inputs were performed by more than 7 testers.

4.4 Experiment Design

Since the characteristics of each allocation input (number of tests, testers available, etc.) can influence the performance of the algorithms, we control this confounding factor by considering each allocation input as a block, in a randomised complete block design.

Hence, we generated, in a random order, 12 automatic allocations for each one of the 100 blocks (allocation inputs) available. Six of these allocations were generated by our allocation systems and other six were generated by the random algorithms. The random algorithms differ from each other only in the value of their seeds and they randomly allocate a tester for a given test case. Random algorithms have zero unassignment rate, since all test cases are always allocated to some tester.

4.5 Experimental Procedure

In this experiment, we performed the following procedure:

1. We collected the allocation inputs from the TTC repository from November 2009 to September 2010;

2. For each allocation input, we saved the date in which that allocation input was used: only data prior to that date were used in order to create the tester profiles. This way we guarantee that the recommender algorithm did not have more information than the manager had at that moment;

3. We run each allocation system (proposed and random) to generate automatic allocations;

4. For each automatic allocation made, we calculated the metrics M_1 to M_5 previously described.

Just before executing task **4** above, we had to define the groups of equivalent testers. In order to define these equivalence groups we asked two test managers to classify the testers who were involved in our experiment.

5. EXECUTION

During the experiment, we noticed that the historical allocation of some test plans seems not to follow a typical allocation done by the TTC's test managers. For example, an allocation input with more than 200 test cases had a particular tester allocated to a single test case. We investigated these scenarios together with the test managers and they confirmed that such allocations did not reflect the initial planning. A particular tester was allocated to some other activity but became available at the end of the day for test execution, being asked to run a particular test case. This allocation was stored in the system as if it was the manager's initial plan. Whenever such cases happened, both the tester and the test case associated to that tester were removed from the allocation input not to influence our analysis. This exceptional situations happened in 11 allocation inputs.

In order to calculate approximate precision and approximate recall, the participants of the experiment defined 3 groups of testers with equivalent skills, where group 1 has eight testers, group 2 has five testers, and group 3 has three testers. Group 1 is the group of most skillful testers, group 2 is the group of the second most skillful testers, and so on.

6. ANALYSIS

This section presents the outcome of our experiment with respect to the metrics M_1 to M_5 described in Section 4.1. We use these metrics to perform graphical analyses, test our statistical hypotheses through ANOVA (Analysis of Variance) + Tukey's test or Wilcoxon/Kruskal-Wallis, as detailed next.

6.1 M_1: Unassignment

Figure 4 shows the boxplot for the rate of unassigned test cases per allocation system. The horizontal lines crossing the boxplot indicates the average, while the dots show how the values spread over the Y-axis. The Exp-Manager, Exp-Blind, and MO-Blind allocation systems achieved the best unassignment rate (zero) for all the allocation inputs, which means that all test cases of the 100 allocation inputs were assigned to some tester. In fact, all allocation systems had zero unassignment rate for at least one allocation input. For the other allocation systems, Eff-Manager, MO-Manager and Eff-Blind, the average unassignment rates were 2.34%,

0.05%, and 0.48%, respectively. The random algorithm is not included in this analysis as it always allocates all test cases.

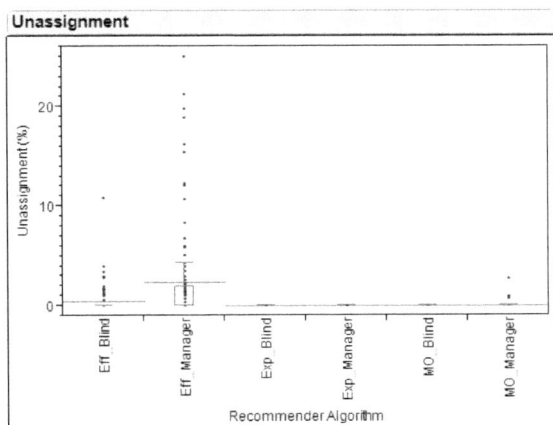

Figure 4: Unassigned test cases per allocation system.

6.2 M_2: Strict Precision

Figure 5 shows the boxplot for the metric M_2 (strict precision). The random algorithms are labelled as Rnd1, Rnd2, ..., Rnd6, and they differ only in the seed used. The average strict precision among our allocation systems varied from 39.32% to 45.41%. The median values ranged from 39.13% to 42.86%. The maximum strict precision value rate achieved was 97.85% (Eff-Blind). Overall, it is clear from Figure 5 that the random algorithms had a lower performance in comparison to our allocation systems.

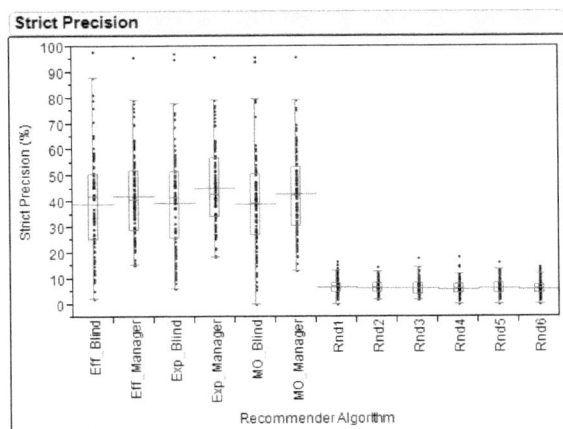

Figure 5: Strict precision per allocation system.

In order to evaluate if any of the allocation systems is significantly different from the others, we run the ANOVA among our recommender systems (without the random algorithms, since we already know they are different). The p-value for the ANOVA was 0.00001, which means that we can reject (at 5% of significance level) the null hypothesis that they have the same mean for the strict precision metric. Therefore, at least one allocation system has a strict preci-

sion mean significantly different from the others. We performed a residual analysis and confirmed that all ANOVA assumptions were met.

Although there is sufficient evidence to reject the claim of equal population means, we cannot conclude which allocation systems are different from the others by considering only the results from ANOVA and the graphical analysis. In order to classify the allocation systems (better or worse), we performed a multiple comparison procedure called Tukey's test.

The left side of table 5 presents the allocation systems classified in levels after the Tukey's test execution. Levels not connected by the same letter have a statistically significant difference. Hence, we can read the data displayed under the column *Strict Precision* in Table 5 as follows. In the average, **A** (Exp-Manager) is better than any system classified as **B** (all Blinds); and it is better than or equal to the systems classified as **AB** (MO-Manager and Eff-Manager). **AB** is better than or equal to the systems classified as **B**; also, it can be as good as any system classified as **A** (more data is needed to better identify these differences). **B** is worse than any system classified as **A**; also, it can be equal to any system classified as **AB** (again, more data is needed to investigate that).

6.3 M_3: Strict Recall

Figure 6 shows the boxplot for the strict recall metric. For our allocation systems, the strict recall means varied from 39.19% to 45.41%. The medians were also very consistent across the allocation systems: they range from 39.13% to 42.86%. The maximum strict recall was 96.97%. Similarly to M_2, the boxplot suggests that all recommender algorithm are better than the random algorithms.

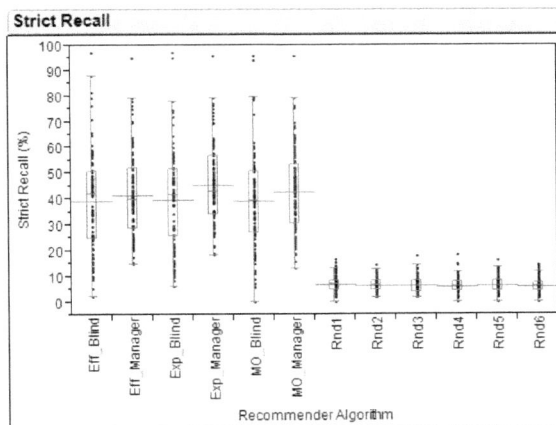

Figure 6: Strict recall per allocation system.

Again, we removed the results from the random allocations and ran the ANOVA. The p-value for the ANOVA was 0.0001, giving us sufficient evidence to reject the null hypothesis and to conclude that at least one allocation system has average performance significantly different from the others. In order to identify the specific means that are different we applied the Tukey's test.

The right side of table 5 presents the allocation systems classified in levels after the Tukey's test execution. The only difference between strict precision and strict recall is

Table 5: Tukey's test - Allocation systems classified in levels.

Strict Precision			Strict Recall		
System	Level	Mean	System	Level	Mean
Exp-Manager	A	45.41	Exp-Manager	A	45.41
MO-Manager	A B	42.91	MO-Manager	A B	42.89
Eff-Manager	A B	42.26	Eff-Manager	A B	41.41
Exp-Blind	B	39.73	Exp-Blind	B	39.73
Eff-Blind	B	39.39	MO-Blind	B	39.32
MO-Blind	B	39.32	Eff-Blind	B	39.19

that MO-Blind and Eff-Blind exchanged positions because of their observed mean values. As both remained in the same group (**B**), the interpretation is the same as described for metric M_2.

6.4 M_4: Approximate Precision

Figure 7 presents the boxplot for the metric M_4 (approximate precision). We can observe that both averages and medians are greater than those for strict precision metric. This was expected, as approximate precision (and approximate recall) do not require the systems to recommend exactly the same pair as allocated by the manager. Notice that the major difference from the results for strict precision is that the performance of the random algorithm has also improved. The average approximate precision for our allocation systems varied from 62.01% to 64.83%. Medians varied from 54.73% to 59.18%. The minimum value for approximate precision was 10% and the maximum value was 100%. The boxplot also indicates that our allocation systems are superior to the random ones.

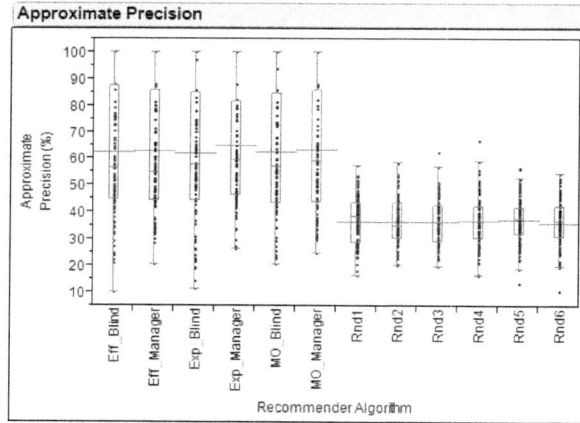

Figure 7: Approximate precision per allocation system.

In order to evaluate if any of the allocation systems was significantly different from the others, we ran the analysis of variance. This time, the Anderson-Darling test showed that the residuals from ANOVA did not follow a normal distribution (or a distribution close enough to a normal one). Hence, we also performed the Wilcoxon/Kruskal-Wallis test, as it does not assume a normal distribution.

By running the Wilcoxon/Kruskal-Wallis test considering only our allocation systems, we found that all allocation systems are similar to each other at $\alpha = 0.05$ (p-value = 0.8509). Therefore, we conclude that they have similar approximate precision means.

6.5 M_5: Approximate Recall

As expected, approximate recall has also improved in comparison to strict recall (see Figure 8). Both average and median increased and all allocation systems reached 100% for some cases. Similarly to approximate precision, the random algorithm also improved markedly in comparison to strict recall. The observed means varied from 61.85% to 64.83% and the medians varied from 54.53% to 59.18%. The maximum value was 100% and minimum value was 9.86%. The boxplot still indicates a superior performance of our allocation systems in comparison to the random ones.

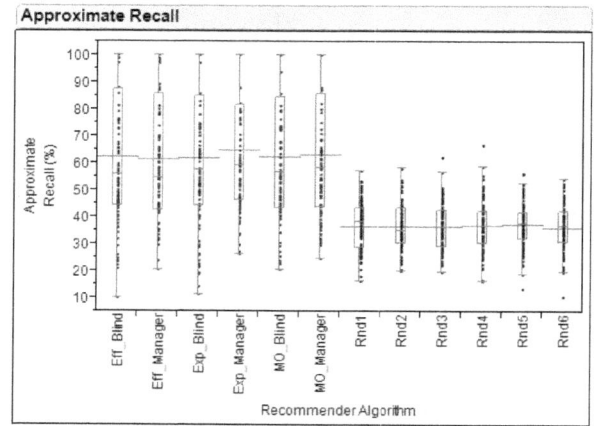

Figure 8: Approximate recall per allocation system.

By running the Wilcoxon/Kruskal-Wallis test over the allocation systems, we found that they are all similar to each other at $\alpha = 0.05$ (p-value = 0.1666). Again, this means that the allocation systems are similar among themselves, but different with respect to the random algorithms.

7. INTERPRETATION

This section discusses the analysis presented in Section 6 and addresses the threats to validity.

7.1 Evaluation of the results and its implications

Unassignment. Three allocation systems (Exp-Manager, Exp-Blind, and MO-Blind) achieved zero unassignment rates: all test cases from the allocation input were assigned to a tester. High unassignment rates (25%) for the other systems indicates that many test cases are poorly documented. Test cases without any information about *component*, *feature* or *category* have a symbolic description built solely from the *description*. This scenario makes some of our allocation systems to assign very low similarities to all testers. It was already expected that the allocation systems based on the effectiveness profile would not perform as well as the ones based on the expertise profile. The preconditions for creating the effectiveness profile are very restrictive: only test cases that failed are used for creating the tester profile. Considering a hypothetical situation in which a tester has run 100 test cases in the past and failed only twice, the expertise profile will be created considering the 100 test cases, while the effectiveness profile will consider only 2 test cases. Tester profiles built from little information results in low similarity rates and, consequently, higher unassignment rates.

Strict Precision. The Manager-based systems achieved better results than the Blind ones with respect to their mean values: this was somehow expected as the Manager-based systems receive the tester's workload before creating the automatic allocations. Although the Manager-based systems performed very well in some cases (95.74%), the average was at most 45.41%. An allocation system does not seem to be capable of identifying the exact person chosen by the manager. This is expected as even a different manager would have difficulties in reproducing the exact results of another manager as there are many possible alternatives for a given test case (the equivalence groups showed that there are many testers with equivalent skills)

Strict Recall. ANOVA and Tukey's test were performed and again the Exp-Manager stood out when compared to the other allocation systems. The results for strict recall are in agreement with the results for the metric M_2 (strict precision). Strict correct pairs seems to be a too restrictive request for a recommender system to detect.

Approximate Precision. With approximate precision all allocation systems reached, for some cases, 100%. The mean approximate precision varied from 62.01% to 64.83%. By inspecting the boxplot we could conclude that the allocation systems performed better than the random algorithm; and the Wilcoxon/Kruskal-Wallis test showed that the allocation systems are similar among themselves.

Approximate Recall. The average recall for the allocation systems varied from 61.85% to 64.83%. Similarly to metric approximate precision, the Wilcoxon/Kruskal-Wallis test showed that the allocation systems are similar among themselves. Again, the visual analysis of the boxplot indicates that the allocation systems are better than the random algorithm.

7.2 Threats to Validity

We identified the following threats to validity:

Analysis of compromised data. The pressure for meeting the deadlines and other daily problems at TTC may have resulted in an ineffective allocation (by the managers) for some allocation inputs. As a consequence, the results can show a lower effectiveness of our approach, as our base of comparison (the manual allocation) may be partially compromised. This threat was controlled by careful filtering the historical data to remove inconsistent test plans.

Test cases poorly documented. The existence of poorly documented test cases in the TTC's database may have resulted in low similarity rates between the test cases and testers, thus leading to higher unassignment rates for some allocation inputs.

Specific industrial setting. We analysed test data from a single test company of a particular application domain (mobile phone testing). Hence, results may vary in different industrial settings.

8. RELATED WORK

This section presents an overview of previous work on recommender systems applied to testing, debugging or people recommendation. As far as we know, there are no recommender systems to allocate test case to testers.

Anvik *et al.* [1] use a machine learning system to allocate developers to bugs. By looking at past allocations, the system infers the best developer to fix a bug. The precision achieved was 57% for the Eclipse project and 64% for the Firefox project. Eclipse and Firefox were used to tune their approach. The application of their system to a different project (GCC) resulted in precisions varying from 6% to 18%. Recall rates were very low, varying from 3% to 10%. Mockus and Herbsleb [14] proposed a system to identify expertise. The tool uses data from version control systems in order to locate people with desired expertise in a given tool or technology. Fault Invariant Classifier [5] is a tool that uses machine learning techniques in order to generate a ranking of program properties likely to lead to errors. For the C programs, the precision was 45% on average and, for the Java programs, the precision was on average 59%. Giger *et al.* [6] look at the history of bug tracking systems to estimate how long it takes to fix a given bug. The precision for the Eclipse project, for example, was 65,4% and the recall was 69,2%. Kpodjedo *et al.* [11] proposed a metric to evaluate, in an object oriented system, which classes deserve more attention from the tester (or from the test manager) to distribute resources and assign testing effort. The system was applied to the development of Mozilla and identified 6 critical classes from a total of 9,000 classes.

9. CONCLUSIONS

We proposed 6 allocation systems to allocate test cases to be run manually by testers. Three of them are manager-based ones, which take as input the tester's workload. The other three algorithms are the blind algorithms that allocate the amount of test cases per tester solely based on similarity. For each of those two categories (manager-based and blind), the algorithms run over three different tester's profiles: the effectiveness profile, the expertise profile and the combination of the two (multi-objective).

The introduction of a tool for test case allocation can help in two ways. The allocations are performed in a much faster way as the managers can now use the automatic recommendation as a starting point of their allocations. And, the arrival of new managers is not impacted as the tool provides them with some knowledge of test cases, testers and previous allocations. With the aid of a recommender tool, managers can perform better allocations faster.

We ran all algorithms over 100 allocation inputs. In our experiment, the ANOVA plus the Tukey's test showed us that the Exp-Manager outperforms the other systems with respect to the strict precision and the strict recall metrics. For *approximately correct pair* the Wilcoxon/Kruskal-Wallis test revealed that all allocation systems are similar among themselves with respect to approximate precision and approximate recall. By analysing the boxplots, all the allocation systems demonstrated to be superior to the random algorithm. For unassignment three of our six allocation systems presented a better performance by achieving zero unassignment rate for all the allocation inputs, namely Exp-Manager, Exp-Blind and MO-Blind.

As all allocation systems presented similar performance (especially for approximate precision and recall), we provide the following guidelines for helping the managers to decide which allocation system to choose. If the manager needs to speed up a particular test execution, then the "Expertise" profile is the best choice as experienced testers run test cases faster. On the other hand, if quality is important, then the "Effectiveness" profile would fit better. If a combination of both (time and quality) is needed, then the manager can use the "Multi-objective" profile. Choosing between Blind or Manager-based depends on whether the manager already knows the workload of the testers.

Our results have already shown that our tool, if it is not as good as the manager, can achieve similar results in most of the cases. Moreover, it automates part of the job that is currently being manually performed. At least good suggestions can be given to the managers to be used as a starting point of their allocations; new managers can benefit even more from our tool as it can provide them with some knowledge of test cases, testers and previous allocations.

As future work, we plan to perform a new experiment to evaluate the managers allocation. We intend to use the equivalence groups of testers defined by the managers (Section 5) and associate a different amount of *points* to the testers based in the group in which they belong. For example, a tester classified in the group of the most talented testers values *3 points*, a tester classified in the group of the second most talented testers values *2 points*, and so on. This allows us to calculate the total amount of points of each allocation and to eventually infer propositions as "*Algorithm X is 65% similar to the manager; and in the 35% it is different, it allocates 50% more testers from the group of the most talented testers than the manager does*". Of course this experiment also has some threats to its validity. For example, *does a high score really characterise a good allocation?* In this future experiment, we assume that the equivalence groups are sound, which seems to be more reasonable than relying on past allocations done (possibly) in a rush.

Acknowledgment

This work was partially supported by FAPERN and the National Institute of Science and Technology for Software Engineering (INES[5]), funded by CNPq and FACEPE, grants 573964/2008-4, 560256/2010-8 and APQ-1037-1.03/08.

10. REFERENCES

[1] J. Anvik, L. Hiew, and G. C. Murphy. Who should fix this bug? In *Proceedings of the International Conference on Software Engineering*, pages 361–370, New York, NY, USA, 2006. ACM.

[2] V. R. Basili, G. Caldiera, and H. D. Rombach. Goal Question Metric Paradigm. In *Encyclopedia of Software Engineering*, volume 1, pages 528–532. John Wiley & Sons, 1994.

[3] B. L. D. Bezerra and F. T. de Carvalho. Symbolic data analysis tools for recommendation systems. *Knowledge and Information Systems*, pages 1–34, 2010.

[4] L. Billard and E. Diday. *Symbolic Data Analysis – Conceptual Statistics and Data Mining*. John Wiley and Sons Ltd, 2006.

[5] Y. Brun and M. D. Ernst. Finding latent code errors via machine learning over program executions. In *Proceedings of the 26th International Conference on Software Engineering*, pages 480–490. IEEE Computer Society, 2004.

[6] E. Giger, M. Pinzger, and H. Gall. Predicting the fix time of bugs. In *Proceedings of the International Workshop on Recommendation Systems for Software Engineering*, pages 36–40, Cape Town, South Africa, 2010.

[7] S. Holzner. *Eclipse*. O'Reilly Media, Inc, 2004.

[8] G. Jeong, S. Kim, and T. Zimmermann. Improving bug triage with bug tossing graphs. In *Proceedings of the European Software Engineering Conference and the International Symposium on Foundations of Software Engineering*, pages 111–120. ACM, 2009.

[9] Juristo and Moreno. *Basics of Software Engineering Experimentation*. Kluwer Academic Publishers, Norwell, MA, USA, 2001.

[10] J. A. Konstan. Introduction to recommender systems: Algorithms and evaluation. *ACM Transactions on Information Systems*, 22(1):1–4, Jan. 2004.

[11] S. Kpodjedo, F. Ricca, P. Galinier, and G. Antoniol. Not all classes are created equal: Toward a recommendation system for focusing testing. In *Proceedings of the International Workshop on Recommendation Systems for Software Engineering*, Atlanta, Georgia, USA, 2008.

[12] M. Lutz. *Programming Python*. O'Reilly Media, 2006.

[13] S. Minto and G. C. Murphy. Recommending emergent teams. In *MSR*, page 5. IEEE Computer Society, 2007.

[14] A. Mockus and J. D. Herbsleb. Expertise browser: a quantitative approach to identifying expertise. In *Proceedings of the International Conference on Software Engineering*, pages 503–512, New York, NY, USA, 2002. ACM.

[15] T. A. B. Pereira, V. S. dos Santos, B. L. Ribeiro, and G. Elias. A recommendation framework for allocating global software teams in software product line projects. In *Proceedings of the International Workshop on Recommendation Systems for Software Engineering*, pages 36–40, Cape Town, South Africa, 2010.

[16] J. Ramos. Using TF-IDF to Determine Word Relevance in Document Queries. Technical report, Department of Computer Science, Rutgers University, 23515 BPO Way, Piscataway, NJ, 08855e, 2003.

[17] I. Sommerville. *Software Engineering*. Addison Wesley, 8th edition, 2006.

[18] C. R. Turner, A. L. Wolf, A. Fuggetta, and L. Lavazza. Feature engineering. *Proceedings of the 9th International Workshop on Software Specification and Design*, page 192, 1998.

[19] C. Wohlin, P. Runeson, M. Host, C. Ohlsson, B. Regnell, and A. Wesslén. *Experimentation in Software Engineering: an Introduction*. Kluver Academic Publishers, 2000.

---

[5]http://www.ines.org.br

Testing Highly Complex System of Systems: An Industrial Case Study

Nauman Bin Ali
School of Computing
Blekinge Institute of
Technology
37179 Karlskrona, Sweden
nauman.ali@bth.se

Kai Petersen
School of Computing
Blekinge Institute of
Technology
37179 Karlskrona, Sweden
kai.petersen@bth.se

Mika V. Mäntylä
Department of Computer
Science
Lund University
22100 Lund, Sweden
mika.mantyla@cs.lth.se

ABSTRACT

Context: Systems of systems (SoS) are highly complex and are integrated on multiple levels (unit, component, system, system of systems). Many of the characteristics of SoS (such as operational and managerial independence, integration of system into system of systems, SoS comprised of complex systems) make their development and testing challenging.

Contribution: This paper provides an understanding of SoS testing in large-scale industry settings with respect to challenges and how to address them.

Method: The research method used is case study research. As data collection methods we used interviews, documentation, and fault slippage data.

Results: We identified challenges related to SoS with respect to fault slippage, test turn-around time, and test maintainability. We also classified the testing challenges to general testing challenges, challenges amplified by SoS, and challenges that are SoS specific. Interestingly, the interviewees agreed on the challenges, even though we sampled them with diversity in mind, which meant that the number of interviews conducted was sufficient to answer our research questions. We also identified solution proposals to the challenges that were categorized under four classes of developer quality assurance, function test, testing in all levels, and requirements engineering and communication.

Conclusion: We conclude that although over half of the challenges we identified can be categorized as general testing challenges still SoS systems have their unique and amplified challenges stemming from SoS characteristics. Furthermore, it was found that interviews and fault slippage data indicated that different areas in the software process should be improved, which indicates that using only one of these methods would have led to an incomplete picture of the challenges in the case company.

Categories and Subject Descriptors

D.2.5 [**Testing and Debugging**]: Diagnostics

Keywords

System of Systems, Software Test, Case Study

1. INTRODUCTION

System of systems (SoS) recently received vast attention in the software engineering research literature. A system of systems is characterized through operational and managerial independence in the development of the individual systems that should later on act together, and is characterized by an integration of many different systems into a new system. System of systems are also generally very complex, and there exist suppliers that deliver them for integration [16, 7]. Literature (cf. [19, 8]) distinguishes different types of SoS, namely virtual, collaborative, acknowledged, and directed SoS.

It is acknowledged that SoS development and quality assurance is very challenging, e.g. due to involvement of many parties, it is not easy to integrate systems continuously, and so forth [19, 16, 17, 7]. However, so far there is a lack of empirical studies that explore the challenges and possible solutions of how to test such complex system of systems. In response to this research gap this case study makes the contribution to investigate the challenges and potential solutions of SoS development in an industrial case study of a large-scale system of systems from the telecommunication domain with over 5,000,000 Lines of code. The following contributions are made by this study:

- Understand how SoS testing is done by describing and characterizing how system of systems are currently tested based on a case having the typical characteristics of directed SoS development.

- Identify the challenges of SoS testing observed in the case and categorize them to three classes: a) challenges that are not different in SoS context and other contexts, b) challenges that are amplified in SoS context but that can also be found in other contexts, and c) new challenges specific only to SoS context.

- Identify possible solutions of SoS testing based on the challenges.

The remainder of the paper is structured as follows: Section 2 presents the related work. Section 3 describes the research method, followed by the results in Section 4. Section 5 concludes the papers by presenting the observations and implications given by the results.

2. RELATED WORK

The Systems Engineering Guide [11] defines SoS *"set or arrangement of systems that results when independent and useful systems are integrated into a larger system that delivers unique capabilities"*. Maier [19] and Dahman et al. [8] classify SoS into Virtual, Collaborative, Acknowledged, and Directed. Virtual means that there is no central management or agreed purpose of the SoS, purposes emerge as systems are combined. This reflects the philosophy of service-oriented architecture, which is a way of implementing SoS [17]. Collaborative SoS have an agreed purpose and interact voluntarily. How systems should interact is collectively decided between system owners. Acknowledged SoS are characterized by common objectives, and there exists a designated manager that assures resources for SoS development. The System Engineering Guide stresses that the individual systems still have independent ownership, objectives, funding, and development. Directed SoS are built to fulfil specific purposes and they are managed around those purposes. There exist a central management for the SoS. However, the system development organizations contributing individual systems are still independent, but subordinate to the purpose. The SoS in this study is characterized as directed.

The System Engineering Guide [11] also highlights some engineering challenges that are particular to SoS, namely (1) Management issues with respect to governance of system development across organizational boundaries, (2) the increased complexity, scope, and cost of processes for planning and engineering, (3) achieving and maintaining interoperability, and (4) likelihood of unpredicted behaviour, and hence the lack of predictability of behaviour.

Lewis et al. [16] point out that SoS challenges are related to collaboration, in particular who collaborates and what everyone has to provide so that the collaboration would work. Furthermore, there are particular challenges if systems do not evolve in a similar pace or manner, which makes their integration challenging. Hence, if there are some dependencies (one system cannot fulfil its service without another) then there is a need for synchronization, which makes collaboration essential. How the SoS is built in an enterprise affects the severity of the challenge of collaboration. They distinguish SoS in an enterprise where a single or multiple organizations develop, and where multiple enterprises develop.

Columbi et al. [7] characterizes SoS as systems that operate synergistically, however, SoS can operate and be managed independently. They acknowledge and highlight that these characteristics make testing and evolution of SoS very challenging. In other words, they have amplifying character, or even lead to completely novel challenges. In their experience report from a SoS development at the Department of Defense (DoD), they suggest a number of challenges: (1) organizational structures do not support testing in a SoS framework; (2) No steps in testing that evaluate the overall SoS capabilities, rather the focus is very much on individual systems (no obligation for the project manager to scope testing on the SoS level), (3) Rate of incoming requirements has drastically increased on the SoS, leading to an exponential increase of test events, complexity, and expense with respect to testing; (4) No overarching test scenarios across different systems due to coordination and communication breakdowns. In response to the challenges, they provided

a number of solutions: (1) only test interoperability with respect to changes made, and do not test everything, but rather *"built a little, test a little"*, (2) use risk assessment to prioritize the ever growing number of tests, (3) focus tests on interfaces as there the greatest risk of mistakes lie, but do not neglect internal behaviour of systems, (4) provide designated environments and people for integration.

Furthermore, we identified other studies that have a focus on SoS quality assurance (see e.g. [13, 5]), but those are solution proposals without an industrial partner involved.

Overall, we found that there is a lack of systematic empirical evidence that investigates how to conduct testing in a SoS context, and relates that to challenges and solutions.

3. RESEARCH METHOD

As a research method we used case study research, following the guidelines provided in Yin [24] as well as Runeson and Höst [22].

3.1 Purpose and Research Questions

The purpose of the study is to gain an in-depth understanding of testing practices, challenges, and potential solutions when testing very large SoS.

RQ1: How is SoS testing done in industry? We first need to gain a deep understanding and rich description of the current situation, as SoS testing is not well described in literature. The case being studied in that sense provides an interesting case as it fulfils the characteristics of directed SoS development very well.

RQ2: What are perceived and measured challenges when testing SoS and how are they different from testing challenges of other contexts? Given testing in SoS is not well explored in industry the first step should be to understand the challenges in order to find useful solutions.

RQ3: What potential solutions do practitioners see in order to address the challenges identified? The identification of the solutions is based on experiences made in the SoS context. They provide useful input for future evaluations to test their actual impact in the studied context.

3.2 Case and Context

The case being studied is a development site of a large Telecom vendor, engaging in SoS development. The case and context are described, as this allows for generalizing the results to a specific context. Other companies in a similar context are likely to find the results transferable to their context [20].

The process used at the company follows a SoS approach. There is no common definition of system of systems, as the term has been defined in different domains, such as military, enterprise information systems, or education [15]. The term has been recently established in the software engineering field, where a system of systems should fulfil several of the characteristics. These characteristics and their presence in the case company are shown in Table 1.

The overall architecture of the system of systems studies consists of 12 systems, which are operationally independent and can also provide services independently of each other. The process used at the company is shown in Figure 2. In the first step the high-level requirements for the overall SoS are specified. Before the requirements are handed over to compound system development a so-called "Go"-decision is taken, meaning that development resources are allocated to

Table 1: System of Systems Approach Characteristics (cf. [15])

ID.	Characteristic	Case Company
C1	Operational independence	(√)
C2	Managerial independence	(√)
C3	Integration of system into system of systems	(√)
C4	SoS comprised of complex systems	(√)
C5	System suppliers deliver systems for integration	(√)
C6	Complete technical overview of SoS and system supply	(√)

the high-level requirement. When the decision is positive, teams specify a detailed requirements specification, which then is handed over to the concerned system(s). The requirements are then implemented for a specific development system, and they are integrated (also called system level test).The development is done in sprints run by agile development teams (AT Sprints in Figure 2). Each system can be integrated independently of another system, which provides them some degree of operational and managerial independence (see Table 1). However, the versions of two systems have to be compatible when the system of systems is integrated (Compound System Test). Each of the systems is highly complex, the largest system having more than 15 development teams. The size of the overall system of systems measured in lines of code (LOC) is 5,000,000 LOC. This fulfils the characteristics of SoS development related to system complexity and integration. In order to make sure that the system of systems is working together in the end an overall system structure and design is developed, referred to as the anatomy. This allows having an overview of the overall SoS, also making explicit how each system in the SoS contributes to the overall system goals.

Looking at other context elements [20] the following should be added as information:

- All systems and the SoS are older than 5 years.

- On principle level the development process is incremental with projects adding increments (e.g. new functionality) to the code base-line on system and compound system level.

- Within the teams and in the testing activities agile practices are used, such as: continuous integration, time-boxing with sprints, face-to-face interaction (stand-up meetings, co-located teams), requirements prioritization with product backlogs, re-factoring and system improvements

3.3 Data Collection

We used multiple data sources for triangulation to increase the validity of the results. In order to answer RQ1 and RQ2 we used documentation, interviews as well as quantitative data as input. For RQ3 we used interviews to gather opinions of how to best improve SoS testing.

Process documentation of the test process is obtained in order to capture the specified test strategies and test levels conducted at the company. This information is used for triangulation purposes as an additional source to the interviews. Furthermore, the documentation aided the researchers to gain better domain knowledge and familiarity with the test specific terminology used at the company before conducting the interviews. In addition we consulted

official templates for reporting (e.g. forms for documenting defect data).

Interviews It is important to point out that the sampling procedure here is not to get a representative sample of a population, but rather having a diversity of perspectives to be able to contrast alternatives in the evaluation step. We notice that with each additional interview there was a high overlap in the views and we decided to stop after five interviews. Even though the practitioners had diverse roles the number of challenges and improvement suggestions stabilised after the third interview, which indicates a good coverage of the interviews (refer to Figure 1).

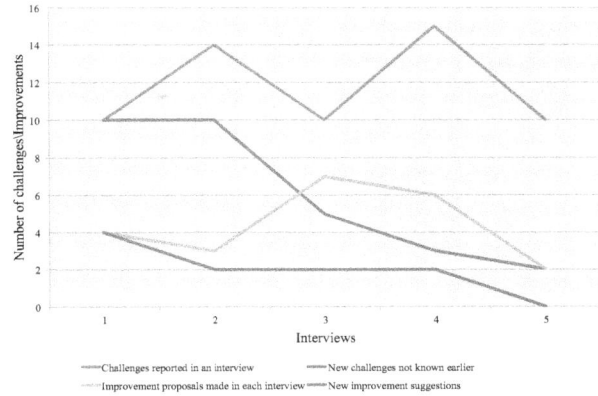

Figure 1: Stability in challenges/improvement suggestions identified in interviews

Test Managers who have the knowledge about their team members supported us in interviewee selection ensuring diversity and coverage of various test levels in the company. In the following a short profile of the testers is provided in Table 2.

Table 2: Practitioners' profile

ID	Description
1	The interviewee is currently working with test improvement with a particular focus on FT and ST, and has experience from working in testing teams before. Furthermore, the interviewee has more than five years of experience focused on testing.
2	The interviewee is working in software development since 1995 and is currently a technical coordinator. In the past the interviewee also worked as a tester, and had a leading role in design teams with responsibility for product and test code.
3	The interviewee is a technical expert assisting software developers in solving technical problems, in particular the problems that occurred in testing. Hence, the interviewee is directly exposed to review and BT in the daily work.
4	The interviewee is working with the company since 1994, and has been involved in software testing, development, support, and system management. She has worked as a developer for several systems in the company, currently leading a development team investigating new enhancements to the main system. The interviewee has experience of conducting reviews, BT, and FT.
5	The interviewee is currently working in ST and CST. Before that the interviewee had various technical roles, including support and software design. Overall, she has over 10 years of experience in designing software.

Interview structure: The interview is structured in four themes, namely: (1) interviewee knowledge and experience, (2) when and where to detect what type of defects, (3) how the tester conducts tests, and (4) strengths and liabilities of the current testing approach. The interview is semi-structured and consists of mainly open-ended questions, hence allowing to follow and discuss interesting issues, or change the order of questions. The interviews approximately took 90 minutes to complete. The contents of the interview were as follows:

- **Part I: Interviewee knowledge and experience:** This theme focuses on obtaining information about the testers knowledge and practical experience (professional background and education, explaining current role at the company, roles before current role).
- **Part II: Understanding test levels and their responsibilities:** This theme focuses on determining which types of defects are detected at which test level, using a defect classification scheme for telecommunication systems from Damm and Lundberg [9].
- **Part III: Understanding how testing is done and its related challenges:** This theme focuses on how testing is done and what challenges occurred, including characterization of test objects at different levels, input used to derive test cases and the quality of the input used (e.g. requirements), tool support, and general strengths and challenges observed.
- **Part IV: Closing:** The interviewees were asked whether they want to add something important that was not covered in the interview questions yet.

Before starting the actual interview, the purpose of the study and the reasons for the selection of the interviewee were provided. Furthermore, the interviewee was asked whether we were allowed to record the interview for transcription. The interviewee was also informed that all information collected was treated anonymously and will be aggregated with the information provided by the other interviewees.

Quantitative Data: With respect to defects we look at distribution of types of defects and defect criticality per test level, and fault slippage. The types of defects discovered at the test levels reveal which types of defects the test level is actually able to capture given the current test practices employed. Fault slippage measures indicate whether each testing phase is able to detect the defects it is supposed to detect (see [10]). The data is available through a company internal and proprietary defect reporting system. For this study we focus on recent defects (in the past 12 months) that reflect the current test strategy employed at the company.

3.4 Data Analysis

Interviews Audio recordings of all five interviews were transcribed. We used colour coding for initial data extraction from transcribed interviews where one unique colour was assigned to each one of the following:

- Challenge, problem, malpractice, limitation and missing information for testing
- Benefit or strength of current practices, tools or processes
- Current practice, way of doing work or tools used
- Improvement suggestions
- Definitions of terms, test levels and artefact descriptions

While colour coding, brief notes were made about the statements making use of the context of the statements and reducing misinterpretation later on. These colour coded statements and their brief descriptors were extracted and were put in a spread-sheet verbatim while maintaining traceability to the source. At this point these were assigned codes (according to Table 3) to capture their relation to the respective test level. A separate spread-sheet was created for each of the five items above. Next step was to aggregate the repeating statements which was done by repeating the following this process for all five sheets:

Step-1: For the first statement create and log a code.
Step-2: For each subsequent statement identify if a similar statement already exists. If it does log the statement with the same code, otherwise create a new code.
Step-3: Repeat Step-2 until the last statement has been catalogued.

A short description was given to each of the resulting clusters with same code. As traceability was ensured between the clusters, their summary/description, individual statements and audio recordings, second author was able to review the results of the process whether the statements were correctly clustered together. The disagreements were resolved by discussion.

Documentation was analysed through the same coding scheme as the interviews (as explained above).

3.5 Threats to Validity

While designing and conducting this case study various conscious decisions were taken to strengthen the validity of results. Using the checklist proposed by [22] we evaluated the case study protocol. This ensured that we had addressed all the critical requirements of case study design including aims of the study, defining the case, unit of analysis and data collection methods among others. Another researcher who has extensive knowledge and experience in case study research also reviewed the protocol. Furthermore, this detailed protocol was kept up-to-date, reflecting the actual course of the case study.

Construct validity: Both methodological (interviews and archival data analysis) and data source (practitioners and defect database) triangulation were used to strengthen the evidence generated in this case study. Using appropriate amount of raw data and through clear chain of evidence (maintaining traceability between the results, qualitative data and sources), this validity threat was minimized.

Internal validity: In this case study, the challenges were examined in the context of SoS, and the relation of SoS context to challenges was discussed. However, given the complexity of a real world organization and the fact that confounding factors are always a challenge when studying real world systems, the isolated effect of SoS characteristics can not be established, and requires further investigation.

External validity: There are too few empirical studies yet to make general claims, but the case in this study represents a typical complex SoS based software product development situation and is likely to apply to similar contexts w.r.t. system complexity, domain, etc.

Reliability: By involving more than one researcher, each actively engaged in the design, review and execution of the study, where case study protocol was the means of communication and documenting the agreement. Thus we believe that the resulting detailed protocol serves as a good means to replicate this study. The detailed documented steps of data collection, processing and analysis also increase the reliability of this study.

4. RESULTS

The results present the current practices of testing SoS, the challenges and their relation to SoS characteristics, as well as SoS solution proposals.

4.1 SoS Testing Process and Practices (RQ1)

Test Process: We found that overall there are six Test levels at the case company. These were visible in both the test process documentation in the company and the interview results. Furthermore, the organization of testing teams and responsibilities is roughly organized around these levels as well. We found additional test levels in the defect database, however, based on the defect reports from the last two years these levels were not used at all in reporting. This hints redundancy of some of these levels. One explanation for no faults reported to "Regression test" is that regression testing is performed within other phases of testing and therefore is not considered a separate phase. Based on the congruence between the latest documents, interview results and defect reports we found six levels as shown in Table 3. These test levels are depicted in the overall development process in the Figure 2.

Table 3: Test levels in the case company

Code	Description of test levels
Rev	Reviews using static analysis and Visual "Diff" tools are performed by the development teams.
BT	Basic test is done in the Agile Team (AT) sprint by the development teams and uses implementation as the test reference. It includes unit testing with JUnit [1] and TestNG [4]. Input for tests are user stories, protocol specifications, component descriptions, dimensioning requirements, and traffic models.
FT	Function test focuses on testing isolated functions and is done in AT sprint by the development teams using Testing and Test Control Notation (TTCN) [3].
ST	System test tests the integration of the AT sprints (teams) in pre-defined cycles. Test cases created in FT and previous releases are used. No new test cases are written. The testing is done on a different branch along with regression testing using self-contained test cases (each test case sets up configuration, executes test scenario, and removes configuration once it is done). In addition, the company uses traffic models and simulates the system behaviour under load.
CST	Compound system test, tests the integration of systems into the overall system. Here, the emphasis is on making sure that the system functionality when integrated, still fulfils non-functional requirements (e.g. load), and is installable.
FOA	After system test is completed, the product is tested by installing it on a trial customer network. After this the product is launched to the general market.

Test Levels and their responsibilities: We used interviews to explore the practitioners' perception as to which defects are found at each of these test levels. The results are presented in Table 4. The first column depicts the fault classification used in the case company and the numbers in each row show how many of the five practitioners interviewed consider that this defect type is often found at this level. From the opinions expressed in the interviews most of the defects are found at ST. For certain defect types this is an expected behaviour e.g. quality assessment at system level is not possible before this level. Perhaps that is why there is a consensus that Quality related issues (performance, robustness and concurrency) are found in ST. One practitioner said, *"the single biggest place where we find faults is in ST"*. Prac-

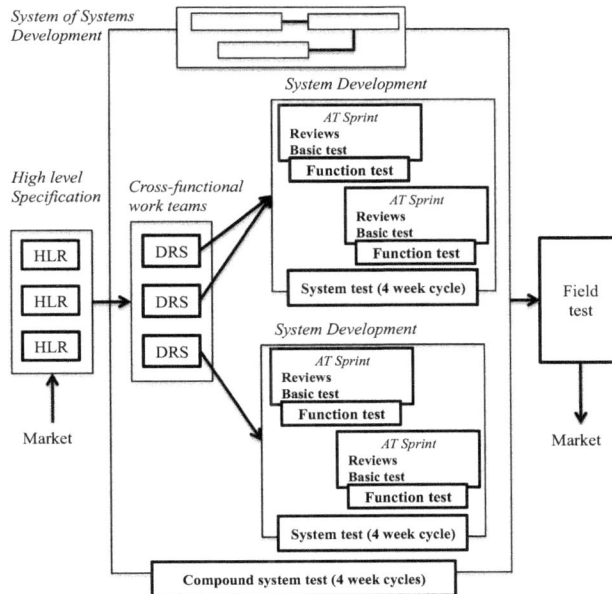

Figure 2: System of Systems development process with test levels at the case company

titioners perceive that programming faults are discovered in basic testing which is an expected behaviour. Although reviews are recognised as a good practice and are used in the company but in practitioners' opinion it is not effective in discovering defects. Only one practitioner was satisfied with the effectiveness of current reviews.

Table 4: Fault Classes [9] and where Practitioners find them based on Interviews

	Rev	BT	FT	ST	CST	FOA
Internal Interface	2	2	2	2		
External Interface			2	2	1	
Human Interface			2	3	1	2
Coding Errors / Coverage	1	4	1	2		
Performance	1			5	3	
Robustness				5	2	
Redundancy				4	4	
Concurrency				5	3	
Configuration				3	2	2
Missing Functionality				2	1	1
Wrong Behaviour			1	1	1	1

Test Efficiency in the current situation: As a measure of test efficiency the company uses fault slippage, indicating whether a fault is found in a later test level than the one where it ought to be found. From Table 4 we observed that there is some fault slippage in the testing process. For example, consider the defects triggered from "internal interfaces" and "Coding errors" that should ideally be found in the early test levels like reviews or basic test. However, in practitioner's opinion these defects often slip through to later stages.

To assess the validity of these observations and look at the effectiveness of testing quantitatively we used the FST data. We analysed the defect reports for the last calendar year since 01.01.2011- 01.02.2012 (see Table 5 for the results).

In Table 5 the values on the diagonal (in bold face) represent the percentage of defects that were found exactly where

Table 5: Fault slip through data

'Should' to 'Did' detect	Rev	BT	FT	ST	CST	FOA	Total slippage
Rev	**30.76**	7.69	30.76	19.23	0.00	11.53	25.71
BT	*6.15*	**26.15**	32.30	18.46	4.61	12.30	62.85
FT		*7.14*	**50.00**	28.57	14.28		8.57
ST				**88.88**	11.11		1.42
CST					**100.00**		0.00
FOA							**0.00**

they are ought to be found. The percentage points in the last column "Total slippage" accounts for the percentage of slippage from each level compared to the total slippage from all test levels. In terms of overall slippage from one test level Basic test (with 62.85%) and Reviews (with 25.71%) have a lot of potential for improvement. From these results ST and CST are the top performers in terms of catching the right faults. As pointed out by one of the practitioners, *"The single biggest place where we find faults is in function test"* we can see that most of the slippage from Reviews and BT are caught in Function test (30.76 % and 32.30% respectively).

In Table 5 there are some unexpected values below the diagonal (in italics). There could be a number of explanations for it, the simplest one that it was a mistake in reporting the data or that although the test strategy states that the defect should have been found later but it was found in an earlier phase, thus requiring an update to the strategy or it was just a coincidence that this defect was found earlier and doesn't warrant a strategy update. However, we did not confirm or reject any of the explanations for this small percentage of defect reports.

We can see some congruence between results from Table 4 and Table 5. The majority of the defects are found in the later test levels especially in FT and ST. Top two levels with maximum slippage are BT and reviews respectively.

Table 6: Fault slip through to customer

'Should' to 'Did' detect	Percentage found by Customer
Rev	15.27
BT	63.88
FT	6.94
ST	11.11
CST	1.85
FOA	0.00
Customer	0.92

Looking at the problems found by the customer (as shown in Table 6) we can see that a high percentage of slip through is from Basic testing and Reviews. Having triangulated the practitioners' observations with quantitative data, we delved deeper to understand the practical challenges and their influence on these symptoms.

4.2 Challenges (RQ2)

From the interviews and defect databases we found three main undesired results with respect to outcome variables in testing, namely fault slippage, long turnaround time and maintenance of test suite. These outcomes are influenced by various issues and challenges, which were also identified from the interviews. In total we identified 30 different challenges that were mapped to three levels: 1) challenges that

are not different in SoS context and other contexts, 2) challenges that are amplified in SoS context but that can also be found in other contexts, and 3) to new challenges specific only to SoS context (see Figures 3 , 4 and 5). We do not claim cause-effect relations, as those would have to be established in controlled environments. Hence, the relation between challenges and outcome variables should be seen as indicators in this exploratory study. The challenges in levels "2" and "3" as described above are also mapped to the characteristics of SOS (presented in Table 1) that aggravate or cause these challenges.

Figure 3, shows the challenges that influence the undesired result of fault slippage. In the related work (Section 2) it was highlighted that the independence of system development leads to challenges in collaboration. As there are many organizations integrating their interacting system and there are many levels of testing (see C1, C2, and C3 in Table 1), the challenge of unclear responsibilities of test levels is apparent. Collaboration challenges and independence (C1 and C2) also affect knowledge sharing, and hence lack of compliance to processes, lack of shared guidelines for testing at various levels and tools. It also leads to a lack of responsibility for test suits that are shared by different systems when they are integrated. SoS affects testability of requirements due to its complexity (C4), and that a requirement concerns multiple systems and in order to interpret them reasonably well a wide domain expertise across system boundaries is needed. There is also a lack of thorough analysis and selection of test cases, which is influenced by the SoS complexity (C4). Other influencing factors (e.g. early evaluation of quality attributes [14], time to market pressure and influence on test [6], difficulties in basic test, and lack of independent verification (people who code also write the test cases) [18] are rather generic challenges.

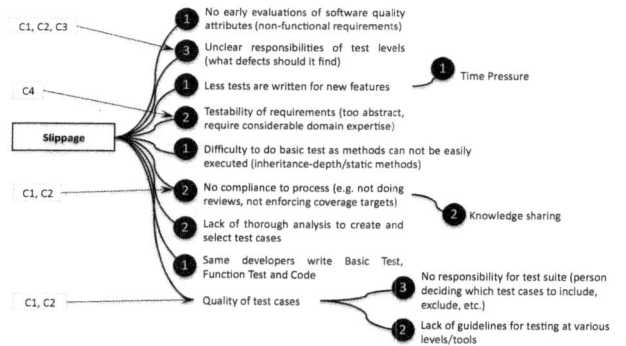

Figure 3: Challenges influencing fault slippage in the case company

In Figure 4 the challenges to the maintenance of regression suite are visualized. Because of the growing number, size and complexity of systems (C4) put together in the SoS (C3 and C5) it is imperative that the system test will get more and more test cases related to FT in regression suite. Furthermore, there is no formal responsibility for maintenance of the test suite given characteristics C1 and C2, which also leads to no detection of redundant and obsolete test cases. The sheer amount of test cases added makes it a difficult problem to address. Any centralized solution is likely to be overwhelmed and with no shared standards (difficult to achieve in a SoS with managerial and operation independence) the current decentralized approach is not working, as the quality of test cases in terms of design, implementation and readability is a major issue for maintenance. Challenges such as test case readability (e.g. addressed to behaviour driven development [23]), company proprietary code due to lack of tool awareness, and lack of separation between test code and test data [12] are rather generic. However, non-compliance is aggravated in SoS due to difficulties in spreading news about good tools.

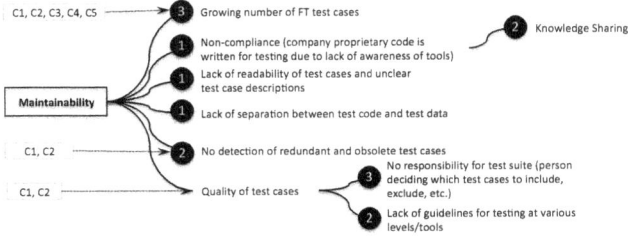

Figure 4: Challenges influencing maintenance of FT regression suite

The challenges contributing to a long turnaround time for regression test are shown in Figure 5. The number of growing number of FT test cases affects the maintainability of the test suite, and is significant due to the SoS context, as was discussed for Maintenance. The difficulty of doing basic testing leads to the misuse of the FT framework, which is amplified by the SoS complexity (C4) and lack of communication and interaction (C1 and C2) as the framework now includes many BT tests, that take more time to be executed due to the limitations of the FT framework. It should also be emphasized that many of these challenges influence multiple problems and have some interactions between them as well. The platforms inefficiency is one dimension of the problem because it is not easy to switch to a different framework because of the cost of migration of existing test cases and retraining the resources. Therefore the solutions to improve the turnaround time may take a multi pronged approach e.g. reducing the number of test cases to run by prioritization, selection or using the framework for its strengths. Another option is to think about smarter ways to design to specifically improve the turnaround time. Prioritization of test cases [25, 21] and TTCN as a test framework [26] have been addressed generically in research contributions.

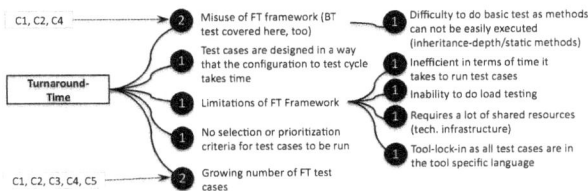

Figure 5: Challenges influencing the turnaround time of FT regression suite

4.3 Improvements (RQ3)

We identified 14 improvement actions in order to reduce/mitigate the negative impact of the issues on fault slippage,

maintainability of test cases, and turn-around time. The improvement suggestions have been organized to five groups based on which area they affect. The groups are developer quality assurance, function test, testing at all levels, requirements engineering and communication.

Table 7: Improvement Ideas and Effected Testing Processes

Improvement ideas	Rev	BT	FT	ST	CST	FOA
Reviews	✓					
Basic Testing		✓				
Maintenance of FT reg suite			✓			
Controlling size of FT reg suite			✓			
Feedback time for FT reg suite			✓			
Guidelines for FT tool usage			✓			
Tech improvements to FT tool			✓			
Improving test case quality		✓	✓	✓	✓	✓
Definitions of test levels	✓	✓	✓	✓	✓	✓
Increase tool usage:	✓	✓	✓	✓	✓	✓
Early quality evaluations	✓	✓	✓	✓	✓	✓
Requirement testability			✓	✓	✓	✓
Feature status tracking	✓	✓	✓	✓	✓	✓
Improved interaction	✓	✓	✓	✓	✓	✓

4.3.1 Developer quality assurance

The improvement suggestions in this group affect the work practices of individual developers and the results produced are not used outside of individual AT.

Reviews: Code reviews have helped in early detection of coding fault, however, there is a need for organization wide adoption of the practice. Reviews should be supplemented with tools that support visualization of code changes in the artefact under review. To utilize the human resources effectively, automated static code analysis should precede reviews. This will enable the reviewers to focus on the defects that the tools cannot find. These tools are generally easy to use and if configured properly can reduce the number of false positives. Thus, reviews can help avoid certain fault slippage and provide means for early evaluation.

Basic testing: Practitioners from development teams believe that increased basic testing has reduced the number of faults that slip through to the function test. They acknowledge that these improvements in basic test have been possible because of inclusive discussions with various development teams. This is a clear indication of why it is necessary to have stakeholder involvement and buy-in/consensus on decisions. Furthermore, some teams set and enforce coverage goals. They use code coverage tools, as these tools help to see the extent of testing. However, there is a need for wider adoption of these tools through out the company. Some practitioners also suggested that test-driven development and use of mock object techniques could offer avenues for improvement.

4.3.2 Function Test

The improvement suggestions in this group focus on the function test level.

Maintenance of FT regression test suite: There was a consensus on having persons with formal responsibility for maintenance of the test suite. This seems plausible, but considering the size of the organization and amount of test cases it will require a lot of skills, effort and coordination between teams. However, the current practice of having a distributed mechanism has not really worked either. Perhaps in the SoS context the only viable solution is that of shared responsibility with some central governance. Thus, having multiple levels of control on what is contributed to the regression suite. For example, first the individual teams assess the quality of FT and suggests an inclusion to the suite, and then the tests are only included if the person(s) with formal responsibility approves them. Furthermore, improving the readability of test cases and enforcing design principles when developing test code will reduce the maintenance cost as well.

Controlling the size of FT regression suite: By improving the effectiveness of reviews and BT (see suggestions in Section 4.3.1) the unnecessary load on FT will be reduced. Similarly having responsible person(s) for test suite maintenance will give an opportunity to have a filter on new test cases being added. Similarly such person(s) may also review existing test cases and remove redundant or obsolete test cases from the suite, thus reducing the number of test cases.

Reducing the feedback time for FT regression suite: Practitioners believe that having prioritization or selection criteria will bring significant improvement to feedback time for the regression suite. So rather than running all the test cases all the time, two suggestions for prioritization criteria were: to run the most relevant tests first or to run the tests that fail frequently before others in the suite. Another step in the right direction is that the test cases have been tagged at a high-level based on the protocols and features they test. This is useful to select relevant test cases and to identify which parts of the system are being neglected in testing and which other parts have a high overlap in test cases. Removal of redundant and obsolete test cases and using the framework for FT (instead of BT) will also alleviate the problems aggravated by having a large regression suite in ST where all the FTs are added, as well as the problems related to an inefficient testing framework.

Guidelines for FT tool usage: We found that TTCN, i.e. the tool used in FT, is sometimes misused for unit testing which is not the strength of the framework. In large organizations dealing with SoS there is a Lock-in with respect to tools and it is very costly to switch to a different tool, especially when it is as embedded as TTCN. Therefore, the practitioners suggested to use TTCN for FT only as it has following strengths:

- Ability to test multiple protocols: is a major strength of TTCN over other testing frameworks.
- Automation helps save time: with use of TTCN for testing the time taken for test has reduced considerably. As one practitioner said, *"For us, for instance if we want to test a Product Customization, with say 30 test cases. Just executing them may be takes about 15 minutes. But doing it manually will take may be 3-4 hours"*.
- Useful for protocol verification: the ability to manipulate at bit level gives better control of protocol messages and parameter verification. This makes it very useful for external interface testing.

Thus, by taking steps in Section 4.3.2 to manage the suite size we can use the resource intensive TTCN for the testing that cannot be tested without it.

Technical improvements to FT tool: Many of the maintenance problems of the FT suite stemmed from the technical shortcomings of the TTCN tool used in the company, thus various improvement ideas for it were suggested in the interviews. Practitioners had complaints about the inability of TTCN to support load and GUI testing. There is also a need to improve the TTCN editor to identify multiple test headers in the same file and improve the readability of test cases. It should be easy to write TTCN test cases without having to repeat a lot of things, and to write configurations in the test cases so that verification is facilitated. One suggestion was to develop wrappers or high-level language constructs for setting up complex configurations, which will reduce the requirements on knowledge about subsystems and intricate details of how the protocols work. This will not only make writing test cases easier, which means even under time constraints it is still possible to develop test cases without the threat of mistakes in configuration.

4.3.3 Testing in all levels

The improvement suggestions in this section affect testing at all levels of testing from basic testing (BT) to field tests (FOA).

Improving the test-case quality: Having templates and guidelines for writing test cases particular to various test levels and tools used will help improve the quality of test-cases. This will enforce a consistent structure in test-cases and help teams following best practices to enabling readability, good design and high coverage. Furthermore, improving the quality of test cases will significantly improve the confidence in the testing suite's ability to find faults. The current mechanism of writing configurations at the bit level results in test cases that are error-prone. In the complex SoS context it is almost impossible to have such detailed knowledge about all the systems. Thus, having a wrapper (which also addresses the technical issues of the FT tool) to provide abstraction for the low level configurations will facilitate writing test cases and reduce the necessity of in-depth domain knowledge about various systems in SoS. Having test-case templates, documented best practices, and high-level constructs to specify test cases will also alleviate the effects of employee turnover as the knowledge will be embedded in the artefacts. Furthermore, reducing fault slippage by writing tests in pairs and/or review test cases by another team member will reduce chances of misinterpretation of requirements.

Definitions and responsibilities of test levels: Practitioners identified the need for better organization wide definitions of test levels with clear strategies of what should be verified at each test level. They also think that a better analysis of what we want to verify in each test level can reduce the overlap in testing. It is important to make a trade-off between early detection and cost of set-up. One may identify certain faults in basic test but the cost of setting up the environment to test may be too high. It is an encouraging sign that the testers understand this e.g. while commenting on the role of basic testing one practitioner said, *"We are aware that we can't test everything and may be we shouldn't in basic test"*.

Increase tool usage: Practitioners were aware of many improvements that could be gained by wider usage of test tools. For example, generating tests instead of manual coding, while talking about the benefits of a tool used to create trees and simulation test cases the practitioner said, *"then you can run a lot of logic in the tree without writing in TTCN"*. Similarly, use Mock tools as suggested in Section

4.3.1 instead of statically programming the interfaces. Also, it was suggested to use tools to generate test data that helps in e.g. boundary value analysis, thus maintaining a differentiation between test code and data.

One practitioner highlighted the importance of tools that can provide a management view by summarizing and presenting data to support decision-making. This aligns well with the need of technical overview in a SoS. SONAR [2] is one such tool that can help providing:

- a management view of measurements and status.
- feedback on test cases, where there are less test cases or too many.
- and highlight, which test cases are not designed properly.

Early quality evaluations: The practitioners expressed the need to run non-functional tests sooner than currently possible. One solution is to look for performance issues that can be identified earlier without running the non-functional tests. This could be done by reviews or static code analysis to e.g. design and complexity of algorithms, memory management that is likely to result in performance degradation. Yet another complementing solution is to have early architectural evaluations for quality requirements e.g. by using prototyping.

4.3.4 Requirements engineering and communication

The large size of the SoS context can easily lead to communication gaps. Furthermore, requirements form the bases against which tests are developed. Thus, it is natural that practitioners suggested how improvements in requirements engineering and communication would help the case company.

Improving the testability of requirements: In a typical case in SoS context, requirements are written to describe a system service that involves multiple systems. It therefore helps when the feature lead (person owning a feature) does a pre-analysis of requirements to understand which systems will be affected and helps testing teams to anticipate workload. Similarly, having concrete user-stories that describe one standard scenario and not the whole service is useful for testing. It should describe a standard scenario with internetworking description (the interactions with other systems) without delving into everything that can go wrong. Another suggestion is that the requirement owner should write function test on at least external interfaces so that the requirement will be documented in a testable manner.

Feature status tracking: There should be a mechanism in the development process to document and communicate the decisions regarding consciously delayed features as it otherwise will create false positives in testing. Currently, the test team creates a defect report for missing functionality and it goes through an expensive process to handle them. Furthermore, there is no distinction between unintentionally and intentionally missing features.

Improved interaction between teams and cross-functional teams: System management is in between the customer and design/test teams and they have a good understanding of the customer needs. So they can be helpful to ask for missing information or explanation to avoid misinterpretation.

Similarly, a new initiative to involve ST teams early on in the process was welcomed by the practitioners. Now the testing team has a better understanding of features and can estimate the expected workload better. This early involvement has led to improved planning and reduced the time it takes the test team to understand the deliverables. If we have a cross-functional team then there will be opportunities to have early deliveries to test and have feedback sooner about problems and avoid expensive opinion/question defect reports.

5. CONCLUSIONS AND DISCUSSION

We made four contributions in this paper. First, we presented a study that focuses on testing challenges in SoS context. We mapped the challenges we found to three categories, 1) challenges that are not different in SoS context and other contexts, 2) challenges that are amplified in the SoS context but that can also be found in other contexts, and 3) to new challenges specific only to SoS context. To our knowledge, only Columbi et al. [7] has addressed this topic previously. In comparison to their SoS challenges we can say that their challenges (2) and (4) in Section 2 are not true in our case as the case company has tests to evaluate overall SoS capabilities and overarching test scenarios in compound system tests and field tests (see Figure 2). Their challenge (1) is partially true in our case as the current organizational structure does not support testing in SoS context, for example the lack of regression test suite maintenance can be traced back to the organization of our case company. Finally, their challenge (3) indicating that SoS systems have a high number of requirements leading to a high number of tests is completely true in our case. Reflecting their solutions proposals with the light of our case we can state that their proposal (2) using risk assessment to prioritize testing would be useful in our case as well. Their solution proposal (3) suggest focusing tests on interfaces might be applicable in our case but we think that other test focusing criteria should be used as well. Their solution proposal (1) "build little, test little" has already been applied and even exceeded in our case as the testing is following agile software development pace and testing with high coverage is performed continuously on different levels (see Figure 2). Their final proposal (4) to provide designated environments and people for integration does not seem that useful in our case as testing integrations did not seem to be a big problem and on the other hand designated people craved more support to regressions test maintenance rather than integration test.

Second, we found a contradiction between the software process improvement focus areas stemming from the fault slippage measure and interviews with practitioners. The fault slippage of internal processes and from customers clearly pointed to improving the areas of review and basic test that resulted in the highest fault slippage numbers (see Tables 5 and 6). However, the challenges and improvement ideas from practitioners pointed mostly to improving the functional tests and the system test suite that had poor maintainability and turnaround time, but high fault detection capability (see Figures 4 and 5 , and Table 7). On the other hand the reasons for problems in FT were caused at least partly by the fact that people did not do basic testing, but implemented the same test as functional tests because BT offered a poor technical support for testing. In the end, we cannot be certain if the company is better off improving functional or basic tests. We believe this can be generalized to the questions whether companies are better off in improving the practices that are already strong, but still have good improvement potential, or the practices that are weak.

Third, we found an interesting circular relationship between the maintenance and turnaround time of functional test. It is difficult to improve turnaround time if the test code has low maintainability. However, the low maintainability also increases the turnaround time when developers add new test cases rather than modify the existing test cases to complement for new features. We believe that circular relationship can be attributed to the SoS context and the managerial independence that each development team has.

Fourth, we found that test case maintainability and maintenance are a big problem in SoS context. Future work should see how could the techniques and practices for regular software maintenance help test code maintenance in SoS context.

6. ACKNOWLEDGMENTS

This work has been supported by ELLIIT, the Strategic Area for ICT research, funded by the Swedish Government.

7. REFERENCES

[1] JUnit: A programmer-oriented testing framework for Java. http://www.junit.org/. [Acc. Mar. 2012].

[2] Sonar - an open platform to manage code quality. www.sonarsource.org. [Accessed Mar. 10, 2012].

[3] Testing and Test Control Notation Version 3 (TTCN-3). http://www.ttcn-3.org/. [Acc. Mar. 2012].

[4] TestNG - a testing framework. http://testng.org/doc/index.html. [Acc. Mar. 2012].

[5] M. C. B. Alves, D. Drusinsky, J. B. Michael, and M. T. Shing. Formal validation and verification of space flight software using statechart-assertions and runtime execution monitoring. In *Proceedings of the 6th International Conference on System of Systems Engineering*, pages 155–160. IEEE, 2011.

[6] J. Christie. The seductive and Dangerous V-model. *Testing Experience*, pages 73–77, 2008.

[7] J. Colombi, B. C. Cohee, and C. W. Turner. Interoperability test and evaluation: A system of systems field study. *The Journal of Defense Software Engineering*, 21(11):10–14, 2008.

[8] J. Dahmann and K. Baldwin. Understanding the current state of us defense systems of systems and the implications for systems engineering. In *Proceedings of the 2nd Annual IEEE Systems Conference*, pages 1–7. IEEE, 2008.

[9] L. O. Damm and L. Lundberg. Identification of test process improvements by combining fault trigger classification and faults-slip-through measurement. In *2005 International Symposium on Empirical Software Engineering, 2005*. IEEE, Nov. 2005.

[10] L.-O. Damm, L. Lundberg, and C. Wohlin. Faults-slip-through - a concept for measuring the efficiency of the test process. *Software Process: Improvement and Practice*, 11(1):47–59, 2006.

[11] DoD. Systems and software engineering. systems engineering guide for systems of systems, version 1.0. Technical Report ODUSD(A&T)SSE, Office of the Deputy Under Secretary of Defense for Acquisition and Technology, Washington, DC, USA, 2008.

[12] M. Fewster and D. Graham. *Software Test Automation*. Addison-Wesley Professional, Sept. 1999.

[13] R. A. Gougal and A. Monti. The virtual test bed as a tool for rapid system engineering. In *Proceedings of the 1st Annual IEEE Systems Conference*, pages 1–6. IEEE, 2007.

[14] J. E. Hannay and H. C. Benestad. Perceived productivity threats in large agile development projects. In *Proceedings of the International Symposium on Empirical Software Engineering and Measurement (ESEM 2010)*, 2010.

[15] J. A. Lane and R. Valerdi. Synthesizing sos concepts for use in cost estimation. *Systems Engineering*, 10(4):297–307, 2007.

[16] G. Lewis, E. Morris, P. Place, S. Simanta, D. Smith, and L. Wrage. Engineering systems of systems. In *Proceedings of the IEEE International Systems Conference (SysCon 2008)*, 2008.

[17] G. A. Lewis, E. J. Morris, S. Simanta, and D. B. Smith. Service orientation and systems of systems. *IEEE Software*, 28(1):58–63, 2011.

[18] R. O. Lewis. *Independent verification and validation [Elektronisk resurs] : a life cycle engineering process for quality software*. Wiley, New York, 1992.

[19] M. W. Maier. Architecting principles for systems-of-systems. *Systems Engineering*, 1(4):267–284, 1998.

[20] K. Petersen and C. Wohlin. Context in industrial software engineering research. In *Proceedings of the Third International Symposium on Empirical Software Engineering and Measurement (ESEM 2009)*, pages 401–404, 2009.

[21] G. Rothermel, R. H. Untch, C. Chu, and M. J. Harrold. Test case prioritization: An empirical study. In *Proceedings of the International Conference on Software Maintenance (ICSM 99)*, pages 179–188, 1999.

[22] P. Runeson and M. Höst. Guidelines for conducting and reporting case study research in software engineering. *Empirical Software Engineering*, 14(2):131–164, 2009.

[23] C. Solís and X. Wang. A study of the characteristics of behaviour driven development. In *Proceedings of the 37th EUROMICRO Conference on Software Engineering and Advanced Applications (SEAA 2011)*, pages 383–387, 2011.

[24] R. K. Yin. *Case study research: design and methods*. Sage Publications, Thousand Oaks, 3 ed. edition, 2003.

[25] S. Yoo and M. Harman. Regression testing minimization, selection and prioritization: a survey. *Software Testing, Verification and Reliability*, 2010.

[26] B. Zeiss, H. Neukirchen, J. Grabowski, D. Evans, and P. Baker. Refactoring and metrics for ttcn-3 test suites. In *Proceedings of the 5th International Workshop on System Analysis and Modeling: Language Profiles (SAM 2006)*, pages 148–165, 2006.

Application of Kusumoto Cost-Metric to Evaluate the Cost Effectiveness of Software Inspections

Narendar R. Mandala,
Gursimran S. Walia
North Dakota State University
IACC Bldg 258-A14
Fargo, ND 58108
+1 701-231-8185

{narendar.mandala,
gursimran.walia}@ndsu.edu

Jeffrey C. Carver
University of Alabama
2019A Shelby Hall
Tuscaloosa, AL 35487
+1 205-348-9829

carver@cs.ua.edu

Nachiappan Nagappan
Microsoft Research
One Microsoft Way
Redmond, WA 98052
+1 425-722-7817

nachin@microsoft.com

ABSTRACT

Inspections and testing are two widely recommended techniques for improving software quality. While testing cannot be conducted until software is implemented, inspections can help find and fix the faults right after their injection in the requirements and design documents. It is estimated that majority of testing cost is spent on fault rework and can be saved by inspections of early software products. However there is a lack of evidence regarding the testing costs saved by performing inspections. This research analyzes the costs and benefits of inspections and testing to decide on whether to schedule an inspection. We also analyzed the effect of the team size on the decision of how to organize the inspections. Another aspect of our research evaluates the use of *Capture Recapture* (CR) estimation method when the actual fault count of software product is unknown. Using data from 73 inspectors, we applied the *Kusumoto* metric to evaluate the cost-effectiveness of the inspections with varying team size. Our results provide a detailed analysis of the *number of inspectors* required for varying levels of cost-effectiveness during inspections; and the *number of inspectors* required by the CR estimators to provide estimates within 5% to 20% of the actual.

Categories and Subject Descriptors

D.2.1 Requirements/Specifications

Keywords

Kusumoto Metric, Capture Recapture, Cost-effectiveness.

1. INTRODUCTION

The Success of a software development organization depends on their ability to deliver high quality products on time and within budget. To ensure software quality, researchers and practitioners have devoted considerable effort to help developers find and fix faults right after their insertion (i.e., in requirements and design documents) in order to reduce its impact in subsequent stages. In addition, finding and fixing faults earlier rather than later is easier, less expensive and reduces avoidable rework [1-4].

Among various methods used for early detection and removal of

faults, software inspections have been empirically validated [1, 3, 14-16]. Inspections are a process whereby software artifacts are examined by a group of inspectors to ensure that they meet a set of quality constraints by uncovering faults in the artifact.

The main idea of the inspection as defined by Fagan [14] is as follows. Once the author completes a software artifact, which could be a requirements document, design, or code, they submit it for inspection. The inspection consists of multiple steps. The inspection leader first chooses a team of skilled individuals who will perform the inspection. Then, the document/code to be inspected is distributed to these team members. The team-members individually review a software work-product to identify faults and meet together to consolidate the faults into a list, which is returned to the document/code author who then fix these faults. Since the initial definition of the inspection process, many variations have been made on it (e.g., placing more emphasis on individual review). Still, the main goal of the software inspection is to remove the faults in the software work product and enable: 1) saving of cost and time, which needs to be expended if the faults pass to later stages of software development; and 2) improving the quality of software product by enhancing its reliability, maintainability and availability [14-16].

Similar to inspections, testing is also widely recommended technique for improving software quality. While both are effective fault detection techniques, testing cannot be conducted until software has been implemented, whereas inspections can be applied immediately after software documents have been created and help avoid costly rework. Empirical evidence suggests that a majority (50% to 80%) of the development effort is spent during the testing stage of project [3, 16]. Furthermore, it is estimated that 40-50% of the development effort is spent on fixing problems that should have been fixed during the early stages of the development [15-16]. There is little empirical evidence regarding the percentage of rework cost-savings that can be achieved by performing the inspections of early work products. Therefore, an empirical evaluation of the cost-effectiveness of the inspections can help understand the costs and benefits of inspections (against the testing cost that would be spent if no inspections are performed) to decide on whether to schedule an inspection.

Additionally, evidence suggests that adding more inspectors to an inspection improves the fault coverage effectiveness. However, adding more inspectors increase the cost and may have an impact the investment decision. This paper evaluates the effect the inspection team size bears on the cost savings to decide whether the cost involved in adding more inspectors is worth the benefits.

To evaluate the cost-effectiveness of software inspections, several metrics have been proposed (e.g., [2, 12, 17]). In light of our research goals, we applied the *Kusumoto* metric [17] that analyzes the cost effectiveness of the inspection in terms of the testing costs that are reduced by the inspection. In this paper, we applied the *Kusumoto* metric on fault data from 73 inspectors who all reviewed the artifact that was seeded with 30 faults. Using this data, the effect of varying team size (1-73) on the reduction in the testing costs was evaluated. Discussion of cost-metrics and the evaluation process is presented in Sections 2.2 and 4.3.

Additionally, the total number of faults present in a software product (required for measuring the inspections' *cost-effectiveness*) is unknown during the development. In that case, an accurate estimate of the fault count can aid the project managers to evaluate the cost-effectiveness of an inspection. To that end, our prior research has shown that, among the different approaches that are available for estimating the number of faults in the artifact (e.g., defect density, subjective assessment, historical data, capture-recapture, curve-fitting), capture-recapture (CR) method is the most appropriate and objective approach [8, 22]. In this paper, we evaluate the CR methods' ability to accurately estimate the cost-effectiveness of an inspection process by comparing the *Kusumoto* metric values obtained from the CR estimates of the total fault count against the values obtained from the actual fault count with varying number of inspectors. More detail of the different CR models and estimators is provided in Section 2.3.

To summarize, this paper evaluates a) the cost effectiveness of inspections with varying number of inspectors on a data set from 73 inspectors, b) the cost effectiveness of inspections for the same data set using the CR estimates, and c) compare the difference in the results from a) and b). These evaluations will benefit the project managers in making a cost effective decision on how the inspection needs to be performed, the number of inspectors to be employed, and which CR estimators to be used.

The paper is structured as follows: Section 2 describes the inspection cost model and metrics, the basic principles of CR models and their application to software inspections. Section 3 discusses the results from the literature review used for the evaluation study. Section 4 describes the design of the evaluation study. Section 5 describes the analysis and results. Section 6 discusses the threats to validity. Section 7 summarizes the results. Section 8 contains the conclusions and future work.

2. BACKGROUND

This section provides information regarding the inspection costs and savings, surveys different cost-metrics that have been proposed, the basic principles of the use of CR models in software inspections, and a summary of the results from the evaluation studies related to the cost-effectiveness of software inspections.

2.1 Inspection Cost Model

The traditional software inspection cost model [17] (shown in Figure 1) consists of the following components:

a) D_{total} - total number of faults present in the software product;
b) C_r – cost spent on an inspection;
c) D_r - number of unique faults detected during the inspection;
d) C_t – cost to detect remaining faults in testing;
e) ΔC_t – testing cost saved by inspection;
f) C_{vt} - Virtual testing cost;

Sections 2.2 discuss various cost-metrics that utilizes a subset of these components to evaluate the inspection. Here in, this section, we describe the process of calculating each of these components:

C_r – *Cost spent on inspection*, is measure of the time taken (in staff-hours) to perform the individual review of a software artifact. This is the total cost invested during the "individual review/preparation" stage of the inspection

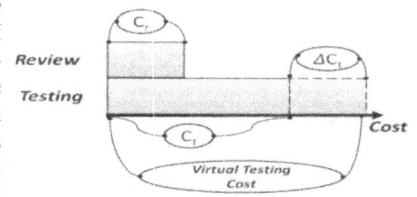

Figure 1 Inspection Cost Model

and is calculated by adding the time taken by each inspector during inspection. To clarify, this cost does not include the time spent during the planning and the team meeting stages of the inspection process.

C_t- *Testing cost*, is the cost required to detect the remaining (*i.e.*, $D_{total} - D_r$) faults post inspection. If we consider c_t as the average cost to detect a fault in the testing stage, then from Figure 1, the testing cost can be measured as the product of total number of faults remaining post-inspection and the average cost to detect a fault during testing. That is, $C_t = (D_{total} - D_r) * c_t$

D_{total} – *Actual fault count*, can be determined by using an artifact that is seeded with a known number of faults. Otherwise, the overlap in the faults found by multiple inspectors can be used to estimate the total fault count using the CR estimators.

c_t – *Average cost to detect a fault in testing*, is not available during the inspection. Therefore, it is measured as a factor of an average cost to detect a fault during an inspection. To process of deriving the cost ratio of detecting a fault during inspection versus testing is described in Section 3 (based on the literature survey).

ΔC_t – *Cost saved by inspections*: By spending cost C_r during inspection, the cost ΔC_t is being saved during the testing. It is calculated as the product of number of unique faults found during an inspection (D_r) and the average cost to detect a fault in testing (c_t). That is, $\Delta C_t = D_r * c_t$

Finally, C_{vt} - *Virtual testing cost*, (*i.e.*, testing cost expended if no inspections are performed) is the sum of the testing cost required to detect the faults remaining post-inspection (C_t) and the testing cost saved by inspection (ΔC_t). That is, $C_{vt} = (C_t + \Delta C_t)$.

2.2 Software Inspection Metrics

This section discusses different proposed metrics and their limitations to select the most relevant metric for evaluating the cost-effectiveness of software inspections:

Myers Metric (M_m): Myers proposed this metric to calculate the effectiveness of design and code reviews, and is equivalent to the number of unique faults detected by all the inspectors [19]. Myers metric is inappropriate to compare results across different projects, since different products have different fault counts.

Fagans Metric (M_f): Fagan evaluated the effectiveness of design, code, and unit test reviews using the metric M_f, called *Error Detection Efficiency*. M_f is defined to be the number of faults found by reviews over the total number of faults existing in the product before its reviews [14].

Our current research focuses on evaluating the cost effectiveness of inspections rather than just finding the fault detection effectiveness and efficiency of inspection techniques. Therefore, the literature review on inspection metrics that didn't take cost factors into consideration are not discussed in this paper anymore.

Collofello's Metric (M_c): Collofello et al., [12] proposed a cost-effectiveness metric that is defined as the ratio of the *cost saved by inspections* (ΔC_t) to the *cost consumed by inspections* (C_r). Although Collofello metric consider the cost factors, it does not take into account the total cost to detect all the faults in the software work product by inspection and testing. As such, the Collofello metric, can be problematic if we compare the results across different projects as illustrated using following example:

Example: Suppose two projects with two quality improvement activities: inspection and testing. Assume further, that in both projects, if inspections had not been performed, the costs of testing would be 1000 units. The first project consumes 10 cost units for their inspections and saves 100 units. Thus, the total cost for defect detection is 910 units. In the second project, inspections cost 60 units and save 600 units. Thus, the total cost for fault detection is 460 units, which is far smaller than the cost in the first project of 910 units. However, the value of M_c in both projects is 10, which doesn't recognize the economic advantage of inspections in the second project. The metric that overcame this problem was proposed by Kusumoto [17] as discussed follows:

Kusumoto Metric M_k : Kusumoto et al. proposed a metric for evaluating the *cost effectiveness* of the inspection in terms of reduction of cost to detect and remove all defects from software product. It is a ratio of the reduction of the total costs to detect and remove all faults from the software product using inspections to the virtual testing cost (testing cost if no inspection is executed). The model proposed by Kusumoto normalizes the savings by the potential fault cost. Hence, it can be compared across different inspections and projects, and is deemed most appropriate for our research purpose and can be calculates as:

M_k is a ratio of the reduction of the total costs to detect and remove all faults using inspections in a project to the virtual testing cost. The testing cost is reduced by (ΔC_t - C_r) compared to the virtual testing cost ($Ct + \Delta Ct$) if no inspection is executed. According to Figure 1, the kusumoto metric can be derived as

$$M_k \quad = (\Delta C_t - C_r) \; / \; (C_t + \Delta C_t) \text{ -------- } Eq\ 2.2.1$$

$$= ((Dr * c_t) - (Dr * c_t)) / (D_{total} * c_t) \text{ -------- } Eq\ 2.2.2$$

$$= (Dr / D_{total}) * (c_t - c_t) / c_t \text{ -------- } Eq\ 2.2.3$$

$$= M_f \; (1 - 1/M_c) \text{ -------- } Eq\ 2.2.4$$

Eq 2.2.4 interprets the M_k as a combination of Fagan (M_f) and Collofello metric (M_c). M_k is intuitive as it can be interpreted as the percentage of fault rework savings due to inspections. Using, M_k, cost-effectiveness can also be compared across inspections on different projects. Hence, this research uses the Kusumoto metric, to evaluate the cost effectiveness of the inspections.

2.3 Use of CR to Estimate Actual Fault Count

Capture-recapture (CR) is a statistical method originally developed by biologists to estimate the size of wildlife populations. To use CR, a biologist captures a fixed number of animals, marks them, and releases them back into the population. Then another trapping occasion occurs. If an animal that was 'marked' during the first trapping is caught again, it is said to have been recaptured. The process of trapping and marking can be repeated multiple times. The size of the population is then estimated using: 1) the total number of unique animals captured across all trappings, and 2) the number of animals that were re-captured. A larger overlap between different trappings indicates a smaller population [10-11].

Using the same principle, the CR method can be used during the inspection process to estimate the number of faults in an artifact. During an inspection, each inspector finds (or captures) some faults. If the same fault is found by more than one inspector it has been re-captured [8, 22]. The total number of faults is estimated using the same process as in wildlife research, except that the *animals* are replaced by *faults* and the *trappings* are replaced by *inspectors*. The inspection team can use the estimate of the total fault count along with the number of faults already detected to estimate the number of faults remaining in the artifact.

The use of the CR method in biology makes certain assumptions that do not always hold for software inspections. The assumptions made by CR method in biology include: 1) a closed population (i.e. no animal can enter or leave), 2) an equal capture probability (i.e. all animals have an equal chance of being captured), and 3) marks are not lost (i.e. an animal that has been captured can be identified) [8, 22]. When using the CR in software inspections, the closed population assumption is met (i.e., all inspectors review the same artifact independently and it is not modified) and the assumption that marks are not lost is met (i.e. it can be determined if two people report the same fault). However, because some faults are easier to find than others and because inspectors have different abilities, the equal capture probability assumption is not met [3, 23].

To accommodate these different assumptions, four different CR models are built around the two sources of variation: *Inspector Capability* and *Fault Detection Probability*. Table 1 shows the four CR models along with their source(s) of variation. Each CR model in Table 1 has a set of estimators, which use different statistical approaches to produce the estimates. The estimators for each CR model are also shown in Table 1.

Table 1 Capture-recapture models and Estimators [8, 22, 26]

Model	Variation Source	Estimators Belonging to Each CR Model
M_o	All inspectors have the same detection ability, and all defects are equally likely of being detected.	Unconditional Maximum Likelihood (M_o-UMLE); Conditional Maximum Likelihood (M_o-CMLE); Estimating Equations (M_o-EE)
M_t	Inspectors differ in their defect detection abilities, but all defects are equally likely of being found.	Unconditional Maximum Likelihood (M_o-UMLE); Conditional Maximum Likelihood (M_o-CMLE); Estimating Equations (M_o-EE)
M_h	Inspectors have the same detection ability, but defects differ in their probability of being found.	Jackknife Estimator (M_h-JK); Sample Coverage (M_h-SC); Estimating Equations (M_h-EE)
M_{th}	Inspectors differ in their detection ability, and defects differ in their probability of being found.	Sample Coverage (M_h-SC); Estimating Equations (M_h-EE)

The mathematical details of CR estimators are beyond the scope of this paper but can be found in provided references. The input data used by all the CR estimators is organized as a matrix with rows that represent faults and columns that represent inspectors as shown in Figure 2. A matrix entry is 1 if the fault is found by the inspector and 0 otherwise.

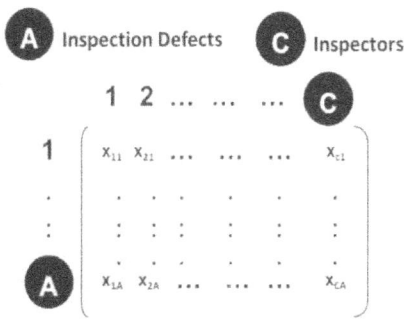

Figure 2 CR Data Input Matrix

CR was introduced to software inspections by Eick, et al. by applying it to real defect data from AT&T. A major result from this study was the recommendation that an artifact should be re-inspected if more than 20% of the total faults remain undetected [8, 13]. Following this study, various empirical studies in SE evaluated the use of CR models on artifacts with a known number of seeded defects [22]. In addition, our prior research evaluated the ability of CR estimators to accurately predict the need of a re-inspection using artifacts with real development faults (as opposed to seeded faults) [24]. A common finding from our evaluation studies is that the CR models generally underestimate the true fault count, but their estimation accuracy improves with more inspectors (or captures) [22]. However, the prior CR research has neglected the cost spent and cost saved by adding more inspectors to an inspection.

This current research extends our prior work by evaluating the cost-effectiveness of the inspection process using the CR estimates with varying inspection team sizes. The results from this research will provide guidance on how to appropriately use the CR estimators to evaluate the cost-effectiveness of software inspections when the actual count of faults present in the software document is not known prior to the inspection.

3. LITERATURE REVIEW

As described in Section 2.2, calculating the *Kusumoto* metric of the inspection requires: a) a count of the unique faults found during the inspection, b) the total time taken to complete the inspection, c) a count of faults remaining post-inspection, and d) the testing cost saved from an inspection. Among these, a) and b)

can be obtained using the fault reporting forms that contains the fault and timing information. The c) can be known if the document is seeded with a known number of faults. Otherwise, the CR method can be used to estimate the remaining faults. However, to calculate d), we need the value of average cost spent to find a fault during the inspection (which can be calculated from the inspection results), and the average cost that will be expended to find a fault during testing if no inspections were performed (which is not available at the end of inspection). On that end, this section presents the literature findings from different software organizations that reported the data on the average time (in hours) spent to find a fault during the inspections versus testing. These results were used to arrive at a ratio of the average cost spent to find a fault during inspections and the average cost spent to find a fault during testing when no inspections occur. This cost ratio is then used to calculate the cost-savings (ΔC_t), and evaluate the cost-effectiveness (M_k) of the inspection process with varying inspection team sizes in our study (described in Section 4).

3.1 Testing Cost Saved by Performing Early Reviews

Table 2 summarizes major results regarding the cost spent (in staff hours) to find a fault during inspections versus the cost spent to find a fault during testing. These results are based on actual reported data across different studies and show a cost ratio of 1:6.

Also, Lionel Briand [7], based on the published data has provided probability distribution parameters for the average effort using different fault detection techniques according to which the minimum, most likely and maximum value for design inspections are 0.58, 1.58 and 2.9 hours per fault respectively and, for testing are 4.5, 6 and 17 hours per fault. These values were summarized and derived from various studies on the cost and effort of finding faults in design, code reviews and testing.

Combining the various experiment results, historical data and assumptions made by different studies, it was hard to arrive at a definite estimate for average cost to detect a fault in testing when no inspection occurs. Different studies in the literature give different estimates because of the differences in study settings, software processes, severity of the faults, review techniques and other factors. In order to find the most appropriate value, we computed the median of the reported cost ratio values resulting from precise data collection. We did not consider approximations, estimates, or data whose origins were unclear. As a result, the median cost ratio is 1:5.93. Therefore, for this research, we used the inspections to testing cost ratio of 1:6.

Table 2 Summary of Inspection vs. Testing Cost Ratio

#	Author	Context and Findings
1	Kitchenham [19]	Reported on industrial experience that the average cost of finding a defect during design inspections was 1.58 work hours and the cost of finding a defect without inspection was 8.47 work hours. (*cost ratio of 1:5.36*)
2	Boehm [3]	Reported that the cost ratio for inspections to testing at a corporation involved in aerospace, automotive, credit reporting businesses was 1:6. (*cost ratio of 1:6*)
3	Briand [7]	Reported findings from an the industrial study that, the average effort to find a defect by inspections is 1.4 staff-hours as compared to 8.5 staff-hours of effort it took to find a defect during testing. (*cost ratio of 1:6.1*)
4	Weller [25]	Reported data from a project that performed a conversion of lines of code for several timing-critical routines. While testing the rewritten code, it took 6 hours per defect. During the pilot project they had been finding defects in inspections at a cost of 1.43 hours per defect. Thus, the team stopped testing and inspected the rewritten code detecting defects at a cost of less than 1 hour per defect. (*cost ratio of 1:6*)
5	Madachy [18]	Based on the results at Litton Data Systems, author estimated that the average cost to detect a defect in testing is 3.3 times the average cost to detect a defect when inspections are performed. However, these results were mostly based on the approximations or estimates. (*cost ratio of 1:3.3*)

4. STUDY DESIGN

Prior research has validated the fault coverage of inspections at the early stages of development. However, there is a lack of empirical research on the benefits of inspections in terms of the extent to which the testing costs can be reduced by performing the inspections. Furthermore, there is lack of empirical evidence on the factors (e.g., inspection team size) to consider while planning the inspections to achieve varying levels of fault rework savings.

While inspections are effective, they cannot certify the absence of faults. To support inspections, the CR method has been evaluated to provide a reliable estimate of the faults remaining post-inspection. Evidence suggests that increasing the *number of inspectors* improves the accuracy of CR estimates [22]. However, the prior research does not provide information on the costs and benefits of adding inspectors using the CR method.

To address these issues, this paper reports the results obtained from evaluating the cost effectiveness of software inspections with varying inspection team size using data set of 73 inspectors on an artifact that was seeded with 30 faults. We also report the relative error in the cost-effectiveness results obtained when using the CR estimates, against the results obtained using the actual fault count.

4.1 Research Goal

This study has two main goals. The first goal is to evaluate the cost-effectiveness of the inspection with varying inspection team sizes using the actual fault count whereas the second goal evaluates the cost-effectiveness of the inspection process using the CR estimates. The goals are stated using the GQM format as:

Goal 1: Evaluate the *cost effectiveness of software inspections* for the purpose of *characterizing the impact of the number of inspectors* from the point of view of *project managers* in the context of *document with a known number of faults*.

Goal 2: Analyze the *CR estimators* for the purpose of *evaluating the cost-effectiveness of inspections with increasing inspection team size* from the point of view of *project managers* in the context of *document with unknown number of faults*.

4.2 Data Set

The data was drawn from an earlier inspection study that was conducted at Microsoft Research to investigate the impact of educational background on the effectiveness of an inspector.

Artifact: The artifact inspected in this study was a requirements document describing the requirements for the Loan Arranger financial system (LAFS). LAFS is responsible for grouping loans into bundles based on user-specified characteristics. These loan bundles are then sold to other financial institutions. For use in previous study, researchers seeded the document with 30 realistic faults. The authors of this paper were not involved in fault seeding process. The faults were seeded prior to the design of the study. Therefore the seeded faults are not biased to benefit our study.

Inspectors: The 73 inspectors were drawn from a training course taught by the Microsoft Engineering Excellence group. The participants came from all major product groups within Microsoft. About 70% had bachelor's degrees with the other 30% having Master's degrees.

Inspection Process: First, the participants received training on the basic concepts involved in an inspection process. Then, the participants inspected the requirements document. To guide their review of the document, the participants used a standard fault-checklist. During the inspection, each participant worked alone to identify and record as many faults as possible. The participants had 70 minutes to complete the inspection task. At the end of the inspection, the 73 fault lists were collected and processed to determine which of the 30 faults were found by each inspector.

4.3 Evaluation Procedure

This section describes the evaluation procedure relative to the two research goals presented in Section 4.1.

4.3.1 Goal 1: Inspection Team vs. Cost-effectiveness

The cost-effectiveness of software inspections with varying team sizes was evaluated by: a) creating virtual inspection teams for each inspection team size (1-73), and b) calculating the *Kusumoto* metric (M_k) for each virtual inspection at all team sizes. The process of creating virtual inspections and calculating the cost-effectiveness of the inspections is described as follows:

Process of Creating Virtual Inspections: This process consisted of randomly selecting the appropriate number of inspectors from the overall pool of inspectors while keeping the fault count constant. For example, to create the 15 member inspection teams, 15 inspectors were randomly selected from a pool of 73 inspectors. Then, a matrix of the inspection data (containing 15 columns representing the inspectors and 30 rows representing the total faults) from these 15 inspectors was created. Using this approach, 10 virtual inspection teams were created for each team size, i.e. 10 virtual inspection teams of size two, another 10 virtual inspection teams of size three, and so on. This process resulted in the creation of 10 inspection teams for each inspection team size (1- 72) and one that combines all the 73 inspectors.

Calculating the Cost-Effectiveness of Virtual Inspections: The following costs and savings were calculated to compute the cost-effectiveness of each virtual inspection team (from above step):

a) **Average cost to detect a fault in inspection (c_r)**: Adding all the faults found by the inspectors, the average number of faults found by an inspector is calculated. From the available values of time taken by each inspector and the average number of faults found by an inspector, c_r is calculated using the following equation:

$c_r = C_r / D_r$ (i.e; Cost spent on inspection / Total faults found during the inspection)

   a. The "C_r - **Inspection cost**", is calculated by adding the total time spent by all the inspectors employed during the inspection. Recall that each inspector spent 70 minutes to perform the inspection.
   b. The "D_r", is the total number of unique faults found by all the inspectors during an inspection cycle.

b) **Virtual Testing Cost (C_{vt})**: is calculated as the product of the average cost to defect a fault in testing (i.e., c_t) and the total number of faults present in the product (i.e., D_{total}).

   a. The "c_t - **Average cost to detect a fault in testing**", is calculated as 6 times of average cost to detect a fault during the inspection (c_r). The average cost to detect a fault during the inspection (c_r) varies with the inspection team size as it is dependent on the time taken by inspectors and faults found by fixed number of inspectors. However, testing is independent of the inspection and inspection team size, and considering all the faults to be of the same severity, the average cost to detect a fault during testing (c_t) is kept constant for the the evaluation regardless of the inspection team size.

b. The "D_{total} - *Total fault count*", is the total number of faults present in the document. The artifact used this study was seeded with a total of 30 faults.

c) *Cost saved from inspection (ΔC_t)*: The testing cost saved from inspection is the product of the number of unique faults found during the inspection (D_r) and the average cost to find a fault during the testing (c_t). That is, $\Delta C_t = Dr * c_t$.

The difference in the testing cost saved by the inspection and the cost spent on the inspection provides the reduction of the total costs. **Kusumoto Metric** (M_k) is then obtained as follows:

M_k = *Reduction of total costs to detect all faults (i.e., $\Delta C_t - C_r$) / Virtual testing cost (i.e., C_{vt})* -------- Eq 4.3.1

By computing the cost of the inspection, cost saved from the inspection and the virtual testing cost in similar fashion as described above; the M_k values of 10 virtual inspections for team of 15 inspectors is shown in Table 3. Similar process was followed for deriving the Mk values for all the 10 virtual inspection by varying the inspection team size (1-73).

4.3.2 Goal 2: Cost-Effectiveness Using CR Estimators with Varying Inspection Team Size

We followed the same process (as described in Goal 1) to evaluate the cost-effectiveness of software inspections assuming we do not know the actual fault count (which is a more realistic situation). The same virtual inspections (created in Goal 1) were used in this analysis. The only difference is that, to calculate the M_k value of each virtual inspection, we used the estimates of the fault count from different CR estimators. In order to estimate the fault count for each virtual inspection, we used the automated tools CAPTURE [10, 26] and CARE-2 [11]. So, using these tools, the virtual inspections for each inspection team size were used as input to the CR estimators to produce estimates of the total number of faults. For each virtual inspection, the virtual testing cost (C_{vt}) is calculated using the estimate of the total fault count. The M_k values are then determined for each virtual inspections at all team sizes and each CR estimator combination using the same process as described for Goal 1. The calculations of the M_k values of same 10 virtual inspections (as shown in Table 3) using estimates from a particular CR estimator (M_h-SC) is shown in Table 4. The columns in Table 4 whose values are different from the values in Table 3 are shaded.

4.4 Evaluation Criterion

For Goal 1, using the actual count of 30 faults, ten M_k values are used to calculate the median and the variance for each inspection team size (1-73). The Mk value ranges from -1 to +1. The Mk value of 1 means the most cost effective inspection. A positive M_k value indicates a cost-effective process (i.e., cost saved outweighs the costs spent on inspection). A negative M_k value indicates a cost ineffective process, and M_k value of 0 is when the cost saved from inspection is equal to the cost spent on inspection.

For Goal 2, using the CR estimates, ten M_k values are used to calculate the median and the variance for each inspection team size and estimator combination. The estimators are then evaluated using three parameters: accuracy, precision, and failure rate.

The **accuracy (bias)** is measured as the relative error (R.E) in the M_k values based on the estimated fault count relative to the M_k values based on the actual fault count:

Table 3 Calculation of Kusumoto Metric (Mk) for Goal 1

Virtual Inspection #	Total Defect Count (D_{total})	Defects Found (Dr)	Cost Of Inspection (Cr)	Avg. Cost to detect a defect in Testing (c_t)	Testing Cost Saved by Reviews ($\Delta C_t = c_t * D_r$)	Virtual Testing Cost C_{vt}	Kusumoto Metric Mk = $(\Delta C_t - C_r)/C_{vt}$
1	30	21	1050	105	2205	3150	0.366666667
2	30	21	1050	105	2205	3150	0.366666667
3	30	22	1050	105	2310	3150	0.4
4	30	22	1050	105	2310	3150	0.4
5	30	24	1050	105	2520	3150	0.466666667
6	30	21	1050	105	2205	3150	0.366666667
7	30	20	1050	105	2100	3150	0.333333333
8	30	20	1050	105	2100	3150	0.333333333
9	30	25	1050	105	2625	3150	0.5
10	30	20	1050	105	2100	3150	0.333333333

Table 4 Calculation of Kusumoto Metric (Mk) for Goal 2

Virtual Inspection #	Estimated Defect Count (D_{total})	Defects Found (Dr)	Cost Of Inspection (Cr)	Avg. Cost to detect a defect in Testing (c_t)	Testing Cost Saved by Reviews ($\Delta C_t = c_t * D_r$)	Virtual Testing Cost C_{vt}	Kusumoto Metric Mk = $(\Delta C_t - C_r)/C_{vt}$
1	25.3	21	1050	105	2205	2656.5	0.434782609
2	26.7	21	1050	105	2205	2803.5	0.411985019
3	27.3	22	1050	105	2310	2866.5	0.43956044
4	27.5	22	1050	105	2310	2887.5	0.436363636
5	32.8	24	1050	105	2520	3444	0.426829268
6	24.3	21	1050	105	2205	2551.5	0.452674897
7	23.7	20	1050	105	2100	2488.5	0.421940928
8	23.5	20	1050	105	2100	2467.5	0.425531915
9	35.7	25	1050	105	2625	3748.5	0.420168067
10	23.4	20	1050	105	2100	2457	0.427350427

Relative error = (M_k using the estimated fault count – Mk using the actual fault count) / M_k using the actual fault count

A R.E of zero means absolute accuracy (i.e., M_k values based on the estimated fault count is same as those based on the actual fault count), a positive R.E. means an underestimation of actual fault count, and a negative R.E means an overestimation of actual fault count. The accuracy of the estimator is measured by calculating the median relative error for each inspection team size. The accuracy of an estimate is considered satisfactory when the R.E. is within +/- 20% of the actual value [8, 13]. In this paper, we evaluated the estimation accuracy of the CR estimators at different levels of R.E (e.g., +/- 20%, +/- 10%, +/- 5%, 0% etc.).

The **precision** of an estimator is measured by calculating the variability of the R.E. estimate of M_k values for each input size (e.g., 1-73). R.E variability around the median value is measured using the inter quartile range of the 25th percentile to the 75th percentile. The **failure rate** of an estimator is defined as the number of time an estimator fails to produce any result.

5. Analysis and Results

This section reports the cost-effectiveness results organized around the two research goals. Section 5.1 evaluates the impact of the inspection team size on M_k values obtained using the actual fault count. Section 5.2 evaluates the CR estimators and the R.E in their ability to accurately predict the M_k values with varying inspection team size.

5.1 Goal 1: Inspection Team Size vs. Cost-Effectiveness Using Actual Fault Count

This section analyzes the effect the inspection team size had, on the cost-effectiveness of the inspection of an artifact under inspection. To provide an overview, Figure 4 shows the median M_k values (from 10 virtual inspection teams) across all team sizes (1-73) using actual count of 30 faults. Some general observations from Figure 4 are as follows:

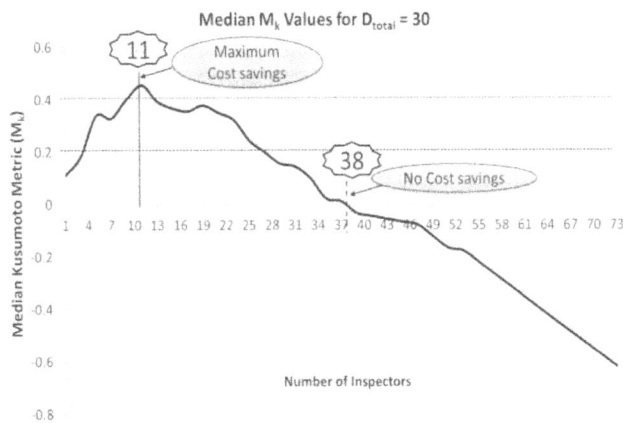

Figure 3 Median Mk Values at all Inspection Team Size

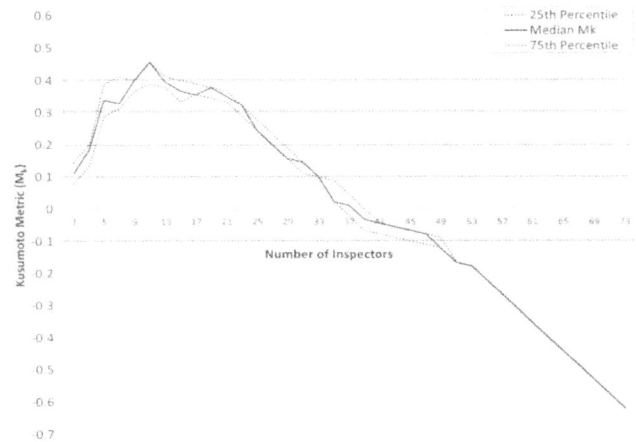

Figure 4 Median and Variance in the Mk Values for Data Set 1

a) There is a consistent improvement in the cost-effectiveness (i.e., median M_k) of an inspection process with increase in the inspection team size from 1 to 11 inspectors;

b) The inspection process was most cost-effective with a team of 11 inspectors (with a median M_k value of 0.46). Adding more number of inspectors (i.e., team size of 12 and more) did not further increase the cost-effectiveness of the inspection;

c) While the inspection process is still cost-effective (i.e., a positive median M_k value), there is a consistent decrease in the median M_k values for inspection team size varying from 12 to 37 inspectors; and

d) For inspection process involving 39 and more number of inspectors, the cost spent during the inspection outweighs the testing cost saved from it. Furthermore, there is a consistent decrease in the median M_k values (going from - 0.03 for an inspection with 39 inspectors to - 0.62 for an inspection with 73 inspectors).

Based on these results, increase in the number of inspectors had a positive impact on the improvement in the cost-effectiveness of inspections to a certain point. Beyond this point, additional quality improvement comes at the expense of the cost spent in adding more number of inspectors (to find additional faults).

While, the above results are only based on the median M_k values, we also examined the variance in the Mk values (across an array of 10 M_k values) at each inspection team size to gain additional insights. An approach for combining the analysis of median and variance of M_k is to calculate the following three different values for each inspection team size (1 -73): a) The *median* M_k value (50th percentile), b) The *seventh largest* M_k value (75th percentile), and c) The *third largest* M_k value (25th percentile). Together b) and c) define the interquartile range and is essentially the range of the middle 50% of the M_k values.

Figure 4 shows these three values with the median M_k value appearing between the upper (75th percentile) and lower bound (25th percentile) at all inspection team sizes. Figure 4 doesn't show a huge variance in the M_k values. To quantify the results shown in Figure 4, we analyzed the *median*, the *seventh largest*, and the *third largest* M_k values to determine the number of inspectors that are required to achieve varying levels of cost-

effectiveness in the inspection process (as shown in Table 5).

Table 5 shows the range of inspectors required to achieve cost savings greater than 40%, 30%, 20%, 10% and less than 0%. The inspector count for varying levels of cost-effectiveness was determined so that beyond that point, all the three Mk values (median, 75th percentile, and 25th percentile) are greater than the given cost saving range. For example, an inspection process of 7 to 22 inspectors are required to achieve all the three Mk values greater than 0.3. Similarly, 5 -26 inspectors achieved cost savings greater than 20% and so on.

Based on the results shown in Figure 4 and the inspector count shown in Table 5, main observations are listed as follows:

Table 5 Cut-off Points for Varying Levels of Cost Savings

Cost Savings	> 40%	>35%	>30%	>25%	>20%	>15%	>10%	>5%	>0%	< 0%
Inspector Count	Never	9 to 17	7 to 22	5 to 23	5 to 26	5 to 29	3 to 31	1 to 33	1 to 35	37 to 73

a) These results confirm previous research findings that performing inspections of early software documents helps save costly rework to find and fix problems later in the development process. The result shows that having even a single inspector review the requirements document saves some testing cost (i.e., cost savings > 0).

b) Regarding the minimum inspector count required to achieve varying levels of fault rework cost savings,
   a. A minimum of 3 inspectors are required to achieve cost savings greater than 10%;
   b. A minimum of 5 inspectors are required to achieve cost savings greater than 15% ; and
   c. A minimum of 7 inspectors and 9 inspectors achieved cost savings greater than 30% and 35% respectively.

c) Adding more inspectors increases the cost rework savings upto 11 inspectors. A software inspections yields positive cost savings up to 36 inspectors. Finally, performing an inspection with 37 or more inspectors does not save any testing cost.

Overall, these results showed that performing software inspections with even few numbers of inspectors (e.g., 9 to 17) save testing costs in excess of 35%. The inspector count for varying level of cost savings is dependent on the cost-spent during the inspection and the number of additional defects found by employing additional inspectors. For example, an inspection process of 36 inspectors found an average of 84% of total faults (across 10 virtual inspections) and the cost spent by adding more number of inspectors is more than the cost saved by them.

We anticipate that these results are dependent on several factors (e.g., inspector's fault detection abilities and the nature of the faults) and may vary across different inspection settings. However, the project managers can employ the *Kusumoto* metric in their organizations to evaluate the cost-effectiveness of their software reviews and the number of inspectors to be employed when scheduling the inspections.

5.2 Goal 2: Using CR Models to Estimate the Cost Effectiveness of Software Inspections

The cost-effectiveness results presented in Section 5.1 were calculated using the actual fault count of software product. In real settings, we don't know the actual fault count. To that end, an accurate estimate of the actual fault count can help project managers evaluate the cost-effectiveness of the inspection. This section analyzes the cost-effectiveness results based on the CR estimates (from all CR estimators) at all inspection team sizes. We also evaluate the error in the M_k values based on the estimated fault count relative to the M_k values based on actual fault count.

To provide an overview of the results, Figure 5 shows the median M_k values at all inspection team sizes (1 to 73) using the estimate of the total fault count from all CR estimators. Figure 5 also shows the median M_k values at all team sizes using the actual count of 30 faults (as highlighted by dotted line).

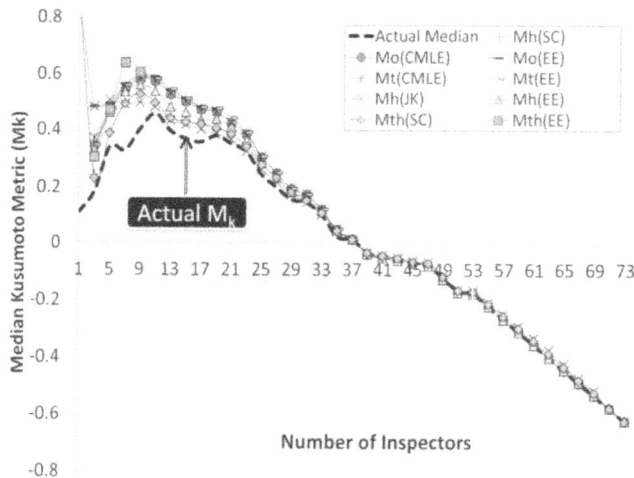

Figure 5 Median Mk for all the Capture Recapture Estimators

Major observations from Figure 5 are listed as follows:

a) For all the CR estimators with a small number of inspectors, there is a huge difference in the estimated median M_k values and the actual median M_k values. This is because the CR estimators generally underestimate the actual fault count with a small number of inspectors which reduces the true virtual testing cost (i.e., C_{vt}, the demoniator of Kusumoto metric formula in *Eq 4.3.1*), and thereby returns a higher M_k value.

b) For all the CR estimators, the estimated median M_k value is closer to the actual value with increase in the number of inspectors. This is because the quality of the CR estimates improve (i.e., the estimated fault count is closer to the actual count) with the increase in the number of inspectors.

c) The median Mk values for some of the CR estimators is closer to the actual Mk values with fewer number of inspectors as compared to the other estimators. This is becase some estimators (i.e., estimators belonging to the M_h and M_{th} models) produce more accurate results with fewer number of inspectors than the other estimators (i.e., estimators belonging to M_o and M_t models). More details on the relative improvement for the CR estimators is discussed later.

To quantify the results provided in Figure 5, Figure 6 shows the relative error (R.E) percentage in the median M_k values produced by each CR estimator at all inspection team sizes. The dashed lines in Figure 6 show the region of +/- 20% within which the estimation results are considered satisfactory [8, 13].

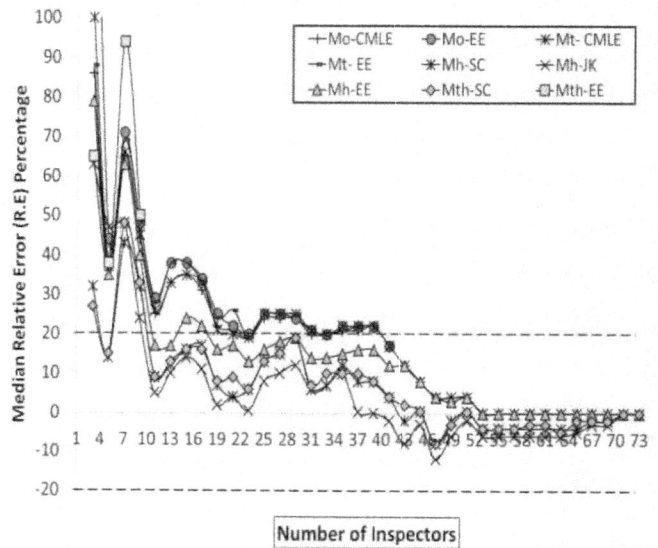

Figure 6 Relative Error in Median Mk for the CR Estimators

The major observations from Figure 6 are discussed as follows:

a) The R.E. in the median M_k values is greater than 20% for all the CR estimators for inspection team size of 1 upto 9 inspectors. Therefore, the CR estimators are not recommended for estimating the cost-effectiveness of the inspections with less than ten inspectors;

b) The CR estimators belonging to Mh and Mth models improve faster. Consequently, the R.E. in the median Mk values obtained from these CR estimators is less than 20% with fewer number of inspectors (11 inspectors) than the estimators belonging to Mo and Mt models (41 inspectors).

c) The same trend is true for R.E. in the Mk values at level +/- 10%, where the SC estimators for Mh and Mth models are better than all the other CR estimators;

d) The EE estimators for all models (M_o-EE, M_t-EE, M_h-EE, and M_{th}-EE) fail often and even for the larger number of inspectors. We don't recommend the EE estimators for use.

To better understand the relative performance for different CR estimators at varying levels of R.E. in the Mk values, Table 6 provides the number of inspectors required by each estimator to obtain Mk values within 0%, +/- 5%, and so on up to +/- 40% of the actual Mk value. The inspector count for each R.E percentage shown in Table 6 is the minimum number of inspectors for which the estimate falls within the given R.E. range and never goes outside the range as the number of inspector increases. For example, the number 19 in the M_o-CMLE row in the +/- 30% column means that for all team sizes greater than or equal to 19, the R.E. is never greater than + 30% and for at least one team size less than 19, the R.E. exceeds + 30%.

Table 6 Number of Inspectors Required to Achieve Different Levels of Relative Error in Median Mk Values

Estimators	+/- 40%	+/- 30%	+/- 20%	+/- 10%	0%
Mo-CMLE	11	19	41	45	53
Mo-EE	11	19	41	Failed	
Mt-CMLE	11	19	41	45	53
Mt-EE	11	19	41	Failed	
Mh-SC	9	11	11	31	43
Mh-JK	9	11	11	49	71
Mh-EE	11	19	19	45	53
Mth-SC	9	11	11	31	45
Mth-EE	Failed				

The CR estimators that achieved estimates at R.E ranging from +/- 0% to +/- 40% with least number of inspectors are highlighted in Table 6 and discussed as follows:

a) Across all CR estimators, 11 to 41 inspectors are required to achieve a satisfactory estimate of the cost-effectiveness of an inspection process (i.e., within R.E. of +/- 20%)

b) The estimators M_h-SC, M_h-JK, the M_{th}- SC require fewest inspectors to obtain an estimate within +/- 20% R.E. (11 inspectors) as compared with the estimators for the M_o and M_t models (19 or 41 inspectors);

c) The SC estimators (Mh-SC and Mth-SC) achieved results within -10% and at 0% R.E. with least number of inspectors.

Based on these results, the accuracy of the SC estimators (for the M_h and M_{th} models) is most positively affected by increasing the inspection team size compared with the other CR estimators. Therefore, based on the R.E values, SC are the best estimators to evaluate the cost-effectiveness of software inspections.

6. THREATS TO VALIDITY

In this study, we were able to address some threats to validity. To reduce the external validity, the data used this study came from an industrial strength requirement document that contained realistic faults and was inspected by Microsoft software professionals (as opposed to students). To reduce the threat of using small data set, the number of inspectors used in this study was the largest in any prior studies of this type. In addition, while the faults were seeded into the document rather than being naturally occurring, the defects were seeded by researchers who had no knowledge that results would be used for this study. Therefore, the defects were not seeded in such a way to specifically benefit our analysis

However, there were also some threats that we could not address.

The cost spent during the inspection only included the time spent during the individual review of software document. In reality, the costs spent in scheduling an inspection would also include other costs (e.g., planning of review, inspection team meeting, project delays due to inspections). In addition, all inspectors completed the inspection in 70 minutes, which is the standard amount of time used for inspections at Microsoft. In the future, we will specifically study these factors in more detail.

7. DISCUSSION OF RESULTS

This section first provides a summary of the major findings of the study. Then, it describes how these findings can be relevant to software development organizations.

7.1 Summary of Major Findings

This section discusses the major finding and recommendation of the *number of inspectors* required for to maximize the cost-effectiveness of inspections; the *number of inspectors* required by the CR estimators to provide reliable estimates of the cost-effectiveness of inspections; and the best CR estimator (s). A summary of major results follows:

a) The cost spent on inspecting requirement document after its development returns significant cost savings by finding faults right after its insertion and by avoiding costly rework;

b) The increase in cost savings is positively correlated with increase in the *number of inspectors*. This was true up to certain team size beyond which the cost spent by adding more number of inspectors doesn't return additional cost savings. We anticipate that this point of maximum cost-effectiveness (team size of 11 inspectors in our study) can vary depending on the product and inspectors abilities;

c) Our results provided the minimum *number of inspectors* that can achieve varying amount of positive cost-savings. A minimum of 1, 3, 5, 7, and 9 inspectors achieved cost savings > 5%, > 10%, > 15%, >30% and > 35% respectively;

d) The CR methods produce M_k values that are different from the actual M_k values for a small number of inspectors (1 to 9), but their estimation accuracy improves as the number of inspectors increases;

e) The results showed that the SC and JK estimators for the M_h model, and the SC estimator for M_{th} model requires a minimum of 11 inspectors (fewest for all the CR estimators) to accurately predict the cost-effectiveness of inspections (i.e., at +/- 20% R.E.) . The SC estimates for M_h and M_{th} models are recommended for use.

7.2 Relevance to Software Organizations

The results provided in this paper can benefit software practitioners when evaluating the use of inspections in their organizations. While our research study used a cost ratio for inspection to testing of 1:6, project managers can use local fault data from their organizations to determine the correct level of testing costs reduced by performing inspections in their projects.

The results regarding the minimum number of inspectors can aid managers to help decide upon the baseline number of inspectors to use when planning an inspection process. Furthermore, managers and developers can vary the inspection team size (using the same process as described in this paper) to evaluate the improvement in the cost-effectiveness of inspection results to decide if additional inspectors need to be employed for saving further testing cost are worthwhile. Although further empirical investigation is necessary, practitioners can use the CR estimates from the SC estimators to evaluate the cost-effectives of inspections and to help make cost-effective decision of the need of a re-inspection.

8. CONCLUSION AND FUTURE WORK

Based on the results in this paper, project managers can apply the *Kusumoto* metric using the CR estimate of the total fault count can be used when the actual fault count is not known during the development to evaluate the cost-effectiveness of the software inspections and to make objective post-inspection decisions. Further research would investigate the effect of other factors (e.g., time spent during the inspection planning and during the inspection team meetings) that can impact the cost investment decisions during inspections. Also, further research will investigate the cost-effectiveness of inspections using artifacts (other than the requirement documents) that contain naturally occurring faults (as opposed to seeded faults).

9. ACKNOWLEDGMENTS

We thank the employees of Microsoft who participated in the inspection that provided the data for this analysis.

10. REFERENCES

[1] Ackerman, A., Buchwald, L., and Lewski, F., "Software Inspections: An Effective Verification Process." *IEEE Software*, 1989. **6**(3): 31-36.

[2] Bernardez, B., Genero, M., Duran, A., and Toro, M. "A controlled Experiment for Evaluating a Metric-Based Reading Technique for Requirement Inspection". In Proceedings of the 10th International Symposium on Software Metrics. 2004: IEEE Computer Society: 257-268

[3] Boehm, B.: *Software Engineering Economics*. Prentice-Hall, 1981.

[4] Boehm, B. and Basili, V.R., "Software Defect Reduction Top 10 List." IEEE Computer, 2001. 34(1): 135-13.

[5] Biffl, B. Freimut, O. Laitenberger, "Investigating the Cost-Effectiveness of Reinspection in Software Development", Proceedings of the 23rd International Conference on Software Engineering (2001) 155-164.

[6] Briand, L.C, Emam, K.E, and B.G.Freimut. "A Comparison and Integration of Capture-Recapture". In *Proceedings of the 9th International Symposium on Software Reliability Engineering*. 1998. Paderborn, Germany: 32-41.

[7] Briand, L.C, Emam, K.E., Laitenberger, and Fussbroich, Using Simulation to Build Inspection Efficiency Benchmarks for Development Projects, in Proceedings of the 20th International Conference on Software Engineering, pp. 340-349, 1998.

[8] Briand, L.C., Emam, K.E., Freimut, B.G., Laitenberger, O., "A Comprehensive Evaluation of Capture Recapture Models for Estimating Software Defect Content" *IEEE Transactions on Software Engineering*, 2000. **26**(6): 518-539.

[9] Burnham, K.P. and Overtom, W.S., "Estimation of the Size of a Closed Population When Capture Probabilities Vary Among Animals." *Biometrica*, 1978. **65**: 625-633.

[10] Chao, A., "Estimating Animal Abundance with Capture Frequency Data." *Journal of Wildlife Management*, 1988. **52**(2): 295-300.

[11] Chao, A. and Yeng, H.C., Program CARE-2 (for Capture-Recapture Part.2), http://chao.stat.nthu.edu.tw, 2003.

[12] Collofello, J.S., Woodfield, S.N., Evaluating the Effectiveness of Reliability-Assurance Techniques, Journal of Systems and Software 9 (3) (1989) 191-195.

[13] Eick, S., Loader, C., Long, M., Votta, L., and Weil, S.V. "Estimating Software Fault Content Before Coding". Proceedings of the 14th International Conference on Software Engineering. 1992. Australia: ACM Press: 59-65

[14] Fagan, M. E., "Design and Code Inspections to Reduce Errors in Program Development". *IBM Systems Journal*, 15(3):182–211, 1976.

[15] Fagan, M. E., "Advances in Software Inspections," *IEEE Transactions on Software Engineering*, Vol. SE-12, No. 7, July 1986, pp. 744-751.

[16] T. Gilb, D. Graham, Software Inspection, Addison-Wesley, 1993.

[17] Kusumoto, T, Matsumoto, K., Kikuno, T., Torii, K., A New Metrics for Cost Effectiveness of Software Reviews, IEICE Transactions on Information and Systems E75-D (5) (1992) 674-680.

[18] Madachy, R., "Process Improvement Analysis of a Corporate Inspection Program," *Seventh Software Engineering Process Group Conference,* Boston, MA, May 23, 1995.

[19] Meyer, G., "A Controlled Experiment in Program Testing and Code Walkthroughs/Inspections". In *Communications of the ACM*, 21(9):760-768, September 1978.

[20] Miller, J., 1999. "Estimating the Number of Remaining Defects after Inspection". Software Testing, Verification, and Reliability, Vol. 9, No. 3, pp. 167-189.

[21] Olson, T., "Piloting Software Inspections to Demonstrate Early ROI," Notes from Presentation given at the 1995 SEPG Conference

[22] Petersson, H., Thelin, T., Runeson, P., and Wohlin, C., "Capture-Recapture in Software Inspections after 10 Years Research - Theory, Evaluation and Application." *Journal of Systems and Software*, 2003.

[23] Giedre SABALIAUSKAITE: "Investigating Defect Detection in Object-Oriented Design and Cost-Effectiveness of Software Inspection" January 2004.

[24] Walia, G., and Carver, J. "Evaluation of Capture-Recapture Models for Estimating the Abundance of Naturally Occurring Defects." Proceedings of the 2nd ACM-IEEE International Symposium of Empirical Software Engineering and Measurement. October 9-10, 2008. Kaiserslautern, Germany. p. 158-167

[25] E. Weller: "Lessons from Three Years of Inspection Data". In *IEEE Software*, 10(5):38–45, September 1993.

[26] White, G.C., Anderson, D.R., Burnham, K.p., and Otis, D.l., Capture-Recapture and Removal Methods for Sampling Closed Populations, Los Alomos National Laboratory, 1982.

Effects of Four Distances on Communication Processes in Global Software Projects

Tuomas Jaanu, Maria Paasivaara, and Casper Lassenius
Aalto University School of Science
Software Business and Engineering Institute
P.O.Box 19210, FIN-00076 AALTO, Finland
tuomas.niinimaki@aalto.fi

ABSTRACT

Global distribution of software engineering introduces geographical, temporal, cultural and organizational distance into teamwork. Globally distributed software projects need to use electronic communication tools to collaborate across these distances. Communication media differ in properties and capabilities to overcome the challenges imposed by these distances.

In this paper, we examine the effects of these four distances to communication in software engineering projects. We use Media Synchronicity Theory as a framework to analyze the capabilities of different communication media to support software engineering across distances. We report our findings on the relationship between communication media and distance from three distributed software projects. Based on the results, we aim at providing conclusions on choosing communication media for globally distributed software projects.

Categories and Subject Descriptors

D.2 [**Software Engineering**]: Management

General Terms

Human Factors, Management

1. INTRODUCTION

Global software development (GSD) projects face several "distances" between teams and individual team members. Such distances arise from geographical and organizational distribution of work. As communication is a key success factor for software projects [1], the introduction of such distance between team members will affect the success of the project. We are interested, how these distances affect the communication in GSD projects, as any negative impact on communication will have consequences in the performance of GSD projects.

As successful communication in GSD projects requires team members to overcome the challenges imposed by distance, and as we believe Media Synchronicity Theory (MST) provides a useful framework for understanding the media choice and communication tool support in GSD projects, we are faced with the following research questions: 1) How do the four distances in GSD affect conveyance within the project team? and 2) How do the four distances in GSD affect convergence within the project team?

2. THEORETICAL FRAMEWORK

For this study, we build our theoretical framework on Media Synchronicity Theory (MST) [2] and distances of global software development (GSD) [3].

2.1 Media Synchronicity Theory

MST suggests effective media use requires a match between media capabilities and the fundamental communication processes needed to perform the task. The theory defines two communication processes: *conveyance* (exchange of information), and *convergence* (development of shared meaning for the information). MST defines media synchronicity as *the extent to which a communication environment encourages individuals to work together on the same activity, with the same information, at the same time; i.e. to have a shared focus.* [2].

MST suggests communication performance to be better if media of low synchronicity is used for tasks requiring conveyance and media providing high synchronicity for tasks requiring convergence. Furthermore, successful completion of more complex tasks requires both conveyance and convergence.

The ability of a communication medium to support these processes is based on the characteristics of the communication tool in question. MST evaluates communication media based on following five capabilities: immediacy of feedback, symbol variety, parallelism, rehearsability and reprocessability [2]. Table 1 summarizes how media capabilities support communicative processes.

2.2 Distance in Global Software Development

Distribution of software work introduces several types of distance between individuals and teams within the distributed project. Much of the earlier work has focused on geographical and temporal distance (see e.g. [4], [5]). Holmström et al [3] have formalized a model of three distances — geographical, temporal and socio-cultural distance — within GSD projects; by adding the socio-cultural distance, they

Table 1: Communicative processes and media capabilities, adapted from [2]

	Conveyance	Convergence
Immediacy of feedback	Low	High
Parallelism	High	Low
Symbol variety	Low	High
Rehearsability	High	Low
Reprocessability	High	Low

are able to address the diversity in cultural conventions and social behavior of teams and individuals. However, in this paper, we want to explore the effects of social and cultural differences in GSD in more detailed level. We argue that ethnic/national culture and organizational culture are — albeit similar in their appearance — different in the way they affect communication and how issues raised by cultural or organizational differences can be alleviated by communication tool use. Therefore, we will use the following four main categories ("distances") to study communication and media choice in GSD projects: geographical, temporal, cultural and organizational distance.

Geographical distance between team members requires mediated communication between team members, as frequent face-to-face communication is not a feasible option for people working in distinct sites. The decline of face-to-face communication as a viable communication medium puts forth several challenges on planning and implementing communication practices within a distributed team and project.

Temporal distance — distance in time — further limits the possibilities for communication and collaboration between distributed team members. The difference between time zones of different sites decreases the number of common working hours for both sites, thus constraining the opportunities for having shared, synchronous communications. Moreover, the lower number of common working hours limits the maximum length of common meetings, which in particular affects planning sessions in iterative and incremental software development projects.

Cultural differences manifest themselves as differences in tacit assumptions and expectations, as diverse working practices, and varying preferences for communication and collaboration methods. Cultural diversity within a team also potentially increases the language diversity, introducing further challenges to communication between team members.

By organizational distance, we mean phenomena resulting from working across organizational boundaries, whether they are caused by differing working practices, organizational culture, different roles and responsibilities, financial rivalry or technical impediments for collaboration. Organizational culture is often emergent in especially organizations with a longer history: organizations both decide formally and converge informally into certain ways-of-working, conventions and practices, and also may exhibit and encourage certain set of values in their operations.

3. METHODOLOGY

We used purposeful sampling [6] for choosing the case projects to be studied: the companies studied in this research were participating in our research project. All se-

lected companies were engaged in GSD, interested in improving their capabilities in global software development, and able to provide several on-going GSD projects for the study. The projects for this study were selected in collaboration with the company managers and the researchers.

Table 2 shows an overview of the selected cases. All three projects were using English as working language, even though practically no team member spoke English as their native language. Two projects were intra-organizational, i.e. all sites were part of the same company, while one case project was partially made by a subcontractor. The reason for utilizing global resourcing in these projects was both cost benefits and lack of suitable personnel at on-site location.

We collected the data using semi-structured, open-ended interviews. We selected a subset of team members to interview in collaboration with project managers of case projects, to include both on-site and off-site personnel as well as different roles, and to reach data saturation. The interviewees represented different roles, ranging from higher management to software developers.

The question set contained open-ended questions on 12 themes related to software engineering and GSD. We asked our interviewees to tell in their own words about their project context, processes and practices in use in the project, and group relations within the project. Interviews were conducted in Finnish or in English. All interviews were recorded and transcribed. Transcripts were then codified by the first author with predefined codes for each of the four distances and used communication tools and processes.

4. RESULTS

4.1 Case A

Case A is a project developing enterprise resource management solution for a single customer organization. The solution is built on commercial-off-the-shelf (COTS) products, with considerable integration and customization to customer needs.

Main communication forum for the project is weekly team meeting, with both sites participating. The team meeting takes place on Friday afternoon and lasts for about two hours. The time difference between sites limits the scheduling of the meeting, and as a result, team members at Indian site need to stay later at the office to participate in the meeting. The time difference also somewhat limits the maximum length for the meeting.

Both the poor audio quality of teleconferencing and the language skills — understanding different dialects — was challenging during weekly meetings. The team used instant messaging to overcome these difficulties. Instant messaging was also considered an efficient tool for communicating across teams, as one could participate in one or more discussions at once, while resuming other activities at the same time.

Cultural distance between Finland and India has been a challenge for the project. Discussion on problems and status reporting has been particularly difficult, as the two cultures have different conventions of communicating such issues. The team has tried to solve the issues by creating explicit procedures for status reporting and distribution of work. The difference in power distance, while itself a cultural difference, caused the conventions related to assignment and management of work to differ between sites, even

Table 2: The case projects

	Domain	On-site	Off-site	Team size	Interviews	TZ dist.	Org. dist.
A	Enterprise resource management	Finland	India	14 + 25	3 + 1	3.5h	intra
B	Information system	Finland	Lithuania	11 + 6	8 + 4	0h	intra
C	Engineering software	Finland	Malaysia, Romania	45 + 7	5 + 6	0–6h	intra+inter

though there was an effort to harmonize these conventions by using task tracking systems and by assigning tasks directly to developers. It also seemed that the Indian team members saw Finnish team as customers for their work. Combined to cultural differences, this may be seen as evidence of organizational distance as well. In general, Indian team wanted to try solve issues themselves first, before contacting any Finnish team members on the issue.

4.2 Case B

Case B was developing an information system for governmental use. Project was distributed between Finland and Lithuania. This project was the first one conducted by the Lithuanian site of the company; while some of the Lithuanian team members had previous working experience in other companies, most of the team was relatively young and had little working experience in software engineering prior this project. As the development of the product in question required a high level of domain knowledge, and as previous versions of the system, all documentation and background information for the system were in Finnish due to customer requirements, a lot of collaboration and knowledge transfer was needed between Finnish and Lithuanian teams.

Initially, the team mainly used email and occasional team teleconferences to communicate across sites. As Finland and Lithuania are located on the same time zone, there was no temporal distance between the teams, but the use of email — combined with limited availability of key personnel — in this project was a source of delay in communication. In addition to email, they were actively using instant messaging with some of the Finnish team members. Due to communication needs teleconferences shortly changed into regular weekly video conference meetings, in which all team members from Lithuania and some key members from Finland were present.

The only cultural difference noted by team members was about the power distance: the Lithuanian team members seemed to have a preference to express their concerns and their lack of knowledge less openly when their own superiors were present.

4.3 Case C

In case C, the company was developing and maintaining software for computer aided engineering. Case C was inter-organizational: Finnish and Malaysian sites were internal sites, while Romanian site was provided by the subcontractor.

Geographical distance between the teams caused less awareness of competencies and skills of remote team members, as well as caused delay in communication between the sites. Teams in Finland, Romania and Malaysia had multiple communication media — both synchronous and asynchronous — at their disposal. They had a weekly meeting over teleconferencing, but beyond that they used mainly email and chat to communicate with each other. For technical tasks, chat was considered to be sufficient, as it could be used to collaborate on technical problems. Temporal difference caused however some limitations to the synchronous communication: using instant messaging with team members in Malaysia was only possible until noon Finnish and Romanian time.

Cultural differences between Finland and Malaysia were also hampering communication between sites. Different cultural conventions — and potentially also lack of teamness between sites — required product management to poll the status of tasks and issues frequently from the remote team, just to find out the remote site had been struggling with the issue for a longer period of time. Working with different cultures also brings in the language barriers. In this case, it seems that the language skills of some of the Malaysian developers were sometimes not adequate for communication, causing either delay in asking questions or even questions not asked.

Romanian site was part of another company, so there was steeper organizational boundary between Finnish and Romanian site than between Finnish and Malaysian site. This organizational distance seemed to make some aspects of the collaboration more difficult. Especially the technical aspects seemed to be challenging, as they would have needed to expose some of their internal servers to the subcontractor.

5. DISCUSSION

Physical separation between team members raises the need for mediated communication between team members, as frequent face-to-face communication is not a feasible option for people working in distinct sites. The decline of face-to-face communication as a viable communication medium puts forth several challenges on planning and implementing communication practices within a distributed team and project.

Physical co-presence provides team members with awareness of many aspects related to their team and project. Overall project awareness — the comprehension about what is going on in the project — can be much more difficult to attain when people are not sharing the same physical space.

For distributed projects, there are several practices and tools, which aim for improving the project level awareness, such as task and issue trackers, group chat and frequent regular team meetings. Increased project awareness makes it easier to coordinate the overall effort and work-in-progress within the team, and therefore reduces the risk of duplicate or erroneous work within the project. The use of such tools in geographically distributed team forces the team to conduct their communication in reprocessable way, which should increase the potential for conveyance, sharing and internalizing information within the team.

Temporal distance limits the possibilities for communication and collaboration between distributed team members, as the overlapping working time is usually the only point of time in which the use of synchronous communication is possible; outside common working time asynchronous communication must be used instead.

Table 3: The negative impact of distance on communication and tool recommendations

	Conveyance	Convergence	Suggested tools
Geographical	Low	Low	Instant messaging, teleconferencing
Temporal	Low	High	Email, task management system
Cultural	High	High	Instant messaging, task management system, video conferencing
Organizational	High–Low	Low–High	Face-to-face, task management system, instant messaging

As the use of synchronous communication is limited, communication overhead is increased due to use of asynchronous communication tools as more context needs to be communicated. This additional amount of information per message adds to overhead both in the sending and receiving side of the communication. However, more emphasis on building the messages increases both the ability to reprocess and to rehearse the message, potentially providing more support for conveyance of information.

Cultural differences manifest themselves as differences in tacit assumptions and expectations, as diverse working practices and varying preferences in communication and collaboration. The diversity of working practices can be one consequence of working in cross-cultural teams, as different underlying cultures will inevitably affect the way people think and feel about different issues. Some cultural traits may be more present when using certain communication media, e.g. a tool providing less social presence may help when working with cultures with differing views on power distance, avoiding conflicts caused by this cultural difference.

The main consequence of organizational distance arises from the loss of teamness: it can be difficult to build teams across organizational boundaries, especially if there are potential conflicts-of-interest or lack of trust. Organizational borders also limit the knowledge whom to contact on the other organization; such issues can often be solved by defining the organization chart, and providing all stakeholders with information on people involved in the project.

As organizational distance can often be explicitly enforced, there is not much that can be done to alleviate it, other than building trust and transparency between the two organizations. Beyond that, communication across organizational boundaries will benefit from tools supporting both efficient information sharing and building common understanding.

6. CONCLUSIONS

As an answer to research question 1 (How do the four distances in GSD affect conveyance within the project team?), we argue that while geographical and temporal distances do make it slightly more difficult to share information within the team, cultural differences and organizational boundaries will have much larger impact on information flow. Some cultural traits, such as power distance, do affect the way problems are communicated, and there can be explicit rules for not sharing all information across organizational borders. Our findings are aligned with earlier research reporting cultural and organizational distance to decrease the frequency and amount of communication in general [7].

For research question 2 (How do the four distances in GSD affect convergence within the project team?), we found temporal and cultural distances as main impediments for convergence. Time zone distance increases the delay in communication, making it more difficult — or even impossible — to collaborate interactively on building shared understanding of the issue at hand. Our findings on this seem to be in line with earlier research [7, 3]. Cultural differences may make it difficult to converge understanding quickly, as concepts need to be explicated and discussed before actual building of understanding may commence. The impact of organizational distance is less clear, but we argue that especially when starting collaboration with a new partner, the challenges in grounding may be similar to the ones with cultural differences.

Table 3 summaries our findings on the impact geographical, temporal, cultural and organizational distance may have on conveying and converging information in GSD projects. In the table, we present the impact of distance to both process with options "low" and "high". This "quantification" of impact is purely relative to other distances, and the actual extent of impact will depend also on the "quantity" of the distance.

Our findings do call for more research on the effects of all these distances on communicative processes. Firstly, our study was limited on only three case projects, and we were not able to study each of the distances in isolation. Secondly, the analysis is based solely on interview data, and as such, we have only subjective assessment of both the distances and their effect on communication. Furthermore, as our results were indeterminate especially on the effect of organizational boundaries in distributed software development, the subject should be investigated further.

7. REFERENCES

[1] R. E. Kraut and L. A. Streeter, "Coordination in software development," *Communications of the ACM*, vol. 38, no. 3, pp. 69–81, 1995.

[2] A. R. Dennis and J. S. Valacich, "Rethinking media richness: Towards a theory of media synchronicity," in *32nd Hawaii International Conference on System Sciences*, 1999, pp. 1–10.

[3] H. Holmstrom, E. Ó. Conchúir, P. J. Ågerfalk, and B. Fitzgerald, "Global software development challenges: A case study on temporal, geographical and socio-cultural distance," in *IEEE International Conference on Global Software Engineering*, 2006.

[4] J. D. Herbsleb, A. Mockus, T. A. Finholt, and R. E. Grinter, "Distance, dependencies, and delay in a global collaboration," in *Proceedings of the 2000 ACM conference on Computer supported cooperative work*, 2000, pp. 319–328.

[5] J. D. Herbsleb and A. Mockus, "An empirical study of speed and communication in globally distributed software development," *IEEE Transactions on Software Engineering*, vol. 29, no. 6, 2003.

[6] M. Q. Patton, *Qualitative Research and Evaluation Methods*. Sage Publications, Thousand Oaks, California, 2002.

[7] J. A. Espinosa, W. DeLone, and G. Lee, "Global boundaries, task processes and is project success: a field study," *Information Technology & People*, vol. 19, no. 4, pp. 345–370, 2006.

Inter-team Coordination in Large-Scale Globally Distributed Scrum: Do Scrum-of-Scrums Really Work?

Maria Paasivaara
Aalto University
P.O. Box 15400
00076 Aalto, Finland
maria.paasivaara@aalto.fi

Casper Lassenius
Aalto University
P.O. Box 15400
00076 Aalto, Finland
casper.lassenius@aalto.fi

Ville T. Heikkilä
Aalto University
P.O. Box 15400
00076 Aalto, Finland
ville.heikkila@soberit.hut.fi

ABSTRACT

Scrum-of-Scrums meeting is mentioned in the literature as the mechanism for handling inter-team coordination in large-scale Scrum. However, how to implement it in projects with tens of teams is not explained. In this paper, we present a multiple case study on how Scrum-of-Scrum meetings were applied in two large-scale, globally distributed Scrum projects both employing at least twenty Scrum teams. We conducted 58 semi-structured interviews of project personnel, including managers, architects, product owners, developers and testers. Our results show that Scrum-of-Scrum meetings involving representatives from all teams were severely challenged: the audience was too wide to keep everybody interested and the participants did not know what to report that might be valuable to other teams, often ending up not reporting anything. As a solution, one of the case projects introduced feature-specific Scrum-of-Scrums meetings for 3-5 teams working on the same feature, which turned out to work well. However, challenges with coordination at the project level remained. The other case organization tried a site-based SoS structure that still did not work well.

Categories and Subject Descriptors

D.2.9 [**Software Engineering**]: Management

Keywords

Agile Software Development; Distributed Scrum; Global Software Engineering; Inter-team Coordination

1. INTRODUCTION

Agile methods were originally designed for small collocated teams. Due to their popularity, they are nowadays also applied by large companies in large software development projects employing multiple teams that are distributed to several geographical locations. Scaling agile methods to this new context introduces new challenges, such as inter-team coordination, distribution of work without a defined architecture or properly defined requirements, as well as all the challenges of distributed projects [6]. Despite the challenges, companies have applied agile practices in large projects [5,

7]. While a few case studies and experience reports on taking agile methods into use in projects involving several teams and several geographical locations do exist, most are from small projects involving only a few teams and the number of developers in a project is often under thirty.

Practitioner literature contains some advice on scaling, [4, 6], but studies on how these scaling practices really work in practice, what kind of challenges there might be, and how to overcome the challenges are still rare [3].

In this paper we focus on scaling practices for Scrum [11], which is one of the most widely adopted agile methods. For inter-team coordination and collaboration, the Scrum literature proposes and reports on the use of so-called Scrum-of-Scrum (SoS) meetings [11], but does not discuss how the SoS meetings are applied nor their benefits or challenges.

Research on experiences from larger projects consisting of more than ten teams is currently limited, and thus how to handle inter-team coordination in-the-large in globally distributed Scrum is not well understood. In this paper, we help shed some light on this by presenting a study on how Scrum-of-Scrums meetings were applied in two large distributed Scrum projects.

The paper is structured as follows: Section 2 presents the previous work, Section 3 describes the research goals and methods, Section 4 presents the results, and finally Section 5 discusses the results and presents our conclusions.

2. PREVIOUS WORK

The *Scrum-of-Scrums* meeting (SoS) is basically the only practice Scrum offers for inter-team coordination [10]. Recommendations for how to arrange SoS meetings can be found in the practitioner literature [2, 4, 11]. The basic format of the SoS resembles the Daily Scrum meeting, except that it deals with teams instead of team members. It is recommended that the SoS be arranged daily [10], or 2–3 times a week [2].

It has been suggested that the three questions answered in Daily Scrums [10] could be changed slightly to keep the SoS meeting interesting and effective [4]: 1) What did your team do since the previous meeting that is relevant to some other team? 2) What will your team do by the next meeting that is relevant to other teams? 3) What obstacles does your team have that affect other teams or require help from them? A fourth question to facilitate future coordination might be added: 4) Are you about to put something in another team's way? [2]

The SoS meeting is suggested to be time-boxed to last a maximum of 15 minutes, just like the Daily Scrums [4]. Cohn [2] suggests booking 30–60 minutes for SoS meetings in the calendar, so that if big problems show up at the meeting they could be discussed and solved right away, when all relevant people are present. Another suggestion is to arrange self-organized follow-up meetings after the strictly timeboxed SoS [4]. Each team sends their representative to the SoS meeting. This member is normally rotating, either every time or after a couple of iterations. However, sending a Scrum Master (SM) is considered a bad practice, since it easily leads the Scrum Master role to slip towards that of a traditional project manager [4]. Another challenge of the SoS meeting is not make it into a status reporting meeting for management, but to keep it as a synchronization meeting between the teams [4].

Experiences reported in scientific articles of the usage of SoS meetings are very limited, and most of the articles discuss the usage of SoS meetings in projects with only a few Scrum teams [1, 14, 13]. We found only three research articles briefly reporting experiences from projects over ten Scrum teams [5, 8, 12].

For scaling up the SoS meetings when having a lot of teams, nested Scrum meetings, i.e., Scrum-of-Scrum-of-Scrum meetings (SoSoS) have been suggested [2]. For example, one could arrange normal SoS meetings with representatives from seven Scrum teams, after which each SoS meeting sends their representative to a higher level SoSoS meeting. However, whether this suggested structure has worked anywhere in practice is not reported in the paper describing it [2]. Also Schwaber [11] suggests that SoS meetings may be arranged in large organizations at multiple levels, with progressively higher levels of staff meeting less frequently. A case study presents a project with 14 teams, distributed to four time-zones that had scaled their daily SoS meetings to a two-level nested structure, where they had multiple daily SoS meetings led by senior SMs, who then reported in the project SoSoS [12]. The biggest challenge was the information flow up and down the nested structure. Another case study reports the usage of weekly two-level nested SoS meetings in a project consisting of 21 teams, and mention the weekly SoS as the best way to mitigate the problem of having two teams solving the same problem that a third team had already solved [5].

As an alternative to SoS meetings, consultants report on suggesting arranging a weekly Open Space to a client with 30 teams that was dissatisfied with the SoS. However, the authors do not report whether the client was more satisfied with the Open Space than the SoS [4].

As neither the scientific articles nor the practitioner literature report detailed experiences on using SoS meetings, there seems to be a clear gap in the literature that we hope to partly bridge with this multiple case study.

3. METHODOLOGY

3.1 Research Goals and Data Collection

For this multiple case study, which is part of a larger study on adopting Scrum in-the-large, the goal was to understand how the case organizations handled inter-team coordination in large-scale distributed Scrum. We purposefully selected two information-rich case projects [9] from two companies participating in a joint research program. Both projects were globally distributed and were developing similar large telecom infrastructure systems, consisting of both software and hardware. Our study was purely focussed on software development. We collected the data using 58 semi-structured interviews, see Table 1. We selected the interviewees jointly with management at the case organizations, aiming for people with different length of experience and working in different roles.

All interviews were recorded. In addition, one researcher took detailed notes. The interviews were relatively loosely structured and conversational in order to maintain adaptability to the roles and individual experiences of the employees in different roles.

Table 1: Case Projects and Data Collection

	Case A	Case B
Product	Telecommunications, started from scratch	Telecommunications, 10-years old
Process	Scrum	Incremental change from waterfall to Scrum
Scrum experience	2,5 years	1,5 years
Sites and # of teams	Finland (10 dev. teams), India (6 dev. teams), Germany (2 test teams), Greece (2 test teams)	Finland (18 teams), Hungary (7 teams)
Interviews	19 (Finland 16, Greece 3)	39 (Finland 28, Hungary 11)
Roles[a]	Managers (4), Agile coach (1), Scrum Master (1), Developers (5), Testers (2), Line managers (2), Area Product Owners (4), Architects (1)	Managers (6), Agile coach (1), Scrum Masters (6), Team members (13), Line managers (3), Product/Proxy product owners (7), Technical management / architecture (5)
Interview length	Managers, coach: 1.5–3h, others 1–1.5h	Managers, coach: 2–3h, others 1–2h

[a]The sum exceeds the total number of interviews, as some line managers had double roles, e.g. also worked as Scrum Masters

In this paper, we focus on the experiences of inter-team coordination, for which both case organizations used Scrum-of-Scrum meetings. The research questions we aim to answer are:

1. How have Scrum-of-Scrums meetings been applied in large-scale distributed Scrum projects?
2. What are the benefits and challenges of Scrum-of-Scrums meetings?

3.2 Data Analysis

All interviews were transcribed by a professional transcription company. While waiting for the transcriptions, we did a first round of coding based on the interview notes, creating preliminary categories for coding of the transcripts. We then coded the transcribed interviews in Atlas.ti using the preliminary categories, adding a few more while coding. Two researchers did this coding together, agreeing on and discussing codes while coding and using the same hermeneutic unit. For this paper, we extracted the codes and related quotations for "SoS", "SoS Grande", "SoS Feature", as well as combined them with the codes "Problem" and "Positive" to find out what were seen as problematic or positive in Scrum-of-Scrum meetings.

3.3 Validation

We validated our findings by presenting them to both case companies in feedback sessions to which all interviewed persons were invited. During the sessions, questions were asked and the audience was eager to discuss. The companies found the feedback valuable, and while, e.g., management challenged some of our (less flattering) findings, personnel in other roles confirmed them, and no corrections to our findings came out of the sessions.

4. RESULTS

4.1 Scrum-of-Scrums in Case A

Case project A, developing a telecom product from scratch using Scrum from the outset, had grown from 2 teams to 20 teams distributed to four sites in 2,5 years. Teams were site-specific. Initially, while located at a single site in Finland, SoS meetings were held face-to-face daily, with one representative from each team present. The teams decided themselves who would represent them in the SoS meetings, using e.g. a round-robin approach. When teams from a second site (India) were added to the project, initially the project held daily project-wide SoS meetings using teleconferencing, using the same principle for participation.

However, these meetings were not considered to work properly, and were replaced by a structure consisting of two separate meetings: a *Finnish SoS* followed by a *Global SoS*, both led by the Finnish project manager. The project manager became a communications bridgehead, as he was the only one participating in both meetings. The project manager created a short memo in each meeting, and sent it to all project personnel by email. Later, when even more teams were added from two new sites, they also participated in the Global SoS, that now had team representatives from three sites, as well as the project manager from the fourth site.

Initially, the representative of each team answered the four SoS questions on the behalf of his or her team. However, when the number of teams grew larger, the meetings took longer and longer and the teams gave feedback in the retrospective that they were not that interested in what the other teams were doing. As a result, the first questions were left out, and teams only report if they have impediments or plan to put impediments in the way of other teams.

This has led to a situation in which the meetings are short — 5–15 minutes — and many teams report "No problems", which is not always entirely true, but the result of assuming that the other teams do not have to know or are not interested in their problems.

> "...it would be good if people would really tell about the problems there. Sometimes it feels like everybody just says 'No problems', that everything is going ok, but later on comes up that this and this does not work. (...) And many are fighting with the same problem at the same time." — Tester

Another problem and one of the reasons that the teams did not report problems seemed to be that they did not feel that they would receive help in the meeting:

> "Maybe part of the reason is that in general you don't find solutions from there anyway. Now we are scattered around the world, so we don't have an absolute Scrum of Scrums." — Developer

In Case A, managers admitted that inter-team communication and the SoS meetings did not work properly, and that they did not know how to improve it. The majority of the interviewed team members saw the SoS meetings as poor or even useless. Despite this fact, when we recently visited the company again, there was still no improvement to the situation.

4.2 Scrum-of-Scrums in Case B

Case project B consisted of 25 site-specific Scrum teams distributed to two sites, developing a 10-year old telecommunications product. The organization had started a transformation from waterfall to Scrum 1,5 years ago, and at the time of the interviews all software development teams were using Scrum.

In this project, SoS meetings were initially held using videoconferencing three times a week. Each team send a representative of their choice, most teams opting for a round-robin model. In this meeting, each team could report what they found important to share with the other teams. The problem was that the teams did not seem to know what to share, thus often ending up just reporting "Nothing to share". As a result, participants did not find these meetings useful, and some of our interviewees even claimed that it was a waste of time.

Therefore, after a while the project added another set of meetings called *Feature SoS* meetings. These were held by 3–5 teams working on the same feature[1]. The Feature SoS meetings took place once a week. In addition, the project still arranged the project wide SoS meeting once a week, which now was called the *Grande SoS*.

All interviewees found the Feature SoS meetings useful, since there a small group of people with common interests and goals could share, discuss and even solve problems together:

> "This [Feature SoS] is a good meeting, since this is the only place where we are all together at the same time (...) Here we can discuss everything. We have tried to keep it this way, that we don't have agenda, but discuss what is done at different teams, if there are any problems or other common topics."
> — Proxy Product Owner

> "Feature SoS meetings are pretty good, because people there do the same things, talk "the same language" and have a common goal." — Proxy Product Owner

However, the Grande SoS meetings were seen as problematic according to most interviewed persons, as evidenced by the following quotations:

> But the [Grande] SoS meetings between features, it's very difficult to see the added value, because people do not talk about the same things, it just doesn't work, it's too big." — Proxy Product Owner

> "It [Grande SoS] has not worked well. (...) We are still looking for the role of this meeting and things that should be discussed there." — Developer

Participants of the Grande SoS meetings did not clearly know what to share with each other, they were not interested in what others were doing and sometimes could not even understand each other's problems, since technologies used in different parts of the product differed. On the other hand, another frustration was that the weekly rhythm for the meeting was too slow for dealing with real problem situations requiring daily communication between the teams.

> "I think that teams have not recognized the things that would be really interesting and useful to share with others. (...) And the features are quite separate from each other, and teams have done things that are internal to one feature and thus felt that it might not be interesting to other features. There just have not been enough connecting points." — Scrum Master

5. DISCUSSION AND CONCLUSIONS

Our results can be summarized as two main findings: SoS meetings seem to work poorly when they have too many participants with disjoint interests and concerns; and smaller, focussed inter-team meetings with participants having joint goals and interests, seem to have a better chance of being perceived as successful.

Both case projects started by applying the SoS meetings "by the book", as advised by the agile consultants they employed — "This is the Scrum way". Doing it this way, they answered all the 3-4

---

[1]In this context, a *feature* is a big development task, comprising several epics, often involving several teams and taking several months to develop.

SoS questions and involved representatives from all teams in this common meeting for the whole project.

However, when the number of teams grows, it is clear that all 20 team representatives cannot answer all the Scrum questions in the 15 minutes allotted for the meeting. Instead of lengthening the meeting, both case projects started using a model in which only one issue was discussed: impediments. However, this solution did not turn out well — people did not know what to report, were not interested in what teams working on other parts of the product were doing, or could not understand the other areas if they were discussed.

To help alleviate the problems with the project-wide SoS, both case projects adopted a kind of multiple-level model. Case A used a site-and-size based approach, having one daily face-to-face SoS in Finland, where half of the teams were located; and another daily SoS by teleconferencing involving the Finnish project manager and the teams from the other sites. Case B used a model in which the weekly project-wide "Grande SoS" was augmented with weekly feature-specific SoS meetings. Of these two models, quite logically, the content/architecture-based model rather than the geographically-based one seemed to work much better. However, interestingly, both case projects still recognized the need for project-wide inter-team synchronization, but did not have any good solutions to the problem.

People in both projects had a history of working in waterfall type development, in which global visibility was neither needed nor required from the developers. However, in Scrum everybody should care about the whole product, and according to Scrum, teams are responsible for inter-team coordination. Maybe the change of mindset was not yet successful.

One could also argue that our case projects just did not practice the SoS meetings long enough to get them working properly. However, both projects had already used and improved this practice for a quite a long time and still kept trying. Both projects were all the time looking for improvements.

The literature suggests multi-level SoS meetings, but in reality there are almost no reported experiences on how they should be arranged nor whether they really work. In this kind of nested structure literature mentions information flow up and down the structure as a challenge. Our projects had challenges already with this very low hierarchy structure: What to report in a SoS meeting? What to report back to the team? The team representative often "forgot" to report back to his team or did not find anything important to report back.

Our overall findings — at least in retrospect — seem more or less obvious, and we were frankly a bit surprised at getting such results from our case companies. Both companies are "best in class" in their own field, and have a long history of successful software development. In addition, Case A was one of the organizations the consultants writing one well-known book on how to scale agile worked with. Despite this, the organization had serious issues (among other things) with inter-team coordination, and expressed frustration that neither consultants nor the literature really had provided any real help. This gives an indication that claims in the practitioner literature might be exaggerated and solutions over-simplified.

5.1 Limitations

The paper is based on only two case projects from two organizations, which limits the generalizability of the results. The results are based interviews during which we collected data on many topics, SoS practices being only one of the them. Thus, we could have received even more detailed information if we could have put more emphasis on SoS meetings. Unfortunately we have not yet had the chance of observing the actual SoS meetings in the organizations.

5.2 Future Work

More empirical research is needed on how to tackle inter-team coordination in large-scale agile projects. We plan to follow our case organizations to see how their SoS practices evolve, collecting more detailed data about their SoS meetings by observations, analyzing the meeting notes, as well as by additional interviews. We are also interested in performing additional case studies.

6. REFERENCES

[1] P. L. Bannerman, E. Hossain, and R. Jeffery. Scrum practice mitigation of global software development coordination challenges: A distinctive advantage? *Hawaii International Conference on System Sciences*, 0:5309–5318, 2012.

[2] M. Cohn. Advice on conducting the scrum-of-scrums meeting., May 2007.

[3] E. Hossain, M. A. Babar, and H.-y. Paik. Using scrum in global software development: A systematic literature review. In *Proceedings of the 2009 Fourth IEEE International Conference on Global Software Engineering*, ICGSE '09, pages 175–184, Washington, DC, USA, 2009. IEEE Computer Society.

[4] C. Larman and B. Vodde. *Practices for Scaling Lean & Agile Development: Large, Multisite, and Offshore Product Development with Large-Scale Scrum.* Addison-Wesley Professional, Boston, MA, USA, 2010.

[5] E. C. Lee. Forming to performing: Transitioning large-scale project into agile. In *Proceedings of the Agile 2008*, AGILE '08, pages 106–111, Washington, DC, USA, 2008. IEEE Computer Society.

[6] D. Leffingwell. *Scaling Software Agility: Best Practices for Large Enterprises.* Addison-Wesley Professional, 2007.

[7] M. Paasivaara, S. Durasiewicz, and C. Lassenius. Using scrum in distributed agile development: a multiple case study. In *Proceedings - 2009 4th IEEE International Conference on Global Software Engineering, ICGSE 2009*, pages 195–204, 2009.

[8] M. Paasivaara and C. Lassenius. Scaling scrum in a large distributed project. In *Proceedings - 2011 5th International Symposium on Empirical Software Engineering and Measurement, ESEM 2011*, pages 363–367, 2011.

[9] M. Q. Patton. *Qualitative evaluation and research methods.* Sage Publications, Newbury Park, Calif., 2nd edition, 1990.

[10] K. Schwaber. *Agile Project Management with Scrum.* Microsoft Press, Redmond, Washington, USA, 2004.

[11] K. Schwaber. *The Enterprise and Scrum.* Microsoft Press, Redmond, Washington, USA, 2007.

[12] H. Smits and G. Pshigoda. Implementing scrum in a distributed software development organization. In *Proceedings of the AGILE 2007*, AGILE '07, pages 371–375, Washington, DC, USA, 2007. IEEE Computer Society.

[13] J. Sutherland, G. Schoonheim, and M. Rijk. Fully distributed scrum: Replicating local productivity and quality with offshore teams. *Hawaii International Conference on System Sciences*, 0:1–8, 2009.

[14] J. Sutherland, G. Schoonheim, E. Rustenburg, and M. Rijk. Fully distributed scrum: The secret sauce for hyperproductive offshored development teams. In *Proceedings of the Agile 2008*, AGILE '08, pages 339–344, Washington, DC, USA, 2008. IEEE Computer Society.

Alignment of Business, Architecture, Process, and Organisation in a Software Development Context

Stefanie Betz
Blekinge Institute of Technology
371 79 Karlskrona, Sweden
+46-(0)455-385852

stefanie.betz@bth.se

Claes Wohlin
Blekinge Institute of Technology
371 79 Karlskrona, Sweden
+46-(0)455-385820

claes.wohlin@bth.se

ABSTRACT

In this paper we investigate the current state of work regarding alignment of Business, Architecture, Process, and Organisation (BAPO) perspectives in a software product development context. We planned to do that by conducting a systematic literature study to capture the state of the art in alignment of BAPO in software development. But, as it turned out we found that almost no substantial information is available about the alignment of BAPO in software development. Thus, based on the available literature and a small qualitative study, we defined a conceptual model of the alignment of BAPO including five levels of alignment that can be used as a basis for future empirical studies.

Categories and Subject Descriptors

D.2.9 [**Software Engineering**]: Management – *Life cycle, Software process models, Software quality assurance.*

General Terms

Management, Measurement, Documentation, Economics.

Keywords

BAPO, Business, Architecture, Process, Organisation, Alignment, Decision, Software Engineering.

1. INTRODUCTION

In [1] it is stated how the ideal process in terms of alignment of BAPO in software product development should look like and that the BAPO perspectives are dependent on each other. Meaning if one perspective is altered the other perspectives will be affected.

Thus, we assume that dependencies between the BAPO perspectives exist and as such the different perspectives affect each other. But, they are not necessarily aligned to the level where the other perspectives are fully taken into account before taking a decision with respect to one of the perspectives. Representatives of other perspectives are not involved in the decision-making process so that a proactive alignment between the perspectives can take place e.g. architectural design needs to be taken into account when going global [2]. So, the question is what the consequences are if the alignment is missing and what the actual level of alignment present in a company is and what measures are taken to align them, or if it is assumed that they will eventually align as they are affected. In order to study that we developed a

conceptual model of the alignment of BAPO with five levels of alignment based on an aborted Systematic Literature Study (SLR) and a small interview study.

In our SLR we found that almost no substantial information is available about the alignment of BAPO at least not in (global) software product development. But, it is stated that it is important to understand the dependencies between the BAPO perspectives [2]. Therefore, it is important to define the different BAPO perspectives and their level of alignment. Thus, we provide a conceptual model of BAPO including five levels of alignment to provide a basis for a common understanding of the BAPO perspectives and their possible level of alignment.

The remainder of the paper is structured as follows. The next section describes the aborted SLR. In Section 3, we present our interview study. Section 4 contains a detailed description of the developed conceptual model including the five levels of alignment and the paper ends with a summary and future work.

2. SYSTEMATIC LITERATURE REVIEW

The goal of our SLR was to find out if there has been "any work" done regarding the alignment of BAPO in a global software product development context. Any work can be: empirical studies, models, frameworks or theories [3]. Thus, our research question was:

RQ: What is the state-of-the-art regarding the alignment of the four perspectives business, architecture, process, and organisation in a global software product development context?

We added the global software development (GSD) context because we thought in a distributed setting the alignment is even more important for example architectural design needs to be taken into account when going global [2]. Furthermore, adding GSD is a possibility to narrow the scope in the literature study because business, architecture, process and organisation are words which are used quite often and in a lot of different contexts (e.g. development processes, business processes, process improvement, process maturity and so on).

2.1 Search strategy

To answer the research question a systematic review was conducted. As a first step we looked for search strings. We aimed at finding the state of the art regarding alignment in a global software development product context. Thus, we included the four perspectives business, architecture, process, and organisation in our search strings. In addition, we were looking for alignment and its synonyms and we used GSD and its synonyms as well as embedded systems and its synonyms for further refinement of the search in our pilot study. But, the plan to use Google scholar did not work the way we intended, because Google scholar is not able to handle the search string with several ANDs and ORs. This means only one group of words can be chosen as "one of the given synonyms should match". Therefore we got very different results, because we either needed to add the group with an AND to the search string by choosing only one of the synonyms (e.g. AND "Alignment") or we had to put the whole group in the section "only one of the words" (e.g. OR "Alignment", "Traceability", "Goals", "Integration", "Bridge", "Harmony", "Linkage") but then we could not add any other groups to the OR section because there is only one OR section for all. Due to that problem with the search string the results were very different given the number of hits and the general output. In general, it could be shown the outcome had a strong variation in terms of hits as well as in terms of research directions. As a cross check we tested the original search string using the database *SciVerse Scopus*, but the result was also not useful, we only got 28 hits and the papers have not been relevant for our search, as we judged based on the titles. Thus, we decided to reduce the search string. In doing so, we finally found one search string that at least included one of the known key papers [1] in the first 10 hits. Thus, we decided to use this search string to create a set of papers to be used for snowballing, i.e. given that we did not really find a good way of identifying the most relevant papers through searching databases. In addition, snowballing is found to be effective in identifying relevant research [4]. So, the final search string was:

"Business", "Architecture", "Process", "Organisation", "Alignment", and "Embedded Systems" in the AND section and "Global Software Development" OR "Global Software Engineering" OR "Distributed Software Development" OR "Distributed Development" OR "Offshoring" OR "Outsourcing" OR "Software Transfer" (number of hits 426).

In addition, the search strategy was based on the following parameters [5]:

Spatial parameters: global due to the actual setting

Temporal parameters: As we do snowballing, we cannot use the only most recent papers, due to references search on that paper. We will search backwards through references and we have no time limits there as well as in the initial search. In addition, we are looking on any work done in our specific topic.

Disciplinary parameters: We are aware that we are conducting an interdisciplinary search and expect that the software product line, the requirements engineering and the information system communities have done some work regarding the alignment of BAPO. But, we want to find out what work is available on our specific topic. Later, we are planning to compare existing approaches from the mentioned disciplines

Formal parameters: We are taking into account journals, conference and workshop proceedings (=peer reviewed).

Search applied on: Full text. We did choose the full text in order to get access to all the papers that do not include our keywords in title or abstract, although they may be relevant.

Language: English

Searched databases: Google scholar

Our search strategy was to take the 20 best hits from Google scholar as a start for snowballing.

2.2 Assessment criteria and quality criteria

As a second step before conducting the search and the literature selection we invented relevance assessment and quality criteria in

order to be able to conduct a relevance analysis upon full text and conduct inclusion or exclusion [6]. Our relevance assessment criteria are shown in Table 1. In order to measure the relevance we used the following scoring: 1 point for yes (main questions), 0 point for unclear (main questions and sub questions), 0 point for no (main questions and sub questions), ¼ point for one of the areas of BAPO (sub questions), ½ point for aligning two areas (sub questions), and ¾ point for aligning 3 areas (sub questions). If the full paper had more than 3 points, then it was considered as relevant and included.

Table 1. Relevance assessment criteria

1. Are the areas to align (BAPO) discussed in the paper?
If not which of the following areas are included?
a) Business; b) Architecture; c) Process and d) Organisation
2. Is the paper dealing with (any kind of) alignment of all four areas (BAPO)?
If not, is the paper dealing with the alignment of some of the areas?
Two at the time: a) B – A; b) B – P; c) B – O; d) A – P; e) A – O; f) P – O;
Three at the time: g) B – A – P; h) A – P – O; i) B – P – O; j) B – A – O;
3. Is the setting a global software development project?
4. Is the regarded product embedded?
5. Is the paper concerned with software development

For the quality assessment we used the criteria in Table 2.

Table 2. Quality assessment criteria

1. Is the research aim clearly stated?
2. Is the research methodology clearly described?
3. Is the method chosen appropriate (e.g. answers the RQ)?
4. Is the setting the study/method/theory applies to thoroughly and clearly described
5. Are limitations and or validity threats discussed?
6. Does the empirical data and or results support the conclusion?

In order to measure the quality we used the following scoring: ½ point yes, ¼ point partially, and 0 point for no. We did not define a threshold, because the quality assessment was not used for selecting papers. An external researcher with experience in performing SLRs checked our assessment criteria and the scoring. In addition we piloted the protocol.

2.3 Literature selection

In this phase, the aim was to choose the papers to be used as the basis for the actual snowballing. The literature selection was performed in three steps (see Table 3).

Table 3. Literature selection based on [6]

Analysis Steps	Inclusion Criteria	Researchers involved	Papers left
1. Selection based on search	Search strategy parameters	Leading researcher	20
2. Exclusion based on title and abstract		Two researchers	10
3. Exclusion based on full paper	Relevance assessment	Two researchers	0

Using the search string defined in Section 2.1, we got 426 hits. From these hits we took the first 20 hits fitting our search strategy parameters (see step 1). In the next step, step 2, we conducted the exclusion based on title and abstract. In order to do so both researchers separately assessed the titles and abstracts of the 20 papers. This was followed by a discussion between the two researchers to obtain consensus on inclusion and exclusion. The researchers agreed on 14 out of 20 papers and decided for the 6 papers not in agreement to include all papers with at least one "inclusion" for the full text analysis. In step 3, we conducted a relevance analysis of the full text based on the relevance assessment criteria. Therefore, three papers have been randomly chosen as an input, none of the papers passed the relevance threshold. Then the "key paper" [1] has been chosen for relevance assessment but even there we did not find the paper relevant for the objectives of our SLR. Thus, being not able to find any relevant papers with our search strategy, we decided to check how the outcome of the search would be if we search without the GSD focus (search string: "Business", "Architecture", "Process", "Organisation", "Alignment", and "Embedded Systems"). We got more then 10.000 hits and in the list of the first 30 hits we found couple of identical papers to the ones found with the search string including the GSD focus. But, in general there was a stronger focus on software product lines and on business. Nevertheless, the papers either have already been assessed or not relevant for our search, as we judged based on the titles. At that stage we decided to abort the SLR because we could not find any relevant papers.

So, we found evidence that there is a lack of research regarding the alignment of the four perspectives business, architecture, process, and organisation in a software product development context. But, we found hints in the literature that dependencies between the different perspectives exist [1] and that alignment is needed between different perspectives [2]. Consequently, we conducted an interview study with a software product developing company to find out if there is a need to conduct research in this topic.

3. INTERVIEW STUDY

3.1 Design of study

To understand the level of alignment and challenges related to any misalignment, an interview study was conducted at a large company developing software-intensive systems for an international market. The interviews were planned to be semi-structured in the sense that several areas should be covered in the interviews, but it was also important to allow the interviewees to express their opinions and experience in particular in relation to their specific expertise. In total, 11 people coming from a mixture of roles were interviewed. The roles include system architects, product managers, line managers on different levels and technical experts. The starting point for the interviews was the assumption that alignment of the different perspectives in BAPO is beneficial. Furthermore, it is assumed that it is preferable if the order of the letters in BAPO reflects the starting point for alignment, which is also argued in [1], although some iteration is most likely needed.

3.2 Main findings

Bellow, the findings in relation to the BAPO perspectives are summarized:

Business: There is an agreement that the business is changing quickly, although it is expressed slightly different by different interviewees. This puts requirements on the other letters in BAPO, i.e. APO.

Architecture: The development processes have changed over the last five years from supporting large plan-driven project to becoming more agile and lean. However, system and software architecture has not changed sufficiently with the processes. This also includes that the architecture is not necessarily well suited for distributed development. At the same time there is too little focus

on the actual architecture (lack of long-term investments), and hence the development is too much driven by the need to deliver new features. Development becomes reactive and not proactive.

Process: To respond to the requirements from the market in terms of being faster to the market and being able to react to change quickly, agile and lean methods have been adopted. However, the consequence is that agile and lean software development is introduced without necessarily the business becoming agile as a whole or for that matter the system being ready for being developed using agile and lean software development.

Organisation: This perspective was mentioned the least by the interviewees than the other perspectives. There is a perception that the organisation indirectly decides too much, i.e. the "O" in BAPO becomes too powerful. The organisation was originally designed to fit the system architecture, but now it is the other way around, i.e. the organisation governs the architecture.

From the interviews, we conclude that the perspectives are not taken into account as much as needed and that alignment between the BAPO perspectives would most likely be beneficial. All perspectives have challenges regarding alignment with the other perspectives, e.g. architecture does not fit to a business decision, processes are agile but the business is not, and organisation governs architecture. Thus, to mitigate misalignment and to be able to make informed decisions there is a need to achieve a certain level of alignment. Based on the insights gained by literature and the conducted interview study, we decided to build a conceptual model of BAPO alignment including different levels of alignment. The aim of the model is it to use it as a basis for future empirical studies on the alignment of BAPO in a software product development context.

4. CONCEPTUAL MODEL OF BAPO

First, we are defining the four different perspectives business, architecture, process, and organisation. We tried to define the perspectives based on existing work as well as keeping the definitions short but precise in order to use them in an industrial context. As such the first two definitions are based on the definitions of [1], the third one is a shorter version of the definition of business processes from [7] and the fourth one is based on [8] and [9].

Business: how to make money from products and services,

Architecture: the structure to build the software,

Process: a set of structured activities to achieve a specific goal,

Organisation: a set of people organized in a specific structure to achieve a common goal.

Our conceptual model consists of the four BAPO perspectives, their dependencies, their attributes, and the levels of alignment. Figure 1 gives an overview over the BAPO perspectives and their dependencies. The attributes and levels of alignment are further elaborated below.

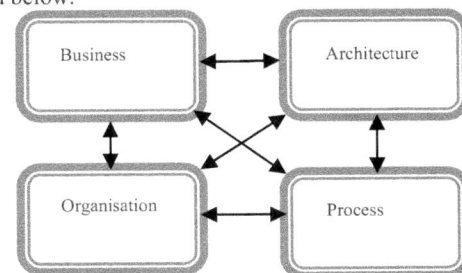

Figure 1. The BAPO perspectives

The links between the different perspectives show the dependencies between the different perspectives. In our view the different perspectives are all dependent on each other, but often they are not well aligned as shown through the interview study. This implies that when a decision has been taken in one of the perspectives, for example, taking a business decision to develop a software system globally instead of at one site may have implications for the other perspectives. With a lack of alignment and a limited awareness of the dependencies the decisions may be made without taking the other perspectives into account. As a consequence a reactive process starts now, where the other perspectives will slowly align with potential (negative) effects on cost, quality and time as illustrated by the architecture perspective in the interview study in Section 3.2. Thus, we assume dependencies exist and alignment will eventually be achieved through being affected but a conscious alignment is preferable to be proactive towards changes caused by the dependencies. In our model each of the four perspectives has the following attributes to capture the decisions associated with them:

- Drivers: What are the drivers of the decisions?
- Responsible: Who is responsible for the decisions?
- Constraints: What are the constraints of the decisions?
- Objectives: What are the objectives of the decisions?
- Timeline: What is the timeline for the implementation of the decisions?
- Challenges: What are the major challenges of the implementation of decisions?
- Dependencies: What are the dependencies of the decisions?

Additionally, we developed five levels of alignment going from reactive to proactive decision-making.

1. Not aware or aware and ignored: none of the other perspectives is taken into account,
2. Aware: other perspectives are taken into account by the decision-maker, but no further actions are taken,
3. Informed: other perspectives are taken into account by the decision-maker and other stakeholders are informed that changes are needed after the decision is taken,
4. Communication: other perspectives are taken into account by the decision-maker and others are informed before the decision is taken that changes are needed,
5. Discussion: other perspectives are taken into account by the decision-maker and representatives of the other perspectives are involved in the decision-making process.

The levels are classified in reactive levels and proactive levels.

- Levels 1 and 2: reactive
- Level 3: from reactive to proactive – neutral
- Levels 4 and 5: proactive

The goal is to use the levels to classify the current situation of alignment of the BAPO perspectives in a company. Therefore, we also classified them according to their reactive and proactive level. Level 3 is on the borderline where the level is actually changing from reactive to proactive decision alignment.

5. SUMMARY AND FUTURE WORK

In this paper we described an aborted SLR on what research has been done regarding the alignment of the four perspectives business, architecture, process, and organisation in a (global) software product development context as well as a small interview study on the topic. As we found a research gap regarding the alignment of BAPO in software product development we presented a conceptual model of the alignment of the four BAPO perspectives including five levels of alignment of BAPO. With the help of the conceptual model we want to investigate decisions in relation to BAPO to understand if decisions made within one of the BAPO perspectives are taking the other perspectives into account. Thus, in our future work we want to investigate the actual state of the conscious alignment of the BAPO perspectives, or if the alignment is a slow process based on being affected. The objective is to capture this empirically. Moreover, we want to give companies the possibility to take the consequences of decision-making on the different perspective of BAPO into account as early as possible in the decision-making process. The goal is that the company is able to increase the level of alignment and as such evolve from taking reactive decisions to proactive decisions.

6. ACKNOWLEDGMENTS

This work is part of the BESQ+ research project funded by the Knowledge Foundation (grant: 20100311) in Sweden.

7. REFERENCES

[1] Linden, F. v. d., Bosch, J., Kamsties, E., Känsälä, K. and Obbink, H. 2004. Software Product Family Evaluation. In *Software Product Line Conference (SPLC)*, 110-129.

[2] Mustapic, G., Wall, A., Norström, C., Crnkovic, I., Sandström, K.; Fröberg, J. and Andersson, J. 2004. Real world influences on software architecture - interviews with industrial system experts. In *4th Working Conference on Software Architecture (WICSA'04)*, 2004, 101-112.

[3] Webster, J. and Watson, R. T. 2002. Analyzing the past to prepare for the future: Writing a literature review. *MIS Quarterly*, vol. 26, no. 2, 13-23.

[4] Greenhalgh, T. and Peacock, K. R. 2005. Effectiveness and efficiency of search methods in systematic reviews of complex evidence: audit of primary sources. *BMJ - Information in Practice*, no. 331, 1064-1065.

[5] Duff, A. 1996. The literature search: a library-based model for information skills instruction. *Library Review*, 14-18.

[6] Kitchenham, B. and Charters, S. 2007. *Guidelines for Performing Systematic Literature Reviews in Software Engineering*. Software Engineering Group, School of Computer Science and Mathematics, Keele University, EBSE Technical Report Version 2.3.

[7] Davenport, T. H. and Short, J. E. 1990. The New Industrial Engineering: Information Technology and Business Process Reedesign. *Sloan Management Review*, Vol. 31, no. 4, 11-27.

[8] Daft, R.L. 2003. *Organization Theory and Design*, 8th ed., South-Western College Pub.

[9] Oxford University Press. 2012. Oxford Dictionaries. http://oxforddictionaries.com/definition/organization

Software Quality Modeling Experiences at an Oil Company

Constanza Lampasona &
Jens Heidrich
Fraunhofer IESE
Fraunhofer-Platz 1
67663 Kaiserslautern, Germany

{constanza.lampasona |
jens.heidrich}@iese.fraunhofer.de

Victor Basili
University of Maryland,
Fraunhofer CESE, and
King Abdulaziz University
825 University Research Court Suite
1300, College Park, MD, USA
basili@fc-md.umd.edu

Alexis Ocampo
ECOPETROL S.A.
Calle 37 No 7-43
Bogotá, Colombia

alexis.ocampo@ecopetrol.com.co

ABSTRACT

The concept of "software quality" is often hard to capture for an organization. Quality models aim at making the concept more operational by refining the "quality" of software development products and processes into sub-concepts down to the level of concrete metrics and indicators. In practice, it is difficult for an organization to come up with a reliable quality model because quality depends on numerous organizational context factors, and the model as well as the metrics and indicators need to be tailored to the specifics of the organization. This paper presents experiences in developing custom-tailored quality models for an organization, exemplified by Ecopetrol, a Colombian oil and gas company. The general approach taken is illustrated and excerpts from the initial model are presented.

Categories and Subject Descriptors

D.2.8 [**Software Engineering**]: Metrics – *Product metrics*

General Terms

Measurement

Keywords

Quality measurement and assurance, Industrial experience.

1. INTRODUCTION

Quality is defined as "the totality of characteristics of an entity that bear on its ability to satisfy stated and implied needs" (ISO 8402). Typically, the term "software quality" is hard to capture for an organization. In order to make the concept more operational, software quality models have been defined. These models try to refine the abstract term "quality" of software development products and processes into sub-concepts down to the level of metrics and indicators to allow quality measurement. One of the most popular product quality models is ISO 9126 and its successor ISO 25000.

When applying these models in practice, the problems are that (1) there exist a huge number of different quality models for different purposes, (2) the abstraction level is too high for applying the model, and most of all, (3) it is very difficult to come up with reliable metrics and indicators for an organization. One of the major reasons is that quality depends on stakeholders, application context, usage purpose, and other context factors of an organiza-

tion and the models as well as the metrics and indicators need to be tailored to the specifics of the organization.

This paper describes first steps towards creating a quality model for the IT department of Ecopetrol, a Colombian oil and gas company. One major goal of Ecopetrol is to become one of the 30 most important companies in the oil and gas domain by 2020. IT plays an important role in supporting the business processes necessary to establish Ecopetrol's top-level goals. Equally, it is important to align the incorporation, acquisition, and development of IT solutions with the company's landscape so that the goals achieved by IT directly impact the business goals. The company supports standardization of business processes and IT based on the premise that standardization will help it to expand and grow faster and be more agile. The paper presents the ongoing work of defining a quality model for the software that is acquired, maintained, or developed by external suppliers of Ecopetrol's IT department. The major goal related to developing the quality model was to improve software quality, reduce the issues caused by unknown/probably poor software quality, and in turn contribute to the ability to develop and maintain software faster and support Ecopetrol in becoming more agile. The quality model will support the definition of baselines for software quality at Ecopetrol and will become part of its IT landscape. It will help Ecopetrol define policies to be followed by the organization in order to achieve the goal of standardization of quality requirements.

This paper presents our practices and experience in developing quality models for an organization's specific needs. Section 2 presents related work in the field of quality modeling and the problems with the application of standardized quality models. Section 3 presents the approach taken to develop the model and introduces an excerpt of the developed model. The approach consisted of a survey of key stakeholders, a highly interactive GQM workshop, and the extraction of the model based upon the identification of problems and potential mitigation strategies. This led to the definition of the local meaning of quality and set the stage for evaluating the product based upon that definition. Suggestions for mechanisms for improving quality within the organization were also derived. Finally, Section 4 presents a short summary and conclusion and highlights future work aimed at completing the model and introducing the model into the organization.

2. RELATED WORK

Many quality models specify a prescriptive set of quality characteristics or metrics. ISO 25010 [8], for example, provides a structure for defining a set of quality attributes and sub-attributes. However, the direct use of this model is difficult because it is not easy to operationalize, which is an issue we also observed for other well-known models such as [4], [7], and [9]. Nevertheless, they provide a useful reference for defining high-level quality attributes.

Besides these general focus models, there exist many models explicitly developed for specific domains. Some examples are [2], which presents a maintainability model for embedded systems; [5], which presents a model for object-oriented design; and [6], which is a quality model specialized for European aerospace projects.

Kläs et al. [10] studied approaches for tailoring quality models and offer an approach for adapting existing quality models. We could not use the approach because we did not have an existing, worked-out model; Ecopetrol decided to only use an excerpt of the ISO25010 standard and develop their metrics from scratch.

We found only one model for measuring the quality of software in the oil industry [11]. Although the model's domain coincides with our domain of interest, we did not use it because it focuses only on the evaluation of discrete-event simulation software.

Because of the flexibility provided by the GQM paradigm [1], which allows for specifying a customer-tailored measurement program connecting high-level measurement goals and metrics, we chose to apply it to derive a quality model for Ecopetrol. The main reason for applying the GQM paradigm was its ability to provide a model that connects high-level quality aspects (as found in common standards, such as maintainability or reliability) with concrete metrics found on the operational level of the organization. Further advantages of applying GQM are that it can be used for (1) evaluating all artifacts from all development phases; 2) identifying strengths and weaknesses of the current product; 3) deriving a quantitative baseline; and 4) selecting and evaluating improvement measures.

3. METHOD AND QUALITY MODEL

We developed the GQM-based quality model in two steps: a survey on the relevance of various quality characteristics, and a workshop to identify issues related to the identified quality characteristics, derive GQM measurement goals, and determine concrete metrics for the identified goals. The survey asked the key stakeholders at Ecopetrol to rate the importance of each quality characteristic proposed in ISO 25010 for their projects. Based on their answers, the goal was to focus on the most important quality characteristics during the workshop.

3.1 Survey

The survey included a list of 30 items corresponding to the ISO 25010 quality sub-characteristics, which the responders had to rate using a scale from 1 (very unimportant) to 10 (very important), i.e., a rating of less than 6 indicated minimal importance. The 14 participants were technical leaders from the company's IT department and external software suppliers. To analyze the answers, we simply aggregated the ratings given to the sub-characteristics for the corresponding quality characteristic (Figure 1). Besides the importance of the quality characteristics, we collected data about the type of software developed, the programming languages used, and the areas addressed by the products (Figure 2).

However, we were unable to determine which quality characteristics to focus on because they were all considered very important, with the possible exception of portability. Also, neither a deeper analysis on the level of sub-characteristics nor the grouping of data according to different context factors (such as those listed in Figure 2) revealed any significant difference. Even though the definitions for all quality characteristics and sub-characteristics were provided, it became clear from the feedback of the participants that the different terms were understood in different ways

when it came to the technical impact of the quality characteristics on their software. This tends to be a problem with standardized quality models in general; stakeholders understand their particular quality needs but are unable to map them to the general terms provided by the models. So, from the abstract definition of the terms, it was not clear which characteristic is more important than others.

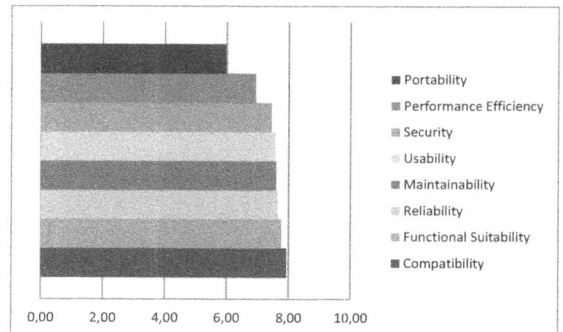

Figure 1. Aggregated rating for quality aspect importance

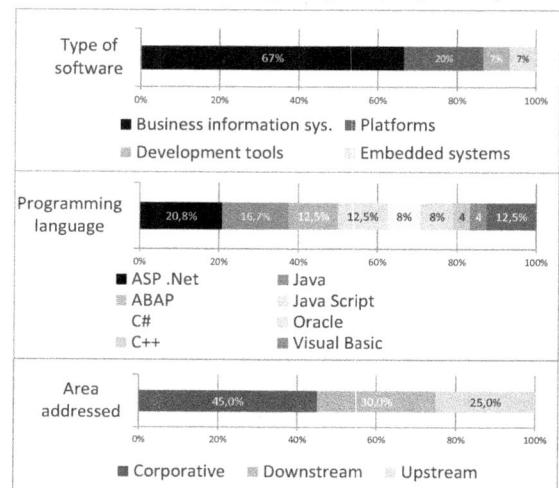

Figure 2. Software type, programing language, and area

For further discussion, we limited the scope of the quality model and characterized the context by asking the following questions:

- What is the application scope of the measurement model?
  - Customization of commercial products and in-house development
  - IS systems only
  - Corporate, upstream, downstream development
- Which organizational units are involved in the measurement?
  - Shared services
- Which stakeholders are involved in the measurement?
  - Architects, technical leads, information leads
- What is the context/environment for the measurement model?
  - Project types: maintenance, new development, integration
  - Development processes: RUP and ASAP (based on SAP)

The next steps, which were carried out during the on-site workshop, were to determine the organizational objectives, prioritize the goals, and develop GQM measurement goals and finally metrics for creating an overall quality model.

3.2 Workshop

Since the survey provided little differentiation among the quality characteristics, it was difficult to prioritize and identify the most important quality needs. So we chose to take a different approach to gain some more insight into the Ecopetrol "quality" issues of importance. We turned the problem upside down and asked the nine workshop participants to come up with specific issues related to software quality that should be avoided. To this end, we informally applied the UMD approach [3] for eliciting such requirements, which essentially revolves around asking the stakeholders the following questions: What do you see that should not happen, i.e., what causes you the most trouble? What should be done to mitigate this problem? The problem may abstract to several standard quality aspects, e.g., reliability and maintainability, creating some confusion in identifying a particular quality aspect, even though the stakeholder knows what the real quality problem is. So in that sense the defined quality aspect is too abstract to be of value since we cannot map the aspect back to the real problem.

This generated a lively discussion. It was clear that there was a problem with the dynamic nature of requirements elicitation and on-demand implementation of the rules, as business rules and requirements were introduced at random by various levels of stakeholders and multiple implementation teams developing the software solutions. This led to a variety of issues focusing on requirements stability, design and implementation, and code reuse. Some of the issues and the suggested mitigations were:

Requirements Stability:
- **Issue:** Constantly evolving requirements and business rules.
- **Mitigation:** Improve the requirements elicitation process from the customers using more focused reviews and inspections at the right point in time. Try to identify potential future change requests.

Design and Implementation:
- **Issue:** External and internal dependencies of components create problems (if one interface is changed, the whole system does not work or, even worse, the set of information systems interacting with each other).
- **Mitigation:** Make the dependencies (of interfaces) transparent; consider doing an impact analysis.
- **Issue:** Hard-coded parameters in the code.
- **Mitigation:** Identify and eliminate hard-coded parameters; make use of a business rules engine to access the parameters, make better use of the MDM (Master Data Management) system.
- **Issue:** It is difficult to deal with and maintain a very large number of public interfaces between the information systems interacting with each other.
- **Mitigation:** Minimize the number of public interfaces by eliminating deprecated interfaces and unifying the way information systems are interacting with each other.

Code Reuse:
- **Issue:** There can be more reuse; maybe some reuse is achieved, but the process is not transparent.
- **Mitigation:** Create a dictionary of reusable components made visible to all stakeholders.

Once we understood the major issues related to software development, we were able to better identify the quality needs and prioritize where measurement should be applied. From the application of the GQM paradigm [1], we derived ten goals (Table 1).

Other goals were identified based on the issues, but these are not included in the first version of the quality model because measurement data collection for these goals involves a high degree of manual work, e.g., requirements completeness, requirements

redundancy, and cost and size of change requests. The focus of the initial model was on goals for which measurement data can be collected at least semi-automatically from existing sources of information. For all ten goals, we applied the GQM approach and derived questions, metrics, and identified variation factors. Table 2 shows an example of a GQM abstraction sheet.

During the discussions in the workshop, many variation factors were identified, including development and support practices, as well as management practices, such as project team fluctuation, regulation changes, operational incidents, project time constraints, number and type of change requests, application performance constraints, application domain knowledge and skills of project team, communication and team work skills of project team, and disciplined requirements management.

Table 1. Overview of GQM measurement goals

Name	Object	Purpose	Quality Focus
G1: Requirements stability	Application requirements	Characterization	Stability
G2: Hard-coded parameters in code (constants, literals)	Application code	Characterization	Hard-coded parameters
G3: Design of internal dependencies	Application design	Characterization	Internal dependencies
G4: Design of external dependencies	Application design	Characterization	External dependencies
G5: Code reusability	Application code	Characterization	Reusability
G6: Code defect density	Application code	Characterization	Defect density
G7: Enterprise architecture coupling	Enterprise architecture	Characterization	Coupling
G8: Test coverage	Traceability matrix	Characterization	Test coverage
G9: Conformance of design to implementation	Design	Characterization	Conformance
G10: Traceability	Traceability matrix	Characterization	Traceability

Viewpoint	Context
Architects, technical leads, information leads	Maintenance, new development, and integration projects, based on RUP or ASAP.

During the workshop discussion we noted that personnel fluctuation and application domain knowledge and skills have the greatest influence on quality. Since the company's software is developed by external suppliers, managing personnel fluctuation is especially important since it takes time to acquire knowledge and experience regarding the specifics of the oil and gas domain. Personnel fluctuation is one factor for success in a software development project in terms of effectiveness and efficiency. If people with high domain experience/knowledge leave or move to different projects, they will be replaced by people with less domain experience and knowledge and the risk of being less productive typically increases dramatically. In general, it is recommended that personnel fluctuation should be limited as much as possible. As a minimum, a key personnel group should be established that can act as a multiplier of domain experience/knowledge and as advisors for "new" members of the development team.

For each of the ten GQM goals, an abstraction sheet (as shown in Table 2) was developed. After that, all goals, questions, and metrics were integrated into a comprehensive quality model. The initial quality model developed consisted of 10 measurement goals, 17 questions, 36 metrics, and 10 variation factors.

Table 2. GQM abstraction sheet for the design of external dependencies

Object	Purpose	Quality Aspect	Viewpoint		Context
Design	Characterize	External dependencies	Architects, technical leads, information leads		Maintenance, new development, integration projects
Quality Focus (Questions and Metrics)				**Variation Factors**	
What do you want to know regarding the quality focus? **Q1:** How many of the provided external interfaces are used by other applications per interface type? **M1:** Number of external interfaces provided used by other applications per interface type **Q2:** How many external interfaces are provided per type? **M2:** Number of external interfaces provided per type **Q3:** Which is the proportion of interfaces provided and used by other applications? **M3:** Ratio M1/M2				What explains variations in the quality focus? − Team experience − Team knowledge − Time constraints − Performance constraints	
Baseline Hypotheses				**Impact of Variation Factors**	
What are known baselines for metrics in the quality focus? (Confidential information)				What is the impact of factors? (Not clearly specified)	
Interpretation Model					
How to interpret and assess the data? (Confidential information)					

Moreover, for each goal, the corresponding quality characteristics from ISO25010 were identified and related to the corresponding goals.

4. CONCLUSIONS AND FUTURE WORK

This paper presented our practices and experiences in developing a custom-tailored quality model for Ecopetrol using the classical GQM approach for identifying and measuring information needs. First, a survey was conducted to identify quality characteristics of interest. Second, a workshop was conducted to identify the current top-priority issues and the techniques that can be used to mitigate those problems and improve the quality of the products. Based on this discussion, a set of measureable quality goals that define the oil company's quality focus was defined and agreed upon. For each goal, abstraction sheets were developed to derive concrete metrics that characterize software quality at Ecopetrol. Finally, these metrics were integrated into a comprehensive quality model. Some lessons learned from building the model include:

- Building a quality model is neither a pure top-down nor a pure bottom-up process, and it was easy to use GQM in this context.
- The main drivers for building the quality model were the issues and mitigation strategies identified, rather than the ISO 25010 quality characteristics. The major reasons were that people understood various terms in different ways and the technical impact of the general quality characteristics was hard relate to their specific quality problems. It was easier for people to say what they did not want to happen.
- Using this approach results in a model that may not be compatible with the ones found in other companies (in fact one would assume they would all be different), so it is difficult to do benchmarking across companies. However, the resulting model was understood by and useful to the Ecopetrol stakeholders. Discussion centered on real problems and it was clear when progress was being made in addressing these problems. This reduced the complexity of the quality model and increased acceptance among the Ecopetrol experts participating in the development of the model.

Current work focuses on applying the quality model to a set of selected software development projects at Ecopetrol. Therefore, a tool chain is being created that will automate large parts of the measurement data collection. We are also working on visualizing the analysis results in an intuitive manner, thus allowing for data exploration and identifying root causes for quality issues. In the future, the first analysis of the results will trigger initial recommendations for further improvement of software quality

and will lead to the identification of reliable target values for the creation of quality gates as a mechanism for checking software quality as early as possible in the development process. Future work might include further application of the UMD approach for the development of quality models.

5. REFERENCES

[1] Basili, V., Caldiera, G., Rombach, D. 1994. Goal question metric paradigm. In J. Marciniak, editor, Encyclopedia of Software Engineering, Volume 1, pages 528-532. John Wiley & Sons, Inc., New York.

[2] Deissenboeck, F., Wagner, S., Pizka, M., Teuchert, M., and Girard, J.F. 2007. An activity-based quality model for maintainability. In Proceedings of the IEEE International Conference on Software Maintenance, 184-193.

[3] Donzelli, P., Basili M. 2006. A practical framework for eliciting and modeling system dependability requirements: Experience from the NASA high dependability computing project. Journal of Systems and Software, 79, 1 (January 2006), 107-119.

[4] Dromey, G.R. 1995. A model for software product quality. IEEE Transactions on Software Engineering, 21, 2 (Feb. 1995), 146-162.

[5] Dumke, R. 1998. An OO framework for software measurement and evaluation. In proceedings of the Conference on Quality Engineering in Software Technology, 52-61.

[6] ECSS, ECSS-Q-30A. 1996. Space product assurance: dependability.

[7] Grady, R.B. and Caswell, D.L. 1997. Software metrics: establishing a company-wide program: Prentice Hall.

[8] ISO/IEC 25000-1. 2005. Software engineering - Software product quality requirements and evaluation (SQuaRE) - Guide to SQuaRE.

[9] Kitchenham, B.A. 1987. Towards a constructive quality model: part 1: software quality modeling, measurement and prediction. Software Engineering Journal, 2, 4 (July 1987), 105-113.

[10] Kläs, M., Lampasona, C., Münch, J. 2011. Adapting software quality models: Practical challenges, approach, and first empirical results. 37th EUROMICRO Conference on Software Engineering and Advanced Applications (SEAA), 341-348

[11] Rincón, G., Alvarez, M., Perez, M., Hernandez, S. 2005. A discrete-event simulation and continuous software evaluation on a systemic quality model: An oil industry case. Information & Management, 42, 8 (Dec. 2005), 1051-1066.

Managing Technical Debt in Practice: An Industrial Report

Clauirton A. Siebra
Center of Informatics
Federal University of Paraiba
Joao Pessoa – PB – Brazil
+55 83 3216 7093

cas@di.ufpb.br

Graziela S. Tonin, Fabio Q. B. da Silva, Rebeka
G. Oliveira, Antonio L. C. Junior, Regina C. G.
Miranda, Andre L. M. Santos
CIn/Samsung Project – Federal University of Pernambuco
+55 81 3454 3300

{gst,fabio,rgo2,alocj,rcgm,alms}@cin.ufpe.br

ABSTRACT

The Technical Debt (TD) metaphor has been used as a way to manage and communicate long-term consequences that some decisions may cause. However the state of the art in TD has not culminated yet in rigorous analysis models for large-scale projects. This work analyses an industrial project, from the perspective of its decisions and related events, so that we can better characterize the existence of TD and show the evolution of its parameters. The project in study had a life cycle of six years (2005-2011) and its data for analysis was collected from emails, documents, CVS logs, code files and interviews with developers and project managers. From this analysis, we identified the factors that had influence on the project decisions and their impact on the system along the time. Furthermore, we were able to extract a set of lessons associated with the characterization of TD in projects of this port.

Categories and Subject Descriptors

D.2.9 [**Management**]: Cost estimation

General Terms

Management, Measurement, Documentation.

Keywords

Technical debt, maintenance, software evolution.

1. INTRODUCTION

The development process of large software systems certainly requires several types of project decisions, which affect future development activities. The use of the Technical Debt (TD) metaphor [1] is well suitable to support this decision process. In fact, TD provides both abilities of monitoring the evolution of decisions effects and representing low level development aspects in a more comprehensive and straighter language for stakeholders. Thus, TD could be seen as, or has the potential to be, a powerful tool for management and communication activities. Unfortunately, the state of the art in TD has not culminated yet in rigorous analysis models, mainly for large-scale projects, and we have a substantial lack in formal theories about it [2].

Considering this context, our research group is leading an exploratory investigation to identify sources of technical debt and understand its evolution. The object of study is the SMB (Samsung Mobile Business) system, a commercial mobile software application that runs on different Samsung mobile phone platforms and woks as a client for Microsoft Exchange™ e-mail service (MS Exchange). SMB has a total of 63.218 logic code lines, according to the Unified Code Count tool. The SMB system was developed in J2ME language, using RUP as development methodology, and translated to 17 languages to be released in the European, South American and Asian markets. This application was started at 2005 and was maintained during 6 years. Its first official release was in March 2006 and the system was finished in March 2011. Consequently, there is a considerable amount of documents and code versions. The development was carried out by a consortium stabilized between Samsung Brazil and Informatics Center, at the Federal University of Pernambuco, and involved an average of 20 specialists per month. An important feature of the SMB development was its number of requirement modifications, regarding its adaptation to the very dynamic mobile technology and market. As this application was constantly modified, the process of maintenance and evolution presented several difficulties. We argue that a TD theory could have been used to attenuate such difficulties. This was the main Samsung's motivation to invest in this exploratory study, so that its results could be used in future projects.

2. SCENARIOS

We could identify three main scenarios for our investigation. Such scenarios are summarized as follows.

2.1 Scenario 1: Persistence Layer

The first scenario is associated with the persistence layer. The SMB version 1.0 was based on a client-server architecture and its persistence layer was very simple and defined to only support functions associated with the management of emails, calendar and contacts. This approach was latterly changed to a version without a server component (SMB V1.1), which employed the Webdav protocol due to its simplicity and support to Microsoft Exchange 2003. In this decision moment, the team was aware that Microsoft was going to release a new version of the Microsoft Exchange, called Microsoft Exchange 2007.

The SMB V1.1 presented serious persistence problems, such as low efficiency, adaptability and bad use of memory. Then, a specialist in persistence was allocated in the project and a new architecture to persistence was planned on. Meanwhile, Microsoft informed that the release of *Microsoft Exchange 2007* was going to be on 30th November 2006 and that this new version was not going to support the Webdav protocol. The decision to still using the Webdav protocol was maintained and the persistence layer was almost completely reimplemented. In this new version (V1.2), the communication and protocol layers presented a strong logical coupling. In November 2007, the team decided to change the protocol, once the market was already using the Microsoft Exchange 2007. The ActiveSync protocol was chosen to be used. However, due to the strong logical coupling between the persistence and communication layers, a total refactoring was required in the persistence Layer.

2.2 Scenario 2: GuiFramework

In V1.1, the team decided to develop its own GUI (Graphic Unit Interface) framework, which did not consider the touch functionalities because the team did not believe that the touch technology could be so popular at a short term. However, in November 2008, the team identified a higher probability about the future use of the touch technology, based mainly on trends of the market. A first porting to a touch device was planned and the touch project was started on 24/11/2008. However, such development branch was cancelled three days later due to a mandatory decision of the client. In August 2009, the client sent a new request to porting the system to a touch screen device. According to evidences from emails sent back to the client, three alternatives were evaluated to implement the touch screen support: via fixe virtual command bar (simplest), via implementation of a touch engine in the GUI framework (hardest) and via a hybrid solution. The team decided for the first option as an urgent solution and after the release, they could work in a complete solution to the touch technology. However the client declined this decision and requested the implementation of the hybrid solution. The final version with this feature was released in January 2010 and it was discontinued in the beginning of 2011.

2.3 Scenario 3: New Language Inclusion

In some moment of the development (April 2007), the inclusion of a language became a hard task, so that the team considered to create an automation solution for this task. However, as they believed in a low probability to use other languages in the application, a simple manual process was implemented. In December 2009, the client requested the translation of the application to 7 European languages (Germany, French, Italian, Dutch, Hungarian, Serbian and Slovakian). According to the interviews, at this moment the team had again considered the implementation of a complete automation solution. However this was not carried out due to time constraints, once the team should prepare versions of the application with such languages. In February 2010, the client informed the need of translating the application to Turkish and that new translations were going to be required, once the application was going to be delivered in the Asian Southeast and Medium Orient markets. After that, the team received the request to translate the application to 6 other languages: Farsi, Chinese, Thai, Vietnamese, Malaysian and Indonesian. In February 2010, the automation of new languages inclusion was implemented. Thus, the process of including a new language, which used to spend 2 days with one allocated resource, could be carried in 2 hours.

3. Data Collection and Analysis

The activity of collecting information was based on the parameters presented in the Cunningham metaphor [1]. In this way, concepts such as debt, interests and benefits were mapped to more concrete concepts, such as impact in quality, recoding difficulty and refactoring. The data was collected in a systematic way, considering all the identified changes associated with each scenario. The collected information for each change is: facts of influence, motivation and impact in terms of effort (persons per hour). Regarding decisions, we have collected data associated with possible alternatives, motivations, facts of influence, description and decision identifier. The aim of this data collection was to characterize the moment when a decision was taken. This means, the moment when the debt was created, the impact of this decision in the scenario on investigation (in terms of effort) and the benefits that could be motivated such a decision. The main sources of information were emails, development documents and interviews. The data collection was carried out to each scenario and the results are discussed in the next subsections.

3.1 Analysis of Scenario 1

The analysis of Scenario 1 (Persistence Layer) has stressed three main decisions to be characterized:

- Decision 1: implementation of a simple persistence layer, just to support the current demand;

- Decision 2: complete redefinition of the persistence layer, with a strong logical coupling with the communication layer;

- Decision 3: redefinition of the persistence layer, once the previous version could not be used with the new protocol and such layer was strongly coupled with the communication layer.

After the identification of the motivations to each decision, we could trace some conclusions The Decision 1 could be considered correct because, at that moment, the team was not able to predict, in a long term, the way that the application was going to. The Decision 3 could also be considered correct because the marked was already requiring a new communication solution and the Webdav protocol was not supporting such a solution. We have found strong evidences of technical debt in Decision 2. Thus, such decision was detailed as follows:

- Benefit: to evolve the persistence layer as so as possible to V1.2 of the application;

- Debt: accept the risk of not implementing the persistence layer with an architecture more independent of the communication layer, which could simplify future changes;

- Interest: accumulation of efforts, since the moment of the decision of coupling the persistence layer to the communication protocol, until the moment when the debt was paid;

- Payment: effort spent to carry out reimplementations in the persistence layer.

According to evidences, the debt was created in the moment of Decision 2, when the team decided to implement the new persistence with dependent layers. The total of 12 months was required to plan, implement and test the application with this new architecture. Using the documentation (chronograms, backlogs and register of code lines modifications) along this period, we were able to estimate the total effort, in terms of hours per person, to implement Decision 3 at the moment when Decision 2 was taken. The documentation was also important to identify the effort of the architecture reimplementation, associated with Decision 3. Regarding the values, the effort to implement Decision 3 at the moment of Decision 2 (estimation) was 345 h/person, while the effort to implement Decision 3 (real) was 1416 h/person. Thus we have an interest of 1071 h/person.

We concluded that the scenario where the team consciously decided for implementing a persistence layer strongly coupled to the communication layer (Decision 2), even with the information that the protocol was going to be changed in the future, incurred a debt that needed to be paid some months later. This payment is associated with Decision 3 and it had a high cost of 1071 h/person.

3.2 Analysis of Scenario 2

This scenario also presented three main decisions to be characterized:

- Decision 1: implementation of the GUI framework without touch support;

- Decision 2: non implementation of the full touch support at the moment when the requests for SMB porting to touch devices started to appear;

- Decision 3: implementation of just some few touch functions, considering particular features of the device that was going to receive SMB.

The Decision 1 could be considered correct, once the touch technology was not popular in the market. The risk to consider this technology versus the time required to implement such technology could probably result in a significant delay to deliver the SMB. The Decision 2 could also be considered correct, once the application was finished in March 2011 and few portings to touch devices were performed. The Decision 3 could again be considered correct because the team needed a small effort to its implementation and any new porting was carried out to touch devices. In this context, we can better analyze details about saved effort related to Decisions 2 and 3 and prove that such decisions did not incur TD:

- Benefit: (Decision 2) to prioritize the porting process that was being carried out at that moment, once such porting was strategic to the client; and (Decision 3) carry out a faster implementation, so that the touch device could be released in a short time;

- Debt: (Decision 2) accept the risk of not implementing the touch full support, even with a strong trend of the mobile market in using this technology; and (Decision 3) accept the risk of a future GUI framework adaptation, so that it could support a full touch set of functionalities;

- Interest: (Decision 2) effort accumulation, since the moment of the decision of not implementing touch support, until the moment that this implementation was required; and (Decision 3) accumulation, since the moment of the decision of not implementing a full touch support, until the moment when it was required.;

- Payment: (Decision 2) defined as the effort spent to implement the full touch support; and (Decision 3) the effort to adequate the full touch support to a specific device.

At the first moment, when the team considered to implement the full touch support (November 2008), the effort was estimated to 1567 h/person. However this implementation was not carried out and, later on, the client requested the implementation of some few functions to support part of the touch technology to a specific mobile model. According to emails and chronogram, the effort was estimated to 96 h/person. This application was sent to client in January 2010 and discontinued in early 2011. Regarding the

values, the effort for implement a full touch support was estimated to 1576 h/person, while the effort to just adapt a specific mobile model was 96 h/person. Then, we had a saved effort of 1480 h/person (185 work days, considering one person)

Thus, the decision of not implementing the full touch support did not incur technical debt and has saved 1480 h/person. This is a type of decision that avoids unnecessary costs and did not incur technical debt because, in this scenario, the system was discontinued before the need of a touch implementation. We did not simulate the situation where the system is not discontinued and the touch support is implemented in the future.

3.3 Analysis of Scenario 3

We have identified three relevant decisions associated with this scenario:

- Decision 1: implementation of a manual approach to include new languages;

- Decision 2: maintenance of the manual approach for inclusion of new languages at the moment when the translation to 7 new languages was requested;

- Decision 3: implementation of an automatic inclusion process at the moment when the translation to 9 new languages was requested.

The Decision 1 could be considered correct, once the system was initially translated only to three languages and the team could not predict the use of the system in so many countries. We have found evidences of TD in Decision 2, while the Decision 3 could also be considered correct, once a significant amount of effort was saved. Thus, we can detail the features of Decision 2 as follows:

- Benefit: saving of effort;

- Debt: accumulation of effort related to the manual language translation/inclusion;

- Interest: effort accumulation, related to new languages that may be included, from the moment when the automation process was not implemented, until the moment that is was implemented;

- Payment: effort to include new languages.

According to Decision 1, the process of including a new language was carried out in a manual way and the team believed in a low probability of new inclusions. In this scenario, the cost to include two languages (English and Spanish) was 32 h/person. According to Decision 2, the team maintained the manual translations. However, 7 new languages were translated with a total cost of 171 h/person. If the automation process had been implemented, the effort should be 14 h/person. Thus, the saved effort could have been about 157 h/person. However we are not considering here the additional effort associated with the implementation of the automation process, which was 40 h/person. Consequently, if we add this cost to the cost of the automated translations and decrease the resultant value from the manual effort, we could have a final saved effort of 117 h/person.

The value of 117 h/person is also the debt associated with Decision 2. In this case, the debt is fixe (interest is null) and it will only increase if new languages are included. Thus, the cost of payment is also fixe. However, if we extend the TD concepts to other aspects, beyond effort analysis, this cost could increase due to the modifications in the value/hour associated with the work of each collaborator, which tends to increase along the time. Thus, the fact of not implementing the automated approach was not a correct decision (Decision 2), incurring technical debt because the team had an additional cost of including 7 manual translations. In other words, an effort of 117 h/person was wasted.

4. DISCUSSION AND LEARNED LESSONS

According to the analysis of our scenarios, the use of decisions appears as an adequate approach to characterize the historical evolution of a technical debt. The principal aspect of this approach was to identify related decisions, so that we could define the timeline of technical debts and monitor their evolution. A deep study of these timelines raised up important lessons that must be considered, from the start, in any other project.

The first lesson is related to the advantages of incurring a debt. Works about TD [3] comment that intentional debt incurs for strategic reasons and list the time to market and preservation of startup capital as main examples. We have observed, in practice, another important reason. When a system is discontinued, all of the system's technical debt is retired with it. Once a system has been taken out of production, there is no difference between a "clean and correct" solution and a "quick and dirty" solution. The Scenario 2 (GuiFramework) represents this situation in a practical manner, when the decision of not implementing the full touch support did not incur technical debt and has saved 1480 h/person. Thus, this decision, which could normally be considered a TD, brought advantages to the project. This experience shows the importance in predicting the discontinued time of modules and systems, so that the decision of paying a TD could be written as a function that considers its start and discontinued time. In fact, the principal reason to monitor TD is to know the best moment to pay the debt, or part of it [4]. However, this decision makes more sense when we know the remainder life time that the system/module still has before its retirement. Unfortunately, this discontinued time is not generally so easy to predict.

The second lesson is related to what we should consider as a source of TD. In the literature, TD is mostly associated with implementation aspects [5]. However, our experience shows the importance to extend this concept to other aspects. For example, consider the Decision 3 of Scenario 1 (Persistence Layer). According to some interviews, the use of a unique specialist could lead the development team to solutions that he/she wants and believes that are correct. This could be dangerous once some problems may not be identified and covered by the experience of this specialist. In this scenario, the use of a second specialist was essential to take the Decision 3. This was a typical case where modifications in the team had influence on the project decision and, consequently, in the technical debt values. Thus, the conscious use of a team that is not ideal could also be considered a case of technical debt.

A third lesson is related to additional facts that should be considered during the monitoring process of a TD. The Scenario 3, for example, shows the importance of considering the valorization of collaborators to calculate the real interest in terms of financial cost. In order, all our studies are limited just to the development cost analysis (development effort) due to access restriction to financial information of the project. We believe that even if we had access to such information, we probably still have the challenge of estimating what could have been the depreciation of product value due to delays in its release, and how much the product could have been appreciated if it had immediately met the customers demand for mobile solutions for MS Exchange 2007 clients. In both cases, external factors such as the occurrence of competing products can significantly affect this value. Another factor that could be difficult to estimate is the return if the extra effort had been invested in new features such as support for touchscreen technology.

The major contribution of our investigation is its practical perspective. This means, these lessons were extracted from a real project and based on several documents, interviews and coding statistics. Finally, several research directions can be derived from this work. Currently we are working in two main directions. First, the development of empirical studies that could support the development of methodologies to monitor technical debt. This could be important, for example, to identify the ideal moment to pay the debt. Second, applications of financial mathematic techniques in technical debt, so that we can define a methodology to demonstrate the financial viability of changes in a project.

5. ACKNOWLEDGEMENTS

The authors would like to thank all the software engineers from CIn/SIDI-Samsung Development Unit, which have provided the technical details about the SMB application and documentation. The team is also very grateful for the support received from Samsung/SIDI team, in particular from Helder Piho, Miguel Lizarraga, Ildeu Fantini and Vera Bier. Professor Fabio Q. B. da Silva holds a research grant from the Brazilian National Research Council (CNPq), process no. 314523/2009-0. CNPq has also provided valuable support to the project through the Brazilian Federal Law no. 8010/90.

6. REFERENCES

[1] Cunningham, W. 1992. The WyCash Portfolio Management System, *Addendum to the proceedings on Object-oriented programming systems, languages, and applications*, pp.29-30, Vancouver, British Columbia, Canada, doi:10.1145/157709.157715

[2] Seaman, C. and Guo, Y. 2011. Measuring and Monitoring Technical Debt, *Advances in Computers*, vol. 82, pp. 25-46, doi: 10.1016/B978-0-12-385512-1.00002-5

[3] Brown, N. *et al.* 2010. Managing Technical Debt in Software-Reliant Systems", *Proceedings of the FSE/SDP workshop on Future of software engineering research*, pp. 47-52, New York, NY, USA, doi:10.1145/1882362.1882373

[4] Buschmann, F. 2011. To Pay or Not to Pay Technical Debt, *IEEE Software*, vol. 28, no. 6, pp. 29-31, doi: 10.1109/MS.2011.150

[5] Klinger, T., Tarr, P., Wagstrom, P. and Williams, C. 2011. An enterprise Perspective on Technical Debt", Proceedings of the 2nd Workshop on Managing Technical Debt, pp. 35-38, New York, NY, USA, 2011, doi: 10.1145/1985362.1985371

Assessing the Impact of Real-Time Machine Translation on Requirements Meetings: A Replicated Experiment

Fabio Calefato, Filippo Lanubile
University of Bari
Dipartimento di Informatica
Bari, Italy

calefato,lanubile@di.uniba.it

Tayana Conte
Universidade Federal do Amazonas
Instituto de Computação
Manaus, Brazil

tayana@dcc.ufam.edu.br

Rafael Prikladnicki
Pontifícia Universidade Católica do
Rio Grande do Sul
Porto Alegre, Brazil

rafael.prikladnicki@pucrs.br

ABSTRACT

Opportunities for global software development are limited in those countries with a lack of English-speaking professionals. Machine translation technology is today available in the form of cross-language web services and can be embedded into multiuser and multilingual chats without disrupting the conversation flow. However, we still lack a thorough understanding of how real-time machine translation may affect communication in global software teams.

In this paper, we present the replication of a controlled experiment that assesses the effect of real-time machine translation on multilingual teams while engaged in distributed requirements meetings. In particular, in this replication we specifically evaluate whether non-English speaking groups benefit from communicating in their own native languages when their English is not fluid enough for a fast-paced conversation.

Categories and Subject Descriptors

D.2.9 [**Management**]: Programming teams

H.4.3 [**Communications Applications**]: Computer conferencing, teleconferencing, and videoconferencing.

I.2.7 [**Natural Language Processing**]: Machine translation.

General Terms

Experimentation, Human Factors.

Keywords

Controlled experiment; global software engineering; machine translation; requirements meetings.

1. INTRODUCTION

Global Software Development (GSD) is characterized by the dispersion of stakeholders across different countries, continents and time zones. Requirements engineering is one of the most communication-intensive activities in software development and, thus, it suffers much from language difficulties in global software

projects [10], [11], [20]. Language is indeed an important factor that largely accounts for the success of offshore IT work in countries with strong English language capabilities, such as Ireland, the Philippines, India, and Singapore [6], [15].

However, there are several other countries, considered followers in global competition, which are increasing their presence in the global IT market. Brazil is one real example of this situation [7]. Brazil's IT industry is large – A.T. Kearney consultancy estimates that the sector employs 1.7 million people, including programmers, systems analysts, and managers [17] – and it is growing by 6.5% a year on average since 2005 [2], although the vast majority of the IT companies are focused on domestic clients and do not export. For those who export, US companies are the main clients, accounting for over 80% of demand, followed by Latin America (especially Argentina, Chile, Colombia and Mexico), and Europe (especially Germany, Spain, France, England and Portugal). Nearly 100% of Brazil's IT export clients have time zone overlap with this country [10]. However, in order to take full advantage of the time zone overlap, Brazilian sites should create richer interactions with their foreign partners. This could avoid problems such as coordination breakdown, asynchronous and not so frequent communication, lack of interactive work, among other problems that lack of rich interaction may cause. And one key element for this is more effort on the English. Unfortunately, A.T. Kearney estimates that Brazil has only 10.2 million of English speakers, or 5.4% of the population. Chile, for example, has 34.7% of English speakers; India has 8.2% (which represents 90.6 million). Another study published by KPMG in 2009 indicated that one of the disadvantages of Latin American countries is the lack of English speaking professionals [18]. In this context, there are several initiatives going on, for example, in order to include English in the qualification of the IT professionals in Brazil [7]. However, this may be not enough and, to stay competitive in the global IT market these countries we will have to search for alternative solutions. For this reason, distributed project meetings, such as requirements workshops, can benefit from machine translation, as this technology is today available in the form of cross-language chat services and it might be used in countries, such as Brazil, where there are at the same time opportunities for global projects and the lack of English speaking professionals.

Machine translation (MT) is an established technology that uses software to translate text or speech from one natural language to another. The idea of using digital computers for translation of natural languages was proposed 50 years ago [14]. The technology available today – i.e., real-time, online conversation – is experiencing tremendous growth of interest, mostly because of the Internet continuous expansion. The rise of social networking has also contributed to this growing interest, allowing users of social media to speak different languages to communicate with each other. Despite the recent progress of the technology, we still lack a thorough understanding of how real-time machine translation affects communication.

In our previous works, we first run a simulated study, which proved that state-of-the-art machine translation services, such as Google Translate, could be embedded into synchronous text-based chat with a negligible extra time [3]. However, the simulation could not say anything about completing complex group tasks while communicating with multiple native languages.

Then, we conducted a controlled experiment to investigate whether real-time machine translation could be successfully used instead of English in distributed multilingual requirements meetings [5]. We could observe that, despite far from 100% accuracy, real-time machine translation was not disruptive of the conversation flow and, therefore, accepted with favor by participants. However, since we involved only groups with high English proficiency, we concluded that stronger effects could be expected to emerge when language barriers are more critical.

Now, we have replicated the former study by means of a controlled experiment which involves participants who are not proficient in English, that is, they are not able to communicate in English as in their mother tongue. With respect to the initial study, other than changing the level of English proficiency, Portuguese-speaking participants came from the North of Brazil rather than the South Region of Brazil. From the initial experiment, we reused the research questions, the experimental plan, the variables and the instrumentation.

The remainder of this paper is structured as follows. Section 2 describes the experiment, including the design, the variables, the instrumentation and execution. Section 3 presents the results from data analysis. Section 4 discusses the results and the differences between the two replications. Threats to validity are described in Section 5. Finally, conclusions and future research activities are presented in Section 6.

2. THE EXPERIMENT

We are interested to further evaluate the effect of real-time machine translation on multilingual groups of individuals. Thus, the research questions we inherit from the previous study are the following:

RQ1: *Can machine translation services be used in distributed multilingual requirements meetings, instead of English?*

RQ2: *How does the adoption of machine translation affect group interaction in distributed multilingual requirements meetings, as compared to the use of English?*

Since a better command of language provides better opportunities of steering communication during meetings, one could reasonably argue that machine translation is more useful to those who are not proficient in English. Therefore, we add the following research question:

RQ3: *Do individuals with a low English proficiency level benefit more than individuals with a high level when using their native language, assisted by real-time translation?*

We have investigated these research questions by means of a replication of the original controlled experiment. The 16 participants involved in the replication were graduate and undergraduate students from Brazil and Italy. The former were from the Federal University of Amazonas in Manaus, while Italian students were from University of Bari. In particular, students interacted in groups of four people, two from Italy and two from Brazil, using two different communication modalities, that is, their respective native language (i.e., Italian or Portuguese), with the help of machine translation (*MT*), and English (*EN*), as a common, non-native *lingua franca* [22].

During the experiment, the multilingual groups were involved in a Planning Game activity, a requirements prioritization technique used in agile development. In particular, they had to complete two tasks. During the first task (*T1*), acting as customers, they separated a few vital requirements from the many elicited in a software development effort. Then, during the second task (*T2*), acting as developers, they completed a release plan. The task material, adapted from a previous work by Berander [1], was selected because the domain chosen for task execution is that of mobile phones, about which students typically have a rather equal knowledge gained through daily usage.

In order to assess whether machine translation is more beneficial to individuals with low English skills, we measured the English proficiency level for each study participant. We chose a placement test made publicly available online by Cambridge University[1], which includes 40 questions to be answered within 20 min. The test originally placed subjects into one of four distinct categories. In this replication, we selected participants at the *Low* level (scores 0-20), which will be then compared to the *High* level (scores 21-40) participants from the former experiment.

2.1 The Study Design

We followed a fractional factorial design [19] (see Table 1) in which each group participated in two meetings (Run 1 and 2), using a combination of the *communication mode* (MT and EN) and *task* (T1 and T2). Each multilingual group included 4 subjects, 2 speaking Italian and 2 speaking Portuguese as native language. As in the original experiment, each planning task in the replication was executed by two groups (i.e., 8 subjects), one group using MT (4 subjects) and one group using EN (also 4 subjects).

Table 1. Experimental plan

	Original experiment		Replicated experiment	
	MT	EN	MT	EN
Run 1	Gr1, Gr3 execute T1	Gr2, Gr4 execute T1	Gr6, Gr8 execute T1	Gr5, Gr7 execute T1
Run 2	Gr2, Gr4 execute T2	Gr1, Gr3 execute T2	Gr5, Gr7 execute T2	Gr6, Gr8 execute T2

---

[1] www.cambridge.org/us/esl/venturesadulted/placement_test.html

In each run, each participant used different communication modes and different tasks. For example, a group that communicated through MT in the first run, used English language (EN) in the second run and vice versa. In addition, a group that executed task T1 in the first run executed task T2 in the second run.

The design allows an experimenter to do two comparisons, namely: in run 1, between the groups that executed task T1, and in run 2, between the groups that executed task T2. In addition, with this design, it is possible to analyze the influence of the communication mode both at the team and individual level.

2.2 Instrumentation, Training & Execution

Multilingual group meetings were run using eConference [4], a tool built on Eclipse RCP, the primary functionality of which is a closed group chat, augmented with agenda, meeting minutes editing, and typing awareness capabilities. In addition, we extended the tool developing an *ad hoc* plugin that enables the automatic translation of incoming messages, using the Google Translate APIs. In fact, whenever a new message is processed by eConference, the MT plugin invokes the MT web-service in order to show the translated messages, along with the original text, as shown in Figure 1.

Before each meeting, the group involved was trained to use the tool. First, a half-hour demo was given to students by one of the researchers. Then, a training session was set up, during which involved groups had to perform two training tasks, interacting first using their native language, exploiting the MT plugin, and then in English. As for the training tasks, we selected two riddles, described in English, which had to be completed within half an hour each.

During the training, two of the four students involved in each session were randomly selected to act as moderator or scribe. The extra duties of being a moderator include starting the meeting once every participant is online, keeping track of time limit, and so forth. The session scribe, instead, is enabled by the moderator to edit the tool whiteboard, a shared editor where all the group decisions and the final task solution were logged. We note that the groups of students were kept the same in the training sessions and in the actual experiment.

Each meeting required two hours in order to complete the experimental run. Two of the researchers, one in Brazil and one in Italy, were available to students during the runs, in order to provide technical help and prevent undesired interactions to occur outside of the tool, as pairs were collocated at each site.

During each run, groups were required to solve one of two tasks adapted from [1]. Both tasks were described in English. The first one (T1) was a requirements prioritization task to be completed within 30 minutes. Group's participants received a list of 16 features that described the desired functionalities of a mobile phone (e.g., alarm, calendar, MMS, notes, etc.). Then, they acted as a distributed group of customers who had to produce a prioritized list of requirements by dividing them into three distinct piles (i.e., less important, important, and very important). Further task constraints required that requirements within each pile were ranked by importance, and that no more than 13 requirements were assigned to one pile (85%).

The second task (T2) was about release planning and consisted of two consecutive steps, which had to be executed from a developer's perspective and completed within 60 minutes. In the first step, group participants had to distribute an overall amount of 1000 story points between the same 16 requirements from task T1, thus assigning the relative costs of implementing each of them. In the second step, the goal was to plan three releases of the product, based on the priorities, obtained from the outcome of T1, and the cost estimates, just assigned in the previous step. The following constraints were also given to participants. For the first release, they were allowed to assign 150-200 story points, whereas, for the second and third releases the ranges were 300-350 and 450-550, respectively.

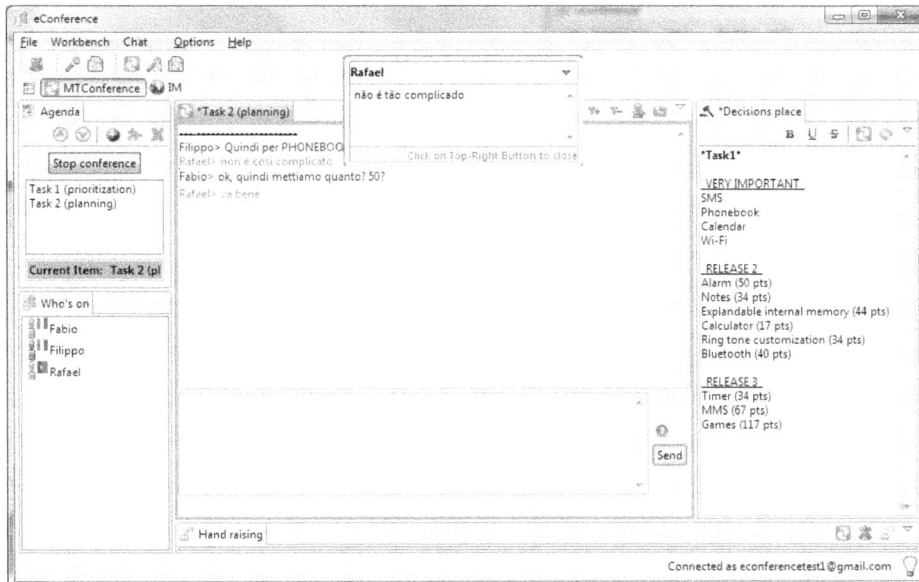

Figure 1. eConference with MT plugin

Finally, we note that, no matter what the language/task combination was, for each run the shared solutions were always edited in English.

2.3 Dependent Variables and Measures

The data sources considered in this study are the questionnaires, which were administered to the students upon the conclusion of the two tasks, and the meeting logs.

A large existing body of research on Group-Decision Support Systems (GDSS) identified domination, peer pressure, and social consensus among the problems faced in group communication. For example, according to DeSanctis & Gallupe [12], the health of group communication is observed through the equality of participation and the levels of satisfaction perceived with respect to process interaction and outcome. Such problems are expected to be even harder in multilingual groups, due to language barriers.

Therefore, for the two post-task questionnaires, inherited from the first study and written in English, we adopted a 4-point Likert scale (anchored with '4=strongly agree' and '1=strongly disagree' values), which was formulated with the aim of assessing the subjects' perception about the two constructs of i) *engagement and comfort with communication*, and ii) *satisfaction with task performance*. The questionnaires listed 16 closed questions, plus an open question, where subjects could freely report any thought or consideration about the whole experience, and a few "control" questions, in order to ensure that task execution was not hindered by the tool flaws or by unclear instructions and objectives. In addition, the post-T2 questionnaire also contained four extra questions that aimed at assessing the differences between the overall subjects' perception when using machine translation and English, at the end of both experimental runs.

From the chat logs collected at the end of the meetings, the *# of utterances* entered by group participants were counted to assess equality of participation. We also note that the chat logs were collected at both the Italian and the Brazilian site, since tasks executed using native languages produced two versions of the same discussion, one in Italian and one in Portuguese.

Finally, to gain more insight on the effects of machine translation, we looked at the very basic goal of communication, which is establishing a shared understanding. In fact, although machine translation helps people to cope with language barriers, it also poses hurdles to establishing mutual understanding due to translation inaccuracies and errors, which may cause both lack of mutual understanding (i.e., being aware that there is a problem that must be clarified) and misunderstandings (i.e., realizing that something that was initially considered understood correctly was actually wrong) [23]. In such situations, people become aware that there is a problem of a *lack of common ground*. Common ground is the knowledge that participants have in common when communicating and the awareness of it [8]. A common ground is dynamically established through grounding, an interactive process in which participants exchange evidence about what they do or do not understand over the course of a conversation. One the one hand, one could expect more *clarification requests* to emerge during MT meetings due to translations errors and inaccuracies. On the other hand, however, it could also be argued that low proficiency in a non-native language can be the cause of mistakes and inaccuracy, as well. Therefore, we need to investigate whether it is MT technology inaccuracy or low English proficiency to cause more clarifications requests by participants in a conversation. To quantify our construct of clarification requests, we performed a content analysis of the meeting logs.

3. RESULTS

In this section, we report the results from the analyses of the quantitative and qualitative data collected from the eight experimental runs. We first present quantitative analysis of the meeting logs. Then, we illustrate the findings from the quantitative analysis of the questionnaires. Finally, we report the results obtained from the content analysis performed on the logs. For the sake of clarity, where necessary, new results from this replication and findings from the original study are reported side by side.

3.1 Quantitative analysis of meeting logs

Table 2 provides some descriptive measures of the new meetings executed in the replication (i.e., with low proficiency groups Gr5-Gr8), along with those executed in the original experiment (i.e., with high proficiency groups Gr1-Gr4). To characterize them, we computed the time (in minutes) spent for executing the tasks, the overall number of utterances presented by participants, the frequency (expressed as utterance per minute – upm), and the average delay between two consecutive answers (in seconds).

Looking at the amounts of time spent for executing tasks, we note that results vary for run 1, whereas they are all somewhat comparable for run 2, for which all the groups took the whole time allowed (1 hour). In fact, the amounts time spent for run 1 range between 16 (Gr2) and 40 minutes (Gr1 and Gr7), who took about 10 extra minutes to complete the prioritization. As for Gr1 and Gr7, looking at the transcripts we realized that the delay was not related to the communication mode. Instead, the larger amount of time spent was due to the fact that group both group decided to adopt a time consuming approach. As such, every participant came up with a priority list, from which they eventually built a shared solution. The other groups, instead, adopted a more practical approach, that is, one participant proposed an initial priority list and the others suggested amendments until a shared solution was reached through discussion. With respect to Gr6 and Gr3, instead, we note that they took 35 and 67 minutes to execute run 1 and run 2, respectively. In both cases, the few extra minutes were granted to recover from a brief network disconnection that occurred at one site. Besides, Gr3 and Gr7 proved to be the most "active" groups overall, as they exhibited the highest frequency (6.33 and 6.90 upm; 6.44 and 6.75 upm, respectively) and the lowest average delay at typing utterances (10 and 8 sec.; 9 and 9 sec., respectively) over the two tasks. With respect to delays, the comparisons between the average delays in English meetings (mean 13.2 sec.) and MT meetings (mean 11.6 sec.) confirm that the subjects spent a little extra time in elaborating messages using the non-native English language.

Table 2. Descriptive measures for the eight meetings

Group		Communication mode	Time (min.)	# Utterances	Frequency (upm)	Average delay (sec.)
Gr1 (High)	Run 1	MT	40⁺	159	3.95	15
	Run 2	EN	61	322	5.28	11
Gr2 (High)	Run 1	EN	16	68	4.25	15
	Run 2	MT	59	346	5.86	10
Gr3(High)	Run 1	MT	30	190	6.33	10
	Run 2	EN	67*	462	6.90	8
Gr4 (High)	Run 1	EN	16	52	3.25	20
	Run 2	MT	54	169	3.13	14
Gr5(Low)	Run 1	EN	28	92	5.41	11
	Run 2	MT	59	358	6.17	10
Gr6(Low)	Run 1	MT	35*	140	4.38	14
	Run 2	EN	59	164	2.83	21
Gr7 (Low)	Run 1	EN	41⁻	264	6.44	9
	Run 2	MT	60	405	6.75	9
Gr8 (Low)	Run 1	MT	43⁻	240	5.58	11
	Run 2	EN	67⁻	354	5.28	11

* *Extra minutes granted to recover from network disconnection*
⁺ *Exceeded the time limit for the task*

Table 3. A breakdown of participation level of subjects during task executions

Group (level)	# Utterances (%) – English				Δ Most - Least prolific member	# Utterances (%) -- Machine Translation				Δ Most - Least prolific member
	Member 1 (mod)	Member 2	Member 3	Member 4		Member 1 (mod)	Member 2	Member 3	Member 4	
Gr1 (High)	181 (56%)	61 (19%)	52 (16%)	28 (9%)	47%	64 (41%)	43 (27%)	26 (16)%	25 (16%)	25% ↓
Gr2 (High)	16 (24%)	28 (41%)	15 (22%)	9 (13%)	28%	71 (21)%	117 (34%)	91 (26%)	67 (19%)	15% ↓
Gr3 (High)	133 (29%)	106 (23%)	76 (16%)	147 (32%)	16%	60 (32%)	47 (25%)	39 (21%)	44 (23%)	11% ↓
Gr4 (High)	24 (43%)	12 (23%)	5 (10%)	11 (21%)	33%	65 (38%)	39 (23%)	24 (14%)	41 (24%)	24% ↓
Gr5 (Low)	29 (32%)	19 (21%)	24 (26%)	20 (22%)	11%	94 (26%)	130 (36%)	61 (17%)	73 (20%)	19%
Gr6 (Low)	33 (20%)	37 (23%)	53 (32%)	41 (25%)	12%	38 (27%)	38 (27%)	36 (26%)	28 (20%)	7% ↓
Gr7 (Low)	136 (52%)	46 (17%)	40 (15%)	42 (16%)	37%	212 (52%)	65 (16%)	56 (14%)	72 (18%)	38%
Gr8 (Low)	127 (36%)	79 (22%)	81 (23%)	67 (19%)	17%	71 (30%)	55 (23%)	62 (26%)	52 (22%)	8% ↓

In order to verify equality of participation during meetings (i.e., no domination by any group participants), we computed the number of utterances presented by each participant during a meeting to see how the use of machine translation affect the participation extent of subjects (see Table 3). We also computed the percentages because the release planning task executed during run 2 takes longer than the prioritization task of run 1, and so, regardless of the communication mode, any participant is supposed to have contributed more utterances during the former. We then computed the deltas between the percentage of utterances presented by the most and the least prolific subjects for each task execution. Comparing the two columns, we observe that: 1) there is an increase of participation (i.e., a smaller delta) of the least prolific subject, always at expense of the most prolific member during MT-enabled tasks, both for high and low proficiency groups; 2) the deltas are usually higher in high proficiency groups from the original experiment than in low

proficiency groups from this replication; 3) the deltas from high proficiency groups always decrease when using MT, whereas, as for low proficiency groups, Gr7 delta remain unchanged after the communication mode switch, and Gr5 delta even increased by 8 percentage points when using MT.

Finally, we compared the percentages of utterances presented by group members with the lowest English proficiency skills during the EN and MT meetings (see Table 4). The new results with low proficiency groups confirm the same general tendency observed in our previous study with high proficiency groups, that is, the percentage of utterances presented by the least proficient subjects tend to increase when switching from English to their native language, with one exception (Gr7 and Gr3, respectively).

3.2 Questionnaires analysis

In this section we report the findings from our quantitative analysis of post-task questionnaires administered to low proficiency groups in the replicated experiment.

In order to measure the *satisfaction with task performance*, we defined a 4-item 4-point Likert scale to assess participants' perception of whether tasks were performed positively, with participants feeling actively involved in group communication when reaching shared decisions. In other words, we aimed to verify that information exchanged, and optionally translated, was properly processed when using both communication modes.

As a nonparametric alternative to the t-test for two paired samples, we performed a Wilcoxon signed rank test [9] on the responses to the four questions shown in Table 5. The test failed to reveal any difference in the levels of satisfaction with performance perceived by low proficiency subjects when using English rather than their native language.

Likewise, to measure the levels of *engagement and comfort with communication mode* perceived by low proficiency subjects, we used a 6-point Likert scale to assess discussion contentment. Again, we performed a Wilcoxon signed rank test, as shown in Table 6, which failed to reveal any difference between the use of

English and MT in terms of being involved in an open and useful discussion with others.

Table 4. Gain in participation of the least proficient subject for each group when using native language with machine translation

Group (level)	Least proficient subject (nationality)	% of utterance	
		EN	MT
Gr1 (High)	Student #7 (Brazilian)	19%	27% ↑
Gr2 (High)	Student #4 (Brazilian)	22%	26% ↑
Gr3 (High)	Student #16 (Brazilian)	32%	23%
Gr4 (High)	Student #12 (Brazilian)	10%	14% ↑
Gr5 (Low)	Student #17 (Italian)	21%	36% ↑
Gr6 (Low)	Student #22 (Italian)	20%	27% ↑
Gr7 (Low)	Student #27 (Brazilian)	15%	14%
Gr8 (Low)	Student #32 (Brazilian)	23%	26% ↑

Table 5. Evaluation of satisfaction with performance for the four low proficiency groups Gr5-Gr8 (N=16)

	EN > MT	EN < MT	EN = MT	Wilcoxon Signed Rank Test
Q8. *"I actively participated in the discussion"*	4	1	11	Z = -1.41 p =.157
Q12. *"I had the sensation of wasting time"*	7	4	5	Z = -1.4 p =.163
Q13. *"It was easy to reach a common decision"*	3	4	9	Z = -1.28 p =.26
Q16. *"I had a positive global impression of the performance"*	3	1	12	Z = -1.0 p =.317

Table 6. Evaluation of engagement and comfort with communication mode for the four low proficiency groups Gr5-Gr8 (N=16)

	EN > MT	EN < MT	EN = MT	Wilcoxon Signed Rank Test
Q1. *"I had enough time to perform the activity"*	2	3	11	Z = -.707 p =.48
Q6. *"It was easy to communicate with others"*	4	5	7	Z = -.183 p =.855
Q7. *"I had adequate opportunity to participate in the discussion"*	4	3	9	Z = -.378 p =.705
Q9. *"I was encouraged to discuss contrasting solutions with others"*	5	2	9	Z = -1.265 p =.206
Q10. *"Other participants adequately answered my questions"*	6	2	8	Z = -1.613 p =.107
Q11. *"I felt involved in the discussion"*	0	1	15	Z = -1.0 p =.317

Finally, we asked four questions (Q17-Q20) to collect subjects' overall perceptions and preferences for each communication mode (i.e., "*Group activity has benefited from the suggested translations / chatting directly in English*", "*If I should choose a meeting environment, I would prefer a tool with the MT service / without the MT service*"). We again applied a Wilcoxon signed-rank test. The results, reported in Table 7, show that, overall, subjects perceived no particular benefit from using MT. Conversely, the test revealed a statistically significant difference at the 1% level ($Z = -2.801$, p=.005) only for low proficiency groups who showed a preference towards using MT-enabled communication rather than English.

3.3 Content analysis

Measuring the level of common ground that people achieve in group communication is generally a challenging task [8]. However, to determine if the adoption of machine translation affects group interaction in multilingual group meetings, we rather looked at evidence of lack of common ground. We operationalized the construct of lack of common ground in terms of clarification request. Receivers provide negative evidence during communication when messages are improperly or incompletely understood. Therefore, the higher the number of ill-defined messages presented, due to either MT inaccuracy or poor English proficiency, the more negative evidence presented by receivers and, consequently, the more requests for clarification.

To quantify our construct of clarification requests, we performed the content analysis of some logs collected from low proficiency group meetings. Content analysis, also called coding [21], is a mix of quantitative and qualitative analysis that transforms qualitative data (e.g., written text, as in our case) into quantitative data by applying a coding schema, which classifies content according to a finite set of possible thematic units (i.e., categories). We applied the same coding schema that was proposed as a result from our original study, but here we augmented the original set of nine categories with an extra one, called *Unknown*, to cope with those cases when poor English or an inaccurate translation made a message incomprehensible and, consequently, its categorization impossible. Two of the researchers performed the content analysis separately and then, intercoder agreement was measured by Cohen's Kappa to ensure the concordance level between the resulting categorizations. We opportunistically performed such analysis only on the logs from low proficiency groups Gr5 and Gr7, for which some subjects reported on comprehension difficulties in the questionnaires.

In addition, as one can observe in Table 3, these two are the only cases where equality of participation was not affected or even decreased when using MT.

Table 8 shows the breakdown of the content analysis performed. We note that unit percentages are reported, rather than occurrences, as a necessary normalization due to the large differences in the lengths of task discussions. Also, for the sake of space, we only report results for those thematic units that contribute to quantify the construct of clarification requests, namely *Check Misunderstanding*, *Check Provisional*, and *Unknown* categories. In particular, the Check Misunderstanding unit categorizes any utterance providing evidence that a previous message was not fully accepted (e.g., *"Not sure I get your question..."*, *"What?"*). The Check Provisional unit, instead, categorizes utterances that explicitly look for confirmation of acceptance through provisional, try-marked statements (e.g., *"So*

we decided for color screen, right?"). Finally, the *Unknown* unit categorizes utterances that could not be coded by the raters, because the meaning was unclear, and, at the same time, misunderstood by other meeting participants.

Table 7. Evaluation of overall communication mode preference for both high and low proficiency groups (N=16)

	A vs. B	A > B	A < B	A = B	Wilcoxon Signed Rank Test
High group	"*Group activity benefited from using...*" MT vs. English	7	4	5	$Z = -.711$ p =.477
	"*Another time, I would rather communicate using...*" MT vs. English	11	3	2	$Z = -1.904$ p =.057
Low groups	"*Group activity benefited from using...*" MT vs. English	4	5	7	$Z = -.061$ p =.951
	"*Another time, I would rather communicate using...*" MT vs. English	11	1	4	**$Z = -2.801$ p =.005***

* Statistically significant results at the 0.05 level are indicated in bold

As compared to EN runs, the results show a higher number (8%) of Unknown (i.e., unclassifiable) utterances and checks for misunderstandings during MT runs. Although only partial, these results seem to suggest that the inaccuracy of state-of-the-art machine translation technology poses more hurdles to common ground than language barrier.

4. DISCUSSION

Table 9 compares the context variables and the results between the original study and the current replication. The original study involved only subjects with a high proficiency level of English, thus suggesting that the usefulness of MT would improve when used by individuals who are not able to communicate in English as in their mother tongue. Therefore, in the replicated experiment, we only involved subjects with a low proficiency level in English.

Table 8. The result of content analysis on Gr5 and Gr7 logs

	EN (Run 1)			MT (Run 2)		
	Check Mis.	Check Prov.	Unk.	Check Mis.	Check Prov.	Unk.
Gr5 (Low)	0%	2.2%	0%	2.9%	5.9%	4.3%
Gr7 (Low)	1.9%	3.8%	.9%	1%	1.2%	3.2%

Table 9. Comparison with the original experiment

		Former experiment	Current replication
Context	number of data points	4 teams, 16 subjects	4 teams, 16 subjects
	Subjects	(South) Brazilian students Italian students	(North) Brazilian students Italian students
	Proficiency level in English	High level	Low level
	number of tasks	2 tasks in 2 consecutive runs	2 tasks in 2 consecutive runs
Results	frequency of messages & delay between utterances	MT = EN	MT = EN
	equal participation	EN < MT	EN < MT
	checking misunderstanding and provisional	* NA	EN = MT

* Data not available

In the following, we compare the findings from the two studies, with respect to the research questions presented earlier. In general, the new results confirm prvious findings.

More specifically, regarding the first research question RQ1 (*Can machine translation services be used in distributed multilingual requirements meetings, instead of English?*), Table 2 shows that in both the original study and in this replication the frequency of presented messages (measured by utterance per minute rate – upm) is substantially similar between EN and MT runs. This is also confirmed by the average delay between two consecutive utterances, a measure that is correlated to message frequency, since faster interaction means lower delay. However, we are not able to distinguish between the delay due to message comprehension and message production.

Results in Tables 3 and 4 are more interesting because they confirm that, no matter what their English proficiency level is, members of multilingual groups participate in more balanced discussions when using their native language with the help of MT, instead of English. In fact, Table 3 shows that the delta (i.e., the difference in participation) between the most prolific and the least prolific subjects tends to reduce in MT-enabled discussions. In addition, especially the least proficient subject of a multilingual group seemed to benefit from machine translation, as their percentage of contributed messages grows when language switched from English to native (see Table 4).

Overall, these findings from the two studies allow us to affirm that machine translation is not disruptive of the conversation flow, even during the execution of complex group tasks, such as distributed requirements meetings, and that it is accepted with favor independently of subjects' English proficiency level.

With respect to the research question RQ2 (*How does the adoption of machine translation affect group interaction in distributed multilingual requirements meetings, as compared to the use of English?*) one of the results from our original study was the definition of a coding schema that emerged from the inspection of meeting logs in the original experiment. In this replication, we opportunistically applied that coding schema to a couple of the logs of the low level groups. The results of the related content analysis are shown in Table 8. In one case (Gr5) we can observe a higher number of utterances coded as checks to avoid misunderstandings during MT meetings than in English meetings. However, the opposite happens in the other case (Gr7). These findings suggest the need to further our understanding by completing the content analysis of logs from both high and low proficiency groups. Instead, we can observe a higher number of utterances that could not be coded because the meaning was unclear, during the two runs with native language. Such finding suggests that inaccurate translations may impair the development of shared understanding more than low English skills. In addition, a percentage as high as the 4% of utterances that cannot be coded due to poor performance of the MT service raises questions on the feasibility of supporting multilingual groups with real-time translation in professional contexts for executing crucial tasks. More specifically, although such inaccuracies neither break the communication flow nor impair interaction to the extent that a task cannot be carried out, they force participants to fix them nonetheless. And, even if such a lack of common ground can be resolved by exchanging further utterances, this requires extra time, thus decreasing the efficiency of a meeting.

Finally, with respect to the research question RQ3 (*Do individuals with a low English proficiency level benefit more than individuals with a high level, when using their native language assisted by real-time translation?*), in terms of the levels of satisfaction and comfort perceived during the experimental runs, questionnaire analyses failed to reveal any difference (see Tables 5 and 6), which, on the one hand confirm findings from the original study with highly proficient subjects. On the other hand, however, these results (surprisingly?) suggest that, as of now, state-of-the-art MT technology is no more beneficial to individuals with low English proficiency than it is to people with high skills in a foreign language. The only statistical significant difference observed is that people with low English skills are more incline to use MT again in multilingual group interaction, despite some flaws of the current technology (see Table 7).

5. THREATS TO VALIDITY

One of the key issues in experimentation is evaluating the validity of results [22]. In this section we discuss the potential threats that are relevant for our study and how they are addressed.

5.1 Construct Validity

Construct validity concerns the degree of accuracy to which the variables defined in the study measure the constructs of interests. We identified a couple of such kind of threats.

We acknowledge the need to perform factor and scale reliability analyses on the responses to the questionnaires, in order to determine the validity of the constructs of *engagement and comfort with communication* and *satisfaction with task performance*. Instead, to ensure the validity of the *clarification requests* construct, two of the researchers independently applied the coding schema to chat logs. Then, inter-rater agreement was measured by Cohen's K index. The computed indexes are .88 and .91, meaning almost perfect agreement between the raters.

5.2 Internal Validity

Threats to internal validity influence the conclusions about a possible causal relationship between the treatment and the outcome of a study. The following rival explanations for the findings have been identified.

A learning effect occurs when subjects learn more about how to perform the required task, and are better the next time. The experimental design minimized this threat. We assigned the groups in such a way that, for each run, we are able to compare MT and EN on the same task (T1 in run 1, T2 in run 2) between different groups. Thus, for each comparison, the subjects have the same amount of accumulated experience.

An instrumentation effect occurs when differences in the results may be caused by differences in experimental material. Because in this study there are two different planning tasks, we cannot exclude that task complexity could have been a confounding factor, since subjects experience a communication mode with one task only. A selection effect occurs due to the natural variation in human subjects' performance. Random assignment of subjects to experimental conditions usually reduces this threat, but our experimental design is heavily influenced by the small amount of groups. We control this threat by design, restricting the level of groups to high and low proficiency (respectively, in the original study and its replication), and consequently assigning to groups any student whose proficiency do not alter the designed level.

5.3 External validity

External validity describes the study representativeness and the ability to generalize the results outside the scope of the study.

We identified the following threats to external validity. For any academic laboratory experiment the ability to generalize results to industry practice is restricted by the usage of students as study participants. Although the students may not be representative of the entire population of software professionals, it has been shown that the differences between students and real developers may not be as large as assumed by previous research [14]. Another issue with the representativeness of subjects is related to their familiarity with the use of synchronous, text-based communication. Computer science students are very accustomed with text-based interaction. Nevertheless, synchronous, text-based communication tools, such as chat and IM, are increasingly being adopted in the workplace, not only in the field of software development, to complement email [13].

5.4 Conclusion validity

Conclusion validity is concerned with the relationship between the treatment and the outcome.

We acknowledge that the small number of data points is not ideal from the statistical point of view. Small sample sizes, especially when the key experimental unit is at the team level, are a known problem difficult to overcome, especially for cross-country controlled experiments with participants interacting from different time zones.

6. CONCLUSIONS

The work presented here is part of an ongoing research, the purpose of which is understanding to what extent real-time machine translations can be beneficial for distributed, multilingual teams located in countries where professionals are not proficient in one common language. In particular, in this replication we specifically assessed whether non-English speaking groups benefit from communicating in their own native languages when their English is not fluid enough for a fast-paced conversation.

The results of this replication confirmed that real-time machine translation is not disruptive of the conversation flow, is accepted with favor, and grants a more balanced discussion. However, the findings also show that state-of-the-art MT technology is no more beneficial to individuals with low English proficiency than it is to people with high skills in a foreign language. Content analysis suggests that this might be due to machine translation inaccuracies, which slow down the development of a common ground.

As future work, we plan to (a) analyze the results in order to learn about the effects of human typos on machine translation accuracy; (b) execute further runs to obtain more data points and strengthen the conclusion validity; (c) replicate the experiment involving professionals.

ACKNOWLEDGMENTS

This research is partially funded by the Rio Grande do Sul State funding agency (FAPERGS), by the FTS-Brasil Project CNPq (483125/2010-5), and by the European Territorial Cooperation Operational Programme "Greece-Italy 2007-2013" under the project Intersocial. We also thank the PDTI program, financed by Dell Computers of Brazil Ltd. (Law 8.248/91), and all the students who took part in the experiment.

REFERENCES

[1] P. Berander, "Using Students as Subjects in Requirements Prioritization," *Int'l Symposium on Empirical Software Engineering (ISESE'04)*, pp. 167-176, 2004.

[2] Brazil IT-BPO Book 2008-2009, published by Brasscom, Brazilian Association of Information Technology and Communication Companies, São Paulo, SP, Brazil, 2010.

[3] F. Calefato, F. Lanubile, and P. Minervini, "Can Real-Time Machine Translation Overcome Language Barriers in Distributed Requirements Engineering?", *Proc. 5th Int'l Conference on Global Software Engineering (ICGSE'10)*, Princeton, NJ, USA, Aug. 23-26, pp. 257-264, 2010.

[4] F. Calefato and F. Lanubile, "Using Frameworks to Develop a Distributed Conferencing System: An Experience Report", *Software: Practice and Experience*, 2009, vol. 39, no. 15, pp. 1293–1311.

[5] F. Calefato, F. Lanubile, and R. Prikladnicki, "A Controlled Experiment on the Effects of Machine Translation in Multilingual Requirements Meetings", *Proc. 6th Int'l Conference on Global Software Engineering (ICGSE'11)*, Helsinki, Finland, August 15-18, 2011.

[6] E. Carmel, and R. Agarwal, "Tactical Approaches for Alleviating Distance in Global Software Development," *IEEE Softw.*, vol. 18, no. 2, pp. 22-29, Mar. 2001.

[7] E. Carmel and R. Prikladnicki, "Does Time Zone Proximity Matter for Brazil? A Study of the Brazilian I.T. Industry." Technical Report, 2010, available at http://ssrn.com/abstract=1647305.

[8] H.H.Clark, and S.E. Brennan. *Grounding in Communication, in Perspectives on Socially Shared Cognition*, American Psychological Association, Wash. DC, 1991, pp. 127-149.

[9] W.J. Conover, *Practical Nonparametric Statistics*. Wiley, New York, 1980.

[10] D. Damian and D. Zowghi, "Requirements Engineering Challenges in Multi-Site Software Development Organizations", *Requirements Engineering Journal*, 8-3, 2003, pp. 149-160.

[11] D. Damian, "Stakeholders in Global Requirements Engineering: Lessons Learned from Practice", *IEEE Software*, 24-2, 2007, 21-27.

[12] G. DeSanctis and R. B. Gallupe, "A Foundation for the Study of Group Decision Support Systems", *Management Science*, 33(5): 589-609, May 1987.

[13] J.D. Herbsleb, D.L. Atkins, D.G. Boyer, M. Handel, and T.A.Finholt, "Introducing Instant Messaging and Chat into the Workplace." *Proc. Int'l Conference on Computer-Human Interaction (CHI '02)*, Minneapolis, MN, USA, 2002.

[14] M. Höst, B. Regnell, B. and C. Wohlin. "Using Students as Subjects - A Comparative Study of Students and Professionals in Lead-Time Impact Assessment." *Empirical Software Engineering*, Vol. 5, No. 3, 2000, pp. 201-214.

[15] Y. Hsieh, "Culture and Shared Understanding in Distributed Requirements Engineering," *1st Int'l Conf. on Global Software Engineering (ICGSE'06)*, Florianopolis, Brazil, Oct. 2006.

[16] D. Jurafsky and J. H. Martin, *Speech and Language Processing* (2nd ed), Prentice Hall Series in Artificial Intelligence, Prentice Hall, 2008.

[17] A.T. Kearney. "Destination Latin America: A Nearshore Alternative, Technical Report, 2007.

[18] KPMG, Nearshore Attraction: Latin America Beckons as a Global Outsourcing Destination, Technical Report, 2009.

[19] D.C. Montgomery. *Design and Analysis of Experiments*. J. Wiley & Sons, New York, 1996.

[20] B. Nuseibeh, and S. Easterbrook, "Requirements engineering: a roadmap," *Proc. Int'l Conf. on the Future of Software Engineering* (ICSE '00), pp. 35-46, June 2000.

[21] S. Stemler, "An Overview of Content Analysis", *Practical Assessment, Research & Evaluation*, vol. 7, no. 17, 2001.

[22] C. Wohlin, P. Runesson, M. Höst, M.C. Ohlsson, B. Regnell, and A. Wesslén. *Experimentation in Software Engineering, An Introduction*. Kluwer Academic Publishers, 2000.

[23] N. Yamashita, R. Inaba, H. Kuzuoka, and T. Ishida. "Difficulties in establishing common ground in multiparty groups using machine translation." *Proc. 27th Int'l Conf. on Human Factors in Computing Systems (CHI '09)*, Boston, USA, April 4-9, 2009, pp, 679-688.

Does the Prioritization Technique Affect Stakeholders' Selection of Essential Software Product Features?

Hans Christian Benestad
ExpertWare AS
NO-0274, Oslo, Norway
benestad@expertware.no

Jo E. Hannay
Simula Research Laboratory
Pb. 134, NO-1325 Lysaker, Norway
jo@simula.no

ABSTRACT

Context: To select the essential, non-negotiable product features is a key skill for stakeholders in software projects. Such selection relies on human judgment, possibly supported by structured prioritization techniques and tools. *Goal*: Our goal was to investigate whether certain attributes of prioritization techniques affect stakeholders' threshold for judging product features as essential. The four investigated techniques represent four combinations of granularity (low, high) and cognitive support (low, high). *Method*: To control for robustness and masking effects when investigating in the field, we conducted both an artificial experiment and a field experiment using the same prioritization techniques. In the artificial experiment, 94 subjects in four treatment groups indicated the features (from a list of 16) essential when buying a new cell phone. In the field experiment, 44 domain experts indicated the software product features that were essential for the fulfillment of the project's vision. The effects of granularity and cognitive support on the number of essential ratings were analyzed and compared between the experiments. *Result*: With lower granularity, significantly more features were rated as essential. The effect was large in the general experiment and extreme in the field experiment. Added cognitive support had medium effect, but worked in opposite directions in the two experiments, and was not statistically significant in the field experiment. *Implications*: Software projects should avoid taking stakeholders' judgments of essentiality at face value. Practices and tools should be designed to counteract biases and to support the conscious knowledge-based elements of prioritizing.

Categories and Subject Descriptors

D.2.1 [**Software Engineering**]: [Requirements/Specifications]

Keywords

Requirements, Prioritization techniques, Essential features, Stakeholders, Field experiment, Robustness

1. INTRODUCTION

Making sound judgments about the importance of proposed product features is a key skill for stakeholders in software projects, from project inception, through construction and evolution. In this study, we wish to draw attention to *essential* product features (denoted *essentials* in this paper); i.e., those product features that, according to stakeholders, cannot be left out if the product vision is to be fulfilled.

Different stakeholders may have different perspectives and interests and may assess the importance of a given feature differently. With prioritization techniques and tools, individual stakeholders' assessments are collected in a structured manner; the goal being to support experts in setting priorities that reflect their knowledge and best judgment.

However, it is well known that expert judgments are subject to contextual biases. For example, in software cost estimation, question format and irrelevant information have been shown to affect estimates significantly [17, 18], and there are a host of other general biases from the judgment and decision-making literature [19, 1] that have been shown to apply also to software estimation [11]. Due to general unconscious cognitive factors that underlie cost estimation, priority judgments, and judgments in general, it is expected that judgments of priorities of product features are subject to similar biases. However, judgment research has also uncovered conscious factors that are task specific and that can be manipulated through training and the building of expertise [29, 7]. There is little empirical evidence on how and when both conscious and unconscious factors affect priority judgments in software engineering.

The goal of this study is to investigate how different prioritization techniques affect stakeholders' threshold for judging product features as essential. A lower threshold means that more features are rated as essential. Therefore, a natural outcome measure for the study is the number of features rated as essential from a list of candidate features.

Prioritization techniques may be classified according to how they vary in terms of *measurement scale*, *granularity*, and *sophistication* (e.g., *cognitive support*) [3]. Our study focuses on techniques that elicit priorities on an ordinal measurement scale, according to granularity (low, high)—which is predicted to trigger unconscious biases, and according to cognitive support (low, high)—which is predicted to trigger conscious processes. We will elaborate on these characteristics below. The research question for the study is:

> *Does granularity and cognitive support in prioritization techniques affect stakeholders' thresholds for judging software product features as essential?*

	high granularity	low granularity
low cognitive support	*Simple dropdown* (T1)	*Sortable table* (T3)
high cognitive support	*Drag into bins* (T2)	*Pairwise comparisons & ranking* (T4)

Table 1: Investigated Prioritization Techniques

In two controlled experiments we investigated four ordinal prioritization techniques representing the combinations of low/high granularity and low/high cognitive support. We denoted the techniques *Simple dropdown, Drag into bins, Sortable table,* and *Pairwise comparisons & ranking.*

In addition to offering input to the reflective practice of software practitioners, this study offers input to empirical software engineering research. First, the study contributes a new objective outcome measure for prioritization studies. Objective outcome measures are important for the validity of empirical studies investigating judgmental biases, and such measures have been scarce in earlier prioritization studies. Second, the study uses underlying characteristics of prioritization techniques as independent variables, rather than the technique itself. This is important, because it facilitates a deeper understanding of the results by making it possible to draw lines from theories in behavioral judgment and decision science. We suggest these research design elements as complements to a proposed framework for prioritization studies [5]. Methodologically, the study demonstrates the viability of conducting a decently scaled controlled experiment in a live software engineering context, and illustrates the usefulness of comparing results (effect sizes in particular) with replications in a more artificial context.

Section 2 presents the investigated techniques, Section 3 reviews related work, Section 4 discusses effects underlying the techniques from a theoretical perspective, Section 5 describes the experiment and results, Section 6 discusses implications, Section 7 discusses validity issues, and Section 8 concludes.

2. THE INVESTIGATED TECHNIQUES

Prioritization techniques can be classified in terms of the following three characteristics [3]:

1: The *measurement scale* used for prioritizing features. Priorities given on an ordinal measurement scale hold information simply about the relative ordering of features (A is more important than B). Interval or ratio scale priorities add information about the magnitude of differences between features (A is three units more important than B, C is three times more important than D).

2: The *granularity* of the scale denotes how many categories or values are available on which to rate features. For example, on an ordinal scale, higher granularity means that the expert can choose from a larger set of possible ratings (e.g., "Essential", "Important", "Not important" rather just "Essential", "Non-essential")

3: The degree of *cognitive support* for the technique. Several modes of cognitive support exist, and many of them are designed to help the expert prioritize more reliably or consistently. For example, prompting for multiple and overlapping pairwise comparisons should reduce the likelihood for accidental inaccurate assessments.

In this study, our focus is on essentials. This entails that it suffices to offer experts an ordinal scale. The study is

designed to investigate if there are effects of varying granularity and cognitive support. For this purpose, it suffices to vary each of these two independent variables binomially (high and low) which gives 2x2 factorial design with four distinct techniques T1–T4, as indicated in Table 1.

The four techniques were implemented using the tool EstimationWeb (`estimationweb.com`), a publicly available web-based tool for estimation, prioritization, and scheduling, developed by our research group. The functionality and visual appearance of the techniques are presented below. In Section 4 we will discuss the theory underlying the design of the techniques, and in Section 5 we will present details on how the techniques were used in the experiment.

2.1 Simple dropdown

With *Simple dropdown* (T1), each line on the prioritization page contains a feature description and a dropdown box offering choices to give the priorities "Essential", "Significant", "Limited", and "Insignificant". Figure 1 shows the tool page in EstimationWeb for *Simple dropdown* configured for the general experiment.

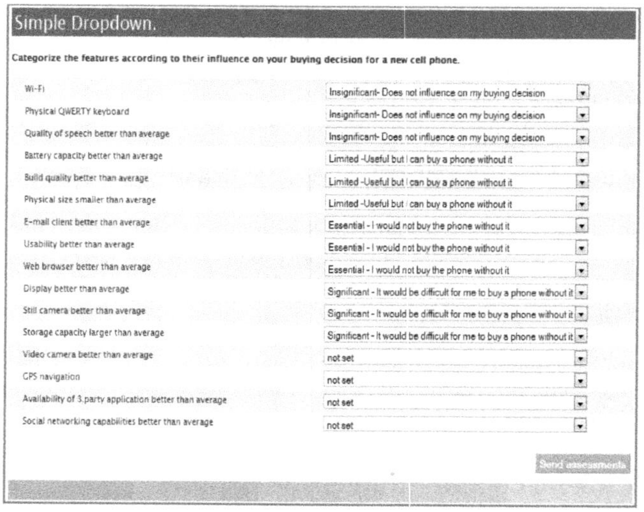

Figure 1: Simple dropdown (T1)

2.2 Drag into bins

With *Drag into bins* (T2), the user drags features into or between categories. The categories and their descriptions in T2 were identical to those in T1, implying equal granularity for these techniques. However, the spatial grouping of features may lead the expert to repeatedly compare features of equal or adjacent ratings, possibly resulting in more reliable priorities. Therefore, T2 is said to offer more cognitive support than T1. Figure 2 shows the tool page for *Drag into bins* configured for the general experiment.

Figure 2: Drag into bins (T2)

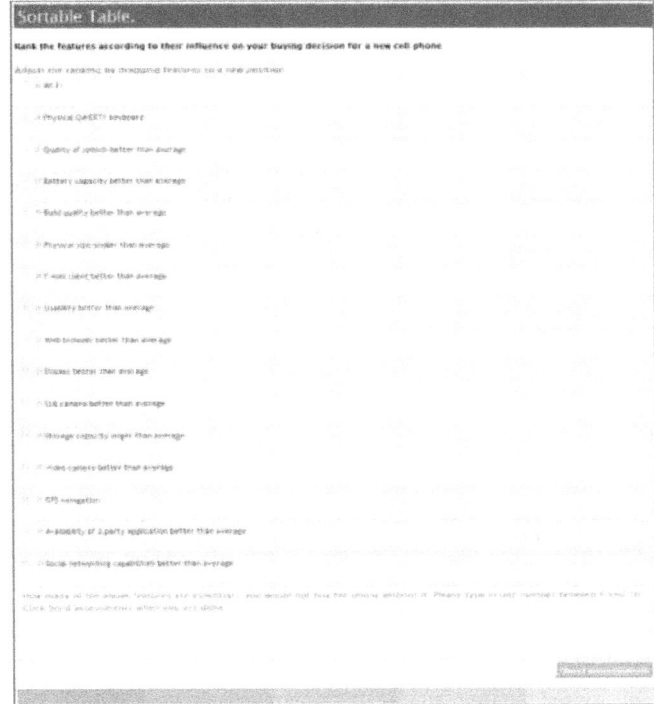

Figure 3: Sortable table (T3)

2.3 Sortable table

With *Sortable table* (T3), the features are presented in a table view in which the rows can be dragged and re-arranged according to priority. After sorting the table, the subjects in our experiments used a simple input field to indicate the number of essential features in the now prioritized list. Implicitly, this method classifies features into two categories, "Essential" and "Not essential". Figure 3 shows the tool page for *Sortable table* configured for the general experiment.

2.4 Pairwise comparisons & ranking

Figure 4 shows the tool page for *Pairwise comparisons & ranking* (T4) configured for the general experiment. With *Pairwise comparisons & ranking*, the user is presented with pairs of features and is prompted to indicate the difference in importance on a scale from 1 (equal) to 9 (extreme difference) in either direction of the two features. After these pairwise comparisons, the tool computes a global ranking and displays the results in the table to the right. In this table, the user can adjust the calculated ranking. After any adjustments, the subjects in our experiments indicated the number of essentials in the now sorted table. As with T3, this method implicitly classifies features into two categories, "Essential" and "Not essential". With the pairwise comparison step, some degree of redundancy is introduced, leading to reduced sensitivity for accidentally inaccurate or arbitrary assessment. Also, through the repeated contrasting of feature pairs, users can possibly uncover important criteria relevant for the prioritization. Technique T4 is therefore assumed to offer more cognitive support than T3.

The tool's calculations of ranks in T4 uses the algorithms of the analytical hierarchy process (AHP) [34, 33], complemented with Harkers method to calculate weights and ranks from incomplete pairwise comparisons [15]. AHP is designed to reduce the sensitivity for accidental inaccurate

assessments by prompting for redundant pairwise comparisons. The tool was configured to fix the number of pairs to compare to $1.5n$, with n candidate features, i.e., the subjects were asked to perform 24 pairwise comparisons with 16 features. With complete pairwise comparisons, 120 comparisons would have been required. The chosen number was a compromise between obtaining more stable rankings by way of more comparisons, and avoiding fatigue and experiment drop-outs due to too many comparisons. Simulations have shown stable ordinal ranks even below $1.5n$ [15].

3. RELATED WORK

A number of case studies [4, 21, 22, 23, 27, 28] and controlled experiments [6, 24, 25, 31] have been conducted to evaluate prioritization techniques with respect to outcome variables such as time usage and accuracy, but none of the studies directly address our research question. However, since our interest is in the accuracy of essential ratings, studies on the effects of prioritization techniques on the overall accuracy of priorities are still relevant.

The results from such studies do not yet give grounds for strong conclusions. For example, techniques based on pairwise comparisons performed well in some studies, e.g., [23], while in other studies simpler techniques performed equally well [25]. One problem with comparing results for prioritization techniques may be the possible confounding impact of tool support [25]. Another problem is that no objective measures of accuracy have been used in the studies. Subjective measures of accuracy fall short when measuring effects due to factors of which subjects are not consciously aware.

Our study relates to theories developed in the field of judgment and decision-making, and we also investigate this link

263

Figure 4: Pairwise comparisons & ranking (T4)

explicitly by replicating the experiment in field and artificial settings. We discuss relevant theoretical work and effects predicted by theory in the next section.

4. THEORETICAL PROPOSITIONS

If properties of the prioritization technique do not affect subjects in their assessment, there should be no difference in the judgment of essential features between techniques. However, based on a substantial body of research on unconscious factors that produce biases in related domains and on related tasks [11], we propose that unconscious factors produce biases also in prioritization, and, further, that various prioritization techniques embody these factors. However, we also propose that cognitive support represents a counterweight to these unconscious mechanisms, in that it strengthens the deliberate and conscious part of the prioritization task. In the following, we discuss the theoretical foundation underlying this study's variation in granularity and cognitive support.

4.1 Effects of granularity

The theoretical basis for effects of variation in granularity is *range-frequency theory* [30, 32], with links to psychophysics, a discipline within psychology that investigates the relationship between physical stimuli and perceptions, see, e.g., [9]. This theory explains judgments of a set of stimuli as a compromise between two mental principles: Distributing features equally over categories (the frequency principle) and distributing categories over equally sized ranges of features (the range principle).

The frequency principle gives rise to the *equal frequency bias*, by which there is a tendency in people to distribute stimuli equally over available categories in a rating situation. This equal frequency bias affects judgments in the presence of *contextual skewing* [30]: Consider a distribution of features according to a person's unbiased view of importance. If this distribution is positively skewed so that more features are viewed as less important than more important,

this will induce a tendency in the subject (a bias) to rate a given feature higher (to equalize the distribution), than if the same feature occurred in the context of a balanced or negatively skewed distribution. Figure 5 exemplifies a positively skewed distribution. In our setting, it is reasonable to expect positive skewing in unbiased priorities, since we are asking for essentials, but this is not known *a priori*.

As a counterpoint to the frequency principle, the range principle induces a tendency in people to perceive categories as constituting equal ranges of features. This entails that categories are spaced out equally along a person's perception of ranked features, and thus the "Essential" category will be perceived as smaller and more extreme the more categories are introduced. The range principle also pertains to the stability of the perception of "Essential". If the term is not solidly based in a person's mental model [8, 16], it is more likely that the category denoting "Essential" and the rating scale itself will change meaning in different circumstances. Roughly, for skewed distributions and with few available categories, more weight is put on the frequency principle, rather than the range principle [30].

Together with variations in granularity, the frequency principle and range principle produce the *category effect*. This effect is the tendency of the effect of contextual skewing to diminish when increasing the number of categories. Thus, the count of features in the highest category (essential) would decrease with higher granularity, because of the tendency to distribute equally. This effect is directly relevant in our study because the number of available categories differs between the treatment groups. The use of an explicit "Essential" threshold in T3 and T4 may increase the influence of the range principle on these techniques, since they prompt the user to set this category boundary explicitly.

If subjects distributed features uniformly across categories, twice as many essentials for two-category techniques (T3 and T4) than for four-category techniques (T1 and T2) would be measured. We note that in situations where categories are described with relative labels, e.g., 1 to 4 or low to very high, such a result could be considered rational, rather than biased. In contrast, our observation in many software engineering contexts is that one attempts to assign a precise definition to categories, particularly to the category for essentials. (Assigning specific meanings to ordinal categories actually gives the categories a nominal flavor.) The tendency to distribute features equally over the available categories in such cases is correctly denoted a bias.

Even when influenced by the equal frequency bias, subjects may be able to reliably (i.e., consistently) rank the features on an ordinal scale. In contrast, imagine a situation where features were allocated to available categories by a random process. The predicted result of such a process would be a uniform distribution over the available categories. Hence, *randomness* and the equal frequency bias are distinct effects that coincide. It is reasonable to assume that more randomness will be present when people have less knowledge or weaker opinions about the subject matter. In software projects, where the assumption is that people know product goals and the features needed for their realization, indications of substantial randomness in priorities would be a cause for concern.

4.2 Effects of cognitive support

The theoretical basis for the cognitive support expressed in

T2 and T4 is the *selective accessibility process* [29, 37]. This process explains the cognitive steps in comparisons as an initial holistic judgment in which a person determines whether two things to be compared are holistically similar or dissimilar, followed by a step in which a person's knowledge is accessed in a confirmatory way according to the holistic judgment, which then leads to either an assimilation or a contrast as the end result of the comparison. As in many cognitive mechanisms, there are unconscious mechanisms at play in this process as well, but a substantial distinction is that the strength of the effects of this process depend on domain-specific knowledge. In contrast to the unconscious biases-inducing factors in this study, which relate to general psychological mechanisms that are robust, the unconscious mechanisms of the selective accessibility process are influenced by knowledge of the features under judgment and can therefore be modified to improve performance. This is arguably the basis for building deliberate and conscious processes (i.e., expertise) in planning tasks such as estimation and prioritization [12].

Comparisons are the essence of virtually all judgment tasks, and T2 and T4 prompt explicit comparisons. One would therefore expect stronger signals over randomness by this fact alone, and therefore more reliable ratings. For example, with T2 the subject can more easily compare a feature with features of equal ranking. In addition, T2 and T4 prompt repeated comparisons which should successively make feature-relevant knowledge more accessible. With less randomness, it can be predicted that the average number of essentials will decrease in the case of a bell-shaped or positively skewed distribution of features to importance.

4.3 Summary

Figure 5 summarizes the discussed effects. First, the graph exemplifies a skewed distribution, where the proportion of tasks is shown as a function of feature importance; the latter measured by some objective measure, such as the return of investment for implementing a feature.

When a subject sets a threshold for what constitutes an essential feature with a low-granularity technique (dashed line), the equal frequency bias, the category effect, and randomness pull in the direction of a larger number of essentials, i.e., a larger area under the curve, when compared to a judgment made with a high-granularity technique (rightmost solid line). These effects are to an unknown extent counteracted by the cognitive support of the techniques and by the definition of "Essential" being kept constant.

The figure is not intended to suggest a precise position for the dashed line; rather it illustrates that its actual position is some context-dependent compromise between the effects illustrated as arrows, with a higher barrier at the rightmost solid line and a lower barrier at a position corresponding to a uniform distribution over categories (leftmost solid line).

5. EXPERIMENT

5.1 Overview

The cognitive mechanisms that underlie prioritizing, are basic mechanisms in the sense that they have been demonstrated to exist in artificial settings where other effects are controlled for. In naturalistic settings, however, such effects might interact with other effects to give combination effects, emergent effects [36] or cancellation of effects [35].

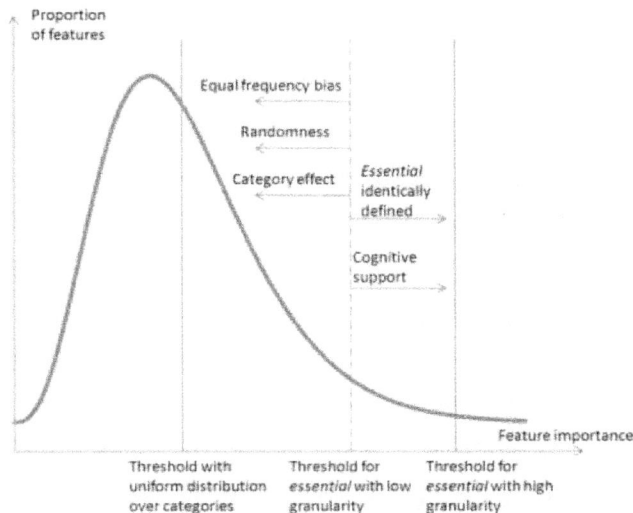

Figure 5: Summary of proposed effects

This brings uncertainty to what one is observing in field settings [10, 26] in terms of such biases. In field studies, it is therefore important to control for the variation in artificiality by subjecting the experiment design to both an artificial setting and the intended field setting. If proposed effects that are demonstrated in the artificial setting recur in the field setting, it is likely that the effects are robust. If the proposed effects do not recur, or other effects manifest themselves in the field setting, then this gives grounds for further deliberations [14].

We therefore conducted both an artificial experiment and a field experiment using the same prioritization techniques. The experiment material was prepared so that subjects across treatments received identical definitions of what it is that a feature is essential. In the first experiment, 94 subjects were asked to rate the importance of 16 cell phone features that would pertain to their decision for purchasing a new phone. In the second experiment, 44 subjects were recruited from the pool of functional experts at a large development project in the public sector in Norway. The subjects were asked to assess the contribution of 16 proposed features to the fulfillment of the project's vision for the software product. In both experiments the subjects were randomly allocated to one of four treatments groups, corresponding to the four prioritization techniques investigated.

The experiments followed a 2x2 factorial design, with Granularity (low, high) and Cognitive support (low, high) as independent variables and the count of features judged as essential as dependent variable. Two-way ANOVA on the rank-transformed dependent variable was used to analyze the data.

5.2 Recruiting subjects

Experiment 1. The subjects were convenience sampled. We explained the goal and the basics of the experimental design to the head of administration of our research institution. All 120 employees were invited by email, explaining the overall goal and the relevant procedures. This population represents employees in the domain of ICT research. The average age of the invited employees was 39 years, and they represented 25 nationalities. Fifty-nine colleagues agreed to participate. Concurrently, we contacted a Polish software house with which our research group has collaborated. The same procedures were followed. The average age of the invited developers was slightly below 30 years, and all of them were Polish nationals. Thirty-five developers agreed to participate. We offered compensation based on standard hourly rates and an estimate of 20 minutes time usage per subject.

Experiment 2. We recruited participants from a large agile development project which was about to engage in feature prioritization for an upcoming release. The authors already had a research collaboration established with this project [2, 13]. We sent a request to the project manager, explaining the goal and the basics of the experimental design. The request was forwarded to one of the project's three product owners who suggested a list of 60 project members who participate in prioritization activities on a regular basis. An email was sent to the potential subjects, explaining the purpose of the experiment and the procedures to follow. We explained that neither agreeing to, declining, or ignoring the invitation would have negative consequences for the invited person. We did not offer incentives for participation other than contribution to project-relevant research and experience with prioritization techniques and tools. Eventually, 44 people agreed to participate in the experiment. The subjects were free to perform the task at the time and location of their own choice within 8 days.

5.3 Experimental material

Experiment 1. 16 features of modern cell phones were identified by the authors based on the authors' judgment of what might be important to the experimental population in a buying situation. The actual features are displayed in Figure 1.

Experiment 2. We selected 16 features from the product queue recorded in the project's issue tracker. The product owner assisted in making the selection based on two criteria.

1: Expected effort is in the same order of magnitude for all features because it makes less sense to prioritize between features at different abstraction levels [3].

2: It is possible for the subjects to understand the basics of the feature through a brief description.

This was to ensure that experimental conditions w.r.t. time and restrictions in collaboration were identical over the two experiments, while at the same time ensuring realism in the field setting. The short description already given in the issue tracker could be used almost unchanged, but some of the texts were improved with respect to clarity and consistency. Three examples follow, translated from Norwegian:

> *As a user/employer, I can execute a check of the salary file for logical errors so that these can be corrected before the file is submitted to the system.*

> *As an agency official, I can reconstruct NAV and AORD information so that I can see which data was registered at a certain point in time.*

> *As a customer service operator I want to have phone calls automatically recorded in the person log when members call SPK and identify themselves with a social security number, so that I spend less time recording the call.*

Table 2 outlines the instructions given to the subject for the four techniques in the two experiments.

5.4 Execution

In both experiments, subjects were randomly allocated to four equally sized treatment groups, corresponding to each of the four techniques under investigation. The study administrator sent an email containing a brief general description of the study and a personalized link to the web form containing the experimental material:

> *[intro]...The purpose is to investigate whether the format of various prioritization techniques affects the priorities. The participants have been divided into four groups, and through random allocation you have been assigned the technique [Simple dropdown | Drag into bins | Sortable table | Pairwise comparisons & ranking]. Once you have started, it is important that you complete without interruptions. Please spend the time needed for you to feel comfortable about your answers. We ask that you work individually and not use other sources than the material we present. Click the link below to start.*

Technique Experiment	Prioritization instruction	Categorization
T1 and T2 Experiment 1	*Categorize the features according to their influence on your buying decision for a new cell phone*	Essential – I would not buy the phone without it Significant – It would be difficult for me to buy a phone without it Limited –Useful but I can buy a phone without it Insignificant– Does not influence my buying decision
T3 and T4 Experiment 1	*Rank the features according to their influence on your buying decision for a new cell phone*	How many of the above features are essential – you would not buy the phone without it. Please type in one number between 0 and 16
T1 and T2 Experiment 2	*Categorize the tasks according to their contribution to the project's vision, the way you perceive the vision*	Essential– The vision will not be fulfilled without it Significant – The vision will be hard to fulfill without it Limited – Useful, but the vision can be fulfilled without it Insignificant–Does not influence the fulfillment of the vision
T3 and T4 Experiment 2	*Rank the tasks according to their contribution to the project's vision, the way you perceive the vision*	How many of the above elements are essential – the vision will not be fulfilled without it. Please type in one number between 0 and 16

Table 2: Experiment instructions (translated from Norwegian for Experiment 2)

In Experiment 1, all 94 subjects submitted their priorities within 8 days. Reminders were sent by e-mail to nonrespondents after 3 and 7 days. In Experiment 2, 44 out of 60 invited subjects replied within 8 days. One reminder was sent to nonrespondents after 6 days. Sixteen invited subjects did not submit their responses. A web-based experiment that gives subjects freedom to choose time and place for completing the experimental tasks imposes some threats to validity, as further discussed in Section 7. Such validity threats would have been reduced or eliminated had all subjects been under our supervision. However, having 44 domain experts from one project meet at the same place and time to participate in an experiment was neither possible, nor desirable, in the field setting.

5.5 Analysis

In the analysis, the two independent variables are denoted gr (granularity) and $cogn$ (cognitive support), and the dependent variable is denoted ess (the number of features judged as essential). Two-way ANOVA is used to identify effects and interaction effects of the independent variables on ess. A rank-converted measure of ess was used to avoid sensitivity to the ANOVA normality requirements. A *post-hoc* Normal Q-Q plot indicated a non-normal distribution of residuals in Experiment 1 but not in Experiment 2. However, we employed rank-converted measures of ess in the ANOVA for both experiments. The analysis was executed using the statistical analysis package R, Version 2.10.1.

5.6 Deviations

In three cases (Experiment 1) and four cases (Experiment 2), the subject misunderstood the instruction of providing the number of essential features. We noticed this misunderstanding on reception of the web forms (within a few minutes after submission) and asked the subject by e-mail to update the response.

5.7 Results

Descriptive statistics for variable ess in the two experiments are shown in Tables 3 and 5, while the ANOVA results are shown in Tables 4 and 6.

Experiment 1: The average number of essential ratings increased by 56% (statistically significant) with low-granularity techniques (T3 and T4) compared to high-granularity techniques (T1 and T2). The effect size measured by Cohen's d is 0.73, which is in the medium category of effect sizes reported in software engineering experiments [20].

The average number of essential ratings increased by 32% (statistically significant) with low cognitive support (T1 and T3) compared to high cognitive support (T2 and T4). The effect size measured by Cohen's d is 0.43, which is in the lower end of medium effect sizes reported in software engineering experiments [20].

Statistic	Overall	T1	T2	T3	T4
Mean	4.1	3.4	2.9	5.8	4.1
Stddev	2.7	1.8	1.8	3.1	2.9
Range	0-12	0-7	0-7	1-11	0-12

Table 3: Descriptive statistics for *ess* Experiment 1

Experiment 2: The average number of essential ratings increased by 195% (statistically significant) with low-granularity techniques (T3 and T4) compared to high-granularity techniques (T1 and T2). The effect size measured by Cohen's

	Df	Sum sq	Mean sq	Sq F value	Pr(>F)
gr	1	7458	7458	11.18	0.0012**
cogn	1	3812	3812	5.71	0.019*
gr : cogn	1	574	574	0.86	0.36
Residuals	90	60057	667		

Table 4: ANOVA results for Experiment 1

d is 2.40, which is in the highest category of effect sizes reported in software engineering experiments [20].

The average number of essential ratings increased by 33% (not statistically significant) with high cognitive support (T1 and T3) compared to high cognitive support (T2 and T4). The effect size measured by Cohen's d is 0.50.

Statistic	Overall	T1	T2	T3	T4
Mean	5.8	3.0	2.9	7.8	9.50
Stddev	3.75	2.22	2.18	2.15	2.78
Range	0-14	0-7	0-7	5-10	5-14

Table 5: Descriptive statistics for *ess* Experiment 2

	Df	Sum sq	Mean sq	Sq F value	Pr(>F)
gr	1	4420	4420	64.20	<0.001***
cogn	1	55	55	0.80	0.38
gr : cogn	1	110	110	1.60	0.21
Residuals	40	2754	69		

Table 6: ANOVA results for Experiment 2

In summary, the results showed that the number of essential ratings significantly increased with lower granularity. The effect size was greater in Experiment 2 (the software engineering context) than in Experiment 1. Added cognitive support affected the number of essential ratings in both experiments but in opposite directions and with statistical significance only in Experiment 1. The results showed no interaction effect between granularity and cognitive support. Re-doing the analysis with the original outcome measure ess (the ANOVA analyses used a rank-converted measure) did not change any of the significance levels.

6. DISCUSSION

The results showed that with lower granularity significantly more features are rated as essential, in line with the equal frequency bias. In Experiment 1, the effect on essential ratings was of a magnitude that could be predicted from the discussion in Section 4 and summarized in Figure 5. Halving the granularity increased the essential ratings, but not by 100% as a pure uniform distribution strategy would have predicted. It may be the case that the definition of "Essential" (*I would not buy the phone without it*) is relatively stable in people's mental models, thus helping in limiting, e.g., the category effect that pulls in the direction of more reported essentials. Also, a higher level of cognitive support had the predicted direction in Experiment 1.

The result for granularity in Experiment 2, on the other hand, is extreme. The effect of reducing granularity is larger than even a full adherence to the principle of equal distribution over categories would have accounted for. In this case it seems that the definition of "Essential" (*The vision will not be fulfilled without it*) is more volatile and perhaps subject to the category effect. In the studied project, the term "vision" is central in the release planning and prioritization processes. Project management assumes that the vision is understood and shared between the key stakeholders; however, the present result indicates that this assumption may not be met. Indeed, in a post-hoc analysis, we measured the inter-rater agreement of the priorities by Kendalls W, giving values of 0.39 and 0.33 for the two experiments, respectively. These are both in the range of low to medium correlation, and it is interesting to note that individuals ranking their personal cell phone preferences agree more than do software project stakeholders assumed to share a common vision. A qualitative study confirms that there may be challenges in maintaining a common vision in the project [13]. The effect of cognitive support was negative in the field experiment, but not statistically significantly so.

In summary, the correspondence in results between the artificial experiment and the field experiment support the proposition that general biases also occur in our field setting. The differences between the two experiments give valuable insight into the specificities of the field setting that should be investigated further.

An important question is whether the subjects were able to assess reliably the relative importance of features. If so, the results can be explained by the equal frequency bias. Alternatively, the results were influenced by a high degree of randomness, which would be a cause for larger concern. With reliable ordinal rankings, the most important features would still be selected for development, but this would not necessarily be the case with randomness in priorities.

The differences in effect sizes between the two experiments could possibly be explained by extensive randomness in the priorities given in Experiment 2. Future plans are to re-execute the experiment sessions, which would allow us to measure the inter-rater agreement scores of the essentiality ratings. A lower score in the field context than in the phone feature context would support the proposition that more randomness was present in the field.

At the outset, the implications of the study results seem important. If stakeholders' threshold for judging features as essential is sensitive to the prioritization technique and perhaps also to the questioning format in general, this could be an important obstacle against collecting trustworthy judgments as input to release planning. Indeed, it is possible that the results point to a root cause for software failure archetypes such as "Unable to meet the user's needs".

It is important to note that any direction of bias can be harmful. Too strict thresholds for judging features as essential can imply that required functionality is not prioritized over more dispensable features or even gold-plating features. Thresholds set too loosely could lead to projects being prematurely stopped due to outlooks of severe cost overruns or could mean that falsely reported essentials take the place of true essentials when the project budget becomes tight.

In practice, projects have mechanisms to compensate for judgmental biases of the kind demonstrated in this study. First and foremost, group discussions and other forms of broad-banded communication can enable stakeholders to counteract the biases through group discussions and clarifications. Such communication is more difficult to achieve in the largest projects and in projects where stakeholders cannot meet frequently. Unfortunately, these are exactly the kinds of projects that are already considered at risk.

The results are also relevant for discussions on how to handle change and feature requests in the context of a commercial development contract. Such contracts sometimes describe different procedures and conditions for handling change or feature requests of different importance. For example, a contractor might commit to expediting the development of essentials or to develop them as part of a fixed-price contract. Biases in judgments of essentiality could therefore easily have commercial and legal consequences.

Providing recommendations concerning the biases are not straightforward. Since biases in both directions can be harmful, and the "correct" prioritization is generally not known, it is not possible to give normative recommendations, such as "Use a large number of categories". Furthermore, improvements in the accuracy of essential ratings are more difficult to assess then in the context of cost estimation. While cost estimates can be compared with an objective measure of actual expenditure, it remains a matter of subjective opinion to determine whether a requirement was eventually essential. Currently, our best advice would be to triangulate priorities by combining different prioritization techniques. On major deviations between stakeholders or between techniques, stakeholders should meet to clarify their views so that the responsible product owner can make the final decisions based on more and better information. Being as precise as possible in the priority guidelines, category definitions, and descriptions of features is likely to help, but as the results from the present study demonstrate, such measures are unlikely to fully remove the biases.

On the other hand, more effort should be spent on investigating ways to improve cognitive support so as to influence the cognitive elements that rely on knowledge and expertise. This would strengthen the conscious signal in prioritization to overcome the noise of unconscious biases [12]. This would also open up the possibility to train people in prioritizing, by deliberatively targeting [7] the appropriate elements in the selective accessibility process [29].

7. VALIDITY ISSUES

Conclusion validity. Unreliable measurement induced by the unsupervised experiment context can be a threat to conclusion validity. With unsupervised execution, subjects may more easily break the rules by collaborating, answering at random, answering destructively, or consulting information outside of the experimental material. We have no explicit reason to believe such problems were prevalent, given the well-willingness to participate and the professionalism of the participants. To some degree, the use of robust methods of analysis would have counteracted effects of outliers in the data due to such problems.

Internal validity. At present, we have not identified large threats to establishing internally valid treatment-outcome relationships from the experiment. However, future investigations may reveal confounding or missing variables that should have been included in the analysis. We cannot obtain more information about underlying relationships from the experimental results. We would have liked to have gathered qualitative data to complement the quantitative analyses; however, we preferred to concentrate our limited time of access to subjects on collecting better quantitative data.

Construct validity. Although our study is theoretically based, our constructs are only very informally defined; if at all. This is a general short-coming in empirical software engineering. In particular, there are many ways of adding cognitive support to prioritization techniques, and effects might differ between different operationalizations of the concept. Further research is needed to establish valid constructs for the informal concepts involved in our study. For now, the results can only very informally be generalized through construct validity. However, the results from Experiment 1 strengthens the case that the observed effects are indeed domain independent and instances of robust psychological effects between meaningful constructs, at least for variations in granularity.

External validity. For Experiment 2, the population was restricted to one specific development project. Hence statistical inference can be used to generalize to this population but not automatically to other software development projects. For granularity, we have shown effects of varying between two and four categories. Whether similar effects occur for other specific levels of granularity remains to be investigated. We do not believe the experimental material or context have provoked or exaggerated the results. On the contrary, we paid significant attention to articulating the instructions, the category definitions, and the feature descriptions precisely and in an understandable manner. It is likely that our observations can cautiously be transferred to variations over our experiment variables; hence we postulate a modest degree of external validity.

It is also possible to use the logic of case studies to discuss external validity [38]. Earlier, we have argued that the investigated project can be seen as a critical case in the class of large and agile software development projects [13]. The project is a prestige project in the Norwegian public sector, attracting the best skilled workers, both on the client and contractor side. Great attention has been put on sharply defining the scope and vision for the project. Critical case logic implies that other, less fortunate projects in the same class are likely to face similar or more severe challenges.

8. CONCLUSIONS

We have conducted two controlled experiments to investigate whether certain attributes—granularity and cognitive support—of prioritization techniques affect stakeholders' thresholds for judging product features as essential. In an experiment asking subjects to pick essential mobile phone features, the number of reported essentials increased by around 50% when granularity decreased from four to two categories. The effect was extreme—195% in the experiment conducted in a realistic software engineering context.

It seems that subjects in both experiments had a tendency to distribute features equally across available categories (known as the equal frequency bias), despite a clear and constant definition of what "essential" means across treatments. The extreme effect in the software engineering context indicates that stakeholders were able to make absolute judgments of essentiality only to a very limited degree and instead resorted to, at best, ordinal ranking. Additionally, randomness in assigned priorities can explain such results.

For cognitive support, the results are less conclusive. In the phone feature experiment, adding cognitive support resulted in a statistically significant decrease in the number of essential ratings. An opposite, but not statistically significant, effect occurred in the field experiment. The most immediate explanation is that the potential effect of cognitive support was overshadowed by the equal frequency bias and randomness in the latter context.

Incorrectly picking essential product features can have harmful effects for software projects. This study has shown that contextual biases can have large effects when stakeholders assign priorities to software product features. We believe this study has shown the importance of designing and employing practices that counteract or manage such effects, and also the necessity to strengthen the conscious elements of the task of prioritizing.

Acknowledgments

The authors are grateful to Krzysztof Rolak, Mona Hegreberg, and Ottar Hovind for accepting and helping us to conduct the experiment in their organizations and to the participants from PGS Software, the SPK/Perform project, and Simula Research Laboratory, respectively. We thank Torleif Halkjelsvik at the Department of Psychology, University of Oslo, for pointing out relevant empirical studies within psychology. The work was partly funded by the Simula School of Research and Innovation.

9. REFERENCES

[1] J. S. Armstrong, editor. *Principles of Forecasting: A Handbook for Researchers and Practitioners.* Kluwer Academic Publishers, 2001.

[2] H. C. Benestad and J. E. Hannay. A comparison of model-based and judgment-based release planning in incremental software projects. In *Proc. 33rd Int'l Conf. Software Engineering (ICSE 2011)*, pages 766–775. ACM, 2011.

[3] P. Berander and A. Andrews. Requirements prioritization. In *Engineering and Managing Software Requirements*, chapter 4, pages 69–94. Springer, 2005.

[4] P. Berander and P. Jönsson. Hierarchical cumulative voting (hcv) prioritization of requirements in hierarchies. *Int'l J. Software Engineering & Knowledge Engineering*, 16:819–849, 2006.

[5] P. Berander, K. A. Khan, and L. Lehtola. Towards a research framework on requirements prioritization. In *Proc. 6th Conf. Software Engineering Research and Practice in Sweden*, pages 39–48, 2006.

[6] A. S. Danesh and R. Ahmad. Study of prioritization techniques using students as subjects. In *Int'l Conf. Information Management and Engineering*, pages 390–394. IEEE Computer Society, 2009.

[7] K. A. Ericsson. The influence of experience and deliberate practice on the development of superior expert performance. In K. A. Ericsson, N. Charness, P. J. Feltovich, and R. R. Hoffman, editors, *The Cambridge Handbook of Expertise and Expert Performance*, chapter 38, pages 683–703. Cambridge Univ. Press, 2006.

[8] D. Gentner and A. L. Stevens, editors. *Mental Models.* Lawrence Erlbaum Associates, Inc., 1983.

[9] G. A. Gescheider. Psychophysical scaling. *Annual Review of Psychology*, 39:169–200, 1988.

[10] G. Gigerenzer and P. M. Todd, editors. *Simple Heuristics that Make Us Smart*. Oxford University Press, 1999.

[11] T. Halkjelsvik and M. Jørgensen. From origami to software development: A review of studies on judgment-based predictions of performance time. *accepted to Psychological Bulletin*, 2011.

[12] J. E. Hannay. Better software effort estimation—a matter of skill or environment? *Submitted to IEEE Trans. Software Engineering; available at* `simula.no/people/johannay/bibliography`, 2012.

[13] J. E. Hannay and H. C. Benestad. Perceived productivity threats in large agile development projects. In *Proc. 4th Int'l Symp.Empirical Software Engineering and Measurement (ESEM)*, pages 1–10. IEEE Computer Society, 2010.

[14] J. E. Hannay and M. Jørgensen. The role of deliberate artificial design elements in software engineering experiments. *IEEE Trans. Software Eng.*, 34:242–259, Mar/Apr 2008.

[15] P. T. Harker. Incomplete pairwise comparisons in the analytic hierarchy process. *Mathematical Modelling*, 9(11):837–848, 1987.

[16] P. N. Johnson-Laird. *Mental Models: Towards a Cognitive Science of Language, Inference, and Consciousness*. Cambridge Univ. Press, 1983.

[17] M. Jørgensen and S. Grimstad. The impact of irrelevant and misleading information on software development effort estimates: A randomized controlled field experiment. *IEEE Trans. Software Eng.*, 37(5):695–707, 2011.

[18] M. Jørgensen and T. Halkjelsvik. The effects of request formats on judgment-based effort estimation. *J. Systems and Software*, 83(1):29–36, 2010.

[19] D. Kahneman and S. Frederick. A model of heuristic judgment. In K. J. Holyoak and R. G. Morrison, editors, *The Cambridge Handbook of Thinking and Reasoning*, pages 267–294. Cambridge Univ. Press, 2004.

[20] V. B. Kampenes, T. Dybå, J. E. Hannay, and D. I. K. Sjøberg. A systematic review of effect size in software engineering experiments. *Information and Software Technology*, 49(11–12):1073–1086, Nov. 2007.

[21] J. Karlsson. Software requirements prioritizing. In *2nd Int'l Conf. Requirements Engineering (ICRE'96)*, pages 110–116. IEEE Computer Society, 1996.

[22] J. Karlsson, S. Olsson, and K. Ryan. Improved practical support for large-scale requirements prioritising. *Requirements Engineering*, 2:51–60, 1997.

[23] J. Karlsson, C. Wohlin, and B. Regnell. An evaluation of methods for prioritizing software requirements. *Information & Software Technology*, 39(14–15):939–947, 1998.

[24] L. Karlsson, M. Höst, and B. Regnell. Evaluating the practical use of different measurement scales in requirements prioritisation. In *Proc. 2006 ACM/IEEE Int'l Symp. Empirical Software Engineering*, ISESE '06, pages 326–335. ACM, 2006.

[25] L. Karlsson, T. Thelin, B. Regnell, P. Berander, and C. Wohlin. Pair-wise comparisons versus planning game partitioning—experiments on requirements prioritisation techniques. *Empirical Software Engineering*, 12:3–33, 2007.

[26] G. Klein. Developing expertise in decision making. *Thinking & Reasoning*, 3(4):337–352, 1997.

[27] L. Lehtola and M. Kauppinen. Empirical evaluation of two requirements prioritization methods in product development projects. In T. Dingsøyr, editor, *Software Process Improvement*, volume 3281 of *Lecture Notes in Computer Science*, pages 161–170. Springer, 2004.

[28] L. Lehtola and M. Kauppinen. Suitability of requirements prioritization methods for market-driven software product development. *Software Process: Improvement and Practice*, 11:7–19, 2006.

[29] T. Mussweiler. Comparison processes in social judgment: Mechanisms and consequences. *Psych. Review*, 110(3):472–489, 2003.

[30] A. Parducci and D. H. Wedell. The category effect with rating scales: Number of categories, number of stimuli, and method of presentation. *J. Experimental Psychology: Human Perception and Performance*, 12(4):496–516, 1996.

[31] A. Perini, F. Ricca, and A. Susi. Tool-supported requirements prioritization: Comparing the ahp and cbrank methods. *Information and Software Technology*, 51(6):1021–1032, 2009.

[32] E. C. Poulton. *Behavioral Decision Theory: A New Approach*. Cambridge University Press, 1994.

[33] T. L. Saaty. *The Analytic Hierarchy Process: Planning, Priority Setting, Resource Allocation*. McGraw-Hill, 1990.

[34] T. L. Saaty. *Multicriteria Decision Making: The Analytic Hierarchy Process: Planning, Priority Setting, Resource Allocation*. RWS Publications, 1990.

[35] W. R. Shadish, T. D. Cook, and D. T. Campbell. *Experimental and Quasi-Experimental Designs for Generalized Causal Inference*. Houghton Mifflin, 2002.

[36] H. A. Simon. *The Sciences of the Artificial*. MIT Press, third edition, 1996.

[37] F. Strack and T. Mussweiler. Explaining the enigmatic anchoring effect: Mechanisms of selective accessibility. *J. Personality and Social Psychology*, 73(3):437–446, 1997.

[38] R. K. Yin. *Case Study Research: Design and Methods*, volume 5 of *Applied Social Research Methods Series*. Sage Publications, third edition, 2003.

How can Open Source Software Development Help Requirements Management Gain the Potential of Open Innovation: An Exploratory Study

Krzysztof Wnuk, Dietmar Pfahl
Department of Computer Science
Lund University
Box 118, SE-221 00 Lund
Sweden
+46 46 222 45 17
Krzysztof.Wnuk@cs.lth.se,
Dietmar.Pfahl@cs.lth.se

David Callele
Department of Computer Science
University of Saskatchewan
110 Science Place
Saskatoon, Canada
+ 1 (306) 966-2073
callele@cs.usask.ca

Even-André Karlsson
Add a Lot, Sweden
Gråbrödersgatan 8
211 21 Mamlö
Sweden
even-andre.karlsson@addalot.se

ABSTRACT

A key component in successfully managing software products is to properly, and in a timely manner, identify and secure competitive advantage by innovation via feature differentiation. Although open source software (OSS) is not a new idea, several product development companies that operate in a market-driven context have started to use open source solutions as core software components in their products. Adopting open source core components implies a lower degree of control over software development and increased business risk associated with integrating differentiating contributions into the core release stream. Whether and how to adjust the current requirements management practices after the adoption of OSS components to fully benefit from the concept of open innovation has not yet been empirically explored. We outline experiences and challenges related to leveraging open innovation via engaging in OSS identified during 19 interviews with practitioners occupying different roles in the requirements management process at a large company followed by four validation interviews with other practitioners. We then propose a research agenda for requirements and decision management in the open innovation context and suggest which challenges in requirements engineering open innovation affects.

Categories and Subject Descriptors

D.2.1 [**Software Engineering**]: Requirements/Specifications;

General Terms

Documentation, Management

Keywords

Case study, open innovation, open source software, software requirements management,

1. INTRODUCTION

The principal goal of commercial software companies is to generate profit by actively exploiting viable business opportunities. Achieving and sustaining competitive advantage is becoming more and more challenging due to frequent (and uncontrollable) technology changes [1], shifting market needs and ubiquitous globalization of software production [2]. From the perspective of maximizing *return on investment* (ROI), software companies should focus on identifying and implementing the most profitable functionality, a goal that is strongly correlated with identifying requirements that fulfill customers' needs [1]. Unfortunately, this relationship appears to be underestimated: during the software engineering process, requirements are not necessarily ranked or prioritized from the perspective of value creation; rather, every requirement is often considered equally important [3].

Requirements engineering practice is predicated, in part, upon the belief that successful software product definition is inevitably related to accurate identification and implementation of customer needs, needs represented as various types of requirements [4]. Traditional requirements identification has focused on internal (from within the company) stakeholder interaction – analysis, research and development activities followed. This approach, called *closed innovation* by Chesbrough [5] is threatened by the need to adapt to a world of rapid change and fierce market competition. As noted by Chesbrough [5], companies need to "learn how to play poker as well as chess" with their innovation processes. Searching for, experimenting with, and ultimately using externally generated innovation can be a good short-term provider of growth opportunities [6], extending the lifecycle of existing products.

Companies can no longer rely only upon their internal resources to source innovation. Instead, they may be forced to look to the surrounding environment. Chesbrough [5] identifies the act of identifying and adopting externally generated innovations as *open innovation*, arguing that it may lead to new sources of technology and growth (open innovation is not open source). The open innovation approach supports both the adoption of externally acquired innovation and the active commercialization of internally generated innovations that are not aligned with the current business model (*e.g.* via licensing or sale). This approach attempts to address issues exemplified by the well-known "PARC Problem" experienced by the Xerox company [5]; the inability to assess and capture value for (technology) innovations that were not directly related to Xerox products. A similar problem exists in some requirements engineering contexts (e.g,. market-driven requirements engineering) where not all requirements can be implemented [14], [15] in the products, potentially *wasting* those ideas that could not be commercialized due to, for example, a lack of alignment with the overall product portfolio of a company or limited resources.

The open innovation paradigm has been addressed by several researchers including explorations from the business management perspective [5], in terms of corporate venturing and valuation using a real options model [6], technology transactions [7] and finally to determine if open innovation is unique to large companies in so-called 'high-technology' industries [16]. However, to the best of our knowledge no study has attempted to investigate the role of open innovation in the requirements management process or to identify possible new challenges and process adjustments that the introduction of open innovation may enforce. As there appears to be a strong relationship between requirements engineering, the value creation process [1] and the innovation process, this study investigates open innovation in the requirements engineering context, simultaneously exploring "requirements management to sustain innovation", one of the future research topics identified by Kaupinnen [8].

The open innovation paradigm appears to be of interest to innovation management in large organizations [5], particularly in the context of maintaining a competitive position. In this paper, we investigate open innovation in a large organization that recently transitioned to an open innovation model by abandoning the development of a purely proprietary code base for their software product and making use of an *open source software* (OSS) project or code base (referred to here as a "platform") as a source of innovation (in both knowledge and technology). The code base is the main component of the company's products – embedded systems developed for the global market. The code base is also non-exclusive – it is also available to, and used by, competitors to the case company. In this scenario, each organization develops differentiating features based upon the common open source platform.

To investigate whether and how much the adoption of OSS components in the context of requirements management helps companies take advantage of the open innovation paradigm, we investigated the strengths and weaknesses of the requirements engineering practices in our case company. We formulated the following research question:

> *RQ1: Is the current requirements process in the case company designed to facilitate from open innovation?*

To tackle our research question, we conducted an exploratory interview study at a large-company that develops embedded systems for a global market using OSS components. In 19 interviews we explored challenges related to adjusting their current requirements management and decision-making processes to better benefit from the open innovation paradigm. The findings from 19 in-depth interviews were discussed, validated and complemented by four additional interviews at the case company. In particular, we focus in this study on requirements management and decision making processes [17]. The paper identifies research opportunities in creating effective contribution strategies as well as revisiting current prioritization and release planning methods to better benefit from open innovation. Furthermore, we analyzed the approach to innovation at the case company and identify which challenges in requirements engineering are impacted by open innovation and how the impact occurs.

In the remainder of this paper we present background and related work in Section 2; in Section 3 we outline the methodology and the case company context. Section 4 discusses the validity of the study. Section 5 presents the results of the study. The results are discussed in Section 6 and the paper is concluded in Section 7.

2. BACKGROUND AND RELATED WORK

Open innovation was defined by Chesbrough [5] as "the use of purposive inflows and outflows of knowledge to accelerate internal innovation, and expand the markets for external use of innovation, respectively." Lichtenthaler [7] proposed this refinement: "An open innovation approach refers to systematically relying on a firm's dynamic capabilities of internally and externally carrying out the major technology management tasks, *i.e.*, technology acquisition and technology exploitation, along the innovation process. Thus, open innovation processes involve a wide range of internal and external technology sources, and a wide range of internal and external technology commercialization channels." Both Chesbrough and Lichtenthaler set their work in the context of medium to large organizations, organizations that perceive innovation as one means (among many) to maintain or expand market share [16].

Lichtenthaler [7] surveyed the innovation environment within 154 European companies and plotted the results in the context of source of technology (internal *vs.* external) versus technology exploitation mechanism (products and services *vs.* licensing). Approximately 68% of the respondents were deemed *closed innovators* generating technology internally and exploiting that technology in products and services. A further 9% were *absorbing innovators,* acquiring technology externally and exploiting that technology in products and services. Approximately 6% were *desorbing innovators*, licensing internally developed technologies to third parties without developing related products or services and 8% were *open innovators*, acquiring technologies for use in products and services while also actively pursuing further technology commercialization such as licensing. Finally, 8% were *balanced innovators*, illustrating no significant bias in any direction.

To illustrate the range of perspectives on the issue, we note that Vanhaverbeke *et al.* [6] model innovation in terms of a *real option*, the right, but not the obligation, to take an action in the future. Instead of the commercialization strategies identified by Lichtenthaler, Vanhaverbeke *et al.* [6], [7] consider both closed and open innovation as considered risk management tactics that keep the organizations options open, postponing the need to make a decision until later in the development process. While sourcing innovation can be expensive, they consider this expense to be small compared to the overall costs of introducing the innovation to the organization or the marketplace.

Requirements engineering is a key activity of software engineering and management decision processes are cornerstones of business success [1], [4], [15]. After the requirements are captured, analyzed, specified, and sent to implementation, decision-making processes become the dominant activity [1], [14], [15]]. In the studied case company, the innovation is represented as identified needs (in the form of requirements) for technology acquisition followed by technology exploitation, typically on a commercial basis. Closed technology exploitation occurs when the technology is held as a proprietary advantage and offered to third parties only in the form of a product or service.

Open technology exploitation occurs when a technology is available to a third-party, via licensing or some other means. The company under study has recently transitioned from the closed innovation to open innovation exploitation.

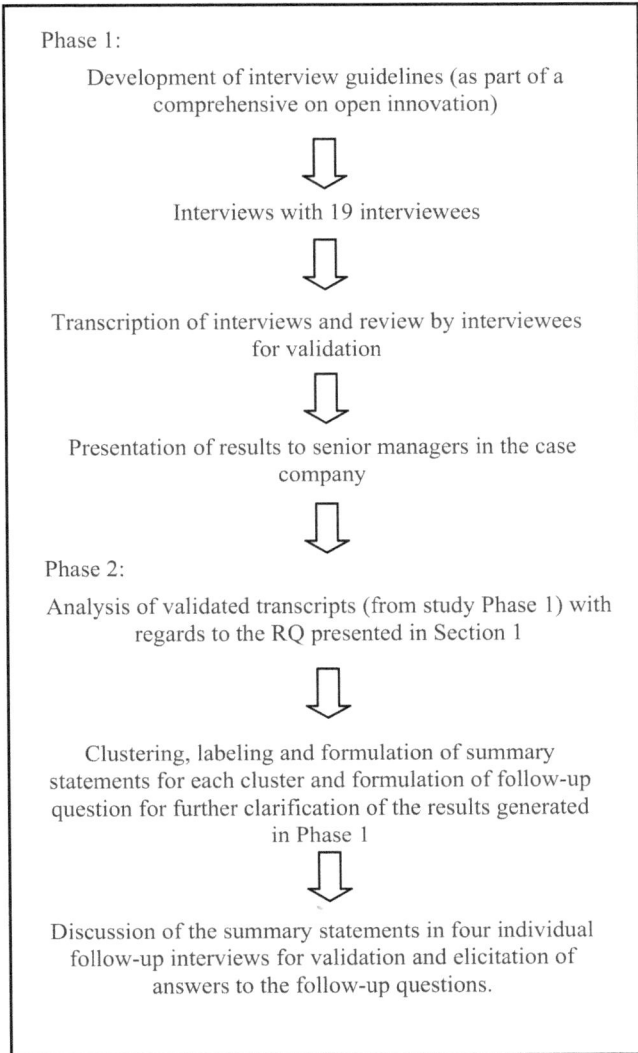

Phase 1:

Development of interview guidelines (as part of a comprehensive on open innovation)

⇩

Interviews with 19 interviewees

⇩

Transcription of interviews and review by interviewees for validation

⇩

Presentation of results to senior managers in the case company

⇩

Phase 2:

Analysis of validated transcripts (from study Phase 1) with regards to the RQ presented in Section 1

⇩

Clustering, labeling and formulation of summary statements for each cluster and formulation of follow-up question for further clarification of the results generated in Phase 1

⇩

Discussion of the summary statements in four individual follow-up interviews for validation and elicitation of answers to the follow-up questions.

Figure 1. The phases of the study

An integral part of the *market-driven requirements engineering* (MDRE) context, in which our case company operates, is the constant flow of new requirements arriving from multiple sources [15]. MDRE also presents other challenges, e.g., balancing between market pull and technology push, cost-value estimation and release planning as well as overloaded requirements management [15]. Making decisions about which of the incoming requirements to implement is a vital part of developing software systems that meet stakeholders' needs and expectations [14], [15]. Given that only some requirements can be implemented due to limited resources, prioritization techniques need to be applied to find the most valuable requirements [14]. The task of prioritizing requirements; although considered generally challenging; could be further complicated in an open innovation context due to several reasons. Firstly, in a closed innovation model, the cost for implementation is estimated (e.g., by experts) and the market-value is estimated using market research or business intelligence

activities. In an open innovation context (e.g., when a company uses an OSS solution as the basis for its software products), the cost could be low (only the integration cost must be incurred). However, the market value of the innovation could be limited by the fact that competitors may be using the same open source solution as the company.

The company must decide which version of an OSS project to use, how to make it compatible with the rest of the software and hardware elements of the product, and which new (differentiating) features to add in order to create or maintain competitive advantage (especially when competitors use the same open source code base). The decision is quite complex as there may be: (1) necessary features to continue to participate in a marketplace, (2) non-differentiating *vs.* differentiating features (differentiating features can confer a competitive advantage), (3) evolutionary *vs.* revolutionary features (*e.g.* abandon the current open source solution and move to another one).

In this case it appears to be critical to properly identify and prioritize the differentiating features that offer a competitive advantage. The lack of full control over the features and contents of releases of the OSS code base complicates software product management activities, especially scoping [11] and release planning [18] compared to the closed innovation context. Past research has not yet focused on these emerging issues [14], [11], [18], [17], [4]].

As the role of innovation is related to creating or eliciting requirements, several researchers have explored the role of innovation in requirements engineering. Kauppinen *et al.* observed six companies and discovered that creativity was not emphasized in their current RE processes [8]. According to Kaupinnen *et al.*, better support of innovation can be secured by ensuring that ideas about innovative features are not removed by the process constraints, as well as by discovering and developing hidden customer needs. Grube and Schmid [9] reviewed creativity techniques for the purpose of devising a systematic approach to those techniques in the requirements management process. Still, there is little empirical work on how requirements management processes can support innovation in general and open innovation in particular also in the case when open source software is used as a source of open innovation.

Open innovation based on OSS can be considered a tool for uncertainty reduction and risk management: if the requirement is already in the open source project, it can't be used as a differentiator by a competitor. However, OSS is also an unpredictable and only loosely controllable source of innovation. The innovation comes for free and is available to anyone using this solution. A company that uses open source can inject new requirements into the community to outsource the cost of prototype development. The company can 'contribute' by licensing outside of organization area of interest (as a *desorbing innovator* [6]) and can 'interfere' by deliberately placing an innovation in the freely available open context, thereby removing the contribution as a differentiator for any competitor. The company can simply 'extract' the already identified requirements and in this way reduce the risks related to their identification and implementation. Further, adopting an open source platform may not be a matter of choice: competitors may attempt to take competitive advantage via the platform, thereby forcing the organization to follow rather than lead. While related papers described the requirements processes in open source software forums [19] or identified which industry sectors are significantly penetrated by open source software [20], little research has been conducted into identifying and understanding the new requirements engineering and decision making challenges posed by the open innovation paradigm.

3. CASE COMPANY DESCRIPTION AND RESEARCH METHODOLOGY

In this paper we investigate open innovation in the requirements management context at a case company using OSS and performing both requirements scoping and requirements management activities. Requirements scoping is defined as a process of deciding: (1) which version of the OSS product (*platform*) should be utilized, (2) what should be added to the platform in order to create product differentiation and competitive advantage, (3) what shall be contributed to the open source community (and when), and (4) how to influence the open source community and become the leading stakeholder to maximize ROI and reduce uncertainty. The associated requirements management aspects are related to understanding which customer requirements are going to be satisfied when a certain open source product is selected and how to ensure that previously satisfied customer requirements (and, therefore, no longer considered innovative) are implemented in the new version of the OSS platform.

Due to the exploratory nature of this study, we decided to use a combination of maximum variance and convenience sampling [12] to gather the data. A case company sample population of different roles that are related to the requirements management process was created. The 19 study participants who came from requirements engineering, product planning, high-level management, and portfolio management. The requirements-related experience of interviewees varied between 6 months and 10 years. Given the limited related work and the exploratory nature of this study, a qualitative interview study was used to understand the issues raised by the change in the experimental context [10], 12].

The interviewees are employees of a global company with approximately 5,000 employees currently undergoing a transition from a waterfall-based methodology to an agile methodology [13]. As a part of the transformation to the agile methodology the company introduced the following innovations: continuous release planning flow, cross-functional development teams, iterative detailing of requirements and integrated requirements engineering. The company uses *software product line* (SPL) management [11] in the embedded systems domain and there are more than 20,000 feature and system requirements defined across all the product lines. New projects on the product line typically add 60 to 80 new features with an average of 12 new system requirements per feature. Approximately 20 to 25 different development teams (with 40 to 80 developers per team) work on implementing these features. At the same time as undergoing this methodology transformation, the company started using an open source solution as a base for software products. The open source solution, referred to here as the *platform*, is the base for the software product line projects and derived products.

The research process is outlined in Figure 1. In the first part of the study (Phase 1), each of the 19 participants was interviewed. The first author of this paper interviewed each participant individually. Each interview was recorded and transcribed. The transcripts were returned to the participants for validation before coding and grouping the transcribed responses. The transcripts were later analyzed using the content analysis technique by

marking interesting section of transcripts and identifying patterns [12] by the first authors based on his subjective judgment. Next, the categories were grouped into 12 clusters, labeled, and assigned summary statements S1 to S12 as described in Section 5 below. These statements serve as the basis for developing a better understanding of the interplay between requirements management, engaging in OSS development, and facilitating open innovation. The completeness and consistency of the clusters and their summary statements were discussed between three authors of this paper. One concern was, for example, that statements S7 and S11 as well as statements S3 and S12 had seemed to have some overlap. The argument to keep them as separated categories, nevertheless, was that they approach the issues raised by our research question from different angles, either from the process or contribution angle or from the release planning and prioritization angle.

At the end of Phase 1, the study results were summarized in a presentation and presented to high-level management at the case company and their feedback was collected.

Table 1. Interview questions used in study Phase 1, grouped into topics (with topics related to the study reported in this paper highlighted in gray)

1. Background
1.1 What is your role?
1.2 How long have you been working with this role?
1.3 How much experience do you have working with requirements?
1.4 How much experience do you have working with scoping and scoping processes?
2. The business goal of the current requirements management process
2.1 What is according to you the goal of the business goal of the current requirements management process?
2.2 How the part of the process you are mostly involved in can contributes to this overall business goal?
2.3 How do we know that the overall business goal of the requirements management process is achieved?
3. Current metrics of the requirements management process
3.1 Do you have any metrics to measure the performance of the process?
3.2 Can the exiting metrics be traced to the business goal of the process?
3.3 How much time do you spend on the metrics right now?
3.4 How do you collect the metrics? Manually or automatically?
3.5 How do you analyze and interpret the metrics? Do you have any issues with analysis and interpretation?
4. Desired metrics of the requirements management process
4.1 What metrics would you like to have to better measure the process?
4.2 How much time would you spend on collecting and analyzing these metrics?
5. Visualization of the requirements management process
5.1 Do you see the need to visualize the requirements management and especially the scoping process?

6. Requirements management and open innovation
6.1 Do you think that the current requirements management process is designed to facilitate open innovation?
6.2 What actions you suggest to improve the current requirements management process to better benefit from open innovation?

The interview questions used in Phase 1 of the study are listed in Table 1. The questions were sent to each of the participants in advance to help them prepare for the interview. The results reported in this paper are exclusively related to the questions under topics 1 and 6. The remaining topics discussed during the interviews will be reported in a separate publication. The questions directly concerned with open innovation are questions 6.1 and 6.2. The open nature of these questions allowed interviewees to express their opinions about the readiness of the current process to support open innovation as well as to provide their views of the process improvements that are required to fully benefit from open innovation.

In the second part of the study (Phase 2), additional interviews were conducted with one high-level business development manager, two requirements engineers performing feature scoping, and one process manager. The 4 respondents were presented with the list of 12 statements S1 to S12 derived from the 19 interviews in Phase 1 of the study and were asked to agree or disagree with the 12 statements and to provide comments if they were so inclined. The meaning of each statement was described in detail to the interviewees and additional clarifications based on the findings from Phase 1 were provided to the interviewees if requested. In addition, the interviewees were also asked to classify their company using the classification scheme reported in [6] – both as it currently operates and how the respondent would like their company to operate. Finally, the respondents were asked to assess whether open innovation impacts requirements engineering challenges and, if so, in what way.

Table 2. The interview instrument used in study Phase 2

1. Please agree or disagree with the following statements related to open innovation and requirements management and to provide comments if they were so inclined
Contributions to the OSS community
(S1) Unclear content and contribution strategy
(S2) Contribution timeline unclear
(S3) Minimize modifications to the open source code
(S4) Unclear relationship between the benefits from contributions in terms of strategy and business goals
(S5) Be strategic when adopting innovative features
Relation between process and innovation
(S6) Augmenting the requirements management process
(S7) Manage innovative features in a separate process
(S8) Top-down or bottom-up open innovation
Release planning and prioritization
(S9) Prioritization process needs modifications

(S10) Challenging acceptance criteria kills innovative features
(S11) Need for special flow for innovative features to evolve to meet acceptance criteria
(S12) Release planning even more challenging
2. Please assess whether open innovation impacts the following requirements engineering challenges and, if so, in what way
2.1 Identify stakeholders needs
2.2 Requirements traceability
2.3 Changing requirements
2.4 Quality requirements
2.5 Communication
2.6 Release planning
2.7 Requirements prioritization
2.8 Requirements overload
3. Please classify your company using the following classification scheme (based on [6])
Closed innovator – generating technology internally and exploiting that technology in products and services
Absorbing innovator – acquiring technology externally and exploiting that technology in products and services
Open innovator – acquiring technologies for use in products and services while also actively pursuing further technology commercialization such as licensing
Balanced innovator – illustrating no significant bias in any direction

4. VALIDITY ISSUES

Following the typology suggested by Maxwell for qualitative studies [21] we briefly discuss the five categories of validity relevant for qualitative studies: description validity, interpretive validity, theoretical validity, generalizability and evaluative validity.

Description validity is concerned with the factual accuracy of our account of what the interviewees actually said. In order to mitigate threats to description validity, we recorded the interview sessions, transcribed them, where necessary removed repetitions or obviously irrelevant statements, and then asked our interviewees to check the accuracy of the cleaned transcription.

Asking interviewees to check the cleaned transcriptions was a measure to mitigate threats to *interpretive validity*.

Theoretical validity is concerned with the relationship between the researchers' observations during the study and their attempts to relate their observations to existing theories, e.g., for the purpose of confirmation, or for the purpose of modifying existing and generating new theory. In other words, theoretical validity has to do with reasoning about the descriptions and interpretations. It has two aspects, firstly, the application of theoretical constructs to the descriptive and interpretive understanding of what has been observed, and secondly, the creation of semantic relationships, narrative structures, and causal relationships that help explain what has been observed. The first aspect of theoretical validity is often called *construct validity*; the second aspect is often called *internal* or *causal* validity. We tried to mitigate threats to theoretical validity. For example, to avoid bias due to unclear questions, we had our interview guideline and the list of statements we presented to the interviewees reviewed by four experienced researchers and practitioners familiar with both open innovation and requirements management research and practice. This contributed also to minimizing the risk of response bias, i.e., the possibility that questions or our list of statements are formulated in a way that they impose a particular answer. We also were aware of the risk of reflexivity during the interview session, i.e., the possibility that an interviewee responds according to a perception of what the interviewer wants to hear. We took precautions that the interviewer expressed neutrality when, for example, talking about the concepts mentioned in our list of summary statements S1 to S12 during the second interview round (Phase 2). Since the study was purely exploratory, we did not have specific hypotheses, theories, or conceptual frameworks in mind to which we tried to connect the responses given by the interviewees. However, we tried to develop an understanding of how the adoption of OSS in the context of requirements management facilitates open innovation. To what extent our conceptualizations and conclusions derived from the interviews are correct (e.g., the generation and clustering of statements S1 to S12) remains to a certain degree unclear and calls for inspection by other researchers in the field as well as follow-up studies conducted to corroborate or disprove our findings. The least we can claim, however, is that the investigated problem is authentic as it originates directly from the company under study.

Generalizability has two sides, internal generalizability, concerned with generalizing within the case company studied to persons that were not directly observed or interviewed, and external generalizability, concerned with generalizing to other companies. These two sides of generalizability correspond to what is often called statistical conclusion validity and external validity in quasi-experimental research. Both aspects of generalizability are – as it is typical for qualitative studies - strongly limited, since our study was conducted in one single company, involving a relatively small number of interviewees. Nevertheless, we can say that we took care through our contacts within the case company to sample representative individuals as interviewees. Furthermore, our case company is comparable to their direct competitors and thus could be considered typical case for that group of companies.

Finally, we can say that evaluative validity didn't play a role in the context of our study, since our study was purely exploratory, and we didn't refer to any kind of evaluative framework when investigating our research question.

5. RESULTS

After we had transcribed and interpreted responses from the first round of interviews, we extracted key statements and grouped them into 12 clusters. For each cluster, a summary statement was synthesized for use in the second round of interviews. We present the summary statements and our observations below and briefly sketch the opinions shared by the interviewees participating in the validation sessions (second interview round, Phase 2 of the study).

5.1 Contributions to the OSS community

(S1) Unclear content and contribution strategy. In our study context, contribution strategy is defined as a management strategy defining when and what to contribute back to the OSS community. The contribution unit is in this case features. Several interviewees mentioned issues and challenges in relation to the contribution process and contribution strategy; four respondents stressed the lack of a clear contribution strategy. One respondent stated that there exists a contribution process description at the case company, a statement supported by three out of four respondents in the validation phase. For one respondent (the business development manager) the contribution strategy was clearly identified. This suggests that the contribution strategy may be present at the case company but not clearly communicated to the operational levels of the company.

(S2) Contribution timeline unclear. One interviewee expressed uncertainty as to when the developed innovative features should be contributed back to the open source community and all four validation respondents agreed. Given that guidelines do not exist, we take this as evidence that deciding when to contribute is challenging.

(S3) Minimize modifications to the open source code. Two interviewees pointed out that adopting the open source code, making changes, and not contributing these changes back to the community creates a risk of creating additional effort to perform maintenance and gap analysis. One interviewee stressed that, regardless of the risk of losing a competitive advantage, the company should contribute as much as possible to the open source community in order to minimize the maintenance effort. Two of the validation respondents agreed, one expressed a neutral opinion and one suggested that this is *not* an issue since the current requirements management process prevents too much code differentiation during the architecture analysis phase.

(S4) Unclear relationship between the benefits from contributions in terms of strategy and business goals. One interviewee expressed the concern that some competitors are more successful in the market even though the company is contributing more than they are contributing. All validation interviewees agreed, explaining that the company actually contributes many low level features that may not be directly recognized as short-term business value. Further, contribution to the community is a long-term investment.

(S5) Be strategic when adopting innovative features. Another interviewee stated that sometimes the company shouldn't be the first one to release certain features based upon open source code but should instead wait for the open source release to provide the functionality and be the second company on the market. The participants of the validation interviews partially agreed or disagreed with this statement – explaining that it depends on whether the features are a part of differentiating technological advance. In this case, the company should be the first one to release new technology or functionality to the market. In areas not considered of *core technological advantage*, being second in the market would probably not harm profitability. In other words, early commitment to customer requirements seems to be not beneficial for non-core technological features as OSS may provide these features in the next release minimizing the effort required to implement them.

5.2 Relation between process and innovation

(S6) Augmenting the requirements management process. Most interviewees suggested that the process needs to be upgraded to fully benefit from open innovation, but some interviewees disagreed. For example, commitments to customers' requirements early in the development process and delivery time agreements were felt to hinder open innovation: the current process is tailored for well-defined features for a specific product definition and "you get locked in, with the agreed functionality, sometime ahead". However, the validation interviewees disagreed with this statement explaining that the current requirements management process is *independent* or *agnostic* to the innovative features as long as they are technically feasible and could prove to have the market potential required to by the demanding prioritization process.

(S7) Manage innovative features in a separate process. One interviewee stated that their process is designed for handling mature feature concepts that can be designed and implemented by developers in a straightforward manner. This interviewee proposes a separate process for maturing innovations so that they can be implemented when ready. All four participants of the validation interviews agreed with this statement, we reckon the interviewer to their response to S6 as the reason (see above).

(S8) Top-down or bottom-up open innovation. Two interviewees stressed that, to enable more contributions, open innovation should be handled at the developer's level; the company should be much more technology-driven, asking the developers "what can be done next with the same code base". The respondents of the validation interviews disagreed with this statement explaining that the developer may have difficulties understanding the overall business and product portfolio strategy. Therefore, open innovation should, according to them, be handled both by developers and managers. These results complement the viewpoint of Chesbrough who focused on introducing open innovation in a top-down fashion [5].

5.3 Release planning and prioritization

(S9) Prioritization process needs modification. One interviewee stressed that the business value prioritization currently used by the case company, designed for handling mature concepts within a defined product, hinders the acceptance of innovative features. Although the problem of applying wrong prioritization criteria doesn't seem to be specific only for OSS and open innovation contexts, in the studied context the challenges seems to be related to the fact that the values for the selected criteria may change depending on what the next release of the OSS provides and the contribution strategy.

(S10) Challenging acceptance criteria kills innovative features. According to another interviewee, the company has tried to include the innovative features in the normal feature decision making and release planning flow but this resulted in an inability to meet the tight deadlines dictated release planning as well as by the market and competitors. Therefore, only mature features are currently considered.

(S11) Need for special flow for innovative features to evolve to meet acceptance criteria. Two interviewees suggested extending the current process to have a special process for handling these features, perhaps by giving them more time to mature (see Section 4.2). All four participants of the validation interviews agreed with statements S9, S10 and S11 – pointing out that the current feature management process is a "controlled factory" that

facilitates the development of the features with greatest potential value, a defined customer, and reliable estimates of system impact and development effort. All respondents supported a separate process for introducing and maturing innovative features to prepare them for joining the tight release deadlines of the "controlled factory" process.

(S12) Release planning even more challenging. One interviewee considered release planning more challenging in the open innovation context, stressed the inherent difficulties. She provided an example where it turned out to be a better business decision to just adopt the open source code, perform minimal adaptation, and sell it rather than spending time and effort on creating differentiating features. The lack of control over release planning was cited as a complicating factor. Two validation respondents agreed with this statement but the other two pointed out that release planning is not more difficult if the innovative features are releasable (possible to implement within budget and hold promising business potential). To summarize, the respondents felt that release planning could be more challenging in the open innovation context.

5.4 Challenges in requirements engineering

The four interviewees that participated in the validation interviews were asked to suggest which requirements engineering challenges [8] are addressed by, impacted by, or made more challenging by the open innovation context. Three out of four interviewees indicated that open innovation makes the challenge of identifying stakeholders' needs more manageable and one indicated that this challenge is not related to open innovation. Regarding the challenges of requirements traceability and release planning, two interviewees thought that it is more challenging while the other two felt that this challenge is not related to open innovation. Further, all four respondents confirmed that the challenges of changing requirements and requirements overload are more manageable in the open innovation context. Regarding the challenge of managing quality requirements, two interviewees indicated that this challenge would become more manageable in the open innovation context (since the company will use open source code with potentially fewer bugs) while the other two respondents suggested that this challenge is not related to the open innovation context. Further, three out of four interviewees indicated that the challenge of communication in requirements engineering is unrelated to open innovation and all four interviewees suggested that requirements prioritization is more challenging in the open innovation context.

The validation interviewees were asked to identify which type of innovative company the case company is and which type of innovative company it should be. All four interviewees suggested that the company is currently mostly an *absorbing innovator* [6] and one interviewee also suggested that the company is behaving a bit like a *desorbing innovator* when releasing the implemented features back to the open source community. All interviewees pointed out that the ultimate goal for the company is to become an *open innovator*.

6. DISCUSSION

Answering our research question RQ1 (see Section 1), based on the results presented in the previous section, we found that the current requirements management process isn't designed to fully benefit from open innovation context. In the following, we summarize and discuss the suggestion for adaptations of the current requirements management process in the case company and actions that should be taken in order to better benefit from open innovation.

The overall results from both sets of interviews suggest the need for creating a contribution strategy that clearly identifies what should be contributed, when, as a part of the requirements management process. Further we identified a need for finding the right balance for contribution that secures successful product differentiation. Moreover, our respondents suggested that *open innovation* should be introduced in both a top-down and bottom-up fashion.

When it comes to the requirements management process, our results highlight the need for introducing a separate requirements process for handling (often immature) innovative feature concepts. Further, our interviewees expressed the need for creating a method for prioritizing requirements (or features) that is more suitable for the open innovation context. Our interviewees suggested that release planning and prioritization methods should be revisited and optimized for the open innovation context as planning releases is definitely more challenging in this context. Finally, our results suggest that challenges of identifying stakeholders' needs, changing requirements and requirements overload are more manageable in an open innovation context while release planning and requirements prioritization are more challenging.

Based on the results from the two rounds of interviews we highlight two areas where we believe further research should be focused on:

- *Requirements management processes for open innovation (this area emerged based on summary statements S1, S2, S3, S6 and S7).* Our respondents clearly state the need for improved requirements management that supports planning and execution of feature contributions that will be sent back to the open source community. Early or frequent contributions create a risk of losing competitive advantage while late or rare contributions can greatly increase the maintenance cost. Thus, further research is needed to better understand the balance between limited and generous contribution strategies. Moreover the right level of adjustments and differentiations has to be preserved in order to minimize the maintenance costs. Additionally, there seems to be a need for augmenting the requirements management process by a separated flow for introducing innovative features where they can mature and become integrated into the main process pipeline.

- *Revisit release planning and prioritization models (this area emerged based on summary statements S3, S9 and S11).* There is a need for revisiting current release planning and prioritization techniques with the goal of understanding how those two tasks can be performed in the open innovation context. For example, the market value and the implementation cost commonly used as criteria in the Analytic Hierarchy Process (AHP) method [14] should be considered in the context of both the company and the open source community. The cost of functionality developed individually by a company and later contributed back to the open source community will be decreased by sharing the ongoing maintenance effort (the dominant cost factor in the case company). Moreover, the release planning methods should be reviewed and possibly augmented by the necessary risk and dependency analysis when features provided by open source products (with release times that can't be controlled) are key components of a company's software products.

7. CONCLUSIONS

We have presented initial results from a study that explores challenges regarding requirements scoping and requirements management in the open innovation context. The results obtained through a first set of 19 interviews followed by a second set of 4 interviews, highlight that managing requirements in an open innovation context is challenging as requirements are freely available for several potentially contributing companies and, even more interestingly, their implementation is freely available.

Future work includes further empirical studies in understanding the impact of open innovation on requirements engineering processes, tools and techniques. In particular, it would be interesting to apply some of the grounded theory principles to further analyze the qualitative material from the interviews. Further, we also plan to focus on exploring new ways of prioritizing requirements that could potentially be more suitable for the open innovation context.

8. ACKNOWLEDGMENTS

This work was supported by VINNOVA (Swedish Agency for Innovation Systems) within the UPITER project. Special thanks to the anonymous informants for their valuable time and knowledge.

9. REFERENCES

[1] Aurum, A., Wohlin C. 2007. A Value-Based Approach in Requirements Engineering: Explaining Some of the Fundamental Concepts. In *Proceedings of the REFSQ 2007 Conference* (Montpellier, France, June 20-23, 2007). 109-115. Springer, Heidelberg (2007) 109-115. DOI = 10.1007/978-3-540-73031-6_8.

[2] Herbsleb, J. D. 2007. Global Software Engineering: The Future of Socio-technical Coordination. In: Procceedings of the *FOSE'07 Future of Software Engineering* (Minneapolis, MN, United states, May 23, 2007 - May 25, 2007). IEEE Computer Society, Washington, DC, USA, 188-198. DOI = 10.1109/FOSE.2007.11.

[3] Biffl, S., Aurum, A., Boehm, B., Erdogmus, H., Grunbacher, P. (eds.). 2005. *Value-Based Software Engineering.* Springer, Heidelberg, ISBN 3-540-25993-7.

[4] Sommerville, I., Sawyer P. 1997. *Requirements Engineering: A Good Practice Guide.* John Wiley & Sons Ltd., Chichester.

[5] Chesbrough, H. 2003. *Open Innovation The new Imperative for Creating and Profiting from Technology*, Harvard Business School Press, USA.

[6] Vanhaverbeke, W., Van de Vrande, V., Chesbrough, H. 2008. Understanding the Advantages of Open Innovation Practices in Corporate Venturing in Terms of Real Options. *Creativity and Innovation Management.* 251 (Mar. 2008), 251-258. DOI: 10.1109/IEEM.2008.4738011.

[7] Lichtenthaler, U. 2008. Open Innovation in Practice: An Anlaysis of Strategic Approaches to Technology Transactions. *Trans on Eng Management* 55 (May 2008), 148-156. DOI: 10.1109/TEM.2007.912932.

[8] Kauppinen, M., Savolainen, J., Mannisto, T. 2007. Requirements Engineering as a Driver for Innovations. In *Proceedings of the 15ᵗʰ IEEE International Requirements Engineering Conference* (New Delhi, India, 15--19 October 2007). IEEE Press, New York, 15-20. DOI: doi: 10.1109/RE.2007.47.

[9] Grube, P., Schmid, K. 2008. Selecting Creativity Techniques for Innovative Requirements Engineering. In *Proceedings of the Third International Workshop on Multimedia and Enjoyable Requirements Engineering - Beyond Mere Descriptions and with More Fun and Games* MERE '08 (Barcelona, Spain 3 September), IEEE Press New York, 32-36. DOI: 10.1109/MERE.2008.6.

[10] Myers, M. D., Avison D. 2002. *Qualitative Research in Information Systems.* Sage Publications, USA.

[11] Pohl, C., Böckle, G., Linden, F. J. van der. 2005. *Software Product Line Engineering: Foundations, Principles and Techniques.* Springer-Verlag, New York USA.

[12] M.Q. Patton. 2002. *Qualitative Research and Evaluation Methods.* Sage Publications, USA.

[13] Agile manifesto `http://agilemanifesto.org/`, accessed January 2012.

[14] Karlsson, J., Ryan, K. 1997. A cost-value approach for prioritizing requirements. *IEEE Softw.* 14 (Sept. 1997), 67-74. DOI: 10.1109/52.605933.

[15] Regnell, B., Brinkkemper, S. 2005. Market–Driven Requirements Engineering for Software Products. In: *Aurum, A., Wohlin, C. (Eds.), Managing and Engineering Software Requirements*, 287-308. Springer- Verlag, Heidelberg.

[16] Chesbrough, H., Adrienne Kardon C. 2006. Beyond high tech: early adopters of open innovation in other industries. *R&D Management.* 36 (June 2006), 229-236. DOI: 10.1111/j.1467-9310.2006.00428.x.

[17] Hood, C., Wiedemann., S., Fichtinger, S., Pautz, U. 2008. *Requirements Management: The Interface Between Requirements Development and All Other Systems Engineering Processes.* Springer, Berlin.

[18] Svahnberg, M., Gorschek, T., Feldt, R., Torkar, R., Bin Saleem, S., Usman M. 2010. A systematic review on strategic release planning models. *Inf. Softw. Technol.* 52 (Mar 2010), 237-248. DOI: 10.1016/j.infsof.2009.11.006.

[19] Laurent, P., Cleland-Huang, J. 2009. Lessons learned from open source projects for facilitating online requirements processes. In *Proceedings of the 15th International Working Conference Requirements Engineering: Foundation for Software Quality* (Essen, Germany, 25 – 28 march 2009). Springer Verlag, Berling, 240-55. DOI: 10.1007/978-3-642-02050-6_21.

[20] Glynn, E., Fitzgerald, B., Exton C. 2005. Commercial adoption of open source software: An empirical study. In *Proceedings of the International Symposium on Empirical Software Engineering*, (17-18 November, Noosa Heads, Australia , 2005), IEEE Press, New York , 225-234. DOI: 10.1109/ISESE.2005.1541831.

[21] Maxwell, J. A. 1992. Understanding and validity in qualitative research. *Harvard Educational Review, 62*(Fall 1992), 279-300.

Towards a Model to Support *in silico* Studies of Software Evolution

Marco Antônio Pereira Araújo
COPPE/UFRJ
Caixa Postal: 68511
Rio de Janeiro, Brazil
+55 21 2562-8712
maraujo@cos.ufrj.br

Vitor Faria Monteiro
COPPE/UFRJ
Caixa Postal: 68511
Rio de Janeiro, Brazil
+55 21 2562-8712
vitorfaria@cos.ufrj.br

Guilherme Horta Travassos
COPPE/UFRJ
Caixa Postal: 68511
Rio de Janeiro, Brazil
+55 21 2562-8712
ght@cos.ufrj.br

ABSTRACT

Software evolution is recognized as one of the most challenging areas in the field of Software Engineering. The observation of evolution is time-dependent, reducing opportunities for actual observations in short periods of time. Usually, maintenance cycles are proportional to the software life cycle. Therefore, the amount of research has not been enough to deal with all the issues related to the evolution of software. However, simulation through confident models represents an interesting strategy to support software decay observation in short period of time. Towards that, this paper describes a model aimed at supporting the software decay simulation through systems dynamics. The Laws of Software Evolution and ISO 9126 were used as initial knowledge to support the discovery of software characteristic (size, periodicity, complexity, effort, reliability, and maintainability) relationships. Next, evidence to strengthen the existence of such relationships was acquired through quasi-systematic literature reviews. In sequence, the model was applied to support the simulation of industrial software decay. The results suggested its feasibility and correctness, making it an interesting candidate to support future software decay studies.

Categories and Subject Descriptors

K.6.3 [**Management of Computing and Information Systems**]: Software Management – *software development, software maintenance, software process.*

General Terms

Management, Measurement, Experimentation.

Keywords

Software Evolution, Software Maintenance, Object-oriented Software, Simulation Model, *in silico* Study, Experimental Software Engineering.

1. INTRODUCTION

Experience and practice in software development allows the understanding that change is an intrinsic and almost inevitable characteristic in the software development process. Software evolution has been recognized as one of the most problematic and challenging areas in the field of Software Engineering. It has been observed that over 80% of the development life cycle costs have been spent after system delivery [1].

According to Lehman and Ramil [2], the greater the understanding of systems evolution the greater the possibility will be of improving methods and processes towards its planning, management, and implementation.

Despite its importance and all the effort put in this topic, results are not enough to support its full comprehension. In general, researchers and practitioners have neither sufficient information nor the understanding as to why and how systems gradually change over time [3]. Therefore, software engineers usually face unknown risks when dealing with the planning and managing of the software evolution processes.

In a Software Engineering context, the term evolution can be interpreted in two ways. One view considers that important topics regarding the evolution of software are the ones that describe the means through which evolution occurs, i.e., the mechanism, instruments, and tools used in this process. In this case, the focus is the understanding of how software is modified. Another view seeks to understand the nature of the evolution phenomenon, its causes, properties and characteristics, consequences, impacts, management, and control. In this case, the focus is to investigate what software evolution is and why it happens. In this context, the Laws of Software Evolution (LSEs) mean to support the understanding of the evolutionary process of software [3].

The technical literature has offered several papers in this area. Most of them discuss the evolution of software usually on a conceptual level, or by observing the evolution of versions of a particular system, considering the source code of legacy systems or free software [4]. In contrast, Smith and Ramil [5] presented an initial model of System Dynamics for Software Evolution through qualitative analysis, without providing a tool to support model execution. Stopford and Counsell [6] presented the only study we were able to find in the technical literature which consists of a framework for simulating the evolution of software based on a fictitious simulation process.

Accepting that all LSEs [7] are valid (Table 1) and dependent on each other, they can be used to organize a conceptual environment to support the definition and execution of *in silico* studies of software decay throughout the software development process activities. It's not the purpose of this work to prove or reject any of the Laws of Software Evolution but use them to prepare a conceptual environment to support the definition of experimental studies concerned with the different object-oriented software development process phases. We are using, as a basis for our research, the Requirements Specification, High and Low Level Design and Coding phases, usually present in most of the OO software development processes.

Considering this, Araújo [4] introduced a model to support the observation of software evolution for *E-type systems* [9] through simulation, using systems dynamics. An *E-type system* represents software for solving a problem or addressing an application in the real word. More specifically, the model intends to allow the observation of software quality decay along the execution of maintenance cycles and thus aims at providing a better understanding of how the software can be affected by various changes throughout its life cycle. The LSEs and ISO 9126 [11] represent the starting points to build such model. A set of software characteristics and possible relationships among them has been established based on interpreting the LSEs formulations (Table 1).

To strengthen the confidence in the model's validity and investigate the possible influences amongst software characteristics, a series of secondary studies has been done [8]. It allowed identifying evidence in technical literature on the following software characteristics relationships: Size, Periodicity, Complexity, Effort, Reliability and Maintainability. Besides, to increase our confidence in the model, it was used to simulate consecutive maintenance cycles (*in silico* study) concerned with a large-scale Web-based application (*E-type systems*) using System Dynamics.

Table 1 – The Laws of Software Evolution [2]

Laws of Software Evolution
Law I - Continuing Change: An E-type system must be continually adapted or it will become progressively less satisfactory in use
Law II - Increasing Complexity: As an E-type system evolves its complexity increases unless work is done to maintain or reduce it
Law III – Self Regulation: Global E-type system evolution processes are self-regulating
Law IV - Organizational Conservation: Average activity rate in an E-type process tends to remain constant over system lifetime or segments of that lifetime
Law V - Conservation of Familiarity: In general, the average incremental growth (growth rate trend) of E-type systems tends to decline
Law VI - Continuing Growth: The functional capability of E-type systems must be continually increased to maintain user satisfaction over the lifetime of the system
Law VII – Declining Quality: Unless rigorously adapted to take into account changes in the operating environment, the quality of an E-type system will seem to decline as it evolves
Law VIII - Feedback System: E-type evolution processes are multi-level, multi-loop, and multi-agent feedback systems

This paper presents the definition and initial assessment of such model to support *in silico* studies of software evolution (quality decay). Thus, such study aims to understand the mechanisms through which one software product is submitted when in a maintenance process in order to better accommodate the changes that have to be made. The observation of this evolution process would allow assisting in accommodating changes, providing the Software Engineer with a mechanism to support decision-making to get higher quality and maintainability in future versions of a software product, extending its useful life, and producing greater investment efficiency.

Apart from this introduction, this paper is organized as follows: Section 2 presents the basis to organize the software evolution observation model. Section 3 offers an explanation on how model confidence has been strengthened through a secondary study. In Section 4 the model assessment in an industrial software application is described. Finally, Section 5 presents conclusions, including the limitations and future work on the model.

2. SOFTWARE DECAY MODEL

Model building was done through the selection of software characteristics [10] representing both system quality and LSEs' features, aiming at providing a better understanding of what would affect software decay. The selection of software characteristics took into account the ISO 9126 [11] standard, as follow [4]:

- Size, the magnitude of artefacts produced in each life cycle phase of the proposed software (e.g., the amount of lines of code in the source code or the number of requirements in the requirements specification document);
- Periodicity, the time interval between each release version of a produced artefact (e.g., software or documentation versions);
- Complexity, the elements that can measure the structural complexity of an artefact (e.g., cyclomatic complexity of methods, or number of classes in the class diagram);
- Effort, the amount of work performed to produce a version of some artefact (e.g., measured in terms of man-hour or equivalent unit);
- Reliability, the number of defects identified per artefact in each software version;
- Maintainability, the time spent in identifying, removing and fixing defects.

After identifying the software's characteristics, each one of the LSE was interpreted according to its possible decay influence in the selected software characteristics. The results were represented through truth tables describing the expected behaviour of each software characteristic regarding a particular item of the LSE. It led to logically formulate a set of assumptions suggesting the behaviours that could be observed under the perspective of the existent linkage among the LSE and software characteristics. So, logical formulations describe software characteristic trends (increasing - ↑, decreasing - ↓ or no changing - ↔) [10] when some LSE can be observed in the software project, or not. So, these assumptions become the observational decay hypotheses regarding the LSE as described in Table 2. These hypotheses are used to verify the behaviour of the LSE on a given system, from the measurements collected for each software characteristic.

Table 2. Observing software decay through LSEs

Observational Hypotheses
$(\neg\uparrow$Periodicity **AND** $\neg\downarrow$Effort$) \Rightarrow$ **Continuing Change**
$(\uparrow$Size **OR** $\uparrow$Complexity **OR** $\uparrow$Effort **OR** $\downarrow$Modularity **OR** $\downarrow$Maintainability$) \Rightarrow$ **Increasing Complexity**
$(\neg\uparrow$Size **AND** $\neg\downarrow$Reliability **AND** $\neg\downarrow$Efficiency$) \Rightarrow$ **Self Regulation**
$(\leftrightarrow$Effort **AND** $\leftrightarrow$Efficiency$) \Rightarrow$ **Conservation of Organizational Stability**
$(\leftrightarrow$Size **AND** $\leftrightarrow$Complexity **AND** $\leftrightarrow$Effort$) \Rightarrow$ **Conservation of Familiarity**
$(\uparrow$Size **AND** $\neg\uparrow$Periodicity$) \Rightarrow$ **Continuing Growth**
$(\uparrow$Complexity **OR** $\uparrow$Effort **OR** $\downarrow$Modularity **OR** $\downarrow$Reliability **OR** $\downarrow$Maintainability$) \Rightarrow$ **Declining Quality**
(Collection of relative measures to Size, Periodicity, Complexity, Effort, Modularity, Reliability, Efficiency, Maintainability) $\Rightarrow$ **Feedback System**

3. STRENGHTENING MODEL REPRESENTATION

3.1. Study Protocol Overview

Generally, technical literature reviews are done through with informal and subjective methods for collecting and interpreting studies. Therefore, researchers may tend to selectively quote studies reinforcing pre-estimates, that is, following a chain of reasoning, giving bias to research results. On the other hand, the systematic literature review (SLR) focuses on executing a comprehensive and thorough search to find studies related to a formally defined research question. Furthermore, it uses well defined criteria to select studies, their quality assessment and also to present a summary of the results according to predetermined procedures [12].

According to Travassos et al. [13], the concept of *quasi* SLR represents a systematic literature review where the PICO's Comparison dimension [12] is represented by an empty set, thus reducing the possibility of executing meta-analysis or any kind of more elaborated research synthesis. Therefore, such reviews represent an intermediate level between mapping studies [14] and systematic literature reviews. The definition of a research protocol containing guidelines for the execution and delivery results of the *quasi* SLR, such as research question definition, inclusion, and exclusion criteria for study selection, criteria for assessing study quality and results, amongst others, give a high degree of formality to this type of secondary study. This formality brings great benefits to the community, as related to the research area under study, such as the reuse of the results achieved as a reference for other surveys, and especially the possibility of re-executing the research protocol for a possible evaluation of the results obtained or to update it.

Therefore, a *quasi* SLR research protocol was organized, to seek evidence on the linkage amongst software characteristics, thus reinforcing the existence of the relationships amongst them, including their mutual influence [8]. The goal is to reduce a threat to the validity of the study based on the number of relationships considered, together with the question that these relationships are processed on different levels of abstraction and at different moments in the lifecycle of a software product, as it is necessary to evaluate the results obtained in the observation of evolving systems and the reality presented by these systems over successive cycles

of maintenance. A relationship between two software characteristics shall be considered to exist if it could be identified in any object-oriented software development stage [15]: Requirements Specification, High Level Design, Low Level Design, and Coding. The testing stage is not being directly considered as it generates information (failure detection) that will support the finding of defects to be fixed in some of the previous stages, which will generate possible evolution opportunities. Measurements allow the observation of software characteristics. Each measurement has been separately taken, according to the software development stage. For example, size may be measured as number of requirements at the Requirements Specification stage or as number of lines of source code in the Coding stage. More details on how measurements can be associated with each characteristic software at different stages of the process are described in [4].

So, model building [4] consisted of answering 15 different research (capturing relationships) questions, aiming at investigating the existence of linkages amongst each of the selected software characteristics.

Aiming to investigate all the research questions, considering each software development stage, a meta-protocol for the *quasi* SLR was produced [4]. Each pair $\{C_a, C_b\}$ of software characteristics was used in the composing of three questions (1 primary and 2 secondary):

Q_i: Is there any influence between the software characteristics $\{C_a, C_b\}$ in the OO software development process?

$\quad Q_{i.1}$: What is the direction of influence between the software characteristics $\{C_a, C_b\}$?

$\qquad Q_{i.1.1}$: What is the intensity/rate of influence between the software characteristics $\{C_a, C_b\}$?

All the three questions for each pair of software characteristics (questions $Q_1..Q_{15}$) were separately analyzed for the software development stage considered, as follows:

- Q_1: *Size* and *Complexity*;
- Q_2: *Size* and *Reliability*;
- Q_3: *Complexity* and *Effort*;
- Q_4: *Effort* and *Reliability*;
- Q_5: *Complexity* and *Maintainability*;
- Q_6: *Effort* and *Maintainability*;
- Q_7: *Effort* and *Periodicity*;
- Q_8: *Periodicity* and *Maintainability*;
- Q_9: *Size* and *Effort*;
- Q_{10}: *Size* and *Maintainability*;
- Q_{11}: *Periodicity* and *Size*;
- Q_{12}: *Complexity* and *Reliability*;
- Q_{13}: *Periodicity* and *Complexity*;
- Q_{14}: *Maintainability* and *Reliability*, and,
- Q_{15}: *Periodicity* and *Reliability*.

The basic sources of information were represented by digital libraries including conferences and journals. Additionally, the search for conference proceedings whose themes are concerned with software maintenance or evolution was also considered, such as the *International Conference on Software Engineering (ICSE)*, *International Conference on Computer Science and Software Engineering (CSSE)*, *International Conference on Software Maintenance,* and *European Conference on Software Maintenance and Reengineering.*

EI Compendex and *Scopus* were used as the main search engines to look for technical papers published until October 2010. The reason for choosing them is the coverage they provide in the field. For instance, the *Scopus* search engine indexes the vast majority of papers published in the field of Software Engineering, such as, *IEEE, ACM, Cite Seer, Elsevier*, and *Springer*. The *quasi* SLR considered only sources available in the Web, in English, including theoretical papers, proof of concept, and especially experimental studies. The studies should also consider the relationship between software characteristics and metrics for *E-type systems*. Optionally, the articles should present influences between software characteristics, influence and direction of this intensity or rate of influence among the software characteristics.

Each research question consists of four searches related to the four development process stages. Thus, 60 different search strings were executed regarding questions $Q_{i,i=[1..15]}$. The structure of the search strings e follows a pattern, considering the development stage and the corresponding software characteristics. Therefore, the search strings have many similar keywords which can affect the results with respect to the number of duplicate papers.

The execution of all search strings in both search engines returned a total of 6,753 papers, most of them duplicated. It led us to group them by research question. Even among the different questions, there were duplicate papers, as one same software characteristic was present in different research questions and some papers are concerned with several of the analyzed software characteristics. It represents a kind of expected behaviour that we were not able to eliminate. Nevertheless, the use of the JabRef tool (http://jabref.sourceforge.net/) to organize and classify the papers made this task easier.

To build the search strings the following general keywords were used: Software Characteristic, metric, relation, relationship, correlation, dependency, influence, effect, direction, primary study, experimental study, empirical study, intensity, and rate. For instance, (1) represents the search string for Q_1 on coding stage:

(Relationship OR Relation OR Correlation OR Influence OR Dependence OR Effect OR Linkage) AND (size OR LOC OR {lines of code} OR {source lines of code} OR {methods per classes}) AND (complexity OR {Depth of Inheritance per Class} OR {Coupling between Objects} OR {Response for a Class} OR {Lack of Cohesion in Methods} OR {Children per Class} OR {Cyclomatic Complexity per Method}) AND (Codification OR Programming OR Building OR Construction OR Implementation OR Coding) AND ({Software Characteristic} OR {Software Metric} OR {Software Development Project} OR {software project} OR {software measure} OR {software measurement}). **(1)**

An information extraction guide was defined to keep track of the necessary data to answer the research questions and also to support paper assessment. The following data was extracted from the papers: title, author, source, publication date, type of study (experimental, case study, survey, technical report), category (conference or journal), context, applied technologies, stages of development involved, measures or software characteristics used, and description of influence (direction and rate or intensity) amongst the software characteristics analyzed.

A set of inclusion and exclusion criteria was defined for selecting the studies. The criteria consider papers written in English, available in the Internet and presenting studies on the relationship between software characteristics or correspondent metrics. Moreover, they should consider object-oriented software systems

defined as *E-Type Systems* [9], and preferably present studies on the direction and rate or intensity of the relationship amongst software characteristics.

The process to select the studies was done by two experienced researchers and consisted of two analyses. The first one was guided by the reading of the title, abstract, and conclusions. The second and more detailed analysis consisted of a full reading. On both analyses, the inclusion and exclusion criteria of studies were applied.

With the removal of the duplicate papers, a total 884 papers remained that cleared the first analysis process [4]. After this, there remained 98 papers which cleared a second and more detailed analysis. Based on the results it was possible to choose 27 papers able for inclusion as possible evidence to support our model. Therefore, these papers passed through the information extraction process. The results and the complete definition of this process can be found in [16].

After information extraction, an assessment of the papers was performed. The assessment criteria applied to the papers selected were defined to identify whether methods or procedures were applied in order to provide higher quality study results. Eight items were defined as criteria for assessing the papers and they are related to the data analysis used in the study (identification and treatment of outliers), the application of methods of sensitivity or residual analysis, the use of appropriate statistical methods, the presentation of information on the projects used, methods of comparison applied, the accuracy of results and presentation of the methods used to achieve the results. Amongst the criteria used, those related to data treatment and applied statistical methods were considered as more important [16]. So, it resulted in 22 papers that could be accepted (5 papers were excluded). Table 3 shows the amount of evidence found for each pair of characteristics.

Table 3. Relation between research questions and evidence

Research Question	Evidence from paper
Q_1	[17] [18] [19] [20] [21]
Q_2	[18] [19] [22] [23] [24] [25] [26] [27] [28]
Q_3	[1] [21] [29] [30] [31]
Q_4	[32]
Q_5	[29] [30] [33] [34] [35] [36] [37] [38] [39] [40]
Q_6	[36] [41]
Q_7	[42]
Q_8	Not found
Q_9	[18] [30] [31] [43] [44] [45] [46] [47] [48] [49] [50] [50]
Q_{10}	[33] [34] [36]
Q_{11}	[24] [50]
Q_{12}	[18] [23] [30] [37] [52] [53] [54] [55]
Q_{13}	[56]
Q_{14}	[57]
Q_{15}	[57]

Each paper was evaluated according to the questions shown in Table 4, assigning a score per article, which was used to prioritize evidence to be considered in the model. Some questions produced few evidences, especially those related to software characteristics related to the process, such as reliability, where a few studies were found in the technical literature. Further details on the protocol for the *quasi* SLR used in this work and the study implementation are available in [16].

Table 4. Criteria for Paper Assessment

Questions
1. Is the data analysis appropriate? (Yes/No)
1.1. Was the data investigated to identify outliers and to assess distributional properties before analysis?
1.2. Was the result of the investigation used appropriately to transform the data and select appropriated data points?
2. Did the studies carry out a sensitivity or residual analysis? (Yes/No)
2.1. Were the resulting estimation models subject to sensitivity or residual analysis?
2.2. Was the result of the sensitivity or residual analysis used to remove abnormal data points if necessary?
3. Were accuracy statistics based on the raw data scale?
4. How good was the study comparison method?
5. Is it clear what projects were used to construct each model?
6. Is it clear how accuracy was measured?
7. Is it clear what cross-validation method was used?
8. Were all model construction methods fully defined (tools and methods used)?

3.2. Visualizing and Supporting Model Use

Based on evidence, a Cause and Effect Diagram [58] describing the model was built. It represents the basis of an infrastructure to allow the observation of software evolution [4]. This model is shown in Fig. 1. To support it, 25 evidence items from technical literature have been catalogued and evaluated $\{Q_1..Q_7, Q_9, Q_{10}..Q_{15}\}$. No evidence has been found to support $\{Q_8\}$, therefore there is no marked relationship between *Periodicity* and *Maintainability* in Fig. 1. All of the used evidence supports the existence of a correlation amongst the software characteristics. These correlations were seen through experimental studies using historical data on software projects, as reported in their original papers (references in Table 3). A similar approach has been used by [59] to create a model to support a project manager to trade-off the resources used against the outputs in a software project.

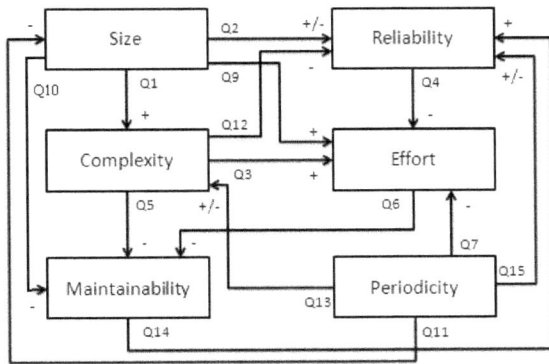

Figure 1. Cause and Effect Diagram from [4]

The use of a Cause and Effect Diagram does not imply causality in the presented relationships. According to its notation [58], a connection between two variables (software characteristics) indicates the existence of a relationship (possible influence) between them. The connection arrow indicates the relationship direction between software characteristics. The signals associated with each relationship indicate the suggested software characteristic trend (increasing +, decreasing -, increasing/decreasing depending on a threshold +/-) in that relationship. The signals were also obtained from the evidence found by reviewing each pair of software characteristics. For example, complexity positively influences effort, that is, the higher the complexity (e.g., measured by cyclomatic complexity) the greater the effort will be to develop or maintain the system. This way, the model allows observations of software evolution done over different software development stages, with the use of appropriate metrics for each stage. The observation will be done separately for each stage, that is, for a given stage only the same chosen metrics related to it must be consistently collected to allow consistency and contextualization.

Based on these principles, an environment was built comprising a set of activities for its operation. Initially, the software engineer collects data (representing the software characteristic measurements) from a real system in which one would like to observe the evolution process. It is important that the measurements are consistent and similar for a given system, keeping the same unit for a particular software characteristic. This information can be used to generate the equations used in the simulation with linear regression. It is appropriate to use linear regression, despite the possibility of a greater error margin on the basis of such observations being typically performed using semi-quantitative analysis for the analysis of data, where the trend is the focus, more than the precision of actual values. The generated set of equations can be computed by a tool providing support for dynamic models, such as, for example, System Dynamics, simulating the behaviour of software systems in evolution. Finally, through this tool, we can see the result of the decay process and the simulation software, also indicating the state of each one of the LSE, depending on the trends for behaviour of the software characteristics.

From this perspective, it is possible to perform *in virtuo*[1] and *in silico*[2] experimental studies. *In virtuo* studies are accomplished with the collection of metrics and analysis of the presented software characteristics from the observation of real systems. *In silico* studies are executed from the simulation of metrics and software characteristics behaviour, regarding the different software development process stages. Therefore, an environment has been constructed, as shown in Figure 2.

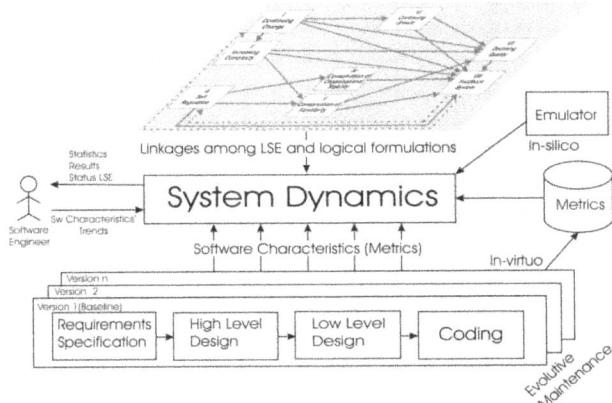

Figure 2. Architecture of the environment

---

1 *In virtuo* experiments: Experiments that involve interaction amongst participants and a computerized model of reality.
2 *In silico* experiments: Studies are marked for both subjects and real world, being described as computer models.

4. MODEL ASSESSMENT

This Section shows the results of an *in silico* study [4] using the model to track software decay. Historical data regarding a Web-based information system was used to extract the measurements for software characteristics used by the model. It represents a large-scale Web-based application controlling the business workflows of research projects, both in financial and administrative aspects. Geographically distributed teams took part in the development using Java and JSF platforms. The development team is stable, with about 12 developers. The development cycle was iterative and incremental, organized according to CMMI level 3 suggestions. Software quality is an ongoing concern, promoting the use of verification, validation, and testing techniques throughout the software development.

To support observation, 13 different system releases were considered. The historical data on these releases was available in version control system repositories, bug tracking services, and effort registration spreadsheets, whose measurements are relevant to the observation of system evolution.

This study analyzed the coding stage. The following measures were considered: *Size* in KLOC; *Periodicity* is the interval in days for delivering a new system release; *Complexity* is represented by the cyclomatic complexity of class methods; *Effort* is the total time spent (in hours) to develop a new release; *Reliability* is the number of defects identified per release; and *Maintainability* is the total time spent to identify, remove, and fix defects. Table 5 shows actual data on the 5 first system releases.

Table 5. Data Collected [4]

Version	1	2	3	4	5
Size	62,183	62,578	62,524	62,537	62,551
Periodicity	0	1	6	2	7
Complexity	11.338	11.407	11.391	11.391	11.392
Effort	6	0.25	30.75	13.75	1
Reliability	1	1	7	2	1
Maintainability	0	0.25	15.75	3.75	1

To increase the simulation process accuracy some statistical analyses were done on the historical data, through graph visualization, analysis of outliers and calculation of the measurements of central tendency, linear regression, and least squares. The standard deviation was cumulatively calculated for each software characteristic in each system release supporting the definition of the smallest number of necessary releases to calibrate the model. An outlier analysis was also done. To observe the trend for each software characteristic, scatter plots were constructed, as shown in Fig. 3, which portrays an increasing trend for *Size*.

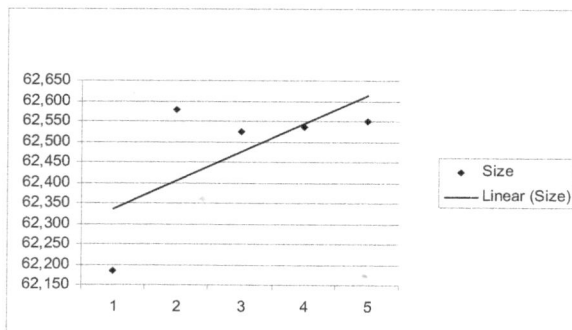

Figure 3. Scatter plot for software characteristic Size

After this, equations (linear regression + least squares method) were generated from historical data for each relationship involving the software characteristics presented in the model. For instance, **(2)** represents the equations for this system. The constants are the regression line slope calculated through linear regression, using the least squares method. The first one was calculated by considering *Size* and *Complexity* and the second used *Periodicity* and *Complexity* measurements:

$Size = 0.10 * Periodicity;$
$Complexity = 0.33 * Size + 0.05 * Periodicity;$
$Maintainability = 13.12 * Complexity + 0.17 * Effort + 3.87 * Size;$
$Reliability = 0.49 * Size - 0.04 * Periodicity + 0.28 * Complexity + 0.13 * Maintainability;$
$Effort = 18.65 * Size + 2.82 * Periodicity + 57.82 * Complexity - 2.01 * Reliability;$ **(2)**

With all equations and based on the Cause and Effect Diagram shown in Fig. 1, a System Dynamics model was built [4], as presented in Fig. 4.

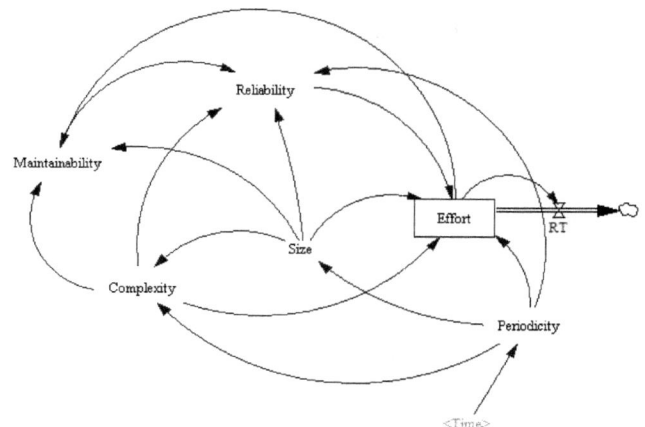

Figure 4. System Dynamics Model [16]

The simulation was mainly performed with the use of the Illium Software Evolution Simulation Tool [4], which uses the Illium Simulation Tool engine [60]. This engine was originally developed to support the simulation of risk analysis in software projects. The Illium engine had been used and evaluated in other studies [61] [62], involving the simulation of dynamic system models. Besides, considering the same System Dynamics model, Illium and an academic version of Vensim PLE [63] present equal results [16], demonstrating that Illium is also a feasible infrastructure to support System Dynamics simulations.

To assess the future behaviour of the evolving system and simulation results, new data was collected over eight new releases (Table 6), representing later versions not previously used to generate the equations.

Table 6. Collected Data from New Versions [4]

Version	1	2	3	4	5	6	7	8
Size	63,990	64,310	64,310	64,370	65,430	65,760	65,960	65,960
Periodicity	14	8	20	7	30	5	16	48
Complexity	11.57	11.63	11.63	11.64	11.85	11.93	11.96	11.96
Effort	4.75	22.50	2.00	29.50	53.50	10.50	3.50	25.75
Reliability	1	4	1	8	8	5	1	5
Maintainability	4.75	2.50	2.00	13.50	6.50	3.50	3.50	3.00

Again, the data was analyzed and scatter plots were constructed to observe the trend of each software characteristic compared with the simulated results. Table 7 shows these trends as observed behaviour, where Expected refers to the observed behaviour of the measures by linear regression, Simulated refers to the behaviour generated by the equations using system dynamics, and Observed is the actual behaviour of the measures collected in the new system releases. Forecast trends for *Size, Periodicity, Complexity, Reliability,* and *Maintainability* were maintained for the new software releases. It is important to emphasize that the purpose of observing the software evolution is to visualize curve trends, from a semi quantitative view, where the curve slope is generated by linear regression, proper for analysis [4]. The grey line in Table 7 highlights the difference amongst expected, simulated, and observed behaviours. Please note that expected results represent the software characteristic trend observed in isolation, as it means only its own historical dataset was used to suggest, based on data behaviour, something that could happen with that software characteristic in future releases.

Table 7. Simulation Results with Original Model [16]

Behaviour	Expected	Simulated	Observed
Size	↑	↑	↑
Periodicity	↑	↑	↑
Complexity	↑	↑	↑
Effort	↓	↑	↑
Reliability	↓	↓	↓
Maintainability	↑	↑	↑

In the first software releases *Effort* showed a downward trend. However, after the simulation process, a reversal in behaviour was seen, with an upward trend, compatible with the actual software characteristic behaviour, which can be seen in the new collected versions. All other behaviours were observed to be consistent with this information system behaviour [4].

These results may assist in decision-making as related to managing the development and maintenance of software processes. It is important to see that the results presented are restricted to the data set used in the experiment and it is not possible to generalize the results to other systems. However, the model is generic enough to be tried in other software projects.

In other words, the simulated behaviour for all characteristics corresponded to actual system behaviour. The results indicate that, for this system, the model of software evolution can be used to support the software development management, something that effectively happened in this industrial project.

5. CONCLUSIONS

This paper presented a model to support *in silico* studies of software evolution. The execution of a *quasi* SLR including 15 primary research questions contributed to identify 34 evidence items in the technical literature concerned with the existence of software characteristics relationships. The increased coverage given by the *quasi* SLR allowed strengthening the conceptual validity of the software evolution observation model, thereby reducing the threats to model construct validity.

The use of the model to support the simulation of a real software project was shown to be feasible and correct. Therefore, the managers of such project started to make use of the model to support their decision-making activities.

The results of the *quasi* SLR lead us to consider the relevance of each one of the relationships presented in the model, as there was no additional evidence to reaffirm all the relationships. Therefore, we would like to suggest, as future work, the examination of the existence of a minimum set of relationships to simplify the model, whilst keeping or increasing the quality of the results obtained from simulations based on it.

The model was built based on the analysis of 2-way interactions amongst the characteristics. Analyses of higher order interactions also represent an interesting future work to improve model confidence.

The execution of additional experiments with other data sets was not possible at this time due our difficulty in finding different data sets with available information (measures) for all the software characteristics presented in the model. This reduces the chance of generalizing the results, which can affect the external validity of the study.

The next steps of our research are concerned with using the model in performing additional *in virtuo* and *in silico* studies to evaluate the model's practical impact on new software projects.

6. ACKNOWLEDGMENTS

The authors would like to thank CNPq and CAPES for their supporting this research. We are also indebted to Profs. Barbara Kitchenham for her support to the initial discussions regarding this research, Márcio Barros for his System Dynamics support and Msc. Breno França for suggestions regarding this paper.

7. REFERENCES

[1] Bocco, M., Moody, D. and Piattini, M. 2005. Assessing the capability of internal metrics as early indicators of maintenance effort through experimentation. *Research Articles. J. Softw. Maint. Evol.* 17, 3 (May 2005), 225-246. DOI=10.1002/smr.v17:3 http://dx.doi.org/10.1002/smr.v17:3.

[2] Lehman, M. M. and Ramil, F. F. 2002. Software Evolution and Software Evolution Processes. *Ann. Softw. Eng.* 14, 1-4 (December 2002), 275-309. DOI=http://dx.doi.org/10.1023/A:102055752590.

[3] Madhavji, N. H., Ramil, J. F., and Perry, D. 2006. Software Evolution and Feedback: Theory and Practice. *John Wiley & Sons.*

[4] Araújo, M. A. 2009. *Um Modelo para Observação da Evolução de Software.* Doctoral Thesis. Federal University of Rio de Janeiro.

[5] Smith, N., Ramil, J.F., 2002. Qualitative Simulation of Software of Evolution Process. In: *WESS'02 Eighth Workshop on Empirical Studies of Software Maintenance.*

[6] Stopford, B., Counsell, S., 2008. A Framework for the Simulation of Structural Software Evolution. *ACM Transactions on Modeling and Computer Simulation*, Vol. 18, No. 4, Article 17.

[7] Lehman, M. M. 1980. Programs, Life Cycle and the Laws of Software Evolution. *Proc. IEEE Special Issue on Software Engineering*, vol. 68, no. 9, pp. 1060 -1076.

[8] Araújo, M. A. P., Travassos, G. H. 2008. A System Dynamics Model based on Cause and Effect Diagram to Observe Object-Oriented Software Decay. *Technical Report ES-720/08*, COPPE/UFRJ.

[9] Lehman, M. M. and Ramil, F. F. 2003. Software evolution: background, theory, practice. *Information Processing Letters*, v. 88 n. 1-2, p. 33-44, 2003. DOI= http://dx.doi.org/10.1016/S0020-0190(03)00382-X.

[10] Araújo, M. A. P., Travassos, G. H.. Kitchenham, Barbara. 2006. Evolutive Maintenance: Observing Object-Oriented Software Decay. *Technical Report*, COPPE/UFRJ.

[11] ISO 9126-1, 1997, International Standard. Information Technology – Software Quality Characteristics and Metrics – Part 1: Quality Characteristics and Sub-Characteristics.

[12] Pai M., McCulloch M., Gorman J., Pai N., Enanoria W., Kennedy G. 2004. Systematic reviews and meta-analysis: an illustrated step-by-step guide. *Natl Med J India*. 2004;17:86–95.

[13] Travassos, G. H., Santos, P. S. M., Mian, P., Dias Neto, A. C., Biolchini, J. 2008. An Environment to Support Large Scale Experimentation in Software Engineering. *In: Proc. of the IEEE International Conference on Engineering of Complex Computer Systems*, ICECCS 2008, p. 193-202.

[14] Kitchenham, B.A., Charters, S. 2007. Guidelines for Performing Systematic Literature Reviews in Software Engineering. *Technical Report EBSE-2007-01*.

[15] Travassos, G.H., Shull, F., Carver, J. 2001. Working with UML: A Software Design Process Based on Inspections for the Unified Modeling Language. *Advances in Computers*, San Diego, v.54, n.1, p.35 - 97.

[16] Monteiro, V. F. 2011. Infraestrutura Computacional para Observação de Evolução de Software. Master Thesis. *Federal University of Rio de Janeiro*.

[17] Aggarwal, K., Singh, Y., Kaur, A. and Malhotra, R. 2006. Empirical Study of Object-Oriented Metrics, in *Journal of Object Technology*, vol. 5. no. 8, November-December 2006, pp. 149-173.

[18] Heijstek, W., Chaudro, M.R.V. 2009. Empirical Investigations of Model Size, Complexity and Effort in a Large Scale, Distributed Model Driven Development Process. Software Engineering and Advanced Applications, 2009. SEAA '09. *35th Euromicro Conference on 2009* , Page(s): 113 – 120. DOI=http://dx.doi.org/10.1109/SEAA.2009.70.

[19] Basili, V.R., Perricone, B.T., 1984. Software Errors and Complexity: An Empirical Investigation. *Communications of the ACM*, 27, 42 – 52.

[20] Ebert, C., 1996. Evaluation and application of complexity-based criticality models. In: *International Software Metrics Symposium, Proceedings*, 174 – 184.

[21] Misic, V.B., Tesic, D.N., 1998. Estimation of effort and complexity: An object-oriented case study. *Journal of Systems and Software*, 41, 133 – 143.

[22] El Emam, K. , Benlarbi, S., Goel, N., Melo, W., Lounis, H., Rai, S. N. 2002. The Optimal Class Size for Object-Oriented Software. *IEEE Transactions on Software Engineering*, v.28 n.5, p.494-509, May 2002. DOI= http://dx.doi.org/10.1109/TSE.2002.1000452.

[23] English, M. Exton, C., Rigon, I., Cleary, B. 2009. Fault detection and prediction in an open-source software project. *Proceedings of the 5th International Conference on Predictor Models in Software Engineering*, May 18-19, 2009, Vancouver, British Columbia, Canada. DOI= http://doi.acm.org/10.1145/1540438.1540462.

[24] Fenton, N.E., Neil, M., Marsh, W., Hearty, P., Radlinski, L., Krause, P. 2008. On the effectiveness of early life cycle defect prediction with Bayesian Nets. In *Proceedings of Empirical Software Engineering*. 2008, 499-537. DOI= http://dx.doi.org/10.1007/s10664-008-9072-x.

[25] Leszak, M. 2005. Software Defect Analysis of a Multi-release Telecommunications System *In Product Focused Software Process Improvement* (2005), pp. 98-114.

[26] Zhang, H. 2009. An investigation of the relationships between lines of code and defects. ICSM, pp.274-283, 2009 *IEEE International Conference on Software Maintenance*, 2009.

[27] Selby, R.W., 1990. Empirically based analysis of failures in software systems. *IEEE Transactions on Reliability*, 39, 444 – 454.

[28] Malaiya, Y.K., Denton, J., 2000. Module size distribution and defect density. In: *Proceedings of the International Symposium on Software Reliability Engineering, ISSRE*, 62 – 71.

[29] Darcy, D., Kemerer, C., Slaughter, S., and Tomayko, J. 2005. The Structural Complexity of Software: An Experimental Test. *IEEE Trans. Softw. Eng.* 31, 11 (November 2005), 982-995. DOI=http://dx.doi.org/10.1109/TSE.2005.130.

[30] Kozlov D., Koskinen J., Sakkinen M., Markkula J. 2008. Assessing maintainability change over multiple software releases. In *Journal of Software Maintenance and Evolution: Research and Practice* 2008; 20:31–58. DOI=http://dx.doi.org/10.1002/smr.v20:1.

[31] Sentas, P., Angelis, L., Stamelos, I. 2008. A Statistical Framework for Analyzing the Duration of Software Projects. *Empirical Software Engineering (Springer)*. 13:147–184. DOI=http://dx.doi.org/10.1007/s10664-007-9051-7.

[32] Bianchi, A. Caivano. D., Lanubile, F., Visaggio, G., 2001. Evaluating Software Degradation through Entropy. *IEEE*.

[33] Canfora, G., García, F., Piattini, M., Ruiz, F., Visaggio, C. A. 2005. A family of experiments to validate metrics for software process models. *Journal of Systems and Software*, v.77 n.2, p.113-129, August 2005. DOI=http://dx.doi.org/10.1016/j.jss.2004.11.007.

[34] Cruz-Lemus, J., Genero, M., and Piattini, M. 2007. Using Controlled Experiments for Validating UML Statechart Diagrams Measures. In *Software Process and Product Measurement*. Lecture Notes In Computer Science, Vol. 4895. Springer-Verlag, Berlin, Heidelberg 129-138. DOI=http://dx.doi.org/10.1007/978-3-540-85553-8_11.

[35] Poels, G., Dedene, G. 2001. Evaluating the Effect of Inheritance on the Modifiability of Object-Oriented Business Domain Models. In *Proceedings of the Fifth European Conference on Software Maintenance and Reengineering* (CSMR '01). IEEE Computer Society, Washington, DC, USA.

[36] Riaz, M.; Mendes, E.; Tempero, E. A. 2009. Systematic Review of Software Maintainability Prediction and Metrics. *Proceeding ESEM '09 Proceedings of the* 2009 3rd International Symposium on Empirical Software Engineering and Measurement. IEEE Computer Society, Washington,

DC, USA, 367-377. DOI= http://dx.doi.org/10.1109/ESEM.2009.5314233.

[37] McCabe, T. J., 1976. A Complexity Measure. *IEEE Transactions on Software Engineering.*

[38] Lindell, J., Hagglund, M., 2004. Maintainability Metrics for Object Oriented Systems. *Software Quality.*

[39] Koten, C., Gray, 2005. An Application of Bayesian Network for Predicting Object Oriented Software Maintainability. *The Information Science Discussion Paper Series.* University of Otago.

[40] Aggarwall, K.K., Singh, Y., Kaur, A., Malhotra, R., 2006. Application of Artificial Neural Network for Predicting Maintainability using Object Oriented Metrics. *Transactions on Engineering, Computing and Technology Volume.*

[41] Nikora, A. P., Munson, J.C., 2003. Developing Fault Predictors for Evolving Software Systems. In: *Proc. Ninth International Software Metrics Symposium – METRICS'03.*

[42] Mockus, A. Weiss, D., Zhang, P., 2003, Understanding and Predicting Effort in Software Projects. In: *ICSE'03.*

[43] Dolado JJ. 2001. On the problem of the software cost function. *Inform Software Technology* 2001;43:61-72. DOI= http://dx.doi.org/10.1016/j.advengsoft.2004.10.001.

[44] Ferrucci, F., Gravino, C., and Di Martino, S.. 2008. A Case Study Using Web Objects and COSMIC for Effort Estimation of Web Applications. In *Proceedings of the 2008 34th Euromicro Conference Software Engineering and Advanced Applications* (SEAA '08). IEEE Computer Society, Washington, DC, USA, 441-448. DOI=http://dx.doi.org/10.1109/SEAA.2008.

[45] Tsunoda , M., Monden , A., Yadohisa, H., Kikuchi, N., Matsumoto, K. 2009. Software development productivity of Japanese enterprise applications. In *Information Technology and Management*, v.10 n.4, p.193-205, *December* 2009. DOI= http://dx.doi.org/10.1007/s10799-009-0050-9.

[46] Zhang, J. 2008. The Establishment and Application of Effort Regression Equation. In *Proceedings of the 2008 International Conference on Computer Science and Software Engineering - Volume 02* (CSSE '08), Vol. 2. IEEE Computer Society, Washington, DC, USA, 11-14. DOI=http://dx.doi.org/10.1109/CSSE.2008.726.

[47] Waltson, C. E., Felix, C.P., 1977, A Method of Programming Measurement and Estimation. *IBM System Journal.*

[48] Boehm, B., 1981. Software Engineering Economics. *Prentice Hall.*

[49] Bailey, J. W., Basili, V., 1981. A Meta-Model for Software Development Resource Expenditures. *IEEE.*

[50] Boehm, B., 1984. Software Engineering Economics. *IEEE Transactions on Software Engineering.*

[51] Premraj, R., Shepperd, M., Kitchenham, B., Forselius, P., 2005. An Empirical Analysis of Software Productivity over Time. In: *11th IEEE International Software Metrics Symposium (METRICS 2005).*

[52] Aggarwal, K., Singh, Y., Kaur, A. and Malhotra, R. 2007. Investigating effect of design metrics on fault proneness in object-oriented systems. *Journal of Object Technology.* v6 i10. 127-141.

[53] Ferneley, E. H. 1999. Design metrics as an aid to software maintenance: an empirical study. *Journal of Software Maintenance* 11, 1 (January 1999), 55-72. DOI= http://dx.doi.org/10.1002/(SICI)1096-908X(199901/02)11:1%3C55::AID-SMR184%3E3.3.CO;2-F.

[54] Schneidewind, N., Hinchey, M. 2009. A Complexity Reliability Model. In *Proceedings of the 20th IEEE international conference on software reliability engineering* (ISSRE'09) on. page(s): 1 – 10.

[55] Basili, V., Briand, L., Melo, W., 1995. A Validation of Object Oriented Design Metrics as Quality Indicators, *Technical Report*, Univ. of Maryland, Dep. of Computer Science, College Park, MD, 20742 USA.

[56] Munson, J.C., 1996. Software faults, software failures and software reliability modeling. *Information and Software Tecnology.*

[57] Schneidewind, N., 1999. Measuring and Evaluating Maintenance Process using Reliability, Risk and Test Metrics. *IEEE Transactions on Software Engineering.*

[58] Forrester, J. W., Industrial Dynamics. *The M.I.T. Press*, Cambridge, Mass., 1961.

[59] Fenton, N., Marsh, W., Neil, M., Cates, P., Forey, S., Tailor, M., 2004. Making Resource Decisions for Software Projects, icse, pp.397-406, *26th International Conference on Software Engineering (ICSE'04).*

[60] Barros, M.O., Werner, C. M. L., Travassos, G.H. 2000. *Illium: Uma ferramenta de Simulação de Modelos Dinâmicos de Projetos de Software*, In XIV Simpósio Brasileiro de Engenharia de Software, Caderno de Ferramentas, p. 355-358, João Pessoa, PB, Brasil.

[61] Barros, M. O., Werner, C. M. L., Travassos, G. H. . A System Dynamics Metamodel for Software Process Modeling. *Software Process Improvement and Practice*, 2003.

[62] Barros, M. O., Werner, C. M. L., Travassos, G. H. 2004. Supporting Risk Analysis on Software Projects. *Journal of Systems and Software.*

[63] Vensim PLE 2010. Ventana Systems, Inc. Avaiable at: <http://www.vensim.com>.

On the Role of Composition Code Properties on Evolving Programs

Francisco Dantas[1], Alessandro Garcia[1] and Jon Whittle[2]
[1]Opus Research Group – Software Engineering Lab, Informatics Department, PUC-Rio, Brazil
[2]School of Computing and Communications, Lancaster University –Lancaster, United Kingdom
{fneto,afgarcia}@inf.puc-rio.br, whittle@comp.lancs.ac.uk

ABSTRACT

Composition code defines the binding of two or more modules in a program. Post object-oriented programming techniques are increasingly providing expressive mechanisms to enable the flexible definition of composition code. Such composition mechanisms are intended to support programmers in factoring out the complexity of a program and facilitate its evolution. However, the properties of composition code might introduce new flavours of complexity, and in turn cause side effects on program evolvability. Unfortunately, the role of composition code properties on evolving software systems is not yet well understood. This gap is mostly due to the lack of a measurement framework to characterize and quantify composition code. Existing metrics suites are focused on quantifying properties of programs and their modules only. Therefore, programmers are not able to analyse and understand the impact of particular composition properties on program evolvability. This paper presents a framework aimed at characterizing and computing composition code properties. The proposed framework consists of terminology and a metrics suite, which can be used in programs structured with diverse sets of composition mechanisms. We also empirically studied the role of the measurement framework through 22 versions of 4 software projects. Our evaluation revealed that the measurement framework provided consistent indicators of program instabilities observed in history of the evolving compositions.

Categories and Subject Descriptors

D.2.8 [**Software Engineering**]: Metrics; K.6.3 [**Software Management**]: Software Maintenance.

Keywords

Composition mechanisms, software metrics, software stability, program evolution.

1. INTRODUCTION

The demand for incremental software development has been increasing over the last decades [1]. As a result of this demand, it is often claimed that expressive programming mechanisms are required to support agile realization of software changes [2][3]. In

fact, post object-oriented programming techniques (e.g. [3][4][5][6][7]) are increasingly providing composition mechanisms to enable the flexible definition of module composition. They are moving away from supporting only simple composition mechanisms, such as message passing [8]. Classical examples of these techniques range from aspect-oriented programming [3] and its dialects [6] to feature-oriented programming [4], and many others [5][7].

Composition code consists of statements used to define the binding of two or more modules in a program. Composition mechanisms are used to define this code, and examples include pointcut-advice [3] and virtual classes [4]. These mechanisms recognizably play a key role in factoring out the complexity of individual modules [9][10]. Therefore, they also promote a shift in the structure of programs: while complexity is factored out of software modules, the derived composition code is much more complex [32]. The use of advanced composition mechanisms implies that: (i) multiple modules are involved in the composition code, (ii) more effort is now required to structure the composition code, and (iii) the structure or behaviour of modules are potentially extended, merged or replaced by elements of other modules [9][10]. Accordingly, programmers have now a new challenge: to devote a large extent of their time to evolve and manage the complexity of composition code [11].

Unfortunately, the effects of composition code structure on evolving programs are not well understood. This misunderstanding is mainly due to a lack of measurement frameworks to quantify composition code properties. Existing frameworks [12][14][15][20] and metrics suite [13] are focused on quantifying properties of programs and their modules only. Some researchers have recently proposed metrics for programs structured with advanced composition mechanisms. However, they are only intended to measure the properties of program modules, such as their coupling and cohesion [9][17][18][31]. As a result, there is not even an understanding about basic characteristics comprising composition code. Without this knowledge, it is not possible to define a metrics suite intended to compute composition code properties. It is not possible either to study their impact on program evolvability.

This paper presents a framework that encompasses basic terminology (Section 2) and a metrics suite (Section 3) for composition code. It is not the intention of our framework to capture all possible properties of composition code; instead, it focuses on three significantly-different dimensions of composition code complexity. We studied the role of the measurement framework to support stability analysis of 22 versions pertaining to 4 software projects (Section 4). The programs were structured with two different programming techniques: aspect-oriented programming and feature-oriented programming. These techniques were chosen as they support a wide variety of composition mechanisms. They enable us to understand the impact of composition code on program evolvability in different contexts.

Our study results revealed that certain composition properties are often detrimental to program stability (Section 5). In particular, our investigation has shown that specific composition metrics were consistent indicators of software instabilities along the analysed project histories. For instance, measures of composition scope were the most strongly correlated with program instability in all the cases. They even outperformed coupling measures, classical indicators of software evolvability in object-oriented programs [19][20]. We also compare our work with related work in Section 6. Threats to validity are discussed in Section 7 and finally, conclusions are presented in Section 8.

2. TERMINOLOGY AND COMPOSITION CODE PROPERTIES

The proposed framework consists of basic concepts, presented in this section, and a metrics suite (Section 3) for composition code. First, we present the basic terminology (Section 2.1) to describe key properties of composition code (Section 2.2) in a consistent manner. The examples provided in this section are based on the CaesarJ [21] (FOP) programming language notation. These languages were chosen because they support a variety of composition mechanisms.

2.1 Terminology

We seek to define a terminology that is, as much as possible, language independent and extensible. We have chosen set theory to formalize our terminology because both it has been largely used in other works for the definition of metrics [13][14] and it has an expressive power that allow us to capture the essence of each composition property. A basic set of concepts related to composition code is presented in Figure 1. It defines the relationships between different components of a program, such as module and programs, and the composition properties.

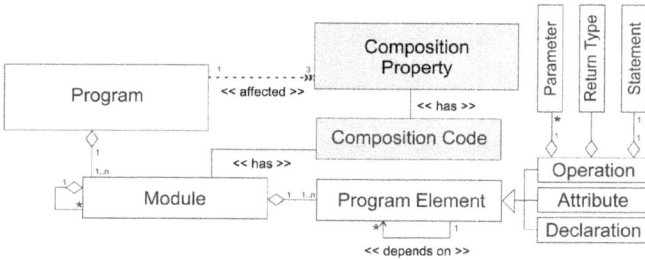

Figure 1. Composition Code Measurement: Basic Terminology

A Running Example. For illustration purposes, Figure 2 illustrates a program in the CaesarJ language. We selected this example as CaesarJ[1] offers a rich set of composition mechanisms; it also supports both aspect-oriented programming (AOP) and feature-oriented programming (FOP). This program consists of a set of modules: classes (E1 to E5 and B1 to B4), aspects A, A1 to A3, interface (I) and virtual classes (V1 to V6). Each module contains a set of program elements. A program element is a sequence of statements. There exist three types of program

---

[1] CaesarJ supports both FOP and AOP composition mechanisms. However, in this evaluation we are taking into consideration only its feature-oriented mechanisms.

elements: attributes, operations and declarations. For instance, methods and advices are classified as operations in CaesarJ; the same applies to AOP-specific languages, such as AspectJ [22]. Pointcut expressions, intertype declarations and mixin composition expressions are classified as declarations.

A *pointcut* selects well-defined points (*joinpoints*) of the program flow that should be extended by pieces of code called *advice*. *Aspect inheritance* provides a simple mechanism of pointcut overriding and advice inheritance. To use inheritance between aspects it is required to define an *abstract aspect*, with one or more abstract pointcuts, and with advice on the pointcut. *Pointcuts-advice* dynamically affects program flow whereas *intertype declarations* operate statically, at compile-time, affecting a program's modules hierarchy. *Intertypedeclarations* may declare members or change the inheritance relationship between classes. In Figure 2 the aspect A2 introduces the method mB( ) in the module B2. As the aspects A1 and A2 intercept the same point in B2 (method getA()), the order of the interception needs to be specified. The aspect A3, using a mechanism of *declare precedence*, defines such an order: A1 has precedence over A2. Besides, there are also several other composition mechanisms to implement FOP concepts such as virtual classes, mixin composition and wrappers. *Virtual classes* are inner classes of another outer class. They behave like virtual methods and thus can be overridden in a subclass of the outer class. In Figure 2, the class E4 has an inner class V1, which overrides V1 in E1 by inheritance relationship. Thus, in CaesarJ, a module can be created by composing several CaesarJ classes using simple and multiple inheritance mechanisms.

The basic concepts of our framework (Figure 1) are formalized through the definitions 1 to 4 and illustrated using the example presented in Figure 2.

DEFINITION 1 (MODULE AND PROGRAM ELEMENT). *A module M is a sequence of program elements, E_M. A program element can be an attribute, an operation or any other form of declaration. Let Att_M be the set of attributes of M, Op_M be the set of operations of M and Dec_M be the set of declarations of M, $E_M := Att_M \cup Op_M \cup Dec_M$.*

By means of composition mechanisms, program elements supported by distinct programming languages can be combined, so that they can work together. Taking in consideration the example illustrated in Figure 2, we can highlight the following composition mechanisms: *pointcut in A1, intertype-declaration in A2, declare precedence in A3* and *virtual classes in E1, E2, E3, E4 and E5.*

DEFINITION 2 (COMPOSITION MECHANISM). *Given two languages, L_1 and L_2, a composition mechanism is a means to combine one or more program elements implemented in either L_1 or L_2.*

A program can be made up of a set of modules from L_1 and L_2, which are combined by means of composition mechanisms. L_1 and L_2 are sets of constructs that are either the same or different depending on the programming language at hand. For instance, L_1 and L_2 are different in most of the AOP languages, such as CaesarJ, AspectJ and its dialects. As far as AspectJ is concerned, L_1 is considered to be formed by Java constructs, used to define the classes; whereas L_2 comprises the set of constructs to define aspects.

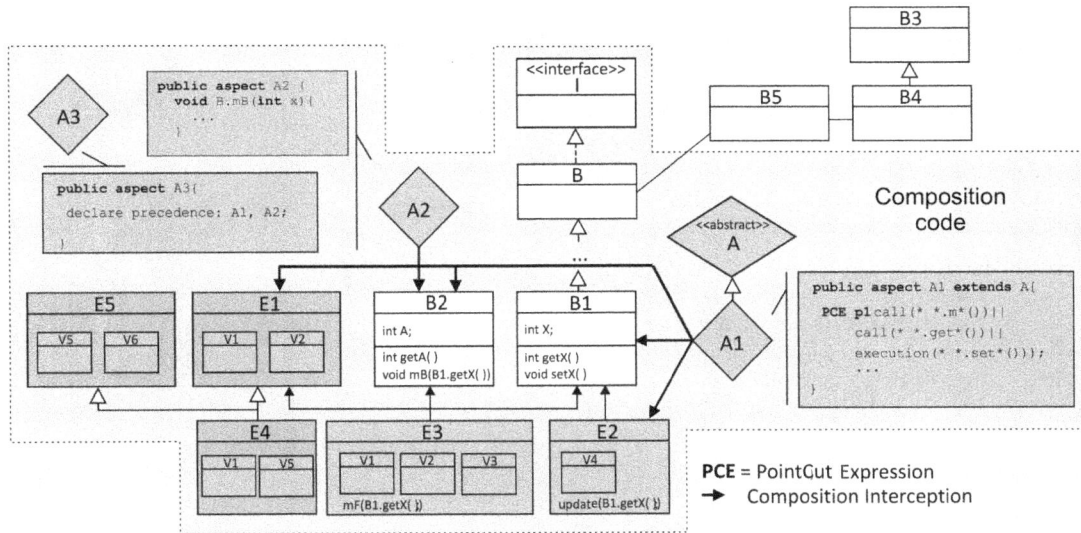

Figure 2. Program in CaesarJ

In subject-oriented programming languages, such as Hyper/J [23], L_1 and L_2 are the same language, i.e. Java; the difference from Java resides on the additional set of composition mechanisms supported by Hyper/J. The code implemented by the use of composition mechanisms is called composition code. In Figure 2, the composition code is made up by the modules in the light grey area.

DEFINITION 3 (PROGRAM AND COMPOSITION CODE). *A program P consists of a set of modules, M. There exist two subsets of modules: M_b, the set of modules of L_1 and M_e, the set of modules of L_2 where $M:=M_b \cup M_e$. A composition, Com, is a set of modules $M_{com}:= M_{cb} \cup M_{ce}$, where $M_{cb} \subset M_b$, $M_{ce} \subset M_e$, $M_{cb} \neq \emptyset$ and $M_{ce} \neq \emptyset$.*

Program elements, which belong to the composition code, depend between them. A composition dependency is an ordered pair of program elements which defines either a direct or indirect relationship between the elements.

DEFINITION 4 (COMPOSITION DEPENDENCY). *A composition dependency, D_{ij}, between two program elements e_i and e_j is defined as a 4-tuple (e_i, e_j, m_i, m_j), where $e_i \square E_{mi} \square e_j \square E_{mj}$. D_{ij} is considered indirect when there is a relationship between e_i and e_j characterizing a transitive closure of D_{ij}. On the other hand, D_{ij} is considered direct when there is direct relationship between e_i and e_j.*

In Figure 2 the composition dependencies are illustrated by the composition interceptions. The dependency between the pointcut p1 (aspect A1) and the method setX() (class B1) is an example of direct dependency as this relationship is declared in the implementation of A1 (* *.set*()). An example of indirect dependency is illustrated between E2 and E3. The method update(B1.getX()) in E2 updates the value of the attribute X in B1. There is no reference to E3 in E2. However, as E3 uses the attribute X, there is an indirect dependency between E2 and E3.

2.2 Composition Properties

Composition code entails new dimensions of complexity in a program. The essence of composition code relies on the understanding of its properties. Therefore, programs are built to have certain properties, which may exert an impact on the quality

attributes, such as software stability (Section 5). Composition code is characterized by at least three basic properties: *diversity, scope* and *volatility*. The realization of such properties on the source code is discussed using the example provided in Figure 2. In order to make our discussion more concrete, we used CaesarJ as example; i.e. L_1 and L_2, are respectively instantiated by Java and the set of CaesarJ constructs to support both AOP and FOP.

Composition Diversity. Composition code encompasses a significant diversity of modules. The term *diversity* refers to the amount and type of different modules that comprise the composition code. The example of Figure 2 illustrates how diverse the composition code can be. In this example, there are different modules supported by L_2 (e.g. virtual classes and aspects) and L_1 (e.g. Java classes and interfaces) used to realize the composition.

Taking into consideration the example illustrated in Figure 2, the composition diversity is characterized by the dependency among different modules: three concrete aspects (A1, A2 and A3), one abstract aspect (A), six virtual classes (V1 to V6) and one interface (I). In order to compose different modules the programmers need to have in their mind the different forms of modules dependency. For instance, direct dependencies are explicit in the code of Java classes and thus their execution order is pre-defined. On the other hand, the aspects can be dependent among them with no explicit reference. This form of dependency among different modules requires a special treatment. Considering the example in Figure2, a precedence mechanism (aspect A3) needs to be defined as the aspects A1 and A2 share a same declaration (*joinpoints*). The aspect A3 is in charge of defining the correct interception order of A1 and A2 in B2. An extensive reasoning about the composition code is inevitable in these cases in order to manage the composition diversity. For instance, the pointcut declaration (PCE call (* .m*()) intercepts all the calls to methods of Java classes whose name begins with m (*.m*()). These calls are scattered through many modules of the program (e.g. B2 and E3). Thus, programmers need to analyse the names of all the methods in order to confirm that the composition was correctly implemented and no wrong method has been picked out. In other words, this means to avoid that implicit rules of the composition (e.g. the set of modules that belong to the composition) are broken.

Composition Scope. Composition code is a set of modules implemented by two programming languages, L_1 and L_2 respectively. In this context, the term scope refers to the extent of the enclosing context where the program elements of L_2 are associated with. In the example illustrated in Figure 2, the composition scope is defined from the modules supported by L_2

In order to understand the scope of the composition in Figure 2, it is essential to understand that the operation `update(B1.getX())` in E2 updates the value of the attribute x declared in module B1. However, the original value of x is used by E3 (operation `mF(..)`). Thus, the update of x by D cannot be ignored by E3 as these two modules depend on the manipulation of the correct value of x. Then, E2 explicitly impacts on B1 and also implicitly impacts on E3. For this reason, we can say that the global scope of E2 is B1 and E3. In addition, there can exist a long dependency chain of some modules connected with the composition code. For instance, the dependency of E2 with B1 is an example of long dependency chain and such a dependency generates a scenario that may affect the quality of the composition code. Changes on the top of the chain tend to be propagated in the other modules.

Composition Volatility. Composition dependencies are established in order to prepare the existing program code; otherwise, the composition of modules from L_1 and L_2, cannot work properly. The term volatility refers to the extent that these dependencies are broken when a single change is made in the composition code.

In order to analyse the composition volatility in Figure 2, it is important to take into consideration the existing composition dependencies. For instance, the use of wildcards (star notation) in A1 creates dependencies among A1 and the Java classes that implement methods get and set. The aspect A1 uses wildcards aiming at intercepting all the methods that begin with m (`* *.m*()`) and get (`* *.get*()`). The PCE is based on the syntax of the source code and during the evolution process the syntax can be changed. In other words, names of methods can change and new methods that begin with m or get can be added. As a consequence, when the application tends to evolve, the PCE needs to be modified.

3. THE MEASUREMENT SUITE

This section presents a metrics suite that relies on the terminology presented in Section 2.1. The metrics are intended to quantify the composition code properties (Section 2.2). The goal is also to provide support for studying and assessing the impact of composition measures on quality attributes of evolving programs, such as software stability (Figure 3). The composition code is the input to the measurement process, which is in turn quantified through the set of composition metrics.

We defined four metrics for composition code, namely: Local Impact (LoI), Global Impact (GoI), Composition Volatility (CoV), and Depth of Dependency Chain (DDC). An overview of these metrics is presented in Table 1. It provides brief definitions of the metrics and their association with the composition properties (Section 2.2), which they are intended to measure. Each metric is described in terms of: (i) an informal definition (Table 1), (ii) a

formal definition based on the terminology presented in Section 2.1, and (iii) a simple example.

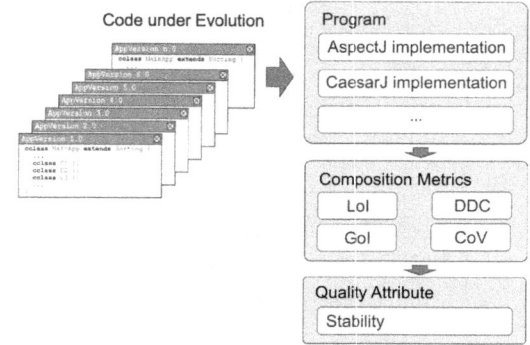

Figure 3. Measurement Framework Overview

The existing relationship between the composition properties (Section 2.2) and the composition metrics are illustrated in Table 1, column 2 respectively. The metrics LoI and GoI are directly associated with the extension of the composition scope in a program. Therefore, they are used to quantify the scope property of the composition code. The broken dependencies in program elements are quantified by the CoV metric. In addition, as the DDC metric quantifies the length of dependency chain it operates as another indicator of volatility. Quantification of breakings in the source code is also a reflection of the diversity of modules involved in the composition. As the number of modules increases, thus the number of dependencies and breakings are expected to increase as well.

Table 1. Composition Metrics

Metric	Composition Property	Metric Definition
LoI	Scope	The ratio between the numbers of program elements affected by the composition divided by the total of program elements.
GoI	Scope	Quantifies the composition scope by counting all the program elements affected through the use of composition mechanisms.
CoV	Volatility and Diversity	Quantifies the dependencies broken in the composition code while preparing it so that composition mechanisms can be properly applied.
DDC	Volatility	Quantifies the depth of dependency chain for each program element.

For the formal definition of the metrics, let's consider $m \in M$ such that (i) DD_m be the set of program elements that represent direct dependencies of m and (ii) ID_m be the set of program elements that represent indirect dependencies of m. In addition, let us also consider that for the set of program element of M, there are sets of added program elements, $E_{add,M}$, removed program elements, $E_{rem,M}$, and modified program elements, $E_{mod,M}$.

Local Impact (LoI) Metric. Given a program P, for each module $m \in M$ the LoI impact of m can be defined $LoI_{P,m} = |DD_m|/|E_M|$. As a result, LoI of a program P can be defined as $LoI_{P,Me} = \Sigma_{m \in Me} LoI_{P,m}$.

Considering the example of Figure 2, we have four modules directly affected by the composition: E1, E2, B2 and B1 as there are explicit references to them. Let's consider program elements as modules affected by the invocation of just one program element. As the whole example has sixteen modules, the ratio between directly affected modules and number total of modules is 0.25, which is equivalent to 25% of the code. Lower values for this metric mean that the code affected by this composition is located in a few modules. For instance, this measure might be useful to indicate that changes in the composition code are likely to impact less modules and, therefore, better sustain the code stability.

Global Impact (GoI) Metric. This metric is a generalization of LoI. Given a program P, for each module $m \in M$ the GoI impact of m can be defined $GoI_{P,m}=|DD_m|+|ID_m|/|E_M|$. As a result, GoI of a program P can be defined as $GoI_{P,Me}=\Sigma_{m \in Me} \ GoI_{P,m}$.

The relative value of this metric considers the total number of program elements involved. For the example illustrated in Figure 2, the entire composition directly affects the modules E1, E2, B2 and B1. The modules E3 and E4 are considered indirectly-affected as the values of parameter X used by it is modified by E2. Thus, the GoI value to the example illustrated in Figure 2 is the sum of the number of affected elements divided by total of elements. This relation is equal to 0.38 (38%). This means that the composition code is impacting 38% of the modules of the program.

Composition Volatility (CoV) Metric. Given a program P, for each module $m \in M$, the CoV of m can be defined as $CoV_{P,m}=|E_{add,m}|+|E_{mod,m}|+|E_{rem,m}|$. As a result, the CoV of an entire program P can be defined as $CoV_{P,Me}=\Sigma_{m \in Me} \ CoV_{P,m}$.

For the example illustrated in Figure 2, in order to add the composition modules (A, A1, A2, A3, E3 and E2) to the program, the module B1 was modified. Thus, the value for this metric is 7, which was calculated from the sum of manipulated program elements. Lower values for this metric is better because this means that less code was necessary to implement the composition which can imply in less modification.

Depth of Dependency Chain (DDC) Metric. Given a program P, for each module $m \in M$, the $DDC_{P,m}$ of m can be defined $length(m)$, where

$$length(m) = \begin{cases} 0, \ if \ m \notin DD \ \vee \ m \notin ID \\ max\{length(m) + 1\}, \ otherwise \end{cases}$$

This metric takes into consideration modules directly and indirectly affected. Each dependence chain has a root and leaves. The depth of dependency of a leaf is always greater than the root. In other words, DDC of a program element is the distance from it to its root, which is the module itself. If multiple dependencies exist, then the DDC is the longest path for the distance. For the example illustrated in Figure 2, the DDC of module E2 is size of the path from it to I.

4. STUDY SETUP

This section presents the study goal and research hypotheses (Section 4.1), the target applications used to evaluate the proposed framework (Section 4.2), and the study procedures (Section 4.3).

4.1 Goal and Research Hypothesis

The goal of this study was to evaluate to what extent composition properties are correlated with stability of evolving programs. In order to achieve this goal, we performed a comparative analysis of how changes are correlated with composition measures (Section 3). Our analysis was performed using the procedures described in Section 4.3. Our research aims were twofold. First, we aim at evaluating whether the composition properties (Section 2.2), as quantified by our metrics (Section 3), are related to stability of evolving programs. Second, we also aim at discussing some implementation factors that were detrimental to program stability. In this sense, this investigation relies on the analysis of one hypothesis (H), whose null (0) and alternative (1) definitions are as follows:

- **H0:** Composition properties are not related to the instability of evolving programs.
- **H1:** Composition properties are related to the instability of evolving programs.

4.2 Target Applications

In order to evaluate the proposed measurement framework, four evolving composition programs were generated to iBatis [24] and MobileMedia [10]: one AspectJ and CaesarJ implementation for each one. Together, these evolving programs encompass 22 versions. The programs have medium-size and are representative from different domains. We selected these systems because they have been evaluated in previous research work with different purposes [9][10][16]. In addition, these programs contain many types of compositions with different complexity degrees. This way, they enabled us to observe the impact of composition properties on their stability along their versions.

iBatis. It is a Java-based open source framework for data mapping. It is composed by more than 60 versions incrementally implemented, where four of them are implemented using AspectJ and CaesarJ programming languages. These versions implement the following functionalities: type mapping, error context, and design patterns. These versions were chosen mainly due to the diversity of their composition code. In addition, they have undergone more frequent and heterogeneous changes through the iBatis history, and their own crosscutting nature and properties (e.g. as occurs with type mapping and error context) call for the composition mechanisms being assessed in our study.

MobileMedia. It is an application that provides support to manage (create, delete, visualize, play, send) different types of media (photo, music and video) on mobile devices. During its development and evolution, the initial core architecture was systematically enriched with mandatory, optional and alternative features. Seven versions of the MobileMedia were analysed. The core features are: create/delete media (photo, music or video), label media, and view/play media. Some varying features, amongst others, are: transfer photo via SMS, count and sort media, copy media and set favourites. Unlike iBatis, which implements mainly new non-functional requirements, the MobileMedia evolution consists of implementing new functional requirements. This distinction allows us to analyse the full range of composition code structures and evaluate the impact of their properties on different evolution contexts.

4.3 Study Procedures

All target application versions (Section 4.2) were analysed according to a number of programming alignment rules. This procedure was applied to assure equal compliance to coding styles and included functionalities. As a second step, we also quantified the degree of stability of the target applications implementation. Program stability was quantified in terms of the program elements changes as proposed by Dantas and Garcia [9]. Change propagation metrics [24] were used with the purpose of quantifying the degree of stability of each program element. This means that the degree of stability is quantified by the number of program elements manipulated (i.e. added, removed and modified) along each program evolution (Section 4.2). Program elements are manipulated in either (i) to improve the program elements while preserving the existing code semantics (e.g. refactoring operations or bug fixes) or (ii) to increment the program in terms of new functionality. The conceptual framework is instantiated in Table 2 for AspectJ and CaesarJ, which are representative examples of contemporary programming languages used in this study.

Table 2. Conceptual Framework Instantiation

Framework component	AspectJ	CaesarJ
Program	AspectJ Program	CaesarJ Program
Module	aspect, interface and class	aspect, interface, class and virtual classes
Program Element	Method, pointcut-advice declarations, intertype declarations expressions and advices	Method, pointcut-advice declarations, intertype declarations expressions, advices and mixin composition expressions
Property	Diversity, Scope and Volatility	Diversity, Scope and Volatility

Our third step consists in applying the composition metrics to the target applications (Section 4.2). The goal is to gather insight about the usefulness of the composition metrics (Section 3). In particular, we analysed whether the composition metrics are related to program stability (Section 5). At this step, we aim at verifying whether composition metrics are able to work as indicators of program instabilities.

5. DATA ANALYSIS AND DISCUSSION

This section discusses the impact of composition properties on program stability (Section 5.1) using our measurement framework. The data of the composition metrics were automatically collected using our prototype tool [25]. The proposed framework has been applied to programs structured with both FOP (CaesarJ language) and AOP (AspectJ language) techniques. The use of both FOP and AOP in the chosen applications (Section 4.2) enables us to analyse the impact of composition properties on different implementation scenarios. We extend this discussion in Section 5.2 by comparing our composition metrics and conventional coupling metrics. We focus our discussion on the most significant results. A complete data analysis can be found at the website of this study [25]. There, the reader can also find additional results of composition metrics as stability indicators.

Statistical Tests. For the statistical tests performed in Section 5.2, we used the R language and environment[2]. We applied the Kolmogorov-Smirnov test to verify if our samples were normally distributed [30]. As our samples were normalized we applied the parametric Pearson's correlation coefficient [30]; the goal is to obtain evidence about the correlation of the composition metrics with stability. We used a confidence level of 95% ($\alpha = 0.05$). The Pearson correlation indicates three cases: values close to +1.0 indicate a strong positive (increasing) linear relationship; values close to -1 indicate a strong negative linear relationship; and finally, values between -1 and 1 indicate the degree of linear dependence between the variables. When the values are close to zero, this means that there is little relationship. The statistical tests were used to accept or reject the hypotheses listed in Section 4.1.

5.1 Composition Properties vs. Stability

The more code changes are required to realize a new program change, the more unstable its design is likely to become [26]. We chose to focus our analysis on stability because it is a key quality attribute on program evolvability [26]. Table 3 shows the correlation results between the composition metrics and the program stability. The Pearson's correlation computation tests the pair (composition metric value, stability value) for each composition metrics per program version. The analysis of these results reveals that the composition metrics have a strong correlation with the observed instabilities. The high correlation is inferred as, while the maximum correlation value is 1, the correlation values obtained from our set of metrics vary from 0.61 (LoI metric) to 0,90 (CoV metric). While the minimum correlation between the metric LoI and stability is 0.61, GoI correlation values vary from 0.78 to 0.99 for AspectJ versions and from 0.83 to 0.86 for CaesarJ versions. The correlation between stability and GoI is more expressive as GoI captures indirect dependencies among programs elements, which are not captured by the LoI metric (Section 3). The metric CoV is also another strong indicator of stability. Its lowest correlation value is 0.70. However, similar to GoI, its highest correlation value is 0.99. As illustrated in Table 3, the correlation values for AOP are closer to 1 than the same values for FOP. This occurs because the AOP composition scope (AspectJ language) has a greater impact on the program when compared with the FOP scope (CaesarJ language). As the correlation values are very close to 1 (maximum), we conclude the composition properties have presented good indicators of stability. Therefore, we can state that the hypothesis H_1 is accepted (Section 4.1).

Even though all the composition metrics (Section 3) were found to be related to stability, those quantifying composition scope tend to work as better indicators. According to the values in Table 3, we could state that the program stability is more strongly related to metrics in the following order (from the most to the least correlated): GoI, LoI, CoV and DDC. This ranking reinforces that the composition scope consistently emerges as the most significant property to explain program instabilities. We observed that this happens because the propagation of changes from a composition program element, for instance, is delimited by its composition code, which is quantified by the composition scope metrics. Figures 5 and 6 illustrate some key results for the interplay of composition code properties and program stability. They are used to support the discussion below.

---

[2] http://www.r-project.org/ (11/03/2012)

Table 3. Correlation of Composition Properties with Stability per System

Composition Metrics	MobileMedia – AOP	iBatis – AOP	MobileMedia – FOP	iBatis - FOP
	Coefficient	Coefficient	Coefficient	Coefficient
LoI	0.71	0.97	0.61	0.86
GoI	0.78	0.99	0.83	0.86
CoV	0.85	0.99	0.90	0.50
DDC	0.76	0.89	0.60	0.86

The Role of "Wide" Composition Scopes on Stability. In order to illustrate a concrete example of modification associated with composition properties, we present a simplified slice of code extracted from iBatis (Figure 4). Considering this example, when a method `m3()` is added to the class `C1` using AspectJ's mechanisms the programmer needs to change the aspect `A1` (pointcut `save`) in a way that `m3()` is not intercepted by the pointcut `save`. However, the scope of the composition implemented by the pointcut `save` embraces 80% of the iBatis' source code. Without knowing the impact of composition scope generated from the pointcut `save`, programmers would tend to change it inadvertently. Fortunately, the GoI metric, when applied to the pointcut `save` provides insights about its composition scope impact on the program, which is 80%. The use of wildcards leads to high GoI values, which explain why these forms of composition are detrimental to program stability.

```
01 class C1 {
02    …
03    int m1( ) { … }
04    int m2( ) { … }
05    …
06 }
```

```
01 aspect A1{
02    pointcut save():call(int *.m*( ));
03    ...
04    after( ): save(){
05        System.out.println("…");
06    }
07    …
08 }
```

Figure 4. Slice of iBatis Code (AspectJ)

We observed that composition code with higher GoI values than 20% are considered detrimental to stability. This information is useful as it works like a warning to programmers. Equipped with this knowledge, programmers are able to have in their mind that changes in both pointcut `save` and its dependent program elements can propagate others changes. This way, instead of changing the pointcut `save` expression to avoid the interception of the method `m3()`, the programmer can start to consider the possibility of creating a new pointcut. The creation of a new pointcut would contribute to the scope from the existing pointcut `save` more constant and in turn minimize the possible changes associated with it. Alternatively, whenever possible, programmers can decide to realize refactoring operations before evolving the program as a strategy for decreasing the GoI percentage and thus decreasing its side effects as well.

The Consistency of Global Scope as Stability Indicator. Figure 5 illustrates the variation in instability promoted by a single composition in a representative CaesarJ scenario. It is possible to observe that the variation in the stability degree is reflected by the values of GoI. The GoI metric was slightly better than the LoI metric due to the type of dependencies is dominated for direct dependencies. It is also possible to observe that low GoI values in one given version Ri indicate better stability in the next version

(R_{i+1}). From R_1 to R_2 the composition scope declined in 31%. Analysing the stability of MobileMedia modules, those affected by the composition code, from R_1 to R_2 we also identified a decrease of 39% in the number of changes. From R_3 to R_4 both composition scope and stability continued together on a downward trajectory.

However, overwhelmingly they increase in R_5. The explanation for this is that in R_6, new types of media (audio and video) were added in MobileMedia. As a consequence, the name of its modules, operations and declarations were prepared through the rename operations, which were reflected by the composition volatility, quantified by the CoV metric (Figure 6). Also in R_5, the depth of the composition dependency chain, DDC metric, reached the total of 9 program elements. Changes in this dependency chain were propagated by all the program elements which make it up. Based on indicators like these provided by the GoI, CoV and DDC metrics, programmers are able to know the risk they are taking when they need to change the program elements that belong to the scope of the composition.

Composition Volatility vs. Composition Scope. We can highlight that to evolve the version R_4, a number of refactoring operations in its program elements was required in order to prepare its code for R_5 (Figure 6). In addition to the modification of existing modules and programs elements, new ones were added to R_5. This variation is captured by the CoV metric (see Figure 6). The CoV metric quantifies the manipulation of elements that occurs within the composition code and it also operates as a consistent stability indicator. On the other hand, GoI goes further since it can be used to predict the stability of a R_{i+1} based on the scope of R_i, when R_{i+1} evolves over the composition code. The composition scope provides insights about the stability variation. We can observe in Figure 6 that the percentage of the composition scope is always aligned with the program instability variation. The propagation of changes from the modification of a program element occurs through its dependencies, which are captured by the composition scope metric.

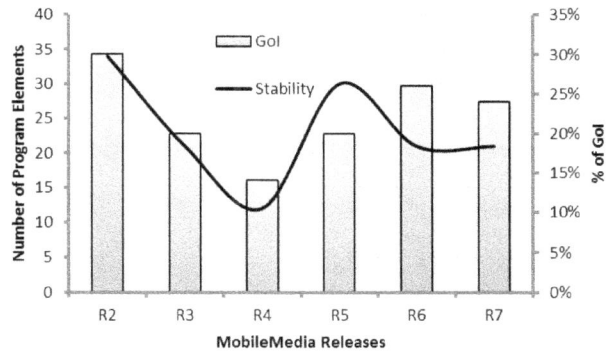

Figure 5. Stabiliy vs GoI for MobileMedia

297

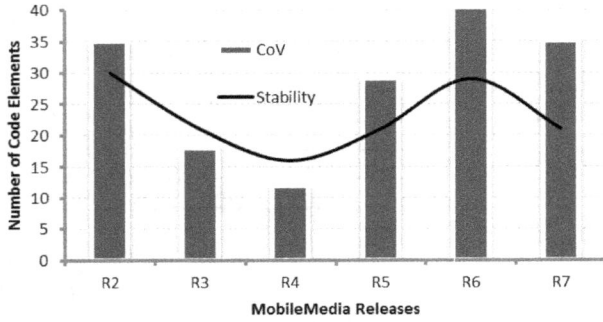

Figure 6. Stability vs. CoV for MobileMedia

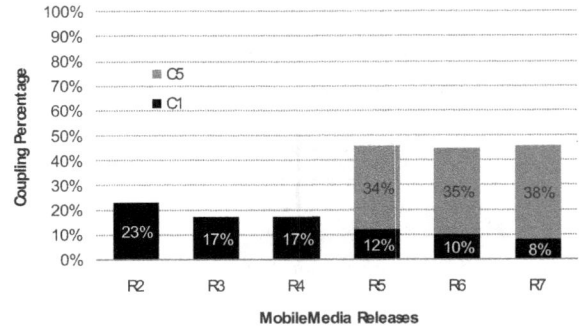

Figure 8. Coupling of the Composition Code (C1 and C2)

Progressive Increase of Composition Diversity over Time. We also observed an interesting phenomenon in all the systems with both AOP and FOP: the composition diversity consistently increases through the history of all the programs. In other words, the number of modules joining the composition code always increases as the programs evolve. This means that the composition code consistently embraces additional modules that were not planned to be in the original version of the composition code. This also means that the number of dependencies between programs involved in the composition code tends to increase. This dependency growth can be translated into: (i) more impact with regard to the composition scope, or (ii) more preparation of the source code to work properly with diverse program elements and modules. This explains why the composition code was often the source of instabilities in both AOP- and FOP-based systems.

5.2 Coupling vs. Composition Measures

We selected coupling metrics to compare with our composition metrics as stability indicator. The reason is that coupling has been widely used as an internal quality attribute to indicate or predict the stability of programs [13][20]. The coupling metric counts the occurrence of dependencies between modules in two directions: afferent and efferent [12][14]. In addition, we have observed that the first quantitative evaluations for advanced composition mechanisms are emerging [27][28]. These studies often rely on metrics that quantify the level of coupling (and other module-driven properties) as the better indicators of program stability.

In order to analyse the existing correspondence between program stability and both coupling and composition properties, we will take into consideration each instance of composition declaration in the code separately. Figure 7 illustrates a MobileMedia change scenario where the evolution behaviour of two different compositions, called C1 and C5, can be observed. C1 was included in R_2 while C5 was included in R_5. We chose these versions because they encompass all changes in MobileMedia for both compositions (C1 and C5). For each composition, we analysed the coupling of modules that are part of this composition. The compositions C1 and C5 were implemented in CaesarJ. For each composition, it is presented its percentage of coupling related to the total coupling in the code (Figure 8). As illustrated the coupling of C1 is almost the same along the evolution. This occurs because the composition C1 does not share code with other compositions. There is only a decrease in its coupling percentage in the last versions (e.g. R_6 and R_7) due to the number of modules that were added to the program. On the other hand, the coupling of the composition C5 presents variation because C5 is coupled with other compositions that need it to work along the evolution.

Coupling Metrics are Agnostic to Indirect Dependencies. However, the key deficiency of coupling metrics is the following: they do not capture most of the indirect dependencies. As a result, they fail to indicate (or predict) the program instabilities sourced on indirectly-related program elements joining a composition. The modules presented in Figure 9, which are associated with compositions C1 and C5, are highlighted by circles (M1, M2, M3 and M4 – Figure 9. Taking into consideration the values for coupling illustrated in Figure 8, we can observe that the compositions C1 and C5 are coupled with less stable modules. However, they do not present a high percentage in terms of coupling (Figure 8), which means that lower coupling may not mean better stability.

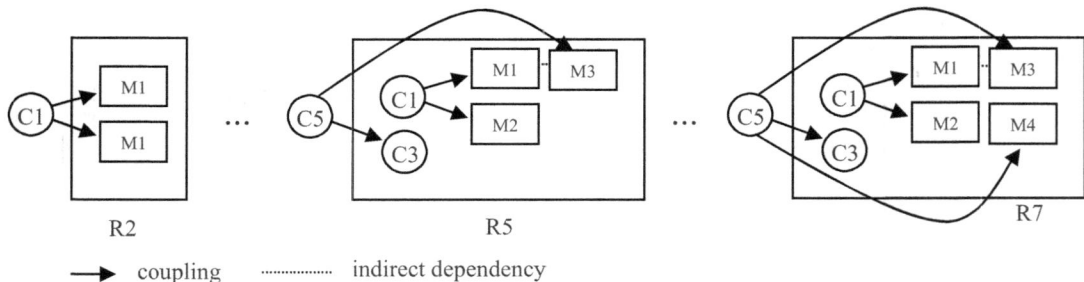

Figure 7. Composition Evolution

298

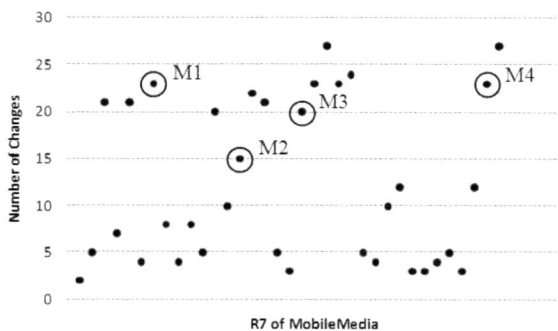

Figure 9. Stability of MobileMedia per modules

6. RELATED WORK

Over the past few years, many measurement frameworks have been proposed [13][14][15][20]. These existing frameworks supported the evaluation of maintainability of AO and OO programs; they were intended to measure specific module-centric or general program properties, such as coupling, cohesion, size [9][10][31]. For instance, Zhao [13] proposed a framework to describe new forms of dependencies between modules in aspect-oriented programs. This framework comprises a metrics suite for only assessing the coupling in AO programs in terms of different types of dependencies between aspects and classes. Bartsch and Harrison [29] extended the framework proposed by Briand *et al.* [20] for AspectJ. They described new types of specific coupling connections in AOP, such as coupling on advice execution, coupling on method call, coupling on field access. Unfortunately, none of these related works focused on composition code properties. They also do not take into consideration different composition mechanisms supported by a wide range of programming techniques. Also, they did not evaluate them in terms of stability of evolving programs.

Bartolomei *et al.* [14] went one step further and proposed a generic framework that captures and takes into consideration the composition mechanisms supported by AspectJ and CaesarJ languages. However, their analysis relies on the coupling created by the use of these mechanisms and how to account for them. Our framework is a further development of their work and, hence, delivers complementary contributions because: (i) we explored different composition code properties (Section 2.2), and (ii) we assessed and discussed the impact of these properties on stability of evolving programs. Our work is different and present novel ideas when compared to related work. This occurs because they do not provide means for quantifying the impact of composition properties, supported by post-OO programming techniques, on program stability. Finally, existing work did not discuss and gather evidence of how the evolving program stability is related to code composition properties.

7. THREATS TO VALIDITY

With respect to the validity of our study (Section 5), the *conclusion validity threats* are related to the data set. In other words, the analysed data set might not be large enough to allow broader statistical analyses. However, we tried to overcome this threat by using systems that were structured with very different techniques and underwent several software evolution scenarios. Threats to *internal validity* reside on the software history and

maturation of the target application designs. The designs and implementations of MobileMedia and iBatis have been evaluated and continuously improved through the last years. Different maturity levels of the investigated systems may impact differently on their stability.

Threats to *external validity* reside on the limited size and complexity of the target applications, which may restrict the extrapolation of our results. However, while the results may not be directly generalized to professional programmers and real-world systems, the chosen projects allowed us to make useful initial assessments whether the composition metrics would be worth studying further. In spite of its limitations, the presented research constitutes an important initial empirical work on the composition metrics.

8. CONCLUSIONS AND FUTURE WORK

Composition code properties lead to the introduction of new flavours of complexity and may cause side effects on the program stability. In this context, this paper has presented a measurement framework for quantifying key properties of composition code. The framework was instantiated and evaluated in the context of a stability study involving four evolving programs, totalling 22 versions being analysed. The programs were structured with two advanced programming techniques: aspect-oriented programming and feature-oriented programming. Our analysis revealed that composition code properties, as supported by our metrics suite, were consistent indicators of program instabilities. Therefore, the results confirmed that the composition code properties are strongly related to program instabilities (hypothesis H1). The confirmation was observed regardless of programming techniques and composition mechanisms being used.

Composition properties exerted more influence on the stability superiority (or inferiority) of a program than a conventional stability indicator, i.e. coupling (Section 5.2). In particular, we identified that the composition scope property is the most strongly associated with stability. Moreover, in many cases, we observed that program instabilities could be avoided if the scope of certain composition declarations (e.g. pointcuts) was decomposed in narrower scopes (Section 5.1.). Therefore, we believe that the use of our composition measurement framework can also better inform programmers to tame possible side effects of composition code structure.

As future work, we believe that our work can be further extended in many ways, including: (i) the evaluation of our framework in the context of analyses involving other post-OO programming techniques, such as Compose* [7] and Hyper/J [23], and (ii) the use and evaluation of our framework in the context of other quality attributes, such as error-proneness. Those evaluations would enable us to reveal any extension needed for our framework. By now, we assessed the usefulness of the framework to study program stability, as reported in this paper, and program reusability (available at our supplementary website [25]).

9. REFERENCES

[1] Lehman, M. 1996. Laws of software evolution revisited. In Proc. of the EWSPT, Springer, London, UK, 108-124.

[2] Mezini, M. and Ostermann, K. 2002. Integrating independent components with on-demand remodularization. In Proc. of the OOPSLA, 52-67

[3] Kiczales, G. et al. 1997. Aspect-oriented programming. In Proc. of the ECOOP, 220-242.

[4] Prehofer, C. 1997. Feature-oriented programming: A fresh look at objects. In Proc. of the ECOOP, 419-443.

[5] William Harrison and Harold Ossher. 1993. Subject-oriented programming: a critique of pure objects. SIGPLAN Not. 28, 10 (October 1993), 411-428.

[6] Rajan, H. and Sullivan, K.J. 2005. Classpects: unifying aspect- and object-oriented language design. In Proc. of the ICSE, 59- 68

[7] Bergmans, M. et al. 1992. Composition filters: extended expressiveness for OOPLs. Position paper for the OOPSLA: The Next Generation, Vancouver.

[8] Mintchev, S. and Getov, V. 1997. Towards portable message passing in Java: binding MPI. In Recent Advances in PVM and MPI. no.1332 in Lecture Notes in Computer Science (LNCS), Springer-Verlag, 135-142.

[9] Dantas, F. and Garcia, A. 2010. Software reuse vs stability: evaluating advanced programming techniques. In Proc. SBES, IEEE Computer Society, Salvador, Brazil, 40-49.

[10] Figueiredo, E. et al. 2008. Evolving software product lines with aspects: an empirical study on design stability. In Proc. of the ICSE, ACM, NY, USA, 261-270.

[11] Endrikat, S. and Hanenberg, S. 2011. Is aspect-oriented programming a rewarding investment into future code changes? A socio-technical study on development and maintenance time. In Proc. ICPC, Kingston, Canada, 51-60.

[12] Figueiredo, E. et al. 2008. On the maintainability of aspect-oriented software: a concern-oriented measurement framework. In Proc. of the CSMR. IEEE Computer Society, Washington, DC, USA, 183-192.

[13] Zhao, J. 2004. Measuring coupling in aspect-oriented systems. In Proc. of the Metrics, 14-16.

[14] Bartolomei, T. et al. 2006. Towards a unified coupling framework for measuring aspect-oriented programs. In Proc. of the SOQUA, ACM, NY, USA, 46-53.

[15] Sant'Anna, C. et al. 2003. On the reuse and maintenance of aspect-oriented software: an assessment framework. In Proc. of the SBES.

[16] Figueiredo, E. et al. 2009. Crosscutting patterns and design stability: an exploratory analysis. In Proc. ICPC, 138-147.

[17] Garcia, A. et al. 2005. Modularizing design patterns with aspects: a quantitative study. In Proc. AOSD, 3-14.

[18] Avadhesh, K., Rajesh, K., and Grover, P. S. 2009. Generalized coupling measure for aspect-oriented systems. SIGSOFT Softw. Eng. Notes 34, 3, 1-6.

[19] Stevens, W.et al. 1979. Structured design. In Classics in software engineering, Edward Nash Yourdon (Ed.). Yourdon Press, Upper Saddle River, NJ, USA 205-232.

[20] Briand, L., Daly, J., and Wust, J. 1999. A unified framework for coupling measurement in object-oriented systems. IEEE Trans. Softw. Eng. vol. 25, n. 1, 91-121.

[21] Aracic, I. et al. 2006. Overview of CaesarJ. Transactions on AOSD I, LNCS, 3880, 135-173.

[22] Kiczales, G., Hilsdale, E., Hugunin, J., Kersten, M., Palm, J. and Griswold, W. 2001. An overview of AspectJ. In Proceedings of the ECOOP, Springer-Verlag, London, UK, UK, 327-353.

[23] Hassoun, Y. and Constantinides, C. 2003. The development of generic definitions of hyperslice packages in Hyper/J. Electronic Notes in Theoretical Computer Science, vol. 82, issue 5, April, 8-20

[24] iBatis Data Mapper - http://archive.apache.org/dist/ibatis/binaries/ibatis.java/. Accessed in March, 2012.

[25] On the Role of Composition Code Properties on Evolving Programs. http://www.inf.puc-rio.br/~fneto/esem12/

[26] Kelly, D. 2006. A study of design characteristics in evolving software using stability as a criterion. IEEE Trans. Softw. Eng., vol. 32, 315-329.

[27] Burrows, R. et al. 2010. The impact of coupling on the fault-proneness of aspect-oriented programs: an empirical study. In Proc. of the ISSRE, 329-338.

[28] Burrows, R. et al. 2011. Reasoning about faults in aspect-oriented programs: a metrics-based evaluation. In Proc. of the ICPC, 131-140.

[29] Bartsch, M. and Harrison, R. 2006. A coupling framework for aspectJ. In Proc. of the EASE, Extended Abstract.

[30] Sheskin, D. 2007. Handbook of parametric and nonparametric statistical Procedures (fourth edition). Chapman & All, 2007

[31] Greenwood, P. et al. 2007. On the impact of aspectual decompositions on design stability: an empirical study. Proc. of the ECOOP, Berlin, Germany, 176-200.

[32] Ferrari, F. et al. 2010. An exploratory study of fault-proneness in evolving aspect-oriented programs. Proc. ICSE, 65-74.

The Effect of Branching Strategies on Software Quality

Emad Shihab
Software Analysis and Intelligence Lab (SAIL)
Queens University, Canada
emads@cs.queensu.ca

Christian Bird and Thomas Zimmermann
Microsoft Research
Redmond, WA, USA
{cbird, tzimmer}@microsoft.com

ABSTRACT

Branching plays a major role in the development process of large software. Branches provide isolation so that multiple pieces of the software system can be modified in parallel without affecting each other during times of instability. However, branching has its own issues. The need to move code across branches introduces additional overhead and branch use can lead to integration failures due to conflicts or unseen dependencies. Although branches are used extensively in commercial and open source development projects, the effects that different branch strategies have on software quality are not yet well understood. In this paper, we present the first empirical study that evaluates and quantifies the relationship between software quality and various aspects of the branch structure used in a software project. We examine Windows Vista and Windows 7 and compare components that have different branch characteristics to quantify differences in quality. We also examine the effectiveness of two branching strategies – branching according to the software architecture versus branching according to organizational structure. We find that, indeed, branching does have an effect on software quality and that misalignment of branching structure and organizational structure is associated with higher post-release failure rates.

Categories and Subject Descriptors

D.2.8 [**Software Engineering**]: Metrics – *Process Metrics*

Keywords

Branching, Quality

1. INTRODUCTION

Coordination is key as software development becomes a more and more complex enterprise. Software projects today range in size up to tens of millions of lines of code, are developed by teams of thousands of developers, and may support multiple releases at different stages of development. Managing all of the changes being made to a codebase is an increasingly difficult task. Software Configuration Management Systems (SCMs, also known as version control systems) are important tools, as they are the primary mechanism used to coordinate the sharing of actual code artifacts, the key output in software products. In large-scale software projects where all changes are immediately seen by all developers (i.e. one "line" of development), changes can lead to a number of significant problems: single changes can cause build breaks and halt the progress of the *entire* project; piecemeal changes to interoperating components can lead to incompatibility,

and finding the change that causes a test to fail can almost be impossible, especially for long-running test suites. While some of these effects are present in smaller projects too, the impact is intensified in large projects; a build break that affects a team of five developers is not as serious as a break that affects thousands of developers.

One of the key features of modern SCMs that helps to mitigate these problems associated with the complexity of software projects is the support of parallel lines of development known as branches [1]. A branch is a virtual workspace created from a particular state of the source code that a developer or team of developers can make changes to without affecting others working outside the branch. Branches provide isolation from other changes; for example a build break on a branch affects only the teams working on that branch and not the entire development team. The use of branches within a project has a profound effect on the processes used during development, from the build processes to release management [1].

However, like any development tool, branching needs to be leveraged correctly in order to be most effective [2]. Teams may choose to work in branches to avoid dealing with the work of other teams, but some coordination *is* required. Branches may introduce a false sense of safety, as changes made in different branches *will* eventually be merged together (either manually or automatically), and bugs may arise if these changes are syntactically or semantically incompatible. The process of moving code between branches represents additional error-prone work for developers. A complex branching structure may hinder the development process, making it hard to track code changes, causing build failures (due to unexpected dependencies), increasing the chances of introducing regression failures and making it difficult to maintain the code base [3]. In fact, some claim that branching is the most problematic area of SCM [4]. Therefore, it is important to understand how branching structures affect software systems and impact their quality. We note that these outcomes are not *caused* by the branches themselves, but rather by the processes and coordination required when employing the use of branches.

However, the relationship between branching structure and quality remains an important open question. With more projects in open source [5] and commercial contexts [6] employing branches in their development, understanding the impact of branching is increasingly relevant. To address this, we perform an empirical study to examine the effect of branch structure on software quality in Windows. We find that many aspects of branch use do indeed affect software quality.

As a prescriptive step, we also examine how to best align branching structures with other aspects of a software project. Specifically, we compare the branch structure with the organization of the teams within the project and also with the architecture of the software itself to determine which is the better branching strategy.

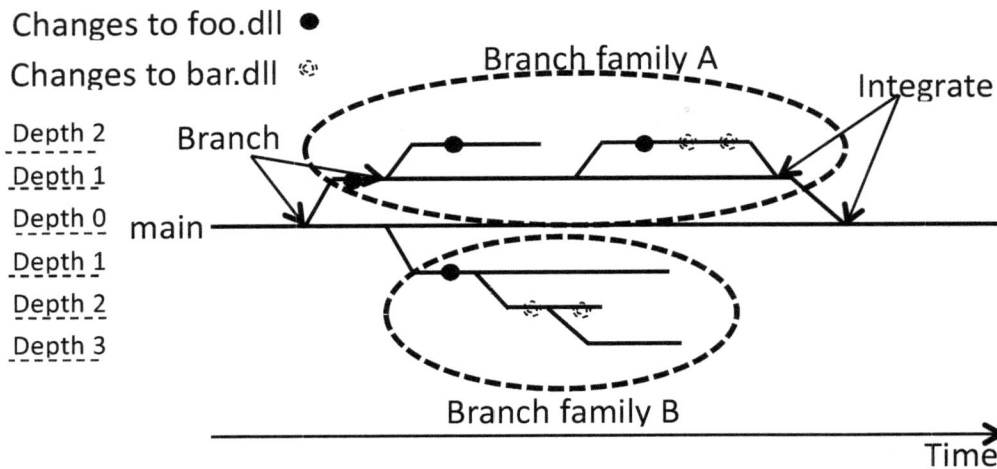

Figure 1: Example branch structure

To the best of our knowledge, this is the first study to empirically examine the effect of branching on software quality. We make the following contributions in this study:

1. We define metrics to capture the effects of branching on software quality.

2. We perform an empirical study and quantify the effects of branching on software quality in two releases of a large industrial project.

3. We examine the effect of mismatch between the branching structure and organizational and architectural structures.

4. We provide recommendations of branch use for projects that heavily utilize branching.

The rest of the paper is organized as follows. We first survey prior work in the area of SCM branching. We then provide terminology and describe our data collection process. Next, we discuss our hypotheses regarding branching strategies and define the metrics used to evaluate these hypotheses. Finally, we present the results of our analysis, discuss implications of these results, and make recommendations based on our findings.

2. RELATED WORK

A number of researchers have studied the role of branching within SCMs. Midha [7] outlined key characteristics of SCMs and their use at Lucent Technologies and iterated the need of future SCMs to facilitate the creation and support of multiple branches (referred to in the paper as streams). Walrad and Strom [1] investigated tradeoffs between several branching models and suggested the use of a branch-by-purpose model which calls for branches to be created only when there is a specific purpose (e.g. when software is released). Wingerd and Seiwald [4] provided best practices for SCMs and suggested branching only when necessary, such as when incompatible policies arise (e.g. when developers have different commit privileges), branching late to make sure as many changes as possible are propagated, and using branching instead of code freezing to allow parallel development. Appleton et al. [2] and Buffenbarger and Gruell [8] studied and proposed branching patterns and best practices to use in order to achieve efficient parallel development.

Perry et al. [9] perform an empirical study to investigate and understand the nature of large scale parallel development and find that multiple levels of parallelism exists (i.e. at the release, MR and IRM levels), that as much as 12.5% of all deltas may be in conflict and up to 50% of files are changed by multiple developers in the same release. Premraj et al. [3] examined the branching and

merging in an industrial agile development setting and found that the roles of branchers (e.g. architects, developers, or testers) and the type of files (e.g. header files or configuration files) they work on dictates the cost of merging. They also presented findings that suggested that programs should be structured not only by the software architecture, but also by the team structure, so that communication about prevention and unnecessary branching could be possible. Bird et al. [6] examined a theory that branches are created to accomplish a goal and groups of developers making changes on a branch represent virtual teams with a common goal. Then, they examined the relationships between files changed in a branch and the people who make changes to the branch and found support for their theory in Windows Vista and Windows 7.

The prior work has focused primarily on providing best practices for branching or studying the role of branching in large teams. It is important to note that most of these best practices suggested are based on experience and theoretical scenarios. In this work, we complement the previous work by empirically studying and evaluating the effects of branching on software quality. In addition, our study proposes and validates metrics that capture general characteristics of branches (i.e. we do not constrain ourselves to one branching model). For example, our findings regarding branch depth can be used to compare two different branching models based on their depth characteristics.

3. TERMINOLOGY AND METRICS

3.1 Terminology

We start by introducing relevant terminology used in this paper. The Windows Vista and Windows 7 teams heavily relied on branching to manage their large code base. Generally speaking, branches are created based on a specific structure that is agreed upon within the development teams. As the project evolves, more branches are created to support development.

To maintain order in the branching structure, related branches are grouped into *branch families*. A branch family is a subtree rooted off of the trunk (a.k.a. main, the release branch). For example, all of the branches used to build tools are grouped into one 'tools' branch family. In some cases, a branch may be added to a branch family in order to provide further isolation. In such cases, the new branch is said to be one level "deeper" in the branch tree. Figure 1 shows an example of two branch families and the different branch depths. In our study, we use the notion of *branch depth* as the measure of how deep a branch is from the main branch. Once a change is checked in on a branch at depth n, it is merged into the parent branch at depth n-1, and eventually is merged into the trunk (level 0).

To differentiate between development and branching activity, we classify changes into two types: changes to the actual code, which we call *development changes* (add, edit and delete operations) and changes which move and merge code between branches, which we call *branching changes*. In our context, a *branch change* is a change that copies or integrates (also known as merges) a file change from one branch to another. These two categories of changes are fundamentally different, as modifying code and moving code require different skillsets and pose different types of risk (e.g. implementation errors vs. integration errors). In practice, these two types of changes are performed by contributors that have different roles and even different job titles within the project.

3.2 Data Collection

To conduct our study, we leveraged data from two releases of one of the largest projects at Microsoft, Windows. Windows is composed of thousands of executable files (.exe), shared libraries (.dll) and drivers (.sys), which we refer to as binaries. We collected historical development data for each binary in Windows Vista and 7 from the release of Windows Server 2003 to the release of Windows 7. We chose to perform our analysis at the binary level because failure data is collected and reported at this level at Microsoft and we have observed cases where a failure caused by a change to one source file for a binary was fixed in a different source file for the same binary. We decided to perform our case study on Windows Vista and 7 because they are two large releases that have a rich development history and heavily use branches.

We collected a number of different metrics for each component. To gather the metrics for each component, we leveraged the commit histories and software failure data of Windows Vista and Windows 7. Each change in the repository contains the change author, the change date, a change log message, the source files modified by the change, the branch and branch family of each source file, the type of change (e.g. development or branching) and the purpose of the change (e.g. bug fix or enhancement). We used a mapping of source files to binaries in order to collect the different metrics at the component level.

As an indicator of software quality, we used the number of post-release failures per binary. Both versions of Windows have been released for multiple years and have an installation base in the hundreds of millions. Most defects are found quickly and the report rate falls off dramatically after the first year, indicating that our results are unlikely to change with time. Various code metrics, such as churn, complexity and size metrics were also gathered from the source code repositories and build process for each component. We use the code metrics in our models as control variables since they are known to also relate to failures [10]. We detail all of the metrics calculated from our data in the next section. Prior research has shown that when characteristics such as size and complexity are not considered, they may affect the validity of other software metrics [11].

As part of our study examines the relationship between branching structure and organizational structure, we gathered snapshots of the Windows organizational hierarchy (who reports to whom as well as job titles) over the course of Windows Vista and 7 development.

Lastly, the binaries within Windows are logically partitioned into systems, subsystems, areas, and (in some cases) subareas. For instance, an mp3 decoding library may be in the audio codec area of the audio subsystem within the multimedia system. We use this hierarchical breakdown for both releases of Windows as the system architecture and use it to determine how well branches span architectural boundaries.

4. RESEARCH QUESTIONS

Our high level research question is "How much and in what ways does branching affect software quality?" To answer this question, we evaluate quality at the component level and the branch level through the use of a number of measures of branch use. In this section we present the testable hypotheses that we evaluate as well as the rationale that underlies each of these hypotheses and the metrics that we use to quantify different aspects of branch use. Each hypothesis is related to the research question in a different way and has different implications for software teams.

Our hypotheses come from discussions with developers, managers, and other stakeholders in Windows and other projects at Microsoft. They have indicated that it is just as valuable to know which branching characteristics (i.e. metrics) *do not* have a relationship with software failures as those that do; both inform stakeholders' decisions and practices.

4.1 Effects on Component Quality

One goal of our research is to examine the effects of branching on software quality. Based on discussions with developers we expect that overly complex branching structures negatively impact the quality of a software system. Since software components that are developed in more complex branching structures require more process overhead in terms of branching and integrating activity as well as more coordination, we expect more opportunities for error and that these components will have more post-release failures. Therefore, we focus our study on three factors that we believe measure the complexity of a branching structure, namely – branch activity, branch scatter and branch depth.

H1. Branch Activity: Software components with high branching activity have more failures.

Branches are meant to provide a level of isolation for development teams to work on parts of the code base without having to worry about affecting others. However, this level of isolation comes at the cost of having to resolve integration conflicts when changes on these branches are finally merged back. Integration changes are risk-prone because a) the developer merging the code may not be the developer that made the code changes (and thus may lack key knowledge), b) the changes represented in a merge are often aggregated and are therefore large and widespread, c) the integration is often temporally distant from the development changes themselves, and d) developers may rely on the invalid assumption that lack of syntactic conflicts implies a lack of semantic conflicts or issues [12]. Therefore, we expect higher levels of branching activity to lead to more post-release failures since higher activity requires more integration. We use the **branching activity** metric to evaluate this hypothesis.

Branching Activity – is defined as a ratio, the number of branching changes divided by the number of development changes, per component. We use the ratio instead of simply using the number of branching changes since components that have many development changes are more likely to have more branching changes as well (we control for total number of changes by using a churn metrics in our models). We use the branching activity metric to evaluate our first hypothesis (H1) that more branching activity reduces software quality.

H2a. Branch Scatter: Software components spread across many branch families have more failures.

In addition to the hypothesis that higher levels of branching activity may lead to more failures, we also hypothesize based on discussions with developers, that components that have changes scattered across different branch families will experience more integration failures. The intuition is that software components that are spread across many branch families have changes that will not integrate until they reach the main branch and will thus happen in larger batches and later in the development cycle. Furthermore, teams working in different branch families are typically organizationally farther apart and have disparate tasks. Prior research has shown that in such cases, awareness is lowered, coordination breakdowns occur more often, and failures result [13] [14]. This measure is different from the branching activity metric. A software component may have high branching activity but only be modified in two branches that are in a single branch family (i.e., it keeps going back and forth). In this case, the branch scatter would be low. We use the **branch scatter** metric to evaluate this hypothesis.

Branching Scatter – is defined as the ratio of unique branch families that a component is in divided by the number of development changes. Again, we use the ratio instead of using the number of branch families that a component touches, to control for the fact that components that have more development changes are more likely to be scattered across branch families. We use the branching scatter metrics to evaluate our hypothesis (H2a) that higher levels of branch scatter reduce software quality.

H2b. Branch Scatter: Software components that are equally developed across multiple branch families have more failures.

In addition to simple branch scatter, we examine the effect of the proportion of scatter across branch families. The intuition is that a component may need to be changed in different branch families; however the majority of the changes to the component should be made mainly within a single branch family. If a component is developed equally across many branch families, then there is more room for missed dependencies and conflicts. We use the **branch scatter entropy** metric to validate this hypothesis.

Branch Scatter Entropy – is defined as the entropy of the scatter of the changes to a component across branch families. In certain cases, a component may need to be shared across different families. The intuition is that if a component is changed equally across the different branch families, this is worse than having a component change mainly in one branch family and lightly changed in the others. For example, a component may need to be modified in two branch families, however, if 95% of its changes happen in one branch family and only 5% in the other that is much better than having 50% of its changes in each branch family. We use Shannon Entropy [15] to capture this effect of distribution (e.g. [16], [17]). Entropy is defined as $H(P) = -\sum_{k=1}^{n}(p_k * log_2 p_k)$, where $p_k \geq 0, \forall k \in 1,2,...,n$ and $\sum_{k=1}^{n} p_k = 1$. Maximal entropy is achieved when all elements in a distribution, P have the same probability of occurrence (i.e. $p_k = \frac{1}{n}, \forall k \in 1, 2, ..., n$). In contrast, minimal entropy is achieved if one element p_i in the distribution, P has probability of occurrence 1 (i.e. $p_i = 1$) and all remaining elements in P have a probability of occurrence 0 (i.e. $\forall k \neq i, p_k = 0$). Since some components are changed in a different number of branch families compared to others, we normalize by dividing the entropy value by $log_2 m$, where m is the number of branch families containing changes to that component.

To illustrate our intuition, we use the example shown in Figure 1. Foo.dll and bar.dll both have equal number of changes (depicted by the solid and hollow dots on the branches). Three of the four

changes to foo.dll are in branch family A. Therefore, developers working on the branches in branch family A are more likely to be aware of the other changes to foo.dll. On the other hand, bar.dll has two changes in branch family A and another two changes in branch family B. Therefore, it is more difficult for the developers working on the branches in the two branch families to be aware of all the changes to bar.dll, possibly causing incompatible changes, leading to a higher number of failures. In this example, foo.dll has lower branch scatter entropy value than bar.dll.

H3a. Branch depth: Software components developed primarily in deeper branches have more failures.

In addition to measuring the branching activity and frequency, software components that are developed in deeper branches are more isolated and must "travel" further to a release branch. Thus, they have a higher likelihood of conflicts upon integration to the release branches. To evaluate these claims, we use the branch depth metrics to examine whether branch depth has an effect on the quality of a component. We use the **low and high branch depth** metrics to validate this hypothesis.

Branching Depth (Low, Medium, High) – is defined as the ratio of development changes to a component in low depth branches, medium depth branches and high depth branches. The choice for using three categories rather than using a continuous measure maintains confidentiality at Microsoft and also allows for generality; a branch structure of any depth can be easily binned into these categories. Furthermore, this allows for a non-monotonic relationship between depth and failure rates. We use the branch depth metrics to evaluate our hypothesis (H3a) that development at deeper branches reduces software quality. In the example, figure 1, foo.dll has 50% of its changes at low depth branches (i.e. branches in depth 1) and 50% of its changes at medium depth branches (i.e. branch at depth 2).

H3b. Branch depth: Software components that are developed evenly across low, medium and high depth branches have more failures.

Similar to the proportion of branch scatter across multiple branch families hypothesis, we also examine whether components that are mainly developed in one depth level have better quality than components that are equally developed at all depth levels. We use the **branch depth entropy** metric to validate this hypothesis.

Branch Depth Entropy – is defined as the entropy of the changes at each depth level (low, medium, and high). This is in an effort to determine whether changing components *evenly* at different depth levels (high depth entropy) is better or worse (in terms of software quality) than a component that changes primarily in *one depth level* (low depth entropy).

Since the depth of the branch reflects its purpose (e.g. core functionality is often developed at lower levels), being distributed across different depth levels may lead to confusion in the purpose of the component. Using the example in Figure 1, foo.dll has 50% of its changes at low branch depth and 50% of its changes at medium branch depth, whereas bar.dll has all of its changes in medium depth branches. In this example, foo.dll may be harder to work with since it does not clearly reside in any one depth level. We use the branch depth entropy metric to evaluate our hypothesis (**H3b**) that even distribution across branch depths reduces software quality. Since different components are changed in a different number of branch depths compared to others, we normalize by dividing the entropy value by $log_2(m)$, where m is the number of branch depths containing changes to that component.

4.2 Architectural and Organizational Congruence

In the previous section, we examined topological characteristics of the relationships between changes to components on branches and post-release failures. An equally important question is how the branching structure should align with the architecture of the system being developed and the organization of the teams developing the system. According to Conway's Law [18], in an ideal setting the decomposition of the system into subsystems and subsystems into components would match the division of the developers into teams. In practice, due to cross-cutting concerns, architectural coupling, and external organizational factors such as geography [19], pre-existing organizational structures, and organizational churn [20], there is rarely perfect congruence between system architecture and organizational structure. Thus, a branching structure can match organizational structure at the cost of spanning subsystem and component boundaries, or it may closely align with the system architecture and cross-cut the organization.

The decision is not clear. Prior work suggests that components with changes spanning organizations increase failures [13]. However, cross-cutting concerns – functionality requiring changes that span system architecture -- also lead to failures [21].

Therefore, in an effort to provide actionable results to software teams to assist them to decide on effective branching strategies, we examine the effect of aligning the branching structure to architectural or organizational structure on branch quality. This leads to two competing hypotheses:

H4a. Branching according to architectural structure: Branches with higher architectural mismatch have more failures.

One strategy to follow when creating branches is to dedicate one branch per component. Doing so, allows software components to be developed in isolation. However, in certain cases multiple components are modified in a single branch, causing branches to cross-cut the architecture (i.e., architectural mismatch). We expect branches that include work on multiple components to have more failures.

Archictectural Mismatch – is the number of individual systems, subsystems, areas, components and subcomponents (forming a hierarchy) that are affected by the changes on a branch. We expect that a branch that contains only changes to one subsystem have fewer failures than a branch that changes many.

H4b. Branching according to organizational structure: Branches with higher organizational mismatch have more failures.

In many cases multiple teams need to coordinate when developing a software component. Therefore, having the branching structure match the organizational structure may be ideal. We expect that branches that are contributed to from multiple organizations (i.e., organizational mismatch) have more failures.

To answer the aforementioned question, we measure the effect that architectural and organization mismatch has on branch quality. To measure architectural and organizational mismatch of the branch, we define the following metrics:

Organizational Mismatch – includes the number of managers, development leads, and engineers (counted and used in our models separately) that make changes to files on the branch. The number of engineers that work in a branch serve to represent the size of the group working in a branch. However, each team has one development lead and a number of leads report to one development manager. Thus, each lead and each manager is indicative of

additional teams working in a branch. We expect a branch with twenty engineers, six leads, and two managers to have more failures than a branch with twenty engineers, one lead, and one manager because the former spans organizational structure.

We quantify branch quality by mapping components (and their post-release failures) to the branches they were changed on. Using a technique similar to the approach used by Ostrand et al. to calculate the failure ratios of developers [22], we use the ratio of a component's changes on a branch (analogous to changes made by a developer in Ostrand's approach) to map post-release failures to that specific branch. For example, assume that a component A had 8 post-release failures and that A had a total of 20 development changes, 15 changes on branch B1 and 5 changes on branch B2. We map 6 ($\frac{15}{20} * 8 = 6$) failures to branch B1 and 2 ($\frac{5}{20} * 8 = 2$) failures to B2.

These metrics enable us to study the effect of mismatch on branch quality. As before, we build linear regression models and use the goodness-of-fit measure to compare which of architectural or organizational mismatch better explain branch failures. We also report direction and magnitude of the relationship to quality (derived from regression coefficients).

4.3 Analysis Techniques and Statistical Modeling

We use multiple linear regression models to study the effect of branching on software quality.

Linear regression models are generally used in empirical studies to model an outcome of a response variable (e.g. model the number of post-release failures) or to model the relationship between an observed phenomena (represented by the model independent variables) and an observed outcome (represented as the dependent variable). In this paper, we use linear regression models to achieve the latter, to study the relationship. *Prediction is not the aim of this paper.* In particular, we use linear regression to examine the relationship of one or more of the branching metrics with software quality, while controlling for code and process metrics.

The independent variables in our linear regression models are the branching activity, scatter and depth metrics; the dependent variable is the number of post-release failures. All of our measurements are performed at the software component level.

One of the assumptions of linear regression is that the residuals must be normally distributed. We observed that, similar to many other software metrics, our control variables and some branch metrics here highly skewed, leading to non-normality of residuals. To alleviate this problem, we used a log transformation on these metrics with high skew and/or kurtosis values.

As our evaluation criteria, we examine the statistical significance, magnitude, and direction of the variable's contribution in the model. In addition, similar to previous work (e.g. [23]) we use model fit (variance explained, also known as adjusted R^2) as evaluation as well. We begin by building a base model, which contains our control variables, and record the adjusted R^2. Then, we incrementally add one variable at a time and measure the improvement in adjusted R^2.

We employed Variance Inflation Factor (VIF) analysis to measure the level of multicollinearity between independent variables [24] and removed highly correlated variables from the linear regression models, i.e. any variables that had a VIF value above 10, as recommended by Kutner et al. [24]. To test for statistical

	Base Model	Model 2	Model 3	Model 4	Model 5
log(Size)	↑	↑	↑	↑	↑
log(Churn)	↑	↑	↑	↑	↑
log(Complexity)	-	-	-	-	-
log(Dev. Changes)	↑	↑	↑	↑	-
log(No. Files)	↑	↑	↑	↑	↑
Branch Activity		↑	↑	↑	↑
log(Branch Scatter)			↑	-	-
Branch Scatter Entropy			↑	↑	↑
Low Branch Depth				↑	↑
log(High Branch Depth)				-	-
Branch Depth Entropy				↓	↓
Branch Groups					↑
R^2	72%	75%	77%	77%	79%

Table 1: Post-release failures model for Vista. Arrows indicate effect on failures. Table 3 shows magnitude of effects.

significance, we performed ANOVA analysis on the models and report the p-value of the independent variables.

5. CASE STUDY RESULTS

We now present the results of our case studies on Windows Vista and Windows 7. We build linear regression models that model the number of post-release failures and examine whether or not adding branching metrics improves the model fit. For each version of Windows, we built five models. We start by building a base model with the control metrics, which in our case are churn, complexity, size, the number of files and the number of development changes to a software component. Then, we build an additional four models where we incrementally add the branch activity, branch scatter, branch depth metrics, and branch families, respectively.

Tables 1 and 2 present the results of our analysis. Arrows (↑ and ↓) are used to denote direction of the effect, a ↑ denotes a positive effect and a ↓ denotes a negative effect. The model fit (R^2) of each model is shown in the last row of the tables. A log transformation was applied to some metrics, indicated in the left column, as discussed earlier. In all cases the effects were statistically significant with a $p < 0.01$.

The base models provide a model fit of 72% and 17% for Windows Vista and Windows 7, respectively. The lower model fit for Windows 7 is likely due to the fact that Windows 7 had both fewer post-release defects and less variance in post-release defects across binaries. Adding the branch activity metric to the base model improved model fit to 75% for Windows Vista and 18% for Windows 7. The model fit is further increased to 77% when the branch scatter metrics are added Windows Vista and 19% for Windows 7. Branch depth metrics added a fractional (less than 0.5%) improvement to model fit in Windows Vista and did not add to the model fit in Windows 7. These model fit values are in the same range as prior work on software quality that achieves model fits values between 22-33% deviance explained [25]. In all cases, we found one or more of the metrics in each metric category (i.e., activity, distribution or depth), except for the case of depth metrics in Windows 7 to be statistically significant and improve model fit.

Furthermore, we divided the changes based on the branch families they were in. The purpose of doing so was to study whether certain branch families are more risky than others. The results are shown in the last column of Tables 1 and 2. Since the sum of the changes in each branch family is equal to the number of development changes, we cannot include both metrics in the model. Therefore, we remove the number of development changes from the model and add the number of changes in each branch family, labeled as Branch Groups in the tables. We see that using the branch families improves the model fit to be 79% for Windows Vista and 36% for Windows 7. This is a large improvement, suggesting that changes in certain branch families leads to more failures compared to other branch families. One explanation for the considerable improvement in model fit in Windows 7 compared to Vista is the fact that Windows 7 had more branch families than Windows Vista. Thus branch families provide more discrimination in Windows 7.

5.1 Quantifying the Effect of Branching on Software Quality

Although model fit is traditionally used to evaluate linear regression models, its importance depends on the context in which it is evaluated. Since our base models were fairly robust (providing a model fit of 72% for Windows Vista for example), we did not expect a large improvement in model fit. Our primary goal was determining which measures had a statistically significant relationship with post-release failures.

Having identified the statistically significant metrics, we are interested in quantifying the relationship of these metrics on post-release failures. For example, we would like to be able to quantify the increase in post-release failures if branching activity increased by 10%. Quantifying the effect is of primary importance to practitioners because it helps them better understand - how and by how much – their branching practices impact their software quality. Quantifying the effect allows practitioners to put a cost on the impact of their branching practices (e.g. mapping an increase of 10% in failures to dollars lost) and argue for process change, if needed.

To practically quantify effect, we study each metric in isolation. We do so by using the fitted model and setting all the metrics

	Base Model	Model 2	Model 3	Model 4	Model 5
log(Size)	↑	↑	↑	↑	↑
log(Churn)	↑	↑	↑	↑	↑
log(Complexity)	↑	↑	↑	↑	↑
log(Dev. Changes)	↑	↑	↑	↑	-
log(No. Files)	↑	↑	↑	↑	↑
Branch Activity		↑	↑	↑	↑
log(Branch Scatter)			-	-	-
Branch Scatter Entropy			↓	↓	↓
Low Branch Depth				-	-
log(High Branch Depth)				-	-
Branch Depth Entropy				-	-
Branch Groups					↑
R^2	17%	18%	19%	19%	36%

Table 2. Post-release failure models for Windows 7. Arrows indicate effect on failures. Table 3 shows magnitude of effects.

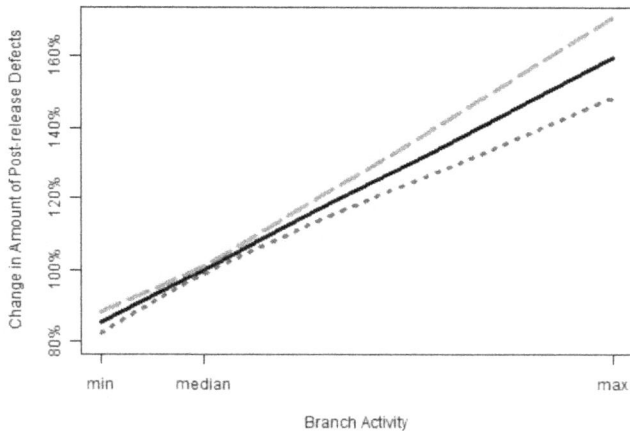

Figure 2: Effect of branch activity on post-release failures in Windows Vista

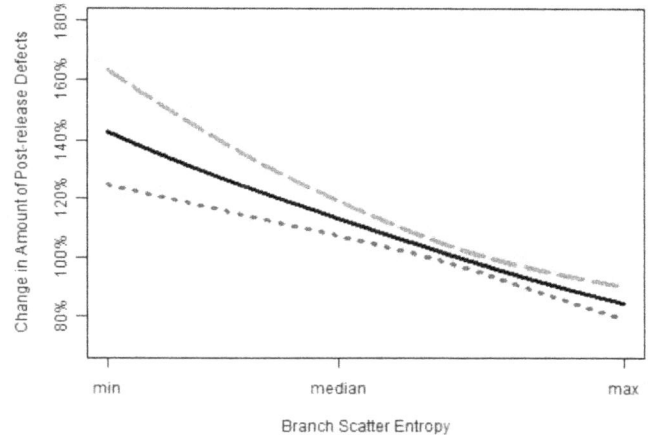

Figure 3: Effect of branch scatter entropy on post-release failures in Windows 7

other than the metric of interest to their median values. Then, we vary the metric we are interested in studying the effect of, from its minimum to its maximum value and observe the change in the projected number of post-release failures. To put the in-crease/decrease of effect into perspective, we normalize the effect of each metric, by its effect at the median value. The direction of the effect can be positive or negative. A positive direction indi-cates that an increase in the metric causes an increase in post-release failures. A negative direction indicates that an increase in a metric leads to less post-release failures.

We illustrate with an example in Figure 2 where we plot the change in effect for the branch activity metric in Windows Vista. The x-axis shows the change in the value of the metric from its minimum to its maximum value. The y-axis shows the change in the amount of projected post-release failures, normalized by the median. We also plot the 95% confidence interval, shown by the dashed lines. At 100% on the y-axis represents the modeled num-ber of post-release failures when branch activity is at its median

value (and all other metrics in the model are also set to their me-dian). Decreasing the branch activity metric to its minimum value would reduce the amount of failures to 85% (± 2.9%) of the value observed at the median. If branch activity was at its maximum value, we expect an increase of up to 59% (± 11%) more failures. Figure 3 shows a similar graph, depicting the effects of branch scatter entropy in Windows 7.

Table 3 summarizes the effects of all metrics at their minimum and maximum values (values below 100% indicate decreases in failures, values above, increases). We find that for Windows Vista, branch activity, branch scatter and low branch depth have the biggest effect, increasing the amount of post-release failures by up to 59%. Branch scatter entropy and depth entropy have a moderate effect. In Windows 7, we find that branch activity and branch scatter entropy both have a large effect (up to 70%), how-ever they also have wide variation.

The majority of the metrics have a positive relationship with post-release failures, except for the entropy metrics, which have a neg-

Release	Metric	Min %	Max %	Direction
Windows Vista	Branch Activity	85±2.9	159±11	Positive
	Branch Scatter	98±1.2	140±10.5	Positive
	Branch Scatter Entropy	83±3.8	111±2.3	Positive
	Low Branch Depth	92±3.8	141±15.4	Positive
	Branch Depth Entropy	86±8.4	111±5.2	Negative
Windows 7	Branch Activity	78±7.4	151±26.2	Positive
	Branch Scatter Entropy	84±58	143±20.8	Negative

Table 3: Summary of metric relationships with failures

ative relationship. This finding makes intuitive sense, since entropy is high when the proportions across the different branches are equal. Therefore, having a low branch scatter entropy value means that software components that are mainly developed in one branch family have less post-release failures than components that are developed an equal amount across different branch families. One exception is branch scatter entropy in Windows Vista, which has a small, but positive effect. One possible explanation is that Windows Vista had few branch families, therefore, branch scatter entropy did not play a major role.

Our results on Windows Vista and 7 can be summarized:

- **H1. Branch activity:** has a negative impact on software quality. It can increase post-release failures by up to 59% in Windows Vista and up to 51% in Windows 7.

- **H2a. Branch Scatter:** has a negative impact on software quality. It can increase failures by up to 40% in Windows Vista.

- **H2b. Branch Scatter Entropy:** has a slight positive impact on software quality in Windows Vista and negatively impacts software quality in Windows 7. It can increase failures by up to 43% in Windows 7.

- **H3a and b. Branch Depth and Branch Depth Entropy:** have very little to no impact on software quality.

6. BRANCHING STRATEGIES

Thus far, we have mainly focused on the three hypotheses surrounding the effects of branching on software quality at the attribute level. Our findings showed that branch activity, and branch scatter effect the software quality of components in Windows Vista and Windows 7 and branch depth only had a moderate effect on quality in Windows Vista.

However, one question that still lingers is *how to best align the branching structure?* Traditionally, branch structures are aligned in one of two ways: to match the architecture of the software system or to match the organizational structure.

Aligning the branching structure with the architectural structure means that each branch will be dedicated to a component of the software. For example, in a layered software architecture, a branch family will be created for each layer. Branches within the

	Vista	Windows 7
Arch mismatch	0.426**	0.308**
Org mismatch	0.543**	0.321**
Org + Arch	0.594**	0.385**

($p<0.01$ **; $p < 0.05$ *)

Table 4: Model fit (R^2) of architectural and organizational mismatch

branch family can be used to develop sub-components and so on. The advantage of matching the branching structure with the architectural structure is that changes to a component mostly happen on the same branch, thereby minimizing integrations.

Aligning the branching structure along the organizational structure means that branches match team boundaries. In such a scenario, each team manager will have his own branch family. The individual branches within the branch family will be assigned to different sub-teams, managed by the different team leads under that manager. The advantage of matching the branch structure with the organizational structure is that the personnel working on the branches are close organizationally, making coordination and communication much simpler.

We built linear regression models that examined the relationship of organizational and architectural mismatch of individual branches with branch quality. All measures of organizational mismatch -- number of development leads and number of managers that made changes on a branch -- and architectural mismatch – number of subsystems changed on a branch – were statistically significant ($p < 0.05$) and had a negative impact; increased mismatch decreased quality.

Table 4 shows the results of our analysis. We find that organizational mismatch provided a better fit (i.e., higher R^2) when modeling branch quality in both, Windows Vista and Windows 7. The effects of our measures of organizational and architectural measures on defects in branches are shown in Table 5 (same format as Table 3). This finding indicates that branches that cross-cut organizational boundaries have a higher correlation with post-release failures than branches that cross-cut architectural boundaries. Therefore, we suggest that, contrary to traditional belief, branching structures should not only align according to architectural structure of the software, but also according to its organizational structure.

Our finding complements prior work that showed organizational metrics outperform the traditional process and product metrics in modeling software quality at the component level [13]. The difference between prior work and ours is that we examine the failures on a *per branch* basis and compare the effects of architectural vs. organizational mismatch rather than examining only organizational mismatch. With regard to our hypotheses, we conclude:

- **H4a: Branching according to architectural structure:** Architectural mismatch increases post-release failures in both releases of Windows.

- **H4b: Branching according to organizational structure:** Organizational mismatch increases post-release failures in both releases of Windows.

- **Architectural vs. Organizational Mismatch:** Organizational structure has a stronger relationship with failures than architectural mismatch.

| | Vista | | Windows 7 | |
Metric	Min %	Max %	Min %	Max %
Managers	100±5	135±24	100±6	146±34
Leads	78±6	201±25	83±8	156±29
Engineers	65±8	217±24	67±14	169±25
Components	92±10	120±8	88±9	119±11
Subcomponents	88±9	130±9	89±9	113±11

Table 5: Summary of organizational and architectural mismatch on branch quality

7. IMPLICATIONS

7.1 Future Research

Our work has implications for future work. Our findings indicate that branching does indeed have an effect on post-release failures. At the same time, we believe that there are scenarios where more branching activity and scatter is expected, and we are not advocating a "branch-free" development process. For example, globally distributed teams, that are not able to communicate frequently may have more branching activity than co-located teams. This increase in branching activity is due to the fact that distributed teams are more concerned about keeping each other up-to-date and avoiding conflicts (since conflicts will require them to communicate). Our experience in talking with developers is that many failures that they deem "caused" by branching are in fact not directly caused by the creation of a branch, but rather by issues such as unmet (and sometimes unknown) coordination needs, poor integration work, and changes that propagate to the rest of the project late, all that result from *how teams work as a result of using branches.*

We have identified which concrete aspects of branching are related to decreased quality. However, changing the branching structure will only affect quality to the degree that they change the malignant behavior and process problems that lead to problems to begin with. Indeed, our experience studying open source projects that use branching heavily [5] [26] suggests that different projects use branches in their development processes differently. Understanding which "branch processes" lead to better outcomes than others in different contexts is a clear avenue for future research, and we exhort others to study this and report their findings (along with contextual details [27]) as we do the same in contexts at Microsoft.

7.2 Practical Implications

Our results have important practical implications. Based on our findings in this study, we make the following recommendations to software practitioners:

- Practitioners should aim to reduce branch activity since it may lead to an increase in the likelihood of failures.

- Practitioners should aim to reduce the scattering of development across many branch families since branch scatter increases the likelihood of failures in Windows Vista.

- When deciding how to best align branch structure, organizational mismatch should be closely considered by practition-

ers since it has a stronger relationship with failures than architectural mismatch.

Based on our findings, we are working with product groups within Microsoft and suggesting that, in addition to aligning branching structure according to architectural structure, branching structures should align with the organizational structure of their teams. When combined with prior work that empirically evaluates Conway's Law ([14] [13]), this study provides further evidence that the makeup and organization of software teams has a direct relationship with quality. Development projects (especially those at large scale) would do well to consider this mounting body of evidence.

8. THREATS TO VALIDITY

Threats to Construct Validity: consider the relationship between theory and observation, in case the measured variables do not measure the actual factors. We use post-release failures to measure software quality. In certain cases, it might be more beneficial to use pre-release failures as a measure of quality since branching may cause integration failures that are often reported as pre-release failures. However, in our case changes were used to identify pre-release failures, therefore, using them to measure quality as well would introduce bias in our study. More importantly, post-release failures represent those failures not caught by QA processes and are more costly as they are customer-facing failures.

When evaluating the effect of architectural and organizational mismatch on branch quality, we measured branch failures as a ratio of development that a component had on that branch times the number of failures for that component. Ideally (and if possible), one would map each failure to the branch that the it was introduced in. However, we were unable to create such a mapping due to lack of data.

Threats to External Validity: consider the generalization of our findings. The studied projects are both developed by Microsoft and follow processes that are defined by the development and management teams at Microsoft. A common misconception about industrial research at large companies such as Microsoft is that the software projects are not representative of other software projects and thus not valuable. This is not true. While projects might be larger in size, most development practices at Microsoft are adapted from the general software engineering community outside Microsoft. Many commercial and OSS projects also use branches to partition work and filter changes based on quality and this study represents a first step in examining the relationship between branching and quality. Therefore, we believe that this study can be replicated on other large software systems that use branches.

Another frequent misconception is that empirical research within one company or one project is not good enough, provides little value for the academic community, and does not contribute to scientific development. Historical evidence shows otherwise. Flyvbjerg provides several examples of individual cases that contributed to discovery in physics, economics, and social science [28]. W. I. B. Beveridge observed for social sciences: "More discoveries have arisen from intense observation than from statistics applied to large groups" (as quoted in Kuper & Kuper [29] p. 95). This should not be interpreted as a criticism of research that focuses on large samples or entire populations. For the development of an empirical body of knowledge as championed by Basili [30], both types of research are essential.

Lastly, a common misinterpretation of empirical studies is that nothing new is learned (e.g., "I already knew this result").

However, such wisdom has rarely been shown to be true and is often quoted without scientific evidence. This paper provides such evidence: Most common wisdom and intuition is confirmed (e.g., "binaries with more branch activity tend to have more failures") while some is challenged (e.g., "branches should be divided along architectural boundaries").

9. CONCLUSION

We have presented the first, but hopefully not last, empirical evaluation of the relationship between various aspects of branch use in a software project and post-release quality. We have demonstrated not only that branch activity and branch scatter lead to decreased quality, but we have also *quantified* the magnitude of the relationship. Further, we have evaluated two differing branching strategies and found that organizational alignment is more important than architectural alignment, thereby allowing software teams to make more informed decisions about their branching structure. This evidence is being used within Microsoft and can be of value to other software projects that use branching, or are considering it, as well.

10. REFERENCES

[1] Walrad, C. and Strom, D. The importance of branching models in SCM. *Computer* (2002), 31--38.

[2] Appleton, B., Berczuk, S., Cabrera, R., and Orenstein, R. *Streamed Lines: Branching Patterns for Parallel Software Development*. Vol. 2002, 1998.

[3] Premraj, R., Tang, A., Linssen, N., Geraats, H., and Vliet, H. To Branch or Not to Branch? In *Proceeding of the 2nd workshop on Software engineering for sensor network applications*. 81-90, (2011).

[4] Wingerd, L. and Seiwald, C. High-Level Best Practices in Software Configuration Management. In *Proceedings of the Sym. on System Configuration Management*. 57-66, (1998).

[5] Bird, C., Rigby, P.C., Barr, E.T., Hamilton, D.J., Germán, D.M., and Devanbu, P.T. The promises and perils of mining git. In *Mining Software Repositories*.1-10, (2009).

[6] Bird, C., Zimmermann, T., and Teterev, A. A Theory of Branches as Goals and Virtual Teams. In *Proceedings of CHASE*. 53-56, (2011).

[7] Midha, A.K. Software configuration management for the 21st century. *Bell Labs Technical Journal*, 2 (1997), 154--165.

[8] Buffenbarger, J. and Gruell, K. A Branching/Merging Strategy for Parallel Software Development. In *System Configuration Management*. 86-99, (1999).

[9] Perry, D.E., Siy, H.P., and Votta, L.G. Parallel changes in large-scale software development: an observational case study. *ACM Transactions on Software Engineering and Methodology (TOSEM)*, 10 (2001), 308--337.

[10] Nagappan, N. and Ball, T. Use of relative code churn measures to predict system defect density. In *Proceedings of the 27th international conference on Software engineering* (2005), 284--292.

[11] Briand, L., Daly, J.W., and Wust, J. A Unified Framework for Cohesion Measurement in Object-OrientedSystems. *Empirical Softw. Engg.*, 3, 1 (July 1998), 65--117.

[12] Brun, Y., Holmes, R., Ernst, M.D., and Notkin, D. Proactive Detection of Collaboration Conflicts. In *Proceedings of ESEC/FSE11*. 168-178, (2011).

[13] Nagappan, N., Murphy, B., and Basili, V.R. *The Influence of Organizational Structure on Software Quality: An Empirical Case Study*. In Proceedings of the International Conference on Software Engineering. 521-530, 2008.

[14] Cataldo, M., Wagstrom, P.A., Herbsleb, J.D., and Carley, K.M. Identification of coordination requirements: implications for the Design of collaboration and awareness tools. In *Proceedings of the Conference on Computer supported cooperative work* (2006), 353--362.

[15] Shannon, C. A mathematical theory of communication. *The Bell System Technical Journal*, 27 (1948), 379--423.

[16] D'Ambros, M., Lanza, M., and Robbes, R. An extensive comparison of bug prediction approaches. In *Mining Software Repositories*. 31-41, (2010).

[17] Hassan, A.E. Predicting faults using the complexity of code changes. In *International Conference on Software Engineering*. 78-88, (2009).

[18] Conway, M. How do committees invent? *Datamation*, 14, 4 (1968).

[19] Herbsleb, J.D., Mockus, A., Finholt, T.A., and Grinter, R.E. An Empirical Study of Global Software Development: Distance and Speed. In *Proceedings of the 23rd International Conference on Software Engineering*. 81-90, (2001).

[20] Mockus, A. Organizational volatility and its effects on software defects. In *ACM SIGSOFT Int'l Symposium on Foundations of Software Engineering*. 117-126, (2010).

[21] Eaddy, M., Zimmermann, T., Sherwood, K.D., Garg, V., Murphy, G.C., Nagappan, N., and Aho, A.V. Do Crosscutting Concerns Cause Defects? *IEEE Transactions on Software Engineering*. Vol. 34, 4. 497-515, (2008).

[22] Ostrand, T.J., Weyuker, E.J., and Bell, R.M. Programmer-based fault prediction. In *International Conference on Predictive Models in Software Engineering*. 1-10, (2010).

[23] Cataldo, M., Mockus, A., Roberts, J.A., and Herbsleb, J.D. Software Dependencies, Work Dependencies, and Their Impact on Failures. *IEEE Transactions on Software Engineering*, 35, 6 (2009), 864--878.

[24] Kutner, M., Nachtsheim, C., and Neter, J. *Applied Linear Regression Models*. , 2004.

[25] Cataldo, M., Mockus, A., Roberts, J.A., and Herbsleb, J.D. Software dependencies, work dependencies, and their impact on failures. *Software Engineering, IEEE Transactions on*, 35 (2009), 864--878.

[26] Barr, E.T., Bird, C., Rigby, P.C., Hindle, A., German, D.M., and Devanbu, P. Cohesive and isolated Development with Branches. In *International Conference on Fundamental Approaches to Software Engineering*. To appear, (2012).

[27] Murphy-Hill, E.R., Murphy, G.C., and Griswold, W.G. Understanding context: creating a lasting impact in experimental software engineering research. *Workshop on Future of Software Engineering*. 255-258, (2010).

[28] Flyvbjerg, B. Five misunderstandings about case-study research. *Qualitative inquiry*, 12 (2006), 219-245.

[29] Kuper, A. and Kuper, J., eds. *The Social Science Encyclopedia*. Routledge, 1985.

[30] Basili, V.R., Shull, F., and Lanubile, F. Building knowledge through families of experiments. *IEEE Transactions on Software Engineering*, 25 (Jul/Aug 1999), 456-473.

How Many Individuals to Use in a QA Task with Fixed Total Effort?

Mika V. Mäntylä
Lund University
Department of Computer Science
22100 Lund, Sweden

mika.mantyla@cs.lth.se

Kai Petersen
Blekinge Institute of Technology
School of Computing
37140 Karlskrona, Sweden

kai.petersen@bth.se

Dietmar Pfahl
Lund University
Department of Computer Science
22100 Lund, Sweden

dietmar.pfahl@cs.lth.se

ABSTRACT

Increasing the number of persons working on quality assurance (QA) tasks, e.g., reviews and testing, increases the number of defects detected – but it also increases the total effort unless effort is controlled with fixed effort budgets. Our research investigates how QA tasks should be configured regarding two parameters, i.e., time and number of people. We define an optimization problem to answer this question. As a core element of the optimization problem we discuss and describe how defect detection probability should be modeled as a function of time. We apply the formulas used in the definition of the optimization problem to empirical defect data of an experiment previously conducted with university students. The results show that the optimal choice of the number of persons depends on the actual defect detection probabilities of the individual defects over time, but also on the size of the effort budget. Future work will focus on generalizing the optimization problem to a larger set of parameters, including not only task time and number of persons but also experience and knowledge of the personnel involved, and methods and tools applied when performing a QA task.

Categories and Subject Descriptors

K.6.3 [**Software Management**]: *Software process*

General Terms

Measurement, Economics, Human Factors, Management

Keywords

Effectiveness, Fixed effort Budget, Effort, Review, People

1. INTRODUCTION

Given enough eyeballs, all bugs are shallow, is known as the Linus Law stated by Linus Torwalds [1]. The statement claims that if we increase the number of people performing quality assurance (QA) tasks we find an increasing number of bugs and if we have the possibility to add people endlessly finally all bugs will be found. Whether this statement is completely true is debatable. However, it illustrates the fact that using a larger group of people in a QA task increases the number of defects found in comparison with a smaller group. For example, data by Jones [2] indicates that beta-testing is the most effective QA measure when a high number of sites is available (>1000). Furthermore, research shows that having large groups can be beneficial, e.g. in data of [3] from software inspections, we can see that the number of defects found

increases when adding more inspectors even after 20 people. We witnessed in our previous research a similar pattern with manual software testing [4].

However, the problem with using large groups in QA tasks is the increasing personnel cost, but one can control this problem by limiting the effort budgets for QA tasks. The question to be answered when doing this how to divide the effort. For example, assume we have an effort budget of 10 person-hours for doing a software review. Then how many people should we use? Should we have one person working for ten hours or ten persons working one hour? Questions of this nature have received limited attention in the prior research on software testing and reviews, which focused more on the different techniques and tools to use.

In this paper, we continue our previous work [4] on understanding how many individuals to use in a QA task when having a fixed effort budget. In this paper, a QA task is any task where the primary goal is to find faults in a product under scrutiny. Section 2 presents the relevant prior work. Then, in Section 3, we discuss implications and present extension based on prior work. Section 4 models defect detection as a function of time, by first formulating defect detection with fixed effort budget as an optimization problem, and then applying this optimization problem to experimental data. Finally, Section 5 discusses the results and possible future work. Section 6 presents conclusions.

2. PRIOR WORK

In prior work, Biffl et al. describe how inspection team performance can be statistically estimated from individual inspector performances [3, 5]. For example, assume we have performed an experiment A with 40 participants and 10 of them found a particular defect $d1$. Then the detection probability for this defect is 0.25 on average for a single individual picked randomly from that population. Furthermore, if we pick two individuals then what follows from is that the detection probability for the particular defect is $0.4375 = 1 - (1 - 0.25)^2$.

We can also pick individuals from populations using different techniques and combine results as originally suggested by Biffl et al. This idea can be extended to other populations as well, e.g., ones having different time budgets, or having different experience. In Section 4 of this paper we discuss the case of fixed time budgets. To illustrate the case of using different techniques, let us assume we perform an experiment B with 40 participants – but using a different technique than in experiment A – and this time 20 individuals find defect $d1$ suggesting an average detection probability of 0.5. Then, from this we can calculate the detection probability of a group consisting of one inspector from each population A and B as $0.625 = 1 - (1 - 0.25)^1 * (1 - 0.5)^1$. In more formal terms, the probability $P(d)$ that a group of size n finds a given defect d is calculated as follows:

$$(1) \qquad P(d) = 1 - \prod_{ps \in \{1,...,Pops\}} (1 - p_{ps})^{n_{ps}}$$

In the formula above, *Pops* is the number of all populations from which group members are picked, *ps* is the index of a specific population, n_{ps} is the number of group members picked from the population with index *ps*, and p_{ps} is the average defect detection probability for defect *d* of group members picked from the population with index *ps*. Note that the sum over all n_{ps} equals *n*. In this paper, the binomial distribution is used to approximate the hypergeometric distribution when sampling from two populations. In more complex settings, the multinomial distribution could be used to approximate the multivariate hypergeometric distribution (assuming large sized populations).

The expected total number of defects detected can be calculated by summing up the defect detection probabilities of each defect. For example, assume that from the population A, 20 individuals found another defect called *d2*. Then for a single individual picked out of population A the expected performance is to find 0.75 defects (0.25 (d1) + 0.5 (d2)) and for groups of two individuals we expect them to find 1.1875 defects, calculated as the sum of $0.4375 = 1 - (1 - 0.25)^2$ and $0.75 = 1 - (1 - 0.5)^2$. Again, in more formal terms, for a given number of existing defects D, the expected number of detected defects E := Exp(D) can be calculated according to [3, 5] as follows:

$$(2) \qquad E = \sum_{d \in D} P(d)$$

In our previous paper [3], we investigated time-restriction in software testing and found that two time-restricted testers with a 2-hour time slot found the same amount of defects as a single tester with no time-restriction, using almost 9.83 hours on average. The results of the study indicate that going slow and being thorough, i.e. using more time, is a good strategy for achieving high defect detection effectiveness for single individual. However, the study also indicates that this is not necessarily true if we consider groups of individuals with time budgets. In fact, we found that if we pool 5 individuals each using 2h testing, i.e., adding up to a total of 10 person-hours effort, the nominal 5-person groups find 71% more defects than a single individual using 9.83 hours of time.

3. IMPLICATIONS AND EXTENSION BASED ON PRIOR WORK

One surprising implication we can deduce from the work and equations proposed by Biffl et al. [3, 5], which they did not mention themselves, is that we should not use the average number of defect detected or any statistical test based on it, e.g. *t-test*, to reason about defect detection performance differences between group. The reason for this is that it uses only the *number* of defects detected per participant and thus ignores the detection probabilities of individual defects. Furthermore, we cannot calculate group performances unless we do know defect detection probabilities for each individual defect. For example, if we consider QA techniques A and B, and experiments show that they both detect 50% of the defects in a given set of four defects, then a classical t-test comparing the average number of defects detected would reveal no difference. Let us further assume that technique A has the detection probabilities of (0.95, 0.05, 0.95, 0.05) for the four defects and that technique B has the detection probabilities of (0.5, 0.5, 0.5, 0.5), i.e., both techniques detect 2 defects on average. Now, if we have a group of two people both using either technique A or B, we find that using technique B is superior. The expected performance of technique B for a group of two people is detecting 3 defects. This can be calculated using equations (1 and 2) in Section 2, i.e., $3 = 4 * (1 - (1 - 0.5)^2)$. However, when using technique A, the expected number of defects found would

be $2.19 = 2 * (1 - (1 - 0.95)^2)) + 2 * (1 - (1 - 0.05)^2)$. In other words, while the average total number of defects detected by a single individual revealed no differences between techniques A and B, the situation in the group settings changes towards favoring the technique that has smaller variation between the defect detection probabilities of individual defects, in our example technique B.

Our decision problem is related to research about the relationship between review speed (or review rate) and defect detection probability, as studied also by Kemerer and Paulk (see fig 6 in [6]). In [6], one individual reviewing 200 LOC/h (or slower) finds 59.2% and an individual reviewing 400 LOC/h (or faster) 50.0% of all defects. To make the effort budget comparable, the setting would be to compare one person reviewing at a speed of 200 LOC/h against two persons reviewing at 400 LOC/h. Ideally, two fast reviewers together with a defect detection effectiveness of 50% each could find up to 75.0% (i.e., $(1 - (1 - 0.5)^2)$ of all defects. Based on this analysis, using two fast reviewers instead of one thorough reviewer seems to be promising.

We can improve the estimate of the defect detection effectiveness of two individuals by using empirical data. In [3] we studied 13 empirical data sets to determine the average increase in defect detection effectiveness when using two individuals instead of one. We found that across all data sets the number of defects detected by two persons is on average 73.6% (range: 59%-89%) of the theoretical maximum minus the theoretical minimum. Applying this average to the data of Kemerer and Paulk, where two fast reviewers (reading at a speed of 400 LOC/h) have a theoretical minimum of 50% defect detection probability (e.g., if both reviewers happen to find exactly the same defects) and a maximum of 75%, we could predict that two fast reviewers find 68.4% (i.e., 0.736*(0.75-0.5)+0.5) of all defects.

4. MODELING DEFECT DETECTION OVER TIME

The defect detection probability of a given defect *d1* can be understood as a function of time, derived from the defect detection times of individuals performing a QA task. For example if we have 40 reviewers and 10 of them find defect *d1* then the detection probability of *d1* is 0.25 after they all individuals have completed their reviews. At the beginning of the review time is zero (*t=0*) and so is the detection probability of *d1* (*d1p=0*). As time passes, *d1p* changes from 0 to its maximum of 0.25. In Figure 1, we illustrate this by presenting how the defect detection probabilities of two defects (D5 and D36) change over time based on data we got from a previous experiment [7].

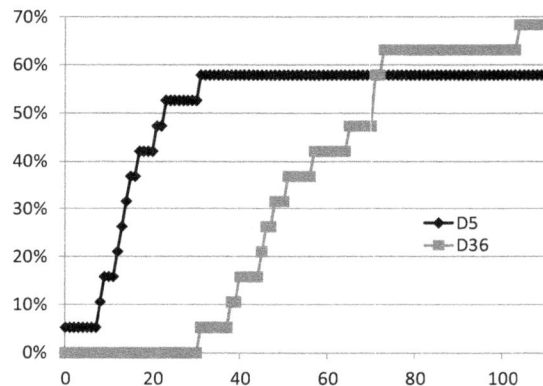

Figure 1. Detection percentages of two defects (D5 and D36) over the course of an inspection

Based on the graph we can now answer questions like the following: How many defects, on average, would 2 individuals find, if they both used half of the given time $2 * {}^t/_2$? Depending on the graph, the performance of the two individuals using 50% of the time could be worse or better than that of one individual using 100% of the time. In the illustrated case, considering only the two depicted defects, a single individual finds on average 1.21 of those defects when t=100 min. Two individuals using $2 * {}^t/_2$, i.e. 50 min each, would find 1.35 defects.

4.1 Formalization in mathematical terms

If n is the number of individuals working independently on a QA task and t is the time used by each individual to perform the QA task, then we can formulate an optimization problem that aims at finding the largest defect detection effectiveness, expressed in terms of the expected number of defects $E(n, t)$ found by all individuals n in time t with fixed effort budget $t * n = c$, where c is a constant, as follows:

$$(3) \qquad E(n,t) = \sum_{d \in \{1,...,D\}} (1 - (1 - p(d,t))^n) \to max$$

with:

- $n \in \{1, ..., N\}$, with N maximum number of individuals,
- $t \in (0, T)$, with T maximum duration of QA task,
- $d \in \{1, ..., D\}$, with D total number of defects,
- $p(d, t) \in [0, 1]$, average probability of detecting defect d at time t by any individual,
- $t * n = c$ with c is a constant effort budget

Since the probability $p(d,t)$ that a defect d is found by an individual within a time period of length t is a continuous function over time which we cannot derive analytically from a corresponding mathematical formula, we must base the calculations of optimality on empirical data, similar to that shown in Figure 1.

4.2 Application using empirical data

To illustrate our idea, we use a data-set from a previous experiment [7] were inspection techniques, time-controlled reading and usage-based reading, were studied in an experiment involving 19 students who detected in total 31 defects. In that study, no statistically significant differences between the compared techniques were found. Therefore, for our study, we pooled the data and treated it as one data set. It was important for our study that the original experiment recorded the exact time in minutes when each defect was found by each individual. This allowed us to construct figures like Figure 1 and applying the formulas presented in Section 0.

In the original experiment, the time was split into preparation time (40 min used in average) and inspection time (125 min used in average). During the preparation time, the students were instructed to do an overview reading of the inspected document, but also to read instructions on the inspection techniques that were tested. This preparation time would be shorter in the industrial context when inspectors would already be trained in a given technique and familiar with the product. Thus, the long preparation time in the student case represents a situation when beginners come to inspect a product they know nothing about. Since we do not know the values for more realistic preparation time we present the following extremes cases: *case 1* where only the inspection time is considered, and *case 2* where the preparation time is added on top of the inspection time. The maximum inspection time used by an inspector was 125 minutes and the maximum inspection + preparation time was 165 minutes.

Table 1. Defect detection effectiveness (= expected number of defects E)

n	Case 1: fixed budget of 125 min (inspection time only)			Case 2: fixed budget of 165 min (inspection+preparation time)		
	t/n [min]	E(n,t)	t [min]	t/n [min]	E(n,t)	t [min]
1	125	9.16	125	165	9.21	165
2	62	9.78	124	82	6.70	164
3	42	7.89	126	55	3.94	165
4	31	7.25	124	41	1.66	164
5	25	6.43	125	33	0.24	165
6	21	6.33	126	27	0.28	162
7	18	6.21	126	24	0.32	168
8	16	6.02	128	21	0.35	168

We used the maximum inspection times of each case as our base values for the fixed effort budgets, i.e., 125 min for case 1, and 165 min for case 2. Table 1 and Figure 2 show the number of expected defects $E(n,t)$ for case 1. From the table, we can see that for case 1 the optimal configuration is to use 2 inspectors who split the time budget of 125 min. Choosing 3 or more inspectors results in declining performance. When we use the multiples of the base time budget of 125 min, as shown in Figure 2, we can see that in all cases the optimal number of inspectors is n+1 when n is the minimum number of inspectors that could be used to consume the effort budget. Also, with effort budgets from 250 min to 500 min, n+2 inspectors perform better than n inspectors.

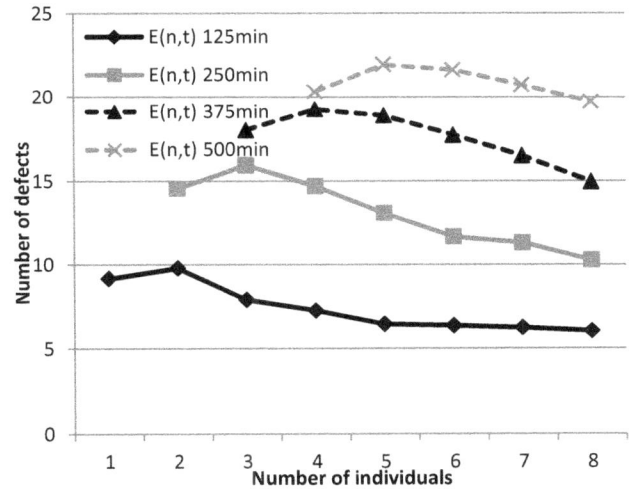

Figure 2. Defect detection effectiveness with fixed budgets of 125, 250, 375, and 500 min (case 1: inspection time only).

Table 1 and Figure 3 show the results for case 2 where both preparation and inspection times are taken under consideration. The table shows how using a single individual is superior when the preparation time is accounted for and having the smallest time budget of 165 minutes. However, from Figure 3, we can see that using the smallest possible number of inspectors is not beneficial for the time budgets of 495 minutes and 660 minutes and in such cases it would be the best to use n+1 inspectors when n is the minimum number of inspectors that could be used to fill the time budget.

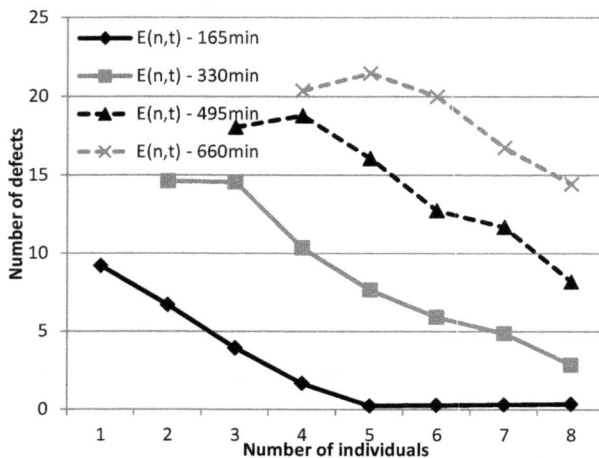

Figure 3. Defect detection effectiveness with fixed budgets of 165, 330, 495, and 660 min (case 2: inspection+preparation time).

5. DISCUSSION AND FUTURE WORK

This paper describes our ongoing work on trying to understand how many individuals to use in QA tasks where the primary goal is defect detection, e.g. inspections or testing, when having a fixed effort budget.

Prior work had indicated that using several fast readers could be more beneficial than using a single thorough reader. In this work, we could not find support for this finding. We would like to point out that our usage of the data is purely illustrative since it did not contain actual data of fast readers, i.e., readers forced to work under defined time-restrictions. To compensate the lack of data on actual fast readers we used the defect detection probabilities of uncompleted reviews. In the future, we plan to fix this shortcoming, by using the same experimental material as in [7], but by applying time-pressure and by forcing the students to perform the whole reviewer in a shorter time and then compare the results with data of previous experiments.

Whether to use multiple readers with shorter individual total time is context dependent and, in this paper, we could see how the number of reviewers that should be assigned changed whether we included or excluded the individual preparation time, and with different effort budgets. In the future, one should look at how much preparation time is actually needed in industrial settings. Furthermore, plenty of mathematical optimization techniques have already been applied in other areas of software engineering such as release planning [8] and they can undoubtedly be applied to this optimization problem as well.

As a next step, the optimization problem presented here will be generalized to include cases where not all inspectors are given an equal time slot, e.g. one could divide 90 minutes into three reviewers by giving one reviewer 60min and two others 15min each. We could also add other dimensions to the optimization problem. For example, higher expertise would make of individuals better in detecting defects, but in industrial setting people with higher expertise would also be more expensive to use. Thus, in such case, the total budget would be monetary and there would be tradeoff in choosing between more and less expensive individuals and the time their use. Furthermore, defect detection techniques could represent yet another dimensions that could be added to the optimization equation.

Furthermore, we aim to generalize the optimization problem to help design QA processes with stages. For example, would it be beneficial to first have one fast reader to find the easy defects, and then have a pair of thorough readers to dig out the defects that are more difficult to find? Such generalization would require that the defect detection rate of a subsequent task depend (partly) on the defect detection effectiveness of the predecessor task. This line of work could lead to giving practical recommendations for designing industry QA-processes based on solid empirical research.

6. CONCLUSION

In this paper we have made three contributions. First, we have described how defect detection probability should be understood as a function of time. Furthermore, we have formulated it as an optimization problem and showed the results of using the formulas on previously collected empirical data set of [7]. Second, based on this we have shown numerous avenues for future work in Section 5. Third, we showed that using number of defects detected per individual and statistical tests relying on such numbers, e.g. *t-test*, should not be used to reason between different techniques in-group settings. This is because defect detection probabilities of individual defects are needed to study group performance. It is still correct to use the number of defects detected per individual if one is only interested in the performance difference between singles. However, we believe this is actually rarely the case as software development and QA are often collaborative activities.

7. ACKNOWLEDGMENTS

This work has been supported by ELLIIT, the Strategic Area for ICT research, funded by the Swedish Government.

8. REFERENCES

[1] E. Raymond, "The cathedral and the bazaar," Knowledge, Technology & Policy, vol. 12, no. 3, 1999, pp. 23-49.

[2] C. Jones, "Software defect-removal efficiency," Computer, vol. 29, no. 4, 1996, pp. 94-95.

[3] S. Biffl and M. Halling, "Investigating the defect detection effectiveness and cost benefit of nominal inspection teams," Software Engineering, IEEE Transactions on, vol. 29, no. 5, 2003, pp. 385-397.

[4] M.V. Mäntylä and J. Itkonen, "The Effect of Adding People and Restricting Time in Software Testing – Power of the Crowds," Submitted to a Journal, Under review,

[5] S. Biffl and W. Gutjahr, "Influence of team size and defect detection technique on inspection effectiveness," Software Metrics Symposium, 2001. METRICS 2001. Proceedings. Seventh International, 2001, pp. 63-75.

[6] C.F. Kemerer and M.C. Paulk, "The impact of design and code reviews on software quality: An empirical study based on PSP data," IEEE Trans.Software Eng., vol. 35, no. 4, 2009, pp. 534-550.

[7] K. Petersen, K. Rönkkö and C. Wohlin, "The impact of time controlled reading on software inspection effectiveness and efficiency: a controlled experiment," Proceedings of the Second ACM-IEEE international symposium on Empirical software engineering and measurement, 2008, pp. 139-148.

[8] G. Ruhe and M.O. Saliu, "The art and science of software release planning," Software, IEEE, vol. 22, no. 6, 2005, pp. 47-53.

The Impact of Process Maturity on Defect Density

Syed Muhammad Ali Shah
Politecnico di Torino
Corso Duca degli Abruzzi, 24 10129
Torino, Italy
syed.shah@polito.it

Maurizio Morisio
Politecnico di Torino
Corso Duca degli Abruzzi, 24 10129
Torino, Italy,
maurizio.morisio@polito.it

Marco Torchiano
Politecnico di Torino
Corso Duca degli Abruzzi, 24 10129
Torino, Italy
marco.torchiano@polito.it

ABSTRACT

Context: A common assumption in software engineering is that a more structured process delivers higher quality products. However, there are limited empirical studies that support this assumption. *Objective*: In this paper we analyze 61 projects looking for a relationship between process structured and quality of the product. The structure is considered under two dimensions: level of maturity (as measured by the CMMI assessment model) and type (e.g. TSP, RUP). The quality of the product is measured in terms of Defect Density (DD) defined as the number of delivered defects divided per size. *Results*: We found a small and statistically not significant difference of DD between the projects developed under CMMI and those that are not developed under CMMI. Considering the CMMI levels, the pair (CMMI 1, CMMI 3) is characterized by a statistically significant different DD. CMMI 1 exhibiting higher DD than CMMI 3. By comparing different software processes with each other we found that Hybrid process exhibits statistically significant lower DD than Waterfall. *Conclusion*: Software process in either dimension, level of maturity and type has an impact on the software quality but smaller than one might expect.

Categories and Subject Descriptors

D.2.9 [**Management**]: Software process models, Software quality assurance

General Terms

Reliability, Standardization

Keywords:

Software quality, Software process, Defect density,

1. INTRODUCTION

The relationship between quality of the product and quality of the process is a key issue in all the engineering disciplines. In software engineering the attention to process started to be widespread from the 90's thanks to the work of Watts Humphrey, who applied to software engineering process concepts developed in other disciplines [1]. The CMMI [2], main result of this work, proposes a capability assessment model and an improvement path for organizations. On a parallel track, a large variety of software processes have been proposed over the years, starting from the Waterfall model up to the Team Software Process (TSP), Rational Unified Process (RUP), and Agile, just to name a few.

Behind many of these proposals stands the assumption that more sophisticated processes leads to higher quality products. This view has been later challenged by the Agile movement that insists more on *low ceremony* approaches. Our research is focused on finding empirical evidence of the effect of process choices on product quality. Product quality can be measured in several ways: reliability at function or system level, user satisfaction, defect density. In this study we take the pragmatic, view of quality in terms of defect density. Defect density (DD) is defined as the total number of delivered defects divided by the size of the software [3]. The paper is organized as follows; Section 2 discusses the related work. Section 3 presents the research design of the study. Section 4 presents the results. Finally, results are discussed and conclusions are presented in Section 5.

2. RELATED WORK

The Capability Maturity Model Integration (CMMI) has been widely adopted as a guideline to improve the overall software quality. There is research evidence that a higher CMMI level is linked to better quality [4][5]. Li et al, highlighted the experience of Neusoft Group, where defect density decreased from 0.85 defects per KLoC in 2000 to 0.1 defects per KLoC in 2005 as a result of CMMI adoption [6].

To date, there are various software development processes and an even larger numbers of Hybrids (RUP+TSP etc) in use. Software development process research literature contains different claims about quality. As reported in [7], if a well structured TSP is used, it has a positive impact decreasing the DD, in particular, and increasing the software quality in general. Abrahamsson and Koskela obtained the system defect density of 1.43 defects per KLoC from a controlled case study on extreme programming in Agile setting [8]. The study [9] reported the IBM experience of the Agile software process that reduced the DD and increased the overall quality. The survey conducted by Ramasubbua and Balan [10] on 112 projects showed that the combination of CMMI 5 with Agile had a significant and mostly positive impact on the project DD. Mohan et al. suggested the use of RUP to achieve increased reliability with higher productivity and lower defect density [11]. Bhat and Nagappan observed a significant increase in quality of two Microsoft projects developed using TDD (Test Driven Development) compared to same projects developed in a non-TDD fashion [12]. In one review study, Mitchell and Seaman [13] performed a systematic review comparing Waterfall vs. Iterative and Incremental development but the data set did not demonstrate any difference in quality.

Jones et al. [14] classify CMMI not assessed, CMMI level 1 and Waterfall projects under the low quality category. For average quality, they classify CMMI 1, 2 and Agile projects. For high quality, they classify CMMI level 3, 4, 5, Hybrid process, TSP and RUP projects.

3. RESEARCH DESIGN

In this section, we present the research questions, the data set and the metrics used.

3.1 Research Questions

Two primary research questions were formulated for this research.

RQ1: Does process maturity (i.e. different CMMI levels) affect defect density?

The goal here is to first characterize the defect density for different CMMI levels, and then check if these levels are significantly different.

RQ2: Do different software processes types affect defect density?

The goal is to characterize the effect of a different software process on defect density.

3.2 The Software Project Selection

We selected 61 software projects from the "Overview of United States Software Industry Results CIRCA 2011" [15], a survey conducted by Capers Jones & Associates LLC[1] in June 2011. The inclusion criterion was the availability of required metrics (DD figures, CMMI adoption levels and Software Process types) to answer our research questions. The projects that did not satisfy the inclusion criteria were excluded. Data was collected from the client companies of different domains (web based, embedded, military, civilian etc) in an exploratory manner (primarily on-site interviews of software projects). All the projects are considered to be large with average size of above 69 KLoC.

3.3 Metrics

The CMMI levels are expressed on an ordinal scale 1 to 5. However, the dataset contains also companies that were not assessed. In practice we have two merged scales: a nominal scale (assessed, not assessed) and an ordinal scale 1 to 5, only for assessed companies. The software process is expressed as a nominal scale (TSP, PSP, RUP, Hybrid). The studied defects are of high severity, major and minor nature however other non defects items like issues, warnings and further enhancements are not included. All the projects go through the same level of test removal activities i.e. unit test, system test and beta test. Defect density (DD) is calculated by dividing the number of delivered defects, by the code size in lines of code (LoC).

3.4 Analysis Method

To answer our research questions we adopted both visual analysis and statistical hypothesis testing. For the purpose of visual representation, we use box plots: as they allow for an immediate comparison. The research questions are addressed by means of statistical hypothesis testing; therefore we formulated null and alternative hypotheses as follows.

Concerning RQ1

$H0_0$:   There is no significant difference in terms of DD between projects assessed under CMMI and projects not assessed under CMMI.

$H0_a$:   There is significant difference in terms of DD among projects assessed under CMMI and projects not assessed under CMMI.

$H1_0$:   There is no significant difference in terms of DD among projects developed under different CMMI levels.

$H1_a$:   There is a significant difference in terms of DD among projects developed under different CMMI levels.

Concerning RQ2

$H2_0$:   There is no significant difference in terms of DD among projects adopting different software processes.

$H2_a$:   There is a significant difference in terms of DD among projects adopting different software processes.

If the above null hypothesis $H1_0$ and $H2_0$ can be rejected, we can conduct a post-hoc investigation of the pair wise differences; in this case, the Bonferroni correction for multiple tests shall be applied. For any pair of CMMI levels (L1, L2) and software processes (P1, P2) we can formulate the hypotheses as:

$H1.1_0$: $DD_{L1} = DD_{L2}$ (Projects developed in L1 have the same defect density as those developed in L2)

$H1.1_a$: $DD_{L1} \neq DD_{L2}$ (Projects developed in L1 have not the same defect density as those developed in L2)

$H2.1_0$: $DD_{P1} = DD_{P2}$ (Projects developed in P1 have the same defect density as those developed in P2)

$H2.1_a$: $DD_{P1} \neq DD_{P2}$ (Projects developed in P1 have not the same defect density as those developed in P2)

According to the recommendations in [16] we use the Kruskal-Wallis test for differences between three or more groups and the Mann-Whitney test for pair wise differences. The assumption to select was the not normal distribution of data sets. To evaluate the practical difference comparing different groups, we use the standardized effect size measure like Cohen's d. In the statistical testing, the significance level is checked by the given p-value. For rejecting or accepting the null hypothesis, we used the significance value $\alpha = 5\%$ / number of tests (Bonferroni correction).

4. RESULTS

RQ1: Do different CMMI levels affect defect density?

The data set contains 33 projects from companies that are certified under CMMI and 28 projects from companies that have not been assessed. Figure 1 shows the box plot of DD vs. project category (CMMI certified, CMMI not assessed). Table 1 in its first section, reports the descriptive statistics of DD of the two project categories. For RQ1, observing the box plots in Figure 1 it appears that they overlap. We test the hypothesis $H0_0$ with Mann-Whitney test for differences. The test reports a p-value = 0.7013 which is above the α threshold. Therefore, we cannot reject the null hypothesis, indicating that there is no significant difference of DD between the projects certified under CMMI and those not assessed.

As a next step, we focus our attention on projects with CMMI certification. The data set contains 9 CMMI 1 projects, 15 CMMI 3 projects, and 9 CMMI 5 projects. Figure 2 contains the box plot of DD vs. CMMI levels. It shows that higher levels of CMMI seem to have a lower DD, but higher variance. Table 1 in its second section reports the corresponding descriptive statistics. To test $H1_0$ we select the Kruskal-Wallis test. The test reports a p-value = 0.009, which is below the α threshold. Therefore, we can reject the null hypothesis that there is no difference in terms of DD among projects developed under different CMMI levels.

---

[1] http://www.namcook.com/

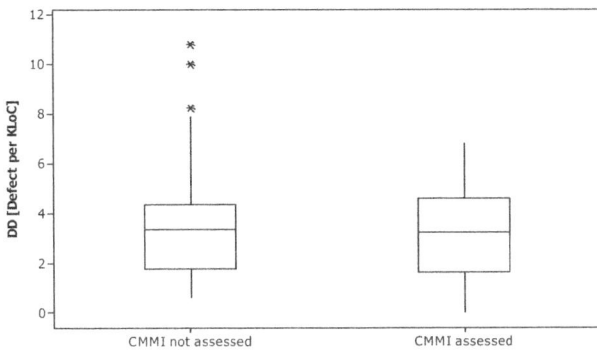

Figure 1 Box plot of DD of projects assessed under CMMI vs. projects not assessed under CMMI.

Table 1 Descriptive statistics of DD of projects

Group		N	Mean	Median	Std Dev
CMMI	Assessed	33	3.1	3.2	1.6
	Not Assessed	28	3.8	3.3	2.66
Maturity Level's	CMMI 1	9	4.3	4.1	0.79
	CMMI 3	15	3.1	3.0	1.25
	CMMI 5	9	2.0	1.25	2.2
Software Process	Unstructured Cowboy dev	4	6.0	5.8	3.4
	Agile (scrum)	6	4.9	3.4	3.2
	Water Fall	10	4.1	4.0	0.9
	Rational Unified Process	7	2.7	2.8	1.1
	Team Software Process	4	2.2	2.2	1.1
	Hybrid Process	5	0.8	0.7	0.7

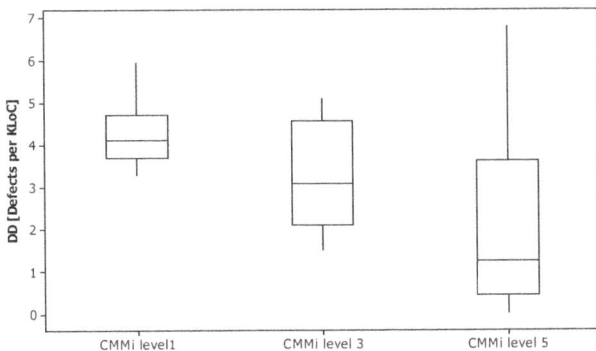

Figure 2 Box plot of DD of different CMMI levels

Given the above results we precede with the pair wise comparisons. In particular, we test the $H1.1_0$ for the two possible adjacent pairs of CMMI levels, i.e. (CMMI 1, CMMI 3), (CMMI 3, CMMI 5) by means of the Mann-Whitney test. In assessing the

test results, we adopt an α divided by 2 (0.025) according to the Bonferroni rule. For the pair (CMMI 3, CMMI 5) we obtained the p-value 0.06, which is larger than 0.025, therefore we cannot reject the corresponding null hypotheses. For the pair (CMMI 1, CMMI 3) the p-value is 0.023, therefore we can reject the null hypothesis. The significant difference can be considered large (Cohen's d = 1.14), CMMI 3 projects have a DD that is on average 1.2 defects per KLoC smaller than CMMI 1 projects.

In summary, concerning CMMI levels, there is evidence that the defect density of CMMI 3 projects is lower than CMMI 1 projects.

RQ2: Do different software process types affect defect density?

The data set contains 4 projects using unstructured 'Cowboy' development, 6 projects using Agile (scrum), 10 projects using Waterfall, 7 projects adopting RUP, 4 projects using TSP and 5 projects using Hybrid (RUP+TSP+Agile (scrum)) process. Figure 3 contains the box plot of DD vs. process type. Apparently TSP and Hybrid process exhibit the lowest DD. The third section of Table 1 reports the descriptive statistics of DD of projects by software process type. To test $H2_0$ we selected Kruskal-Wallis test. The test reports a p-value = 0.001, which is below the α threshold. Therefore, we can reject the null hypothesis.

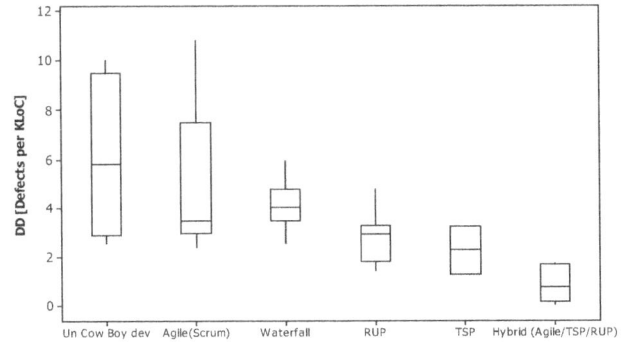

Figure 3 Box plot of DD for different processes

Given the above result, we precede with the pair wise comparisons. In particular, we test the $H2.1_0$ for all possible pairs of software processes i.e. (Cowboy, Waterfall), (Cowboy, Agile(scrum), (Cowboy, RUP), (Cowboy, Hybrid), (Cowboy, TSP), (Waterfall, Agile(scrum)), (Waterfall, RUP), (Waterfall, Hybrid), (Waterfall, TSP), (Agile(scrum), RUP), (Agile(scrum), Hybrid), (Agile(scrum), TSP), (RUP, Hybrid), (RUP, TSP) and (Hybrid, TSP), by means of Mann-Whitney test.

In assessing this test, we adopted an α divided by 15 according to the Bonferroni rule. For all pairs except (Waterfall, Hybrid) we obtained p-values > 0.003, therefore we cannot reject the corresponding null hypotheses. For (Waterfall, Hybrid) we obtained p–value = 0.0027 < (0.003) therefore we can reject the corresponding null hypothesis indicating that they have statistical different DD. The significant difference can be considered of large size (Cohen's d = 4.1), Waterfall projects have a DD that is on average 3.3 defects per KLoC higher than Hybrid projects.

4.1 Threats to Validity

We discuss in this section validity threats using the classification proposed by [16]. As for internal validity, we have two levels of indirection and possible sources of error. First we rely on a data set collected by others, who in their turn rely on how companies have maintained the data. Unfortunately, as any secondary study, we have no control on these aspects. As for construct validity, there are concerns about the conformance of projects classified according to CMMI levels and process types. As authors we acknowledge that no degree of process assessment was made by ourselves but we believe the authenticity of the collected data and its prior usage. We concede that there are also other factors (domain, expertise of developers) that have influence on the DD but for this work we only focus on process related factors. As for external validity we face the problem of generalizing the results. The study samples 61 projects, which are not a negligible absolute number but may offer a limited representation of industrial projects in general.

5. DISCUSSION AND CONCLUSIONS

The extraction of DD figures from industrial projects allowed us to publish a summary of DD data available. Table 1 presented the essential descriptive statistics. These results can be useful to both researchers and practitioners. Overall these results confirm that having a process (as suggested by CMMI, RQ1, or by any process type, RQ2) has a positive effect on quality measured in terms of DD. Higher CMMI levels have an effect on quality, but probably smaller than one might expect, especially considering that we couldn't find any difference between levels 3 and 5. Also adopting a specific process (Waterfall, Agile (scrum), TSP....) does not produce specific effects on quality. To this respect the most surprising comparison is Waterfall vs. Agile (scrum), where again there seem to be no difference in product quality. Of course we acknowledge that our analysis is partial: a process may have an effect on other properties (cost, time to market, customer satisfaction, etc). Further studies should be dedicated to analyze the effect of processes on those qualities.

This study has performed a statistical analysis of the product DD along two dimensions of process quality - i.e. level of maturity and type - in 61 industrial projects. Our results could not completely confirm some previous studies [1][6] that reported a steady quality increase with higher process capability levels. Our results partially support the observed increase in quality, by moving to the higher levels of maturity e.g. CMMI 1 to CMMI 3. However, the results corroborates the findings from previous study [7] where increase of quality is observed with the adoption of increasingly more structured software processes. After a survey on the literature we believe that empirical research on process characterization is limited. There is a need of further empirical evidence with precise methodology to give managers a broad perspective in making appropriate decisions when selecting software processes. The authors would like to extend grateful thanks to Capers Jones & Associates LLC, for providing the required study material for the analysis.

6. REFERENCES

[1] W. S. Humphrey, *Managing the Software Process*, Addison Wesley Professional. 1989.

[2] D. M. Ahern, A. Clouse, and R. Turner, *CMMI Distilled: A Practical Introduction to Integrated Process Improvement*, 3rd ed. Addison-Wesley, 2008.

[3] P. D. Ronald and B. Finkbine, "Metrics and Models in Software Quality Engineering," *SIGSOFT Softw. Eng. Notes*, vol. 21, no. 1, p. 89, 1999.

[4] M. M. Hinkle, "Software Quality, Metrics, Process Improvement, and CMMI: An Interview with Dick Fairley," *IT Professional DOI - 10.1109/MITP.2007.57*, vol. 9, no. 3, pp. 47–51, 2007.

[5] I. Sommerville, *Software Engineering*, 8th ed. Pearson Education, 2007.

[6] Meng Li, He Xiaoyuan, and A. Sontakke, "Defect Prevention: A General Framework and Its Application," in *Quality Software, 2006. QSIC 2006. Sixth International Conference on*, 2006, pp. 281–286.

[7] B. O. Sussy, J. A. Calvo-Manzano, C. Gonzalo, and S. F. Tomas, "Teaching Team Software Process in Graduate Courses to Increase Productivity and Improve Software Quality," in *Computer Software and Applications, 2008. COMPSAC '08. 32nd Annual IEEE International*, 2008, pp. 440–446.

[8] P. Abrahamsson and J. Koskela, "Extreme programming: a survey of empirical data from a controlled case study," in *Empirical Software Engineering, 2004. ISESE '04. Proceedings. 2004 International Symposium on*, 2004, pp. 73–82.

[9] J. C. Sanchez, L. Williams, and E. M. Maximilien, "On the Sustained Use of a Test-Driven Development Practice at IBM," in *AGILE 2007*, 2007, pp. 5–14.

[10] N. Ramasubbu and R. K. Balan, "The impact of process choice in high maturity environments: An empirical analysis," in *Software Engineering, 2009. ICSE 2009. IEEE 31st International Conference on*, 2009, pp. 529–539.

[11] K. K. Mohan, A. K. Verma, A. Srividya, G. V. Rao, and R. K. Gedela, "Early Quantitative Software Reliability Prediction Using Petri-nets," in *Industrial and Information Systems, 2008. ICIIS 2008. IEEE Region 10 and the Third international Conference on*, 2008, pp. 1–6.

[12] T. Bhat and N. Nagappan, "Evaluating the efficacy of test-driven development: industrial case studies," in *Proceedings of the 2006 ACM/IEEE international symposium on Empirical software engineering*, Rio de Janeiro, Brazil, 2006, pp. 356–363.

[13] S. M. Mitchell and C. B. Seaman, "A comparison of software cost, duration, and quality for waterfall vs. iterative and incremental development: A systematic review," in *Empirical Software Engineering and Measurement, 2009. ESEM 2009. 3rd International Symposium on*, 2009, pp. 511–515.

[14] C. Jones, J. Subramanyam, and O. Bonsignour, *The Economics of Software Quality*, Addison-Wesley Professional. 2011.

[15] C. Jones, "Overview of United States Software Industry Results Circa," Capers Jones & Associates LLC, 2011.

[16] C. Wohlin, P. Runeson, M. Höst, M. C. Ohlsson, B. Regnell, and A. Wesslen, *Experimentation in software engineering: an introduction*. Norwell, Massachusetts. USA: Kluwer Academic Publishers, 2000.

Language Interaction and Quality Issues: An Exploratory Study

Antonio Vetro', Federico Tomassetti, Marco Torchiano, Maurizio Morisio

Politecnico di Torino,
Dept. of Computer and Control Engineering
C.so Duca degli Abruzzi 24
Torino, Italy
{firstname.lastname}@polito.it

ABSTRACT
Most software systems are complex and composed of a large number of artifacts. To realize each different artifact specific techniques are used resorting to different abstractions, languages and tools. Successful composition of different elements requires coherence among them. Unfortunately constraints between artifacts written in different languages are usually not formally expressed nor checked by supporting tools; as a consequence they can be a source of problems. In this paper we explore the role of the relations between artifacts written in different languages by means of a case study on the Hadoop open source project. We present the problem introducing its terminology, we quantify the phenomenon and investigate its relation with defect proneness.

Categories and Subject Descriptors
D.2.8 [**Software Engineering**]: Metrics – *product metrics.*

General Terms
Measurement, Experimentation, Languages.

Keywords
Languages interaction, cross language modules, polyglot programming.

1. INTRODUCTION AND BACKGROUND
Most software projects nowadays are polyglot, i.e. files written using different languages interact with each other. Wampler et al. [1] introduced a special issue on this topic writing "Most teams are by necessity MPP [Multi-Paradigm programming] teams now. No one writes in a single language anymore. Even trivial applications have a general-purpose language, SQL, JavaScript, CSS, and dozens of frameworks, each of which includes an external DSL [Domain Specific Language] (usually in XML) that is its own mini language (the syntax is XML, but the XMLSchema defines the semantics)".

Given this scenario our team seek to study the effects of language interaction and eventually evolve development techniques and

supporting tools to consider these aspects. Nowadays tools used by developers help them only to verify the consistency internal to a language, i.e. consistency within a set of artifacts written in the same language. For example, editors check that an expression in Java code invokes a Java method which exists in the codebase, either in the same file or in another Java file. On the other hand there are major limitations in verifying the consistency across the language boundaries. For example can tools help the developer to understand immediately if a piece of XML code used for configuration refers to a really existing Java class? Normally currently available tools cannot do this because they are not aware of the cross-language semantics.

While the issue of language interaction is already very relevant today, the appearance of language workbenches [2] let us suppose that this issue is going to become even more important in the future. For example, with Xtext [3] and GMF [4] we can create, textual and graphical DSLs with custom editors integrated in the Eclipse platform with a minimal effort. Other tools like Intentional Software [5] and the Meta-Programming System [6] fully support the Language Oriented Programming paradigm [7] and are based on projectional editing. The existence of these tools and their usage in industrial projects [8] seem to indicate that the interaction between languages in projects will increase in the future.

Pfeiffer et al. [9] conducted a study related to language interaction. They realized a tool named *GenDeMoG* to mine inter-languages interaction based on text analysis. Their work was motivated by observing the amount of errors introduced by undocumented relations that cross the language border (i.e., they involve modules written in different languages) and the resulting complexity.

Our hypothesis is that in the long run we need to support cross language development, including design, modeling, and validation. To reach this goal we first need to start understanding the effects of languages interaction: this work is intended as a first step in that direction.

2. DEFINITIONS
Before stating our goals and translating them into actionable research questions, we define how we do identify and measure the languages interaction. We provide here a list of definitions used throughout the rest of the paper.

Module: we considered a module each single file.

We consider a commit[1] as a unit of work, consequently we suppose that files committed together are related.

Intra-language commit (*ILC*): a commit containing a set of modules with the same extension.

Cross-language commit (*CLC*): a commit containing modules with different extensions.

Cross-language commit for an extension (*CLC_{ext}*): a CLC containing that includes modules with the extension *ext*.

Defect fix: a commit executed to fix a defect.

We consider a module to be *cross language* when it is related to modules written in a different language (e.g., a Java file loading the configuration from an XML file). To measure how much a module is cross language we analyze its history: if the module was frequently committed with files written in other languages we consider that as an indicator of interaction between the module and those files. This interaction is measured through different variants of the *cross language ratio* (CLR).

Cross language ratio of a module (*CLR_m*): the CLR of a module *m* is the fraction of cross-language commits in which *m* was involved with regard to the total number of commits regarding the module (both intra-language and cross-language):

$$CLR_m = \frac{\# \, CLC}{\# \, CLC + \# \, ILC}$$

Cross language ratio of a module with regard to an extension (*$CLR_{m,ext}$*): the CLR of a module *m* considering as CLC only the commits involving *m* and a module with extension *ext*:

$$CLR_{m,ext} = \frac{\# \, CLC_{ext}}{\# \, CLC_{ext} + \# \, ILC}$$

Cross language ratio of an extension (*CLR_{ext}*): for each extension *ext* we compute its cross language ratio as the mean of the CLR_m considering all modules having extension *ext*:

$$CLR_{ext} = \frac{\sum CLR_m \, , m \in ext}{\# * . ext}$$

Cross language ratio of an extension *extA* with respect to an extension *extB* (*$CLR_{extA,extB}$*): the mean of $CLR_{m,extB}$ among all modules *m* with extension *extA*:

$$CLR_{extA,extB} = \frac{\sum CLR_{m,extB} \, , m \in extA}{\# * . extA}$$

Cross Language Module (*CLM*): a module is cross language if its CLR is $\geq t_{CLM}\%$, where t_{CLM} is a threshold to be defined.

Intra Language Modules (*ILM*): a module is intra language if its CLR is $< t_{ILM}\%$, where t_{ILM} is a threshold to be defined.

3. GOALS, RESEARCH QUESTIONS AND METRICS

The goal of this preliminary study is two-fold. Firstly we investigate the level of languages interaction in a common project. Secondly, we verify whether the level of interaction is related to quality problems. We look at defects as a proxy of software external quality. We identify two research questions related to the first goal.

RQ1 How much interaction is there among the languages present in a project?

The interaction is computed as the percentage of CLC among a set of commits. First we consider all type of commits (RQ1.1), then (RQ1.2) we consider separately the commits related to a particular activity (e.g., improvement, bug fixing, new feature).

Once we have defined the size of the phenomenon by answering to RQ1, we will go deeper considering the behavior of each single extension.

RQ2 Which extensions interact more?

The second research question is answered at two levels, i.e. firstly investigating the relationship between one extension versus all the other extensions (RQ2.1), then analyzing the most interacting pairs of extensions (RQ2.2).

We answer RQ2.1 computing the CLR_{ext} for each extension, while we answer RQ 2.2 computing the $CLR_{extA,extB}$ for all pairs of extensions.

The last research question is related to the second goal, i.e. investigating whether a high interaction between languages might result in higher defect proneness.

RQ3 Are Cross Language Modules more defect-prone?

We answer RQ 3 computing the number of Cross Language Modules (CLM) with and without defects, and the number of Intra Language Modules (ILM) also with and without defects. Then we compare the two proportions with/without defects by means of the F-test to see whether the proportion of Cross Language Modules with defects is different from the one of Intra Language modules.

This metric is computed at three granularity levels:

- considering all files regardless of their extension (RQ3.1),
- considering for each single extension its level of interaction with all the other extensions as aggregate (RQ3.2),
- considering interaction between specific ordered pairs of extensions (RQ3.3).

4. CASE STUDY

This exploratory study aims at understanding the phenomenon of language interaction and derived quality issues. We also use it to investigate whether the methodology defined above is applicable. We selected as a case study Apache Hadoop[2], which is a set of libraries to support distributed data processing. We selected Hadoop because it is a mature project (it is supported since April 2006) and it is used in many industrial applications (e.g., Yahoo, and Facebook).

Our methodology for computing the metrics defined above is based upon the fact that Hadoop uses SVN[3] to manage artifacts versions and JIRA[4] to track not only defects but any other activity that can be associated with software artifacts. Those elements are called "JIRA issues", and each project has its own set of issues. Example of JIRA issues are the implementation of a new feature, a single implementation task, a bug report, and so on. Hadoop developers established links between commits in the SVN code repository to JIRA issues by systematically including issue ids in their SVN commit comments.

We downloaded the SVN log from the Hadoop repository (last revision retrieved is the 1233090, from 01/18/2012, the first

---

[1] We refer to the term commit as used in the context of version control systems.

[2] http://hadoop.apache.org

[3] http://subversion.tigris.org/

[4] http://www.atlassian.com/software/jira/overview

Table I. Percentage of cross language commits (RQ 1)

All	Bug	Improvement	New Feature	Sub task	Task	Test
0.53	0.12	0.26	0.30	0.45	0.26	0.05

Table II. CLR_{ext} (RQ 2.1)

CLR_{ext}	Nr files	Extension
0.96	49	c
0.87	114	sh
0.72	75	properties
0.71	320	xml
0.59	4328	java

Table III. $CLR_{extA,extB}$ (RQ 2.2)

extA/extB	C	Java	Properties	Sh	XML
C	-	0.51	0.10	0.50	0.83
Java	0.01	-	0.28	0.04	0.48
Properties	0	0.54	-	0.36	0.46
Sh	0.09	0.22	0.24	-	0.47
Xml	0.04	0.52	0.43	0.24	-

Table IV. Odds ratio of the defectivity in respect to the relation between pairs of extensions (RQ 3.3)

	C	Java	Properties	sh	XML
C	-	**Inf**	0	0	**Inf**
Java	2.79	-	0.32	0.43	**0.96**
Properties	**Inf**	1	-	12.08	**0.94**
Sh	**3.55**	4.45	17.17	-	7.44
Xml	3.83	**0.95**	3.22	4.73	-

available revision is the 776174 from 5/19/2009). We also extracted all JIRA issues from the Apache JIRA database.

We computed all modules CLR_m and observed their distribution: about 30% of modules have CLR_m between 0 and 0.1, and about 55% files have CLR_m between 0.9 and 1. Given these percentage and given that the remaining files have a positive (right) skewed distribution, we decided to use as thresholds $t_{CLM}=t_{ILM}=50\%$ to define CLM and ILM modules.

5. RESULTS AND DISCUSSION

Table I reports the percentage of cross language commits in the Hadoop repository: 53% of all commits (first column) are CLC, i.e. containing files of different languages. Looking at the portion of CLC related to the different activities (i.e., JIRA issues), we observe that their percentage varies with respect to the type of issue (from 2nd to last column in Table I). It goes from a minimum of 5% in commits related to Test up to a maximum of 45% in Sub Tasks (since not all issues are linked to JIRA issues, the mean "All" in the first column is not related to the other means in the following columns).

RQ 1.1 answer: the 53% of commits in Hadoop are cross language.

RQ 1.2 answer: looking at the single activities, we derive that writing/modifying tests or fixing bugs are activities that involve mainly a single language, while adding new features is an activity that involves multiple types (or at least extensions).

We now proceed to RQ 2.1 and 2.2. Table II contains the top 5 extensions in terms of number of files: c, sh, properties, xml and java. Among them, four extensions correspond to programming languages and one is used for configuration files. Subsequently, we compute the $CLR_{extA,extB}$ for all combinations of the five extensions . Table III reports the $CLR_{extA,extB}$.

RQ 2.1 answer: all most common extensions in Hadoop are highly interacting with other extensions (i.e., CLR_{ext}, > 0.50).

RQ2.2 answer: the most frequent interactions ($CLR_{extA,extB} \geq 0.50$) are: C-XML (0.83), Properties-Java (0.54), XML-Java (0.52), C-Java (0.51), C-sh(0.50). Border values are: Java-XML (0.48), sh-XML (0.47) Properties-XML (0.46), and XML-Properties (0.43).

We observe that the only pairs with frequent interactions in both directions are Java-XML and Properties-XML. All the other pairs have frequent interactions in only one direction. For instance, $CLR_{XML-C} = 0.04$ and $CLR_{C-XML}=0.83$ means that most of the commits involving C contain also XML files, but not the other way around.

We now focus on the last RQ, i.e. on the relation between languages interaction and defect proneness. Table V contains metrics to answer RQ 3.1 (first line) and RQ 3.2 (from 2nd to last line). The following columns contain, in the order: the number of ILM with no defects and then with at least one defect, the number of CLM with no defects and then with at least one defect, the p-value of the F-test and finally the odds ratios (which is greater than 1 when CLM are more defect prone than ILM).

RQ 3.1 answer: considering all extensions, ILM are more defect prone that CLM (about 5 times less).

RQ 3.2 answer: considering the five most common extensions, we observe that three extensions (XML, Properties and C) have CLM with higher defect proneness, while two extensions (Java and Sh) exhibit the opposite relation.

Among the above differences, only *all extensions* and *Java* are statistically significant (p-value ≤ 0.05).

Finally, Table IV contains the odds for each pair of extensions to answer to RQ 3.3. We report in bold the values for which we obtained a p-value ≤ 0.05. We observe 7 pairs for which ILM are less defect prone than CLM, 12 pairs with CLM more defect prone than ILM and one pair with odds ratio =1. We consider only values with p-value ≤ 0.05 to answer RQ 3.3.

RQ 3.3 answer:

four extension pairs have CLM more defect prone then ILM (C-Java, C-XML, Properties-C, Sh-C),

five extension pairs have ILM more defect prone then CLM (C-Properties, C-sh, Java-XML, Properties-XML, XML-Java)

one extension pair have exactly same defect proneness (Properties-Java).

We notice that interactions where CLM results more defect prone involve always the C files. While interactions where ILM results more defect prone involve mainly XML, however C is also present. An interesting fact is that the pair Sh-C is in the first set, the pair C-sh is in the second.

Table V. Relation between classification in ILM and CLM and presence of defects (RQ 3.1 and 3.2)

	RQ	MN	MY	CN	CY	P	Odds
all	2	1891	225	2875	89	0.000	0.26
c	2.1	2	0	46	1	1.000	Inf
java	2.1	1692	201	2239	25	0.000	0.09
properties	2.1	19	1	45	7	0.429	2.92
sh	2.1	10	5	64	13	0.162	0.41
xml	2.1	96	11	184	24	0.851	1.14

Besides these considerations, we do not have an unique answer for RQ3. However, we observe that having languages interacting with other languages is related to higher defect proneness for certain languages (mainly C) and specific interactions.

6. THREATS TO VALIDITY

Internal: in this exploratory case-study different aspects were not considered. In particular we did not examine all the possible confounding factors influencing the defect proneness of the modules. Among them the age and the size of modules (expressed in LOC, for example) are the most relevant ones.

We discriminated between modules on their names while the same module can change name in the course of the project. We grouped the files by their extension while a different extension could not always indicate a different language.

Construction: we are unable to measure directly the interaction between modules written in different languages and consequently we use as a proxy their concurrent presence in the same commits, which may be an imprecise approximation.

External: another threat is due to selection bias: we have no particular reason to believe that Hadoop is representative of other software projects. Of course having considered only one project generalization of the results presented is not possible at all.

7. CONCLUSIONS AND FUTURE WORK

Although we do not have unique answers, the results and observations from this exploratory study let us understand that the problem is worthy to be investigated. In fact we observed that more than half of the commits in Hadoop are cross language (at least according to our definition). However we also observed that this property depends on the type of the activities and the extensions of the modules.

Commits related to testing or fixing bugs involve mainly a single language, while adding new features or doing implementation sub-task are activities which involve multiple languages (or at least extensions).

Looking at the single extensions, we verified that the most common extensions are frequently changed together with files with different extensions. Frequent interactions are generally not symmetric, and many of them involve XML.

When we look at defect proneness, we observe that for Java modules the interactions with other languages (as an aggregate) is not problematic at all: we observed that Java CLMs files are ten times less defect prone than ILMs. However, when looking at single pairs of interactions, we notice that several pairs have CLM significantly more defect prone then ILM, especially C modules.

Finally, the widespread interaction between Java and XML apparently is not related to defect proneness.

This study represents a first step in understanding the phenomenon of languages interaction. We should address in future work the threats that limit the scope and the validity of the study. However this study let us hypothesize that the interaction of languages might be problematic for specific languages interactions. We would like also to study other effects of languages interactions, for example on the development speed.

8. REFERENCES

[1] Wampler, D.; Clark, T.; Ford, N.; Goetz, B.; , "Multiparadigm Programming in Industry: A Discussion with Neal Ford and Brian Goetz," Software, IEEE , vol.27, no.5, pp.61-64, Sept.-Oct. 2010 doi: 10.1109/MS.2010.121

[2] Fowler, M. 2011. Domain Specific Languages. Addison Wesley Signature Series.

[3] Moritz Eysholdt and Heiko Behrens. 2010. Xtext: implement your language faster than the quick and dirty way. In Proc. of the ACM int. conf. Object oriented programming systems languages and applications companion (SPLASH '10). ACM, New York, NY, USA, 307-309. DOI=10.1145/1869542.1869625

[4] Fredrik Seehusen and Ketil Stølen. 2011. An evaluation of the graphical modeling framework (GMF) based on the development of the CORAS tool. In Proc.of the 4th int. conf. on Theory and practice of model transformations (ICMT'11).

[5] Charles Simonyi, Magnus Christerson, and Shane Clifford. 2006. Intentional software. SIGPLAN Not. 41, 10 (October 2006), 451-464. DOI=10.1145/1167515.1167511

[6] Markus Volter. 2011. From Programming to Modeling - and Back Again. IEEE Softw. 28, 6 (November 2011), 20-25. DOI=10.1109/MS.2011.139

[7] Sergey Dmitriev, 2004. Language Oriented Programming: the next programming paradigm http://www.jetbrains.com/mps/docs/Language_Oriented_Programming.pdf.

[8] Markus Völter and Eelco Visser. 2010. Language extension and composition with language workbenches. In Proceedings of the ACM int. conf. companion on Object oriented programming systems languages and applications companion (SPLASH '10). ACM, New York, NY, USA, 301-304. DOI=10.1145/1869542.1869623 .

[9] Rolf-Helge Pfeiffer and Andrzej Wąsowski: "Taming the Confusion of Languages" In: ECMFA 2011. Published in: ECMFA'11.

A Comparison of Database Fault Detection Capabilities Using Mutation Testing

Donald W. McCormick II
Computer Science, Virginia Tech.
7054 Haycock Road
Falls Church, VA, USA - 22043
Ph: +1-703.538.8371
dmccormick@heitechservices.com

William B. Frakes
Computer Science, Virginia Tech.
7054 Haycock Road
Falls Church, VA, USA - 22043
Ph: +1-703.538.8371
wfrakes@vt.edu

Reghu Anguswamy*
Computer Science, Virginia Tech.
7054 Haycock Road
Falls Church, VA, USA - 22043
Ph: +1-703.538.8371
reghu@vt.edu

ABSTRACT

Mutation testing involves systematically generating and introducing faults into an application to improve testing. A quasi-experimental study is reported comparing the fault-detection capabilities of real-world database application test suites to those of an SQL vendor test suite (NIST SQL) based on mutation scores. The higher the mutation score the more successful the test suite will be at detecting faults. The SQLMutation tool was used to generate query mutants from beginner-level sample schemas obtained from three popular real-world database test suite vendors – MySQL, SQL Server, and Oracle. Four SQLMutation operators were applied to both real-world and NIST SQL vendor compliance test suites - SQL Clause (SC), Operator Replacement (OR), NULL (NL) and Identifier Replacement (IR). Two mutation operators, SC and NL generated significantly lower mutation scores in real-world test suites than for those in the vendor test suite. The IR operator generated significantly higher mutation scores in real-world test suites than for those in the vendor test suite. The OR operator produced roughly the same mutation scores in both the real-world and vendor test suites.

Categories and Subject Descriptors: H.2.3

[Information Systems]: Database Management – Language (SQL)

Keywords: SQL, database testing, test adequacy criteria, mutation testing

1. INTRODUCTION

Mutation testing involves systematically generating and introducing faults into an application to improve testing [1]. The mutations, or faulty versions of the code, are derived from a systematic application of mutation operators. A mutation operator mutates the original code, for example, by modifying integer constants at boundary values, negating if-then and while decisions, deleting code segments, etc. Application of the mutation operators is designed to produce errors similar to those introduced in real-world applications through human error. Research has demonstrated that the ability for a test suite to detect mutated faults approximates its ability to detect real-world faults [2].

A survey of SQL query usage in industry revealed problems inherent to the SQL language suggesting that database applications are good candidates for mutation testing. SQL is a declarative computer language for use with "SQL databases" [3]. When it comes to querying databases, its strength lies in the interoperability

of its component parts or clauses: (1) SELECT, (2) FROM, (3) WHERE, (4) GROUP BY, (5) HAVING and (6) ORDER BY. This also makes it too easy for novices to formulate queries where they have no confidence in the results [4] [5] [6]. An example is improper use of the Cartesian Join that over-utilizes the CPU, returning all possible combinations between 1 or more tables.

2. Background and Motivation

2.1 SQLMutation Tool

The *SQLMutation* tool automatically generates query mutations designed to emulate errors made by professional database developers [7]. The mutations are designed to assess the adequacy of the query schema and test cases at revealing faults. If a mutant generates a different result than the original query then the mutant is "killed" and the test data is considered sufficient to reveal the inserted fault. If the mutant result is equivalent to the original query then either the query schema prevents a different result or the test data is insufficient to reveal the fault. *SQLMutation* automatically generates mutants for: (1) the main SQL clauses, (2) operators in conditions and expressions, (3) handling of NULL values and (4) replacement of identifiers such as column references, constants and parameters.

2.2 Mutation Operators

The original set of SQL mutation operators, designed to mutate SQL Data Manipulation Language (DML) SELECT commands, or queries, were first introduced in a paper by Tuya et al. [8], hereafter referred to as the Tuya-study. It presented SQL Clause (SC), Operator Replacement (OR), NULL (NL) and Identifier Replacement (IR) mutation operators that were designed to anticipate the errors resulting from the ambiguity of the SQL language, complexity of table joins, and challenges that handling NULL field values introduce.

- The SC mutation operators include subtypes like Select (SEL) that replaces each occurrence of either the SELECT or SELECT DISTINCT keywords with the other
- The OR mutation operators include subtypes like Unary Operator Insertion (UOI), that replaces each arithmetic expression or number reference e with –e, e + 1, and e-1, and Arithmetic Operator Replacement (AOR) which replace each arithmetic operator (+, -, *, /,%) with all of the other possible arithmetic operators.
- The NULL mutation operators include subtypes like Null check predicates (NLF) that replaces each occurrence of either the keywords IS NULL or IS NOT NULL with the other.
- The IR mutation operators include subtypes like column replacement (IRC) that replaces each column reference with each of the other column references, constants and parameters of like type in the query.

Each mutation operation generates a mutant or variation of the query that is designed to emulate the faults found in real-world SQL applications. The majority of the SQL mutation operators are syntactic since they rely exclusively on the existence of SQL keywords when generating mutants. For example, the JOI operator is a syntactic operator that replaces every occurrence of a JOIN type with all other possible JOIN types. Only token replacement is used. Some SQL mutation operators are syntactic and semantic. The Null in the Select List (NLS) operator, for example, first checks the query schema for fields that can store a null value, or are null-eligible. This indicates semantically to the operator that the application should be able to handle null values for that field. If the NLS operator syntactically identifies a null-eligible field in the SELECT list, it mutates it so its results are guaranteed to be different than the original query when a null value exists for that field.

2.3 The Tuya-study

Test cases from the SQL Test Suite, available for download from the NIST Conformance Test Suite Software web site [9], were used to demonstrate the mutant generating capabilities of the mutation operators from the Tuya-study [8]. The SQL Test Suite includes Data Definition Language (DDL) for creating the test database schema, as well as the Data Manipulation Language (DML) for populating and querying the schema. The test suite is divided into modules designed to validate commercial vendors' conformance to ISO, ANSI and FIPS SQL standards. Each module focuses on a particular feature of the standard and includes one or more queries and their expected results.

In the Tuya-study each of the mutation operators was run against all of the queries from the test suite. The resulting mutants were then executed against the test database. A mutant was considered to be dead if the mutant query result differed from the original query result. If execution of the mutant resulted in a run-time error, the mutant was considered to be dead. If execution of the mutant produced an equivalent result then the mutant remained alive.

The queries from the research test suite used in the Tuya-study were designed to verify vendor compliance with 141 different SQL features. In the Tuya-study mutation scores from Table 3 provided some clues. The average mutation score for all operator types from the Tuya-study was almost 70% but these scores varied by 26. Analysis of the scores revealed a distribution skewed to the left with a peak between 80-90%. At first glance it appeared that some operators consistently generated mutants that were killed more often than others regardless of the test suite. Would the converse be true – some operators consistently generated mutants that were killed less often than others regardless of the test suite? In our study, a quasi-experiment was planned to compare the fault detection capability of mutated queries from real-world test suites against the fault detection capability of mutated queries from the Tuya-study.

3. Hypothesis

The overall mutation adequacy score (**AM**) for *real-world* test suites, defined as the ratio of mutants detected to the total number of non-equivalent mutants [10], will be significantly lower for all commonly observed mutant operators than the **AM** from those using the NIST (*research*) vendor compliance test suite in the Tuya-study. The real-world test suites considered are from: MySQL, SQL Server, and Oracle.

$$AM_{real\text{-}world} < AM_{research} \qquad (1)$$

This is a quasi-experiment because there was no random assignment of subjects to treatments [11]. The dependent variable is the mutation adequacy score (**AM**). The independent variable is the test environment (real-world and research). The comparison is done for the four mutation operators from the Tuya-study – SC, OR, NL, and IR.

The basis for the hypothesis was that both the test data and test queries from the Tuya-study would be more comprehensive than those from the real-world test suites. The research test suite was designed to exercise all 141 features of the SQL standard and provide guaranteed query results while real-world test suites are generally designed to support a specific application such as a shopping cart, library search, etc. Moreover, the test data adequacy of the NIST test suite is expected to be better than the test data in the real-world test suites. In the NIST test suite, queries were constructed first and then the data was backfilled to provide the expected results. However, in most real-world test suites the data exists before the queries are developed, either because it has been inherited from another system or has never been mined. Based on these assumptions the experimental model for this hypothesis was that a test suite's overall mutation adequacy score (**AM**) depends on the set of mutation operators used and the test suite environment. The mutation adequacy score (**AM**) is referred to as the 'mutation score' hereafter.

4. The Quasi-Experiment
4.1 Generating Mutants and Mutant Scores

The set of mutation operators used in the real-world experiment was the same set used in the Tuya-study. Real-world test suites were selected at random from a pool of entry-level test suites so as to compare with the entry-level test suites from the original experiment. The queries, and consequently their query schemas, were also selected at random from the real-world test suites. Otherwise the test data from the real world test suites were left to vary naturally.

Database vendors typically include sample databases with their product releases. These are intended to demonstrate new and existing features of the database. Beginning database developers often leverage the tables, views, stored procedures, functions and constraints from the entry-level samples when designing their first database. Vendors also include intermediate and advanced level schemas for developers to use according to their own experience level with the product. The Tuya-study included separate entry level and intermediate level test suites separated by data module number. For this study, one each of the entry-level sample schemas available from Microsoft SQL Server [12], Oracle [13] and MySQL [14] were selected as the real world test suites. Available resources prevented testing more than three sample schemas so the schemas were selected at random in order to minimize bias due to the small sample size.

The SQL, Oracle and MySQL sample schemas were installed on 2005 Express Edition (XE), 10g R1 Personal, and 5.0 versions of the databases, respectively. Each query from all of the sample schemas was run against SQLMutation. SQLMutation can be automated through a web service or run in a browser using an online interface. The query text and query schema are required elements before mutants can be generated. The query schema must be entered in an XML-like format that includes the table name, as well as each field's name, type, null eligibility, and primary key status. XDBSchema is a tool that automates generation of a query schema for use with SQLMutation [15].

A repeatable process was developed for each database environment to run the mutant queries and count the dead mutants. Mutants were "killed" when they generated a result different from the original query, or they produced a run-time error.

The process for executing the MySQL mutants involved running the original query in the MySQL Query Browser, opening a new result pane, running the mutant query and then selecting to compare the results. A row that appears in one result set but not the other appears in green, while the missing row appears in red. If the result sets contain matching rows but different field values, the mismatched fields appear in blue.

The process for executing the SQL Server mutants involved executing a SELECT EXCEPT clause comparing the original query with each mutant and recording the results in a log file. The comparison query was wrapped inside of a stored procedure so that run-time errors could be trapped and recorded as dead mutants. The DDL script for the stored procedure was saved as a template and the template was customized for each query mutant and saved as a batch file that was executed against the database.

The process for executing the Oracle mutants was similar to that for SQL Server. The Oracle PL/SQL equivalent to the SQL Server EXCEPT clause is MINUS. Using the same logic principals as with SQL Server, a DDL script was constructed for each mutant that included the MINUS clause, error handling and recording for dead mutants. These scripts were saved to a batch file and executed against the Oracle database.

Table 1 lists the total mutants generated by each mutation operator and type for the Tuya-study and all three real world test suites. Real world testing generated 1070 mutants. Table 1 also lists the mutation scores in parentheses. The mutation score is a ratio of the number of mutants that were killed (dead mutants) divided by the number of mutants that were generated, by mutation operator and type. The absence of a mutation score does not indicate a score of zero (0) rather it indicates that there were no mutants generated for that type and therefore the mutation score cannot be calculated.

4.2 Results

The results in Table 1 allow us to compare an overall mutation score, or percentage of dead mutants, of 70% for mutants generated in a research environment with 57% for mutants generated in a real world environment. The missing values in the real-world for the mutation scores from Table 1 demonstrate how the total query space was more adequately represented in the research test suite than in the real-world test suites. This is to be expected since the research test suite contains over 100 varied queries in the beginner-intermediate modules alone, designed to guarantee software vendor compliance to ISO, ANSI and FIPS standards, whereas the real-world test suites target particular applications.

Figure 1 displays matched pairs of box plots comparing the research and real world mutation scores of mutants generated from the four commonly observed mutation operator categories: SC, OR, NL, and IR. Understanding and interpreting box plots can be found in [16]. Data points for the SC-Research and SC-Real World plots are mutation scores for the SEL and JOI subtypes from Table 1. Mutation scores are a ratio of the total number of dead mutants divided by the total number of non-equivalent mutants.

Two SC-Research data points were calculated from the 325 mutant results in Table 1. Five SC-Real World data points were calculated from the 41 mutant results in Table 1.

Table 1. Total Mutants and Mutation Scores

Mutation Operator	Type	Tuya-Study #Mutants (Mutations Scores)	Real World Mutants		
			MySQL	SQL Server	Oracle
SC	SEL	241(0.05)	2(0)	2(0)	1(0)
	JOI	84(0.62)	28(0.46)	8(0)	0
	SUB	379(0.85)	0	0	0
	GRU	72(0.89)	0	0	0
	AGR	560(0.73)	0	0	0
	UNI	23(0.87)	0	0	0
	ORD	39(0.82)	0	0	0
OR	ROR	1211(0.7)	49(0.43)	17(0.57)	35(0.57)
	LCR	145(0.82)	0	0	17(0.24)
	UOI	741(0.69)	57(0.56)	69(1)	33(1)
	ABS	510(0.45)	40(0.3)	46(0.61)	22(0.51)
	AOR	253(0.91)	0	25(1)	0
	BTW	76(0.55)	0	0	0
	LKE	33(0.58)	0	0	0
NL	NLF	8(1)	0	0	0
	NLS	153(0.72)	1(0)	7	9(0.56)
	NLI	92(0.98)	0	0	3(0)
	NLO	276(0.88)	0	0	9(0.67)
IR	IRC	989(0.81)	90(0.93)	129(1)	260(0.99)
	IRT	200(0.88)	24(1)	25(1)	0
	IRH	238(0.83)	0	0	0
	IRP	562(0.67)	0	0	0
	IRD	0	35(0.49)	8(1)	19(1)
Total Mutants (Overall Score):		6,885(0.7)	326(0.46)	336(0.69)	408(0.55)

The features of each box plot can be explained in part by the small sample sizes. For example, the large inter-quartile spread for the SC-Research plot is based on a 5% mutation score and a 62% mutation score. Similarly, the flat SC-Real World box plot is based on three zero percent (0%) scores out of five total scores. A comparison of the notched boxplots reveals that the confidence intervals do not overlap, indicating a significant difference between the groups.

Data points for the OR-Research and OR-Real World plots from Figure 1 are mutation scores for the ROR, LCR, UOI, ABS and AOR subtypes from Table 1. Five OR-Research data points were calculated from the 2860 mutant results in Table 1. Eleven OR-Real World data points were calculated from 400 mutant results in Table 1. The large inter-quartile spreads for both box plots can be explained in part by the reduced sample size. A comparison of the notched pair reveals that the confidence intervals overlap, indicating no significant difference between the groups.

Data points for the NL-Research and NL-Real World plots from Figure 1 are mutation scores for the NLS, NLI and NLO subtypes from Table 1. Three NL-Research data points were calculated from the 521 mutant results in Table 1. Four NL-Real World data points were calculated from the 29 mutant results in Table 1. As with the other subtypes, the features of each box plot can be partly explained by the reduced sample size. A comparison of the notched pair reveals that the confidence intervals do not overlap, indicating a significant difference between the groups.

Data points for the IR-Research and IR-Real World plots from Figure 1 are mutation scores for the IRC and IRT subtypes from Table 1. Three IR-Research data points were calculated from the 1189 mutant results in Table 1. Five IR-Real World data points were calculated from the 528 mutant results in Table 1. As with the other

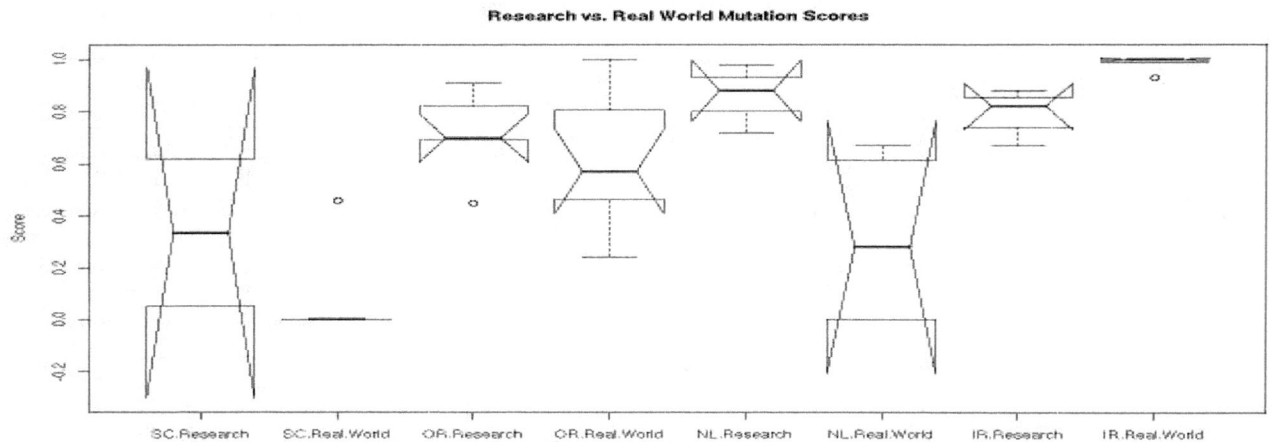

Figure 1. Research vs. Real-world Mutation Scores

subtypes, the features of each box plot can be partly explained by the reduced sample size. A comparison of the notched pair reveals that the confidence intervals do not overlap, indicating a significant difference between the groups.

Threats to validity: This is a quasi-experiment because there was no random assignment of subjects to treatments [11]. Only three of the real-world test suites are considered. Future studies will involve more real-world test suites. There are missing data points (mutation scores) for the real-world test suites. This is because there were no available mutants for some types of queries to generate the mutant scores. Also, the sample size is small. However, we have generated all the possible mutants from the real-world test suites.

5. Conclusions and Future Work

A quasi-experiment was reported comparing the fault-detection capabilities of real-world database application test suites to those of a NIST SQL test suite (research) based on mutation scores. One each MySQL, SQL Server, and Oracle sample schema was selected for the real-world test suites. Queries from these sample schemas were run against the mutation operators from the Tuya-study in order to produce a set of real-world mutants. These mutants were then executed in their native database environments and mutation scores were generated based on the results. The SC, and NL mutation operator scores were demonstrated to be significantly lower in the real world environment than in the research environment. The IR mutation operator scores were demonstrated to be significantly higher in the real world environment than in the research environment. The only mutant category that was not significantly different between environments was OR. Therefore the hypothesis investigated can be accepted only for 2 out of 4 commonly observed mutation operator categories. The results thus show that the choice of database type is a relevant factor for mutation testing. Future work will involve more real-world test suites.

6. References

[1] M. R. Woodward, "Mutation testing--its origin and evolution," *Information and Software Technology,* vol. 35, pp. 163-169, 1993.

[2] J. H. Andrews, *et al.*, "Is mutation an appropriate tool for testing experiments? [software testing]," in *Software Engineering, 2005.*

ICSE 2005. Proceedings. 27th International Conference on, 2005, pp. 402-411.

[3] ISO, "Information Technology - Database Language - SQL," in *ISO/IEC 9075:1992* vol. 3rd Edition, ed. Maynard, MA: Digital Equipment Corporation, 1992.

[4] H. Lu, *et al.*, "A survey on usage of SQL," *SIGMOD Rec.,* vol. 22, pp. 60-65, 1993.

[5] H. C. Chan, *et al.*, "User-Database Interface: The Effect of Abstraction Levels on Query Performance," *MIS Quarterly,* vol. 17, pp. 441-464, 1993.

[6] S. Brass and C. Goldberg, "Semantic errors in SQL queries: A quite complete list," *J. Syst. Softw.,* vol. 79, pp. 630-644, 2006.

[7] J. Tuya,, Suarez-Cabal M. J, and de la Riva C., "SQLMutation: A tool to generate mutants of SQL database queries," presented at the Proceedings of the Second Workshop on Mutation Analysis, 2006.

[8] J. Tuya, *et al.*, "Mutating database queries," *Inf. Softw. Technol.,* vol. 49, pp. 398-417, 2007.

[9] NIST. (2008, April 2008). *Conformance Test Suite Software.* Available: http://www.itl.nist.gov/div897/ctg/software.htm

[10] A. Namin, *et al.*, "Sufficient mutation operators for measuring test effectiveness," in *Proceedings of the 30th international conference on Software engineering,* Leipzipg, Germany, 2008, pp. 351-360.

[11] T. Campbell Donald and C. Stanley Julian, "Experimental and quasi-experimental designs for research," ed: Chicago: Rand McNally, 1963.

[12] Microsoft. (Accessed: 18 May, 2012). *Northwind and Pubs sample databases for SQL Server 2000.* Available: http://www.microsoft.com/downloads/details.aspx?FamilyID=066 16212-0356-46a0-8da2-eebc53a68034&DisplayLang=en

[13] Oracle. (Accessed: 18 May, 2012). *Installing the sample schemas and establishing a connection.* Available: http://www.oracle.com/technology/obe/obe1013jdev/common/OB EConnection.htm

[14] MySQL. (Accessed: 18 May, 2012). *Sakila database download file.* Available: http://downloads.mysql.com/docs/sakila-db.zip

[15] XDBSchema. (Accessed: 18 May, 2012). *Generation of a Database Schema in XML.* Available: http://in2test.lsi.uniovi.es/sqltools/xdbschema/

[16] R. McGill, *et al.*, "Variations of box plots," *American Statistician,* pp. 12-16, 1978.

Author Index

327

www.ingramcontent.com/pod-product-compliance
Lightning Source LLC
Chambersburg PA
CBHW080916220326
41598CB00034B/5590